THE CRITICAL EYE

THE CRITICAL EYE

Thematic Readings for Writers
Second Edition

Sally T. Taylor
Brigham Young University

Harcourt Brace College Publishers

Fort Worth Philadelphia San Diego New York Orlando Austin
San Antonio Toronto Montreal London Sydney Tokyo

Publisher	Ted Buchholz
Acquisition Editor	Michael Rosenberg
Developmental Editor	Laurie Runion
Project Editors	Barbara Moreland / Annelies Schlickenrieder
Production Manager	Debra A. Jenkin
Art Director	Jim Dodson
Permissions	Julia Stewart / Van Strength
Compositor	P&M Typesetting, Inc.
Cover	*Daniel-Henry Kahnweiler* by Pablo Picasso, Courtesy of the Art Institute of Chicago

ISBN: 0-15-500589-8

Library of Congress Catalog Card Number: 93-77821

Address Orders to:
6277 Sea Harbor Drive, Orlando, FL 32887
1-800-782-4479, or 1-800-433-0001 (in Florida)

Address Editorial Correspondence to:
301 Commerce Street, Suite 3700, Fort Worth, TX 76102

Printed in the United States of America

3 4 5 6 7 8 9 0 1 2   090   9 8 7 6 5 4 3 2 1

Preface to the Instructor

The initial impetus for writing the first edition of *The Critical Eye: Thematic Readings for Writers* came from an extensive search for a textbook for our first-year English classes at Brigham Young University. Although many readers contained good rhetoric, fine selections, and supplementary aids, none of the ones we examined had exactly what we needed. We wanted comprehensive coverage of basic reading and writing skills—not exhaustive coverage, but enough to build on in classroom discussion; we wanted a section on critical thinking skills that included analysis, argument, and persuasion; and we wanted a group of readings covering the three genres—essays, stories, and poetry—arranged thematically. The first edition successfully filled these needs and was widely used at schools throughout the country. For the second edition, we wanted to retain the best features of the first edition, but we also wanted to update it. We knew that several areas needed more emphasis—most especially critical thinking skills and classical argument.

The Critical Eye was initially based on the premise that communication skills should be consciously interactive. This concept is retained in the second edition, but critical thinking skills have been placed in Chapter 1 to give them more emphasis. Additionally, critical thinking skills have been divided into introductory critical thinking skills—including the analysis of facts, inferences, assumptions, and claims—and more complex critical thinking skills—including tracing the history of rhetoric and argumentation and analyzing the logical fallacies that can distort an argument.

Much of the useful information on interaction, reading, and writing skills given in the first edition has been retained. The Introduction shows the interaction among communication skills and their interdependency. Although the concept of interaction is not new—since aspects of interaction can be traced to classical rhetoric—this section is a reminder of the means to increase learning proficiency.

Chapters 2 and 3 on critical reading and writing have proven invaluable to students and have been retained with the addition of clarifying information and many new examples. New models for organization replace the outdated five-paragraph essay structure and additional graphic elements and cartoons make the chapters more "reader-friendly."

A new section in Chapter 4—the argumentation chapter—provides two sets of readings: one that focuses on classical texts and one that focuses on the pro-con issues of gun control and global warming. Chapter 5 is an expansion on the use of figurative language and offers additional explanations of why and how figures of speech are used to enhance reading.

The readings—essays, stories, and poems by thematic arrangement—are found in Chapters 6 through 13. Twenty-nine new selections have been added, specifically, more work by women and minority writers. Introductions to the chapters explain the focus of each chapter and how each selection fits that focus.

The new selections that have been added reflect current issues, cultural diversity, and popular new writers. Randy Shilts's careful investigation of the history of the AIDS epidemic offers the first recorded incident of an AIDS death—ironically a white female health care worker. A follow-up article on AIDS by Lori Oliwenstein describes the testing of the AIDS virus on primates. New horizons in science are explored in James Gleick's work on chaos and in Stephen W. Hawking's clearly written introduction to scientific theory. Two very moving stories drawn from Native American culture (''Lullaby'') and Japanese American culture (''Seventeen Syllables'') demonstrate the universality of human emotions. New essays and poems from African American, Hispanic, and Native American cultures enrich the diversity of the second edition. Popular writers such as Katherine Anne Porter, Allan Bloom, Stephen Jay Gould, Richard Selzer, Alice Walker, Tess Gallagher, Garrison Keillor, Annie Dillard, and Mary Oliver are also represented.

Although new selections bring exciting insights, many familiar selections have been retained in order to make readers feel ''at home'' with the book: Dorothy Canfield's ''Sex Education,'' Tillie Olsen's ''I Stand Here Ironing,'' Nathaniel Hawthorne's ''Young Goodman Brown,'' E. M. Forster's ''My Wood,'' Walt Whitman's ''When I Heard the Learn'd Astronomer,'' and Virginia Woolf's ''What If Shakespeare Had Had a Sister.''

Three tables of contents allow the reader to find material in several different ways: by theme, by mode, or by discipline. The cross-curricular table of contents, divided into twenty-one disciplines, is especially useful in such areas as women's studies or ethics.

An instructor's manual is available to help instructors use *The Critical Eye* more effectively in the classroom. It offers suggestions for classroom discussion, activities, and vocabulary for each chapter as well as sample syllabi. To obtain a copy, contact your local Harcourt Brace College Publishers sales representative.

Much valuable assistance in preparing *The Critical Eye* came during the writing of the first edition, including the help of research assistant Beth Ann Chun, numerous in-house reviewers, and sixteen reviewers from around the country. With the second edition, many excellent suggestions were given by twelve additional reviewers: Marla Allegre, Allan Hancock College; Suzanne Blaw, Southern Methodist University; David Chapman, Samford University; Pamela Collins, State University of New York at Cobleskill; Margaret Deys, Broome Community College; Ruth Dorgan, University of Wisconsin at Stevens Point; Scott Ellsworth, Ricks College; Magdalena Gilewicz, California State University at Fresno; Joan Gilson, University of Missouri at Kansas City; Carol Jamieson, Niagara County Community College; Linda Palumbo, Cerritos College; Elizabeth Walquist, Brigham Young University.

In addition to the student help given in the first edition, two additional students allowed me to use their papers in the second edition: Jonathan Freedman and Adam Sowa. Richard and Jason Walker have also graciously allowed me to reprint their Letter to the Editor in the pro-con discussion on gun control.

My sincere thanks also goes to those at Harcourt Brace College Publishers who made an extra effort to support and encourage me during the preparation of the second edition, especially my developmental editor, Laurie Runion. I also wish to thank Michael Rosenberg, Barbara Moreland, Annelies Schlickenrieder, Jim Dodson, Van Strength, and Julia Stewart.

Finally, I would like to thank my husband, David A. Taylor, for his patience and support through this difficult project.

Contents

Contents

CHAPTER 2   INTRODUCTION TO CRITICAL READING   32

CHAPTER 3   INTRODUCTION TO CRITICAL WRITING   67

PART II   READINGS

CHAPTER 6   PERSPECTIVES ON SCHOOLING: CHALLENGING MODERN EDUCATION   224

CHAPTER 7   THE AMERICAN HOME IN TRANSITION: EXAMINING FAMILY RELATIONSHIPS   294

CHAPTER 8   HUMAN MINDS AND BODIES: UNDERSTANDING OURSELVES   343

CHAPTER 9   DIFFERENT FACES IN THE CROWD: DEVELOPING CULTURAL AWARENESS   399

CHAPTER 10   THE UNEXPLORED REALM: BECOMING AWARE OF THE SPIRITUAL LIFE   440

CHAPTER 11   RINGS AND BEAUTIFUL THINGS: CREATING NEW PERCEPTIONS THROUGH THE ARTS   490

Rhetorical Contents

G. Cause and Effect

H. Persuasion and Argumentation

Cross-Curricular Contents

FINE ARTS

GEOLOGICAL SCIENCES

HISTORY

HUMAN DEVELOPMENT AND FAMILY RELATIONS

HUMANITIES

LAW AND ETHICS

MEDICINE

PHILOSOPHY

POLITICAL SCIENCE AND PUBLIC AFFAIRS

SCIENCE AND ECOLOGY

SOCIOLOGY AND CULTURAL ANTHROPOLOGY

SPEECH AND ORATORY

TECHNOLOGY AND INFORMATION SCIENCES

THEATRE AND PERFORMING ARTS

WOMEN'S STUDIES

1 part

Principles and Practices

ve so
ow clear
should be
e thesis state-
o start. The five-

statement
, examples
act, proof, examples
ng fact, proof, examples

on, pulling facts and thesis statement together
nowing why your thesis statement is correct

facts seem to be a good number because they are not as
ould seem, but they are not too many to remember. However,
s work well—or two very strong ones, and you can have more
graph per fact—so you don't really need exactly five paragraphs in

ganizing the Five-Paragraph Essay. To organize your materials, prepare
utline with your thesis statement, an introduction. Fit the research and ideas under
major heading, and a place for a conclusion. Each major heading should have two
the major headings. Subdivide the ideas. Watch for only one subheading under a major heading.
or more subheadings. Usually, one subheading is just a restatement of the heading and you will need
to either integrate the subheading into the heading or expand that part of your
paper to be more balanced.

Using Notecards. It helps to have the information on separate notecards so
you can physically divide the information. Then you can see if one pile outweighs the others. You will want to balance your paper by going back for more

Introduction

Human Communication

Although many living creatures communicate, human beings are the only ones that question or analyze. Lower species may use mating calls, distress calls, and other signals to express basic instinctive needs; they may even reason in some elementary ways, such as when a cat or dog contrives to communicate its wishes (standing at the food bowl when it is hungry) or participate in simple games (chasing a ball). Yet humans seem to be the only ones with the ability to use critical thinking to analyze problems, communicate detailed information, and exchange abstract ideas. Without these abilities, humans would have advanced no further than the primates.

Nonverbal and Complex Communication

Although humans are not baboons, some of the thinking and communication they use demonstrates their close tie to the instinctive and nonverbal elements of the animal kingdom. We know when others are tired, bored, angry, delighted, or unhappy by the position or movement of the body, by facial expressions, or by other nonverbal means. Our instincts and previous experience give clues to these nonverbal messages. But without critical thinking—the ability to analyze problems, language, and the complex communication it makes possible—our understanding of other human beings and of the world would likely remain on this instinctive level.

Complex Communication at Work

Complex communication involves skills in reading, writing, speaking, and listening and requires critical thinking as the central focus of all these activities (note the diagram on page 4). The interaction between these fundamental communication skills, based soundly on the principles of critical thinking, is what accelerates learning beyond the instinctive level.

The Interactive Nature of Critical Thinking and Communication Skills

Cross-Pollination of Skills

Critical thinking and all of the communication skills work together. None is separated from the others. They might be said to "cross-pollinate" each other, to overlap and influence each other.

Thinking begins every activity because we must think about anything we do, making *inferences* and *assumptions* (for definition and explanation of these terms, see pages 12–21) and reaching decisions on every aspect of our lives. When people write, they are speaking with themselves as they think out what they want to write and how to put it into words. They also are reading the words as they write.

The Interaction or Recursiveness of Communication

All of the communicative behavior is interrelated—"cross-pollinated." All such behaviors *interact,* or are *recursive*—we go back and forth between the forms of communication, interpreting and evaluating as we go. Similarly, when people read complex material, they sometimes make notes on their reading (they *write*) or they *annotate* (write in the margins in their own book, one hopes, not the library's!) to understand or to remember what they read. Sometimes, as people *read* words, they *speak* them (or recount the main ideas of the reading) in their minds and they *listen* to themselves, although many people read so fast, they simply do not have time to speak or listen to every single word. However, they remember (or speak in their minds) major ideas and concepts. This speaking, or retelling what they read, helps people to sort out, put ideas together, reach conclusions, and finally understand what they are reading. Some readers, especially beginning readers, move their mouths as they read, silently speaking the words they see, although doing so slows their reading speed and comprehension considerably. As readers gain speed, they no longer have time to form the words with their mouths as they read. Nonetheless, early reading practices emphasize the close link of reading, listening, and speaking in the communication process.

Social/Personal Communication Activities

Speaking and listening can be social (group) or personal (individual) activities, depending on who the audience is. One of the great pleasures of life is social interchange—talking and listening to people; other pleasures are solitary—meditation or private reading, thinking deeply by ourselves, or quietly reading what we enjoy. Critically listening to another (a teacher, for example) may stimulate critical thinking, leading to speaking or further reading and, perhaps, writing. Connections between the skills or forms of communication are important in the process of learning.

Levels of Learning

Children learn rapidly by using their senses and getting feedback on their reactions from others and from the world itself. Adults continue learning in this basic manner,

Figure 1 Interactive Nature of the Communication Circle

4 Writing			1 Reading
	THINKING		
3 Speaking			2 Listening

but add the more sophisticated communication skills of critical thinking as reflected in critical reading and writing. Adults become gradually more proficient in these skills as they gain knowledge and begin to combine skills to increase their proficiency. All skills interact to aid the learning process; a conscious combining of skills can speed an increase in the level of understanding. Figure 1 illustrates the interaction of communication with critical thinking at the center.

Using the Communication Circle

The movement sequence within this illustration may follow a clockwise pattern or any of several other patterns, always with critical thinking at the center of communication. Note that the communication circle may start at any point, especially in casual learning (people are constantly listening and responding to their environment). Class discussions often follow a clockwise pattern. Students begin by (1) *reading* a selection from the text. As they are (2) *listening* to a discussion of that selection in class, they may do some (3) *speaking* when they add their comments to the class discussion. They then may finish the circle by (4) *writing* an essay or taking notes about the ideas found in the selection and heard in the discussion. When others read what has been written by classmates, the circle has come around to *reading* again.

When students help each other in the classroom in peer response groups, they may try (1) *reading* to one another (or silently) what another classmate has written, (2) *listening* to what others in the group have to say, and (3) *speaking* to one another to help improve the classmate's writing, analyzing, and organizing skills. They may also (4) *write* critiques for their classmate. Again they have completed the circle. During this entire process, they have used critical thinking to analyze and interpret ideas, to question and determine answers and arguments, to make connections between abstract and concrete ideas, and to identify facts and fallacies.

Also included in the communication circle is another set of divisions in communication: oral and written communication.

Oral and Written Communication

The lower half of the communication skills listed in the circle deal with the spoken word and the upper half with the written word. Literacy statistics are more concerned with the second part of these skills, but all are important. Individuals can be proficient in any one of the four, any set of two or three, or all of the skills. Both oral and written skills also have varying degrees of proficiency.

Combining the Skills with Critical Thinking

In daily life people frequently combine communication skills, informally making connections and drawing upon elements of critical thinking to help them function in society. They use such interaction more formally when they consciously combine skills. When they wish to remember something they are listening to, they may take notes. Often, upon reading or hearing something controversial, they mentally (if not actually) respond by thinking of arguments, writing a scathing rebuttal, or hotly debating the issue. For example, several readings in Chapter 4 focus on gun control. This topic is especially controversial in the West, where deer hunting is a common sport and gang warfare or big-city crime is minimal. An avid hunter might see an article or hear a program advocating gun control and assume that increased government control may limit hunters' rights. The concern may be manifested in an emotional discussion with friends, a letter to the editor, or a petition.

Some common combining of skills include:

Shopping: reading (labels), speaking (to clerks), listening (to clerks' responses), critical thinking (evaluating choices)

Preparing tax forms: reading (forms), writing (to get an extension), critical thinking (calculating)

Contacting a friend: writing (a letter), speaking (conversation), listening (to a friend)

Participating in drama: reading (scripts), speaking (the lines), listening (to the director/other participants)

Preparing for an exam: listening (to instructor), reading (texts/notes), critical thinking (studying)

Writing an essay: reading (background material), writing (drafts of the essay), critical thinking (organizing, evaluating)

Driving a car: reading (street signs), listening (for sirens), critical thinking (evaluating road/traffic conditions)

Political debates: speaking (arguing a point of view), listening (to candidates), critical thinking (In detail: A political debate may involve the participants in reading and writing in preparation for the debate, or their writing during the debate in the form of notes; however, when listeners experience the debate, they see and hear mainly the obvious speaking ability of the candidates, their answers and rebuttals to questions and arguments, and the conduct of the other candidates and the audience.)

Note that critical thinking is at the heart of most activities.

Conscious Combining of Skills

If using and combining communication and thinking skills comes naturally, why be concerned about it? Communication may be natural, but controlling and focusing it are not so natural and are seldom easy. Critical thinking must be worked on throughout a lifetime and though seldom, if ever, fully mastered, it has a great impact on how well people communicate.

All communication skills can be improved, especially when they are practiced in combination. When we consciously use more than one form of communication, we improve out ability to understand, learn, analyze, and remember, just as when we use more than one sense (touching plus seeing) we enhance our awareness and memory of the thing experienced. Consciously writing (taking notes) as we listen or read increases retention of the subject matter. Similarly, consciously talking out a problem, seriously listening to others analyze it (as in Alcoholics Anonymous meetings), studying and reading about a problem, or carefully writing solutions to that problem (as suggested by some psychiatrists) helps people solve their problems. Reading and discussing facts, inferences, and assumptions, and carefully forming logical arguments can help one function more responsibly in society and in one's personal life.

Although this text focuses on critical thinking, reading, and writing, because they are the most complex of the skills, the natural interaction of all forms of communication will suggest many ways to combine critical thinking with reading, writing, speaking, and listening. Above all, and always, people should *think* carefully about their work since critical thinking is at the heart of all other communication skills.

Example: *James, Manuel, Yoneko, Thomas, Kai, Susan, Jasbir, Louise, and Kening have gathered in a study group to prepare for an examination. They pool the notes they have taken in class and discuss the important points of each class period. In a previous session, they each have taken the assignment of one chapter to read and review carefully and provide written outlines to the rest of the group. As they meet together for a final time, they orally present each chapter and discuss the key points while the rest make additional notes on the printed outline. The session is interrupted with good humor and heated discussions of salient questions. Then they all go out for pizza. When they finish the session, they all feel confident and prepared for the examination—and comfortably full. The following day, all received high scores on the examination.*

The Learning Process

The above example shows how interaction of communication skills helps students in their class preparation. In the following pages, we will be working to develop increased proficiency in critical thinking, reading, and writing. Because each person is different in ability, some exercises may not apply to every individual, but trying them all will help readers discover which ones best serve their needs. Although this text gives a good start toward developing critical thinking, reading, and writing skills, no single class or text or teacher can satisfy every need. Readers should use the text as a springboard for learning and then continue to work on reading, writing, and thinking throughout their lives because each skill can be challenging, complex, or difficult depending on the information to be learned.

Introduction to Critical Thinking

The very act of reading these words and thinking about them indicates that skills of communication are taking place. What is different, then, about critical thinking? Is that not what every reader is doing right now? Yes, every reader is reading and thinking, but *critical* thinking is a more highly developed skill by which we creatively make connections between ideas. When we need to determine the accuracy of a statement and respond to its claims with reliable, logical criteria, we are in the realm of critical thinking.

Critical thinking skills of high quality are needed in many aspects of our lives if our decisions are to be more than habitual, conventional, or emotional reactions; they help us to evaluate which products to buy, to judge a political issue or candidate, to decide the merits of social activities or attitudes, and to shape arguments. They also can help us to use creativity to solve problems. The quality of a person's opinions and actions depends largely on his or her proficiency in critical thinking.

Individuals want to be able to think for themselves using sound criteria, without being manipulated by faulty perceptions. They want to construct sound arguments to persuade others by clear and effective logic. They want to find or invent solutions to problems. To do these tasks, they must be able to understand the principles of critical thinking and to apply those principles in their everyday interaction with others. They must be able to analyze the difference between facts and inferences, recognize unwarranted or hidden assumptions, know when language is used in nonliteral ways, and support claims.

Although making strict categories may be problematic, for the purpose of simplifying the concepts, we can say that critical thinking has two aspects: analytical and creative. Analysis involves looking at facts (truth—or those things we think we know for sure), inferences (guesses to the truth), assumptions (our interpretation of the truth), and claims (our statements of the truth as we see it), to see if perceptions and understanding are accurate. Creative thinking looks at connections between things which may not be quite so obvious. Understanding figurative language, for example, involves making connections between objects and ideas which may be dissimilar. Critical thinking skills come into play when these connections bring new insights. More about creative thinking later, but first, a look at analytical thinking.

Analyzing Facts

Part of our perception of what is called reality is based on tangible objects and empirical facts. What we can see or verify through observation or witnesses becomes the basis for our perception of truth. Most people are comfortable with something they know "for sure," something that can be objectively demonstrated or proved.

The Reality We Know

Although modern theorists question the facts of reality, we need to begin somewhere to understand the world. Suppose a person is walking to a mall. She sees the solid evidence of civilization around her—buildings, pavement, automobiles, traffic lights. These objects seem to represent the reality she knows because they behave in certain consistent ways. She does not give this behavior a second thought because she *knows* what to expect. She is comfortable with this kind of reality. It is the reality upon which she bases her decisions and ideas. Names, dates, places, processes, behavior can all be factual in this way. We know where the nation's capital is located, the current date, at what temperature water freezes, why dogs have become a favorite human pet, or how we feel when we have a pleasant experience. These facts seem easy to assess, but our sense perception is not always accurate. It is colored by individual beliefs and attitudes. For example, after a week of sub-zero temperatures, we may think that 32-degrees F is not so cold. But our personal perception does not change the fact. Facts, as things we perceive through the senses, are the closest things to reality that we have.

Ideas as Facts

Ideas are more slippery. Some people consider ideas to be hypotheses or theories, rather than facts. Some ideas that we accept as facts can, indeed, be proved repeatedly: mathematical formulas and operations, for example. But some ideas are subject to change. Political, religious, social, psychological, or economic facts are notoriously unstable. Examples of this instability can be seen especially in the political arena. Ideas supporting communist political systems recently have crumbled; but ideas about human behavior, religious dogma, or governmental policy also are often under attack.

Facts that Change

Facts do not change, but many things that are *held to be* facts, or *thought of* as facts will change because they are based on perceptions, and perceptions can change. History shows us many examples of previously held "facts" which were faulty: stereotypes so strongly held that they became fact for groups of people, scientific principles based on incomplete observation or measurement, medical practices which may have actually harmed the patients, or some religious or educational ideas once thought to be beneficial which, in actuality, were hurtful.

Facts Limited by the Senses

People's conceptions of facts are limited first by their senses, and their senses are not always alert. Sharp observation skills are important in accurate perception, yet even careful observation may need additional proof. Then we must use other means and methods to prove the "observed" fact. Some of these methods of proving are verification by witnesses, measurement, or documentation; verification by reliable and adequate data; or verification by reasonable, or logical, judgment.

Methods of Verifying Facts

Verification by witnesses refers to facts which are observed by more than one person. For example, after a bank robbery, police try to find as many people as possible who saw what happened. If everyone comes up with the same observations about the events of the robbery, the police can feel confident about making a valid report. Those wishing to know any fact or set of facts may assume that although one witness might lie, many witnesses would verify the truth of a fact.

Verification by measurement is a method that commonly uses instruments to prove a fact. Scales, rulers, measuring cups, or more complicated measuring devices such as spectrographs or transits can all be used to verify size, weight, quantity, distance. Such measurements can be taken repeatedly with almost identical results, verifying a fact of a physical nature.

Verification by documentation is a process of finding written witness of a fact. Previous researchers may have used measurements or questionnaires of many witnesses to verify some idea, process, or event. That verification is discussed in a respected journal. As students or other researchers investigate that fact, they may look for this documented evidence to validate their observations.

Verification by reliable and adequate data can combine all three methods of verification (witness, measurement, documentation) to prove a fact. However, the witness, measurement, or documentation must first be reliable—meaning that the witnesses are not lying or misrepresenting the facts, the measurements must be done with accurate, valid equipment, and the documentation must be by authorities in the field. The data must also be adequate; that is, more than one reliable witness may be required, the measurement should be repeated more than once to avoid the chance of error, and documentation by more than one authority may need to be examined.

The last method of verification, reasonable or logical judgment, draws heavily upon individual critical thinking skills. Using good judgment in decisions and behavior is easier to do in the abstract than in practice. However, we are often called upon to judge and make decisions based upon our experience. If, for example, we have found by experience that sweeter cantaloupes have a distinctive odor at the stem end, we make it a practice to sniff carefully each time we purchase a cantaloupe. Our judgment may prove to be valid, cantaloupe after cantaloupe. More complex examples of logical judgment and reasoning can be found later in this chapter and in Chapter 4.

Student Exercises: Facts

A. Name five facts that are discovered through the following senses:

1. sight

2. hearing

3. touch

4. taste

5. smell

B. Name one method of verification that can establish the following facts:

1. The number of deaths from AIDS during a certain year. _____

2. The damage to life and property in an automobile accident. _____

3. The chemical behavior of a certain element. _____

4. The intensity of a storm. _____

5. Reaction of a child to a strange food. _____

C. Which of the following are statements of fact?

1. One inch is equal to approximately 2.54 centimeters.

2. Maize is the native corn of America.

3. Mount Everest is the tallest mountain in the world.

4. Broccoli tastes terrible.

5. Ecuador is located at the southern tip of South America.

6. Everyone should have measles vaccinations.

D. Why are some of the above statements false?

Suggestions for Discussion: Facts

1. Choose a local problem that needs a solution. Discuss the problem, its background, severity, and proposed resolution. Find at least three facts which have an impact on this problem. Example: A local stream is polluted. A particular industry seems to be the major culprit. The community needs to be alerted to the danger. One fact which would convince them would be professional testing of the water; another might be photographs of dead fish or foam on the water.

2. Discuss a "fact" that previously has been considered true, but in recent years has been found to be incorrect or faulty (e.g., everyone should have immunizations to prevent the spread of communicable diseases).

3. Find three "facts" that are suspect in a newspaper. Tell why you do not believe them to be facts.

Inferences

Facts, however, cannot cover every aspect of daily living. We must make inferences when the facts are inadequate. An inference is a judgment, a mental act, which is based on fact, but which goes beyond fact and into the unknown.

George Price's cartoon shows a character being thrown out of an automobile dealership—that is the only fact we know by observing the cartoon. The humor in the cartoon comes from what we guess, or infer. We can infer, or judge, from the four signs in the window that the character has made an offer for a car that has angered the sales force. We can infer that the offer was so absurd that it insulted them, causing the anger expressed on their faces.

However, not enough facts are given to allow us to be certain that this interpretation is accurate. True, most people who examine the cartoon may make the same inferences about it, but still their conclusion is only a guess. It is not a fact, but an inference, which creates the humor in the cartoon. The man *may* be being thrown out because he is a poor salesperson (i.e., he is being fired), or maybe he's a squatter, or

from THE WORLD OF GEORGE PRICE. Copyright © 1988 by George Price. All rights reserved. Reprinted with permission.

perhaps he has just attempted an abortive robbery, or admitted to embezzlement, or perhaps he is merely the bearer of evil tidings. Maybe the two men in the doorway have no connection with the dealership at all. These are, of course, all possible interpretations, but none of them allows the cartoon to be funny—indeed, not one of them necessitates a cartoon. Even though they may cover the facts, they give no reason for the facts to be addressed in the first place.

Inferences to Explain the Nonobvious

Inferences are used to explain the nonobvious aspects of life. Often the use of creative thinking is a part of making inferences. Suppose we were to see an automobile sitting atop the roof of a house. Two facts would be obvious: the car is on the roof, and somehow the car got on the roof. We infer that some means or instrumentality is responsible for the location of the car. Beyond the fact of its location, we might make various explanations about how the car got on the roof: pranksters had disassembled the car and reassembled it on the roof, the car had been lifted to the roof by a crane for advertising purposes, or a natural disaster had lifted the car to the roof and left it there. Both how and why the automobile was on the roof are inferences.

Making Incorrect Inferences

Inferences can easily be wrong. Suppose one saw a strange person walk into a neighbor's house. If one suspects foul play, one might have the police come—only to have them falsely arrest a relative of the neighbor. Inferences cannot always be categorized rigidly as true or false, right or wrong. Sometimes they are strong or weak—without the dramatic polarity. But, since inferences are always based on incomplete facts, we need constantly to gather additional facts and ask additional questions to reach more reliable or stronger conclusions. Some questions may take a long time to answer—if they are *ever* answered completely. Without inferences and the curiosity these guesses generate, no progress can be made.

Student Exercises: Inferences

Determine two correct and two incorrect, strong or weak inferences from the following facts:

1. A large lake nearby is beginning to dry up.

2. As a woman sits in a doctor's office, she hears music coming in through the window.

3. You smell the scent of cinnamon.

4. After a very long day of automobile driving, the driver feels the car starting to lose power.

Suggestions for Discussion: Inferences

1. Discuss and illustrate possible danger or other problems in making faulty inferences when you see an unusual occurrence, such as an animal acting in a strange way, or an unusual storm, or silence where there should be sound.

2. Discuss how important inferences can be in some area of science, biology, human behavior, or business (e.g., a researcher may guess that a certain area may contain an oil field).

3. Compare three similar facts with the different inferences which can be made from those facts. For example, *facts:* a dog (a) has stopped eating (b) doesn't want to get up (c) has lost her enthusiasm for life; *inferences:* (a) she is sick (b) she is very old (c) she misses someone in the family who is gone.

4. Describe the reasoning pattern that illustrates how a faulty inference begins and develops.

5. Compare two individuals' reactions to a murder trial. Show how their differing conclusions are the result of different patterns of inference.

Example: *Antonia awakened in the night to the sound of a car engine. It sounded very close. Soon she heard muffled voices. Someone is going to break into my home, she thought fearfully. She lay very still, hoping they could not see she was awake in case they came into her bedroom. Her heart pounded so loudly that she was afraid they could hear it. She could hear the sound of soft footsteps. Her fear became intense. Then she heard the car door shut softly and the car drive away. The next day she discovered that her neighbors had left very early for a vacation. Her inferences had been incorrect. She had gone through a traumatic experience needlessly.*

Assumptions

An assumption is an opinion or belief that is accepted without requiring explanation or proof. Most assumptions are generalizations—general statements about some aspect of the world or the people in it—such as, men are better mechanics than women, or the laws of physics are constant in any area of investigation, or dogs are more friendly than cats. Anything that we believe or take for granted without requiring evidence is an assumption. All reasoning contains assumptions, so understanding depends on being aware of what is being assumed and rejected as faulty or accepted as valid.

Although it is not always easy to differentiate between inferences and assumptions or to fit inferences and assumptions into neat categories (indeed, many inferences eventually become assumptions), here is an approximate but useful distinction between the two terms. Inferences are judgments, but assumptions are taken to be fact even though they may or may not be fact.

Warranted and Unwarranted Assumptions

When a person purchases a new compact disk (CD), she would expect it to play clearly and smoothly. Her expectation probably would be based on a warranted assumption (an assumption she has good reason to trust: new items should work correctly). If, however, the CD had uneven sound, she would expect the store to take it back and give her a refund or replacement. Her expectation would be based on another warranted assumption: reputable dealers treat customers fairly.

On the other hand, if she were to expect the CD to last forever, her assumption probably would be unwarranted. We live in a society of planned obsolescence. Nothing is built to last forever.

Whereas warranted assumptions are justifiable and are valuable parts of the thinking process, unwarranted assumptions are not, as noted in the above example. However, assumptions are not always entirely right or wrong; rather, like inferences, they may be strongly or weakly grounded—more or less warranted by the facts and principles on which they are based. We may assume that the presence of certain kinds of clouds foretell rain. Our assumption may be warranted or unwarranted—depending on what we know of clouds and weather patterns—or it may be *more* or *less* warranted.

Often the facts and principles behind an assumption are out of sight. Perhaps there are other assumptions that we have so taken for granted that we act on them out of habit. For example, we may assume that going to a dentist is going to be a horrible experience, so we avoid going. Critical thinking involves tracking down these hidden assumptions, making ourselves aware of them, and evaluating their reliability in the thinking process. Our assumption about the dentist may be based on one experience or on hearsay—someone's exaggerated tale of horror. We need to track down or evaluate our assumption about the dentist to see if we are using logical thinking and reasonable behavior.

Stereotyping, as noted above, is also a kind of unwarranted assumption about a certain group of people, type of behavior, or set of attitudes that is built on faulty perception of facts. Red-haired people have been stereotyped as having hot tempers; overweight people as being jolly; blonds as being dumb; people who wear glasses as being intellectual. These assumptions are unwarranted because superficial physical characteristics are usually not linked to personality traits. We could find just as many blonds and brunets who have hot tempers as "redheads," and probably as many redheads who have placid temperaments.

Using Critical Thinking to Discover Assumptions

As we try to discover assumptions and interpret meaning, we look at three things: what is said (literal meaning), what is not said but is implied (hidden or implicit assumptions), and what is said in an indirect way (figurative language).

The Literal Meaning

When a person speaks or writes, what others probably notice first are those things observed or said directly, including stated assumptions; they see the literal, obvious meaning. An idea can be expressed quite literally (factually), although totally avoiding assumptions is almost impossible. Understanding the literal part of an idea is often no more than a simple, superficial understanding—the assumptions are generally open and clear. When we watch television or listen to a conversation, the literal meaning may be mostly what the speaker intends us to hear. If so, we should try to understand that literal meaning clearly and honestly. If the speaker is giving information straight—nothing significant hidden—the viewers should understand it in that way. For example, we would have no reason to question the television report of the number of dead in an airline disaster, unless the announcer indicated that the number was in question. The Richter scale measurement of an earthquake is a fact that is literal. Our assumption follows that we are receiving truthful information.

Biased Motives and Hidden Agendas

Most of the time, even speakers who try to be honest and objective are somewhat biased about their subjects—at least enough to want to talk about them. But sometimes a speaker may have motives other than honesty and objectivity, and that speaker's approach may be anything but straightforward. He or she may deliberately twist facts or make unwarranted assumptions just to persuade the audience. When we suspect someone of hidden motives (e.g., dangerous self-interest or power plays), we must call upon further critical thinking skills to find these motives. We need to look for hidden (not merely unstated, but intentionally concealed) assumptions—a hidden agenda—to determine how far we are willing to trust the speaker.

Example: *While watching a television program, Emil noticed that the product advertised was to prevent sun damage to the skin, yet the model showing the product was deeply suntanned. He knew that although a sunburn is obviously dangerous, any prolonged sun damage can eventually cause cancer. Knowing that people who stay out of the sun entirely, or use protective clothing instead of lotions, would not buy as much (if any) of the product advertised, the company was promoting the very thing it was saying it tried to prevent. It wanted its customers to stay out in the sun. Emil told his sunbathing roommate about the irony of the advertisement.*

Stated and Unstated (Including Hidden) Assumptions

Assumptions can be either stated (explicit) or unstated (implicit). Stated assumptions are generally written or spoken statements which a speaker assumes no one will question, so no supporting facts or examples are given. Perhaps in conversation or a talk show, the speakers may not have time to give extended support, and so they assert their general assumptions without support or elaboration. Or a speaker may feel that an assumption is so evident that verification does not have to be stated. For example, at an environmental rally, the speaker may assume that the audience has positive feelings toward legislative measures to clean up air pollution. She may not, therefore, take time to justify the existence of the Environmental Protection Agency. But in addition to this kind of unsupported, stated assumptions, most discussions contain several unstated assumptions.

Unstated assumptions can be unconscious (even the speaker is not aware of what he or she is taking for granted) or conscious (the speaker is aware of the unstated assumption but for some reason *chooses* not to state it). Unstated assumptions, whether conscious or unconscious, are usually not so buried that a careful listener with reasonable judgment cannot find them. Deliberately hidden assumptions may be harder to spot. Politicians and advertisers often become very good at hiding assumptions which, if seen, would cause the viewer or listener immediately to reject what is being said or sold. For example, for many years, cigarette advertisers hid the assumption that smoking may be bad for one's health. Their campaign focused on the assumption that consumers would enjoy smoking.

Unstated assumptions, then, may be conscious or unconscious. If conscious, they may be well meaning or intentionally deceptive; if unconscious, they merely may reflect the trustworthy thinking habits of a sound mind, or they may betray the accidental, incomplete thought of a careless or uncritical mind. Most people probably leave assumptions unstated for various reasons. The example below contains no maliciously hidden, nor ignorantly unstated assumptions. Rather, it uses unstated assumptions as a kind of shorthand, expecting those who hear or read the message to fill in the gaps.

> Automobile accidents are the leading cause of death in the United States for every age group under 50. Statistics report more than 60,000 highway deaths per year and more than 35 million traffic accidents annually. But the majority of people are still not wearing seatbelts.

Although it is not stated, the major unstated assumption of this passage is that the wearing of seatbelts would prevent highway deaths. If this assumption is warranted, the implied message that we should wear seatbelts is probably worth paying attention to; if it is unwarranted, the message may safely be ignored.

Most people would accept both the unstated assumption and the message, although some people may legitimately question how far the assumption can be reasonably extended and object that seatbelts are only one of many ways to reduce traffic fatalities. This unstated assumption is relatively safe; sometimes, however, such assumptions can be treacherous.

The Dangers of Hidden Assumptions

Faulty hidden assumptions can weaken a discussion and cause anger or frustration. Without looking at the ramifications behind their assumptions, some people may fail to allow critical thinking skills to serve them. Look at the hidden assumptions behind the following statements:

1. Home schools are better than public schools for children.
   Hidden assumptions:

   - Public schools are not adequate.

- Untrained parents know more than trained teachers.
- The home always creates a learning environment.
- Children learn more from parents than from others.

Some of these assumptions may have some validity, but others may be false. Without some explanation or qualification, some of the assumptions can weaken the discussion and cause feelings of resentment.

2. College sports figures are not good students.
   Hidden assumptions:

- Players are chosen only for their ability at sports, not for their intellectual ability.
- Students cannot make good grades if they are involved in sports.
- One can excel in scholastics or sports, but not both.
- All college sports figures are the same.

In a discussion of college sports, a person who gives the above statement would risk offending fine scholars who happen to be on athletic scholarships. The faulty assumptions might cause a loss of friendships or valued acquaintances.

3. Homeless people are either drunks or former mental patients.
   Hidden assumptions:

- Alcoholism and/or mental illness are the only reasons people lose housing.
- People without homes are somehow impaired.
- Normal people would not be homeless.

Recent surveys of the homeless make this assumption invalid. People would show their ignorance by making this faulty assumption.

When a statement contains a questionable hidden assumption, the audience may feel uneasy or confused. Something is not quite right, but the generalization is hidden so that the audience is not able to confront it directly. Questionable hidden assumptions can be found anywhere, but here are two examples:

Do unto others before they do unto you. (A wry rephrasing of the golden rule which makes the faulty hidden assumption that everyone is out to get you.)

If one is good, two is better. (The faulty hidden assumption is that greater quantity means greater worth. Instead, inappropriate quantity of drugs means overdose; excessive quantity of food means obesity; and excessive dieting, stress, or exercise can mean death.)

Some faulty hidden assumptions are soon unmasked. However, many hidden assumptions are not recognized as faulty. Prejudice is often based on faulty hidden assumptions. Unfortunately, prejudice is often deep-seated and almost impossible to remove once it has taken a firm hold. The hidden assumptions in prejudice are held as fact. The "enemy" remains the enemy.

Problems with hidden assumptions also occur when two readers have different set of assumptions about the same idea. Such statements as "all old people should be confined to rest homes" or "all young people should be allowed to drive automobiles" would be interpreted very differently by people of different age groups. "Old" or "young" can be any age, depending on a person's perspective.

The hidden assumption in the following cartoon is that this woman (and therefore all women) is not real, that she is like a statue or a figure on a pedestal (notice her stiff posture). The assumption comes from the stereotype of the "perfect wife" who is idealized into unreality. The tone of the cartoon is ironic, suggesting that this attitude is not only wrong but absurd.

" SWEETHEART, YOU'VE FALLEN OFF YOUR PEDESTAL AGAIN!"
Freeway to Perfection. Copyright © 1978 The Sunstone Foundation.

Student Exercises: Assumptions

A. Identify either unwarranted or warranted assumptions in the following statements:

1. Except on special occasions, clothing stores in America usually are open on a 10–6 schedule.

2. All fresh-water streams contain trout.

3. With some variations, the seasons follow a regular pattern.

4. Anyone can make big money in the stock market.

5. Books are the best source of knowledge.

B. Discuss what assumptions would be warranted or unwarranted about the following topics:

1. the death penalty

2. national health insurance

3. year-round schools

4. pesticides

5. medical experiments with animals

C. Name four hidden assumptions in each of the following statements:

1. The United States has always been the aggressor in the last four wars. Its politicians see war as a way to stabilize the economy and raise the standard of living for its citizens.

2. Sex education should not be taught in the schools. It is the parents' responsiblity to teach morality.

3. Pollution is the major concern of the American public. Without governmental control, you would be drowning in garbage.

4. Learning a second (or third) language is the top priority in today's schools. Without a second language, civilization moves toward decay.

5. Since people are the controllers of their own bodies, they should have a choice in the way they die, especially in the case of terminal illnesses.

Examining Assumptions

We would be wise to look at some of our own assumptions to see if they are warranted or unwarranted. After we have given them voice, we need to think about them in a critical way. Where do they come from? Do they correspond to known facts? Do we have enough facts to understand the problem clearly? Should we find more factual information to support our assumption? Does our assumption need to be discarded or altered? Look at the following list to see if any of these assumptions are familiar:

1. All students should hold a part-time job while going to college because it teaches them the work ethic.

2. A car is essential to help build self-esteem as well as for transportation.

3. Natural rain forests should be preserved at all costs.

4. Smoking should be banned in all public buildings because of secondhand smoke.

5. Everyone should keep a diary or journal to make a record of his or her life.

6. Rest homes are the worst places an old person can be put.

7. Physical attraction is the most important factor in choosing a partner.

8. This country is going to the dogs.

9. Television is a total waste of time.

10. Government intervention is always wrong.

Suggestions for Discussion: Assumptions

1. Find a recent newspaper or magazine advertisement and analyze the hidden assumptions the ad writer expects the reader to make. Also, find faulty hidden assumptions that the advertiser attempts to gloss over.

2. Find a strong letter to the editor. List and discuss the warranted and unwarranted assumptions the author of the letter makes.

3. Discuss assumptions made in daily interaction with people. How may those assumptions be valid? How may they be unwarranted or even dangerous?

Indirect Assumptions

A third way assumptions can be used is a statement which is not literal. Nonliteral assumptions are sometimes called figurative language. As noted on page 8, figurative language (sometimes called figures of speech) is part of creative thinking. It is found in metaphors, similes, personifications, and similar nonliteral language. An example of figurative language is a comparison (simile), such as "he looked like a thundercloud." Using critical thinking skills with figurative language means that the reader must interpret what is meant by the simile. A person obviously is not made of the same material as a cloud, nor is he floating in the air. He cannot possible actually *be* a cloud. Therefore, some aspect of the man must reflect qualities of a thundercloud, such as a dark or angry countenance.

Assumptions used in figurative language are to a certain extent hidden or implicit in that they are not directly given. However, they cannot be taken as explicit descriptions because of their comparative nature. Figurative language will be discussed at more length in Chapter 5.

Analyzing and Evaluating Claims

Critical thinking is also brought into play when we not only find the stated and unstated assumptions, but also analyze and evaluate the claim (or conclusion) drawn from those assumptions. Once a person makes a stated assumption, or an assertion, he or she wishes it to be accepted as valid. That assertion must then be supported by evidence, becoming, as Stephen Toulmin calls it, a *claim*—the conclusion the speaker is trying to prove. Reasoning powers are tested as we support the claims we make because we must determine the logic and evaluate the facts which support the claim to make sure those arguments are not false. Critical thinking involves a careful evaluation of the claims we hear and the claims we are making. Further discussion of the Toulmin method will be found in Chapter 4. At this point, however, note that an important way to approach the evaluation of claims is to turn to logic and reasoning.

Critical thinking encompasses an understanding of logic, its reasoning patterns and pitfalls. A discussion of logic often begins with patterns of reasoning. More extensive discussions of logic and its pitfalls, such as logical fallacies, will also be discussed in Chapter 4.

Patterns of Reasoning

Two general patterns of reasoning come into play in supporting a claim: inductive and deductive reasoning. Both deduction and induction are methods to gather facts and inferences to reach a preliminary inference which then moves to become an assumption—a valid, warranted assumption.

Inductive Reasoning

Generally speaking, induction is the process of reaching a general conclusion on the basis of adequate evidence, in the sense of numbers or quality. Researchers examine specific information or experiences to try to find a pattern in them. In the process of living, we constantly gather facts from our environment, then form them into reasonable conclusions, such as when we learn various traffic laws. When we see these laws violated with the sometimes disastrous consequences, we make conclusions about the importance and need for such laws to protect all of the drivers on the road.

Inductive reasoning leads to probabilities, not certainties, until finally the findings are verified. Inductive reasoning is particularly important in scientific research or statistical reports because scientists' conclusions are usually assumptions based on specific experiments or statistical patterns. Inductive reasoning may deal with *sampling*, *diverse facts*, and the *inductive leap*.

Sampling

Sometimes many pieces of information are used to produce a conclusion. Thousands of experiments may be needed to find a pattern. In one kind of induction, however, the pattern (or conclusion) is a generalization about the nature of the whole class or group by using a smaller, representative number or a *sample* of the group. Although the evidence is limited, the limitation is necessary. Examination of the full group may be impossible. For example, a conclusion that all zebras have stripes may come from several experiences (or facts): picture book illustrations, *National Geographic* articles, trips to the zoo, and wildlife documentaries on television. From this information, the assumption is made that all zebras have stripes, in spite of the fact that not all zebras have been seen. However, trying to build a case on one individual sample or two—unless the samples are of certain kinds and qualities—often is flawed because of inadequate testing. Logic flaws of this kind are discussed in Chapter 4.

Diverse Facts

Sometimes the facts are very different, but by using inductive logic to see patterns and similarities, most people can come to a reasonable conclusion. For example, if a woman enters her home and finds the contents of cupboards and drawers scattered on the floor, the television missing, the basement window broken, and the telephone cord cut, she can reasonably assume that her home has been burglarized.

Inductive Leap

An inductive leap is a conclusion drawn from evidence not readily visible, such as past, present (but not obvious), or future events. Concrete, visible facts may be limited to, perhaps, just a sample. However, those facts lead to a belief that inductive conclusions, generalization, or assumptions may be reasonably drawn. An example of an inductive leap is: "All economic indicators show that next fall will bring an increase in interest rates and a decrease in home sales." Since no one knows the future, we must infer that the conclusion was reached by assumptions based on incomplete evidence. However, it may be a warranted assumption based on a careful study of national trends and financial indicators.

Inductive leaps also can be faulty. Sometimes people gather random facts to reach altogether faulty conclusions. Rather than take a logic problem step by step to its conclusion, they make wild guesses about what may happen. Note the following:

Example: Judy was asked to give the commencement address at her graduation. At first she was delighted at the honor, but the more she thought about it, the more nervous she became. She noted that the graduate date was on Friday the 14th—which was only one day off from Friday the 13th—the most unlucky day of the year. On top of that, her hair needed cutting, but if she cut her hair, it would look terrible for the event. The dress she had chosen to wear was the wrong color for the season, and she was afraid her tendency to mix words would become aggravated by her nervousness. As she tried to write the talk, her computer had problems. It kept giving error messages. The printer ribbon ran out just as she was ready to run off a hard copy. She was sure her talk would be a catastrophe. Her inductive leaps had led her to panic. As a matter of fact, everything went very well, despite her fears.

To test the validity of inductive reasoning, ascertain if the facts are: (1) known (not heresay or absent evidence), (2) sufficient (some generalizations require huge samplings and cannot be proven by inductive leaps), and (3) representative (must be typical of the whole class of facts being used).

Samples of Inductive Reasoning

The cartoon on page 24 is an example of inductive reasoning. Remember that the facts (here, diverse facts) must be formed into a pattern to understand the humor of the cartoon. It may help to know that Charles Addams, the cartoonist, specialized in twisted, strange humor. His type of humor was the basis for the old television series "The Addams Family" and a more recent motion picture, *The Addams Family*. The

"Now let's see—one sashweight, one butcher's cleaver, one galvanized-iron tub, fifty feet of half-inch rope, one gunny sack, one electric torch, one pickaxe, one shovel, twenty pounds of quicklime, a box of cigars, and a beach chair."

Drawing by Chas. Addams; © 1940, 1968 The New Yorker Magazine, Inc.

cartoon lists various items that the man is buying at a country store. Find the humor by using inductive reasoning—that is, by looking at these separate facts to find a conclusion. What is the man intending to do with these items? Mild warning: even after the cartoon is figured out, many people do not think it is humorous.

Scientific investigation frequently uses the inductive method of gathering facts to come to a conclusion: an experiment is performed many times before it is verified. Many tests are made on prospective medicines before they are released to the public. Many separate tests or questionnaires are combined to provide a good sampling of a problem in social interaction. Conclusions can be more accurate with such large samplings.

Deductive Reasoning

Deduction is often said to be the opposite of induction, although that is a simplified definition. Deduction is a process of reasoning from a known to an unknown principle, or from a general to a specific statement. It is a process of moving from premises to logical conclusions. While induction goes from a series of facts to a general conclusion, deduction often begins with two or more existing facts or assumptions, puts them together, and produces a conclusion (which is either an assumption or an inference). For example, the person at the front door who is being overly friendly is carrying a case. Since it looks like a salesperson's sample case, I'm going to be cautious because I'm probably going to get a sales pitch.

Syllogisms

Syllogisms are the classical form of structure used in deduction. One example of deductive reasoning about this scenario, put in syllogistic form, would look like the following:

Salespersons carry sample cases. (major premise)
This person is carrying a sample case. (minor premise)
This person is a salesperson. (conclusion)

Other syllogisms made out of this example could include the friendliness and the possibility of hearing a sales pitch.

Valid syllogisms contain two premises which follow the rules, leading to a conclusion. They begin with an assumption or a generalization (the major premise) and then link related or supporting statements (the minor premise) to come to a conclusion. Syllogisms can be structured to be either valid or invalid. Although the following discussion of syllogisms is in no way definitive or all-encompassing, it gives a brief introduction to the form.

Four patterns for valid or invalid syllogisms are simply demonstrated by the X, Y, and Z symbols, where each letter represents a class of things. For example, X could be the item investigated, such as dog; Y could be a descriptive characteristic, such as warm-blooded animals; and Z could be the specific term, such as mammals.

Valid Syllogism #1.   When the major and minor premises are both true, the conclusion is true.

>All Xs are Ys. (major premise)
>All Ys are Zs. (minor premise)
>Therefore, all Xs are Zs. (conclusion)

Or put the example in this form:

>All dogs are warm-blooded animals.
>All warm-blooded animals are mammals.
>Therefore, all dogs are mammals.

Another example of this type of syllogism is as follows:

>Intelligent students do well in Math 500. (major premise)
>Suzanne is an intelligent student. (minor premise)
>Therefore, Suzanne does well in Math 500. (conclusion)

A common assumption in shopping is that if something fits, people should buy it. Sales personnel play upon that assumption to promote sales. The syllogism may go as follows:

>Customers should buy clothing that fits properly.
>This suit fits.
>Therefore, the customer should buy this suit.

Valid Syllogism #2.   The minor premise and the conclusion can be manipulated (no Zs are Ys in the minor premise; no Zs are Xs in the conclusion) in this syllogism and still maintain the syllogism's validity.

>All Xs are Ys.
>No Ys are Zs.
>Therefore, no Xs are Zs.

This type of syllogism can be demonstrated in the following example:

>All sheep are mammals.
>No mammals are reptiles.
>Therefore, no sheep are reptiles.

Even when manipulated, this syllogism remains valid:

Minor premise changed.   All sheep are mammals.
No reptiles are mammals.
Therefore, no sheep are reptiles.

Conclusion changed.   All sheep are mammals.
No mammals are reptiles.
Therefore, no reptiles are sheep.

Invalid Syllogism #1. This syllogism is invalid because the manipulation in the all–all pattern mixes classes improperly:

> All Xs are Ys.
> All Zs are Ys.
> Therefore, all Xs are Zs.

The difficulty in this syllogism is demonstrated by the following example:

> All refrigerators are appliances.
> All toasters are appliances.
> Therefore, all refrigerators are toasters. (invalid)

Invalid Syllogism #2. A final syllogistic pattern that is invalid also contains manipulation and mixing of classes in the no–no category:

> All Xs are Ys.
> No Zs are Xs.
> Therefore, no Ys are Zs.

The invalidity of this form can be shown simply in the following syllogism:

> All hammers are tools.
> No shovels are hammers.
> Therefore, no tools are shovels. (invalid)

Many problems can mar the validity of a syllogism and, unfortunately, the validity of a syllogism does not necessarily imply truth, merely that the conclusion follows the premise logically.

But validity can be tested. A syllogism is considered reliable if (1) the premises are true, (2) the language (or terminology) is clear, and (3) the form is accurate.

Using Deduction

Deduction is useful when the audience agrees with the major premise. If the audience can be convinced to accept the minor premise, it is likely to agree with the conclusion. Deductive reasoning begins with a known fact as the major premise; thus, much scientific investigation also used this kind of reasoning. Finding the facts to fit the minor premise so the argument will be valid is now the challenge.

Student Exercises: Syllogisms

Put each of the following sentences into one of the above syllogistic forms to see if it is valid or invalid:

1. All primitive people are as innocent as children. Therefore, children are primitive people.

2. All criminals have mothers, but no criminal is honest. Therefore, mothers must not teach honesty.

3. All chairs are to be used for sitting, and all sofas are for the same purpose. Therefore, chairs are sofas.

4. Every human being is a mammal. Mammals are warm blooded, so humans must be warm blooded.

5. He is a skeptic. But no skeptic is a friend of mine. He must not be my friend.

Samples of Deductive Reasoning

Examples of deductive reasoning and syllogisms can be found in many of the selections in this reader. However, three short examples are as follows:

Example A

... I would agree with St. Augustine that "an unjust law is no law at all." ... How does one determine whether a law is just or unjust? ... An unjust law is a code that is out of harmony with the moral law. To put it in the terms of St. Thomas Aquinas: An unjust law is a human law that is not rooted in eternal law and natural law. Any law that uplifts human personality is just. Any law that degrades human personality is unjust. All segregation statutes are unjust because segregation distorts the soul and damages the personality. It gives the segregator a false sense of superiority and the segregated a false sense of inferiority. Segregation, to use the terminology of the Jewish philosopher Martin Buber, substitutes an "I-it" relationship for an "I-thou" relationship and ends up relegating persons to the status of things. Hence segregation is not only politically, economically, and sociologically unsound, it is morally wrong and sinful. Paul Tillich has said that sin is separation. Is not segregation an existential expression of man's tragic separation, his awful estrangement, his terrible sinfulness? Thus it is that I can urge men to obey the 1954 decision of the Supreme Court, for it is morally right, and I can urge them to disobey segregation ordinances, for they are morally wrong.

from Martin Luther King, Jr., *"Letter from Birmingham Jail,"* 1963

Example B

"At least it cannot be your health," said he, as his keen eyes darted over her; "so ardent a bicyclist must be full of energy."

She glanced down in surprise at her own feet, and I observed the slight roughening of the side of the sole caused by the friction of the edge of the pedal.

"Yes, I bicycle a good deal, Mr. Holmes. . . ."

My friend took the lady's ungloved hand and examined it with as close an attention and as little sentiment as a scientist would show to a specimen.

"You will excuse me, I am sure. It is my business," said he, as he dropped it. "I nearly fell into the error of supposing you were typewriting. Of course, it is obvious that it is music. You observe the spatulate finger-ends, Watson, which is common to both professions? There is a spirituality about the face, however"—she gently turned it toward the light—"which the typewriter does not generate. This lady is a musician."

"Yes, Mr. Holmes, I teach music."

"In the country, I presume, from your complexion."

"Yes, sir, near Farnham, on the borders of Surrey."

from Arthur Conan Doyle's The Return of Sherlock Holmes

Example C

"Why, Huck, doan' de French people talk de same way we does?"

"No, Jim; you couldn't understand a word they said—not a single word."

"Well, now, I be ding-busted! How do dat come?"

"I don't know; but it's so. I got some of their jabber out of a book. S'pose a man was to come to you and say Polly-voo-franzy—what would you think?"

"I wouldn't think nuffin; I'd take en bust him over de head—dat is, if he warn't white. I wouldn't 'low no nigger to call me dat."

"Shucks, it ain't calling you anything. It's only saying, do you know how to talk French?"

"Well den, why couldn't he say it?"

"Why, he is a-saying it. That's a Frenchman's way of saying it."

"Well, it's a blame ridiklous way, en I doan' want to hear no mo' 'about it. Dey ain' no sense in it."

"Looky here, Jim; does a cat talk like we do?"

"No, a cat don't."

"Well, does a cow?"

"No, a cow don't nuther."

"Does a cat talk like a cow, or a cow talk like a cat?"

"No, dey don't."

"It's natural and right for 'em to talk different from each other, ain't it?"

"Course."

"And ain't it natural and right for a cat and cow to talk different from us?"

"Why, mos' sholy it is."

"Well, then, why ain't it natural and right for a Frenchman to talk different from us? You answer me that."

from Mark Twain's Huckleberry Finn

Suggestions for Discussion: Samples of Deductive Reasoning

1. How does King structure his argument? Can you make a syllogism with his logic?

2. Which of King's statements are facts and which are assumptions?

3. Does King make a valid claim? Why or why not?

4. Are the questions that Holmes asks of the woman inferences, assumptions, or claims?

5. How does Holmes discover the evidence for his conclusion?

6. How does Huck work through the logic with Jim? Can his questions be put into syllogisms?

7. What is the claim Huck makes?

Questions in Inductive and Deductive Reasoning

As we gather support for inductive or deductive arguments, we need to consider questions the audience might ask. If we want to reach our audience, we need to have the answers to questions which may be raised. A child repeatedly asks "Why?" But even as people mature, they want to know why they should accept another person's claim and reasoning. We seriously ask "Why?" and the related questions: "What is it?" or "How does it compare with . . . ?" and "What is it like?" Even harder to answer are the statements, "Prove it!" or "So what!" We need to gather facts and to know the material well enough to support a claim effectively. Claims are an important part of persuasion and argumentation, which will be discussed in Chapter 4. To give an introduction to supporting a claim, however, note the procedure below.

Supporting a Claim

We can begin with a guess (an inference) about an important issue. It becomes an assumption when we become fairly sure that the idea is valid. We come to a conclusion (make a claim) about the idea. Now we must support the idea with evidence. We investigate physical evidence to help prove the claim. We observe all the data available in the natural world, and now we must use the work of others to support the observations. We need other opinions to help with the claim. We must read the material written by experts on the issue, examining the validity of their claims and assumptions. Facts that they have discovered must come to light. But much of the evidence we need is in complex written material. Now, we discover, we will need critical reading skills to find that evidence. Chapter 2 will help clarify some of the principles of critical reading that are needed in the investigation.

Example: *After eating out at a local restaurant, John became deathly sick to his stomach. In looking back at what he had eaten, he guessed (inference) that the offending food was the large plate of oysters on the half-shell that he had eaten. He decided (assumption) that the oysters may have come from contaminated oyster beds. He felt so sure of his conclusions (claim) that he called the restaurant to complain. The restaurant personnel challenged his claim. They only used the best, they said. John went to the local library and to the local health department for evidence (documentation). He also found out who supplied the restaurant with oysters to see if he could find out where they got the oysters. In his investigation, he discovered that the supply company had been under suspicion by the Food & Drug Administration of getting oysters from off-limits areas. Since John's friend owned a boat, they took a ride to the general area of the oyster beds and noticed for themselves some indication of raw sewage coming into the area (physical evidence). When others in the community heard that John was investigating the problem, several people telephoned John to tell him of similar experiences with the oysters (witnesses). John then went to the newspapers with this findings (conclusion). Shortly thereafter, the people at the restaurant called John with apologies. Because of his efforts, they had changed suppliers. They were also willing to recompense him for his time and problems.*

Critical Thinking at the Center of Communication

Critical thinking does not stop with just an analysis of facts, inferences, assumptions, and logic. As we work though problems in communication in every sense, we must go back to the assumptions made about the world. In reading, writing, speaking, and listening, we begin to see and ask questions about the facts and assumptions we encounter. Our success in analyzing and proving claims will depend on thinking through the problems and making accurate and supportable claims. More advanced critical thinking skills such as preparing arguments and analyzing figurative language will be covered in later chapters.

Suggestions for Discussion: Critical Thinking

1. What is the difference between inferences and assumptions? In what areas are they similar, or overlapping?

2. Are facts always reliable? When could they be unreliable?

3. How do inferences and assumptions lead to a claim?

4. How are inferences and assumptions used in inductive reasoning?

5. How are inferences and assumptions used in deductive reasoning?

6. Why is it important to prove the validity of a claim?

7. Why does investigating inferences, assumptions, claims, and reasoning help you think more critically?

Introduction to Critical Reading

Good reading skills stem from an understanding of critical thinking. Like thinking, reading is something most people have done for a long time. Although nonreaders can and do get along in today's world, much of their progress toward more advanced learning or higher-level jobs is curtailed. For most people, reading is such a natural part of life that it is not a topic of conscious analysis. It is something they simply do when the need arises.

But like critical thinking, *critical reading* in college courses and work situations has dimensions beyond perfunctory levels. College students do not read the same things or in the same way they did a few years earlier. In college they notice that the subject matter and style of presentation are more complex than that which they have previously encountered. Students may need help to build those skills for the rest of their college career and beyond. Where should they begin? Try thinking of reading as a continuum. With the assistance of newly acquired critical thinking skills, students can begin with prereading (or preparation to read critically) by analyzing audience and purpose and by previewing. Then they can begin to work on the critical reading skills.

Prereading: The First Task

Prereading may seem to be a strange idea. Does that just mean picking a book off the shelf and opening its front cover? We do those things, of course. But when we are going to do more complex reading, some preparatory activities will help us focus and clarify our reading. Prereading activities will help us to understand the task of critical reading more easily. We can formulate warranted assumptions early in the task rather than making unwarranted assumptions about what we are to read.

We use critical thinking skills to make assumptions about or to define the audience and the purpose in two senses. First, we need to define our position as audience and our purpose in reading. Second, we need to define the audience and purpose of the author we will be reading. Prereading also includes previewing the material for greater comprehension.

Analysis of Audience for All Communication Skills

The introduction to *The Critical Eye* discusses the interrelationship between communication skills, as well as reading. Analysis of audience accompanies all of the communication skills.

Listening.   Have you ever listened to something intended for other ears? Even unintentionally? Being the wrong audience can make us feel very uncomfortable. When we plan to attend a lecture, a program, or a theatrical performance, we usually find out if it is something we are interested in hearing before we ever buy the tickets. As an audience, we have been aware of what we wanted to listen to.

Speaking.   When we speak, someone else becomes the audience. In speaking to different audiences, we usually plan our speech. What tone of voice or language should we use as we speak to someone important—an employer, the mayor of the city, a senator, or even the president of the country? Is it the same as we used to the dimwit who nearly hit our car this morning on the way to school? How do we address a crying child, someone just learning English, or a mugger? In listening and speaking, we either choose our audience or become the audience, choosing (if possible) what we hear.

Reading.   Reading also varies with the audience. We read a newspaper or magazine in a different way than we read a textbook. Likewise, the authors of those materials plan carefully to suit a certain type of audience. Often much money is spent on audience analysis so that a magazine or book can perfectly suit its intended audience—whether that audience is of a certain age, economic status, gender, political persuasion, interest focus, cultural expectations, or attitude. Different audiences demand different language. Either the writer of that material is determining what should be set in print to suit the audience or we as an audience are determining what we will read.

Writing.   Not only has what we read been prepared for a specific reading audience, but also what we write should be suited to a particular audience. When we write to a specific person, we usually consider carefully what we should say, if we want that person to respond positively.

Example: Ralph shops in a local bookstore for a magazine to help him choose the proper plants for his garden. He finds one with beautifully illustrated photographs of many kinds of flowers. After purchasing the magazine, however, he discovers that the flowers in the illustrations are more suited to a warm, moist climate. Ralph lives in a high desert region. The magazine is geared to a different audience, so he can only look at the pictures and dream—or take the magazine back for a refund.

A Careful Look at Audience

It is important to take a careful look at audience before we attempt formal communication: a written work, a speech, study of a text. Up to this point, we have had many audiences to consider in our speaking and listening skills—parents, siblings, friends, teachers, storekeepers, neighbors, public officials. We probably have spoken to or listened to a wide assortment of people. In reading, we probably read texts and novels which were suited to our age and development (depending on the kind of reader we were—a reader with a wide interest range becomes a member of several audiences).

Different Audience Types

- Children (subdivided by age and skills)
- Second-language individuals (information clear and basic with special attention to idioms)
- Technical specialists (specific materials needed)
- Individuals in positions of authority (knowledge of titles or customs needed)
- Disabled individuals (awareness of special needs)
- Special-interest groups or individuals (concern for specific topics important to these groups)
- Emotionally involved individuals (care of presentation to address the problems)
- Audience desiring specific information (awareness of the requirements of audience)

Defining the Self as the Reading Audience

Specifically focusing on reading, we must first look at ourselves as the audience for what we read. Before we begin to read, we usually make preliminary assumptions: Do we really want to read this book or article? Who is the information written for? Is it a story for children or is it a complex piece of information we do not understand? If we wish to read an article written for a highly technical audience (such as marine biologists), we need to consider our background. Do we know everything we need to know to understand the rostral and neurointermediate lobes of skates and rays? If we do not understand a particular article, we may wish to find one more suited to us as an audience. Or if we are determined to read that article or book, we can use a dictionary or reference books to learn about the subject so we can more nearly match the intended audience.

What do we know about ourselves as readers? Do we read slowly and carefully? Do we like the challenge of difficult ideas? Do we just want to get through the material as quickly as possible? How is our comprehension? Do we understand and remember what we have read? In the following cartoon, Calvin thinks he has solved his reading problem, but we smile at Hobbes' wry comment at the conclusion.

Calvin and Hobbes
by Bill Watterson

from Calvin and Hobbes. Copyright © 1986, 1987 Universal Press Syndicate. Reprinted with permission. All rights reserved.

Patterns.   What are our reading habits? What are we as readers? Some communities and social classes, for example, give credence to narrative and anecdotal information; others might expect expository logical analysis. Do we want a good story or an interesting tidbit, or do we want a serious analysis of material?

Background.   Once we identify our patterns and desires, we have begun the process of defining audience. Next, we must take an honest view of our background and level of understanding. What have we been successful at reading in the past? What level of material can we handle? We need to know what kinds of reading materials would help us the most. To have a successful reading experience, we want to stay interested in the material and to gain the most from the pages we read. Often we can choose materials that are at a comfortable level. But we don't always have a choice. We often are given materials to read with no regard of our background and reading level. If we don't understand an assigned reading, we also may have trouble remembering what we read. Critical reading skills must be developed to help these two problems: understanding and remembering.

Understanding.   Experience with and extensive study of information are the most fruitful ways to increase understanding. Looking up words in a dictionary or subjects in an encyclopedia, talking with knowledgeable people about the information, and investigating the physical aspects (if possible) of a topic can help. (But for initial understanding, note the suggestions later in this chapter.)

Remembering.   If we must remember what we have read, we need to determine ways to help our memory. Suggestions on purpose and previewing which follow will help in these problems, as well as other suggestions given later such as note taking, maps, captures, or summaries.

Here are a few questions to think about as we begin analyzing audience:

1. Why do we need to consider an audience when we read?

2. What are we like as an audience; that is, what kind of reading do we enjoy?

3. How are education and experience different when considering an audience? For example, what special training or experience have we had to suit us for a variety of reading tasks?

4. What is our attitude when we read something not appropriate to us as an audience—something too simple, too complex, too biased, or too confusing?

5. When would political or religious persuasion, gender, or economic status become an issue in reading?

6. What assumptions is an author making about us as readers?

The Author Determining the Audience

After we have decided what kind of audience we are, we need to look at the author of the work we are about to read. An author uses many elements to define the audience:

attitude toward the message, level of position, political agenda, social status, prejudices or preferences, education or experience, gender, age, and so on. An article written for a first-grade student will be boring to an adult. But a technical physics article may not be comprehensible to anyone but a person trained in that discipline.

Professional authors carefully examine the audience for which they are writing. They make inferences and assumptions and base their material on their conclusions. By adjusting vocabulary, selection of facts, method of presentation, choice of examples, and many other elements, they try to suit audience desires perfectly.

Below is a series of examples of reading material on the same topic which is adjusted by the author to different audiences.

Readings for Different Audiences

Audience	Adaptation of Material
1. An article on monkeys	
Small children	Picture book, simplified explanation of feeding habits, humorous anecdotes
Higher education	Complex study on habitat, classification of different species, biological studies on similarities to humans
Environmental group	Threat of extinction of certain species, diseases carried by monkeys, the effect of large populations of primates on environmentally threatened areas
Zookeepers	Feeding and care of monkeys, precautions needed for protection of both primates and zoo patrons, costs of purchasing, breeding habits
2. An article on mercy killing	
General public—pro	Needless suffering of the terminally ill, negative aspects of passive euthanasia, high costs of keeping someone alive who has no hope of recovery
General public—con	The value of human life, the danger of the profit motive, the extension of euthanasia to improper uses
Medical personnel	Ethical issues, appropriate medication for euthanasia, the fine line between active and passive euthanasia, the legal implications of euthanasia

3. An article on marriage

Bride and groom	Personality matching, wedding attire, etiquette for weddings, learning to compromise, top honeymoon sites
Businesses	How to plan for peak times, catering for large groups, the shopping strategies of newlyweds, current trends in wedding decor
Sociologists	Declining statistics of marriage success, the changes in family structure, how to minimize the stress of prenuptial planning, the place of the mother-in-law in successful marriages

In commercial products such as popular magazines, professional authors often succeed; however, they do not control who is going to read the magazine. The reader must make the final audience analysis so it will be a match. Students occasionally feel that some textbook authors go far afield in audience match. With a few exceptions (such as required reading) students must now use their critical thinking skills to make inferences and assumptions that will lead to the best reading for them as an audience. Even in required reading, they can analyze the author's perceptions of audience. That analysis may help them to understand the material better.

Inductive and deductive reasoning also can help by showing students how to analyze a variety of types of materials in order to come to a decision on what to read. Or they can compare a current text to texts they previously read so that they can make a decision on the appropriateness of the materials.

Student Exercises: Audience

1. Make a list of your reading tastes and habits. How will this list help you evaluate the type of books you like to read? How will it help you determine the books you need to read for your school or profession?

2. Make a second list of the kind of reader that will succeed in your chosen field of study or your chosen profession. What do you need to do to make up the deficit?

3. Read two contrasting articles on a controversial subject, such as two articles on the environment written for two different audiences. Compare the differences in tone, language, and approach of the articles.

4. Briefly retell one of the stories or essays in this reader with a different point of view from the one given. Retell it for a different audience. Analyze the difference.

Finding a Purpose

Although audience is extremely important in preparing to read, purpose is equally important. Why did we read the last book or magazine article we read for pleasure, not for an assignment? What drew us to that piece of writing?

We may not think of purpose when we pick up a book or magazine to read. However, the major purposes of communication are to receive and to give information. The authors whose texts we read for classes want to provide us with information that interests them and they think is valuable for others in their disciplines. Others may seek to persuade us to a certain point of view, sometimes without notice of that intention. Certainly, the influence of the written word can be very strong. Books such as *Uncle Tom's Cabin* and *The Origin of Species* changed the world. The "I Have a Dream" speech given by Martin Luther King, Jr., reprinted in Chapter 9 of this text, was one of the most powerful speeches made during the equal rights movement. Other books, such as *Mein Kampf* or the *Communist Manifesto* have led the world in a less positive direction.

Analysis of Purpose

Analysis of purpose, like audience, must be approached from two perspectives: from us as the readers and from the author as writer.

When we pick up something to read, the importance of purpose determines our efforts. Reading merely to fill an assignment lacks the motivation that reading for career advancement provides. Reading for entertainment, on the other hand, provides an entirely different mindset from reading for research or learning.

As students move into their career fields, they may have projects assigned to them. They may need to research these projects and read complex specifications or instructions. Their immediate purpose is to understand—perhaps even for the sake of safety. They will want to complete the project as quickly and as well as possible, if they want to keep the job. They read to learn something vital to their work. That is their primary purpose. If the purpose involves substantial rewards, their efforts will reflect that motive—they will work hard to understand, so they can do the project and do it superbly.

Entertainment as Purpose

Sometimes we may wish to read just for enjoyment. Many people find that reading is a relaxing pastime. Reading can be a great pleasure. Through reading we can be transported to another world where we experience the fantastic, or whisked away to the past or to foreign places to see what we may never see with our own eyes. We learn about values and our cultural heritage through reading. The world opens wide to the reader. If our purposes are to learn and to enjoy, we will be richly rewarded for our efforts. Enjoyment in life comes through many different avenues, but the greatest pleasure in life, for some people, is indeed the enjoyment of books.

Once we are aware of our desires, we can find materials suitable to our tastes. Our purposes may be to laugh, to relax by escaping into light fiction, or to get wry pleasure from political or social satire. Our expectations will probably not be satisfied if we choose a book or magazine with a different purpose from the one we hold.

From the point of view of the author, many works are not written to persuade; they are written to entertain. By using critical thinking skills (inductive or deductive reasoning) to find out the author's purpose as quickly as possible, we can pinpoint the value to us of a particular reading. We then can make assumptions on what we read. The assumptions can also lead to wrong ideas—we may be reading something wrong, taking something seriously that was meant to be humorous. Although some may not laugh at them, both "A Modest Proposal" by Jonathan Swift and "Organ Transplantation: A Modest Proposal" by Warren J. Warwick (contained in Chapter 4) are outrageous humor; yet they are written as if the reader is supposed to take them seriously. They use satire to force the audience to look at problems in a new way.

Looking for Clues to Purpose

As we try to determine an author's purpose, we make inferences and assumptions. Our assumptions may be that the reading material is too complex, too simple, or too out of date. It may contain prejudices or biases that are offensive. It may be written to persuade, but we want something simply to inform. As we read, we should look for stated and hidden assumptions that suggest the purpose the author had in mind. By paying attention to the author's language, handling of the subject, tone, attitude, and style of writing, we get clues to the author's purpose, as well as clues to the author's intended audience. These clues help us to get better acquainted with all authors, and therefore to understand them and to make warranted assumptions about what they are going to say and mean.

Multiple Purposes

An author may have multiple purposes in mind with a particular writing: to establish links with fellow human beings, to entertain, persuade, or assist in making a decision, or to analyze or inform. Monetary needs or career advancement also may motivate reading. People often have more than one purpose in mind. For example, perhaps we read something that interests us but which also will result in a pay raise or a stipend for publication. An author may seek to persuade but also may entertain at the same time. Do not be locked into the idea of a single purpose for every piece of reading, or for every reading task. Multiple purposes can help one start and continue reading with interest and comprehension. For example, Richard Selzer's essay ("The Surgeon as Priest" can be found on page 344 in the text) can have several purposes. It is entertaining because it contains humorous situations and characters. It is instructive: Selzer as a physician gives accurate and detailed information about medical problems and treatments. It persuades the reader to have tolerance and compassion for illness.

Reading with a Purpose

People may be assigned to read certain materials in school or for their employment. For example, they may be asked to learn a computer program or to research a law brief—either in or out of school. In such cases, the purpose and subject of their reading are set. Or they may choose to learn a computer program or research a law brief on their own. They may enjoy browsing through a bookstore or a library to find reading material. Even then, their purpose (recreational reading, finding information on household repairs, etc.) determines their approach and, usually, their subject.

Defining Purpose

As we make note of our purpose in reading, we focus our attention, giving ourselves a direction, and providing a measure for knowing if we have arrived at our destination. Our note may look somewhat like one of the following:

Purpose(s)

1. to fulfill an assignment

2. to learn about the habits of spiders

3. to prepare for an exam on spiders

or

Purpose(s)

1. to relax and enjoy reading

2. to be entertained

3. to see what a favorite author has just written

Revising and Evaluating Purpose

We may revise our purpose or purposes during the reading, but by defining our purposes for reading, our interest, attention, and comprehension are all enhanced. We also know whether we have read with adequate comprehension, or if the author has taken us into an area we did not expect. Defining our purposes requires us to get involved in the reading, to evaluate it as we go along, and to appraise our success at the end of our reading.

Example: Louise needs to find information about growing grapes. She therefore begins to look for information on 1) types of grapes that will grow in her climate, 2) correct placement and support of vines, 3) proper planting methods, 4) proper pruning, and 5) general care of vines. In the library are some fascinating books on the history of grape cultivation. If she decides that her purpose is more historical, she can skip the above information and go directly to sources that will give specific information on the history of grape cultivation. Then, as she evaluates her purpose in research, she can see how she is progressing. Did she get sidetracked on the mythology of Bacchus, god of wine? Did she meet her purposes in reading? Did the authors she read fulfill their purposes in presenting the material? What did she learn from what each author presented?

Once we determine our audience and the purpose in the assignment—whether it is a paper for a college class or a report for our employer—we can begin to move into the material itself.

Student Exercises: Purpose

1. Determine your purpose for reading in the following situations: reading the side of a cereal box as you eat breakfast, reading a magazine at a grocery store as you wait to check out, reading in the library as you prepare to write a report, reading street signs as you travel, reading the set of instructions as you assemble a piece of equipment.

2. Choose one of the essays in this text. Determine the motivation the author had for writing it. What did the author expect the reader to do after reading the essay?

3. Look at a popular magazine. Decide why the publisher included the particular articles and advertisements. Then look at a specific article. Determine the assumptions the author makes to fulfill his or her purpose.

Previewing

After examining audience and purpose, a third prereading activity is previewing. When we preview a motion picture, we take a first look at it. Very often, no one has told us about it. It may be a dud, or it may be terrific—the reviews are not out yet. We watch it and make our judgment.

When we preview our reading, we do the same thing. A preview is a first look. And what do we see first? When we preview a written article or a book, we scan the title, the illustrations or graphic material, and the headings—just to get an overall impression. This preview prepares us to see the big picture and to comprehend the subject being presented, although sometimes we may be surprised. The preview may have given a slightly different impression from what we discover in our actual reading.

The Advantages of Previewing

Previewing is one of the most useful, easy, and time-saving skills, yet it is often overlooked or not done carefully enough. Previewing helps readers get in step with the author even before careful reading is begun; it helps them define their purpose and can get them interested and motivated before drowsiness or inattention sets in. When adequately done, previewing saves a lot of time while it improves comprehension. Such previewing activities can be recorded in a reading journal (more about journals later).

What to Look for in a Preview

We have already done some initial previewing when we have scanned a book or magazine for audience and purpose. We want to know if the article or book is suited to our level of understanding and fulfills our purposes. Then we preview for subject suitability. The sooner we can find the main idea or main topic of the work, the more quickly we can put the parts together to understand what the whole says. When there are no editorial helps such as introductions, summaries, headings, questions, or jacket data, we still can preview effectively. Short stories and essays usually can be previewed successfully by carefully considering the title, then reading the first two or three paragraphs very closely to see what the author is setting up in content, tone, and conflict. It is even all right to read the ending (something unsporting to do with mysteries). Readers will find that they are usually about 75 percent correct in their inferences and assumptions. This type of previewing also helps set purposes for reading because it will show not only the audience and purpose of the reading, but also give an overview of subject matter so that the reader can set her purposes in reading.

Previewing Novels

Novels also can be previewed successfully, but it may take more than the first page or two to do it. The first chapter or two should give a good feeling for the situation, characters, conflicts, and the author's values. Readers of difficult novels often benefit from reading the end of the novel in a preview in order to have a solid idea of what to expect in the book. Those who read light fiction or mystery probably would prefer to leave the end as a surprise.

Previewing Textbooks

Previewing textbooks is the smartest way to study. Textbooks usually are edited to make comprehension as painless and clear as possible.

Steps.   By looking at the chapter title and its relationship to the chapters preceding and following it, readers can get an idea of its place in the scheme of the course. Subtitles and other editorial helps are also useful in helping readers grasp the organization of the chapter. However, we must read with the attitude of being master of the information and organize it according to the main idea, the major supporting ideas, and the details that belong to each major idea. The most important task in previewing a text is to find the major divisions of ideas and recognize how they relate to each other and to the chapter as a whole.

Textbooks are not intended to be read like novels. The support for the main idea usually consists of ideas that are related but do not flow from one idea to the next as events in most novels do. The supporting ideas are separate concepts and must be recognized and dealt with that way. Careful previewing to discover this structure is the key to comprehension, retention, and recall.

Rubric.   Another method of organization is to think about discovering a *rubric*— the part of a document that would be set in red for emphasis. What would the author have done in red lettering? Main ideas, vital information, major divisions are occasionally set in red type. Looking for the rubric (even if it is not in red type) will save time overall. (More about rubrics later.) Previewing with rubrics will improve comprehension by helping the reader understand main ideas before the details are filled in.

Previewing other Writing

Most writing can be previewed by the methods just discussed. Shorter pieces are easily scanned; longer works usually have some kind of structure that can be found and evaluated. If a piece of writing has no headings, no introductory material, or no clear thesis; or if it is not edited, or is poorly done, readers themselves can make the divisions with appropriate headings. (Headings have not been popular until recent decades.) Some less skilled writers or writers with different purposes also may write pages full of material without headings or clear thesis statements. Writing from earlier centuries or from unskilled writers may follow different patterns. Nonetheless, students will be amazed at how well they learn by previewing, even when the work is complex or not well done.

Critical Reading

Now that we have taken a brief look at our prospective reading material, we need to take a serious look at the entire context of the work—not only taste, but swallow and digest the ideas. Some of the problems we will encounter are understanding, interpreting, and remembering what we read.

Understanding and interpreting take time. It would be nice if we had immediate understanding of everything we heard. But we do not always understand at first exposure to an idea. It also takes time to think about what we have learned, to make connections between the new material and the things we already know, to see how knowledge relates and connects. In this time of understanding and interpreting, we start forgetting. Unfortunately, memory does not allow us to remember everything we hear and read. Instead of learning, we constantly lose ideas. In college courses, students usually listen, discuss, and read before they write, although sometimes the time lapse is slight, as in the case of note taking. Note taking helps us record what we hear. But what about reading?

One way to use the interaction of communication, to remember as we understand and interpret, is to keep a journal of the things read. This journal, combined with notes taken in class, will help overcome the memory loss so that we can understand and interpret the things we learn.

Keeping a Reading Journal: Audience and Purpose

A reading journal can contain many things. Audience and purpose of each reading selection can be among the first ideas entered in a journal. Other items—personal impressions in inferences, preliminary assumptions, ideas and later perspectives, summaries, questions, notes, outlines, maps, unfamiliar words, interesting use of language, facts gained by inductive or deductive reasoning, irony or hidden assumptions or messages—also can be kept in a reading journal.

The first entry on audience can determine whether we want to read the selection. It can prepare us for ease or rigor. Or it can send us in search of something different.

For example, Samuel H. Scudder's essay, "Take This Fish and Look at It" on page 244 is written for students, but Lionel Trilling's "Of This Time, Of That Place" on page 255 may be from more of a teacher's perspective. Those who have experienced cultural problems would most fully appreciate some of the selections in Chapter 9, just as a musician might be especially drawn to Chapter 11 or a naturalist to Chapter 12. Yet the audience varies even in these sections. To identify audience we may want to explore some assumptions on the target audience intended by the author of the selection. Then we move on to purpose.

Examples of purpose entries in a reading journal could be in question form as follows:

My Purpose

1. What is the main reason I am reading this selection?

2. What will I gain from careful reading?

3. What facts and assumptions are given that help me respond to this reading?

4. What do I want learn from this selection?

Suggestions for Discussion: Author's Purpose

1. Allan Bloom's essay (page 225): What is Bloom's purpose? Is he trying to persuade? What does he want of his audience?

2. Mencken's essay (page 299): Is Mencken satiric or serious? Is his purpose to make us laugh or to make us change?

3. Forster's essay (page 548): Is Forster's essay simply humorous, or does he have hidden motives?

4. Tillich's essay (page 441): What hidden assumptions are found in this essay? What does Tillich really believe?

5. Hawking's essay (page 601): Where is the deductive logic in this essay?

Students can use the suggestions given earlier to find the purpose and record it in a reading journal. Purpose entries can focus on an author's purpose in writing or on the student's purpose in reading an assignment, or both.

Keeping a Reading Journal: Other Items to Include

After identifying the audience and purpose of a selection, we can record our immediate first impressions. Was the article enjoyable? What was memorable about it?

Another option may be recording our first impression on one side of the page and our later perspectives on the opposite page. Such comparisons give insight into the purpose and skill of the author.

Summaries of the reading also can prove helpful, especially if we must be accountable later for the reading. We can record the rubric we have discovered in our reading. Summaries or outlines become excellent means for review. Questioning our reading is another method for learning. Questions lead to discoveries and insights. Notes, outlines, maps, and other information which can go in a journal also can be extremely helpful. They can dramatically increase retention of the selection. There will be more about these items later. As we prepare to make entries in our reading journal, how do we approach the selection?

Critical reading involves comprehending the whole selection and remembering how the parts fit into the whole. A journal can sort out the parts and the whole. It can record assumptions and inferences, inductive and deductive reasoning for later examination. A journal is the place to begin the combining of communications skills: reading, writing, and thinking.

Example: *Philip purchased a notebook to use as a reading journal for his American Heritage class. As he read the assignments, he made brief summaries of each chapter. On an opposite page to this first set of notes, he added some of his own knowledge, questions, or ideas—as well as insightful comments made by his teacher in class. As he was preparing for his examination, he reread the notebook and then made condensed maps to connect ideas so he could understand the whole picture. To make sure he knew the material thoroughly, he checked on some ideas that seemed incomplete and added those clarifications to his notebook. He went in to his examination with confidence.*

Other skills in helping us read critically are reading rapidly, free writing, and brainstorming. Organizational skills also are important and will be discussed later.

The First Reading of a Text

A first reading of a critical assignment gathers information and ideas. If we have skimmed the material, we probably have some idea now of audience, purpose, and subject. We may have made some notes in our journals. We must now sit down to read the text thoroughly for the first time with our purposes clearly focused. We are looking for an overall understanding of the reading. As we read, we should especially look for facts, assumptions or claims that would give structure. A first thorough reading should be for as complete a comprehension of the text's basic ideas as possible. This first reading does not need to be concerned with hidden assumptions or symbolism. It can be done rather rapidly. It simply puts together substance and structure; it is finding the focus of the work.

Reading Rapidly

The first reading may take the most time, or it may be a rapid skimming. Those who read faster find this process easier. Reading at a reasonable speed increases comprehension and is more enjoyable. Slow readers would benefit from a speed-reading course.

Good previewing is essential to reading more rapidly. If readers have previewed well, they probably will read more rapidly without even being aware of it because they already are somewhat familiar with the material. Readers should pace themselves according to time commitments and reading speed. Pages read while the readers are fresh and alert are much more interesting and comprehensible than those they read after midnight just before the assignment is due and the quiz ready to be taken. If they have ample time, they can draw out the process as long as they want. They may want to read some texts at a more leisurely pace. Some masterworks are more fully appreciated with time to savor and reread, but students may not have the luxury of leisurely reading. They may be on tight schedules and have large quantities to read. Therefore this first reading must go as rapidly as possible. Once readers have read the material through, they can move on to other activities that help them understand what they have read.

Student Exercises: Previewing, Journal Keeping, and Rapid Reading

1. Look over one of the selections in the latter half of this text. Get a first impression of audience, purpose, subject, and focus. Write down those first impressions, then carefully read the selection. See if your preview impressions were correct.

2. Try previewing a chapter of a textbook for another class. Does it help you understand the material better?

3. Use a reading journal for your next reading assignment. Compare the understanding and interpretation of the reading with other members of the class to see if the journal helped.

4. Experiment with items you can put in a reading journal. See what kinds of information are most helpful to your understanding, interpretation, and memory.

5. Work with your reading speed on an assignment. Try rapid reading. See if it helps to follow the process suggested.

6. Have your reading speed tested. Could you benefit from a speed-reading course? Discuss it with your instructor.

Free Writing

Free writing is a useful tool to help sort out personal impressions and preliminary ideas about a selection. It involves another of the communication skills mentioned in the introduction, writing.

The process of free writing is, in essence, writing with no preconceived direction or structure in mind. Free writing is an ideal activity for a journal. It helps readers see what they remember from a preview and rapid reading experiences.

Free writing develops from the association of ideas. Usually we free write using isolated words or sentences in an unstructured manner (some call it stream-of-consciousness), noting ideas just as they come, although some free writing comes in full sentences and complete thoughts. When we are writing about a selection or one particular idea, it is a more focused free writing than just writing about anything that comes into our minds.

The following student samples appear just as the students wrote them. As a more focused free writing, it was done after the students read two selections: Scudder's "Take This Fish and Look at It," (page 244) and "Sex Education" by Dorothy Canfield (page 282). Notice that the first student just uses words and phrases as she thinks about the article. The second student gives personal views in more complete thoughts, in full sentence structure. He also tries to find significance in the story and in the structure.

Student Sample #1

With Dr. Agasee? sp. Looking at fish. Hemalon? sp. Look. Look. Examine with fingers. Teeth. Scales. Sloppy fish in jar of alcohol. Don't allow to dry out. Look. Draw. Exam without being able to look at fish again. Walked by river. A little humor. Key: symmetrical sides with paired organs. More looking—for three days more. The best lesson ever had on observation. Drawing fish on blackboard for fun—hemalons.

Nadia Ramirez

Student Sample #2

When I think of sex education the first thing that comes to my mind is teaching teenagers and children about things they should know and what they should do in certain cases. To me, there is nothing wrong with talking about sex. The one thing we must remember though is how we do it. It is a delicate situation at least I think so because it's one in which most parents avoid and dread talking to their children about. The story was really good but I couldn't understand why Aunt Minnie would keep on changing her story. I think though that it was for effect with each individual group. After all, the first time she told her story was to teenagers when she herself was only thirty. The second time was with women who had teenagers themselves although she was fifty-five and hers were all grown up. The third time was with the one woman who had already heard it two times. Aunt Minnie was in her eighties then. It's also coincidental that as each time she tells the story the season has changed or that is how she feels it to be. The first time was during the summer of her life, then in the fall of her life (when she was aging and changing her lifestyle after her husband died) and finally during the winter when her life was almost at an end. The way she taught each group was significant too. With the teenagers she told them to avoid boys and men and always beware of their every action. With the women who had teenagers she told them to teach their daughters about common sense, knowing what to do and when to do it in case you get lost (as she said) which means having had sex. The third time she wasn't really aware of what was going on. After all, she had gone through her life and helped her kids, especially Jake concerning his problems with women. She had felt she did her job and was glad it to be almost over for her.

Steven Bigney

Focused free writing is not only useful the first time we read a text, it can be helpful at any time to broaden perspectives or revitalize interest in the subject or to look at other avenues which may need to be explored.

How to Begin Free Writing

One useful way to begin focused free writing is to follow these steps: (1) make some time available—five, ten minutes, a half hour, but more if a long paper is expected; (2) take a pencil or pen and paper to a quiet room, if possible; (3) start writing rapidly on the essay, story, or poem that has been read, or on a subject for which you want to generate ideas; (4) do not worry about spelling or structure—make lists or mix words, phrases, and sentences; (5) let the mind range freely and write in brief form anything that comes; (6) keep writing until the time is up, but make sure there is a time limit. At the end of the free writing period, there probably will be many words and ideas that will help the free writer understand her perspective on the reading. She will have made many inferences. She also may have discovered hidden assumptions made by the author of the reading, or she will discover her own assumptions. She will find as she winnows out the ideas that interest her the most, that she has made connections and deepened her understanding, almost subconsciously. She also may have generated excitement about her reading.

Brainstorming

Brainstorming is a process similar to free writing (and sometimes used synony-mously with the term free writing) except that it does not have to be a solitary activity. Brainstorming is usually done with two or more people, and it involves speaking and listening (more interaction of the communication skills). Ideas are thrown out to the group, discussed, added to, dismissed, or expanded. Usually someone in the group acts as scribe to capture the direction of the brainstorming session. Brainstorming can be as useful as free writing because of the diverse input from different members of the group, and brainstorming can help students recognize different elements in a piece of writing. A group can profitably brainstorm ideas about something its members have read, to help understand the work better. Casual brainstorming is often done as friends prepare for an exam; they discuss reading and possible exam questions. Setting a definite time and place—with a compatible group—for brainstorming can help, often measurably, in understanding a reading. Notes from free writing or brainstorming sessions can be placed in the reading journal.

Example: *A group of students needed to prepare an oral report on Martin Luther King, Jr.'s speech, "I Have a Dream." They divided into subgroups. The first group discussed with each other the major assumptions in the writing. Others brainstormed the hidden assumptions upon which some of the claims are built. A third group had a brainstorming session about the figurative language in the essay. A final trio discussed the historical background of the essay. Then they brought their ideas all together and prepared the approach that their oral report would take. By brainstorming about the essay, the group shared many fine ideas which enriched their overall comprehension of King's writing. Those ideas were conveyed to the rest of the class in their oral report. The shared ideas were further enriched as the entire class participated in the discussion.*

Student Exercises: Free Writing and Brainstorming

1. Give free writing a chance. Make time to write about a reading assignment. See what happens.

2. Get a group together for brainstorming about a reading assignment. Have a scribe briefly list the ideas you come up with. See if it makes a difference in your understanding—and, maybe, on your test scores.

3. Critique the brainstorming process and results.

   Now is the time to do a second reading of the assignment. This time we read with a pencil or pen in hand. We will need to look in earnest for the main idea—thesis statement—then watch for the structure developed in the reading.

Introduction to Thesis Statement

   Critical reading involves finding structure in a reading assignment so we can fit the parts to the whole. As we read, we need to find the central point of the article or the main idea around which the essay centers if we expect to understand what we are reading. This central point should be the thesis of the essay and usually is a stated or implied assumption formed into a thesis statement or a claim. Sometimes a thesis statement is easy to spot, sitting in the pond of words like a fat frog, at the bottom of the first paragraph. Sometimes a thesis statement hides at the end of the essay and sneaks up, like the frog suddenly swimming out from under the lily pad. But sometimes a thesis statement is not directly stated—it is implied (like a hidden assumption), so it is not truly a thesis statement yet. It is still the main idea behind the selection, so an implied statement is there. It is like hearing the frog croak and the water splash, but never seeing the frog. All the evidence points to the fact that the frog is somewhere in the vicinity, but we simply cannot see it. And if we never see the frog, we may wonder what all the noise is about.

Definition of Thesis Statement

Those who have tried to find an elusive thesis statement probably are wondering what is really meant by the term. By now, there should be an awareness of the problem of definition, but we must address the problem more directly as we struggle to identify thesis statements. What, exactly, is a thesis statement?

It already has been noted that a thesis statement is the main idea of an essay. But perhaps it may be easier to say what a thesis statement is *not* before we can develop the definition of what it is. A thesis statement is not just the general topic of the essay. Statements such as "This poem is abut music," or "This essay is about education" are not thesis statements. They are just general comments on a subject and they could be stuck on any number of poems or essays. They do not say enough. On the other hand, a sentence like "Thirty percent of a family's annual income is spent on clothes" is not a thesis statement. It is a fact. Unless the fact shows an encompassing idea or the approach an author is going to take, it cannot be a thesis statement. Do not confuse general topics or facts with thesis statements.

Topic:	Herbs
Fact:	The herb called comfrey is used to treat a variety of illnesses.
Thesis Statement:	The herb comfrey can be more useful in treating certain illnesses than chemical agents.
Topic:	Clothes
Fact:	Thirty percent of a family's annual income is spent on clothes.
Thesis Statement:	Stylish clothes can increase teenagers' self-esteem
Thesis Statement:	The fire-retarding materials used in children's pajamas can cause irritation leading to cancer.

Hunting for the Thesis Statement

To understand an essay, readers need to hunt for the implied central idea or stated thesis statement. Think of it as looking for the frog. If readers never find it, they probably will be confused about the subject of the essay throughout the reading. They also may find that the essay is difficult to remember because they did not understand it in the first place—they just swam around in words. Details did not fit together because they had nothing to attach them to. They understood words, but lost the overall idea.

A Three-Step Investigation

The best way to find an elusive thesis statement is to follow a three-step investigation: (1) preview the material; (2) look at the first and last paragraphs to see if the thesis statement is in a familiar place; and (3) then ask, "What is the essay about?"

When we preview an essay, as previously suggested, we may find that a key to the thesis comes in the title or in a heading. Following that clue, check the introductory paragraph, again. Often it includes the thesis statement, or at least an indication of the essay's direction. If we cannot find the thesis statement in the first paragraph, we should take a look at the final paragraph. Is the author giving the thesis as a summation? Very often, an indication of the thesis idea is reiterated in the conclusion. Finally, in asking "What is this essay about?" we are preparing ourselves to look for clues found in the essay. We can read through the essay rather rapidly to get the gist of it. This will usually help separate the croak from the splash (to continue the metaphor). A rapid reading also puts main ideas and details into perspective. What overall sense does the reading convey? Look at key words and phrases. They should help point the way. Besides looking at the key words and phrases, noticing what is repeated or contrasted in words, ideas, or events helps identify the emphasis and intent of the writing.

If the essay is clearly written, students should not have too much trouble identifying the main idea, even if the thesis statement is implied. However, if a reader has gone through the three previously listed steps and still is unable to find a thesis statement (or even guess at one), she or he may be able to get some help by visually putting main ideas and supporting ideas and facts on paper in outlines or other forms to see what is happening in the essay.

The Thesis Statement and Comprehension

Why should we go on this frog hunt to find a thesis statement? An essential part of critical reading is comprehension. Until we know the major focus of an essay we cannot understand how its parts fit together or how the author comes to the conclusion he or she does. Critical reading encompasses the whole. Finding the thesis statement is the beginning of full comprehension.

A Thesis Statement Shows Focus and Development

The thesis statement readers find in their reading encompasses the central idea of the essay. If they are finding and writing down an implied thesis statement, they will need to stick as closely to the ideas of the essay as possible. In addition, the thesis points the way the essay will develop or shows how the organization of the essay fits together. It leads to questions the reader wants answered. Because the thesis statement gives only the author's opinion, the statement is open to challenges and questions. In fact, a good thesis statement stimulates interest in discussion. Even if we identify the thesis statement, we may not agree with it. But we cannot argue fairly with something we have inaccurately identified.

Avoiding Bias

Accurate reading also requires that we see things through the author's eyes as clearly as possible. We often have to put aside our own biases, values, and ideas of "this is the way it is" in order to be reasonably objective and fair in grasping the author's thesis. Her view of the world may be quite different from our own, but, to her, it is valid and sensible. A problem many unsophisticated readers have in discovering another's views and values is either rejecting them outright or bending them to fit their own views and values when they differ markedly. In this text, for example, are two different opinions on gun control. Readers usually will favor one or the other, but not both equally.

Reading objectively about the side opposite to the favored point of view is a challenge for readers, but it is the fair way to approach a topic. A point of view may not be changed, but understanding between people is enhanced.

Putting the Thesis Statement in a Reading Journal

The next step is to write the thesis statement in a reading journal. If the statement is clearly stated in the essay, the task is easy. If the statement is implied, the reader will need to formulate one that fits the whole essay. Sometimes the idea wiggles away from a neat thesis statement, and students do not bother to pursue it. They may say, "I don't understand the thesis!" Then they may not try. But the thesis statement must be found if they want to understand what they are reading.

Topic Sentences

Just as the thesis statement puts the entire essay in a nutshell, a topic sentence gives the main idea of each paragraph. By finding the topic sentences as we are reading, we will be able to see the focus of the paragraph. Other material—facts, assumptions, examples, and details—in each paragraph should support the topic sentence. Not all paragraphs have concise topic sentences, just as not all essays have thesis statements. Nonetheless, if we look, knowing that many paragraphs do have them, we may simplify our work in finding the structure and essence of the text we are reading.

Transitions

Another helpful part of finding structure in a text is identifying transitions or transitional expressions. Transitions are the connections between ideas. They can be words such as *and*, *or*, *however*, *additionally*, *also*, or *nonetheless*; or they can be phrases such as *in addition*, *but at the same time*, *in the first place*, *as soon as*, or *on the contrary*. Transitions also can be seen between ideas in repeating nouns or pronouns that relate to the subject or repeated key ideas or words. A discussion of transitions and a list of transitional words and expression and their functions can be found in almost any English handbook.

Transitions show the reader the direction the text is taking; that is, transitions show whether the author is adding examples or ideas or whether the author is contrasting them. Transitions also show the relationship of ideas and help to provide unity to the text. They help the reader follow the author's train of thought or pattern of development. Together with a thesis statement and topic sentence, transitions form guideposts to show the right direction and to remind readers where they are going as they read.

Example of Thesis Statement, Topic Sentences, and Transitions

It may be useful at this point to look at a thesis statement, topic sentences, and transitions in a specific piece of writing. The following essay by Paul Chance was taken from *Psychology Today*, January 1988. Notice the clarity of the thesis statement given in the first paragraph. In addition, a topic sentence begins nearly every paragraph. The paragraphs explain and give examples to support both the thesis statement and each individual topic sentence. Transitions between paragraphs are made with repeated ideas and between sentences with transitional words and expressions. After Chance looks at each possibility given in the various paragraphs, he makes his own conclusion in the last paragraph. The thesis statement, each topic sentence, and his conclusion have been underlined to show the structure.

Apart from the Animals
by Paul Chance

There is one question about human nature that interests all of us. The barber, the baker, the undertaker; the teacher, the preacher, the innkeeper; the worst, the best and all the rest—all of us want an answer. We want to know what it is that separates us from other animals.

No one denies, of course that we humans differ in degree from other animals in a variety of ways. Most of us, for example, are more intelligent than the apes. But intelligence is not a uniquely human characteristic. We want to know what there is about us that we can point to and say, "This is true of us and of no other creature on Earth. This is what sets us apart from the beasts of the field, the slimy things that swim in the seas and the creepy things that hide under rocks."

People have offered answers to the question for at least a couple of thousand years. The ancient Greeks defined us as the reasoning (not to say reasonable) animal. It was the Greeks, after all, not a troop of chimpanzees, who invented logic. This claim to uniqueness satisfied most people until psychologists came into being, about a hundred years ago, and started studying the matter in a systematic way. They soon found that animals can do many of the same things that we take for evidence of reasoning in humans. Chimpanzees, for example, can figure out how to solve a puzzle on their own, seem to do so in much the same way as humans and, like humans, will do it for no other reward than the satisfaction of having done it. Humans may reason better than other creatures, but they don't hold a patent on it.

Some, in searching for the uniquely human, switched their attention from reasoning to creativity. In the 1950s a few troublemakers placed paper and paint before chimpanzees and obtained a collection of scribbles that some art critics admired. But judgments about art are very subjective. One might place some tubes of oil paint on a blank canvas, put the whole works on the fast lane of the Pennsylvania Turnpike and come up with something that an art critic would like. This would do nothing to prove that cars are creative, however, so the scribbles of apes and, more recently, pachyderms, pose little threat to creativity as the defining essence of human nature. However, in the 1960s, psychologists found that porpoises could be trained not only to perform tricks but to invent tricks of their own. The psychologists began by providing fish whenever the porpoises performed a requisite stunt, such as a backflip. Then they began providing food only when the animals did something novel, something they had not been trained to do. The researchers soon had a pair of finned Baryshnikovs, leaping, spinning and cartwheeling their way into the human world of creative endeavor. In the process they killed the idea that creativity was the private property of people.

A lot of folks had high hopes that the distinctly human characteristic would prove to be our ability to make tools. Other animals might use tools, but only humans actually made them. Unfortunately, the perceptive animal behaviorist Jane Goodall saw a wild chimpanzee take a twig, strip it of leaves and use it to retrieve ants from a nest and make a meal of them. We may look down our collective noses at the chimp's taste in uncooked foods, but we cannot deny that the animal modified a natural object to perform a task. And that's toolmaking.

Many scientists, especially linguists, felt that the human gift for language was our crowning glory and our one sure claim to uniqueness. Parrots can talk, of course, but they do not use speech as people do when they produce original combinations of words to express an idea. Language appeared to be the wall the animals couldn't climb when, in the 1950s, psychologists failed miserably in their attempts to teach a chimpanzee to speak. After years of living in a nice, middle-class home, the object of doting parents, the best the ape could muster was a few grunts that some people thought sounded vaguely like words. But a decade later, two psychologists in Nevada began teaching a chimp named Washoe the sign language of the deaf. Not only did Washoe come to understand hundreds of signs, the animal used them in original ways to express new ideas. Since then, other psychologists have taught sign language to other chimps and to a gorilla and an orangutan. The great apes, it turns out, lack the biological equipment to speak but not the brains to use language. Some experts still wonder whether apes really know what they're talking about, but the case for language as the defining characteristic of humankind seems crushed.

After so many setbacks, it was finally proposed that the search for the distinctly human had been conducted on too high a plane entirely. We had failed because we had focused our search in the humanities and fine arts departments when we should have been looking in the prisons. We were, these cynics said, the only animal to rape, murder our own kind and go to war. While it is arguably true that humans rape, murder and make war with greater diligence and efficiency than any other species does, these are not uniquely human acts. Male apes have been seen forcing their gonadal attentions on unwilling females of their kind. Apes have been known to attack and kill members of their own troop, as well as outsiders, sometimes for trivial reasons. And Goodall, that troublesome ethologist, has even observed organized battles between rival troops of chimpanzees that can justly be called wars. So much for the proud title *Homo violentus.*

The failure to find some trait that clearly separates us from other beasts has not diminished our determination to find such a trait, <u>though we seem to have directed the search toward more trivial distinctions.</u> We read, for example, that we humans are the only animal that cries, that blushes, that gambles, and so on. What is most fascinating, though, is not the question of whether some uniquely human feature will ever be identified but the fact that we persist in the search. We seem determined to find some quality we can point to and say, "This is what separates us from the animals. This is what proves that we are, somehow, not really animals at all."

We have overlooked the obvious. The answer to the riddle "What makes humans different from other animals?" lies buried in the question. <u>We are, so far as anyone can tell, the only creature on Earth that tries to prove that it is different from, and preferably superior to, other species.</u> No ape has ever used its new language skills to ask, "How am I different from all other creatures?" No porpoise, so far as we know, has ever interrupted its acrobatic gyrations to ponder whether it is the only species that breathes through the top of its head. Only we humans ask such questions or, for that matter, show any interest in the answers. As unique qualities go, ours leave much to be desired. But when you're looking for unique characteristics, you can't be too choosy.

Now that we have previewed, done a first reading of the text, discovered ideas by free writing or brainstorming, and found the thesis statement, topic sentences, and transitions, we are ready to use critical thinking to find ideas in the reading, extract them, and put them into our own words; that is, we are understanding and interpreting the ideas. If we use the interactive nature of communication, we can write, briefly noting and organizing some of our impressions of what we have read, thus remembering so we can more fully understand and interpret. Readers may want to use their reading journals, if they have not already done so.

Annotating and Note Taking

As already has been suggested in some of the previous examples, one of the best ways to become well acquainted with a piece of writing, to show our reactions to it, and to find the thesis statement and topic sentences and their support is to make notes as we read, either briefly in the margin of the book or article (annotating), or at length on a separate piece of paper (note taking). We should not mark up a library's or friend's book; however, in our own books or in copies of a magazine article we should actively participate in the reading process by making annotations or by taking notes. Note taking and annotating are aids to understanding, interpreting, and remembering the things we read or hear.

Students also often annotate and take notes when they listen to lectures or class discussions as well as when they read. In both cases, they are letting the interactive (or recursive) nature of communication work for them—learning and remembering better by using two or more skills together.

Annotating and note taking are similar in that both comment on reading or listening, but annotations are usually brief observations written in the margins of a book. Each technique is useful, but sometimes it is better to annotate, sometimes to take notes.

When to Annotate or Take Notes

Annotating and note taking are tools that aid the memory; we will remember what we were reading or hearing whenever we use one of those tools. Although students usually annotate as they read and take notes as they listen, either tool can be used at any time. Both annotating and not taking have specific advantages and disadvantages.

Annotating. Annotating can be done quickly. Not only that, annotating becomes a permanent part of the written text. Whenever we pick up that book or that article, the annotation will be there to remind us of specific points we found in the text. These permanent comments are invaluable when we prepare to give a talk, write a paper, or study for an examination on the material. However, annotating also has disadvantages: annotating must be condensed—margins are usually not very large. In addition, annotating is always handwritten. It is therefore somewhat slow and sometimes not very legible. If a person has large handwriting or has much to say, that person is in trouble.

Note Taking. Note taking has the advantage of space. We have room and time to make more extensive comments. It can be done on a typewriter or word processor, so the writing is more complete and legible. If we take notes in a classroom lecture (although we usually handwrite them, they can be done on a laptop computer), we can pick up key points given orally by the professor but not given in a written text (note the information on keeping a journal found earlier in this chapter). We can make visual reminders or outlines of the text or lecture as part of our note taking. Notes can be saved and filed according to subject and project or rearranged and sorted as we prepare for an examination, for writing a speech or essay. However, notes can get separated easily from the original text. Since they do not have the immediacy of annotated text, they can be lost and forgotten, or they can become so lengthy that they are more trouble to go through than to reread the text.

What to Annotate

Perhaps the first thing we should note in a reading assignment is the thesis statement. Underline it in the text and make a marginal note identifying it. We can then identify the supporting ideas or proofs for the main idea or thesis statement. Other items also would be of value: personal reactions to the reading, questions, flaws in the argument, important points to be remembered, notes which may help to build an outline or visual representation of the ideas, or related ideas by other authors. Annotating can be selective or inclusive; that is, we can make annotations only on our reactions, or we can indicate only the thesis statement. Finally, we can note everything which might help us to remember the reading. Another option is to use one margin or side of a note page for summarizing or paraphrasing and the other side for comments. This arrangement helps to keep the author's ideas and the student's reactions to them from getting muddled. Annotations of meaning are like an inventory of the author's ideas and serve well as the raw materials to organize the structure of the reading. Annotations are also the basic materials for an outline.

Reference to annotated texts in the reading journal can help us so we won't forget where to find information.

Some individuals make extensive annotations; others mark very little. Below is an example of a student's annotation on "Sex Education" found on page 282. The student used phrases or complete sentences to indicate ideas in the text. He also used the ideas found through annotation to make a map to prepare his own thesis statement, and then to prepare to write the paper about his reading.

"SEX EDUCATION"

. . . "Now I ask you, if I'd been told how to do that,

wouldn't it have been a lot better protection for me—if

She should have here taught how to escape
protection was what my aunt thought she wanted to give me—than

to scare me so at the idea of being lost that I turned

deaf-dumb-and-blind when I thought I was?

demystification of sex
"And anyhow that patch of corn wasn't as big as she let on.

Isn't the whole of life
And she knew it wasn't. It was no more than a big field in a

farming country. I was a well-grown girl of sixteen, as tall

as I am now. If I couldn't have found the path, I could have

straight & narrow
just walked along one line of cornstalks—straight—and I'd have

instead of panicking — thinking
come out somewhere in ten minutes. Fifteen at the most. Maybe

```
not just where I wanted to go. But all right, safe, where decent

folks were living. . . ."
```

Gregg Ellsworth

What to Note

Readers may write words or sentences to capture the written or spoken information. Even pictures (related or unrelated to the subject at hand) find their way into notes. But what are the best things to put there? First, identify the thesis statement, if possible. Support for the thesis should follow. Copy key quotations intact (making sure it is indicated that they are direct quotes—and where they can be found). In addition, readers may add related ideas or go off on a tangent. The space is not so limited. When listening to speakers, we would make note of those items they write on a chalkboard or show on an overhead. Those are the points the speaker wants to emphasize. Other items we may include in notes are ideas which strike us as particularly appropriate, unusual, memorable, or important.

As we take notes from our reading, we may want to make summaries or paraphrase paragraphs or whole chapters. If we are preparing to use the information later, a summary or paraphrase enables us to review material more quickly.

Although we can make annotations or take notes at any time and with any topic, once we have discovered the thesis statement in the reading, our annotations and notes will take focus. As we read, we look for support for the thesis statement. We also should make notes on points in the reading that we may want to discuss later in writing. Two questions that help identify the development of an essay, story, or poem are: "What is the author doing here?" and "Why is *this* there?" Because we can take time to ponder and review the larger organization of a reading, these questions will help us understand and remember what we have read. When we begin to write about our reading, then we can make annotations on our own work to assist in rewriting.

Student Exercises: Annotating and Note Taking

1. Try annotating the next story, essay, or poem you are assigned to read. See if this experience helps you understand or remember your reading better.

2. Take notes on your reading.

3. Compare the notes you have made on your reading assignment with a group of other students. How are the notes similar? How do they differ?

Finding Structure

Now that we have material to work with, we need to put that information into some kind of a structure. Some of the most useful structures are outlines, maps, and clusters.

Outlining

Outlining is a structured form of organizing ideas and discovering relationships. We can outline the ideas found in an article or book to help us understand and remember what we have read. In addition, sometimes free writing or brainstorming leads to outlining. Outlining makes a start at classifying ideas and putting them in coordinate and subordinate relationships. When we outline, we put ideas in a structure, like the one suggested in the section on previewing. By outlining, the reader can identify major ideas, subtopics, and supporting details, as in the following example:

> Her bags were filled with many new clothes she had purchased for the long journey: a snug white rabbitskin cap and matching muff for winter; a bright pastel skirt with a coordinating vest, pale hose, and some sandals with open toes for spring; a Hawaiian-print swimsuit with a wrap-around sarong skirt she could wear to and from the beach during the summer; and a woolen cardigan and ribbed knee socks with a plaid skirt and sensible shoes for fall.

The major idea of this sentence is clothes. This major topic is subdivided into seasons; then supporting details make the idea of the paragraph more specific. The paragraph could be outlined as follows:

I. clothes

    A. winter
        1. rabbitskin cap
        2. matching muff

    B. spring
        1. bright pastel skirt
        2. coordinating vest
        3. pale hose
        4. sandals with open toes

    C. summer
        1. Hawaiian-print swimsuit
        2. wrap-around sarong skirt

    D. fall
        1. woolen cardigan
        2. ribbed knee socks
        3. plaid skirt
        4. sensible shoes

During a preview, a reader would see immediately that the general idea concerns clothes. When the reader outlines, classifying and categorizing details, he or she perceives the organization of the reading. However, the initial outline may be different from a final outline, depending on further development of the essay or story.

Mapping and Clustering

Similar to outlining, mapping and clustering are techniques to help readers find major ideas and supporting details in the texts they read. However, maps and clusters do not have to follow the outlining structure (Roman numerals, capital letters, Arabic numbers, etc.). Maps and clusters take open structures, often in the form of lists or groupings. Usually a map contains a one-sentence statement of the main idea. Also, a map's groups are categorized with headings and arranged to show the relationships of ideas in hierarchal order, general to specific usually, as well as the connections between ideas. Clusters mainly show the connections between ideas without as much attention to order. Good maps and clusters, however, represent the structure of the writing.

The Advantages of Maps and Clusters

The main advantages of maps and clusters over formal outlines are the rapid visual comprehension and retention for the reader and the flexibility of design. Maps can be made in several useful structures with lists and connections. Clusters are even more flexible: clusters of main ideas with connecting lines or connecting circles to show related ideas, clusters which look like pictures, clusters which have lines and symbols similar to a road map, or clusters which look like some kind of a flow-chart plotting ideas and action. Any creative maps or clusters which immediately show major ideas at a glance fulfill the purpose. Maps and clusters may take a variety of forms, although informal lists and groupings which show relationships are the most common.

Maps and clusters take the major ideas of a reading and put them in a prominent place on the page. Attached to these ideas are the supporting ideas. Subtopics and information which fill in the supporting ideas are placed appropriately in clear and visual form.

The Purpose of Maps and Clusters

The purpose of maps and clusters is to illustrate in graphic form the major ideas of a text. Mapping and clustering are especially helpful to people who learn more quickly through visual clues than by abstract ideas. Mapping and clustering, as methods of illustration, are used to understand the text as the maps and clusters are being made, or to review the text quickly. The following is a student sample of a map. It corresponds to the story, "Sex Education" by Dorothy Canfield, on page 282.

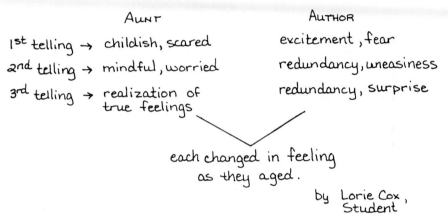

Mapping

(Sex Education)

Aunt Minnie becomes aware of her true feelings about her experience in the corn fields.

CONTRAST OF FEELINGS

AUNT	AUTHOR
1st telling → childish, scared	excitement, fear
2nd telling → mindful, worried	redundancy, uneasiness
3rd telling → realization of true feelings	redundancy, surprise

each changed in feeling as they aged.

by Lorie Cox, Student

A cluster may be shown by the following student example from "Kitsch" by Gilbert Highet found on page 501.

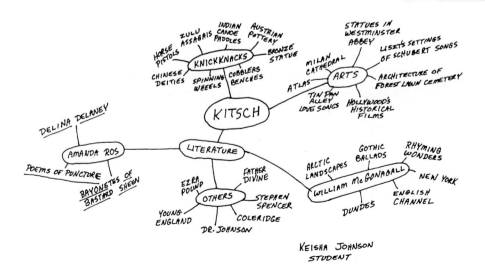

KEISHA JOHNSON
STUDENT

Student Exercises: Outlining and Mapping

1. Using one of the selections in the text, outline an essay, then discuss why you have subdivided it as you have. Has outlining helped you understand the essay? Why or why not?

2. Make a map of one of the selections in the text or use clustering to organize the ideas in one of the essays. How did mapping or clustering affect your perception of the essay?

Capture

Sometimes an even more complete overview of the reading is needed. This overview sometimes is called a "capture." The reader is "capturing" on paper the main ideas of her reading. Captures also are called summaries. However, summaries are a restating of the main ideas of a reading. Summaries follow closely the form and pattern of the original text, condensing the ideas one by one into a shortened version of the whole. The capture can be a bit more creative than a summary since it is giving the reader's impressions rather than adhering only to what is in the text. It also can divide elements of the text into parts.

A capture does not have to be lengthy; in fact, a lengthy capture defeats the purpose. A capture is designed to hit the high points. Writing a capture helps us see if what we are getting is what the author is giving—often with a writing assignment in mind. A capture is, in a way, like the outline or map in that it does not have to be in complete sentences. The reader is setting down the ideas of the reading in whatever form is most useful. Unlike an outline or a map, however, a capture can state ideas more completely and also can be in complete sentences.

The Three Hermits: Capture

Central Message:
In the search for God people often seek after "vain repetitions" (shrines, pride, etc.) and overlook the truth.

Purpose:
To make a statement about seeking God.
—to teach

Validations/Applications
— Pilgrims going to visit shrines
— Crew tries to dissuade
   Bishop from seeking Hermits
— Bishop used to getting his way
— Bishop congratulates self after
   teaching Hermits
— Hermits represent Trinity
— When words not repeated in act
   they're vain—thus forgotten

Values:
1828–1910
Russian
Moral philosopher
Religious conversion
Advocate of nonviolence
Christian

To make a capture, begin with the thesis statement or thesis points the author is making. It also may help to look for topic sentences. Doing a capture can help the reader better understand what she is reading in preparation for her writing task. In the preceding capture, the student finds the thesis statement, which he labels "Central Message," the purpose of the essay, the "Validations or Applications" of the thesis or details (data or backing in Toulmin terms—see Chapter 4 for more information), and the "Values" of the essay.

Searching for Inferences and Assumptions

Once we have used the above techniques to fully understand a reading selection, we can return to the text to further our critical thinking skills. As we read, we have the opportunity to identify and evaluate facts, inferences, and assumptions. By asking ourselves what information is verifiable as factual, what is a guess, and what is assumed, we can sort out stated and unstated assumptions in the text. We can see what the author uses as proof for his or her claim. Then we can evaluate the claim for its validity. Searching for hidden assumptions can be interesting. A reader may begin to see subtexts in her reading—purposes the author seems to have which change her attitude toward the text. She may also agree with hidden assumptions, finding them to be no threat to reading. But we cannot make judgments unless we know what assumptions are there and where they are going. Again, an analysis of audience and purpose will help us understand inferences and assumptions.

Critical Thinking and Critical Reading

Examples of an examination of the facts, inferences, and assumptions of a text could be as follows: Alexander Petrunkevitch, in his essay "The Spider and the Wasp," (page 544) uses careful research to describe natural behavior. He is factual and clear in his presentation. Toward the end of the essay, however, he implies that the spider is stupid. The human perspective does not logically account for the spider's behavior. Since Petrunkevitch cannot get into the mind of the spider, he must make guesses at its behavior. His guesses touch on one of the major questions in natural science: How much of behavior is instinctive and how much is driven by intelligence?

George Gallup, Jr.'s essay, "The Faltering Family," (page 302) shows facts that change and shift. This essay also implies that the traditional family is doomed. He is guessing that elements in society can change nurturing patterns. Some of his ideas move to the area of assumptions. He assumes that statistics follow predictable patterns and that these patterns will result in the conclusion or claims he presents. Some of the hidden assumptions in his essay are that unless traditional patterns remain, society as it now exists will be destroyed.

Richard P. Feynman's essay, "O Americano, Outra Vez!" (page 238) makes assumptions that school systems which stress memorization teach students the wrong way to learn. He uses deductive reasoning to follow the example of faulty thinking in the classroom to a conclusion, with a hidden assumption that the students will not be effective in the workplace because of their learning habits.

Chief Dan George's essay, "My People, the Indians," (page 420) gives deductive structure; whereas, Skolnick's essay, "The Paradox of Perfection," (page 309) and Highet's essay, "Kitsch," (page 501) give inductive structure. By annotating the text of each of these essays and forming an outline or a map of the ideas, the reader can discover the patterns these authors use.

Becoming Aware of Layers of Meaning

Now that we have read the assigned selection twice using all the preliminary help we can get (preview, map, outline, note taking, etc.) we are ready to find some of the things we skipped in the first two readings and to look deeper than surface meaning. What about those words we did not understand but did not take time to look up? Could a mistaken meaning change our perception of the selection? How about some of the subtle inferences or unstated assumptions? Could the author have had some hidden motives or purposes in writing? Could there be symbols in the work? Is the author trying to provoke an emotion in the reader for a different purpose? Are we making the connections the author wants us to make? Do we understand the allusions, the metaphors, or the point of view of the author? The chapters on critical thinking, argument, and figurative language will help sort through some of these questions, but some brief ideas will help us get started.

Helping the Reader Remember

As we think about the selection we have read, we need to consider that most authors give more than a surface meaning to their work. It is not that they want to trip

"My goodness, Harold . . . Now there goes one big mosquito."

from The Far Side Gallery. Copyright © 1980, 1981, 1982, 1983, 1984 by the Chronicle Publishing Company, a division of Universal Press Syndicate. All rights reserved. Reprinted with permission.

up their audience. They want to make the audience remember what they have written. We usually will forget what we read unless it has special significance to us.

That special significance may come through a deeply felt correspondence with the subject. For example, if a person experiences a death in the family, selections on death take on new meaning. But readings can be memorable also if they are enriched with satire, irony, or humor—all of which twist ideas into new shapes. Twisted humor creates such an effect in Richard Armour's poem, and satire is found both in Warren Warwick's and Jonathan Swift's essays—where the ideas are so outrageous that unless the reader recognizes the satirical tone, she is aghast at the suggestions. But she remembers them. Gary Larson's cartoons often carry this same element of twisted humor, as in the one shown on page 64.

Irony is found in "The Three Hermits" when the bishop realizes that he is being taught much more than he teaches.

Unusual approaches to a subject can be found also in student essays. For example, this student picked up and parodied the satire in his paper on Warwick's essay:

The article, "Organ Transplantation: A Modest Proposal," suggests that our society tax its citizens after they die, by retrieving good and usable parts. These good and usable parts would then be transplanted into living human beings. This suggestion is not only reasonable and sound, but it is the best idea since the medical profession began. This will help our society get rid of worthless people, will allow more productive people to live longer, and will open up an entirely new area of medical technology. This new technique can be used not only on unfortunate accident victims, but also on unproductive members of society, such as welfare recipients, aged widows, and many existing government employees. This will "beef up" our remaining citizens and allow our nation to prosper like never before. We could use that extra welfare and Social Security money to pay off the national debt, help freedom fighters in El Salvador, or purchase a million more nuclear bombs—anyway we do it, we come out ahead.

Brian Williams

Like Warwick's and Swift's essays, Brian's essay cannot be read with a surface interpretation. The reader must rethink his suggestions in the light of reason and humanity.

Understanding Words

To fully understand the selections, readers also need to know the denotation—the actual meaning—of some words. Unless they know the actual meaning of words, they will miss knowing the full implications of what they are reading. For example, do all readers know the meaning of the following words or the significance of the following people found in Stephen W. Hawking's "Our Picture of the Universe"?

elliptical

Ptolemy

Copernicus

quantum mechanics

Galileo

Kepler

Kant

antithesis

finite

Newton

Unless readers know what they are reading, they cannot really see what the author has in mind or what he or she is telling them. The article may seem to have no point or is boring to the reader. Not only that, the reader may miss an opportunity to learn and to be excited by new ideas.

Inferences and Unstated Assumptions

Finally, what inferences and unstated or hidden assumptions are found in the reading? What is not being said directly? Much of our perception of life comes indirectly. In our communication with others, we often "read between the lines" of the true message. The same holds true in critical reading. What *is not* stated is sometimes more important than what *is* stated. For example, the message of tolerance and understanding of others is not directly stated, but is an important lesson in several of the selections of the text: "Of This Time, Of That Place" (page 255), "I Stand Here Ironing" (page 328), and "Beauty: When the Other Dancer is the Self" (page 356). As we rethink our reading, we need to look for these hidden messages. Once again, the chapter on critical thinking will help the reader to understand inferences and assumptions.

Conclusion

Although the communication skills interact, the focus in this chapter has been on reading. As we continue our study of reading, writing, and thinking, we will see how much one skill depends on another. Writing depends heavily on good reading skills, and critical thinking is developed from careful reading.

All of the skills discussed in this chapter help the reader perceive and organize what is read. When we record impressions of our reading, we give ourselves a chance to think about and remember the ideas we have found. Use these skills with the selections in this textbook. Most of the essays, stories, and poems contain well-structured ideas and several layers of meaning. We now can find the structure of the readings. The chapter on critical thinking will help the reader to unlock these ideas, and the chapter on writing will help us respond to them.

Introduction to Critical Writing

N ow that we have studied good critical thinking skills and had some experience developing reading skills, we are ready to look at writing skills. Once again the communication skills interact.

When people write, they listen to themselves form ideas, often speaking the ideas silently. Writing is the most complex act of all the communication skills because it uses this interaction. Critical thinking skills, too, must be at their sharpest because writers not only must analyze and evaluate ideas, but also must form, shape, and develop their ideas. The process begins once again with the audience. But audience evaluation takes on a whole new aspect when a writer seeks to appeal to an audience in writing.

Audience

A Writer Looks at Audience

Through the school years, most students have written for two audiences: themselves and their teachers. College brings additional audiences (peers, school newspaper or magazines, wider range of teachers, etc.), and when these same students enter the workplace, their audience becomes even more diverse. To write successfully for different audiences, all writers first must define the audience by making warranted assumptions about it, and then shape the writing to appeal to that audience.

Sensitivity to Audience

Writing for an audience means being sensitive to the audience's needs. If an audience is antagonistic to or unfamiliar with a subject, the writer may have to adjust vocabulary, organization, tone, or style to suit the target audience. Most students have struggled through textbooks that seemed to be more suited to an audience of graduate school professors than to undergraduate students. They know the frustration they felt. Now they must look at their own sensitivity to audience; they should not copy the insensitivity to audiences that they find in some poorly adapted textbooks. Sensitive writers try to communicate, not to impress the audience.

Our goal should be to communicate clearly, not try to overwhelm others with our brilliance. On the other hand, we do not want our audience to be turned off by what it considers to be inadequate writing skills.

What an Audience Expects

Identifying or defining audience is the first step toward preparing to write. We should consider in detail what the audience expects and what we can offer. By using inductive reasoning techniques (looking at individual facts), we can look at the different personality traits and idiosyncrasies of the target audience. Is the audience conservative or flamboyant? Is the audience highly critical? Language and tone should appeal to whichever audience it is. Does the audience already know a great deal about the topic? Then don't bore them with the basics. Is the audience intelligent but uninformed? What knowledge can we assume the audience has? What do we need to explain, carefully using definitions and simplified concepts? Will the audience be antagonistic? Will we need to wear our bullet-proof vest—or at least feel like we should? If so, we certainly should prepare the support with care and anticipate challenges. But avoid stereotyping or making unwarranted assumptions about audience. It is to the writer's advantage to be logical and factual.

Example: *Luis needs to write a letter to apply for an accountant's position at a manufacturing plant. He has heard that the wages and benefits are excellent. The location is also perfect for his situation. Unfortunately, he has heard that he will be competing with many applicants. Although he knows he has excellent qualifications, he has to be very careful in his letter to present himself, so he can be as persuasive as possible. The first thing he needs to know is to whom he is writing. He calls up a friend who works in the plant to find out the name of the personnel director. He also asks her what that person is like. Is the personnel director partial to people with a lot of education, or to people who have had a great deal of experience? What does this person think of minorities? After his friend has told him all she knows, Luis writes the letter, keeping in mind the personnel director's attitudes and preferences.*

The Teacher as Audience

As our own audience, we can write whatever way we want, but as most students have found in the past, the teacher is a very different audience. He or she knows more about many topics than the students do, but they cannot assume the teacher knows exactly what they do or agrees with their conclusions. Additionally, each teacher is a different audience, and some students try to become skilled at writing to suit a particular teacher. But from this time forward, more important than seeing the teacher as an audience, we need to consider who the true audience will be as we write memos, reports, or proposals five or ten years from now. Most people already have noticed different audiences when they speak. They usually have adjusted their communication automatically. However, as we move to more formal communication, we will need to take more time in audience analysis.

Using an Audience Profile Sheet

To reach an audience most effectively, we should know our audience well. Then as we prepare to write, we keep the profile of the audience in front of us.

When we take a stand or make a controversial statement, we use critical thinking skills to make warranted assumptions about how our audience will react. We clarify our inferences and assumptions, trying to base them on as many facts as we know. Wise students make notes. We should make adjustments as we think through possible objections. When we read or listen, we can reject the writer or speaker by putting down the book or leaving the lecture. But when *we* are writing, we may need to modify our approach to the audience by changing our own writing.

To help analyze the audience, both students and professional writers often find the following form useful. It has been used in the classroom and in the workplace to focus a writing task. It also has been used in technical writing to identify audience for technical papers. In fact, it is useful for any audience identification task where an audience profile is desirable.

Audience Profile Worksheet[1]

Intended audience:	Give a general profile, i.e., employees of XYZ company? second-year physics students? third-grade class?
Technical level	
Education:	College degree? Graduate degree? High school diploma? Specialized training?
Experience:	Untrained new employee? A "self-made" person? A new nursing student who has never been in a hospital?
Position	
Job title:	Director of personnel? An immediate supervisor? A psychology teacher?
Organizational relationship:	A subordinate in the work force? A boss? The financial officer who could raise or lower pay? A graduate student who will be giving a grade?
Attitude	
Toward the writer:	Interested in the work? Thinks the writer doesn't know his/her job? Has personality conflicts with the writer? Is a friend?
Toward the subject:	Is bored with the subject? Is neutral—needs to be convinced? Is rushed for time and is not as interested as if he/she had more time to read carefully? Is interested in the subject and has asked to see the paper?

Other factors (if applicable to the task)

General age groups:	Ready to retire—has very set ideas? Six-year-olds? Yuppies? Peers—about the same age?
Political leanings:	Conservative? Liberal?
Economic status:	Blue-collar workers—not enough money is a prime consideration? White-collar workers—not enough time is a prime consideration? Ultra-wealthy—multiple interests?
Sex:	Will this be an issue? Will attitudes and experience within the gender be an issue, e.g., pro-choice versus pro-life?
Religious persuasion:	Orthodox or liberal? Unusual religious beliefs which may impact on the problem?
Other:	Angry about a specific issue? Nationality bias? Any other factors which need to be considered?

[1] Adapted from John S. Harris, *Teaching Technical Writing,* American Teachers of Technical Writing, Potsdam, NY: 1989.

Audience Expectations

We should think about audience expectations when we write. The audience expects:

1. To understand what is written.

2. To be able to follow the author's train of thought or pattern of development.

3. To be given some opinion on the subject and substantial evidence (data) to support that opinion (claim).

4. To see some conclusion from the evidence presented.

We will discuss these expectations at length later. Part of understanding what is written is to know the purpose of writing.

Purpose

Another Look at Purpose

In addition to the problem of audience, we also need to return to the question of purpose. Why are we writing? We may ask ourselves this question many times in the next few years, and our answer will determine what kind of effort we put into the task. Our purpose may be set, but our attitude toward it is entirely in our own hands. If we are writing simply because it is an assignment, we are missing opportunities to fully learn and grow, to have fun, to explore new areas, to challenge ourselves. Attitude is of primary importance.

Example: *Lenore had been working for some time at a newspaper office as one of the sports editors. She loved her job and it showed in her writing. One day Arnold Prescott came into the office and asked for her. He was interested in having a book written about a famous golfer and wanted her to take on the project. He had been so impressed by her writing style that she was the first who had come to his mind when he thought of the project. She was to receive not only a large stipend to get started, she was also to have a substantial share of the royalties. Lenore had known the golfer personally and respected him highly. The topic was one she was excited about. Writing the book was a project she considered to be challenging, exciting, and financially rewarding. Of course, she said, "Yes!"*

On the other hand, work done under duress is always unpleasant. The most delightful writing project can turn sour if we do not think its purpose is valid.

When we write, most of the time we are giving information we want others to receive and understand. If we find that information fascinating, stimulating, exciting, or gripping, we will want our audience to react as we do. But it is not easy to create in them our excitement about this information, so we must give clues to inform the audience of our purpose in our writing. Before we can give clues, we must clearly know for ourselves what the purpose is—from informing the audience of a new procedure or product to instructing the audience on the importance of saving the environment.

The Audience's Purpose in Reading

In addition to our purpose in writing, we must make some careful assumptions about our audience. Why is that audience going to read our work? What must we do to adapt the writing to the audience's needs? Although we need not be intimidated by the audience into changing our own ideas, we need to be sensitive to their purposes. Again, look at the audience profile chart. Judging from who the audience will be, we need to make inferences as to why they will be reading our writing. We must also judge if they, or if we, have more than one motive or purpose.

Multiple Purposes

Multiple purposes are common. One such purpose may be simply to establish links with fellow human beings. Other purposes may be to entertain, to persuade, to assist in making a decision, to analyze, or to become informed. Monetary needs or career advancement also may motivate writing tasks. People often have more than one purpose in mind. Perhaps we are writing something that interests us and we feel will interest others, but which also will result in a pay raise, a stipend for publication, or a grade in class. Look at multiple purposes from the audience's point of view. Is the audience judging the subject of the writing, but judging the writer as well? Is the audience trying to decide whether to use the writer's suggestions, or whether the writer should be promoted, reassigned, or fired?

Writing for Satisfaction

Writing does not just have the purpose of furthering progress at school or in a career. Other important purposes of writing are to clarify thinking, to enrich self-expression, and to find personal satisfaction in writing skills. Once a writer has her ideas on paper, she can support, modify, or dismiss a particular view. Writing is a way of learning and knowing—worthwhile to do in any subject whether the writer hands it in for a grade or not. Writers also may honestly enjoy seeing their ideas on paper, especially if they have written well. As we practice writing, we can find a sense of accomplishment in seeing our skills grow stronger.

Look at the assumptions about purpose. Does the writer or do we have hidden assumptions? Think about them and write them down. In formal communication, we need to identify clearly a major purpose and additional purposes, both for ourselves and for the audience.

Finding Evidence and a Point of View

The audience also wants to know what subject the writer is talking about, how she came to her conclusion, and what her opinion is about the subject. Going back to the list of Audience Expectations on page 70, we see that item three suggests that an audience needs something solid to understand. The audience doesn't want to flounder in a pool of words, wondering whether the writer will throw out a lifeline. Once we have indicated a subject, we need to support our ideas with facts, details, or examples (data) so that the audience will gain a firm understanding of the subject.

As we write, we should think of ourselves as the reader of our own work. What would we want to know? The subject can be either in the title or in the first few sentences. The thesis statement indicates our approach to the subject, the information fills the body of the work (clearly structured with topic sentences in each paragraph), and the tone and language indicate our opinion. When *we* read nonfiction (informational material as opposed to fiction), we want to know the author's main point right away. Our audience asks no less of us.

Finally, our audience expects us to bring our facts and assumptions to a conclusion or some kind of a closure (item four on the Audience Expectations list). Sometimes the facts we have found are inconclusive. Nonetheless, the audience does not want to be left without a feeling of resolution, even if that resolution is only a call to find a solution. When we read, we know when the article ends and we usually know what point the author has been trying to make. We should give our audience the same courtesy.

Finding and Focusing a Writing Topic

Just as an audience and purpose may be given to writers, they also may have a topic given to them, both in school and in the workplace. However, they also may have to find their own topic in either place.

If a teacher or an employer gives a subject (or topic) to write about, we have had part of our problem solved. However, we still will need to narrow the topic, research it, find the central focus and thesis statement, organize, write, and rewrite. This statement is not meant to scare writers with all the things they need to do, but it is important to appreciate the scope of the task.

Having a Topic Given

If the topic has been given, we may have fun exploring approaches to the topic, or we may find it difficult to generate enthusiasm. Sometimes having a topic assigned is more difficult than coming up with our own topic. Many topics we may be given are unfamiliar to us, or, at least, somewhat remote from our personal experience. The topic may be narrowed already, but we still may need to do research if we want to produce a viable product.

In the classroom, we may be asked to write about something we have read. A reading journal is invaluable as a resource in this case. In addition, notes and annotations in the text can assist in writing.

School essays are not the only reports or documents which may be given. They are also not the only writing that requires research. As we move into society at large, we will find that research—"doing your homework"—is necessary in most jobs.

Example: *Ray was working in the advertising division of a large cosmetics firm. During the Christmas season, the company was not getting its share of sales in perfume. The president called Ray in to have him investigate the problem. Ray was to look at advertising and sales of other companies, compare types of advertising media, and write a report on the problem. He was given two weeks. Although the project was necessary, Ray was not excited about the pressure and research it would involve. Nonetheless, he followed through and found flaws in his company's approach, which may have accounted for the loss in sales. His report was thorough, and vital to the company's growth. The final product was satisfying both to himself and to the company president. Shortly thereafter, Ray was promoted.*

Looking for a Topic: Our Own Resources

What if we have to find the topic ourselves? We can look to our own resources or to an external source, such as a library. Our own resources include our thoughts and ideas, our journals or notebooks, and our observations and discussions. Or we can do some research to look for a topic.

Thoughts and Ideas

Some people are brimming with things to write about. They can hardly wait to get paper in front of them to begin pumping out brilliance. In fact, most people, at one time or another, have something they want to say and would like to put it in writing. An idea may come suddenly or take much thinking before it develops. Many people, however, have ideas only occasionally. Most of the time, writing is a "have-to" task—necessary, but not entirely pleasant. However, sudden inspiration can produce some fascinating writing: letters to the editor, complaint letters, personal essays about Aunt Tillie, love poems, or novels. But when a teacher or an employer asks us to write something, our experience still can draw forth ideas which make excellent subjects—if we give those ideas a chance.

Example: *Radhika loved to write. She also was interested in people and wondered what made them act the way they do. Her family jokingly called her "the purple people watcher." One day, however, she saw some disturbing incidents in the park—a group of youngsters was being cruel to a small, lost dog. When she went over to stop them, they ran away. That night, she wrote a letter to the editor, detailing the incident. From her letter, a parent, recognizing the description of her son, wrote to Radhika to thank her for bringing the incident to her attention. She and her son had discussed the problem in a fruitful teaching moment. She felt sure that her son would be more sensitive now to helpless creatures.*

Writing About Our Interests

But why not do the obvious? Write about what we know and are interested in. If a writer is a whiz at beekeeping or repairing small engines or analyzing John Steinbeck's novels, she should use one of those topics. We need to look at our own storehouse of knowledge before we go elsewhere. What do we do and enjoy doing?

Journals and Notebooks

When looking for a writing topic, some people go to diaries and journals to draw upon experiences. A reading journal can be one of these sources. Other people use notebooks of thoughts or ideas gathered from many places. Writers who know they will be called upon to write, or speak on the spur of the moment, or who enjoy creative writing, are wise to consider keeping a writer's notebook specifically for that purpose. My Uncle Fred was a noted speaker and often was asked to give impromptu talks. He kept a small black notebook in his breast pocket and jotted down ideas as they came to him—anytime, anyplace. He was always ready.

Journals are places where we can express our feelings and ideas, as well as write about the things that interest us. Journals also can be used for recordkeeping. We often need to go back for information about important events, and a journal—where we also can practice our writing skills—is an ideal place for information.

Observations and Discussions

If we are asked to write on a topic of our choice, we may wish to take some time on our own—looking, listening, and making note of the world around us: nature, people, the seasons, animal life, technology, science. We can talk to friends about common interests, visit with someone we do not usually talk with, consult a librarian, or listen to a talk which may inspire us. We need to sharpen our listening skills, to be a more sensitive observer. We can schedule interviews or initiate a discussion group. As we listen and look, we should keep in mind our purpose and our audience.

External Sources for Finding a Topic

If we really get stuck for a topic, our best external source is usually close at hand: the library. By checking the *Library of Congress Subject Heading* list, we can browse through the hundreds of thousands of topics listed there. Surely one or even several ideas will be of interest, and each is subdivided to help narrow the topic. In fact, the library is brimming with sources for ideas: encyclopedias, dictionaries, indexes, books, magazines, pamphlets, documents, audio-visual materials. Finding ideas and becoming excited about topics are what a library is for. If we cannot get to the library, we need to look at our resources at hand: textbooks, an ordinary dictionary, related books or magazines, newspapers, people who might have clever suggestions, even the television set.

Make a Decision

Some writers still have problems finding ideas to write about. Topics elude them. They try the suggestions above and still find nothing that interests them. When they have serious decision-making problems, they may have to jump into something that—even if it doesn't fire them up—may light a flicker of interest. With writing that needs to be done, students need to start somewhere. Delaying while they agonize does not make the task easier.

On the other hand, several topics may seem marvelous. Writers may have to flip a coin to make a choice. However, if we as writers find the topic becomes boring or obvious once we get into it, we always can go to another topic (if we have not invested too much time and effort).

Example: *Eric had heard about plastic so strong that it could stop a bullet. He went to a local plastics firm, but it could not tell him much about the kind of plastic he was interested in writing about. In the library, he came upon some government documents which told about the use of super-strong plastic for a security shield when the president spoke. He wrote to the government source listed on the document, curious about the difference between the plastic made by the local firm and that made for government use. Two weeks later, three FBI agents appeared on his doorstep. They wanted to know why he was interested in government security. After a lengthy discussion and a subsequent investigation of Eric's background, Eric was persuaded to change his topic. Unfortunately, it made him late in handing in his paper.*

There is nothing wrong with false starts—if we catch them soon enough. We just need to try again.

A Quest for a Topic

1. Keep a writer's notebook to record observations, personal experiences, and ideas from reading (in addition to or instead of a reader's notebook). Use the notebook in preparation to write.

2. Take 15 minutes outdoors or in a public lobby for observation. Write down everything that may make a good example or a clear detail for an essay.

3. Using the *Library of Congress Subject Heading* list, write down one topic that is interesting and five related topics or subdivisions of that topic. All must come from the *Library of Congress Subject Heading* list.

Narrowing the Topic

Once we have a general topic in mind, we often must reduce its scope to a reasonable size. "Human Life, the Universe, and Everything" is a topic that is unwieldy from sheer bulk. Gardening is a good topic, but it is too big to cover in one student paper. On the other hand, one radish is too little. One of the most difficult tasks we will have is to make our topic exactly the right size to handle in the space and time we have to give it.

A topic can be narrowed by space, by time, or by focus. If an essay is to be short, the topic must be narrower than if the essay is to be longer. A book-length discussion can be even broader. But some subjects take several volumes to cover.

Too Large	More Reasonable
The penal system	Drunk-driving sentences
The environment	Acid rain
Europe	Changes in the Albanian government over the last two years
War	Attitudes of the European community toward the Gulf War
Clothing	Dress styles of the 1920s
William Faulkner	Symbolism in "The Bear"

The Advantages of a Narrow Topic

A narrow topic helps us look closely at a specific thing. It is far too easy to talk about broad, general topics—love, war, beauty—without saying very much of significance. Everyone likes to generalize to some extent. But in careful, planned communication, we need to go beyond the broad generalization and get to specifics. Why? Because broad generalizations are difficult, sometimes impossible, to prove. When we make broad statements without evidence, we risk discrediting ourselves and our views by our naivete or ignorance. Broad generalizations are also often value judgments— war is bad; love is good—which show personal bias but not careful examination.

Limiting the Topic by Space, Time, and Focus

Instead of writing about the entire world, we need to limit our topic by space: continents to countries, countries to states, states to counties, counties to townships,

townships to neighborhoods, neighborhoods to families, families to individuals, individuals to a specific individual or his or her traits, and so on. In limiting by time, we move from all of time down to a specific time period. For example, instead of covering the whole Civil War, take just the last week, or the last battle.

Narrowing by focus limits from all of the large subject to one of its parts. Instead of looking at all of genetic engineering, look at a certain disease passed through the genes, such as macular degeneration (breaking down of the retina). In fact, we may need to narrow by all three (space, time, and focus) depending on what the topic is.

We will do additional narrowing as we construct a thesis statement—giving the topic a point of view and a direction—but before we can begin researching and exploring, we must have limited our topic enough to find specific material.

An Ideal Topic

Perhaps it will help if we can think of the ideal topic as one about which we can discuss three or four specific things—ideas to support it, facts of interest to the audience, examples of the topic, or descriptions—to let the audience see what we see. If we need 15 or 20 examples or ideas to give a good picture of the topic, or if we could write a whole book about the topic, our topic is too large for the kind of essays usually required in first-year college courses. We will not be able to control our material; we will be drowned in information and probably end up back with those vague, broad, biased generalizations.

Letting the Library Sources Help Narrow a Topic

Attention to personal and library sources will help to begin the narrowing process. First, from the *Library of Congress Subject Heading* list, we can start narrowing ideas or getting new ideas as we look at the subtopics and divided categories in the list. Then go to the general encyclopedias to see what they have to say and how they narrow the topic. If we still are interested in one or two topics and need to narrow further, search out an index or a dictionary in those specialized fields. The articles in these indexes and dictionaries about the topic have been narrowed and focused and usually are divided into subheadings. It is helpful to write down the authors of the encyclopedia or index articles and look for other things these authors have written about the proposed topic, in books as well as in magazines or journals. These authors also will have narrowed the subject to a reasonable size, or they will help us see how narrowing can be done. As we are looking for authors, notice that a number of books on a topic is a sure sign that the topic is too big. Note how each of those books in subdivided into chapters and sections, and we will see how we can narrow the topic.

Example   *Jacques wanted to write a paper about Shakespeare. He went confidently to the library, knowing that he could find a book to help him. When he got there, however, he found not just one book, but a whole section on Shakespeare, with shelf after shelf of books. While he was standing, looking, somewhat overwhelmed, he noticed a copy of the* Library of Congress Subject Heading *list on the table next to him. He opened it to the section on Shakespeare and found it subdivided according* *to plays, then further subdivided. This gave him a start. He decided to write on a lesser-known play, and turned to the entries on* Henry VI, Part II. *His topic was beginning to be narrowed.*

Broadening a Topic

On the other hand, the topic is too narrow if we can say everything there is to say about it in two or three sentences. To broaden it, we will need to take the opposite approach from the suggestions above. Look for a broader space, time, or focus. The balance between too much and too little is a fine line. Sometimes the subject will seem too narrow at first, but after researching thoroughly, we may find that it is the right size after all. It is wise to research our first idea before we make decisions on size.

Coming to a balance of the right-sized topic takes experience. At this point of our writing career, we need to get suggestions from others if we are in doubt. A topic which is broad enough to write something substantial about, yet narrow enough to cover in some detail, is the kind of a topic we are looking for.

Prereading Skills Become Prewriting Skills

Some of the skills discussed in Chapter 2 can be used to prepare for writing: previewing, free writing, brainstorming, outlining, mapping, clustering, capturing. We can preview a topic by looking briefly at materials about the topic and seeing the structure in the ideas. We can preview for audience, purpose, topic suitability, or scope. Once we have chosen our topic, we can do free writing about it to see where our interests lie. Free writing develops from associating in our minds a drift of ideas on the general topic we have chosen.

Example: *Sok had a general idea of the topic he wished to explore: roses. But he did not know what aspect of the flower he wanted to talk about. He decided to do some free writing, so he sat down and started to put everything that came into his mind on the paper: roses, pink, red, growing, planting, cultivation, awards, aphids, fragrance, symbolism, decorations. After he had listed these and several other general ideas, he went back over the list and saw the word awards. He decided to find out who chose the annual awards for the best roses of the year, and how they were chosen. His research led both to the library and to the local greenhouse. He was able to get the address of the national rosarian organization to continue his investigation.*

Beginning with the topic which interests us, we should write as fast as we can words or sentences associated with that initial word. These words and ideas will link to other words, and they to others. The important thing about free writing is to make the session spontaneous.

The process of free writing can develop in the following manner. We may be interested in the general topic of disease. As we think of the word *disease,* we may write types of diseases: cancer, chicken pox, flu, hepatitis, AIDS, pneumonia, heart disease. Or we may think of symptoms and write: sore throat, cough, weakness,

THERE! PERFECTLY ORGANIZED FOR MY SPONTANEITY SESSION.

from There Goes The Neighborhood. Copyright © 1991 by Cowles Syndicate, Inc., a division of Universal Press Syndicate. All rights reserved. Reprinted with permission.

bleeding, rash, fever. Another approach is to think of words associated with the prevention or treatment of disease: immunization, doctor, medication, surgery, hospital, etc.

We also may begin with one subject and let the words carry us to linked categories helping to narrow and focus the topic. Linking categories may go from immunizations to drug abuse, drug abuse to child abuse, child abuse to divorce or to single-parent families, divorce to re-entry of women into the work force and to organizations that help with re-entry problems, and finally, to one specific organization and its funding. We may have wandered far afield from our original subject, but in doing so we may have found a more useful topic, one more clearly narrowed or more appealing to our individual interest.

Brainstorming can be followed in the same way as free writing, but with a group. Group members can follow stream-of-consciousness ideas, using a scribe to record. At the beginning of a group-writing project, brainstorming is especially helpful.

Example: *A group of students from English 337 needed to give a presentation on F. Scott Fitzgerald's book,* The Great Gatsby. *They met late in the afternoon to see what approach they could take. Paul was to be the scribe as they threw out ideas. Suzanne wanted to look at the historical approach to the book and focus on the Jazz*

Age. She had been interested in the prohibition era, the Charleston, the flapper mentality, and the beginnings of organized crime. Phillipe contributed ideas about Fitzgerald's life. Juan had thoughts about the characters in the book and showed how they corresponded to Fitzgerald's life. Louise gave ideas about the symbolism in the book. After a couple of hours, they had many ideas from which to draw for their presentation.

Outlines, maps, and clusters are all tools for organizing ideas. Preliminary outlines make a start at classifying ideas and putting them in coordinate and subordinate relationships. By outlining we can tell if a topic has equal parts and if we have a balanced look at the topic. We also can see if we begin at one point and go off on a tangent.

Topic: Magnetic Levitation Trains

Balanced Outline	Imbalanced Outline
I. Introduction	I. Introduction
II. Feasibility	II. Feasibility
Funding	Funding
Available Space	III. Necessity
Safety	Efficiency
III. Necessity	Environmental Concerns
Efficiency	Economic Need
Environmental Concerns	Consumer Response
Consumer Response	IV. Conclusion
IV. Conclusion	

Notice that in the imbalanced outline, the audience is not given adequate information about the feasibility of introducing magnetic levitation trains into the transportation system.

Outlines can show if one category or section of a paper is poorly developed and needs more support, or if another topic or subtopic is getting out of hand with too many ramifications or side issues, and we need to narrow the topic drastically. Maps and clusters can show linking ideas, subordinate ideas, and relationships clearly as we begin developing the topic.

Discovery Writing

Sometimes we have a general idea about a topic and what we would like to explore, but we do not have the exact focus. Discovery writing can be a step toward exploring the topic. A quick draft of ideas can show major interest, interesting examples or incidents, facts which we may use to support the ideas, or side directions which we may take. Sometimes a discovery draft may be sketchy; sometimes it may be more ample. An advantage of discovery writing is that it helps us develop interest in the subject. Having something on paper also gives great motivation. Once we have *something* written, we can begin to shape and change it. Eventually, however, we need to decide on a central focus for our work, and look for a thesis, with its accompanying thesis statement, around which to develop our ideas.

Developing a Thesis Statement

If we have found a good thesis statement in our reading, we know how the statement can draw us into the main ideas quickly and clearly. We may have appreciated the author's consideration in organization. Now that we are writing our own essays, either about our own ideas or about what we have read, we will need to create our own thesis statements.

A Thesis Statement Points the Way

A thesis statement makes a stand on a certain issue and is a personal approach to a topic. A good thesis statement also points the way the essay will develop or shows how the organization of the essay fits together. An example of a thesis statement was given in the previous chapter on the herb comfrey: *The herb comfrey can be more useful in treating certain illnesses than chemical agents.* This thesis first gives the writer's personal opinion on comfrey. It then raises the need to identify the illnesses which are treated by this herb. The thesis also qualifies its claims by stating "comfrey *can be* useful." When is it not useful? Such questions would need to be answered. Development could also include information about the herb and examples of its curative powers. The chemical agents referred to also would need to be identified and discussed. Since the thesis statement expresses the author's judgment or assumption (claim), that judgment must be defended. The audience's opinion might be that comfrey is a useless weed. The writer would need to convince the audience otherwise.

Similarly, essays about readings or literature are the writer's own ideas. Everyone in a classroom may write about one poem, but each thesis statement may be different. Writers bring their personal perceptions and views to their work.

Student approach to a thesis on Robert Frost's "Stopping by Woods on a Snowy Evening":

Celeste—Frost's poem is about suicide.

Anna—The symbolism in Frost's poem reflects death.

John—Rhythm in "Stopping by Woods on a Snowy Evening" and how it heightens the mood of the poem.

Soledad—The horse as an archetypal figure in Frost's poem.

Jorge—Imagery of isolation in "Stopping by Woods . . . "

Alice—Frost's personal reflections on his poem, "Stopping by Woods on a Snowy Evening."

Thesis Statements are Individualistic

Because each thesis statement reflects the individual, no single topic has only one possible thesis statement. Each topic can provide many approaches and interpretations. Writers must work with their chosen topic to find the thesis statement that most clearly reflects the approach they want to take. They need to interpret that topic according to their own observations and feelings, to take a position relative to the topic, and prepare to support their beliefs. Then they write a thesis statement that they believe in and can defend. In doing so, they must be prepared to answer the questions which their thesis statement raises.

Example: *Frederick read an essay on changing family patterns. Since he came from a single-parent family, he was interested in the conclusions made by the author of the article. However, he disagreed that single-parent families were dysfunctional. His own family managed very well. All of his sisters and brothers worked together with their mother to provide financial and emotional support for the family. They had much love in their home and looked forward to being together. His thesis statement reflected his opinion, but he also looked for sources to find if other single-parent families had similar experiences. His thesis was that single-parent families did not need to be dysfunctional if certain attitudes were established in the home.*

Narrowing a Thesis Statement

We must then look at our thesis statement to see if it fits the scope of the paper we will write. Will our paper be three pages, 23 pages, or 83 pages? Our thesis statement must be quite narrow if our paper is three pages but can be broader if we have more pages to work with. We cannot cover the history of the world in three pages. We cannot even cover the history of America, or of Colorado, or of Vail, Colorado, or of an old gold mine in Vail. We need to continue to narrow—perhaps by space, as shown above, or by time, or by specific subject. In three pages, we *might* be able to cover one historical incident—and its significance—which occurred in one particular mine at a specific point in history. For 23 pages, we could cover more than one mine, or more than one time period.

Thesis Statement Problems

Some of the major problems with student papers begin with thesis statements that are too broad. Such essays show that the coverage of data tends to be shallow, at best. When a thesis is too broad, the writer relies too heavily on general statements to prove the points so she loses her focus. She is thin on specific facts, she tries to cover too much, she covers her material unevenly. Because she has so much to say, she sometimes focuses on the parts that interest her instead of giving a balanced picture.

Less common problems are thesis statements which are too narrow (once a writer has stated the problem, he has little else to add), thesis statements which are strongly biased (they lack any objectivity and may be objectionable to the audience), thesis statements which are boring (who cares about the topic?), and thesis statements which are confusing (perhaps they just need restating to make the direction of the paper clear).

Example: *Maya wanted to write a paper about the destruction of rain forests. She felt very strongly about the subject and searched for sources which would condemn the slash-and-burn policy of Third World farmers. Eduardo, one of the other students in her class, came from South America and had friends who had lived in the rain forest area. At first he was highly offended by her one-sided arguments, but then he realized that she simply did not understand the position of subsistence farmers of that area. After he and Maya had discussed the issue— somewhat heatedly—they both began to understand each other's position. Maya's paper was revised to show both perspectives, and Eduardo became more sensitive to environmental issues.*

Student Exercises: Writing Thesis Statements

1. Using an essay, poem, or story from the text, create a thesis statement which could lead to an essay. Write that thesis statement and discuss in class the different approaches to the selection.

2. Using the topic you have chosen, write three thesis statements you could use for an essay.

3. Practice working with a thesis statement—narrowing it, broadening it, making it more or less biased, or clarifying it.

Gathering Information and Ideas

As we were searching for a topic to write about, we went through several different steps and investigated several different sources for information. First, we looked at internal sources such as our own background, ideas, or opinions. Then we went to the library. This process can work once again. We first need to use our memories to draw upon what we already know. What experiences have we had with this topic? What has brought the thesis statement to its present focus? We can stimulate our memories by free writing, then examine the direction our topic seems to be taking. Next, we can ask friends and associates their opinion on the thesis statement. They may give additional insights and directions. We may want to go as far as to interview people whose lives reflect aspects of the thesis statement. We also should keep our observation skills keen. We not only will find answers around us, we also will discover where to find answers, which brings us again to the most obvious place to gather information: the library.

Using the Library

As we were searching for a topic, we checked the *Library of Congress Subject Heading* list for ideas. Now is the time to return there, but not just to the list. General encyclopedias, specialized encyclopedias or dictionaries, books and magazines on the topic can help also. We will be looking for information to support the thesis statement. Now is the time to take notes or make copies, then annotate.

If we find more information than we can possibly use, we may need, even now, to narrow the thesis statement further. We need to keep our thesis statement with us and refer to it often, lest we lose focus as we research. The library is full of fascinating information and it is very easy to get off track. We should try to collect only relevant material, but not ignore information which contradicts a personal view. We may want to include another point of view as part of a counterargument—so we can disprove it.

Analysis of Sources

As we see the thousands of books and magazines before us in the library, how do we decide which ones are the best? These suggestions may help.

1. Check the author of the chosen subject in a current encyclopedia. Publishers of encyclopedias choose the top authorities in the field to write their articles. Even if the papers we are writing are not research papers, the support of authorities who think the way we do can give us confidence, and more ideas.

2. Does the library have anything else written by that author? It probably will. Find that book by the famous author and see who he or she uses as sources. The list of authorities then begins to expand.

3. After finding books or journal articles by the names found in the above search, see who they use as sources.

4. Check the credentials of the authors. Are they truly noted in their fields?

5. Also watch for authorities who have opposing views. Some topics are controversial and do not have one correct answer. Do not use only the authority whose view is closest to a personal one. Show the audience more than one side to the issue. Personal views always can be justified in the conclusion of the paper.

6. Be selective of the types of journals and publishers used. Magazines found at newsstands are usually for a popular audience. Their articles usually do not reflect primary research.

7. Watch for respectable publishers, and books that have gone through many editions (they have passed the test of time and use).

8. Check publication dates. For some topics the material can be outdated in six months. Find the most current material.

9. Use critical thinking skills (evaluating assumptions) to check for blatant bias or partial facts.

Primary and Secondary Sources

We also will need to determine if our source is a primary or a secondary source. That is, can we determine if the book reflects initial research, is a letter, document or newspaper which gives original material, or is significant in the historical perspective? If it does, it is probably a primary source. If the source is a commentary on another source, if it has extensive footnotes, or if it evaluates another source, it is probably a secondary source. Primary sources are sources to use for a paper. We should read the original document before we read what someone else says about it.

Primary Sources	Secondary Sources
Novels	Literary analysis of novels
Letters	Biographies
Newspapers	Historical commentaries
Documents	Documentary analyses
Research reports	Articles about research
Diaries	Articles about people
Poems	Explications of poems

Other Sources of Information

In addition to the library we can find information in many places. Films, videos, recordings, interviews, questionnaires, lectures—all are excellent sources of material for a paper. We should not limit ourselves when we are exploring a topic. Perhaps our most valuable source will come from an unexpected place.

Example: *Domatila wanted to write a paper about archery. She searched the library for information and found many articles and books on the skills and rules of archery competition. Her brother Javier had learned how to make his own arrows, so she decided to narrow her topic in that area. She had her brother teach her the process, using him as an interview source, but also went to a local woodwork plant to see what she could find. The plant had several brochures on the type of wood it used, as well as quality-control information. She was able to use both primary and secondary sources in her paper. For her oral report on the paper, she brought several different arrows to show quality, and she also was able to persuade Javier to come and demonstrate some techniques in construction.*

Limiting Research Time

We also must give ourselves a time limit on research. The process of gathering information and ideas can be the most time-consuming part of writing. It can be the most exciting, but it also can be the part of the process which can bog us down.

We cannot read *everything* on the topic, nor should we try to do so. If we have ample time, we can draw out the process as long as we want, and some writing projects are extensive. Occasionally, graduate students will take several years to produce a thesis or dissertation—much of that time spent in gathering information. But most students have a deadline, which means they must set a limit for themselves: so many hours of research, such and such a date will be the deadline, or so many pages of notes will be the limit. By giving ourselves a deadline or limit on our work, we will avoid getting lost in the research. Deadlines also may keep us from procrastinating until the night before the paper is due. And we know (probably by experience) that last-minute panic does not lead our best effort. If we want an "A" paper, we need to put in "A" effort.

Example: *Mercedes had a paper due in three weeks. She found a topic that absolutely fascinated her. The topic was koala bears. Her local zoo even had a koala bear that she could observe. She asked the zookeeper about koala feeding habits and environment. In the library, she found wonderful material, much of it illustrated as to koala habitat, breeding, diseases, environmental dangers, and socialization. The time went past very quickly for Mercedes, and suddenly she realized that the paper was due in two days, but she had not even started to write. She had a stack of photocopies, many notecards, and a pile of books on her desk. After an all-night session, Mercedes finished the paper, but she was not entirely satisfied with the product because it did not reflect the love and interest she had in the subject.*

Organizing Research Time

Since we usually do not have extra time to work on assignments, we need to evaluate sources carefully, finding the most important information from the most important authorities first. If we need background, we can use the encyclopedias; these articles will give important basic information and terminology, as well as the names of authorities in the field. From this beginning we can explore further. Sometimes it helps to make a list of questions (like a rubric) on the topic so we can narrow the search. If the thesis statement is formulated, it will help shorten the time even more.

We must also stay on focus. Although we may find much material that is *almost* on our chosen topic, we need to set aside extraneous information. Maybe someday we can write another paper on the subtopic we have found.

Taking Notes and Asking Questions

We need to use note-taking skills as we read in preparation for writing. Just as annotating and note taking have helped us understand reading material, these skills also can help us find and record facts and examples for our own writing. Probably we also have been asking questions throughout the process. Now is the time to see if we are on the right track. Try out some of the following questions:

- Why was this particular subject chosen for writing?

- Is the subject narrow enough? How many pages will it take to explore the subject thoroughly?

- Is the thesis statement interesting and clear to others?

- How many different points have been found to support the thesis statement?

- How valid is the support? Do authorities back this point of view?

- Is the subject one-sided? Is there another side not considered?

- Is more research needed to support the statement adequately?

- How much more time is available? When is it time to stop?

- Are subtopics difficult to eliminate?

- Is the first draft ready to begin?

We may not yet have answers to all of these questions, but they should help us see where we are in the process of writing. The questions also can help us become aware of items we may have missed.

We also should use critical reading skills to help us understand and remember the material we have researched.

Student Exercises: Gathering Material

1. Gather information for your paper or talk.

2. Make a time schedule to help you with your reading or writing.

3. List the authorities you have found in your subject. Do any of them have opposing views?

4. Which of your sources are primary sources? Which are secondary? Which will be of most value to you in your writing?

Writing to Develop Ideas

Now that we have gathered information, we need to think about putting that information onto the page. Often, good organization is the crucial factor in the difference between an A or a B grade. Many organizational patterns exist—the introduction/examples/conclusion essay, the quick write (blitz), the rubric pattern, the question pattern, the pro/con pattern. Any of them will help organize ideas into a clear structure.

Organizing Ideas

When we first begin to write, we often put things on paper just as they come into our minds, sort of like free writing. But free writing is sometimes difficult to follow. Now we need to seriously consider the second item of the Audience Expectations given at the first of this chapter: "The audience expects to be able to follow the author's train of thought or pattern of development."

The Basic Structure: Introduction/Information/Conclusion

Although thought processes can move so quickly they sometimes seem jumbled, when we write, we should show clear organization that the audience can follow. Each supporting point should be clearly stated and should be tied to the central focus given in the thesis statement. The traditional basic structure may be one place to start. This basic structure begins with an introduction to the topic—often including the thesis statement, but sometimes giving background, history, or an overall look at the topic. Support information follows, to argue with the thesis, or to explain the thesis. Case studies, facts, inferences, assumptions, examples, detail, or many other ideas can be given to prove (or disprove) the thesis statement. The informational section also can contain material to develop the central idea in many different ways. It can expand or narrow the topic. It can examine different points, argue with major assumptions, or build a case for the major idea. A conclusion ends the essay. The conclusion can include a summary of the statements given, give personal views, recommend action, give the thesis statement again (or for the first time), or simply give closure to the ideas expressed.

Organizing the Basic Structure

To organize materials for a basic structure, one tool we can use is an outline. The structure can begin with the thesis statement at the top, introductory material under the first heading, then informational development under several headings that will constitute the body of the paper, and a heading for a conclusion.

The second step is to subdivide the major headings. What points should be brought up under each informational focus? Each major heading should have two or more subheadings. Watch out for only one subheading under a major heading. Usually, one subheading is just a restatement of the major heading or an inadequate development of that heading. Single subheadings should be integrated into the major heading or expanded into greater development, creating two or more headings to balance the ideas.

A final step is to look carefully at the outline to see if the ideas are in the right order, if they all relate to the thesis or main idea of the paper, if they are logical given the topic of the paper, and if they are balanced and reasonable in their approach.

Example: *Dora had chosen a thesis for her paper about eating disorders that reads, "Eating disorders can lead to obsessive behavior and personality problems." As she researched her material, she found that anorectic behavior began with rejection of* *certain foods, such as sweets and salty foods, then grew to include more healthy foods. Finally, the anorectic rejected most kinds of food until the individual literally starved to death. Bulimic behavior also showed progressive obsession with patterns of overeating, then vomiting. The behavior started gradually, then grew until bulimics were unable to control the physical reactions, vomiting even when they did not want to. She divided her paper into the two major categories of eating disorders, anorexia and bulimia, then subdivided each of these categories into the types of behavior exhibited in each category and the personality problems associated with each. Her conclusion was to find parallels in both the obsessive behavior and personality problems of sufferers of these two disorders.*

Using Notecards

It helps to have the information on separate notecards so that the information can be physically divided. The outline gives a feeling of balance, but a stack of notecards that represents each heading physically illustrates that balance—we can see if one pile outweighs the others. We can balance the paper by going back for more information on the support (pile) that is thin. Separate notecards may seem tedious in the heyday of copy machines and computers, but notecards sometimes still are the best answer for efficient preliminary organization.

Computer Printouts or Photocopies

Support and balance also can be shown by notes taken on a computer or by photocopies of articles or pages from sources. These informational materials can be filed or sorted much like notecards, although they are a bit cumbersome.

Putting Things Together

This preliminary outline is not permanent. It can be changed and adapted as more information is gathered. But it *is* a beginning. It helps bring the paper into focus and to fill in weak points.

Remember, too, we are going to need to tie all those headings and subheadings together when we write, so we should put related ideas together. If we have too many different ideas, it will be like trying to herd cats. The ideas will go off in different directions. In addition, each of those paragraphs should have topic sentences and connections between ideas.

Student Outline Sample

The following student outline corresponds to the the annotation for the story "Sex Education" shown on page 282, which reads, "she should have taught how to escape." The student begins the outline with the thesis statement so it is before the eyes of the audience at all times; it is also a reminder to him as he works on the paper. The three times in which the same incident is retold fall into five main informational divisions.

The Cornfield Experience

Thesis—The experiences of Aunt Millie's life change her view of sex.

```
 I. Introduction

II. The Cornfield Experience:
    The first time she tells the story:

    A. She is trying to scare the children
       into doing what is right.

    B. She tells her story so it will
       relate to the children.

III. The Cornfield Experience:
     The second time she tells the story:

     A. She is in a more mature setting.

     B. She thinks it is best to teach how
        to save oneself instead of
        how to avoid getting lost.

     C. Her son is going through a period of
        being lost, and her
        story reflects this.

IV. The Cornfield Experience:
    The third time she tells the story:

    A. Her husband has died, and she
       misses the relationship.

    B. Maybe the cornfield wasn't so bad after all.

 V. Conclusion
```

Writing the Rough Draft

The first method of writing a rough draft was to work from an outline or map of ideas as the above student has done. We can begin with the thesis statement then write down all the major points. We then develop topic sentences, fill in details, examples, and facts, and remember that the material in each paragraph should support the topic sentence. When we work carefully, we allow the information to grow and fill in the outline we have made. Using a reading journal, library research, and other resources can flesh out the support. If we take information from another writer, we should make sure to give that writer credit. All borrowings should be documented (see section on plagiarism on page 102).

Student Rough Draft Sample

Below is part of a student essay on the article "O Americano, Outra Vez!" by Richard P. Feynman (page 238), with the thesis statement and topic sentences underlined. Notice how his basic structure helps keep the information focused. The essay has been put under major organizational headings for convenience in reading:

I. Memorization is one of the key factors in which a person organizes knowledge. However, acquiring knowledge takes more than mere memorization. In the essay, "Surely You're Joking, Mr. Feynman!" by Richard P. Feynman, we find that students were memorizing everything, but they did not know what anything meant.

II. In order to completely understand a subject one must interpret that which is being taught into his own words and thoughts. In the essay, "Surely You're Joking, Mr. Feynman!" the students were writing down what the professor said exactly word for word. The students would then memorize these words, never knowing what they meant. From personal experience in school, I have learned that when listening to a lecture, it is better to write the important concepts in my own words, than writing exactly what the professor says. In American Heritage, for example, the first lecture that I attended, the professor said that he would test on important concepts and not merely facts. He said that understanding concepts is more effective because concepts can be applied to everyday situations. Facts are concrete and stable and can only be answered true or false. He said that we would never have to memorize dates or events in history because memorization is not the best way to learn. I recall taking the first test in this class and finding that there were no questions dealing with memorization, but that the test consisted of applying concepts to everyday situations and personal experience. Therefore, I have learned to take effective notes by writing down my own words and thoughts and not writing exactly what the professor says and then trying to memorize his words.

III. Another way to learn and understand a subject is by asking questions. In the essay, "Surely You're Joking, Mr. Feynman!" we find that students would never ask questions. They all pretended that they understood the concepts being taught, and if one student asked a question, the others got angry, saying that he was wasting their time. This is not the case in our schooling system. I recall many times being grateful to a fellow student for stopping the teacher to ask a question, because I also had that exact question. Many times a teacher's answer to one student's question answers many of the other students' questions. Asking questions is very important in fully understanding a subject.

IV. Another effective way in understanding a concept or a subject, is by observing, if possible, the concept of subject in action. In the essay Mr. Feynman gives the definition of triboluminescence as the light emitted when crystals are crushed. He said that this was not science because it was just words. If, instead, a student was to ask if you take a lump of sugar and crush it with a pair of pliers in the dark, you can see a bluish flash, then the student would have observed the concept happening and it would be science. My chemistry teacher would use observance as a method in teaching. I recall one time when we were learning about catalysts, he brought his ice cream freezer to class. He showed us how salt acted as a catalyst in lowering the freezing temperature of ice. He explained how this worked while we observed it actually happening. Observance proved to be effective in helping me learn.

V. As one can see, it takes more than just memorizing to learn. Interpreting concepts into a person's own words, asking questions, and observing are only a few of the many ways in which a person acquires knowledge. If we can use these methods to help us learn, along with memorization, we will acquire a great amount of knowledge and become more educated. This will create a pleasant, well-ordered and more efficient society in which to live.

Rod Slater

As we write our first rough draft, we try to get main ideas into words and tie them together with good organization. We may find that returning to a map or outline is helpful in writing. With the outline in front of us, we can fill in ideas and use notes to give examples or prove assertions. Once the outline is filled in , the first rough draft is finished.

Another Writing Method: The Blitz

A second method of doing a rough draft is the blitz. A blitz is a one-time rapid attack and is extremely useful, especially in a paper of five pages or less. To do a blitz, we absorb our outline and research so that our head is full of ideas, then just write nonstop without extensively consulting notes or outline until we are finished with the paper. We do not worry about spelling or grammar; we are just getting ideas down, making major points, giving examples, connecting things, and giving a tentative conclusion. As in free writing, we need to have sufficient time and a place to write without interruption, then we write fast. When we are finished, we have a very rough draft, but it is complete. A blitz is somewhat painful, but not nearly as painful as agonizing over every word. Now we can start working with our essay, adjusting and fine tuning as much as we like. But we have something to work with. A writer cannot rewrite something that has never been written.

Warning: do not make a blitz the final draft. Students who wait to blitz until the night before the assignment is due will be handing in a rough draft, not a quality paper. We are not finished after the blitz. We have just gotten a good start.

Looking at the Rough Draft: Blitz Method

Rough drafts are the most creative (and usually the hardest) part of writing. No one starts with a finished paper. After we have written a rough draft—especially in a blitz, but also in other organizational patterns—we need to prepare an outline or look at a prewritten outline again. Although the traditional basic structure of writing may show intensive care and thought and not need as much revision as the blitz method, the blitz may have flashes of brilliance. But the writer needs to look carefully at the organization in the blitz method. If a writer has made a preliminary outline for the blitz organization, the rough draft may be nothing like that outline. If the writer prepares an outline after the fact, she may find that it does not fit neatly into any organizational structure. Many rough drafts from the blitz method go far afield. So what should be done to them? There are two options: change the rough draft to fit the outline (or fit into some pattern), or change the outline. Both are viable choices.

Using the blitz method can help the writer discover exciting new territory as she writes her rough draft—territory that is much more interesting to her than her original plan. When all that information in her head gets mixed up, new patterns and connections sometimes occur. She can shape the outline to fit this new plan or adjust both the outline and the rough draft. Writers who use the blitz method may have discovered a vitality that eventually will carry the paper to an A, but they need to be willing to chop the rough draft into segments: those that fit the outline, those that are totally off the subject, and those that are possible subtopics if they decide to change the direction of the paper. After all, this is *the writer's* creation. It can be changed all she wants at this point. In fact, most blitz efforts need extensive revision.

Example: *Denzel did not like to have everything neatly structured and mapped out for him because he loved to explore creative approaches to writing. His topic, computer-generated graphics, was one he thought about a lot. He had completed an introductory course in the subject and was preparing do a specialty in computer graphics for his major. When he was asked to write a paper in his English class, his topic was naturally on computer graphics. He went to the library to get some current sources, purchased current journals which discussed the topic, and pulled out some books he had been collecting to research the topic. Although he knew a great deal about the subject already, he did learn some new things from his research. One evening, he set aside the time for writing his paper, turned on the computer, and wrote. It was a blitz of his ideas. Three hours passed, but a draft of the paper was just about finished. During the next week, he reworked his ideas, changed some of the organization of the paper, added a few ideas he had overlooked, and smoothed the transitions between ideas. Then he polished the paper, looking at spelling, grammar, and format.*

Even if a writer has followed the basic structure in his pattern of writing, using an outline carefully as he wrote, he still may want to make additional changes. He probably will want to keep some key sentences, experiences, or examples as he first wrote them, but may change structure, transitions, or arrangement of material.

Student Paper with Revisions

The rough draft of the student paper on Whitman's poem "When I Heard the Learn'd Astronomer" began like a blitz (although it may not have been written in blitz fashion). The emotional response of a personal experience moved with a vitality that needed to be kept. But the student also wanted to show how that personal experience applied to the thesis statement. He kept the personal experience in his paper, but added an introduction and thesis statement. The rough draft and final version are shown below:

Rough Draft	**Final Version**
After I read thru "When I Heard the Learn'd Astronomer" I began to think how I treat people. I'm studying Electrical Engineering and have some pretty tough math and sciences classes. Sometimes I will automatically compute all types of characteristics into a particular system or rather situation and when I do this the people around me sometimes don't understand what I'm doing. This is like the kid who didn't understand what the learn'd dude was talking about. It is ineffective communication and its worthless.	The reading of "When I Heard the Learn'd Astronomer" made me see how knowledge can sometimes inhibit effective communication, distract us away from particular aspects of reality, and cause a lesser appreciation of some things. *Effective Communication*: I began to think of how I spoke with people. I am here studying electrical engineering and am taking some fairly challenging math and science courses. I often find myself automatically computing all types of characteristics of or in a particular system or rather situation. And when I do this, many times the people around me don't understand what I'm doing. This is like the kid who didn't understand what the "learn'd" man was talking about. This is ineffective communication and is worthless.
	Joseph Mower

Rubric or Question Method of Organization

As mentioned previously, a rubric (headings in red) is a method of organization for highlighting main ideas. Rubrics are constructed from major ideas as information is gathered. These major ideas then become the main sections of organization for the paper. These major ideas can be organized into outlines, maps, or clusters to see how the structures fit together.

Rubrics work well if photocopies are used in note taking and free writing is done on the word processor for initial ideas. Shaping can be done electronically with the block function on the computer, as rubrics and their supporting ideas are moved into place.

Sometimes rubrics also are done in question form. Using a rubric, the writer asks what major questions can be explored in a paper. What questions would be so important that they would be written in red lettering? What needs to be answered? Main questions then are arranged either in outline or map form, with additional questions or answers surrounding them.

Lists of questions can create ideas and motivate a search for information. Some of the questions can motivate subquestions. Some can be discarded as being extraneous to the focus that is beginning to take shape in the paper. Questions also demand answers, leading to a search for information to develop the ideas in the paper.

Example: Mary was exploring the idea of euthanasia for her paper. She decided to list the questions she wanted to answer to help her with the organization of the paper. Some of her questions were as follows: When is the quality of life lost? Who should make decisions about withdrawing treatment to a comatose patient? What is the cost of keeping a long-term comatose patient alive? How do living wills work? What are the legal ramifications of mercy killing? What would some abuses of euthanasia be? Mary then let the rubric of questions guide her toward the organization of the paper. Some of the questions led into directions she did not want to take, but the rest of the questions stimulated her interest in researching to find answers.

Rubrics also can be done before the thesis statement is formulated. Both major ideas and questions can be mapped or clustered to show a direction the ideas are taking. Then the major idea can be sorted out from the group and developed into the thesis statement or thesis question.

After an organization pattern is established, we need to consider filling in that structure with a rough draft.

Using Questions for Organization

Questions can be used at any stage of writing—from the prewriting all the way to the finished product. One method of writing is formulated entirely on questions. Each part of the critical thinking and critical writing process goes through a series of questions: what, who, when, why, and so on. These questions lead to organization by forming a pattern of questions and answers. The thesis statement is an answer to What is the main idea? The supporting arguments take Why or What questions. For example, the article by Paul Chance, "Apart from the Animals," (page 53) can be structured by using questions:

Paragraph One:
   1. What separates humans from other animals?

Paragraph Two:
   1. Why isn't intelligence a good measure?

Paragraph Three:
   1. What was the Greeks' answer?
   2. Why isn't the Greeks' answer satisfactory?
   3. What evidence supports this conclusion?

Paragraph Four:
   1. What is the second answer to humans' uniqueness?
   2. What examples can prove this answer?
   3. What examples disprove this answer?
And so on.

In like manner, a series of questions about a research topic can bring not only new ideas, but it also can show how to fit those facts into an organizational structure. Questions that are irrelevant soon can be weeded from the group when the pattern of the essay emerges.

Other Organizational Patterns

These four patterns of organization are not the only ones. Some patterns include two sides to an issue—pro and con. Some use a step-by-step process of explanation. Others use extended definitions to focus on meaning. Organizational patterns are simply tools for the writer. They help put the research onto the page, and they help the reader of the work see how the writer's mind works and how she follows a line of reasoning. However it is done, writers must get their ideas onto the page for their audience to read. But simply getting ideas onto the page in some kind of a pattern is not yet enough.

Rethinking and Revising: Toward a Second Draft

Working Toward a Second Draft

Whatever pattern is used to write the essay, the writer is not finished once she has reached the end of the last page. The writer needs to revise the essay to make it the best it can be. Most papers ar far from complete after one draft. Many need three, four, or even more drafts before they flow smoothly and clearly. Unfortunately, a first draft is usually not perfect—just as the person who wrote it is not perfect. Sometimes it is a relief to know that drafts can be changed and modified. We do not have to be satisfied with the first thoughts on a subject. Imperfection is comfortable.

Revising is also rethinking. As the next step in the writing process, we need to look at our rough drafts with a critical eye. Revising is not just cleaning up the spelling and punctuation errors. Revising begins as we look at the overall structure: ideas, logic, inferences and assumptions, claims and facts. Only then can we move to paragraph structure, then sentence structure, and finally to word choice.

Using Critical Thinking in the Rough Draft

As we take a careful look at the papers we have written, we will need to examine our facts and inferences. Where are these facts and inferences coming from? Are we basing them on solid evidence? Are our guesses reasonable? What about our assumptions? Are they warranted? Are hidden assumptions acceptable or are they getting in the way of logic? How are we gathering our material? Is our sampling adequate and representative? When we read material for support, did we find major ideas, or did we take things out of context—that is, did we ignore a major thesis of the reading and pull out something (a sentence or two) that did not represent the overall idea of the work? How did we find our material? Did we search for reliable sources? Were they primary sources?

Gordon is awash with relief.

from There Goes The Neighborhood. Copyright © 1991 by Cowles Syndicate, Inc., a division of Universal Press Syndicate. All rights reserved. Reprinted with permission.

Revising the Overall Structure

The overall structure could be a traditional or basic structure, or it could be another type. Was it the best one for the purpose? Would another form of development be better? This is the time to make whatever changes are necessary to develop the ideas more fully. If we have used questions, we will need to turn them into topic sentences or let them help us find material. A rubric needs to be filled in. A blitz needs to be shaped. Overall structure is the first thing a reader sees. We want it to clearly reflect our thought processes on the topic.

Example: Hector was struggling to write a paper on the Civil War. He had been looking at the debate the Southerners had in arming their slaves. With a traditional structure as his initial organizational pattern, he noticed that the information he was gathering seemed to be on either side of the issue. Finally, he decided that a pro/con structure would better suit his topic than the traditional structure, although he still began the paper with an introduction and ended with a conclusion.

Revision of Thesis and Topic Sentences

Revision then moves to the thesis statement, which we need to look at again. Does it say what we want it to say? Does it reflect what we have said in our essay? Are things implied in the thesis statement that have not been covered?

Next, we can look at the way the paragraphs fit into the structure and how the topic sentences of these paragraphs reflect their content. Do the points made in these paragraphs support the thesis statement? Does the structure follow the outline? Are there transitions which connect the paragraphs, such as repeated nouns or pronouns, repeated ideas, or transitional expressions? Is the conclusion related to the thesis statement? Does it tie up what has been said in the other paragraphs?

Annotating the First Draft

When we let communication skills interact again, we can reread our writing and make notes on the rough draft. We also can let other people read it, then discuss it with them, listening to their comments and suggestions. If we need to, we can make another outline or map of the essay. Then we can know if we need to do more research. We need to think about the essay in a critical way, to analyze and evaluate what we have done. What can we do better? We may want to put it away for a day or two so we can get some perspective. Then we can get back to work.

Example: *Lisa had worked steadily on her paper for three days. She had finished two drafts but still felt uneasy about the way it was taking shape. She had lost her perspective on the project. She was too close to it. Since she had another week before the paper was due, she set it aside to think about other things for a while. When she picked the paper back up to give it another going-over a couple of days later, she could see where she had not supported one of her ideas well. Her perspective had changed. She was able to work on the paper with renewed vigor.*

Taking Another Look

It is time to read the essay again and make additional notes. Now we look at individual paragraphs and sentences. Does everything in the paper flow smoothly to support the thesis statement? Are the transitions clear? Are the sentences in proper order so that they flow smoothly through each paragraph? Are the paragraphs in proper order so that they move logically to the conclusion?

What about the ideas themselves? Are they logical and sound? Are we missing something vital? Is our argument reasonable? Are portions of the argument weak? Do we need more support? Is our support objective or emotional? Are we coming to a reasonable conclusion?

A good way to approach the second draft of a paper is to consider once more the audience and purpose. We should look at the paper as if we were seeing it for the first time.

Understanding the Words

As we look at our writing, we eventually need to be specific in our analysis— starting with words, structure, punctuation, organization, and so on. Each of the specific parts of writing is geared to audience and purpose. For example, the words used should be suited to the audience. Looking back at the Audience Expectations list on page 70, we notice that the very first statement is: "I understand what is written."

Words are primary to that understanding. In helping the audience understand the words, it is not too much to ask that the writer use plain English. Generally, what we read is written that way. Writing in plain English means that language is used that a general audience will understand. Some audiences will not understand foreign words or expressions, local slang, obscure words, or subject-specific jargon. Other audiences will understand unusual words. But the writer must judge carefully which words are chosen, remembering that the audience needs to understand if communication is to take place. An occasional unfamiliar word does not cause too much distress, but a book or article loaded with unfamiliar words can make readers stop in frustration. When we write, we must realize that not only unfamiliar words cause audience distress, but also misspelled words or words used incorrectly.

Example: *Although she was proficient in English, Alicia sometimes could not understand some of the unfamiliar words in the books she was asked to read. She began to make a vocabulary list of unfamiliar words, just for her own knowledge. The list grew and grew. Soon these words became part of her everyday speaking and writing. When she was asked to write a paper for her English class, she felt confident in using some of her new vocabulary in the paper. However, when she showed the paper to her friend Marcelina, she noticed that Marcelina was confused by some of the words. Alicia chose to change some of the fancier words to more well-known ones so her friends would not be intimidated.*

Using Good Punctuation and Structure

Similarly, correct punctuation helps the reader understand what has been written. Punctuation should be a guidepost in reading. When used incorrectly it creates the wrong traffic signals. Notice the problems that come when a comma is left out of the following sentences.

June Smith is a pretty generous woman. (Is June Smith pretty and generous, or is she quite generous?)

The criminal dropped a bullet in his leg. (Does the criminal have a hollow leg, or did he drop because of a bullet in his leg?)

Should I stick the stamps on myself? (Will I be decorated?)

The opera ended happily. (Was it a happy ending, or were we relieved that it was over?)

The audience wants the structure of sentences and paragraphs to be reasonable to follow, without faulty or tangled syntax that obscures understanding. We should make our writing readable.

Using a Handbook and Dictionary

A writer should keep a good handbook of grammar and a dictionary on the table next to her as she writes. These are her tools of the trade. No one needs to be embarrassed to use them. We need to remember that only specialists remember all of the rules, and no one has memorized the dictionary. We need to use these tools whenever we have a question—whether we are reading, writing, or preparing to speak.

Understanding Structure and Development

Another problem the audience must face is understanding where the writer is going and why. If some kind of structure is not there—no thesis statement, no topic sentences, no transitions—the audience may wonder as it wanders. A confused audience rapidly becomes bored, and a bored audience stops reading or listening. Not only does lack of organization damage the image of the writer for the audience, but the writer also can easily go far afield without structure. An audience wants to be able to follow the train of thought and pattern of development. It feels cheated when it does not understand. The truism is accurate: "It's not what you say, but how you say it."

Editing the Paper

As a final step, a writer will want to edit her paper. Editing, unlike rewriting, is essentially a cleanup process. The ideas already should be developed and in logical order. The ideas should be clear and effective. The introduction and conclusion should be in place and well focused. Now the writer will want the paper to be as free from mechanical error as possible. The first item an audience usually notes is misspelled words. Careless spelling can cause an audience to be turned off about the writing, even if the information is excellent.

Spelling

We can put the essay through a spell-check program in the computer, or look up words we do not often use to make sure of the spelling. Do not forget, though, that the spell-check will not take the place of a careful proofreading. A *not* instead of a *now* will not get picked up by a spell-check since both are spelled correctly, but they certainly have different meanings. Check also for variations in spelling between British and American English (color versus colour). Use the spelling that is appropriate for the area.

Punctuation and Mechanics

Then we need to check the punctuation. We can return to a handbook if we are not sure that the punctuation is correct. Again, we need to be aware that British and American punctuation differ (quotation marks either inside or outside the comma and period), and check such rules in a grammar handbook if we are not sure. Also use the handbook to check on such problems as subject/verb agreement, parallel structure, pronoun use, and so on.

Annotating the Rough Draft

Do not be afraid to annotate and to cut and paste. We may know what we want to say, but we need to make that meaning clear to the reader. Revision usually takes several attempts. Each time we revise, we are fine tuning the writing. We should make sure we give ourselves time to revise several times before the paper is due.

Formatting

Getting the essay on the page in a final draft is as important as writing rough drafts or rewriting. The final draft is the copy the audience will see. If the final product is sloppy or careless, the audience will assume both the research and writing are second-rate.

The handbook will give suggestions on format, but here are just a few points to consider:

1. Make sure the paper is clean and white. Dog-eared or wrinkled paper gives a poor image. Unless otherwise specified, white paper is preferred by most audiences. But avoid erasable or onionskin paper. These are hard to handle and tend to smear. If the writer must use erasable paper, photocopy the final copy onto a better quality paper—preferably a heavier bond paper.

2. The papers should be typewritten unless otherwise specified. The ribbon should be new enough to produce dark letters. If a word processor is used, make sure the print is as close to letter quality as possible. If the type is not standard, check with the audience to see if the print is acceptable before the final draft is turned in.

3. Have adequate margins and some kind of a cover or cover page. Number the pages accurately. If footnotes or documentation is needed, check and recheck the form. Do not guess. Be exact. Use a bibliography if appropriate.

4. Get assistance in the final stages of writing. Find a writing center, a writing tutor, or a friend who will turn a critical eye on the work before the final draft is written.

5. If a word processor is being used, prepare for the system to crash. Remember, Murphy's Law works overtime with sophisticated equipment. Save the work often, have a back-up copy, and do not expect the printer to work at the last minute.

6. Turn the paper in on time. Each writer should pace herself so that she has time to follow the steps and produce a paper she can be proud of.

Benefiting from Discussion and Criticism

When students meet as a class or meet individually with the instructor, they gain knowledge by sharing their ideas and from listening to the ideas of others. One of the criticisms of education in Brazil that Richard Feynman gives in his essay, "O Americano, Outra Vez!" (page 238), concerns the lack of questioning. The student essay by Rod Slater quoted on page 91 also indicates the importance of asking questions and listening to classroom discussions. Now is the time to bring reading into the open and do some rethinking aloud. Letting others help is one of the best ways to learn.

Getting Help on Revision

We also should let others help us on the revision of our paper. Both the instructor and other students can add insights on the topic which may have escaped our notice. They also may see where the structure of the essay is unclear, where paragraphs are not organized, where sentences are weak, or where word choice could be better. But no one can expect *them* to do the work. Suggestions from others can lead in directions we can take, but we *ourselves* must take those directions. Someone else cannot rewrite our paper for us. That is plagiarism.

Plagiarism

Plagiarism is a serious problem; basically, it is cheating to pass off someone else's work as our own. Besides being dishonest, plagiarism takes away an opportunity for learning. We are cheating ourselves of a learning opportunity. To avoid plagiarism, use the following suggestions:

1. Never use someone else's paper as your own. Buying a paper does not make it your own. Unless you write it yourself, it is not yours.

2. If you use someone else's ideas, give that person credit whether you are quoting directly, paraphrasing, summarizing, or synthesizing. Use which-ever type of documentation your teacher suggests to indicate your source, whether it is parenthetical documentation (the name of your source and page or date in parentheses right after the quotation or paraphrase), or footnotes/endnotes.

3. As you do research and take notes, make sure you keep track of which ideas are directly quoted and which are paraphrased. Keep track of book or article titles, author's name, page numbers, and other information you will need for your paper.

4. Learn what information is general knowledge and does not, therefore, need to be quoted. Even if your information is general knowledge, however, make sure you document the source and use quotation marks if you use exact words from your source.

5. Avoid unconscious plagiarism by always giving credit as you search and prepare to write. Often, carelessness in note taking leads to plagiarism.

Although we do not use others' direct words in our papers without giving credit, nor do we have other people write our papers for us, others can give suggestions and feedback on the work. Take criticism with openness. People generally are trying to help, not to put us down. We should not take criticism of our written work as personal criticism but should learn to grow from others' suggestions. Remember, no one likes to be wrong, but no one is right all the time, either. If we are defensive and stubborn about accepting and using criticism, we are only hurting our own writing. However, student helpers can be wrong, too. The writer should be the final judge of what is appropriate.

Using a Writing Center

Many colleges and universities have well-staffed, well-equipped writing centers that can help us on rewriting and revising of our papers. Often, fellow students have been trained to work on a one-to-one basis with us to identify trouble spots. Sometimes, even the writing center director is available for problem situations in our writing. The best way to utilize a writing center is to come with specific questions. If we are unsure whether our thesis is too broad or too narrow, the writing center tutors can give suggestions for making it the right size. If we are not comfortable with the amount of support we are using, or with the organizational structure, we can let the tutors look at what we have done so that they can give us suggestions. Queries about grammar, punctuation, and format also can be answered by writing center personnel.

What we cannot expect of writing center personnel is omniscience. They do not know everything we should do for our classes because they have not sat with us in the classroom. They also cannot write papers for us nor do our proofreading. They cannot research our topic. They cannot type our paper nor prepare the format for us to hand in. But they can be a knowledgeable voice and an understanding second opinion when we do not know where to turn.

Giving Suggestions and Criticism

We also may be asked to give good criticism to others on their work, either in the classroom or in the dormitory. Look at the principles given in this chapter. Help others with their thesis statements, with logic, with assumptions, and so on. When we can give specific suggestions on another's paper, that person can benefit by making the paper clearer and more effective for the audience to read.

Example: *Josh had finished the second draft of his paper, but he still was not entirely satisfied with the way it looked. He knew that he had a few problems with punctuation and organization, but he had corrected all that he could. His friend Cesar told him about the college writing center where he could take his paper for a final check. As Josh entered the center, he was greeted by Katia who had worked in the center for two years. She directed him to a nearby table and they sat down to go over Josh's paper. Josh told her of his concerns, so they looked first at organization. Katia showed him how two of his paragraphs could be reversed to make the paper flow more logically. Then Josh asked about punctuation. He told her how he had always had problems with the use of semicolons. Katia pulled out a handbook with instructions and examples of semicolon use, and together they went through Josh's paper to see if he could utilize the semicolon in his writing. They also saw some commas that were misplaced. As he left the center, he felt much happier with his paper and was ready to write his final draft.*

Conclusion

If we have followed the suggestions thus far, we have begun to understand the principles of good critical thinking, reading, and writing. We also understand the usefulness of being aware of all four aspects of communication, and learn to anticipate the needs of the audience and the place of purpose in our writing. Critical reading and writing may seem like a great amount of work, especially at first, but mastering these skills brings increased satisfaction and more vivid and effective communication. A writer is rewarded for his efforts by achieving confidence in his skills and positive feedback for his writing.

Student Essays in Progress

Several essays written by students follow. They are not model essays—ones that receive A+. The students are simply average students, like most. Their essays show their progress toward the final drafts. Here are drafts that need much additional work; they have logic problems and thesis problems. But they also show normal students' work. As we discuss their essays, we can look at the flaws as well as the good things. We often can learn more by looking at imperfect essays than glossy, perfect ones.

Essay #1 "An Analysis of 'Sex Education'" by Matthew Chase
Example of Annotation

pushing it back and looking around, quick, to make sure one

of the men hadn't found out where I was. Then I thought I saw

a man coming towards me, and I ran away from him—and fell down,

and <u>burst some of the buttons off my dress</u>, and was sick to

my stomach—and thought I heard a man close to me and got up

and staggered around, knocking into the corn because I couldn't

even see where I was going.

"And then, off to one side, I saw Cousin Malcolm. <u>Not a</u>
Different because of position
<u>man. The minister.</u> He was standing still, one hand up to his

face thinking. He hadn't heard me.

probably scared him to death
"I was so <u>terrible</u> glad to see <u>him</u>, instead of one of those

men, I ran as fast as I could and just flung myself on him,
thought she wanted him
to make myself feel how safe I was."

Aunt Minnie had become strangely agitated. Her hands were
she angry, frightened, embarrassed
shaking, her face was crimson. She frightened us. We could not
They were all attention now
look away from her. As we waited for her to go on, I felt

little spasms twitch at the muscles inside my body. "And what
said sarcastically
do you think that *saint*, that holy minister of the Gospel, did

to an innocent child who clung to him for safety? The most

terrible look came into his eyes—you girls are too young to

know what he looked like. But once you're married, you'll find

out. He grabbed hold of me—that dreadful face of his was *right*
Emotional statement
on mine—and began clawing the clothes off my back."

She stopped for a moment, panting. We were too frightened

to speak. She went...

Example of Free Writing

Long drawn-out story. Details change of story over years.

Is story becoming more accurate? Are fine details coming forth

that she was embarrassed to talk about before? Or is she just

rationalizing and making these things up? Early in the story

sounds like classic "tell nothing to kids about sex." Should

have know something any way. All three stories probably wrong.

I think last one probably the best.

Example of Mapping

Aunt Minnie recounts an experience in her past when she wishes she had been more informed about sex education.

1st Time	2nd Time	3rd Time
Cousin got her terrified. She is scared in cornfield. Threw herself at Minister. She innocent and unknowing. He tried to molest her.	She put more blame on herself. She should have known better. He not so aggressive this time.	It just about all her fault now. She'd been watching him. She as much wanted him as she was scared. She only screamed because of his face. She worried about his feelings. She fainted because of tight dress.

Example of Outlining

Thesis statement: Aunt Minnie's story became more accurate with age.

    I. First telling was biased
        A. Happened not so long ago
            1. Tend to exaggerate critical situations
            2. Try to uphold your side of the story
            3. Embarrassed to tell the truth
        B. Talking to young teenagers
        C. Trying to scare same

    II. Second telling not as biased
        A. Talking to older people
        B. Changed blame from minister to cousin
        C. Still not tell total truth

    III. Third telling most accurate
        A. She is old lady
            1. Not embarrassed at all
            2. Looking at situation more realistically
            3. Reminiscing
        B. Blame now switched mostly to her
        C. Somewhat distorted because of time

Rough Draft of "Sex Education"— Nov. 11

In the short story, "Sex Education," by Dorothy Canfield, Aunt Minnie told about an experience that happened to her when she was a teenager. She told this story

Final Draft of "Sex Education" — Dec. 4

In the short story, "Sex Education," by Dorothy Canfield, Aunt Minnie tells about an experience that happened to her when she was a teenager. She tells the same to the narrator on three separate occasions. Many years separate each of the narratives. Accordingly, each time it was told, the story differed. I have come to the conclusion that Aunt Minnie's story became more accurate with age.

I have come to this conclusion due to a number of reasons. I feel these reasons are best summarized by going over each version of Aunt Minnie's story separately, in chronological order.

The first time she told the story, Aunt Minnie was in her thirties. The incident happened to her when she was about sixteen. Thus, in comparison to a person's total lifetime (expected lifetime), not very many years had elapsed between the two. This is a very significant fact. It leads to three distinct defects in Minnie's story the first time it was told.

The first problem is that a person tends to exaggerate many of the details of an extremely emotional and intense situation. The longer it has been since the situation, the less this applies. However, I don't feel that it has been long enough for Aunt Minnie. Especially since this is the first time she has ever told the story. The more times a person tells a story, the less emotional they get about it.

The next problem is that Aunt Minnie probably altered details to uphold her side of the story. this is due to the fact that she is still so emotionally involved with the situation. Both this and

tale to narrator on three separate occasions. Many years separate each of the narratives. Accordingly, each time it is told, the story differs. I have come to the conclusion that Aunt Minnie's story becomes more accurate with age.

I have come to this conclusion for a number of reasons. I feel these reasons are best illustrated by going over each version of Aunt Minnie's story in chronological order.

The first time she tells the story Aunt Minnie is in her thirties.The incident occurs when she is about sixteen. Thus, in comparison to her total expected lifetime, not very many years had elapsed. This is significant because it leads to three distinct defects in Minnie's story.

The first problem with her narration is that a person tends to exaggerate many details of an extremely emotional and intense situation. The longer it has been since the situation occurred, the less this applies. However, I don't feel that fourteen years has been long enough for Aunt Minnie. This is especially true since she claims this is the first time she has ever told the story. Besides the more times a person tells a story, the less emotional they get about it.

The second problem is that Aunt Minnie changes the details of the story as her perception of the incident changes. When she gives her story the first time, she is still very emotionally involved with the situation. But the

the previous problem are both basically subconscious defense mechanisms used to protect an individual in their own mind.

The third problem resulting from the time factor is that Aunt Minnie is still sensitive to the subject of what happened in the corn field on that day. It would be too embarrassing to emit the truth to herself to herself even.

The final major defect with the first version of the story is caused by Aunt Minnie's audience. They were teenage girls. Aunt Minnie was purposely altering the story to try and scare the girls out of sleeping outside. You just didn't talk openly about sex to teenage girls at that time.

The next time Aunt Minnie told the story, she was fifty-five. Also she was talking to women who were apparently in their mid-thirties. Both of these facts caused Aunt Minnie to alter her story.

She is now changes some of the blame for the insident from the minister to herself and even more so to her cousin for getting her paranoid.

She has obviously looked at the situation a little more realistically. She has also probably thought about the incident a great deal. This helps to dispel some of the emotion that clouds what happened.

The final time she tells the story, Aunt Minnie is in her eighties. She is telling the story to just the narrator. Ac-

emotional involvement becomes lessened with time, so that she can see the facts as they truly are. This is clearly seen the first time she tells the story. In this version, the minister is completely at fault: "The most terrible look came into his eyes. . . . He grabbed hold of me . . . and began clawing the clothes off my back" (226). However, by the third time she tells the story, this has all changed.

The third problem caused by time in the first version of the story is that Aunt Minnie is still too sensitive to the subject of what happened. She is too embarrassed to even admit the truth to herself.

The fourth and final major problem with the first version of the story is caused by Aunt Minnie's audience. They are teenage girls at that time. You didn't talk openly about sex to teenage girls at that time. In addition, Aunt Minnie is deliberately altering the story to try and scare the girls from sleeping outside. She is afraid that if the situation arose the girls could fall into the same problem she had. She is aware of the desires and attitudes of young girls and doesn't want them to follow her example.

The second time Aunt Minnie tells the story, she is fifty-five. She is now talking to women who are apparently in their mid-thirties. Both of these facts cause her to alter the story. She is now willing to change some of the blame for the incident from the minister to herself and to her cousin. "Wasn't I the big ninny? But not cordingly, Aunt Minnie is much more "laid back" and open. Being an old lady, she seems to be willing to tell everything without any emabarresment. The truth doesn't bother her now. From her tone, it appears that she has thought about the incident a great deal. This could be due to the problems she has had with her son Jake, and the thoughts that that has induced in her. I'm sure that she now understands the minister's position much better.

so big a ninny as that old cousin of mine. I could wring her neck for getting me in such a state" (228). Time has helped her look at the situation a little more realistically. She has also obviously thought about the incident a great deal. These have helped dispel some of the emotion that clouded what happened.

The final time she tells the story Aunt Minnie is in her eighties. She is telling the story to the narrator alone. Accordingly, Aunt Minnie is much more relaxed and open. Because of her age, she seems to be willing to tell everything without being embarrassed. In addition, she has finally come to terms with herself and accepts responsibility for her actions. She no longer feels the need to cover up her actions, but tells the story as it really happened. She now changes the story so the blame for the incident rests almost totally on herself. "I suppose, if it hadn't been for that dreadful scar, he'd have drawn me up, tight, and—most any man would—kissed me. I know how I must have looked, all red and hot and my hair down and my dress torn open. I might have come out of the cornfield halfway engaged to marry him. Why not? I was old enough . . . But what did I do? I had one look at his poor, horrible face, and started back as though I'd stepped on a snake. And screamed and ran" (231-232).

The reflective attitude she uses as she talks to the narrator indicates deep thought and rationalization about the incident. Through the years and her experiences in dealing with her son,

Jake, and his woman problems, she has gained insight and under-standing in what happened. Now, she can identify with the minis-ter and understand that she could have ruined him.

In summary, it has been said that time heals all wounds. Perhaps this cliche can apply to this story. As time went by, Aunt Minnie's story became more accu-rate as she became emotionally detached from the incident.

Essay #2 "The Three Hermits" by Adam Sowa
Thesis Statement and Outline

Thesis statement: In his characterization of the other characters, and their search of God, Tolstoy defines his audience and shows how their different strategies are "vain."

   I. Pilgrims on boat
      A. Bought passage on boat to shrines
         1. Seeking God at old, "dead" places
         2. Little self-sacrifice
      B. Passive discipleship
      C. Not interested in going out of their way

  II. Ship's crew
      A. Caught up in being successful
      B. Tend to disbelieve reports of hermits
         1. Accuse fishermen of spreading lies
         2. Attempt to dissuade Bishop from seeking hermits
         3. Interested in finances—blinds them

 III. Bishop
      A. Intellectual curiosity
      B. Self-important
         1. Accustomed to shows of respect
         2. Must be obeyed
            a. Changes course of ship
            b. Makes Hermits do as he says
      C. Congratulates self

  IV. Conclusion
      A. Matt. 6:7-8; "vain repetitions"
      B. If you do not search vainly, will be guided to God

First Draft

In Tolstoy's "The Three Hermits" Tolstoy introduces us to three old men who live on an island, "praying for their fellowman and trying to save their souls." The first one is very old and wears "a priest's cassock." The second man is also very old, and wears a "tattered peasant coat." The third hermit is old, with a white beard reaching to his knees. He is stern, and wears a piece of matting around his waist. These three are always together, and seem to know what the other thinks without the first saying it. Tolstoy portrays them as going hand in hand. Tolstoy uses the Hermits to symbolize the Trinity. In his characterization of the others the story Tolstoy makes his audience clear.

Some of the first characters mentioned by Tolstoy were pilgrims travelling on the ship to visit shrines near the Solovetsk Monastery. We are told the pilgrims "lay on deck, eating, or [sitting] in groups talking." These pilgrims are good people intent on seeking God. In their search for God they bought passage on the ship. However, their's is mainly a passive discipleship. They do not do anything beyond going to a place where God was once.

The ships crew, on the other hand, are not interested in travelling to the monastery unless they can get paid for it. They are not seeking for any thing but financial success. Along with this they tend to disbelieve reports of the hermits existence. this is not for lack of witnesses, however, but because of the inconvenience that their existence would cause. When the crew could not convince the

Final Draft

In "The Three Hermits" Tolstoy introduces us to three very old men who live on an island, "praying for their fellowman and trying to save their souls." The first one wears "a priest's cassock." The second man wears a "tattered peasant coat." The third hermit has a white beard reaching to his knees, and he wears a piece of matting around his waist. They are always together, holding hands, and seem to know each other's thoughts. These things, along with the way they walk on water at the end, imply that they are symbolic of the Trinity. In his characterization of the other characters, and their search for God, Tolstoy defines his audience and shows how their different strategies are "vain."

The first characters mentioned by Tolstoy are pilgrims travelling on the ship to visit shrines near the Solovetsk Monastery. The pilgrims are "lay[ing] on deck, eating, or [sitting] in groups talking." Their search for God consists of buying passage on the ship. However, theirs is a passive discipleship. They cannot imagine that God would be anywhere but at these shrines, so they do not seek elsewhere. As a result, they completely miss God, the same way they miss the hermits. The ship's crew, on the other hand, are not interested in travelling to the monastery unless they get paid for it. They are not seeking for anything but financial success. They tend to disbelieve the fisherman's reports of the hermits' existence, because of the inconvenience that the hermits' existence would cause. When the crew cannot convince the Bishop that the hermits don't exist, the

Bishop that the Hermits did not exist, the Captain tried to convince him that seeking them was not worth his time. "They are foolish old fellows, who understand nothing, and never speak a word, any more than the fish in the sea."

The Bishop is the third type of person Tolstoy represents as one who uses vain repetition. First, the Bishop has, primarily, an intellectual curiosity about the hermits. Initially, he wanted to visit the island to "see them," not because he was interested in teaching them. Next, the Bishop is somewhat self-important. He is accustomed to people showing him respect and obedience. Finally, his pride is really emphasized when he sits on the deck congratulating himself for teaching the hermits a better way to pray.

These characters show different ways people who are initially interested in following Christ begin seeking vain repetitions in the end. The pilgrims originally are interested in seeking God, but end up visiting "dead" shrines. The crew are interested only in making a profit, which money, in the end, will be vain. The Bishop has been trained to serve God, by His representative on earth, but ends up putting himself in God's place. Each of these things are "vain" in the quest to find God. Tolstoy teaches that we must follow the Hermits example and humbly seek to emulate God—make "three are ye, three are we; have mercy on us" our own prayer.

Captain tries to convince him that seeking them is not worth his time. "They are foolish old fellows, who understand nothing, and never speak a word, any more than the fish in the sea."

Through the Bishop, Tolstoy teaches how excessive intellectualism and pride are "vain." The Bishop's curiosity about the hermits is primarily intellectual. Initially, he wants to visit the island to "see them," not because he is interested in their "salvation." Next, the Bishop is self-important. He is accustomed to people showing him respect and obedience. His pride is emphasized as he sits on deck congratulating himself for teaching the hermits a better way to pray. These things keep the bishop from "seeing" the spiritual nature of the hermits while he visits with them. His blinded eyes show that this attitude is vain.

In the very beginning of his story, even before the text begins, Tolstoy quotes Matthew 6:7-8. This scripture admonishes to "not use vain repetitions." Tolstoy tells us who uses "vain repetitions," and these repetitions are used through his characterization. Shrines are vain because God is not there anymore; money is vain because it will not bring salvation; pride and intellectual inquiry are vain because they blind us to God. Tolstoy gives examples of what it means to live in those ways. He leaves the reader with hope, however, in the example of the Bishop. If we humble ourselves and shun those things that are vain, we will, as the Bishop does in the end, see a light shining in the darkness of our personal nights showing us where we can find God until finally day breaks.

Introduction to Argument and Persuasion

The History of Argumentation

Critical thinking, reading, and writing—all need to be utilized when a reader or writer approaches argument and persuasion. The conscientious student must develop the "critical eye" in working with sophisticated communication skills. Since the philosophy governing many of these skills stems from early Greek times, perhaps an overview of those beginnings would be helpful to see how critical thinking, along with its expression in reading and writing, developed.

Classical Argumentation and Rhetoric

The basic principles of classical argumentation (logic and debate) and rhetoric (using words effectively to influence or persuade) stem from Aristotle who lived in the fourth century B.C. His methods were shaped and expanded by later writers, but Aristotle's basic principles are still used today. Aristotle studied argument and rhetoric by looking at the patterns of classification or purpose that each speech contained (different kinds of speeches); by looking at the audience for whom the rhetoric was intended (the senate, students, etc.); and by looking at the way that rhetoric was prepared. The five stages of rhetoric preparation are invention, arrangement, style, memory, and delivery. Aristotle also determined that rhetoric could have three forms or modes of persuasion: *logos* (reason), *pathos* (emotion), and *ethos* (authority or ethics).

Purpose and audience were discussed at length in Chapters 2 and 3 as basic considerations in the communication process. The five steps to speech preparation or composing an essay, as an integral part of the study of rhetoric, has shaped discourse (or communication) through the centuries. A discussion of these five comes later, but first let us examine the three modes of persuasion, *logos, pathos,* and *ethos.*

Aristotle's Rhetoric[1]

> Academically speaking, the oldest profession in the world is teaching what we now call composition. The Greeks called it rhetoric. In the fifth century B.C. a group of professional teachers began accepting fees for their public lectures. These

[1]Taken from an unpublished paper, "The Greek Foundation of Composition: Applying Aristotle's *Rhetoric* to the Classroom," by Grant Boswell, Brigham Young University, 1992.

teachers were called sophists, meaning simply wise men. Although each sophist usually had some art or craft that he specialized in, all taught rhetoric or the art of public discourse.

The sophists started an intellectual movement that Socrates, Plato, and Aristotle took up, usually contending against the sophists. But it is as a result of the sophistic interest in rhetoric that Aristotle undertook the first thorough and systematic study of human discourse. [...]

Aristotle begins [his book entitled] Rhetoric *with this statement: "Rhetoric is the counterpart of Dialectic." By "dialectic" he meant something like what we mean by "logic." He also says that rhetoric is a part of ethics and politics: "The truth is, as indeed we have said already, that rhetoric is a combination of the science of logic and of the ethical branch of politics." Rhetoric and dialectic partake of the same qualities in that both deal with probability rather than with truth, and both are generally applicable to all aspects of human knowledge and action. They differ in thoroughness and audience: dialectic is more rigorous, while rhetoric appeals to a general, more diversified audience. Rhetoric is a branch of politics and ethics in that rhetoric deals with matters of significance to citizens in a community and must therefore comprehend and accommodate the habits, mores, and customs of the community.*

In addition to the difference mentioned above, rhetoric differs from logic in two ways that are essential to understand. Aristotle will again be useful here. His three modes of rhetorical proof are ethos, *the speaker's ability to evince a personal character which will make his speech credible;* logos, *his ability to prove a point by means of persuasive arguments; and* pathos, *his ability to discern how the emotional state of the audience will influence its judgment. Dialectic relies only on* logos *while rhetoric relies on all three modes of proof. These three modes of persuasion then provide one basis for teaching a rhetorical approach to composition.*

Invention

In the structure of argument, *logos, pathos,* and *ethos* play an important role. As mentioned previously, the five stages of argument (or rhetoric) preparation are invention, arrangement, style, memory, and delivery. In classical argument, the first step, invention, is weighted toward *logos,* the logical argument. There is an emphasis on the logic of an argument to establish its validity. In the discussion on inductive and deductive reasoning, as well as in the section on logical fallacies, we noted the importance of valid logic.

The second mode, *pathos,* also plays a role in argumentation. During the invention process, emotion usually inspires argument, even if it is controlled and kept in perspective. Aristotle's school acknowledges the value of the popular appeal of *pathos,* emotion used in persuasion, but strongly supports the superiority of *logos.*

Ethos, the third mode, gives validity to an argument during the invention step by authority or by an appeal to universal principles, and includes how the author presents herself to the audience.

All three of the values form the triad of reasonable argument. The triad has been used by many teachers and practitioners of logic as a useful visual representation.

Sometimes other names are given to the corners of the triad as in the communication model below:

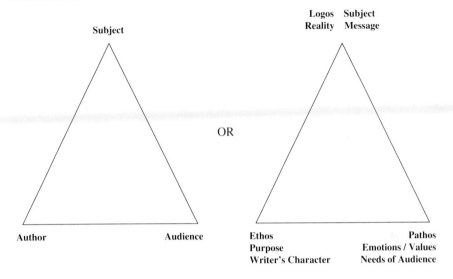

Logos can be related to the subject or message given, *pathos* to the audience needs or values, and *ethos* to the purpose or character of the author. These three aspects must be balanced to make the argument the most effective. Often the center of the triangle includes the medium of communication or language. Without language there is no argument because communication breaks down.

Looking at these three modes, we can return to the earlier discussions on audience and purpose. Chapter 1 discussion on critical thinking also relates to *logos,* or the subject or message by examining assumptions.

Example: *Cynthia became concerned about the vandalism in roadway rest stops which not only cost the taxpayers considerable amounts for repair, but also caused inconvenience to travellers needing to use the facilities. She was asked to write an article about the problem for the local newspaper. During the formulation (invention) of the article, she emphasized the logical consequences of such misbehavior. To add an emotional element to her article, she described a case study of a family who had used the rest stop, but one of the children had become injured on a broken fixture. She used ethos by appealing to the universal principles of honesty and fairness to others. By appealing to statements by the government agency responsible for main-tenance of the rest stops, she also gave validity to her argument.*

Arrangement

In classical structure, the second important step in building an argument is arrangement. Placing the argument in the most effective order, classical rhetoric follows the pattern: the introduction; the statement of the claim or issue; the argument, substantiation (verification or proving) of the claim, or refutation of opposition (answering any opposing arguments); and the conclusion (hence the origin of the traditional structure, as found in Chapter 3). Within the arrangement, *pathos* and *ethos* are often reserved for use in the introduction and conclusion. *Logos* is used to present the argument, substantiate it, and refute the opposition. It usually outweighs the other areas.

Nowadays the classical arrangement seems so natural that we do not think of it as being invented. How else would anyone present an argument but to introduce it, then support it and defend it? Limiting ethics and emotion to the introduction and conclusion probably could use some thought, however. Probably a case could be made for staying with the Aristotelian model in its most basic form.

Example: In writing an argument for support of the homeless, Brad first gave an introduction outlining the problems of the homeless. He used pathos to create sympathy for the plight of the families in crisis who were using the shelter, and he used ethos in the statements by those running the shelter. Logos was used during the substantiation discussion during which he outlined possible solutions to some immediate problems at the shelter. Pathos was again used in the conclusion as he referred to a particular family in need who would benefit by his suggested changes.

Style

One of the major roles of the composing process is the use of words, the language within the argument. As the third aspect of classical rhetoric, it plays a vital role. However, it is a flexible variable because style can include ornate figures of speech or be a straightforward presentation of argument. Style simply reflects the writer's personality and attitudes. But stylists through the centuries have had a heyday with language, compounded with elaborate rules. Current style tends toward the more plain, straightforward presentation of material. Probably the technology of the modern era had a hand in simplifying style. Directions, user manuals, and all aspects of technical writing call for clarity, simplicity, and readability. Much of today's writing follows this pattern.

Of course, more complex and much more individualistic styles can be found with various authors, especially in literature. The writer's choice of words or diction, tone, choice of subject, syntax, or strategies reflect an attitude toward the subject matter, and become that writer's *style.*

Example: Pierre was taking a course entitled Overview of English Literature to 1820. His examinations contained spot passages from the works he had read. To identify the authors, he studied their style. That is, he learned to tell which authors wrote poetry, which used very complex sentences, which wrote on particular topics, and which used such literary devices as allusions or figurative language. Learning the different styles helped Pierre to finish the class in "style."

Inappropriate or illogical approaches or diction, on the other hand, can weaken the argument by showing the author's bias and thus reducing the author's credibility.

Memory

In the centuries before the printing press when only a few documents were available, oral presentation of arguments necessitated extensive memorization. This practice was believed to expand the mind and increase intelligence. As the fourth step in classical rhetoric, memory held a central role in oral persuasion. Its current role in written rhetoric may focus on the mechanics of knowledge, but memory always will play a part in forming arguments and influencing people. Without memory, we cannot pull together ideas that are gleaned at different times and from different places to make a persuasive argument.

Delivery

Effective oral presentation of argument relies on visual support—gestures, facial expressions, vocal interpretations, and body language. In classical rhetoric delivery was the fifth, but also a major, part of argumentation. Currently, delivery still may be part of the communication skill, speaking, but may also focus on reading and writing argument. Delivery can include the structure of an argument on the page; the arrangement of arguments, the substantiation of proof, and the power of the conclusion all influence what an audience will accept. Another aspect of delivery is what an audience sees first—that is, format or how a document looks.

Example: Although she knew that her paper was carefully written with sound logic and good examples, Maureen wanted to make the appearance of the paper as impressive as possible. After doing a final polishing, she ran her paper through the spell-check on the computer and had a friend give it a last going-over. Then she ran the paper off on a laser printer on bond paper, put on a heavy cardstock cover, and had it bound. The paper was presented to the teacher exactly on time. The delivery was then as good as the content.

The Structure of Classical Arguments

Classical rhetoric arguments are formally structured into syllogisms and enthymemes. Syllogisms, with their three-part formal structures, each with a stated major premise, minor premise, and conclusion, were discussed in Chapter 1. Enthymemes are more naturally structured arguments wherein one of the premises or sometimes the conclusion is only implied. The word *enthymeme* comes from the Greek en *within,* thymeisthai *the mind* (but it is a verb), and ma *result.* That is, an enthymeme is an argument wherein part of the result is retained in the mind.

Enthymemes

Aristotle's *Rhetoric* also discusses enthymemes. Quoting from Boswell (see footnote), "Aristotle says that for rhetoric the 'enthymeme' is 'the body of proof.'" By enthymeme he means a statement followed by another causal statement; for example, "It's going to rain today *because* it is cloudy." The implied major premise is thus: If it's cloudy, it will rain.

The difference between a rhetorical enthymeme and the type of syllogism previously discussed is purely formal—the enthymeme has one of its premises suppressed. The enthymeme is a very natural form of reasoning, and our language is set up to construct enthymemes easily. Every time we use "because" or another causal adverb such as "for," "as," or "since"; or every time we use an "If . . . then" or "While this . . . then that" construction; or every time we use words like "therefore," "hence," or "consequently" to signal a conclusion, we are reasoning enthymemically. Often this type of reasoning is called informal logic or practical reasoning, but we also know it simply as common sense. Aristotle's genius was to build a theory of composition around the natural propensity of humans to use reasoned speech (Boswell 3).

Constructing Arguments from Classical Rhetoric

An argument is meant to provide the answer to a problem in question form. Boswell notes, "In rhetorical invention the writer must locate an issue question (a stated problem), provide a thesis, and generate support—all of which meet the criterion of significance to the audience." Classical rhetoric lends itself well to constructing arguments. Facts are presented in either syllogisms or enthymemes, then those facts are defended by support or challenged with opposing arguments. The structure lends itself to analysis of reading as well. Arguments presented in print can be fitted into the patterns and tested for validity.

The thesis or claim is the student's answer to the issue question and is the point to be proven; it is the conclusion *to the paper. The issue question allows us to judge the merit of a writer's thesis because both the issue and the thesis must meet the criterion of significance. To ensure a causal argument the student must state her claim using active, transitive verbs. Example: "Cutting the NASA budget* increases *the likelihood of future space shuttle disasters." The claim must be initially unacceptable to the audience; that is, the reader's response to the claim should be "Why?"*

The supporting statement also uses active, transitive verbs and must be reasonable or probable to the audience.

Example: Encouraging NASA to supplement its budget with commercial ventures increases *its likelihood to take 'business' risks to maintain its research program.*

The complete statement, thesis and support, is the enthymeme: "Cutting the NASA budget increases *the likelihood of future space shuttle disasters because encouraging NASA to supplement its budget with commercial ventures* increases *its likelihood to take 'business' risks to maintain its research program." This enthymeme reflects the student's answer to a topic of interest to her audience and provides a means of supporting her claim.*

Every enthymeme, however, is based on an implicit (or hidden) assumption. Just as the enthymeme "It's going to rain today because it's cloudy" is based on the assumption that clouds bring rain, the enthymeme arguing that cutting the NASA budget increases the chances of future shuttle disasters is also built on an implied assumption. The assumption that clouds bring rain can be challenged: Sometimes clouds do, and sometimes they don't. Just to make sure that her argument has a chance with real readers, the student must test the implicit assumption of the enthymeme on her peers in the class. The implicit assumption is something like "Whenever more risks are incorporated into a program, the probability for problems is increased." This is an assumption that must be subjected to the scrutiny of a representative audience to be validated. In this case the implicit assumption is acceptable to most readers, so the student's argument is couched in an assumption that is acceptable to her audience. The complete enthymeme now can be used as the controlling structure for the entire argument (Boswell 5–7).

Student Exercises: Enthymemes

1. Construct enthymemes from ideas that may develop into an argument paper.

2. Use magazines and newspapers to find enthymemes in modern writing.

3. Write an enthymeme which has questionable hidden or implicit assumption and discuss why it invalidates the argument.

Variations and expansions on the classical modes have helped rhetoricians formulate other patterns of argumentation and persuasion. One of the more popular and useful is the Toulmin method.

The Toulmin Method

Not all principles of argument can be placed under the umbrella of classical rhetoric. Rhetoric has been shaped by many strong voices through the centuries. Stephen Toulmin, who was born in 1922, is one of the more modern of those voices. His theories move logic away from abstract methods of discovering truth and toward clear and flexible structures of argument.

Toulmin begins with a *claim* (a warranted assumption) which is based on *data* (facts). When a claim and data are linked, they need to be supported by rules, principles, or "bridges" called a *warrant*. The claim and data often need *backing* (additional support). The claim may also need a *qualifier* (words like perhaps, likely, might, probably) and may produce a *rebuttal* (exceptions to the claim).

In one of Toulmin's examples of reasoning, the claim (1) is that Harry is a British subject. This claim is based on the data (2) that Harry was born in Bermuda. The warrant (3) establishes that Bermudians are legally British subjects. The warrant is supported by the backing (4) which cites the British Nationality Act for colonies as verification of his citizenship. The qualifier (5) indicates that Harry is *probably* or *likely* a British subject because of the data and the backing, but uses the rebuttal (6) to indicate that there may be exceptions to the claim if Harry's parents were both aliens or if Harry had become a naturalized American.

(from Toulmin, *The Uses of Argument*)

Using the Toulmin Method in Forming Arguments

Arguments can be constructed using the Toulmin model in a similar manner to those constructed using the classical rhetorical method with a few exceptions. Toulmin includes the use of qualifiers and rebuttals. These two additions give flexibility in the argument. For example, note the following example using a qualifier and a rebuttal:

Claim: This mountain stream has unpolluted water.

Backing: All the mountain streams I have seen are unpolluted.

Qualifier: Although not all mountain streams may be unpolluted.

Rebuttal: Sometimes streams become polluted when they contain a dead wild animal upstream.

Conclusion: So this mountain is presumably unpolluted unless it has been polluted by a dead wild animal upstream.

Because the Toulmin model expands the structure of argument to backing and qualifiers, it is especially useful in argument construction to cover a broader range of arguments. We often have to qualify our assumptions to fit conditions. The Toulmin model provides that flexibility. However, none of the above methods of argument is valid if faulty logic is used in the premises or the warrant. Critical thinking demands that we check for flaws that would discredit the argument.

Student Exercises: Toulmin Method

1. Examine an argument to see which method of development is best suited—the classical rhetoric, enthymeme construction, or the Toulmin model. Introduce qualifiers and rebuttals to see if they clarify the issue.

2. Combine reading and writing skills to research an argument. See if it can be presented clearly in skeletal structure, then clothe it with backing and qualifiers. Is there a reasonable conclusion?

Analyzing and Evaluating Arguments

Many people think of argument as a heated discussion where tempers flare and emotion gets in the way of reason—a quarrel, in other words. That definition of argument is a common one; however, argument can be used in another sense. As seen in the analysis of classical rhetoric, argument can be a well-thought-out presentation of a position, given without being clouded with emotional reactions. The purpose of an argument is usually to persuade the audience to a particular position on an issue. Therefore, critical thinking is vital in preparing, supporting, and presenting the issue in such a way that the audience responds favorably.

When the argument is prepared, it should have gone through the processes discussed in Chapter 1; that is, it should be based on facts with warranted assumptions. Then, it should be supported and evaluated using carefully structured inductive or deductive reasoning.

The evaluation of argument can be directed in two ways: we can put ourselves in the position of the reader and evaluate the arguments of those we read, or we can prepare our own arguments in a written composition.

Example: *Tony read a particularly scurrilous article in a newspaper about a political figure he respected. It made him so angry that he wanted to lash back immediately at the writer of the article. So many false statements were made about the person in question, but also there were damaging innuendoes. After Tony had cooled down, he carefully thought through the argument. It helped to place the argument in a syllogistic structure to identify the premises and conclusions. He brought into play his critical thinking skills to look at assumptions and inferences. Following his analysis, Tony carefully constructed an article that refuted the faulty statements and exposed the innuendoes.*

Persuasive Arguments

As we read a newspaper or popular magazine, we often see editorial columns or articles which argue one or the other position of a topic—politics, the environment, social issues, international relations, religion, medical care, and so on. These arguments, often in the form of an enthymeme, try to persuade the audience of the need for a certain kind of belief or action. Most of the arguments are based on facts, such as statistics, case studies, examples, lawsuits. Often the arguments seem so persuasive that the readers must agree, point by point. The assumptions are so well presented, often based on deductive reasoning which, in turn, is tied to a fundamental truth upon which there is little disagreement. The readers cannot find fault, it seems, with the argument. In addition, the argument is clearly and often forcefully written. It has just the right amount of emotional appeal in the right places.

Faulty Arguments

On the other hand, some editorials or other persuasive articles make us uncomfortable, even angry. Sometimes we are disturbed by the argument itself. It challenges a deeply held assumption of our own. At other times the argument uses facts or assumptions that we suspect are distorted or false.

The Distortion of an Argument

An argument may be distorted accidentally. Usually this occurs when the author is so emotionally involved in an issue that he or she uses support that verifies only one side of the position, without considering the ramifications or strengths of the opposite position.

Unintentional distortion is frequently common because people hold certain views that carry a great deal of emotional baggage. They simply will not look at an opposing view. We can find issues of our own that tend to be inflexible. Distancing ourselves from an issue is difficult.

Example: *Barbara intensely disliked the Santa Claus deception. When she had been a child, her parents carried the story far out of proportion and would never admit to the truth. She became disillusioned with everything her parents had taught—including her religious faith—because of what she envisioned to be deception. When she herself had children, she insisted on explaining the Santa Claus myth to them early on. She did not allow them to believe. One day, her young son interrupted her recitation of the myth with the words, "Mama, please don't tell us that story again. I don't like it." The child wanted to believe in Santa Claus.*

Sometimes those emotional issues can trigger excellent articles, especially if an honest attempt for fairness enters the scene. But sometimes the distortion is intentional. Authors deliberately search for material or make claims to present a one-sided view. Or the authors may use evidence in an illogical manner. When such unfair distortion is seen, the argument often becomes discredited—exactly what the author did not want to happen. As readers, we may wish to challenge what we read that seems unfair or wrong.

Discussion Questions: Arguments

1. When have you encountered arguments that persuaded you to change your mind about an issue? What specifically was the method of persuasion used?

2. What kind of arguments do you find most persuasive? How much does emotion play in your response?

3. What approaches to arguments make you uncomfortable? Can you think of a time when you were disturbed or angered by an argument?

4. Why do you think arguments are distorted? What motives could a speaker or writer have to create the distortion?

5. How effective are distorted or faulty arguments? Has anyone you know been taken in by a faulty argument?

Although we may challenge an argument simply because we believe differently, a more effective challenge to an argument examines the second problem: distortion of facts or assumptions. To help work with a challenge, we should be aware of the logical fallacies that often accompany a faulty argument.

Logical Fallacies

Checking for Logical Fallacies

When writers are too emotionally involved with an argument, they may have a tendency to use any method to win the argument. Logical fallacies used to weigh the evidence in one direction may seem appealing. Unfortunately, some authors discredit their arguments by inappropriate use of logical fallacies.

Identifying Logical Fallacies

Flaws in an argument, such as logical fallacies, seriously weaken it, just as structural flaws weaken a building. One purpose for understanding logic is to discover these flaws so that we can distinguish between a good application of proof and a poor one, between truth and distortion. Although not everything that is true is logical nor is everything that is logical true, certain patterns of distortion or logical fallacies are recognizable. The almost endless number of variations in fallacies makes an exhaustive discussion of the subject impractical for this overview. Definitions and examples of some of the more common fallacies are listed below to give a sampling of logical problems. Some examples may be exaggerated or humorous, but flaws in logic can be deadly. Fallacious thinking created the concentration camps of World War II, much of the current civil turmoil in nations, and the international problem of human rights.

Although logical fallacies sometimes overlap, it is useful to make a distinction between some of the more familiar categories. The logical fallacies mentioned in this section are: (1) hasty generalization/sweeping generalization, (2) either/or fallacy, (3) *non sequitur* or "it does not follow," (4) *ad misericordiam* or "appealing to sympathy," (5) begging the question, (6) ignoring the burden of proof, (7) card stacking, (8) *dicto simpliciter* or "simple speech," (9) *argumentum ad hominem* (or *feminan*) or "argument to (against) the man (woman)," (10) poisoning the well, (11) *tu quoque* or "you're one, too," (12) appeal to force, (13) *ad populum* or "argument to the crowd," (14) complex question (a form of circular reasoning), (15) *post hoc, ergo propter hoc* or "after this, therefore because of this," (16) oversimplified cause, (17) red herring, (18) and false analogy.

Hasty Generalization/Sweeping Generalization

These fallacies occur when a conclusion is reached on too little evidence, isolated evidence, or widely accepted general principles applied incorrectly to a specific case. Hasty generalizations are made when insufficient facts are used to draw a conclusion, which is an inductive reasoning problem.

Example: *The increasing number of subway riders in New York and Washington shows that urban dwellers in this country prefer mass transit.*

Even if the conclusion is correct for these two particular cities, the generalization is spread too broadly. Two cities are not an adequate sample to make a valid conclusion about the entire country. In addition, other factors besides preference may be involved in the increase of subway riders—parking problems, the complexion of the work force (who may not be able to afford cars), traffic congestion, or convenience. If one or more of these factors were not present, the urban dwellers might prefer to drive their own cars.

Sweeping generalizations begin with a general principle, often a valid one. However, the generalization may not apply to each specific case because of distortion or irrelevance.

Example: *Christians believe in honesty as one of their basic principles, so we should not worry about hiring Jim Jones since he is a Christian.* Unfortunately, not all Christians exhibit behavior that is exemplary. The argument is too broad to be of value.

Either/Or Fallacy

The world would be much simpler if every decision had only two choices true/false, good/bad, bitter/sweet. However, multiple options are the rule, not the exception. In the either/or fallacy, choice is falsely narrowed to two options. This fallacy is frequently used by salespersons at the close of a sales pitch.

Example: *"Now, which vacuum cleaner should we write up for you, the super deluxe model or the economy commercial model? How would you like to pay for it—by cash or credit?"*

In each case, a third possibility exists of not buying the product. In fact, rarely does anything in life present only two options.

Non Sequitur *(It does not follow.)*

In this fallacy the premises have no connection with the conclusion. The fallacy is often used in advertisements.

Example: *"The striking mountains make a beautiful setting for these beautiful people. Therefore, you should buy a B . . . (brand name)."*

A gorgeous setting and a loving couple have absolutely nothing to do with a particular brand of anything. (This type of *non sequitur* is also called *transfer.*)

By using this type of fallacy, the advertiser hopes to get the prospective buyer to purchase his product by encouraging the audience to transfer their positive feelings about the loving couple to positive feelings about buying a product.

Ad Misericordiam *(appealing to sympathy)*

This fallacy occurs when one appeals to another's emotions and sympathy to gain support for the argument. Rather than using reasonable facts to support a position, the person using this fallacy tries to arouse the sympathy of the audience.

Example: *Asked why she is qualified, Rachel replies that she needs the money. She weeps and tells about her mother's illness and her father's loss of employment. She begs to have the job.*

Money may be Rachel's purpose in seeking the job, but those offering the job want to know about supporting facts such as the person's past experience, previous employment, or so on. The person who weeps or tells tales of woe in support of a position may be falling prey to this fallacy.

The following example was an advertisement for life insurance which also uses this fallacy.

Is Your House In Order?

Five duties line each mortal's path,
That leads to life's far border
To live, to learn
To serve, to earn
To set one's house in order.

You can set your own house in order thru the magic of life insurance with the stroke of a pen. THERE IS NO SUBSTITUTE FOR LIFE INSURANCE.

"A life insurance policy is just a time-yellowed piece of paper with columns of figures and legal phrases until it is baptized with a widow's tears. Then it is a modern miracle. Aladdin's lamp. It is food, clothing, shelter, education, peace of mind, comfort, undying love and affection. It is the sincerest love letter ever written.

"It quiets the crying of a hungry baby at night. It eases the aching heart of a bereaved widow. It is a new hope, fresh courage and strength for the mother to pick up the broken threads of life and carry on. It is a college education for sons and daughters, a chance for a career instead of a need for a job. It is father's parental blessing to the children on their wedding day.

"It is the function of father's hopes and plans for his family's future. Through the magic of life insurance he lives on. There is no death. Life insurance is a plan that exalts life and defeats death. It is the premium we pay for the privilege of living after death."

THERE IS NO SUBSTITUTE FOR LIFE INSURANCE

Begging the Question

This term describes an argument where, instead of giving proof for the solution, the argument simply gives the conclusion. Facts used to support a conclusion must not use the conclusion itself in place of facts. Such statements as "Jean went shopping because she wanted to buy something," or "belief in human rights is universal because everyone believes in human rights" show examples of arguments where proof is lacking. This statement doesn't prove how or why the belief in human rights is universal. *Circular arguments* are a form of begging the question wherein the beginning statement becomes the conclusion and no insight is gained in the interim.

Example: *Uncle Bill is getting old so he is having heart problems. How do you know he is having heart problems? Because he is getting old.*

Ignoring the Burden of Proof

The person trying to prove an argument is the one responsible for the facts and proper logic to reach an adequate conclusion. If that person presents a general statement as truth without supporting the assertion, especially if the statement is controversial, the person must not expect the reader or listener to provide refutation or justification for the assertion.

Example: *The country wastes hundreds of thousands of dollars on projects that are not only unnecessary, but dangerous. If good people were elected to the legislature, we would not have this corruption.*

Questions a reader might ask about this statement are: What projects that waste money is this person talking about? Why doesn't the writer give examples? What projects would be dangerous as well as wasteful? The reader does not have a clue. Also, the last sentence is problematic. It makes the hidden assumption that good people are not elected to the legislature, but gives no examples or verification of this assumption.

Card Stacking

Card stacking is a fallacy in which the writer or speaker provides facts to support his or her argument, but the facts give only one point of view and deliberately ignore the opposite point of view. Advertising and promotional information often use card stacking to sell a product. In fact, most people selling a product, whether it is a commodity or an idea, use card stacking to a certain extent, simply to create an appeal for the product or information.

An example of card stacking occurs when someone tries to set you up for a blind date.

Example: *The matchmaker told Janene that the prospective date was gorgeous, brilliant, charming, lots of fun, great job, loaded with money, dying to meet her, and the list went on and on. What the matchmaker did not tell her was frightening—espe-*

cially as she encounters that date for the first time and realizes that many, many facts were carefully hidden.

Dicto Simpliciter *(simple speech)*

This fallacy is based on an argument which begins with a simple, unqualified statement but reaches a conclusion which must be qualified to be accurate.

Example: *Milk has many vitamins and minerals. It is good for everyone.*

Although the initial statement is true, milk occasionally triggers a violent allergic reaction in some people, and may, therefore, not be good for everyone. The above statement is also a sweeping generalization and a *non sequitur.*

Dicto simpliciter also can be a simple statement which is misinterpreted, such as, "Fifty percent of beginning college students are women; John is a first-year student; ergo, he is 50 percent female."

Argumentum ad Hominem *(or* Feminam*)* *(against the man or woman)*

Argumentum ad hominem, Latin for "argument against the man," is also called "mudslinging." The fallacy occurs when a person is discredited deliberately to lessen the power of his or her argument or influence. Political opponents occasionally use *argumentum ad hominem* in the battle for votes. In court, the fallacy is justifiably used sometimes when a witness presents information he or she is not qualified to give or if his or her personality or habits would prevent him or her from being an adequate witness.

Example: *John Doe has been convicted of fraud on three occasions. His testimony as a character witness is therefore suspect.*

On the other hand, a drunk may be telling the truth when he says your house is on fire. You probably should at least check instead of dismissing what he says.

Poisoning the Well

This fallacy presents an issue in "loaded" terms (words with high emotional connotation), thereby making it difficult for some to consider the issue objectively. Similar to the *ad hominem* fallacy, the fallacy of poisoning the well presents information damaging to the argument even though it is not directly related to the issue.

Example: *Our tyrannical government is eroding the last bastion of society—the home—by raising taxes so high that too many women must work, whether they want to or not.*

The issue in this argument is taxation, but a secondary, emotional issue is eroding the argument by covering the issue with emotionalism (loaded terms). Poisoning the well is sometimes the term used instead of *ad hominem,* discrediting opponents beforehand, so that nothing they say can be accepted. Claiming that opponents have "a hidden agenda" poisons opinions about them before an issue can be discussed.

Tu Quoque *(You're one, too.)*

A free translation of this Latin phrase is, "You're one, too." This kind of argument evades or deflects an attack by making the same charge against the opponent. A roommate, who, when accused of not doing the dishes, replies, "You didn't either," is guilty of this fallacy. Note that such an argument virtually admits the accuracy of the charge while at the same time it diminishes the significance of it.

Appeal to Force

Rather than appealing to logic and reason, an appeal to force (threat) to gain support for an argument creates an emotional reaction that often has immediate and direct results.

Caving in to political or social pressure is another appeal to force. Although physical damage may not occur, social ostracism or ridicule could result.

Example: *If your state passes that law, our organization will boycott the state and make sure every similar organization will do the same.*

Ad Populum *(argument to the crowd)*

Ad populum identifies the kind of argument that appeals to the emotions and biases of the masses. Referring to America as the "greatest land on earth" is a common *ad populum* fallacy. The child who insists he or she should be allowed to do something questionable because "everybody does it" is also using the fallacy of *ad populum.*

Complex Question

Complex question is a question stated in such a way that any direct answer supports the questioner's assumptions. Another name for complex question is *loaded question.* The famous example: "Have you stopped beating your wife yet?" implies that the respondent now beats or has beaten his wife; a positive answer says that he once did beat his wife, but has since stopped. A negative answer indicates that the respondent still beats his wife. The third option, that neither answer is correct, is not mentioned. The cartoon on page 129 illustrates the complex question.

Post Hoc, Ergo Propter Hoc *(after this, therefore because of this)*

Taken from the Latin phrase meaning "after the fact, therefore because of the fact," this fallacy implies that because two events occurred at the same time, or were closely associated, one of them caused the other. A classic post hoc example comes from Mark Twain's *Huckleberry Finn:*

"If elected, would you try to fool some of the people all of the time, all of the people some of the time, or go for the big one: All of the people all of the time?"

from Worst Case Scenarios: A Collection of Cartoons by Jack Ziegler. Copyright © 1990 by Jack Ziegler. Reprinted by permission of Fireside Publishing.

> *I've always reckoned that looking at the new moon over your left shoulder is one of the carelessest and foolishest things a body can do. Old Hank Bunker done it once, and bragged about it and in less than two years he got drunk and fell off of the shot-tower and spread himself out so that he was just kind of a layer, as you may say; and they slid him edgeways between two barn doors for a coffin; and baried him so, so they say, but I didn't see it. Pap told me. But anyway it all come of looking at the moon that way, like a fool.*

(from Chapter 10)

The "Peanuts" cartoon on page 130 also illustrates the post hoc fallacy. Lucy assumes that because Linus gets a sliver in his finger, he has sinned. The conclusion does not follow a logical pattern of reasoning.

Oversimplified Cause

Similar to the post hoc fallacy, oversimplified cause recognizes only one of the several causes of an effect. Unfortunately, the oversimplified cause fallacy is

from Peanuts by Charles Schulz. Reprinted by permission of UFS, Inc.

commonly used to create doubt and unrest among uneducated people. An example of such rhetoric follows:

Example: *Widespread poverty in South America is caused by the greed of large landholders and of capitalists imported from North America. If we were able to get rid of the rich, money-grubbing upper-class leeches and the foreign capitalists, we would have no poverty in South America.*

This argument not only uses loaded terms, but it also ignores the other causes of poverty such as the bare-subsistence, agricultural society, high birth rate, high illiteracy factor, unstable government, and other factors.

Red Herring

The name of this fallacy comes from the herring, a fish which turns brown and red when spoiled. Escaped prisoners used to drag herrings across their trails to throw hounds off the track—the dogs could smell only the herrings. A red herring argument is an irrelevant issue thrown up as a diversionary tactic. Usually the false issue arouses an emotional response which creates a digression.

Example: *Some assert that Ian Smith could not have had any but good intentions for the blacks in Rhodesia because Smith was a good father and devoted husband, as well as a deeply religious man.*

Being a good family man and a religious man has nothing to do with Ian Smith's treatment of other races and proves nothing either way.

False Analogy

False analogy is a comparison that is incorrect. We often use comparisons to aid in providing understanding of an abstract or unknown concept; however, an analogy is false when the difference between the things being compared is greater than, and at odds with, the similarities. Although one cannot reason from analogy, an analogy becomes a logical hindrance when we try to *prove* something from it. It is well and good to draw a helpful comparison between crime and disease ("crime is a disease of society"), but one one can "cure" a culture by inoculation or surgery.

A false analogy occurred with the Mike Tyson incident which brought the boxer to trial. This famous boxer was convicted of rape charges. Those who defended him tried unsuccessfully to equate his success in sports with ethical success. The components of success in the boxing ring are not analogous to the components of success in interpersonal relationships. Force and violence work in one arena but they fail in the other.

The preceding fallacies are only representative of the errors in logic writers can make. This is not a complete list; it may be impossible to list all the ways a writer can err in logic.

The Purpose of Recognizing Logical Fallacies

What, then, is the purpose of learning logical fallacies? Learning a few fallacies should help us to think more critically and to look a little more carefully at our reading and writing. Is every assumption reasonably supported? Is the essay free from any glaring logical fallacies? Is the evidence sound? Finally, are all the arguments carefully planned, accurately verified, and logically fitted into the whole, producing a clear and reasonable conclusion? If critical thinking skills are developed well, we will be able to spot flaws in the argument and distinguish between what is accurately portrayed and what is false. The selections at the end of this chapter will help identify some fallacies. Jonathan Swift's "A Modest Proposal" and Warren J. Warwick's "Organ Transplantation: A Modest Proposal" are satires which twist logic to provide outrageous conclusions.

Student Exercises: Logical Fallacies

1. Find examples of logical fallacies in magazines and newspapers. Bring samples to class to show how logical fallacies are common occurrences.

2. Clip letters to the editor from your local newspaper. Discuss the logical problems of these articles. What would you do to make the arguments more persuasive?

3. Report on logical fallacies you have heard, either on television or radio or in everyday conversation. What do these fallacies make you feel about the program or person?

Developing an Argument

A common aim of writing and speaking is argumentation and persuasion. We often try to convince others of our views when we communicate with them. As we listen and read, we are forming arguments to counter the opinion we are hearing or reading. Effective persuasion or argumentation necessitates critical thinking, logical reasoning, supportive facts, and facility with language.

Looking at Organization and Structure

Good organization or structure of an argument is important. Any argument goes awry if the audience cannot follow it. Be clear on introducing the argument and developing the persuasive points. Getting the facts accurate and paying attention to good logical reasoning are things anyone can do. We need to have honest evidence for our side, and we need to think through that evidence and present it fairly.

Example: *Sherlyn desperately wanted a new carpet in her apartment. She thought the current one was terribly ugly. But how could she persuade her landlord to replace it? She started looking for facts that would help her argument: the carpet was pulling apart at the seams, creating dangerous gaps which could trip someone (maybe the threat of a lawsuit would be convincing); the carpet close to the kitchen sink had begun to rot from a previous water leak; and part of the carpet had pulled away from the wall from all the wet cleaning procedures it had been through. She organized her facts and approached the landlord.*

Plan of Development

All adequate arguments follow a similar development. Although a plan may vary according to audience and purpose, usually we present material in a certain order: (1) *why* this subject should be talked about, (2) a statement of the *problem* and concrete *examples* of it, (3) the *solution* including how and why, if necessary, (4) the *refutation* of anticipated *objection,* and probably (5) a *conclusion.* By being aware of the plan of development, we will read more discerningly and write more effectively. The emphasis on the various parts of the plan changes according to how much in agreement the audience is with the writer, how familiar it is with the problem, and how fundamentally its values may need to change to accept the argument.

Note how much time Swift takes to get to his solution in "A Modest Proposal." Swift was aware of his audience and wrote within a time period of the extended essay. He was also sensitive to the emotions and prejudices of his day and was therefore able to use logical fallacies to his advantage. Every writer has to be aware of the audience and know how to make the argument appealing.

Anticipating Counterarguments

A good argument also includes counterarguments and their rebuttals. Good persuaders anticipate possible objections to both their reasoning and to the implications or ramifications of their arguments. Writers must use critical thinking to consider other possible solutions and how they would implement the solutions and accommodate them in their rebuttal.

Example: *Although Stephen knew that he had some solid facts to support his appeal for a loan, he knew that the loan officer would bring in his record of bad checks. But Stephen was ready for the objections. He had compiled his good credit rating of the past two years, showing how his record had changed. He also had persuaded some friends and colleagues to write supportive letters. Although he knew he would be challenged, he had some ammunition to counter the objections.*

Making the Argument Appealing

In order for the audience to start nodding in agreement, writers or speakers must make the argument appeal to the audience's needs and values. Therefore they must identify the needs and values for the audience as well as for themselves. The most basic or deepest level of hidden assumptions are those of value. This identifying of needs and values ultimately reflects a world view.

Example: *Gordon knew that in his political campaign he would need to focus on family values. Those were the popular issues in his constituency. He knew that if he tied his arguments to these values, he would be more credible in the eyes of his audience. When he thought about it, those were also his own values. He had no problem forming campaign speeches.*

Using Inductive Reasoning in Arguments

The audience may be best persuaded by following along an examination of specific information, moving to logical conclusions. By allowing the facts to build, we persuade with the sheer weight of facts. Sales personnel often use this tactic. They will show each separate feature of the item on display. As they add good feature to good feature, the customer is persuaded the item would be her best buy.

The evidence of sampling also can be used in arguments. Representative information is necessary to make conclusions. If the representative information shows careful research and analysis, the argument gains strength and persuasiveness.

Using Deductive Reasoning in Arguments

Deductive reasoning functions through associations. We connect what we do not know with what we know. Syllogisms and enthymemes help us make those connections, especially when the major premise is a fundamental truth. Critical thinking demands associative thinking. In fact, most intelligence tests are composed of associative thinking questions.

As we prepare an argument, we need to use deductive reasoning to make the kind of associations the audience will accept. The assumption—the major premise—must be clearly stated and based on valid assumptions, whether they are stated or unstated. The supporting statements must be based on facts, and the conclusion should follow logically from the other premises.

Checklist for Arguments

To become more proficient at argument, we need to look closely at many factors, and at many principles we have learned. To establish credibility with audiences and to be persuasive, we will want to recognize faulty logic and reasoning in both the reading and writing. The following checklist may assist in checking reasoning:

1. Make sure that the argument is suited to the audience's needs and values.

2. Determine purpose. What is wanted of the audience?

3. Use the appropriate tone for the subject and audience.

4. Be well prepared with the argument. Get the facts right.

5. Be aware of logic in the arguments. An honest presentation is best. An astute audience usually will pick up fallacies, especially in a written presentation. Speeches sometimes succeed when logical fallacies (such as an emotional appeal) are present.

6. Is the structure of the argument clear? Do transitions move the argument from one logical step to another?

7. Is the conclusion vital and memorable, and is it the *only* one the evidence can support?

8. Is humor or satire used in writing? Is it appropriate for the situation, audience, or subject?

9. Are assumptions made which detract from the main thrust of the argument? Are there hidden assumptions which are inappropriate?

10. Are there logical fallacies in the reading? What is the purpose of the logical fallacy?

11. Are there logical fallacies in the writing?

12. Have objections to the solutions and conclusions been anticipated and answered?

13. Have the ramifications or consequences of the solution been answered?

The Argument Paper

Most people can find all sorts of things to argue about—and every age group has its pet gripes. This student found that his interest turned to recycling. His paper, "It's

Time to Take the Trash Out" is shown in outline stage, rough draft, and final draft as follows:

Outline

I. Trash should be distributed to incinerators and landfills—but first recycled.
   A. Problems with large amounts of garbage
   B. Composition of garbage

II. Incinerators
   A. "Waste-to-energy" plants
   B. Virtually pollution free
   C. Economically effective

III. Recycling
   A. Aids community
      1. Jobs
      2. Environment
      3. Conserves natural resources
   B. Types of materials for recycling
      1. Aluminum
      2. Glass
      3. Yard waste
      4. Plastics
      5. Paper

IV. Enforcement of recycling
   A. Taxes on non-recycled newsprint
   B. Limit trash disposal in homes

V. Conclusion
   A. Respecting environment
   B. Government educate nation on recycling

Rough Draft

Garbage—What Should We Do With It?

American's trash problem is growing every minute and must be controlled. Melissa Beck revealed in a "Newsweek" article, "Americans collectively toss out 160 million tons of garbage—enough to spread 30 stories high over 1,000 football fields, enough to fill a bumper-to-bumper convoy of garbage trucks halfway to the moon. ("Newsweek", Nov 17)" This 160 million tons of waste, about

Final Draft

It's Time to Take the Trash Out

"Americans collectively toss out 160 million tons of garbage [every year]—enough to spread 30 stories high over 1,000 football fields, enough to fill a bumper-to-bumper convoy of garbage trucks halfway to the moon" (Beck 00). The American trash problem is growing every minute and must be controlled. This 160 million tons of waste is thrown into United States municipal garbage systems. This figure breaks down

1,280 lbs of trash per person, are thrown into United States garbage systems. Most of this garbage now goes directly into landfills and other dumps are quickly reaching their capacity. It is becoming more difficult to locate new dumping grounds because of insufficient and non-affordable land, particularly near urban areas.

There are growing concerns about landfill's impact on the environment. The Environmental Protection Agency (EPA) says that there should be an organized distribution of waste to incinerators, landfills, and recycling centers. The EPA has also stated that half of all cities will run out of landfill space by 1998 and a third of all municipalities will run out by 1993. The Citizen's Clearinghouse on Hazardous Waste states: ". . . The technology exists to recycle as much as 80 percent of our solid waste. The issue of what to do is not a technical issue, but a political issue." (Public Citizen, May/June) The government intends to educate the United States on recycling for representatives feel it will solve all these problems.

The biggest percentage of garbage, 41%, in our country is paper. This is mostly computer printouts and phone books. Yard waste is the next largest amount—eighteen percent before recycling, then metal with 9%, glass with 8%, food scraps with just under 8%, plastics 6.5%, and wood about 4%. (Issues in Science and Technology, Nov.2)

Many places have turned to mass burn incinerators. These technologically advance incinerators

to about 1,280 pounds of trash per person every year. Most of this garbage now goes directly into landfills; however, remaining dumps are quickly reaching their capacity. New dumping grounds are becoming increasingly difficult to locate. Insufficient and non-affordable land, particularly near urban areas, makes available space an elevated scarcity. In addition, there are ever growing concerns regarding landfill's impact on the environment. The Environmental Protection Agency (EPA) feels that there should be an organized distribution of waste to incinerators, landfills, but most importantly, the majority of waste should be recycled. According to a survey by the United States EPA, half of all municipalities will run out of landfill space by 1998, and a third of all municipalities will run out by 1993. The Citizens Clearinghouse on Hazardous Wastes sums up the challenge: ". . . the technology exists to recycle as much as 80 percent of our solid waste. The issue of what to do is not a technical issue, but a political issue" (Elberhart 00). The government intends to educate the United States on recycling, for it feels that this is the key to the entire solution.

The biggest percentage of garbage in our country is paper, forty-one percent by weight and it is growing. This quantity is mostly composed of computer printouts and phone books. Yard waste is the next largest source by weight, eighteen percent before recycling. Metals comprise about nine percent, glass about eight percent, food scraps just under eight percent, plastics six and a also are known as "waste-to-energy" plants since they produce steam and/or electricity which can either run the plant or be sold. (Issues in Science and Technology, Nov.2) These burners are large furnaces which burn garbage at very high temperatures, leaving ash that takes up less space than the space of the original trash. A large minority in the U.S. supports the largely self-sufficient incinerators. These supporters believe incinerators should replace landfills for incinerators can accommodate "raw unsorted garbage." This would solve a huge problem without changing waste collection systems. These groups believe that incineration is now safe, that technological improvements achieved during the 1970's have made incineration virtually pollution-free, and that the very high temperatures of the boilers destroy all harmful compounds. Smokestack filters and acid scrubbers also protect against air pollutants.

Although the plants are very expensive to build, incineration has made greater progress than recycling and waste reduction from a monetary standpoint. The U.S. tax code has supported both public and private investment in incinerator plants. The tax code has also allowed cities to issue tax-exempt bonds to finance construction. The Tax Reform Act of 1986 encouraged the trend toward total public ownership of new plants.

The EPA believes that no matter how effective incineration claims to be, that it should only be used as an alternative to recycling. The EPA has set a goal of recy-

half percent, and wood almost four percent (Graff 00).

As an alternative, numerous municipalities have resorted to mass burn incinerators. These burners are large furnaces which consume garbage at very high temperatures, from 1,800 to 3,000 degrees Fahrenheit, leaving ash that takes up as little as 10 percent of the space of the original trash. These technologically advanced incinerators also are known as "waste-to-energy" plants since they produce energy in the form of steam and/or electricity which can be used to operate the plant or sold to local utilities (00). A large minority in the US supports the largely self-sufficient incinerators. These supporters endorse the idea that incinerators should [replace] landfills, for incinerators can accommodate "raw unsorted garbage," solving a huge disposal problem without making any alterations in the framework of the waste collection system. In addition to simplicity, these groups believe, along with industry proponents, that incineration is now safe. Technological improvements achieved during the 1970s have made incineration virtually pollution-free. The very high temperatures of the boilers destroy all harmful compounds. Other technical improvements, such as smokestack filters and acid scrubbers, protect against air pollutants.

Economically, incineration has made greater progress than recycling and waste reduction. Although the plants are very expensive to build, costing anywhere from $100 to $500 million, financing is supported by various cling twenty-five percent of the nations' waste by the end of 1992 which will depend on if people will buy recycled goods. "The trash of a city the size of San Francisco can yield as much copper as a medium-sized copper mine, as much aluminum as a small bauxite mine, and as much paper as a good sized timber stand" (Public Citizen, May/June). Recycling also aids the community by creating new jobs, protecting the environment, avoiding disposal costs, and conserving natural resources. Edward Klein of the EPA says, "Most people think they put out the glass, aluminum, and paper and they've recycled. In fact all they've done is separate. Until those commodities are taken somewhere else and used again, you haven't recycled" (Issues in Science and Technology, Nov. 2).

Aluminum, glass, yard waste, plastic, and paper are the materials that the EPA feels Americans should recycle. These items are cheap and easy to recycle. For example, converting bauxite into new aluminum is ten times more expensive than reprocessing used cans. That is the predominant reason Americans are recycling more than half of all aluminum cans today. Even with this huge amount of can recycling, the United States still disposes of enough aluminum every three months to rebuild our entire airline fleet (Newsweek, Nov. 17).

Reusing old glass also costs less than manufacturing new glass. Today, only a small percentage of glass that Americans use are recycled, but there are advantages to recycling glass. The

government policies. The US tax code has supported both public and private investment in incinerator plants by making private incinerator owners the beneficiaries of investment tax credits, energy tax credits, and accelerated depreciation rules. The tax code has also allowed cities to issue tax-exempt bonds to finance construction. Although the Tax Reform Act of 1986 discouraged private investors, it has encouraged the trend toward total public ownership of new plants.

The Environmental Protection Agency believes that no matter how effective incineration professes to be, that it should only be used as an alternative to recycling. Recycling also aids the community by creating new jobs, protecting the environment, avoiding disposal costs, and conserving natural resources. Annie Elberhart notes that "the trash of a city the size of San Francisco can yield as much copper as a medium-sized copper mine, as much aluminum as a small bauxite mine, and as much paper as a good sized timber stand" (00).

The Environmental Protection Agency has set a goal of recycling twenty-five percent of the nation's waste by the end of 1992. The success of this goal will depend largely on the markets for recycled products. Edward Klein, who leads the EPA's task force on solid waste, says, "Most people think they put out the glass, aluminum, and paper and they've recycled. In fact all they've done is separate. Until those commodities are taken somewhere else and used again, you haven't recycled" (Graff 00).

Aluminum, glass, yard waste,

government encourages Americans to reuse their glass containers at home and work for other purposes because it reduces the large amount of energy and money it consumes to recycle. Glass bottles can be produced in a new form called "glassphalt" which is a combination of glass and asphalt. Glass can take its old shape again in the form of new bottles.

Composting Americans' fertile mounds of leaves and grass clippings could eliminate 1/5 of the nation's waste. Yard waste can contain pesticides and lawn chemicals that pose toxicology problems in compost heaps, but experts quoted in Newsweek say that "markets would grow if more municipalities followed Fairfield, Conn., which opened a three million dollar composting center to create topsoil for parks, playgrounds, and public landscaping" (Newsweek, Nov.17). Many Americans feel that the "fall clean-up" means that all leaves should be removed from homes to look neat and tidy. Actually, some experts say bushes, plants and trees love a warm blanket of leaves around them to protect them from the cold.

The 140 billion dollar a year plastics industry is finally starting to turn to recycling more products. Today, only 1% of plastics is recycled, but manufacturers are scrambling to find new uses, like plastic "lumber" and stuffing for ski jackets because the Environmental Protection Agency intends to pressure large corporations into finding uses for this plastic. Procter and Gamble is making new Spic and

plastic, and paper are the major reusable materials that the EPA feels Americans should be educated to recycle. These items are cost-efficient in the recycling process as they can easily be converted to a raw state for reuse. Converting bauxite into new aluminum is ten times more expensive than reprocessing used cans. That is the predominant reason Americans are recycling more than half of all aluminum cans today, 42.5 billion annually. Even with this fabulous number of recovery, the United States still disposes of enough aluminum every three months to rebuild the nation's entire airline fleet (Beck).

Reusing old glass also costs less than manufacturing new glass items. Today, only a small percentage of glass Americans use is recycled, though, through growing education, people are becoming more aware of the advantages of recycling glass. Glass bottles can be produced in a new form called "glassphalt" which is a combination of glass and asphalt. Naturally, glass can take shape again in the form of new bottles. The government encourages Americans to reuse their glass containers at home and work for other purposes (water storage, food storage, nail holders, etc.) as an alternative to recycling, thus reducing the large amount of energy and money it consumes to recycle.

Composting American's fertile mounds of leaves and grass clippings could eliminate one-fifth of the nation's waste. Yard waste can contain pesticides and lawn chemicals that pose toxicology problems in compost heaps. Still,

Span containers from recycled PET and wants to make plastic trash bags and park benches from Luvs and Pampers. Someday, McDonald's has said that they would like to build entire restaurants out of recycled burger boxes (Issues in Science and Technology, Nov.2). McDonald's in New England began asking customers to toss their polystyrene into separate trash cans and then sent them to recycling centers and made them into plastic pellets to be used in other products.

Industry officials brag that nearly sixty percent of all paper products used in this country are recycled, which is about twenty-six million tons a year. Some of this amount is made into cereal boxes, toilet tissue, even bedding for farm animals. But, more than forty million tons are stuffed in landfills and are burned annually (Public Citizen, May/June). This has caused the EPA to make plans to match supply, demand, and reprocessing capacity at home while exporting some U.S. wastepaper to tree poor nations. The Environmental Protection Agency says that the free market needs to change if recycled is to succeed. America used to be driven by the demand for products and was not worried about the supply of raw materials. Taxes must be placed on non-recycled newsprint to force newspapers to use more recycled paper. Too, it has been much too easy to take out a sixth or seventh bag of trash every week because you knew that the trash man would dump it in someone else's backyard. Except for wars, Americans have not been willing to make individual sacrifices for the common good.

experts say that "markets would grow if more municipalities followed Fairfield, Connecticut, which opened a three-million dollar composting center to create topsoil for parks, playgrounds and public landscaping" (Beck 00). Many Americans feel that the "fall clean-up" means that all leaves should be removed from home properties to have a neat, orderly look. In reality, some experts emphasize, bushes, plants and trees love a warm blanket of leaves around them to protect them from the winter chills. Warm bedding can literally mean the difference between life and death for outside greenery which must fight to endure hard winters.

The 140 billion dollar a year plastics industry is at last waking up to recycling. Today, only one percent of plastics is recycled, but manufacturers are scrambling to find new uses, from plastic "lumber" to stuffing for ski jackets. The Environmental Protection Agency intends to pressure large corporations into finding uses for this plastic. Procter & Gamble is making new Spic and Span containers entirely from recycled PET (polyethylene terephthalate, the material beverage bottles consist of) and hopes to turn even Luvs and Pampers into plastic trash bags and park benches. McDonalds in New England began asking customers to toss their polystyrene into separate trash cans. They were sent to recycling centers and pounded into plastic pellets than can be used in such things as Rolodex file holders, cassette boxes and yo-yos. Someday, McDonalds has said that they would like to build entire restaurants out

If these sacrifices are not make, garbage trucks will stop in everyone's backyard.

The Environmental Protection Agency plans to promote the use of ridding our nation of its raw sewage by incineration rather than landfill. More importantly, the EPA supports a recycling program that will reduce raw waste disposal and believes that recycling products that can be used over and over again will build a stronger sense of practicality in this country and a genuine pride in respecting our environment. Finally, the government want to educate people about recycling by mailing reports every month to every house. By promoting success, the government will try to encourage us to be aware of the need to protect our planet from future ruin.

of recycled burger boxes (Graff 00).

Industry officials are proud that nearly sixty percent of all paper products consumed in this country are recycled, twenty-six million tons appears again in cereal boxes, toilet tissue, even bedding for farm animals. At the same time more than forty million tons are stuffed in landfills and are going up smokestacks annually (Elberhart 00). This is where the EPA steps in. It plans to match supply, demand, and reprocessing capacity at home while exporting some US waste-paper to tree-poor nations like Taiwan and Korea.

In the past, America has been driven by the demand for products, not the supply of raw materials. The Environmental Protection Agency has concluded that the free market needs to change if recycling is to largely dent the nation's garbage piles. Taxes must be placed on non-recycled newsprint to force newspapers to utilize a rising percentage of recycled paper in the near future.

It has been much too easy to take out a sixth or seventh bag of trash in a week and assume that the garbage person will dump the load in someone else's backyard. With some exceptions during wartime, Americans have not been willing to make individual sacrifices for the common good. If these sacrifices are not accomplished, the dumps will cover the country coast to coast and the garbage trucks will stop in everyone's backyard.

In conclusion, the Environmental Protection Agency plans to promote the use of ridding our nation of its raw sewage by incineration rather than landfill, but above and beyond this solution, the EPA supports a recycling program that will reduce raw waste disposal. Recycling products that can be used over and over will build a stronger sense of practicality in this country and a genuine pride in respecting our environment. Finally, the government has proposed to educate the nation about the extreme importance of recycling by issuing monthly progress reports to the nation. By promoting success, the government will encourage more and more Americans to be aware of our country's need to protect our environment.

Jonathan Freeman

BIBLIOGRAPHY

Beck, Melinda. "Buried Alive," Newsweek, November 17, 1989.

David, Phillip A. "Administration Backing Away from RCRA Reauthorization," Congressional Quarterly, September 21, 1991.

Elberhart, Annie. "Turn Trash into Ash," Public Citizen, May/June, 1988.

Graff, Gordon. "The Looming Crisis in Plastic Waste Disposal," Issues in Science and Technology. Washington, D.C.: National Academy of Sciences, 1989.

Okun, Daniel A. "A Water and Sanitation Strategy for the Developing World," Environmental. Falls, Hills, VA: Helen Dwight Reid Educational Foundation, 1991.

Readings in the Classics

from *Phaedrus*

Translated by H. N. Fowler

Plato

*Plato (c.428–c.347 B.C.) was a Greek philosopher and writer who was born
to a noble family in Athens. He was interested in politics and was befriended
by Socrates, becoming his student until Socrates' death in about 399 B.C.
After his mentor's execution, Plato went to Megara and possibly Egypt and
Cyrene, during which time he composed the dialogues of Socrates for which
he is famous. He later went to Italy and Sicily where he may have studied
rhetoric and philosophy. Upon returning to Athens, he founded an Academy
of learning where he wrote and taught for the rest of his life.*

SOCRATES: Since it is the function of speech to lead souls by persuasion, he who is to
be a rhetorician must know the various forms of soul. Now they are so and so many
and of such and such kinds, wherefore men also are of different kinds: these we must
classify. Then there are also various classes of speeches, to one of which every speech
belongs. So men of a certain sort are easily persuaded by speeches of a certain sort for
a certain reason to actions or beliefs of a certain sort, and men of another sort cannot
be so persuaded. The student of rhetoric must, accordingly, acquire a proper knowledge of these classes and then be able to follow them accurately with his senses when
he sees them in the practical affairs of life; otherwise he can never have any profit from
the lectures he may have heard. But when he has learned to tell what sort of man is
influenced by what sort of speech, and is able, if he comes upon such a man, to
recognize him and to convince himself that this is the man and this now actually before
him is the nature spoken of in a certain lecture, to which he must now make a practical
application of a certain kind of speech in a certain way to persuade his hearer to a
certain action or belief—when he has acquired all this, and has added thereto a
knowledge of the times for speaking and for keeping silence, and has also distinguished
the favorable occasions for brief speech or pitiful speech or intensity and all the classes
of speech which he has learned, then, and not till then, will his art be fully and
completely finished; and if anyone who omits any of these points in his speaking or
writing claims to speak by the rules of art, the one who disbelieves him is the better
man. "Now then," perhaps the writer of our treatise will say, "Phaedrus and Socrates,
do you agree to all this? Or must the art of speech be described in some other way?"

PHAEDRUS: No other way is possible, Socrates. But is seems a great task to attain
to it.

SOCRATES: Very true. Therefore you must examine all that has been said from
every point of view, to see if no shorter and easier road to the art appears, that one may

not take a long and rough road, when there is a short and smooth one. If you have heard from Lysias or anyone else anything that can help us, try to remember it and tell it.

PHAEDRUS: If it depended on trying, I might, but just now I have nothing to say.

SOCRATES: Then shall I tell something that I have heard some of those say who make these matters their business?

PHAEDRUS: Pray do.

SOCRATES: Even the wolf, you know, Phaedrus, has the right to an advocate, as they say.

PHAEDRUS: Do you be his advocate?

SOCRATES: Very well. They say that there is no need of treating these matters with such gravity and carrying them back so far to first principles with many words; for, as we said in the beginning of this discussion, he who is to be a competent rhetorician need have nothing at all to do, they say, with truth in considering things which are just or good, or men who are so, whether by nature or by education. For in the courts, they say, nobody cares for truth about these matters, but for that which is convincing; and that is probability, so that he who is to be an artist in speech must fix his attention upon probability. For sometimes one must not even tell what was actually done, if it was not likely to be done, but what was probable, whether in accusation or defense; and in brief, a speaker must always aim at probability, paying no attention to truth; for this method, if pursued throughout the whole speech, provides us with the entire art.

PHAEDRUS: You have stated just what those say who pretend to possess the art of speech, Socrates. I remember that we touched upon this matter briefly before, but the professional rhetoricians think it is of great importance.

SOCRATES: Well, there is Tisias whom you have studied carefully; now let Tisias himself tell us if he does not say that probability is that which most people think.

PHAEDRUS: That is just what he says.

SOCRATES: Apparently after he had invented this clever scientific definition, he wrote that if a feeble and brave man assaulted a strong coward, robbed him of his cloak or something, and was brought to trial for it, neither party ought to speak the truth; the coward should say that he had not been assaulted by the brave man alone, whereas the other should prove that only they two were present and should use the well-known argument, "How could a little man like me assault such a man as he is?" The coward will not acknowledge his cowardice, but will perhaps try to invent some other lie, and thus give his opponent a chance to confute him. And in other cases there are other similar rules of art. Is that not so, Phaedrus?

PHAEDRUS: Certainly.

SOCRATES: Oh, a wonderfully hidden art it seems to be which Tisias has brought to light, or some other, whoever he may be and whatever country he is proud to call his own! But, my friend, shall we say in reply to this, or shall we not—

PHAEDRUS: What?

SOCRATES: "Tisias, some time ago, before you came along, we were saying that this probability of yours was accepted by the people because of its likeness to truth; and we just stated that he who knows the truth is always best able to discover likenesses. And so, if you have anything else to say about the art of speech, we will listen to you; but if not, we will put our trust in what we said just now, that unless a man take account of the characters of his hearers and is able to divide things by classes and to comprehend particulars under a general idea, he will never attain the highest human perfection in the art of speech. But this ability he will not gain without much diligent toil, which a wise man ought not to undergo for the sake of speaking and acting before men, but that he may be able to speak and to do everything, so far as possible, in a manner pleasing to the gods. For those who are wiser than we, Tisias, say that a man of sense should surely practice to please not his fellow slaves, except as a secondary consideration, but his good and noble masters. Therefore, if the path is long, be not astonished; for it must be trodden for great ends, not for those you have in mind. Yet your ends also, as our argument says, will be best gained in this way, if one so desires."

PHAEDRUS: I think what you have said is admirable, if one could only do it.

SOCRATES: But it is noble to strive after noble objects, no matter what happens to us.

PHAEDRUS: Certainly.

SOCRATES: We have, then, said enough about the art of speaking and that which is no art.

PHAEDRUS: Assuredly.

SOCRATES: But we have still to speak of propriety and impropriety in writing, how it should be done and how it is improper, have we not?

PHAEDRUS: Yes.

SOCRATES: Do you know how you can act or speak about rhetoric so as to please God best?

PHAEDRUS: Not at all; do you?

SOCRATES: I can tell something I have heard of the ancients; but whether it is true, they only know. But if we ourselves should find it out, should we care any longer for human opinions?

PHAEDRUS: A ridiculous question! But tell me what you say you have heard.

SOCRATES: I heard, then, that at Naucratis, in Egypt, was one of the ancient gods of that country, the one whose sacred bird is called the ibis, and the name of the god himself was Theuth. He it was who invented numbers and arithmetic and geometry and astronomy, also draughts and dice, and, most important of all, letters. Now the king of all Egypt at that time was the god Thamus, who lived in a great city of the upper region, which the Greeks call the Egyptian Thebes, and they call the god himself Ammon. To him came Theuth to show his inventions, saying that they ought to be imparted to the other Egyptians. But Thamus asked what use there was in each, and as Theuth enumerated their uses, expressed praise or blame, according as he approved or disapproved. The story goes that Thamus said many things to Theuth in praise or blame of the various arts, which it would take too long to repeat; but when they came to the letters, "This invention, O king," said Theuth, "will make the Egyptians wiser and will improve their memories; for it is an elixir of memory and wisdom that I have discovered." But Thamus replied "Most ingenious Theuth, one man has the ability to beget arts, but the ability to judge of their usefulness or harmfulness to their users belongs to another; and now you, who are the father of letters, have been led by your affection to ascribe to them a power the opposite of that which they really possess. For this invention will produce forgetfulness in the minds of those who learn to use it, because they will not practice their memory. Their trust in writing, produced by external characters which are no part of themselves, will discourage the use of their own memory within them. You have invented an elixir not of memory, but of reminding; and you offer your pupils the appearance of wisdom, not true wisdom, for they will read many things without instruction and will therefore seem to know many things, when they are for the most part ignorant and hard to get along with, since they are not wise, but only appear wise."

PHAEDRUS: Socrates, you easily make up stories of Egypt or any country you please.

SOCRATES: They used to say, my friend, that the words of the oak in the holy place of Zeus at Dodona were the first prophetic utterances. The people of that time, not being so wise as you young folks, were content in their simplicity to hear an oak or a rock, provided only it spoke the truth; but to you, perhaps, it makes a difference who the speaker is and where he comes from, for you do not consider only whether his words are true or not.

PHAEDRUS: Your rebuke is just; and I think the Theban is right in what he says about letters.

SOCRATES: He who thinks, then, that he has left behind him any art in writing, and he who receives it in the belief that anything in writing will be clear and certain, would be an utterly simple person, and in truth ignorant of the prophecy of Ammon[1] if he thinks written words are of any use except to remind him who knows the matter about which they are written.

PHAEDRUS: Very true.

SOCRATES: Writing, Phaedrus, has this strange quality, and is very like painting; for the creatures of painting stand like living beings, but if one asks them a question, they preserve a solemn silence. And so it is with written words; you might think they spoke as if they had intelligence, but if you question them, wishing to know about their sayings, they always say only one and the same thing. And every word, when once it was written, is bandied about, alike among those who understand and those who have no interest in it, and it knows not to whom to speak or not to speak; when ill-treated or unjustly reviled it always needs its father to help it; for it has no power to protect or help itself.

PHAEDRUS: You are quite right about that, too.

SOCRATES: No tell me; is there not another kind of speech, or word, which shows itself to be the legitimate brother of this bastard one, both in the manner of its begetting and in its better and more powerful nature?

PHAEDRUS: What is this word and how is it begotten, as you say?

SOCRATES: The word is written with intelligence in the mind of the learner, which is able to defend itself and knows to whom it should speak, and before whom to be silent.

PHAEDRUS: You mean the living and breathing word of him who knows, of which the written word may justly be called the image.

[1]Ammon, or Zeus, delivered his prophecies only orally, as through the murmuring leaves of the Dodona oak. [Ed.]

SOCRATES: Exactly. Now tell me this. Would a sensible husbandman, who has seeds which he cares for and which he wishes to bear fruit, plant them with serious purpose in the heat of summer in some garden of Adonis, and delight in seeing them appear in beauty in eight days, or would he do that sort of thing, when he did it at all, only in play and for amusement? Would he not, when he was in earnest, follow the rules of husbandry, plant his seeds in fitting ground, and be pleased when those which he had sowed reached their perfection in the eighth month?

PHAEDRUS: Yes, Socrates, he would, as you say, act in that way when in earnest and in the other way only for amusement.

SOCRATES: And shall we suppose that he who has knowledge of the just and the good and beautiful has less sense about his seeds than the husbandman?

PHAEDRUS: By no means.

SOCRATES: Then he will not, when in earnest, write them in ink, sowing them through a pen with words which cannot defend themselves by argument and cannot teach the truth effectually.

PHAEDRUS: No, at least, probably not.

SOCRATES: No. The gardens of letters he will, it seems, plant for amusement, and will write, when he writes, to treasure up reminders for himself, when he comes to the forgetfulness of old age, and for others who follow the same path, and he will be pleased when he sees them putting forth tender leaves. When others engage in other amusements, refreshing themselves with banquets and kindred entertainments, he will pass the time in such pleasures as I have suggested.

PHAEDRUS: A noble pastime, Socrates, and a contrast to those base pleasures, the pastime of the man who can find amusement in discourse, telling stories about justice, and the other subjects of which you speak.

SOCRATES: Yes, Phaedrus, so it is; but, in my opinion, serious discourse about them is far nobler, when one employs the dialectic method and plants and sows in a fitting soul intelligent words which are able to help themselves and him who planted them, which are not fruitless, but yield seed from which there spring up in other minds other words capable of continuing the process for ever, and which make their possessor happy, to the farthest possible limit of human happiness.

PHAEDRUS: Yes, that is far nobler.

SOCRATES: And now, Phaedrus, since we have agreed about these matters, we can decide the others.

PHAEDRUS: What others?

SOCRATES: Those which brought us to this point through our desire to investigate them, for we wished to examine into the reproach against Lysias as a speech-writer, and also to discuss the speeches themselves and see which were the products of art and which were not. I think we have shown pretty clearly what is and what is not a work of art.

PHAEDRUS: Yes, I thought so, too; but please recall to my mind what was said.

SOCRATES: A man must know the truth about all the particular things of which he speaks or writes, and must be able to define everything separately; then when he has defined them, he must know how to divide them by classes until further division is impossible; and in the same way he must understand the nature of the soul, must find out the class of speech adapted to each nature, and must arrange and adorn his discourse accordingly, offering to the complex soul elaborate and harmonious discourses, and simple talks to the simple soul. Until he has attained to all this, he will not be able to speak by the method of art, so far as speech can be controlled by method, either for purposes of instruction or of persuasion. This has been taught by our whole preceding discussion.

PHAEDRUS: Yes, certainly, that is just about our result.

SOCRATES: How about the question whether it is a fine or a disgraceful thing to be a speaker or writer and under what circumstances the profession might properly be called a disgrace or not? Was that made clear a little while ago when we said—

PHAEDRUS: What?

SOCRATES: That if Lysias or anyone else ever wrote or ever shall write, in private, or in public as lawgiver, a political document, and in writing it believes that it possesses great certainty and clearness, then it is a disgrace to the writer, whether anyone says so, or not. For whether one be awake or asleep, ignorance of right and wrong and good and bad is in truth inevitably a disgrace, even if the whole mob applaud it.

PHAEDRUS: That is true.

SOCRATES: But the man who thinks that in the written word there is necessarily much that is playful, and that no written discourse, whether in meter or in prose, deserves to be treated very seriously (and this applies also to the recitations of the rhapsodes, delivered to sway people's minds, without opportunity for questioning and teaching), but that the best of them really serve only to remind us of what we know; and who thinks that only in words about justice and beauty and goodness spoken by teachers for the sake of instruction and really written in a soul is clearness and perfection and serious value, that such words should be considered the speaker's own legitimate offspring, first the word within himself, if it be found there, and secondly its descendants or brothers which may have sprung up in worthy manner in the souls of others, and who pays no attention to the other words—that man, Phaedrus, is likely to be such as you and I might pray that we ourselves may become.

PHAEDRUS: By all means that is what I wish and pray for.

SOCRATES: We have amused ourselves with talk about words long enough. Go and tell Lysias that you and I came down to the fountain and sacred place of the nymphs, and heard words which they told us to repeat to Lysias and anyone else who composed speeches, and to Homer or any other who has composed poetry with or without musical accompaniment, and third to Solon and whoever has written political compositions which he calls laws:—If he has composed his writings with knowledge of the truth, and is able to support them by discussion of that which he has written, and has the power to show by his own speech that the written words are of little worth, such a man ought not to derive his title from such writings, but from the serious pursuit which underlies them.

PHAEDRUS: What titles do you grant them then?

SOCRATES: I think, Phaedrus, that the epithet "wise" is too great and befits God alone; but the name "philosopher," that is, "lover of wisdom," or something of the sort would be more fitting and modest for such a man.

PHAEDRUS: And quite appropriate.

SOCRATES: On the other hand, he who has nothing more valuable than the things he has composed or written, turning his words up and down at his leisure, adding this phrase and taking that away, will you not properly address him as poet or writer of speeches or of laws?

PHAEDRUS: Certainly.

SOCRATES: Tell this then to your friend.

PHAEDRUS: But what will you do? For your friend ought not to be passed by.

SOCRATES: What friend?

PHAEDRUS: The fair Isocrates.[2] What message will you give him? What shall we say that he is?

SOCRATES: Isocrates is young yet, Phaedrus; however, I am willing to say what I prophesy for him.

PHAEDRUS: What is it?

SOCRATES: I think he has a nature above the speeches of Lysias and possesses a nobler character; so that I should not be surprised if, as he grows older, he should so excel in his present studies that all who have ever treated of rhetoric shall seem less than children; and I suspect that these studies will not satisfy him, but a more divine impulse will lead him to greater things; for my friend, something of philosophy is inborn in his mind. This is the message that I carry from these deities to my favorite Isocrates, and do you carry the other to Lysias, your favorite.

PHAEDRUS: It shall be done; but now let us go, since the heat has grown gentler.

SOCRATES: Is it not well to pray to the deities here before we go?

PHAEDRUS: Of course.

SOCRATES: O beloved Pan and all ye other gods of this place, grant to me that I be made beautiful in my soul within, and that all external possessions be in harmony with my inner man. May I consider the wise man rich; and may I have such wealth as only the self-restrained man can bear or endure.—Do we need anything more, Phaedrus? For me that prayer is enough.

PHAEDRUS: Let me also share in this prayer; for friends have all things in common.

SOCRATES: Let us go.

---

[2]Isocrates, one of the Ten Attic Orators and a well-known educator, was roughly contemporary with Plato, although he studied with Gorgias while Plato followed Socrates. The retroactive praise of Isocrates here is generally thought to be genuine, if condescending. But Plato's follower Artistotle explicitly condemned Isocrates's teaching on rhetoric. [Ed.]

from *Rhetoric*

Translated by W. Rhys Roberts
Edited by Friedrich Solmsen

Aristotle

Aristotle (384–322 B.C.) was a Greek philosopher born in Stagira, Macedonia. At seventeen or eighteen years of age, he joined Plato's Academy in Athens where he stayed for twenty years first as student, then as teacher in the Academy. At Plato's death, Aristotle left the Academy because he could not become the leader of the Academy—he was not Athenian. About five years later, he became the tutor of Alexander, son of King Philip of Macedonia. When Alexander succeeded to the throne, Aristotle returned to Athens to teach. Much of his writing has been lost, but the fragments which remain contain books on natural philosophy (Physics), two ethical treatises (Nicomachean Ethics and Eudemian Ethics), several volumes of political inquiry (Politics), a book on persuasion (Rhetoric), and one on literary criticism (Poetics). His learning was very broad; in fact, it is said that he mastered every field of learning known to the Greeks.

Book I

Rhetoric is the counterpart of Dialectic.[1] Both alike are concerned with such things as come, more or less, within the general ken of all men and belong to no definite science. Accordingly all men make use, more or less, of both; for to a certain extent all men attempt to discuss statements and to maintain them, to defend themselves and to attack others. Ordinary people do this either at random or through practice and from acquired habit. Both ways being possible, the subject can plainly be handled systematically, for it is possible to inquire the reason why some speakers succeed through practice and others spontaneously; and every one will at once agree that such an inquiry is the function of an art.[2]

Now, the framers of the current treatises on rhetoric have constructed but a small portion of that art. The modes of persuasion[3] are the only true constituents of the art:

[1]"Rhetoric" and "Dialectic" may be roughly Englished as "the art of public speaking" and "the art of logical discussion." Aristotle's philosophical definition of "Rhetoric" is given [on page 153]. . . .

[2]Here and in later passages the term "art" stands for methodical treatment of a subject. [F.S.]

[3]Aristotle here means by ["modes of persuasion"] those attempts at *logical argument* on which he would himself like to see Rhetoric rely. In the next chapter, he gives to the term the wide range it had in current rhetorical usage, and concludes with a reference to the argumentative side. . . . A uniform rendering of the word is hardly possible, but at the outset

everything else is merely accessory. These writers, however, say nothing about enthymemes,[4] which are the substance of rhetorical persuasion, but deal mainly with nonessentials. The arousing of prejudice, pity, anger, and similar emotions has nothing to do with the essential facts, but is merely a personal appeal to the man who is judging the case. Consequently if the rules for trials which are now laid down in some states—especially in well-governed states—were applied everywhere, such people would have nothing to say. All men, no doubt, *think* that the laws should prescribe such rules, but some, as in the court of Areopagus,[5] give practical effect to their thoughts and forbid talk about nonessentials. This is sound law and custom. It is not right to pervert the judge[6] by moving him to anger or envy or pity—one might as well warp a carpenter's rule before using it. Again, a litigant has clearly nothing to do but to show that the alleged fact is so or is not so, that it has or has not happened. As to whether a thing is important or unimportant, just or unjust, the judge must surely refuse to take his instructions from the litigants: he must decide for himself all such points as the lawgiver has not already defined for him.

Now, it is of great moment that well-drawn laws should themselves define all the points they possibly can and leave as few as may be to the decision of the judges; and this for several reasons. First, to find one man, or a few men, who are sensible persons and capable of legislating and administering justice is easier than to find a large number. Next, laws are made after long consideration, whereas decisions in the courts are given at short notice, which makes it hard for those who try the case to satisfy the claims of justice and expediency. The weightiest reason of all is that the decision of the lawgiver is not particular but prospective and general, whereas members of the assembly and the jury find it *their* duty to decide on definite cases brought before them. They will often have allowed themselves to be so much influenced by feelings of friendship or hatred or self-interest that they lose any clear vision of the truth and have their judgment obscured by considerations of personal pleasure or pain. In general, then, the judge should, we say, be allowed to decide as few things as possible. But questions as to whether something has happened or has not happened, will be or will not be, is or is not, must of necessity be left to the judge, since the lawgiver cannot foresee them. If this is so, it is evident that any one who lays down rules about other matters, such as what must be the contents of the "introduction" or the "narration" or any of the other divisions of a speech, is theorizing about nonessentials as if they belonged to the art. The only question with which these writers here deal is how to put the judge into a given frame of mind. About the orator's proper modes of persuasion they have nothing to tell us; nothing, that is, about how to gain skill in enthymemes.

Hence it comes that, although the same systematic principles apply to political as

---

it is important to stress Aristotle's fundamental view . . . that, from the nature of its materials, Rhetoric is, in general, *persuasive* rather than fully *demonstrative*. When in later portions of the treatise a single-word rendering is given, "arguments" will be preferred to "proofs" . . . [Tr.]

[4]Rhetorical arguments.

[5]Highest criminal court of Athens. [F.S.]

[6]Here, and in what follows, the . . . reader should understand "judge" in a broad sense, including "jurymen" and others who "judge."

to forensic oratory, and although the former is a nobler business, and fitter for a citizen, than that which concerns the relations of private individuals, these authors say nothing about political oratory, but try, one and all, to write treatises on the way to plead in court. The reason for this is that in political oratory there is less inducement to talk about nonessentials. Political oratory is less given to unscrupulous practices than forensic, because it treats of wider issues. In a political debate the man who is forming a judgment is making a decision about his own vital interests. There is no need, therefore, to prove anything except that the facts are what the supporter of a measure maintains they are. In forensic oratory this is not enough; to conciliate the listener is what pays here. It is other people's affairs that are to be decided, so that the judges, intent on their own satisfaction and listening with partiality, surrender themselves to the disputants instead of judging between them. Hence in many places, we have said already, irrelevant speaking is forbidden in the law courts: in the public assembly those who have to form a judgment are themselves well able to guard against that.

It is clear, then, that rhetorical story, in its strict sense, is concerned with the modes of persuasion. Persuasion is clearly a sort of demonstration, since we are most fully persuaded when we consider a thing to have been demonstrated. The orator's demonstration is an enthymeme, and this is, in general, the most effective of the modes of persuasion. The enthymeme is a sort of syllogism, and the consideration of syllogisms of all kinds, without distinc. n, is the business of dialectic, either of dialectic as a whole or of one of its branches. It follows plainly therefore, that he who is best able to see how and from what elements a syllogism is produced will also be best skilled in the enthymeme, when he has further learned what its subject matter is and in what respects it differs from the syllogism of strict logic. The true and the approximately true are apprehended by the same faculty; it may also be noted that men have a sufficient natural instinct for what is true, and usually do arrive at the truth. Hence the man who makes a good guess at truth is likely to make a good guess at probabilities.

It has now been shown that the ordinary writers on rhetoric treat of nonessentials; it has also been shown why they have inclined more towards the forensic branch of oratory.

Rhetoric is useful (1) because things that are true and things that are just have a natural tendency to prevail over their opposites, so that if the decisions of judges are not what they ought to be, the defeat must be due to the speakers themselves, and they must be blamed accordingly. Moreover, (2) before some audiences not even the possession of the exactest knowledge will make it easy for what we say to produce conviction. For argument based on knowledge implies instruction, and there are people whom one cannot instruct. Here, then, we must use, as our modes of persuasion and argument, notions possessed by everybody, as we observed in the *Topics* when dealing with the way to handle a popular audience. Further, (3) we must be able to employ persuasion, just as strict reasoning can be employed, on opposite sides of a question, not in order that we may in practice employ it in both ways (for we must not make people believe what is wrong), but in order that we may see clearly what the facts are, and that, if another man argues unfairly, we on our part may be able to confute him. No other of the arts draws opposite conclusions: dialectic and rhetoric alone do this. Both these arts draw opposite conclusions impartially. Nevertheless, the underlying facts do not lend themselves equally well to the contrary views. No; things that are true and things that are better are, by their nature, practically always easier to prove and easier to believe in. Again, (4) it is absurd to hold that a man ought to be ashamed of being unable to defend himself with his limbs, but not of being unable to defend himself with speech and reason,[7] when the use of rational speech is more distinctive of a human being than the use of his limbs. And if it be objected that one who uses such power of speech unjustly might do great harm, *that* is a charge which may be made in common against all good things except virtue, and above all against the things that are most useful, as strength, health, wealth, generalship. A man can confer the greatest of benefits by a right use of these, and inflict the greatest of injuries by using them wrongly.

It is clear, then, that rhetoric is not bound up with a single definite class of subjects, but is as universal as dialectic; it is clear, also, that it is useful. It is clear, further, that its function is not simply to succeed in persuading, but rather to discover the means of coming as near such success as the circumstances of each particular case allow. In this it resembles all other arts. For example, it is not the function of medicine simply to make a man quite healthy, but to put him as far as may be on the road to health; it is possible to give excellent treatment even to those who can never enjoy sound health. Furthermore, it is plain that it is the function of one and the same art to discern the real and the apparent means of persuasion, just as it is the function of dialectic to discern the real and the apparent syllogism. What makes a man a "sophist" is not his faculty, but his moral purpose. In rhetoric, however, the term "rhetorician" may describe either the speaker's knowledge of the art, or his moral purpose.[8] In dialectic it is different: a man is a "sophist" because he has a certain kind of moral purpose, a "dialectician" in respect, not of his moral purpose, but of his faculty.

Let us now try to give some account of the systematic principles of Rhetoric itself—of the right method and means of succeeding in the object we set before us. We must make as it were a fresh start, and before going further define what rhetoric is.

Rhetoric may be defined as the faculty of observing in any given case the available means of persuasion. This is not a function of any other art. Every other art can instruct or persuade about its own particular subject matter; for instance, medicine about what is healthy and unhealthy, geometry about the properties of magnitudes, arithmetic about numbers, and the same is true of the other arts and sciences. But rhetoric we look upon as the power of observing the means of persuasion on almost any subject presented to us; and that is why we say that, in its technical character, it is not concerned with any special or definite class of subjects.

Of the modes of persuasion some belong strictly to the art of rhetoric and some do not. By the latter I mean such things as are not supplied by the speaker but are there at the outset—witnesses, evidence given under torture, written contracts, and so on. By the former I mean such as we can ourselves construct by means of the principles

[7]By "speech" and "reason" the translator here has done justice to the twofold meaning of the Greek word "logos."

[8] . . .["Rhetorician,"] in fact, can mean either a *trained speaker* or a *tricky speaker*.

of rhetoric. The one kind has merely to be used, the other has to be invented.

Of the modes of persuasion furnished by the spoken word there are three kinds. The first kind depends on the personal character of the speaker; the second on putting the audience into a certain frame of mind; the third on the proof, or apparent proof, provided by the words of speech itself. Persuasion is achieved by the speaker's personal character when the speech is so spoken as to make us think him credible. We believe good men more fully and more readily than others: this is true generally whatever the question is, and absolutely true where exact certainty is impossible and opinions are divided. This kind of persuasion, like the others, should be achieved by what the speaker says, not by what people think of his character before he begins to speak. It is not true, as some writers assume in their treatises on rhetoric, that the personal goodness revealed by the speaker contributes nothing to his power of persuasion; on the contrary, his character may almost be called the most effective means of persuasion he possesses. Secondly, persuasion may come through the hearers, when the speech stirs their emotions. Our judgments when we are pleased and friendly are not the same as when we are pained and hostile. It is towards producing these effects, as we maintain, that present-day writers on rhetoric direct the whole of their efforts. This subject shall be treated in detail when we come to speak of the emotions. Thirdly, persuasion is effected through the speech itself when we have proved a truth or an apparent truth by means of the persuasive arguments suitable to the case in question.

There are, then, these three means of effecting persuasion. The man who is to be in command of them must, it is clear, be able (1) to reason logically, (2) to understand human character and goodness in their various forms, and (3) to understand the emotions—that is, to name them and describe them, to know their causes and the way in which they are excited. It thus appears that rhetoric is an offshoot of dialectic and also of ethical studies. Ethical studies may fairly be called political; and for this reason rhetoric masquerades as political science, and the professors of it as political experts— sometimes from want of education, sometimes from ostentation, sometimes owing to other human failings. As a matter of fact, it is a branch of dialectic and similar to it, as we said at the outset. Neither rhetoric nor dialectic is the scientific study of any one separate subject: both are faculties for providing arguments. This is perhaps a sufficient account of their scope and of how they are related to each other.

With regard to the persuasion achieved by proof or apparent proof: just as in dialectic there is induction on the one hand and syllogism or apparent syllogism on the other, so it is in rhetoric. The example is an induction, the enthymeme is a syllogism, and the apparent enthymeme is an apparent syllogism. I call the enthymeme a rhetorical syllogism, and the example a rhetorical induction. Every one who effects persuasion through proof does in fact use either enthymemes or examples: there is no other way. And since every one who proves anything at all is bound to use either syllogisms or inductions (and this is clear to us from the *Analytics*), it must follow that enthymemes are syllogisms and examples are inductions. The difference between example and enthymeme is made plain by the passages in the *Topics* where induction and syllogism have already been discussed. When we base the proof of a proposition on a number of similar cases, this is induction in dialectic, example in rhetoric; when it is shown that, certain propositions being true, a further and quite distinct proposition must also be true in consequence, whether invariably or usually, this is called syllogism in dialectic, enthymeme in rhetoric. It is plain also that each of these types of oratory has its advantages. Types of oratory, I say: for what has been said in the *Methodics*[9] applies equally well here; in some oratorical styles examples prevail, in others enthymemes; and in like manner, some orators are better at the former and some at the latter. Speeches that rely on examples are as persuasive as the other kind, but those which rely on enthymemes excite the louder applause. The sources of examples and enthymemes,[10] and their proper uses, we will discuss later. Our next step is to define the processes themselves more clearly.

A statement is persuasive and credible either because it is directly self-evident or because it appears to be proved from other statements that are so. In either case it is persuasive because there is somebody whom it persuades. But none of the arts theorize about individual cases. Medicine, for instance, does not theorize about what will help to cure Socrates or Callias, but only about what will help to cure any or all of a given class of patients: this alone is its business: individual cases are so infinitely various that no systematic knowledge of them is possible. In the same way the theory of rhetoric is concerned not with what seems probable to a given individual like Socrates or Hippias, but with what seems probable to men of a given type; and this is true of dialectic also. Dialectic does not construct its syllogisms out of any haphazard materials, such as the fancies of crazy people, but out of materials that call for discussion; and rhetoric, too, draws upon the regular subjects of debate. The duty of rhetoric is to deal with such matters as we deliberate upon without arts or systems to guide us, in the hearing of persons who cannot take in at a glance a complicated argument, or follow a long chain of reasoning. The subjects of our deliberation are such as seem to present us with alternative possibilities: about things that could not have been, and cannot now or in the future be, other than they are, nobody who takes them to be of this nature wastes his time in deliberation.

It is possible to form syllogisms and draw conclusions from the results of previous syllogisms; or, on the other hand, from premises which have not been thus proved, and at the same time are so little accepted that they call for proof. Reasonings of the former kind will necessarily be hard to follow owing to their length, for we assume an audience of untrained thinkers; those of the latter kind will fail to win assent, because they are based on premises that are not generally admitted or believed.

The enthymeme and the example must, then, deal with what is in the main contingent, the example being an induction, and the enthymeme a syllogism, about such matters. The enthymeme must consist of few propositions, fewer often than those which make up the normal syllogism. For if any of these propositions is a familiar fact, there is no need even to mention it; the hearer adds it himself. Thus, to show that Dorieus has been victor in a contest for which the prize is a crown, it is enough to say, "For he has been victor in the Olympic games," without adding "And in the Olympic games the prize is a crown," a fact which everybody knows.

[9]Lost logical treatise of Aristotle. . . .
[10]An alternate and perhaps better reading would be "the reason of this."

There are few facts of the "necessary" type that can form the basis of rhetorical syllogisms.[11] Most of the things about which we make decisions, and into which therefore we inquire, present us with alternative possibilities. For it is about our actions that we deliberate and inquire, and all our actions have a contingent character; hardly any of them are determined by necessity. Again, conclusions that state what is merely usual or possible must be drawn from premises that do the same, just as "necessary" conclusions must be drawn from "necessary" premises; this too is clear to us from the *Analytics*. It is evident, therefore, that the propositions forming the basis of enthymemes, though some of them may be "necessary," will most of them be only usually true. Now the materials of enthymemes are Probabilities and Signs, which we can see must correspond respectively with the propositions that are generally and those that are necessarily true. A Probability is a thing that usually happens; not, however, as some definitions would suggest, anything whatever that usually happens, but only if it belongs to the class of the "contingent" or "variable." It bears the same relation to that in respect of which it is probable[12] as the universal bears to the particular. Of Signs, one kind bears the same relation to the statement it supports as the particular bears to the universal, the other the same as the universal bears to the particular. The infallible kind is a "complete proof" (τεχμήριον); the fallible kind has no specific name. By the infallible signs I mean those on which syllogisms proper may be based: and this shows us why this kind of Sign is called "complete proof": when people think that what they have said cannot be refuted, they then think that they are bringing forward a "complete proof," meaning that the matter has now been demonstrated and completed (πεπερασ–μένον); for the word πέρας has the same meaning (of "end" or "boundary") as the word τέχμαρ in the ancient tongue. Now the one kind of Sign (that which bears to the proposition it supports the relation of particular to universal) may be illustrated thus. Suppose it were said, "The fact that Socrates was wise and just is a sign that the wise are just." Here we certainly have a Sign; but even though the proposition be true, the argument is refutable, since it does not form a syllogism. Suppose, on the other hand, it were said, "The fact that he has a fever is a sign that he is ill," or, "The fact that she is giving milk is a sign that she has lately borne a child." Here we have the infallible kind of Sign, the only kind that constitutes a complete proof, since it is the only kind that, if the particular statement is true, is irrefutable. The other kind of Sign, that which bears to the proposition it supports the relation of universal to particular, might be illustrated by saying, "The fact that he breathes fast is a sign that he has a fever." This argument also is refutable, even if the statement about the fast breathing be true, since a man may breathe hard without having a fever.

It has, then, been stated above what is the nature of a Probability, of a Sign, and of a complete proof, and what are the differences between them. In the *Analytics* a more explicit description has been given of these points; it is there shown why some of these reasonings can be put into syllogisms and some cannot.

The "example" has already been described as one kind of induction; and the

---

[11]"Material sources" or even "premises."

[12]I.e., bears the same relation to the conclusion to be reached: to that to which its general probability is directed—to the particular probable case which has to be proved.

special nature of the subject matter that distinguishes it from the other kinds has also been stated above. Its relation to the proposition it supports is not that of part to whole, nor whole to part, nor whole to whole, but of part to part, or like to like. When two statements are of the same order, but one is more familiar than the other, the former is an "example." The argument may, for instance, be that Dionysius,[13] in asking as he does for a bodyguard, is scheming to make himself a despot. For in the past Peisistratus[14] kept asking for a bodyguard in order to carry out such a scheme, and did make himself a despot as soon as he got it; and so did Theagenes[15] at Megara; and in the same way all other instances known to the speaker are made into examples, in order to show what is not yet known, that Dionysius has the same purpose in making the same request: all these being instances of the one general principle, that a man who asks for a bodyguard is scheming to make himself a despot. We have now described the sources of those means of persuasion which are popularly supposed to be demonstrative.

There is an important distinction between two sorts of enthymemes that has been wholly overlooked by almost everybody—one that also subsists between the syllogisms treated of in dialectic. One sort of enthymeme really belongs to rhetoric, as one sort of syllogism really belongs to dialectic; but the other sort really belongs to other arts and faculties, whether to those we already exercise or to those we have not yet acquired. Missing this distinction, people fail to notice that the more correctly they handle their particular subject the further they are getting away from pure rhetoric or dialectic. This statement will be clearer if expressed more fully. I mean that the proper subjects of dialectical and rhetorical syllogisms are the things with which we say the regular or universal Lines of Argument[16] are concerned; that is to say those lines of argument that apply equally to questions of right conduct, natural science, politics, and many other things that have nothing to do with one another. Take, for instance, the line of argument concerned with "the more or less."[17] On this line of argument it is equally easy to base a syllogism or enthymeme about any of what nevertheless are essentially disconnected subjects—right conduct, natural science, or anything else whatever. But there are also those special Lines of Argument which are based on such propositions as apply only to particular groups or classes of things. Thus there are propositions about natural science on which it is impossible to base any enthymeme or syllogism about ethics, and other propositions about ethics on which nothing can be based about natural science. The same principle applies throughout. The general Lines of Argument have no special subject matter, and therefore will not increase our understanding of any particular class of things. On the other hand, the better the selection one makes of propositions suitable for special Lines of Argument, the nearer one comes, unconsciously, to setting up a science that is distinct from dialectic and rhetoric. One may succeed in stating the required principles, but one's science will be

[13]Tyrant of Syracuse.
[14]Tyrant of Athens.
[15]Tyrant of Megara.
[16]Or Topics, Commonplaces.
[17]I.e., the topic of *degree*.

no longer dialectic or rhetoric, but the science to which the principles thus discovered belong. Most enthymemes are in fact based upon these particular or special Lines of Argument; comparatively few on the common or general kind. As in the *Topics,* therefore, so in this work, we must distinguish, in dealing with enthymemes, the special and the general Lines of Argument on which they are to be founded. By special Lines of Argument I mean the propositions peculiar to each several class of things, by general those common to all classes alike. We may begin with the special Lines of Argument. But, first of all, let us classify rhetoric into its varieties. Having distinguished these we may deal with them one by one, and try to discover the elements of which each is composed, and the propositions each must employ.

Rhetoric falls into three divisions, determined by the three classes of listeners to speeches. For of the three elements in speech-making—speaker, subject, and person addressed—it is the last one, the hearer, that determines the speech's end and object. The hearer must be either judge, with a decision to make about things past or future, or an observer.[18] A member of the assembly decides about future events, a juryman about past events: while those who merely decide on the orator's skill are observers. From this it follows that there are three divisions of oratory—(1) political, (2) forensic, and (3) the ceremonial oratory of display.[19]

Political speaking urges us either to do or not to do something: one of these two courses is always taken by private counsellors, as well as by men who address public assemblies. Forensic speaking either attacks or defends somebody: one or other of these two things must always be done by the parties in a case. The ceremonial oratory of display either praises or censures somebody. These three kinds of rhetoric refer to three different kinds of time. The political orator is concerned with the future: it is about things to be done hereafter that he advises, for or against. The party in a case at law is concerned with the past; one man accuses the other, and the other defends himself, with reference to things already done. The ceremonial orator is, properly speaking, concerned with the present since all men praise or blame in view of the state of things existing at the time, though they often find it useful also to recall the past and to make guesses at the future.

Rhetoric has three distinct ends in view, one for each of its three kinds. The political orator aims at establishing the expediency or the harmfulness of a proposed course of action; if he urges its acceptance, he does so on the ground that it will do good; if he urges its rejection, he does so on the ground that it will do harm; and all other points, such as whether the proposal is just or unjust, honorable or dishonorable, he brings in as subsidiary and relative to this main consideration. Parties in a law case

---

[18]A mere onlooker, present at a show, where he *decides* no grave political or legal issue and plays no higher role than that of speech taster or oratorical connoisseur.—*Political* has been preferred to *deliberative,* as being clearer to the English reader. The oratory of the "(parliamentary) counsellor" is meant.

[19]Or: deliberative (advisory) legal, and epideictic—the oratory respectively of parliamentary assemblies, of law-courts, and of ceremonial occasions when there is an element of "display," "show," "declamation," and the result is a "set speech" or "harangue."

aim at establishing the justice or injustice of some action, and they too bring in all other points as subsidiary and relative to this one. Those who praise or attack a man aim at proving him worthy of honor or the reverse, and they too treat all other considerations with reference to this one.

That the three kinds of rhetoric do aim respectively at the three ends we have mentioned is shown by the fact that speakers will sometimes not try to establish anything else. Thus, the litigant will sometimes not deny that a thing has happened or that he has done harm. But that he is guilty of injustice he will never admit; otherwise there would be no need of a trial. So too, political orators often make any concession short of admitting that they are recommending their hearers to take an inexpedient course or not to take an expedient one. The question whether it is not *unjust* for a city to enslave its innocent neighbors often does not trouble them at all. In like manner those who praise or censure a man do not consider whether his acts have been expedient or not, but often make it a ground of actual praise that he has neglected his own interest to do what was honorable. Thus, they praise Achilles because he championed his fallen friend Patroclus, though he knew that this meant death, and that otherwise he need not die: yet while to die thus was the nobler thing for him to do, the expedient thing was to live on.

It is evident from what has been said that it is these three subjects, more than any others, about which the orator must be able to have propositions at his command. Now the propositions of Rhetoric are Complete Proofs, Probabilities, and Signs. Every kind of syllogism is composed of propositions, and the enthymeme is a particular kind of syllogism composed of the aforesaid propositions.[20]

Since only possible actions, and not impossible ones, can ever have been done in the past or the present, and since things which have not occurred, or will not occur, also cannot have been done or be going to be done, it is necessary for the political, the forensic, and the ceremonial speaker alike to be able to have at their command propositions about the possible and the impossible, and about whether a thing has or has not occurred, will or will not occur. Further, all men, in giving praise or blame, in urging us to accept or reject proposals for action, in accusing others or defending themselves, attempt not only to prove the points mentioned but also to show that the good or the harm, the honor or disgrace, the justice or injustice, is great or small, either absolutely or relatively; and therefore it is plain that we must also have at our command propositions about greatness or smallness and the greater or the lesser—propositions both universal and particular. Thus, we must be able to say which is the greater or lesser good, the greater or lesser act of justice or injustice; and so on.

Such, then, are the subjects regarding which we are inevitably bound to master the propositions relevant to them. We must now discuss each particular class of these subjects in turn, namely those dealt with in political, in ceremonial, and lastly in legal, oratory.

It is now plain what our aims, future or actual should be in urging, and what in deprecating, a proposal; the latter being the opposite of the former. Now the political or deliberative orator's aim is utility: deliberation seeks to determine not ends but the

---

[20]I.e., of Complete Proofs, Probabilities, and Signs relating to the three subjects of the expedient, the just, and the noble.

means to ends; i.e., what it is most useful to do. Further, utility is a good thing. We ought therefore to assure ourselves of the main facts about Goodness and Utility in general.

We may define a good thing as that which ought to be chosen for its own sake; or as that for the sake of which we choose something else; or as that which is sought after by all things, or by all things that have sensation or reason, or which will be sought after by any things that acquire reason; or as that which must be prescribed for a given individual by reason generally, or is prescribed for him by his individual reason, this being his individual good; or as that whose presence brings anything into a satisfactory and self-sufficing condition; or as self-sufficiency; or as what produces, maintains, or entails characteristics of this kind, while preventing and destroying their opposites. One thing may entail another in either of two ways—(1) simultaneously, (2) subsequently. Thus learning entails knowledge subsequently, health entails life simultaneously. Things are productive of other things in three senses: first, as being healthy produces health; secondly, as food produces health; and thirdly, as exercise does—i.e., it does so usually. All this being settled, we now see that both the acquisition of good things and the removal of bad things must be good; the latter entails freedom from the evil things simultaneously, while the former entails possession of the good things subsequently. The acquisition of a greater in place of a lesser good, or of a lesser in place of a greater evil, is also good, for in proportion as the greater exceeds the lesser there is acquisition of good or removal of evil.[21] The virtues, too, must be something good; for it is by possessing these that we are in a good condition, and they tend to produce good works and good actions. They must be severally named and described elsewhere.[22] Pleasure, again, must be a good thing, since it is the nature of all animals to aim at it. Consequently both pleasant and beautiful things must be good things, since the former are productive of pleasure, while of the beautiful things some are pleasant and some desirable in and for themselves.

The following is a more detailed list of things that must be good. Happiness, as being desirable in itself and sufficient by itself, and as being that for whose sake we choose many other things. Also justice, courage, temperance, magnanimity,[23] magnificence, and all such qualities, as being excellences of the soul.[24] Further, health, beauty, and the like, as being bodily excellences and productive of many other good things: for instance, health is productive both of pleasure and of life, and therefore is thought the greatest of goods, since these two things which it causes, pleasure and life, are two of the things most highly prized by ordinary people. Wealth, again: for it is the excellence of possession, and also productive of many other good things. Friends and friendship: for a friend is desirable in himself and also productive of many other good

---

[21] . . . Other readings are (1) . . . "for the difference between the greater and the lesser constitutes acquisition of good in the one case and removal of evil in the other"; and (2) . . . "for the acquisition and the removal of the difference between the greater and the lesser amount to the acquisition of good and the removal of evil respectively."

[22] . . ."separately."

[23] I.e., loftiness of mind, greatness of spirit.

[24] As such they are treated in the *Nicomachean Ethics.*

things. So, too, honor and reputation, as being pleasant, and productive of many other good things, and usually accompanied by the presence of the good things that cause them to be bestowed. The faculty of speech and action; since all such qualities are productive of what is good. Further—good parts, strong memory, receptiveness, quickness of intuition, and the like, for all such faculties are productive of what is good. Similarly, all the sciences and arts. And life: since, even if no other good were the result of life, it is desirable in itself. And justice, as the cause of good to the community.

An Overview of the Structure of Rhetoric

Translated by Joseph M. Miller

Boethius

Anicius Manlius Serverinus Boethius (c.480–524 A.D.) was a Roman philosopher who served as consul and teacher under Theodoric the Great until the emperor had him executed in 524 on suspicion of treason. He is best known for his book The Consolation of Philosophy *written while he was in prison awaiting execution. Perhaps his most influential work, which became a textbook during the Middle Ages, is a treatise on logic,* Topica Boetii *(522). He also translated works by Aristotle and other Greek writers.*

It is not easy to analyze the strength of the structural bond which holds rhetoric together; the listener can hardly ever recognize it, and it is certainly not easy to describe. The angry disputes which center about the rules governing each of its parts may lead to a serious error: [Readers] may investigate each of the separate parts of the act and ignore the final product. It is this treatment of the whole, heretofore neglected, to which we now address ourselves as best we can. So we shall treat of the genus of the art, its species, its parts, its tools and the parts of the tools, the duty of its practitioners, and its goals. With this general outline of what is to be covered, we conclude the exordium of this investigation.

By genus, rhetoric is a faculty; by species, it can be one of three: judicial, demonstrative, deliberative. It is clear that the genus is what we have said. What we have said about the species, moreover, is true because rhetoric deals with all these processes. There is one special kind of rhetoric for judicial matters, based upon their special goals; there are other kinds for deliberative and demonstrative purposes. These species of rhetoric depend upon the circumstances in which they are used; all cases deal either with general principles or with the specific application of those principles, in either case using one of the three species we have already identified. For example, judicial rhetoric can treat either of general topics like rendering just honor or demanding satisfaction, or of individual cases, like paying honor to Cornelius or demanding satisfaction of Verres. Likewise, cases which involve deliberation fall under the heading of deliberative rhetoric in the same way: they may deal with general topics like war and peace or with specific issues like the Pyrrhic war and the peace which followed. Similarly, in demonstrative oratory, we deal with what deserves praise or blame; we may do this either in a general way, as when we praise bravery, or in a particular case, as when we praise the bravery of Scipio.

The subject matter for the faculty is any subject at all which can be proposed by speaking; it is usually a question of civil importance. On such a matter, the three species of rhetoric act as molds which shape the topic to themselves; as soon as one of these forms is applied to the question, it is held to that particular structure, as will be evident in what follows. Thus, when a question of public interest which has not yet been given a form is directed at a specific goal, it immediately becomes part of one of the species of rhetoric. So a civil question can take any of the forms: when it seeks the needs of justice in a court of law, it becomes judicial; when it asks in an assembly what is useful or proper, then it is a deliberative act; and when it proclaims publicly what is good, the civil question become demonstrative rhetoric. So the category into which the material falls comes from the rhetoric; otherwise the faulty would be unable to work with the topic which requires special parts of its own; for when those other parts are not present, then rhetoric itself is missing.

But since we are treating of the species of rhetoric and how those species relate to the case being dealt with, we must make clear that they apply to every kind of business which can arise in civil matters. Anything seeking justice for its goal is judicial; anything dealing with what is useful or proper in public actions is deliberative; and anything treating of the propriety, justice, or goodness of an act already performed in a matter of public interest is demonstrative. But enough of this.

And now we must treat of the parts of rhetoric. Rhetoric has five parts: invention, disposition, style, memory, and delivery. These are referred to as parts because if an orator lacks any one of them, then his use of the faculty is imperfect. And clearly it is not absurd to call those elements of the faculty of rhetoric its parts when, if taken together, they make the faculty itself complete. But, since these are the parts of the faculty of rhetoric and since they comprise the whole of that faculty, it is absolutely necessary that wherever rhetoric is to be used, they must be present as well. Now if rhetoric is completely present in each of its species, then all these parts must be present in each of the species. Therefore they all must be used in treating any public business when the issues are clearly assigned to one of the above-mentioned species of rhetoric. It makes no difference whether the matter is treated in a judicial manner, in a deliberative manner, or in a demonstrative manner, invention, arrangement, style, memory, and delivery must all be present.

Since nearly every faculty must use a tool to accomplish what it can do, we must look for some tool here. That tool is the oration, which is sometimes a civil nature, sometimes not. We are speaking now of the [rhetorical], which deals with some such question or is designed to expedite a solution to such a question. When that kind of oration treats an issue of civil importance, it moves forward without a break in continuity; when it does not deal with matters of public concern, it is developed through questions and answers. The former is rhetoric, the latter is called dialectic. They differ because the former treats of civil hypotheses, the latter of theses; the former is an unbroken oration, the latter is interrupted; the former needs both an adversary and a judge, the latter has for a judge the same person who acts as adversary.

The rhetorical oration has six parts: the introduction or exordium, the argument,[1] the partition, the proof, the refutation, and the peroration. These therefore are the parts of the tool of the rhetorical faculty, and since rhetoric is completely present in each of its species, these also must be present in each of them. Nor can they be any more present than to accomplish what they are intended for. And so the structure of introduction and narration and of all the other parts of the tool is necessary in the judicial type of rhetoric, just as it is all necessary in the deliberative and demonstrative types. Now it is the duty of the faculty of rhetoric to teach and to move;[2] the same duty falls no less to the lot of these six elements, which are the parts of the oration. Now the parts of rhetoric, being parts of a faculty, are themselves faculties; therefore the tools which work in the entire oration must also function in each part of the oration, and so they must be present in order to work. For unless the previously mentioned parts of rhetoric are present, that is, unless the author discovers suitable material, clothes it in a good style, arranges it properly, remembers it and delivers it well, he accomplishes nothing. And the same is true regarding the parts of the tool: unless all parts of the oration have them [the parts of rhetoric], they will be useless. And, in conclusion, the practitioner of this faculty is the orator, whose duty it is to speak in such a way as to persuade.

The orator must look for his goal both in himself and in his audience. In himself, because he must be able to say upon completion of the act that he has spoken well—that is, that he has spoken in a way calculated to persuade; in his audience, because he must in truth have persuaded them. For if a deficiency in any of those qualities which are expected of orators causes him to fail to persuade, then, even though the act of speaking be complete, the goal is not attained. And also, one who is truly wrapped up in his work and tied to it, will succeed when the task is done, but one who is unconcerned usually will not succeed. Nor does an orator lessen the dignity of his oratory because he seeks to attain his goal. And all of these factors are all bound together in the same way that rhetoric is complete in each of its species, and each species is a complete piece of rhetoric. Now the parts of cases are known as the *status;*[3] and we must now make a detailed examination of them. How can they be considered parts of a case if "parts of a case" means the same things as "species of a genus"? And how is it possible

[1] In this list of the parts of a speech, the text uses the word *ratio* rather than the traditional *narratio* to indicate the second part. This may be a corrupt reading, since the ms. is unedited; at any rate, all subsequent references are to *narratio.*

[2] For some reason, the text omits the traditional third function: Cicero's *delectare* (to please).

[3] At this point it becomes quite difficult to translate Boethius's explanation. The reason for this is that he uses two terms which should be synonymous, *status* (Quintilian's word for "issue") and *constitutio* (the word used in *Ad Herennium*); at times he seems to consider them synonymous, but at other times he seems to maintain that *status* is the "case" being discussed and *constitutio* the individual issues. Because of this confusion, I shall not attempt to translate the two words, but shall use them as Boethius did.

that in one case there should be many *constitutiones?* The answer is that the species are very closely bound in with one another. There are indeed many *constitutiones* in a case; but they are no more "parts of cases" than *status* is "part of the species." This is all the more clear because no species strengthens another species opposed to itself insofar as content is concerned; however each *constitutio* adds strength to every other *constitutio.* Besides, it is impossible that there should be as many parts of cases as there are parts of an entire oration. Nothing composed of one part can be whole and entire, but a single *constitutio* can be enough to build a whole case.

Then what is there to be said about this? It is clear to one who thinks it out. No *constitutio* can be called a "part of the case" in which it figures, because it is the subject of the dispute and the status establishes it as an issue. This is especially true when we consider that a *status* which is added to the case after one *constitutio* has been settled is not considered principal, but subsidiary. Besides, in one affair there are as many points to be argued as there are *constitutiones,* and there are as many cases as there are points to be argued; and, even granted that one piece of business may need to consider all of them, yet the cases themselves are different, despite the fact that they are so closely related to one another. For example, if a husband sees a young man coming out of a brothel, and a few minutes later sees his own wife coming out of the same place, he may accuse the young man of adultery. This, then, is the one matter to be decided; yet there are two cases: one is a conjectural one, if the young man denies that he has done anything; the other is a case of definition, which hinges on whether an act of intercourse in a brothel can be considered adulterous. But for the man who denies having done anything wrong, the conjectural *status* is not part of the controversy; to the one who is arguing definition, the definition is not part of the controversy: it is the whole controversy. Of course, I am not speaking now of "a case" in the generic sense of that word, but of an argument based on a particular *constitutio.*

The *constitutiones* are, however, parts of the case as a genus in this sense. For if every case were conjectural, and if there were no other status to be investigated, then the conjectural *status* would not be just a part of the case, but would be the very case itself, without exception. But since every case depends partly upon the conjectural, partly upon the end, partly upon the quality, and partly upon objection,[4] the *constitutio* is part of the case—not of the one particular case generically, because it is one of the alternative approaches which can be used independently of the others, like cutting one member off from the others. The *constitutiones* are, therefore, parts in the sense of species of the genus case, but there are not parts of any given case in which they function as necessary to the structure.

---

[4]In identifying these four questions, Boethius ignores the approach of *Ad Herennium,* to which he has adhered thus far, and returns to the *staeseis* as identified by Hermagoras: (1) Conjecture, "Did it happen?"; (2) Definition, "Was it really theft?"; (3) Quality, "Did circumstances justify it?"; and (4) Objection, "Does this assembly have the right to judge?". It seems, moreover, that the text of Boethius' list is corrupt, since it reads, *"partim conjectura, partim sine, partim qualitate, partim translatione,"* while the customary Latin words would have been *conjectura, fine, qualitate,* and *tralatione.* See M. L. Clarke, *Rhetoric at Rome* (London, 1953), pp. 26–27.

In summary, then, the faculty of rhetoric is a genus of which the species are judicial, demonstrative and deliberative. The subject matter is any question of civil importance, called "a case." The parts of this subject matter are the *constitutiones*. The parts of rhetoric are invention, arrangement, style, memory, and delivery. The tool used is the oration, and the parts of the tool are the exordium, the narration, the division, the proof, the refutation, the peroration. The function of the oration is to teach and to move. The practitioner is the orator, his duty is to speak well, and his goal is to have spoken·well and to persuade.

All rhetoric is contained in each one of its species; and the species exercise final control over the content, so that they truly make it their own. We can understand this from the fact that each of the species controls completely all the material which it contains. Thus you may find four *constitutiones* in judicial rhetoric, and in deliberative or demonstrative rhetoric you may expect to find the same four. From this we may conclude that if each of the species has all the parts of a case, speaking generically, that is of a civil question to be decided, then the case is the combination of all those parts. The entire case itself, then, which is the civil question, is determined by the species. It is much like the way a word comes to the ears of many people at once, complete in all its parts, that is in its syllables; for the whole case with all its parts comes under the different species at one time.

But when the species asserts itself over the subject matter, which is the civil question, and imposes itself upon the subject with all its parts, then it brings with it into the question the faculty of rhetoric, and also, in consequence, all the parts of rhetoric. Therefore the parts of rhetoric are necessary in each of the *constitutiones*. But when rhetoric is given authority over the material, it brings in its tool with it: it applies the oration, with all its peculiar parts. So there will be in each *constitutio* an exordium, a narration, and so on. And when the instrument is brought into play, it in turn adds its own function to the civil question; it will, therefore, teach and persuade concerning each *constitutio*. But none of these elements can enter the picture unless there is someone to move them, like an operator or an architect. This person, then, is the orator, who comes into the case and makes it his own project. Therefore he must speak well in every manner of case and in every *constitutio*. The orator also must seek his goal, both to speak well on every *constitutio* and to persuade as well.

We have treated in this discussion, now, everything about rhetoric in general terms. Later, if it is possible, we shall go into greater detail about each item separately.[5]

---

[5]Whether Boethius carried out this promise is not certain. There are no extant tracts about the subjects he has discussed; however, we do have his short treatise on the rhetorical places, as well as tracts on some of the works of Aristotle and Cicero.

Questions on the Classics ▬▬▬▬▬▬▬▬▬

1. Why does Socrates (through Plato's writing) think that an understanding of different kinds of people (audience) is important?

2. How does Socrates use the metaphor of gardening to illustrate his point?

3. How does Aristotle make a distinction between syllogism and enthymemes?

4. What divisions does Aristotle make in the types of rhetoric?

5. How does Aristotle define a "good thing"?

6. What does Boethius see as the five parts of rhetoric? How important are they?

7. Compare the two discussions of rhetoric by Aristotle and Boethius. How does one discussion clarify or amplify the other?

Readings in
Argumentation: Gun Control

Arguments Showing Two Sides

The following advertisements and articles show a variety of approaches to the gun-control issue and to an environmental issue. All of the articles and advertisements seek to persuade the reader to take a side. Some of the logical fallacies are in these articles. There is also a clear development of argument, some articles using the enthymeme approach and others more nearly like the Toulmin method. Of course, arguments do not always need a formal structure—some just develop without formal parts. Look for patterns, or lack of patterns, in the sample essays. Also look for hidden assumptions. Sometimes these assumptions are central to the argument. What conclusions are found? We may discover that the arguments simply do not have easy answers. But, of course, most problems do not.

REP. ALBERTO GUTMAN: Florida Legislator, Businessman, Husband, Member of the National Rifle Association.

"Being from a country that was once a democracy and turned communist, I really feel I know what the right to bear arms is all about. In Cuba, where I was born, the first thing the communist government did was take away everybody's firearms, leaving them defenseless and intimidated with fear. That's why our constitutional right to bear arms is so important to our country's survival.

"As a legislator I have to deal with reality. And the reality is that gun control does not work. It actually eliminates the rights of the law-abiding citizen, not the criminal. Criminals will always have guns, and they won't follow gun control laws anyway. I would like to see tougher laws on criminals as opposed to tougher laws on legitimate gun owners. We need to attack the problem of crime at its roots, instead of blaming crime on gun ownership and citizens who use them lawfully.

"It's a big responsibility that we face retaining the right to bear arms. That's why I joined the NRA. The NRA is instrumental in protecting these freedoms. It helps train and educate people, supporting legislation that benefits not only those who bear arms but all citizens of the United States. The NRA helps keep America free." **I'm the NRA.**

The NRA's lobbying organization, the Institute for Legislative Action, is the nation's largest and most influential protector of the constitutional right to keep and bear arms. At every level of government and through local grassroots efforts, the Institute guards against infringement upon the freedoms of law-abiding gun owners. If you would like to join the NRA or want more information about our programs and benefits, write J. Warren Cassidy, Executive Vice President, P.O. Box 37484, Dept. AG-15, Washington, D.C. 20013.

Paid for by the members of the National Rifle Association of America. Copyright 1986.

Reprinted with permission of the National Rifle Association.

—Mrs. James S. Brady—

"A $29 handgun shattered my family's life."

"Seven years ago, John Hinckley pulled a $29 revolver from his pocket and opened fire on a Washington street. He shot the President. He also shot my husband.

I'm not asking for your sympathy. I'm asking for your help.

I've learned from my own experience that, alone, there's only so much you can do to stop handgun violence. But that together, we can confront the mightiest gun lobby— the N.R.A.— and win.

I've only to look at my husband Jim to remember that awful day... the unending TV coverage of the handgun firing over and over... the nightmare panic and fear.

It's an absolute miracle nobody was killed. After all, twenty thousand Americans are killed by handguns every year. Thousands more—men, women, even children— are maimed for life.

Like me, I know you support *stronger* handgun control laws. So does the vast majority of Americans. But the National Rifle Association can spend so much in elections that Congress is afraid to pass an effective national handgun law.

It's time to change that. Before it's too late for another family like mine... a family like yours.

I joined Handgun Control, Inc. because they're willing to take on the N.R.A. Right now we're campaigning for a national waiting period and background check on handgun purchases.

If such simple, basic measures had been on the books seven years ago, John Hinckley would never have walked out of that Texas pawnshop with the handgun which came within an inch of killing Ronald Reagan. He lied on his purchase application. Given time, the police could have caught the lie and put him in jail.

Of course, John Hinckley's not the only one. Police report that thousands of known criminals buy handguns right over the counter in this country. We have to stop them.

So, please, pick up a pen. Write me to find out how you can help. And support our work with a generous contribution.

It's time we kept handguns out of the wrong hands. It's time to break the National Rifle Association's grip on Congress and start making our cities and neighborhoods safe again.

Thank you and God bless you."

"Don't let it happen to you."

Dear Sarah,

It's time to break the N.R.A.'s grip on Congress once and for all. Here's my contribution to Handgun Control, Inc., the million-strong nonprofit citizens' group you help direct:

☐ $15   ☐ $29   ☐ $35   ☐ $50   ☐ $100 or $_____.
☐ Tell me more about how I can help.

NAME _____

ADDRESS _____

CITY _____ STATE _____ ZIP _____

HANDGUN CONTROL

1400 K Street, N.W., Washington, D.C. 20005, (202) 898-0792
Contributions to Handgun Control, Inc. are not tax deductible.

Reprinted with permission of Handgun Control, Inc.

Why Nick?

Jeanne Shields

When people discuss controversial issues, they sometimes lose sight of how these issues affect individual lives. Gun control has been the subject of national debate for so many years that it may seem of interest only to men and women who are directly involved with guns: those who either own them, sell them, or work with them. But the abstract can become painfully real to anyone who becomes the victim of handgun violence, as this essay by Jeanne Shields reveals. After her son was murdered, Shields became active in the movement to control handguns. Her essay, which originally appeared in Newsweek *in 1978, is both a tribute to the memory of her son and an argument on behalf of stricter laws regulating the sale and possession of guns.*

If the telephone rings late at night, I always mentally check off where each child is, and at the same time get an awful sinking feeling in the pit of my stomach.

Four years ago, April 16, we had a telephone call very late. As my husband answered, I checked off Pam in Long Beach (California), Nick in San Francisco, David in New Brunswick (New Jersey) and Leslie outside Boston. The less my husband spoke, the tighter the knot got in my stomach. Instinctively, I knew it was bad news, but I wasn't prepared for what he had to tell me. Our eldest son, Nick, 23, had been shot dead on a street in San Francisco.

Nick was murdered at about 9:30 p.m. He and a friend, Jon, had come from lacrosse practice and were on their way home. They stopped to pick up a rug at the home of a friend. While Jon went in to get the rug, Nick rearranged the lacrosse gear in the back of their borrowed Vega. He was shot three times in the back and died instantly, holding a lacrosse stick.

Nick was the fourteenth victim of what came to be called the "Zebra killers." Between the fall of 1973 and April 16, 1974, they had randomly killed fourteen people and wounded seven others—crippling one for life. Four men were subsequently convicted of murder in a trial that lasted thirteen months.

My son was tall, dark and handsome, and a good athlete. He was particularly good at lacrosse and an expert skier. Nick was an ardent photographer and wrote some lovely poetry. He was a gentle and sensitive man with an infectious grin and the capacity to make friends easily. It was hard for me to believe he was gone.

The generous support and love of our friends gave us the strength to go on during those days. The calls and letters that poured in from those who knew Nick were overwhelming. In his short life, Nick had touched so many people in so many ways. It was both heartwarming and very humbling.

But always, running through those blurred days was the question. Why? Why Nick? My deep faith in God was really put to the test. Yet, nothing that I could do or think of, or pray for, was ever going to bring Nick back.

Because Nick was shot two days after Easter, the funeral service was filled with

Easter prayers and hymns. Spring flowers came from the gardens of friends. The day was mild, clear and beautiful, and a kind of peace and understanding seeped into my aching heart.

No matter how many children you have, the death of one leaves a void that cannot be filled. Life seems to include a new awareness, and one's philosophy and values come under sharper scrutiny. Were we just to pick up the pieces and continue as before? That choice became impossible, because a meaning had to be given to this vicious, senseless death.

That summer of 1974, the newspapers, magazines and television were full of Watergate. But I couldn't concentrate on it or anything else. Instead I dug hard in the garden for short periods of time, or smashed at tennis balls.

On the other hand, my husband, Pete, immersed himself in a study of the gun-control issue. Very near to where Nick had died, in a vacant lot, two small children found a gun—*the* gun. It was a .32-caliber Beretta. Police, in tracing it, found that initially it had been bought legally, but then went through the hands of seven different owners—most of whom had police records. Its final bullets, fired at close range, had killed my son—and then it was thrown carelessly away.

Pete's readings of Presidential commission recommendations, FBI crime statistics and books on the handgun issue showed him that our Federal laws were indeed weak and ineffective. He went to Washington to talk to politicians and to see what, if anything, was being done about it. I watched him wrestle with his thoughts and spend long hours writing them down on paper—the pros and cons of handgun control and what could logically be done about the proliferation of handguns in this nation.

Through friends, Pete had been introduced in Washington to the National Council to Control Handguns, a citizens' lobby seeking stricter Federal controls over handguns. As Pete became more closely associated with the NCCH as a volunteer, it became increasingly obvious that he was leaning toward a greater involvement.

Consequently, with strong encouragement from me and the children, Pete took a year's leave of absence from his job as marketing executive so that he could join NCCH full time. A full year and a half later, he finally resigned and became the NCCH chairman.

The main adversaries of handgun control are members of the powerful and financially entrenched National Rifle Association, macho men who don't understand the definition of a civilized society. They are aided by an apathetic government which in reality is us, because we citizens don't make ourselves heard loud and clear enough. How many people are in the silent majority, who want to see something done about unregulated sale and possession of handguns? Why are the production and sale of firecrackers severely restricted—and not handguns?

I now work in the NCCH office as a volunteer. One of my jobs is to read and make appropriate card files each day from a flood of clippings describing handgun incidents. The daily newspapers across the country recount the grim litany of shootings, killings, rapes and robberies at gun point. Some of it's tough going, because I am poignantly aware of what a family is going through. Some of it's so appalling it makes me literally sick.

Some people can no longer absorb this kind of news. They have almost become immune to it, because there is so much violence. To others, it is too impersonal; it's always something that happens to somebody else—not to you.

But anybody can be shot. We are all in a lottery, where the likelihood of your facing handgun violence grows ever day. Today there are 50 million handguns in civilian hands. By the year 2000, there will be more than 100 million.

So many families have given up so much to the deadly handgun. It will take the women of this country—the mothers, wives, sisters, and daughters—to do something about it. But when will they stand up to be counted and to be heard? Or will they wait only to hear the telephone ringing late at night?

They Want to Take Our Guns

Joe Foss

The recipient of a Distinguished Flying Cross and a Congressional Medal of Honor, Joe Foss served as Governor of South Dakota from 1954–58. From 1967–74, he appeared regularly on television as the host of The Outdoorsman. *In 1978, he served on the President's Council on Physical Fitness & Sports, and in 1979 he was a member of the White House Conference on Handicapped Individuals. Now President of the National Rifle Association, Foss has also served as Commissioner of the American Football League. "They Want to Take Our Guns" was first published in 1988 by Conservative Digest.*

Criminologists now estimate that every year some 650,000 American citizens use a firearm in defense of their homes, their property, their family, their very lives. These are Americans just like you and me—men and women surprised in their dwellings or businesses or aroused from a deep sleep, possibly by the screams of a loved one. They will be threatened by robbery or rape or the many aspects of domestic terrorism we lump together and call "crime." They will have seconds to react, and they will instinctively choose self-preservation through the only means private citizens have available: They will reach for a firearm, in many instances a handgun purchased expressly for the purpose of self-defense. And each of these law-abiding American citizens will be well within their rights—both morally and according to the Constitution of the United States—when they do so.

It seems unthinkable that anyone would deny Americans the right to defend themselves. Yet at this writing, Congress is being lobbied to do just that. Anti-gun organizations, aided by sympathetic media, continue to push for an ultimate ban on the sale of handguns. Never mind that more women, concerned for their safety, are purchasing self-defense firearms than ever before. Never mind that statistics show crime has continued to flourish—even increased—in cities with rigid handgun ordinances.

Yet the anti-gun push continues. It continues without regard for the lives that would have been lost had thousands of law-abiding citizens been unable to use a personal firearm for self-protection. It continues without regard for public opinion. No national anti-gun measure has ever been approved by American voters. Just this year Nebraska citizens successfully circulated a petition that will place a "right to keep and bear arms" constitutional amendment on a state ballot this fall. And in Maryland, where anti-gun legislators rammed through a law banning handguns, the people have responded. Another successful petition drive will allow the people of Maryland an opportunity to overturn the ban at the voting booth.

Yet somehow the message isn't getting through. A deplorable arrogance exists within the anti-gun camp, an arrogance that shows utter disdain for the reality of life and the will of people. The anti-gun crusade's manipulation of lawmakers, the media, and even some police officials is totally lacking in principle.

For example, in the past several months groups like Handgun Control, Inc., have paraded several high-ranking police officials in front of Congress and the public, prodding them to condemn the National Rifle Association, our nationwide efforts to protect America's Second Amendment rights, and firearms ownership in general. The police chief's message is this: Crime in America is flourishing because American citizens can legally obtain and own firearms. That's as absurd as saying that drunk driving is flourishing because American citizens can legally obtain and drive automobiles.

The propaganda emanating from these police chiefs serves little other than their own political goals. It certainly does not reflect the viewpoint of most law-enforcement professionals, who agree that law-abiding citizens have a right and a need to protect their homes and families. The police can't be everywhere all the time, and any hardworking officer on the beat will be the first to tell you so. Therefore, when men like San Jose Police Chief Joseph McNamara claim to speak for law enforcement, it's much like one renegade general taking it upon himself to speak in behalf of the Pentagon. Now McNamara's ready to consider legalizing drugs. Police officers across America undoubtedly wince when this man claims to represent them.

The difference between thought and deed extends to the liberal media, where famous columnists like Carl Rowan scream out in print for the abolishment of all handguns, yet reach for a pistol when intruders violate the privacy of *their* homes. Rowan now says he'll keep, and continue to use, a handgun to defend himself as long as crime is rife in America. Yet he still favors control for the rest of us.

The fact that Carl Rowan pushes for handgun laws and then chooses to ignore them is representative of the overall anti-gun philosophy. In places where harsh anti-gun laws are in effect, including New York City and Washington, D.C., the rich, the powerful, and the influential are seldom without some means of self-protection. They use their money and prestige to step around the law, while lashing out at the sale of so-called "Saturday Night Specials," the only handguns our nation's elderly and poor can afford.

Crime doesn't prey upon the powerful and the protected. It seeks out the weak and defenseless. Last year some 650,000 Americans decided they didn't want to become victims. Yet if the McNamaras and the Carl Rowans and the membership of Handgun Control, Inc., had been successful, these people would now be either the subject of glaring headlines or the small type in obituary notices. That's too great a price to pay so that a few vocal reformers may bask in their own smugness.

The battle lines have been drawn, and I must admit that the fight appears to be fast becoming bloody. I think it's a contest between idealism and conservative common sense. On one side we have individuals like Senator Howard Metzenbaum (D-OH), a proverbial fountain of anti-gun legislation whose ways are deceitful, to say the least.

Metzenbaum sponsored the recent "plastic gun" legislation that, due to the efforts of men like Senator James McClure (R-ID), cool heads in the Justice Department, and our own NRA lobbyists, was eventually stripped of its thinly disguised anti-gun designs.

The entire "plastic gun" fiasco is an excellent example of how the anti-gun movement has been working its witchery. When the issue first arose, we at the NRA took a common sense approach. For one thing, the entire question was a moot point: There are presently no totally plastic guns being manufactured. Some time in the future America will probably have the technology that enables us to make plastic guns, and then beefed up airport security, with instruments capable of detecting non-metal firearms, would obviously best serve the safety of the American people.

But Metzenbaum was more interested in a *handgun ban.* He also wanted more bureaucratic control over private firearms ownership. His "plastic gun" bill would have banned millions of legitimate self-defense firearms and given the federal government control over the transfer and trade of many of these guns. His scheme was exposed, and the citizens of this country achieved a common sense compromise.

Metzenbaum and his anti-gun comrades wasted little time in reviving their crusade against our Second Amendment rights. Now, under the guise of a national waiting-period law, the Ohio Senator and his sponsors want to create a new and unbelievably cumbersome federal bureaucracy to preside over firearms ownership in America. This new federal monstrosity would decide who could purchase a handgun and when it could be purchased—if at all. It would invade the privacy of law-abiding citizens with background checks. The absurd waiting-period law would also allow the government to block the sale, transfer, or trade of many firearms, and eventually result in gun registration.

Most frightening of all, the measure would invalidate current state laws that guarantee each law-abiding citizen the right to purchase a handgun for sport or self-defense. As a result, a powerful few would gain control over the freedom of millions of Americans—citizens who have never voted to relinquish these rights. When I think of the impact of laws like these, I sense democracy waning. And I renew my resolve to fight against these socialist trends.

Whenever the gun prohibition issue is raised, our opponents cry out that free and legal firearms ownership fosters crime. This is absurd. Criminals do not obtain their guns through legal channels. They do not stand in the lines created by waiting-period laws. Criminals do not submit to background checks. They are not concerned about registration. Criminals operate outside of the law. Doesn't it stand to reason that only the law-abiding obey gun-control laws?

Therefore restrictions on handguns will only undermine the rights and safety of honest citizens, and give criminals even greater opportunity to rape, murder, and terrorize. So why doesn't common sense tell us to quit all this anti-gun nonsense and begin attacking the real issues? Because firearms ownership isn't all that's on trial here.

We are at a crossroads in America, with one path drifting toward a collective, sterile, carefully managed society, the other path reaffirming our constitutional form of government and individual rights. The anti-gun faction is pushing for abolition of the liberties we cherish. That is why the National Rifle Association continues to fight for the right to keep and bear arms, reaffirming American individualism and the grass-roots strength of our system.

Don't Ban Guns

(Taken from letters to the Editor, Tuesday, February 11, 1992, The Daily Herald, *Provo, Utah.)*

Richard S. Walker and Jason Walker

Richard Walker (b. 1956) and Jason Walker (b. 1981) are father and son from Orem, Utah. Richard is a member of the NRA and his son (and two other sons) will become automatic members at 18 years old. They are a sportsman family who enjoy hunting and fishing in the mountains near their home. Richard teaches his sons proper use of guns and also has them take state-sponsored courses in gun safety. They are advocates of the constitutional right to bear arms and support open and responsible discussion on both sides of the issue.

An editorial by Melissa Helquist appeared recently in the Mt. View High School newspaper. My first response upon reading the article called "Gun Control Could Prevent Senseless Slaughter" was anger, not considering that the same Constitution that gives me the right to keep and bear arms also gives her the right to voice her opinion. I have followed the gun-control debate for years and I know that gun control is not the answer.

How interesting it is that the media with its unbiased reporting, forgets to mention that the individuals in the Killen, Texas, incident were presently, or had been, receiving psychiatric therapy and should have been institutionalized, rather than walking the streets. The congressmen that sponsor gun-control legislation sit in their alarm-protected, burglar-proof homes, choosing to ignore the fact that the answer isn't gun control inflicted on honest citizens, but stiffer sentences and punishment for those individuals who use a firearm in the commission of a crime.

More prisons need to be built, and when a person is given 10 years for a crime it should be 10 years not 5 years' reducing the sentence because of "good behavior."

Have the various drug laws stopped the influx of billions of dollars of drugs into this country? Did prohibition work? No. The criminal activity only increased, leaving the honest citizen to "pay the tab" and live with the constant threat of being victimized by some "reformed individual."

It is frightening to think that only the criminals will have guns. Our already overworked police departments need additional jails, funding and judges that enforce stricter penalties, not the added burden of "policing" the honest citizen.

The guaranteed right of life, liberty and the pursuit of happiness can only be assured through personal ownership of firearms, to protect ourselves from criminals or misaligned governments, whose only intentions are to take away freedom.

The N.R.A. recently sponsored a bill as an alternative to the Brady bill, that would conduct an instantaneous criminal background check on any would-be gun purchaser. It was defeated, with its opponents saying the cost for such a system would be staggering. But a similar system, currently in effect in Virginia, Florida and Delaware using state patrol computers, is operating within existing budgets. There are alternatives to gun control that can be made to be effective.

Killing Our Future

Sarah Brady

The head of Handgun Control, Inc., Sarah Brady became active in the fight for gun control after her husband was badly wounded in an assassination attempt upon Ronald Reagan during his first year as President. James Brady was shot in the head, the bullet going through his left eye and crossing his brain. Helping her husband to recover speech and movement though many years of hard work, she also traveled widely to speak on behalf of gun control. She lobbied in particular for national legislation that would require a waiting period after someone applies to buy a gun so that a background check can be made before the purchase is approved. The following 1990 article provides an example of the type of argument Brady made on behalf of the legislation that came to be known as the Brady Amendment.

As America enters the next decade, it does so with an appalling legacy of gun violence. The 1980s were tragic years that saw nearly a quarter of a million Americans die from handguns—four times as many as were killed in the Viet Nam War. We began the decade by witnessing yet another President, Ronald Reagan, become a victim of a would-be assassin's bullet. That day my husband Jim, his press secretary, also became a statistic in America's handgun war.

Gun violence is an epidemic in this country. In too many cities, the news each night reports another death by a gun. As dealers push out in search of new addicts, Smalltown, U.S.A., is introduced to the mindless gun violence fostered by the drug trade.

And we are killing our future. Every day a child in this country loses his or her life to a handgun. Hundreds more are permanently injured, often because a careless adult left within easy reach a loaded handgun purchased for self-defense.

Despite the carnage, America stands poised to face an even greater escalation of bloodshed. The growing popularity of military-style assault weapons could turn our streets into combat zones. Assault weapons, designed solely to mow down human beings, are turning up at an alarming rate in the hands of those most prone to violence—drug dealers, gang members, hate groups and the mentally ill.

The Stockton, Calif., massacre of little children was a warning to our policymakers. But Congress lacked the courage to do anything. During the year of inaction on Capitol Hill, we have seen too many other tragedies brought about by assault weapons. In Louisville an ex-employee of a printing plant went on a shooting spree with a Chinese-made semiautomatic version of the AK-47, gunning down 21 people, killing eight and himself. Two Colorado women were murdered and several others injured by a junkie using a stolen MAC-11 semiautomatic pistol. And Congress votes itself a pay raise.

The National Rifle Association, meanwhile, breathes a sigh of relief, gratified that your attention is now elsewhere. The only cooling-off period the N.R.A. favors is a postponement of legislative action. It counts on public anger to fade before such outrage can be directed at legislators. The N.R.A. runs feel-good ads saying guns are not the problem and there is nothing we can do to prevent criminals from getting guns. In fact, it has said that guns in the wrong hands are the "price we pay for freedom." I guess I'm just not willing to hand the next John Hinckley a deadly handgun. Neither is the nation's law-enforcement community, the men and women who put their lives on the line for the rest of us every day.

Two pieces of federal legislation can make a difference right now. First, we must require a national waiting period before the purchase of a handgun, to allow for a criminal-records check. Police know that waiting periods work. In the 20 years that New Jersey has required a background check, authorities have stopped more than 10,000 convicted felons from purchasing handguns.

We must also stop the sale and domestic production of semiautomatic assault weapons. These killing machines clearly have no legitimate sporting purpose, as President Bush recognized when he permanently banned their importation.

These public-safety measures are supported by the vast majority of Americans— including gun owners. In fact, these measures are so sensible that I never realized the campaign to pass them into law would be such an uphill battle. But it can be done.

Jim Brady knows the importance of a waiting period. He knows the living hell of a gunshot wound. Jim and I are not afraid to take on the N.R.A. leaders, and we will fight them everywhere we can. As Jim said in his congressional testimony, "I don't question the rights of responsible gun owners. That's not the issue. The issue is whether the John Hinckleys of the world should be able to walk into gun stores and purchase handguns instantly. Are you willing and ready to cast a vote for a commonsense public-safety bill endorsed by experts—law enforcement?"

Are we as a nation going to accept America's bloodshed, or are we ready to stand up and do what is right? When are we going to say "Enough"? We can change the direction in which America is headed. We can prevent the 1990s from being bloodier than the past ten years. If each of you picks up a pen and writes to your Senators and Representative tonight, you would be surprised at how quickly we could collect the votes we need to win the war for a safer America.

Let us enter a new decade committed to finding solutions to the problem of gun violence. Let your legislators know that voting with the gun lobby—and against public safety—is no longer acceptable. Let us send a signal to lawmakers that we demand action, not excuses.

Discussion Questions on Gun Control

1. Three of the selections are against gun control (CON). Each of the three makes the same point about guns and criminals. What is this major argument?

2. Each of the three articles uses at least one other argument to support the position. Name these arguments.

3. Three selections are in favor of some type of gun control (PRO). What are the major arguments given by these articles?

4. Both sides of this issue use emotional appeal to persuade the audience to their points of view. How effective is this appeal? Can such an appeal change personal views?

5. Some of the articles use examples to strengthen their persuasive effect. Are they using a deductive or an inductive approach? Which specific article is the most successful in its use of example?

6. What logical fallacies are being used in the articles? Are they effectively used? Give a specific example of a logical fallacy and how it either strengthens or weakens the argument.

7. Can you find the use of irony in any of the articles? Where is it used?

8. What is the strongest argument in this issue? Does it come from the PRO or the CON part of the argument? Defend your position on its strength and validity.

Readings in Argumentation: Global Warming

Endless Summer: Living with the Greenhouse Effect

Andrew C. Revkin

Andrew C. Revkin is a senior editor of Discover *magazine. He is a regular contributor to the magazine, with articles of topical interest. His story on the Florida alligator wars appeared in the September 1988 issue, and "March of the Fire Ants" in the March 1989 issue.*

On June 23 [1988] the United States sizzled as thermometers topped 100 degrees in 45 cities from coast to coast: 102 in Sacramento; 103 in Lincoln, Nebraska; 101 in Richmond, Virginia. In the nation's heartland the searing heat was accompanied by a ruinous drought that ravaged crops and prompted talk of a dust bowl to rival that of the 1930s. Heat waves and droughts are nothing new, of course. But on that stifling June day a top atmospheric scientist testifying on Capitol Hill had a disturbing message for his senatorial audience: Get used to it.

This wasn't just a bad year, James Hansen of the NASA Goddard Institute for Space Shuttles told the Senate committee, or even the start of a bad decade. Rather, he could state with "99 percent confidence" that a recent, persistent rise in global temperature was a climatic signal he and his colleagues had long been expecting. Others were still hedging their bets, arguing there was room for doubt. But Hansen was willing to say what no one had dared say before. "The greenhouse effect," he claimed, "has been detected and is changing our climate now."

Until this year, despite dire warnings from climatologists, the greenhouse effect has seemed somehow academic and far off. The idea behind it is simple: gases accumulating in the atmosphere as by-products of human industry and agriculture— carbon dioxide, mostly, but also methane, nitrous oxide, ozone, and chlorofluorocarbons—let in the sun's warming rays but don't let excess heat escape. As a result, mean global temperature has probably been rising for decades. But the rise has been so gradual that it has been masked by the much greater, and ordinary, year-to-year swings in world temperature.

Not anymore, said Hansen. The 1980s have already seen the four hottest years on record, and 1988 is almost certain to be hotter still. Moreover the seasonal, regional, and atmospheric patterns of rising temperature—greater warming in winters than summers, greater warming at high latitudes than near the equator, and a cooling in the stratosphere while the lower atmosphere is warmer—jibe with what computer models predict should happen with greenhouse heating. And the warming comes at a time when, by rights, Earth should actually be cooler than normal. The sun's radiance has dropped slightly since the 1970s, and dust thrown up by recent volcanic eruptions, especially that of Mexico's El Chichón in 1982, should be keeping some sunlight from reaching the planet.

Even though most climatologists think Hansen's claims are premature, they agree that warming is on the way. Carbon dioxide levels are 25 percent higher now than they were in 1860, and the atmosphere's burden of greenhouse gases is expected to keep growing. By the middle of the next century the resulting warming could boost global mean temperatures from three to nine degrees Fahrenheit. That doesn't sound like much, but it equals the temperature rise since the end of the last ice age, and the consequences could be devastating. Weather patterns could shift, bringing drought to once fertile areas and heavy rains to fragile deserts that cannot handle them. As runoff from melting glaciers increases and warming seawater expands, sea level could rise as much as six feet, inundating low-lying coastal areas and islands. There would be dramatic disruptions of agriculture, water resources, fisheries, coastal activity, and energy use.

"Average climate will certainly get warmer," says Roger Revelle, an oceanographer and climatologist at the University of California at San Diego. "But what's more serious is how many more hurricanes we'll have, how many more droughts we'll have, how many days above one hundred degrees." By Hansen's reckoning, where Washington now averages one day a year over 100 degrees, it will average 12 such scorchers annually by the middle of the next century.

Comparable climate shifts have happened before, but over tens of centuries, not tens of years. The unprecedented rapid change could accelerate the already high rate of species extinction as plants and animals fail to adapt quickly enough. For the first time in history humans are affecting the ecological balance of not just a region but the entire world, all at once. "We're altering the environment far faster than we can possibly predict the consequences," says Stephen Schneider, a climate modeler at the National Center for Atmospheric Research in Boulder, Colorado. "This is bound to lead to some surprises."

Schneider has been trying to generate interest in the greenhouse effect since the early 1970s, although largely unsuccessfully. Frightening as the greenhouse effect is, the task of curbing it is so daunting that no one has been willing to take the necessary steps as long as there was even a tiny chance that the effect might not be real. Since greenhouse gases are chiefly the result of human industry and agriculture, it is not an exaggeration to say that civilization itself is the ultimate cause of global warming. That doesn't mean nothing can be done; only that delaying the effects of global warming by cutting down on greenhouse-gas emissions will be tremendously difficult, both technically and politically. Part of the problem is that predicting exactly what will happen to the local climate, region by region, is a task that's still beyond the power of even the most sophisticated computer model. . . .

The only way to eliminate the greenhouse problem completely would be to return the world to its preindustrial state. No one proposes that. But researchers agree that there is plenty that can be done to at least slow down the warming. Energy conservation comes first: using less coal, finding more efficient ways to use cleaner-burning fossil fuels, and taking a new look at nonfossil alternatives, everything from solar and geothermal energy to—yes, even some environmentalists are admitting it—nuclear power.

Getting the world's fractious nations to agree to a program of remedial measures sounds extremely difficult, but Stephen Schneider sees signs that it may not be impossible. Schneider was one of more than 300 delegates from 48 countries who attended the International Conference on the Changing Atmosphere, which took place in Toronto, coincidentally, just a week after Hansen's congressional testimony. It was, say Schneider, the "Woodstock of CO_2" (an obvious reference to the "Woodstock of Physics" meeting held last year, during which news of the high-temperature superconductors exploded into the public consciousness).

The meeting was the first large-scale attempt to bridge the gap between scientists and policymakers on a wide range of atmospheric problems, including not just the greenhouse effect but also acid rain and the depletion of the protective layer of ozone in the stratosphere. Four days of floor debates, panel discussions, and closed-door sessions produced an ambitious manifesto calling for, among other things, the following:

- A 20-percent reduction in carbon dioxide emissions by industrialized nations by the year 2005, using a combination of conservation efforts and reduced consumption of fossil fuels. A 50-percent cut would eventually be needed to stabilize atmospheric carbon dioxide.

- A switch from coal or oil to other fuels. Burning natural gas, for example, produces half as much carbon dioxide per unit of energy as burning coal.

- Much more funding for development of solar power, wind power, geothermal power, and the like, and efforts to develop safe nuclear power.

- Drastic reductions in deforestation, and encouragement of forest replanting and restoration.

- The labeling of products whose manufacture does not harm the environment.

- Nearly complete elimination of the use of chlorofluorocarbons, or CFCs, by the year 2000.

Of all the anti-greenhouse measures, the last should prove easiest to achieve. Although CFCs are extremely persistent, remaining in the upper atmosphere for decades, and although they are 10,000 times more efficient than carbon dioxide at trapping heat, the process of controlling them has been under way for years, for reasons having nothing to do with the greenhouse effect. Since the early 1970s atmospheric scientists have known that CFCs could have destructive effects on ozone. CFCs were banned from spray cans in the United States and Canada in the late 1970s, and the appearance of a "hole" in the ozone layer over Antarctica in the early 1980s created an international consensus that CFCs must go. Last year 53 nations crafted an agreement that will cut CFC production by 50 percent over the next decade; the chemicals may well be banned altogether by the turn of the century. . . .

Remarkably, the conference spurred some specific promises from political leaders rather than just vague platitudes. Standing before a 40-foot-wide photorealist painting of a cloud-studded skyscape, Prime Ministers Brian Mulroney of Canada and Gro Harlem Brundtland of Norway pledged that their countries will slow fossil fuel use and forgive some Third World debt, allowing developing countries to grow in a sustainable way. Says Schneider, "In the fifteen years that I've been trying to convince people of the seriousness of the greenhouse effect, this is the first time I've seen a broad consensus: First, there is a consensus that action is not premature. Second, that solutions have to occur on a global as well as a national scale."

In the end, the greatest obstacle facing those who are trying to slow the output of greenhouse gases is the fundamental and pervasive nature of the human activities that are causing the problem: deforestation, industrialization, energy production. As populations boom, productivity must keep up. And even as the developed nations of the world cut back on fossil fuel use, there will be no justifiable way to prevent the Third World from expanding its use of coal and oil. How can the developed countries expect that China, for example, which has plans to double its coal production in the next 15 years in order to spur development, will be willing or even able to change course?

And then there is poverty, which contributes to the greenhouse effect by encouraging destruction of forests. "Approximately seventy-five percent of the deforestation occurring in the world today is accounted for by landless people in a desperate search for food," says Jose Lutzenberger, director of the Gaia Foundation, an influential Brazilian environmental group. Commercial logging accounts for just 15 percent of tropical forest loss worldwide. Unfortunately for the atmosphere and the forests themselves, working out an agreement with the tropical timber industry will be far easier than eliminating rural poverty.

Industrialized nations, which created most of the greenhouse problem, should lead the way to finding solutions, says State Department official Richard Benedick, who represented the United States during negotiations for cuts in CFCs and who was a conference attendee. The first priority, he says, should be strong conservation efforts—an area in which the United States lags far behind such countries as Japan. The effect of such measures, Benedick feels, can only be positive and the cost is not great. "Certain things which make sense on their own merits," he says. Technology can be transferred to developing countries. In some Third World nations a partial solution can be as simple as modernizing energy production and distribution system, Benedick says, could double the effective energy output of existing coal-fired power plants.

Addressing the conference, Canadian minister of energy Marcel Masse noted that there is cause for optimism. One need look not further than the energy crisis of a decade ago. From 1979 to 1985, thanks primarily to conservation, substantial cuts were made in the use of fossil fuels by industrialized nations. Only since 1986 and the current oil glut, said Masse, has there been a resurgence in oil use and coal burning.

Michael McElroy concluded, "If we choose to take on this challenge, it appears that we can slow the rate of change substantially, giving us time to develop mechanisms so that the cost to society and the damage to ecosystems can be minimized. We could alternatively close our eyes, hope for the best, and pay the cost when the bill comes due."

What Is the Truth about Global Warming?

Robert James Bidinotto

A staff writer for Reader's Digest, *which published the following article in 1990, Robert James Bidinotto is experienced at writing about cultural and political controversies in terms that can be easily understood by a general audience. In his article on global warming, he offers both a summary of what the greenhouse effect means and an argument against adopting any expensive measures to prevent it until further research confirms that global warming is as threatening as environmentalists believe.*

In the summer of 1988, one of the century's worst heat waves gripped the East Coast and had Midwest farmers wondering if the Dust Bowl had returned. On June 23, at at Senate hearing on global climate change, James Hansen, a respected atmospheric scientist and director of NASA's Goddard Institute for Space Studies, gave alarming testimony. "The earth is warmer in 1988 than at any time in the history of instrumental measurements," he said. "The greenhouse effect is changing our climate now."

Hansen's remarks touched off a firestorm of publicity. A major news magazine speculated that the Great Plains would be depopulated. On NBC's "Today" show, biologist Paul Ehrlich warned that melting polar ice could raise sea levels and inundate coastal cities, swamping much of Florida, Washington, D.C., and the Los Angeles basin. And in his recent book, *Global Warming,* Stephen Schneider of the National Center for Atmospheric Research imagined New York overcome by a killer heat wave, a baseball double-header in Chicago called because of a thick black haze created by huge forest fires in Canada, and Long Island devastated by a hurricane—all spawned by the "greenhouse effect."

In Paris last July, the leaders of seven industrial democracies, including President Bush and British Prime Minister Margaret Thatcher, called for common efforts to limit emissions of carbon dioxide and other "greenhouse gases." To accomplish this, many environmentalists have proposed draconian regulations—and huge new taxes—that could significantly affect the way we live. Warns Environmental Protection Agency head William Reilly: "To slow down the global heating process, the scale of economic and societal intervention will be enormous."

The stakes are high: the public could be asked to decide between environmental catastrophe and enormous costs. But do we really have to make this choice? Many scientists believe the danger is real, but others are much less certain. What is the evidence? Here is what we know:

What is the Greenhouse Effect?

When sunlight warms the earth, certain gases in the lower atmosphere, acting like the glass in a greenhouse, trap some of the heat as it radiates back into space. These greenhouse gases, primarily water vapor and including carbon dioxide, methane and man-made chlorofluorocarbons, warm our planet, making life possible.

If they were more abundant, greenhouse gases might trap too much heat. Venus, for example, has 60,000 times more carbon dioxide in its atmosphere than Earth, and its temperature averages above 800 degrees Fahrenheit. But if greenhouse gases were less plentiful or entirely absent, temperatures on Earth would average below freezing.

Because concentrations of greenhouse gases have been steadily rising, many scientists are concerned about global warming. Researchers at the Goddard Institute and at the University of East Anglia in England foresee a doubling of greenhouse gas concentrations during the next century, which might raise average global temperatures as much as nine degrees Fahrenheit.

What is Causing the Buildup?

Nature accounts for most of the greenhouse gases in the atmosphere. For example, carbon dioxide (CO_2), the most plentiful trace gas, is released by volcanoes, oceans, decaying plants and even by our breathing. But much of the *buildup* is man-made.

CO_2 is given off when we burn wood or such fossil fuels as coal and oil. In fact, the amount in the atmosphere has grown more than 25 percent since the Industrial Revolution began around 200 years ago—over 11 percent since 1958 alone.

Methane, the next most abundant greenhouse gas, is released when organic matter decomposes in swamps, rice paddies, livestock yards—even in the guts of termites and cud-chewing animals. The amount is growing about one percent per year, partly because of increased cattle raising and use of natural gas.

Chlorofluorocarbons (CFCs), a third culprit, escape from refrigerators, air conditioners, plastic foam, solvents and spray cans. The amount in the atmosphere is tiny compared with CO_2, but CFCs are thousands of times more potent in absorbing heat and have also been implicated in the "ozone hole."

What Does the Ozone Hole Have to Do with the Greenhouse Effect?

For all practical purposes, nothing. Ozone, a naturally occurring form of oxygen, is of concern for another reason. In the upper atmosphere it helps shield us from ultraviolet sunlight, which can cause skin cancer. In 1985, scientists confirmed a temporary thinning in the ozone layer over Antarctica, leading to a new concern: if ozone thinning spreads to populated areas, it could cause an increase in the disease.

The ozone hole appears only from September to November, and only over the Antarctic region, and then it repairs itself when atmospheric conditions change a few weeks later. It also fluctuates; in 1988, there was little ozone thinning.

Ozone is constantly created and destroyed by nature. Volcanoes, for example, can release immense quantities of chlorine, some of which may get into the stratosphere and destroy ozone molecules.

But the most popular theory to explain the appearance of the ozone hole is that man-made chlorofluorocarbons release chlorine atoms in the upper atmosphere.

Despite thinning of upper atmospheric ozone over Antarctica, no increase in surface ultraviolet radiation outside of that area is expected. John E. Frederick, an atmospheric scientist who chaired a United Nations Environment Program panel on trends in atmospheric ozone, had dismissed fears of a skin-cancer epidemic as science fiction. "You would experience a much greater increase in biologically damaging ultraviolet radiation if you moved from New York City to Atlanta than you would with the ozone depletion that we estimate will occur over the next 30 years," he says.

Will Destruction of Forests Worsen the Greenhouse Effect?

When trees and plants grow, they remove CO_2 from the air. When they are burned or decay, they release stored CO_2 back into the atmosphere. In nations such as Brazil, thousands of square miles of tropical rain forests are being cleared and burned, leading many to be concerned about further CO_2 buildup.

Worldwide, millions of acres are planted with seedling trees each year, however; and new studies reveal that there has been no reliable data about the impact of forest destruction on global warming. Research by Daniel Botkin and Lloyd Simpson at the University of California at Santa Barbara and by Sandra Brown at the University of Illinois at Urbana shows that the carbon content of forests had been vastly overestimated, suggesting that deforestation is not as great a source of CO_2 as was once thought.

Can We Be Certain that Global Warming Will Occur?

Virtually all scientists agree that if greenhouse gases increase and all other factors remain the same, the earth will warm up. But "the crucial issue," explains Prof. S. Fred Singer, an atmospheric scientist at the Washington Institute for Values in Public Policy, "is to what extent other factors remain the same." Climatic forces interact in poorly understood ways, and some may counteract warming.

At any given time, for example, clouds cover 60 percent of the planet, trapping heat radiating from its surface, but also reflecting sunlight back into space. So, if the oceans heat up and produce more clouds through evaporation, the increased cover might act as a natural thermostat and keep the planet from heating up. After factoring more detailed cloud simulations into its computer models, the British Meteorological Office recently showed that current global-warming projections could be cut in half.

Oceans have a major effect upon climate, but scientists have only begun to understand how. Investigators at the National Center for Atmospheric Research attributed the North American drought in the summer of 1988 primarily to temperature changes in the tropical Pacific involving a current called El Niño—not to the greenhouse effect. And when ocean currents were included in recent computerized climate simulations, the Antarctic Ocean didn't warm—diminishing the likelihood that part of its ice sheet will break up and add to coastal flooding.

How heat travels through the atmosphere and back into space is another big question mark for the global-warming theory. So is the sunspot cycle, as well as the effect of atmospheric pollution and volcanic particles that can reflect sunlight back into space. Such factors throw predictions about global warming into doubts.

So What Is the Bottom Line? Has the Earth Begun to Heat Up?

Two widely reported statistics *seem* to present a powerful case for global warming. Some temperature records show about one degree Fahrenheit of warming over the past century, a period that has also seen a noticeable increase in greenhouse gases. And the six warmest years globally since record keeping began 100 years ago have all been in the 1980s.

As for the past decade, the increased warmth in three of its hottest years—1983, 1987 and 1988—is almost certainly associated with El Niño events in the Pacific.

Paradoxically, the historical records of temperature change do not jibe with the greenhouse theory. Between 1880 and 1940, temperatures appeared to rise. Yet between 1940 and 1965, a period of much heavier fossil-fuel use and deforestation, temperatures dropped, which seems inconsistent with the greenhouse effect. And a comprehensive study of past global ocean records by researchers from Britain and M.I.T. revealed no significant rising temperature trends between 1856 and 1986. Concludes Richard Lindzen of M.I.T.'s department of Earth, Atmospheric and Planetary Sciences, "The data as we have it does not support a warming."

Taking everything into account, few climatologists are willing to attribute any seeming warming to the greenhouse effect. Last May, 61 scientists participating in a greenhouse workshop in Amherst, Mass., declared that "such an attribution cannot now be made with any degree of confidence."

Is There Any Other Evidence of Global Warming?

Atmospheric researchers use complex computer programs called General Circulation Models (GCMs) to plot climate change. But a computer is no more reliable than its input, and poorly understood oceanic, atmospheric and continental processes are only crudely represented even in the best GCMs.

Computer calculations do not even accurately predict the past: they fail to match historical greenhouse-gas concentrations to expected temperatures. Because of these uncertainties, Stephen Schneider says in *Global Warming*, it is "an even bet that the GCMs have overestimated future warming by a factor of two."

In time, the computer models will undoubtedly improve. For now, the lack of evidence and reliable tools leaves proponents of global warming with little but theory.

Should We Do Anything to Offset the Possible Warming Up of the Globe?

Fossil fuels now provide 90 percent of the world's energy. Some environmentalists have advocated huge tax increases to discourage use of coal and other fossil fuels. Some have suggested a gasoline tax. There are also proposals that the government subsidize solar, windmill and geothermal power; that some foreign debts be swapped for protecting forests; and that worldwide population growth be slowed.

The buildup of greenhouse gases is cause for scientific study, but not for panic. Yet the facts sometimes get lost in the hysteria. Stephen Schneider confesses to an ethical dilemma. He admits the many uncertainties about global warming.

Nevertheless, to gain public support through media coverage, he explains that sometimes scientists "have to offer up scary scenarios, make simplified, dramatic statements, and make little mention of any doubts we might have." Each scientist, he says, must decide the "right balance" between "being effective and being honest. I hope that means being both."

The temptation to bend fears for political ends is also ever present. "We've got to ride the global-warming issue," Sen. Timothy Wirth (D., Colo.) explained to a reporter. "Even if the theory is wrong, we will be doing the right thing in terms of economic and environmental policy."

But many scientists are troubled when inconclusive evidence is used for political advocacy. "The greenhouse warming has become a 'happening,' " says Richard Lindzen. To call for action, he adds, "has become a litmus test of morality."

We still know far too little to be stampeded into rash, expensive proposals. Before we take such steps, says Patrick J. Michaels, an associate professor of environmental sciences at the University of Virginia, "the science should be much less murky than it is now."

Further research and climatic monitoring are certainly warranted. If the "greenhouse signal" then emerges from the data, we can decide on the most prudent course of action.

Apocalypse Again

Peter Shaw

A 1958 graduate of Cornell, Peter Shaw received his Ph.D. from Columbia University in 1965. His books include The Character of John Adams *(1976),* American Patriots and the Rituals of Revolution *(1981), and* The War Against the Intellect: Episodes in the Decline of Discourse *(1989). Shaw, who describes himself politically as a "Former Liberal," published the following 1989 essay in* Commentary. *He is currently the Will and Ariel Durant Professor of the Humanities at Saint Peter's College.*

> Some say the world will end in fire,
> Some say in ice.
>
> Robert Frost

Predictions of the end of the world, as old as human history and lately a subject of scholarly inquiry, have by no means abated in our own time. Nor are those who believe in such predictions confined to isolated religious sects, as was the case as recently as the 19th century. While such sects do continue regularly to spring up and disappear, predictions of catastrophe have become the virtual orthodoxy of society as a whole. Journalists, educators, churchmen, and philosophers daily endorse one or another script foretelling the end of individual life, of human civilization, or of the entire earth. Some say the world will end in fire—through the conflagration of a nuclear holocaust; some say in ice—through the same event, this time precipitating a "nuclear winter."

Fire and ice. We need only add earth and air to include within the apocalyptic genre all four of the elements understood as basic by the Greeks, and water to include the biblical account of the flood. Contemporary prophecies of flood are stated in apparently scientific terms: as a result of global warming, the polar ice caps will melt and inundate the world's major cities. As for earth and air, we anticipate the disappearance of the one, thanks to the erosion of farmland and shorelines, while the other is to be depleted of its ozone, if not first saturated with carbon dioxide or poisoned by man-made pollutants.

Pagan man projected his fears outward; contemporary man internalizes. Like biblical man (at least to that very limited extent) he holds himself, or more accurately his own society, responsible for the coming end of the world. Not only the disaster allegedly threatened by pollutants but every prospective modern apocalypse stipulates man rather than the gods or nature as the primal cause. And the charge is always the same: whether it is to be by fire or by ice, mankind faces extinction as a punishment for its impiety.

The continuities and discontinuities between ancient and modern imaginations of disaster would amount to no more than curiosities if it were the case that superstitious fears had been replaced by rational ones. But it is not the case. On the contrary, given the best scientific understanding of reality available to early man, it made sense for him to ascribe natural disasters, present and future, to the gods. Later, it made sense for the Greeks to ascribe such disasters to some wayward or even malign characteristic of matter itself. Nor was Empedocles a simpleton for regarding the personification of the elements by gods as a persuasive account of reality. Would that our own conceptions of apocalypse were similarly founded on the best available scientific understanding. Instead, most if not all of the disasters currently being predicted have gained widespread credence *despite* a lack of scientific basis, or even in the face of definitive counterevidence.

Without question the most spectacular example of such a wholly suppositious theory has to do with the so-called greenhouse effect. The greenhouse effect itself, as every schoolchild knows, is simply the process by which the earth's atmosphere traps enough heat from the sun to create a habitable planet. As for the disaster scenario that bears the same name, it posits, in the words of a *New York Times* editorial, an increased "warming of the atmosphere by waste gases from a century of industrial activity." The *Times* goes on:

> *The greenhouse theory holds that certain waste gases let in sunlight but trap heat, which otherwise would escape into space. Carbon dioxide has been steadily building up through the burning of coal and oil—and because forests, which absorb the gas, are fast being destroyed.*

Now, aside from the mistaken assumption that forests worldwide are decreasing in size (they are not), the theory of a runaway greenhouse effect, otherwise known as global warming, presents even its advocates with a variety of internal contradictions.

In the first place, the earth has a number of mechanisms for ameliorating fluctuations in global temperature: a significant rise in temperature, for example, leads to increased evaporation from the oceans; this is followed by the formation of clouds that shield the sun and then by a compensating drop in temperature. Too, if the greenhouse theory were valid, a global warming trend should be observable in records of temperatures soon after the jump in manmade carbon dioxide that is the result of modern industrial activity. Yet if there has been such a rise over the past one hundred years, it does not follow but precedes the onset of modern industrialism, and anyway it amounts to a barely detectable change of no more than one degree Fahrenheit over the entire period.

Here is a particularly significant problem for any hypothesis—the lack of evidence. Purveyors of the global-warming theory counter it by pointing to computer projections which show a catastrophic upward trend in the *next* century. Once again, however, a known problem presents itself: computer models, writes Andrew R. Solow, a statistician at Woods Hole Oceanographic Institution, "have a hard time reproducing current climate from current data. They cannot be expected to predict future climate with any precision."

Does any of this detract from the persuasive power of the global-warming theory? Apparently not. As in certain forms of religion, the less evidence, the more faith. And in the resultant climate of belief (as it deserves to be called), not only the lack of evidence but even outright counterevidence can work to a theory's benefit. According to the late Leon Frestinger, Henry W. Riecken, and Stanley Schachter, the authors of the classic study, *When Prophecy Fails* (1956), "Although there is a limit beyond which belief will not stand disconfirmation, it is clear that the introduction of contrary evidence can serve to increase the conviction and enthusiasm of a believer." So it has been during the most recent phase of prediction, which itself represents a revival of the great irruption of ecological warnings that dominated the early 1970's.

The central document in that earlier wave was *Limits to Growth,* a report issued by the Club of Rome in 1972 foretelling a world-wide doom brought on by the combined forces of "resource depletion," overpopulation, pollution, and starvation. The future conjured up by computer simulation in *Limits to Growth* bore a certain resemblance to the still more spectacularly stated predictions of Paul Ehrlich in his 1968 book, *Population Bomb*. Ehrlich had offered specific dates for specific catastrophes: 1983, for example, would see a precipitous decline in American harvests and the institution of food rationing, by which time a billion people worldwide would have already starved to death. The Club of Rome, more cautiously, assigned likely years for the exhaustion of specific resources: petroleum (1992), silver (1985), natural gas (1994), mercury (1985), tin (1987).

In 1982 one of the authors of the Club of Rome report had to admit that his predictions were not coming true. Yet he was not repentant. There may have been a postponement, a temporary reprieve, but man and the earth still remained poised on the brink of cataclysm. Presumably Paul Ehrlich, who never recanted, felt the same way. Just so have members of religious sects always responded when their confidently predicted apocalypses pass without incident.

True, the general public and even some members of the sect begin to fall away after such disappointments; in our time, both Paul Ehrlich and the Club of Rome did fade out of the spotlight. But instructively, and in contrast to the sects studied in *When Prophecy Fails,* they did so without having been exposed to the full glare of adverse publicity and ridicule that used to attend the collapse of prophecy. Perhaps that is why so little time elapsed before the public could be brought to credit similar predictions.

For even as the "population bomb" failed to explode on schedule, or ecological disaster to strike, new predictions of not only global but galactic proportions were being prepared. By the late 1980's these were receiving the same respectful, credulous hearing as their forerunners, and were being promoted just as avidly by the press. In the case of nuclear winter, the most publicized apocalypse, the cycle from prediction to publicity to disconfirmation took only a few years, from approximately 1985 to 1988; yet once again the end came without bringing ridicule or discredit to the theoreticians.

Nuclear winter was at once a prediction of what would happen after a nuclear war and the claim that an identical disaster, never detected in the geological record, had already taken place once before, in the age of the dinosaurs. A giant explosion, the theory went, had been caused on earth by a "nemesis" or "death star" wheeling in from far out in the universe and returning so quickly whence it had come as to be invisible to the most farseeing of modern telescopes. The clouds of dust kicked up by that explosion had shielded the sun and thus caused the earth's vegetation to wither, bringing about the extinction of the dinosaurs by cold and starvation. The lesson for the mid-1980's was clear: intermediate-range nuclear missiles should not be emplaced in Western Europe and disarmament should commence forthwith.

As chance would have it, not long after the nuclear-winter theory gained currency there was a giant volcanic eruption at Mount St. Helens in the state of Washington. It was followed by the spreading of just such dark clouds as had been described—but without any hint of the predicted effect on vegetation or climate. At about the same time, too, paleontologists demonstrated that the dinosaurs could not possibly have been the casualties of a single, catastrophic event, since they had disappeared over a period of some thousands of years. Finally, a check of some of the nuclear-winter projections exposed gaping errors of math and physics.

As a result of these and other refutations of the theory, nuclear winter died its own death-by-theoretical-starvation. But so quickly was its place taken by similar predictions, similarly linked to geopolitical issues, that the event seems to have almost entirely escaped notice. Nuclear winter remains today in the public mind as a proven hypothesis, vying for popularity with its mirror opposite, the greenhouse effect.

Actually, not so long ago (as the journalist John Chamberlain has pointed out) we were being assured that we were living not in a warming but in a "cooling world." In the 1970's, as *Science* magazine reported in 1975, meteorologists were "almost unanimous" that such a trend was taking place, and that its consequences, especially for agriculture, were potentially disastrous. Climatologists, according to *Fortune* magazine, warned that the cooling trend "could bring massive tragedies for mankind." A decade later, all of this quite forgotten, the opposite theory of global warming has drifted past the rocks of evidentiary lack, tumbled safely through the falls of skepticism, and sailed triumphantly onto the smooth lake of public respect.

The status of global warming as an unassailable, self-evident truth was recently confirmed by the reaction to a scientific report that challenges its assumptions. This report, compiled at the National Oceanic and Atmospheric Administration and duly described on the front page of the *New York Times* and other newspapers, traces U.S. temperatures since 1895. It shows that the putative one-degree rise in temperature worldwide over the past hundred years, a figure widely accepted even by many of those skeptical of the global-warming scenario, is wrong for the United States. As the *Times* headline put it: "U.S. Data Since 1895 Fail to Show Warming Trend."

The reaction was immediate. All of the experts consulted by the *Times* were in agreement that the report does not set back the global-warming theory by so much as an iota. Prominent among these experts was Dr. James E. Hansen, director of the National Aeronautic and Space Administration's Institute for Space Studies in Manhattan, a leading proponent of global warming and the man who produced the data showing a one-degree rise in global temperature. "We have to be careful about interpreting things like this," he warned, and went on to explain that the United States covers only a small portion of the earth's surface. Besides, the steadiness of the temperature readings could be a "statistical fluke." Note the implicit distinction here: we must be "careful" in interpreting data that appear reassuring, but it is virtually our duty to indulge any strongly felt premonitions of disaster even if they are based on the flimsiest evidence, or none.

The concept of the "statistical fluke" could easily be applied to many current predictions, but is not. Thus, the acidification of a number of freshwater lakes in the eastern United States is considered not a fluke but a definite trend, even though it might be taken to fall well within the range of natural fluctuations. Similarly, the disturbing deaths of numerous dolphins during the summer of 1988 were traced to the same pattern of human depredation of the environment supposed to be causing acid rain and other ecological catastrophes. Later, it developed that the dolphins were killed by a so-called "red-tide" of algae—itself first seen as a man-created scourge but then conceded to be a natural phenomenon. Here, in other words, was a genuine statistical fluke; but it was never labeled as such since it exonerated industrial man.

It does not give pause either to the catastrophists or to their credulous promoters in the media that some predictions cancel out others. Dr. Hansen, for example, suggests that the absence of a warming trend, as shown by the new study, might be "the result of atmospheric pollutants reflecting heat away from earth." Yet these are the same pollutant particles supposedly responsible for global warming in the first place. Now it develops that the particles they carry with them counter the greenhouse effect. In fact, Dr. Hansen is worried that "anti-pollution efforts are reducing the amount of these particles and thus reducing the reflection of heat" away from the earth. It is surely a measure of the power of catastrophic thinking that what may have been the first public revelation of an actual decrease in man-made atmospheric pollutants should prompt the fear that such a decrease itself portends the direst consequences.

What all this suggests is that we have come to depend at any given moment on a constant degree of threat. When times are bad—because of war, depression, or real natural disasters—proximate fears tend to dominate the imagination. When times are good—through the conquest of disease and famine, the achievement of high employment, prosperity, and an upward curve of longevity—apprehension has to be supplied from without. And during extended good times, a supply of fresh disasters is required as each one comes progressively to lose its appeal. Air pollution, rising to disaster proportions in the Club of Rome report, declines in importance but is soon succeeded by loss of the ozone layer, which will supposedly leave mankind vulnerable to the unfiltered rays of the sun and a consequent plague of, among other things, skin cancers and blindness. Continent-wide poisoning of fresh water through the eutrophication of lakes and streams from fertilizer runoff is forgotten only to be replaced by the threat of acid rain. Direct incineration of all mankind by atomic war cedes to a secondary stage of destruction by nuclear winter, and nuclear winter in turn to global warming.

This persistent and insistent imagining of disaster might be no more than a sideshow were it not for its political dimension. But in the 1970's and 80's, successive waves of catastrophism followed and reflected episodes of defeat for radical political movements. The 70's wave succeeded the collapse of the New Left and engaged many of that movement's disillusioned supporters (as well, of course, as many people opposed or indifferent to the New Left). That of the 80's followed the worldwide discrediting of the economic, political, and moral record of Communism. It was as if sanguine hopes of an end to the cold war required a compensatory new fear, one that natural catastrophe alone could supply. And thus, soon after James Baker's nomination as Secretary of State, a bipartisan memorandum from members of the Senate Foreign Relations Committee called his urgent attention to the leading foreign-policy issue he would have to face, a "global problem of unprecedented magnitude." The issue was global warming.

It goes without saying that clean air and water, the retention of farmland and forests, a satisfactory ozone layer, and the avoidance of nuclear war are all desirable things. But the pursuit of these goals through the rhetoric of hellfire renders more immediate political concerns mundane and secondary. Many are the societies that have been distracted from the actual dangers they faced by the allure of disasters wholly imaginary. That consideration aside, though, our obsession with distant and unprovable catastrophe is so stultifying, from both the moral and the intellectual point of view, as to constitute a cultural disaster in its own right.

Healing the Earth?

Jon R. Luoma

A free lance writer and advocate of environmental issues, Jon R. Luoma has published several books on air pollution and animal rights. Troubled Skies, Troubled Waters: The Story of Acid Rain *is a first-person account of the effect of acid rain in Canada and Minnesota. A book published by the US Department of Agriculture—Forest Service in 1990 makes connections between air pollution and forest decline. Luoma's book The Crowded Ark discusses animal rights and conditions. Jon Luoma also contributes articles on his specialty to periodicals.*

The United Nations Conference on Environment and Development in Rio de Janeiro last June was promoted as the greatest environmental diplomacy show on Earth, and it lived up to its billing. On the one hand, the Earth Summit sometimes degenerated into a three-ring political and media circus (with, for example, the Brazilian press characterizing President Bush as "Uncle Grubby"); on the other, the event did amount to the most important international attempt yet to heal the planet.

The extent to which the summit could be called a success falls into the category of the cup that's perceived as half-full or half-empty. The centerpiece of the conference was to be the signing of two major treaties. One was to curb carbon dioxide and other greenhouse gas emissions linked to global warming. The second was to protect biodiversity, meaning not only Earth's totality of plants and animals but also the components of life at smaller scales, as in genetic diversity, and larger scales, as in ecosystems.

The two treaties, negotiated in the months leading up to the summit, wound up falling far short of environmentalists' expectations. At U.S. insistence, the global warming treaty was stripped of provisions that included firm targets and deadlines, and it became little more than a catalog of "guidelines" for reducing gas emissions. Worse, the United States was conspicuous for its outright refusal to sign the biodiversity treaty, despite the signatures of more than 150 other nations, ranging from Japan and Germany to Brazil and India.

Still, the Earth Summit and the treaties did break some new ground. Most notably, they focused on the great conundrum of global environmental issues: the rift between developed and developing nations, or, as the conference often characterized them, North (that is, hemisphere) and South. In cases of global problems like climate change or the threat to biodiversity, developing nations have always resented the prospect of having to suppress their own poor economies in ways that wealthy nations never had to.

The biodiversity treaty tried to close the North-South rift. Most of the millions of land-dwelling species on Earth lie in the developing nations, with as many as half living in the rain forests alone. With the bulk of future population growth expected to come in the South, enormous pressure will be put on already threatened rain forests and even "protected" areas, such as national parks. The biodiversity treaty included predictable mandates calling for nations to strive to protect species within their boundaries and to "establish a system of protected areas where special measures need to be taken to conserve biological diversity." But the treaty went beyond that, calling for nations to become more vigorous in finding what species exist within their borders, and where biodiversity is most at risk. The treaty called for an emphasis on the protection of whole ecosystems rather than individual endangered species, and it emphasized the importance of trying to restore damaged rain forests, wetlands, and other threatened habitats.

Significantly, the treaty also established the "sovereign rights" of nations to profit from protecting biodiversity by virtually allowing them to patent the stuff of the wild. To a poor nation in the species-rich tropics, the economic benefits from controlling access to its genetic resources could be substantial.

In theory at least, the prospect of royalties creates a powerful incentive for poorer nations to inventory and protect biodiversity. "The treaty moves us away from the idea of a global grab bag where anyone can snatch a genetic resource from anybody's backyard and take the profits," says Kenton Miller, the program director for biological resources at the World Resources Institute. "But it also says the sovereign nation must assure that those resources are used sustainably and put mechanisms into place so they can be shared."

The United States objected to portions of the treaty encouraging "transfers of technology," suggesting that the treaty as phrased could compel U.S. companies to transfer their biotechnology patents to other nations. One State Department official close to the negotiations said that most U.S. diplomats were "stunned" themselves at the Bush administration's refusal to sign on such grounds, especially since the treaty did contain language specifically assuring the protection of "intellectual property rights." The United States said the language was ambiguous. In the meantime, though, it has promised to abide generally by the terms of the treaty, suggesting that U.S. companies won't be free to pilfer genetic material outside the nation's borders. Many experts, however, believe the United States will eventually sign the treaty.

The North-South schism is, if anything, more pointed when it comes to global warming. Developing nations point out that the United States, with only 5 percent of the world's population, is nevertheless responsible for 22 percent of carbon dioxide emissions. By contrast, India, with more than three times the U.S. population, produces only about 3 percent of global CO_2.

In negotiations before the Rio conference, diplomats tried mightily to repeat the success of the Montreal Protocol, the 1987 treaty to control chlorofluorocarbons, which are responsible for depleting stratospheric ozone. The innovative ozone treaty gave developing nations relaxed timetables for phasing out CFCs and even allowed them to increase emissions temporarily; the Northern countries meanwhile were obliged to restrict emissions more quickly and to set up a fund to help developing nations pay for CFC control.

But only a few companies produce CFC; other greenhouse gases are produced nearly anywhere combustion occurs, from a coal-fired power plant to a motor scooter. The Bush administration, already skeptical of concerns that global warming poses a real threat, worried about the effects sharp restrictions in the North could have on U.S. industry and hence on jobs and the economy. In the weeks leading up to the summit, Austria, the Netherlands, and Switzerland called for the North to set real targets, rolling emissions back to 1990 levels by the year 2000. But the United States turned down any proposal for targets and deadlines and successfully fought off efforts to require the North to help the South with funding and technology transfer.

In the end the treaty became one of "constructive ambiguities," said Jean Ripert, the French diplomat who chaired the negotiating committee. For example, rather than specifying how much emissions of greenhouse gases should be reduced, the treaty merely states that nations "shall adopt national policies and take corresponding measures" to limit emissions and that by the end of the decade emissions should be reduced to unspecified "earlier levels." On a brighter note, the treaty created a Conference of the Parties, which could negotiate firm targets in coming months. The European Community has already announced that by the year 2000 it will roll emissions back to 1990 levels. It is urging the United States to do the same.

Suggestions for Discussion or Writing

1. How urgent is the crisis of global warming? On a scale of one to ten (one = not urgent; ten = extremely urgent), how does each of the articles rate?

2. What proof does each side give for its position?

3. How does each side see political action in regard to global warming? What do they accuse the government of doing?

4. What effect did the Earth Summit of June 1992 have on the policy of global warming? How did it compare to the 1987 treaty?

5. What suggestions are given to offset global warming? How do these suggestions vary between articles?

6. What direct contradictions in facts and conclusions are found between articles?

7. What assumptions (valid or faulty?) are made in each article? How is deductive reasoning used (or misused) in each article?

8. Can you identify the logical fallacies in the articles? Do they strengthen or weaken the argument?

Readings in Argumentation: Logical Fallacies

A Modest Proposal

Jonathan Swift

English author and satirist Jonathan Swift (1667–1745) was born in Dublin and graduated from Trinity College. He then became the secretary to statesman Sir William Temple, which increased his exposure to politics. He became a minister in the Anglican Church of Ireland and eventually was appointed head clergyman of St. Patrick's Cathedral. As a satirist he ridiculed the customs, ideas, and actions of his society that he considered silly or detrimental. His "A Modest Proposal" (1729) is perhaps the most famous of his satires and defends the Irish against British imperialism. Among his other writings are the ever-popular Gulliver's Travels *(1726),* A Tale of a Tub *(1704),* The Battle of the Books *(1704), and the* Drapier Letters *(1724).*

It is a melancholy object to those who walk through this great town or travel in the country, when they see the streets, the roads, and cabin doors, crowded with beggars of the female sex, followed by three, four, or six children, all in rags and importuning every passenger for an alms. These mothers, instead of being able to work for their honest livelihood, are forced to employ all their time in strolling to beg sustenance for their helpless infants, who, as they grow up, either turn thieves for want of work, or leave their dear native country to fight for the Pretender in Spain, or sell themselves to the Barbadoes.

I think it is agreed by all parties that this prodigious number of children in the arms, or on the backs, or at the heels of their mothers, and frequently of their fathers, is in the present deplorable state of the kingdom a very great additional grievance; and therefore whoever could find out a fair, cheap, and easy method of making these children sound, useful members of the commonwealth would deserve so well of the public as to have his statue set up for a preserver of the nation.

But my intention is very far from being confined to provide only for the children of the professed beggars; it is of a much greater extent, and shall take in the whole number of infants at a certain age who are born of parents in effect as little able to support them as those who demand our charity in the streets.

As to my own part, having turned my thoughts for many years upon this important subject, and maturely weighed the several schemes of other projectors, I have always found them grossly mistaken in their computation. It is true, a child just dropped form its dam may be supported by her milk for a solar year, with little other nourishment; at most not above the value of two shillings, which the mother may certainly get, or the value in scraps, by her lawful occupation of begging and it is exactly at one year old that I propose to provide for them in such a manner as instead of being a charge upon their parents or the parish, or wanting food and raiment for the rest of their lives, they shall on the contrary contribute to the feeding, and partly to the clothing, of many thousands.

There is likewise another great advantage in my scheme, that it will prevent those involuntary abortions, and that horrid practice of women murdering their bastard children, alas, too frequent among us, sacrificing the poor innocent babes, I doubt, more to avoid the expense than the shame, which would move tears and pity in the most savage and inhuman breast.

The number of souls in this kingdom being usually reckoned one million and a half, of these I calculate there may be about two hundred thousand couples whose wives are breeders, from which number I subtract thirty thousand couples who are able to maintain their own children, although I apprehend there cannot be so many under the present distress of the kingdom; but this being granted, there will remain a hundred and seventy thousand breeders. I again subtract fifty thousand for those women who miscarry, or whose children die by accident or disease within the year. There only remain an hundred and twenty thousand children of poor parents annually born. The question therefore is, how this number shall be reared and provided for, which, as I have already said, under the present situation of affairs, is utterly impossible by all the methods hitherto proposed. For we can neither employ them in handicraft nor agriculture; we neither build houses (I mean in the country) nor cultivate land. They can very seldom pick up a livelihood by stealing till they arrive at six years old, except where they are of towardly parts; although I confess they learn the rudiments much earlier, during which time they can however be looked upon only as probationers, as I have been informed by a principal gentleman in the country of Cavan, who protested to me that he never knew above one or two instances under the age of six, even in a part of the kingdom so renowned for the quickest proficiency in that art.

I am assured by our merchants that a boy or girl before twelve years old is no salable commodity; and even when they come to this age, they will yield above three pounds, or three pounds and half a crown at most on the Exchange; which cannot turn to account either to the parents or the kingdom, the charge of nutriment and rags having been at least four times that value.

I shall now therefore humbly propose my thoughts, which I hope will not be liable to the least objection.

I have been assured by a very knowing American of my acquaintance in London, that a young healthy child well nursed is at a year old a most delicious, nourishing, and wholesome food, whether stewed, roasted, baked, or boiled; and I make no doubt that it will equally serve in a fricassee or a ragout.

I do therefore humbly offer it to public consideration that of the hundred and twenty thousand children, already computed, twenty thousand may be reserved for breed, whereof only one fourth part to be males, which is more than we allow to sheep, black cattle, or swine; and my reason is that these children are seldom the fruits of marriage, a circumstance not much regarded by our savages, therefore one male will be sufficient to serve four females. That the remaining hundred thousand may at a year old be offered in sale to the persons of quality and fortune through the kingdom, always advising the mother to let them suck plentifully in the last month, so as to render them plump and fat for a good table. A child will make two dishes at an entertainment for friends; and when the family dines alone, the fore or hind quarter will make a reasonable dish, and seasoned with a little pepper or salt will be very good boiled on the fourth day, especially in winter.

I have reckoned upon a medium that a child just born will weigh twelve pounds, and in a solar year if tolerably nursed increaseth to twenty-eight pounds.

I grant this food will be somewhat dear, and therefore very proper for landlords, who, as they have already devoured most of the parents, seem to have the best title to the children.

Infant's flesh will be in season throughout the year, but more plentiful in March, and a little before and after. For we are told by a grave author, an eminent French physician, that fish being a prolific diet, there are more children born in Roman Catholic countries about nine months after Lent, than at any other season; therefore, reckoning a year after Lent, the markets will be more glutted than usual, because the number of popish infant is at least three to one in this kingdom; and therefore it will have one other collateral advantage, by lessening the number of Papists among us.

I have already computed the chore of nursing a beggar's child (in which list I reckon all cottagers, laborers, and four fifths of the farmers) to be about two shillings per annum, rags included; and I believe no gentleman would repine to give ten shillings for the carcass of a good fat child, which, as I have said, will make four dishes of excellent nutritive meat, when he hath only some particular friend or his own family to dine with him. Thus the squire will learn to be a good landlord, and grow popular among the tenants; the mother will have eight shillings net profit, and be fit for work till she produces another child.

Those who are more thrifty (as I must confess the times require) may flay the carcass; the skin of which artificially dressed will make admirable gloves for ladies, and summer boots for fine gentlemen.

As to our city of Dublin, shambles may be appointed for this purpose in the most convenient parts of it, and butchers we may be assured will not be wanting; although I rather recommend buying the children alive, and dressing them hot from the knife as we do roasting pigs.

A very worthy person, a true lover of his country, and whose virtues I highly esteem, was lately please in discoursing on this matter to offer a refinement upon my scheme. He said that many gentlemen of his kingdom, having of late destroyed their deer, he conceived that the want of venison might be well supplied by the bodies of young lads and maidens, not exceeding fourteen years of age nor under twelve, so great a number of both sexes in every country being now ready to starve for want of work and service; and these to be disposed of by their parents, if alive, or otherwise by their nearest relations. But with due deference to so excellent a friend and so deserving a patriot, I cannot be altogether in his sentiments; for as to the males, my American acquaintance assured me from frequent experience that their flesh was generally tough and lean, like that of our schoolboys, by continual exercise, and their taste disagreeable; and to fatten them would not answer the charge. Then as to the females, it would, I think with humble submission, be a loss to the public, because they soon would become breeders themselves; and besides, it is not improbable that some scrupulous people might be apt to censure such a practice (although indeed very unjustly) as a little bordering upon cruelty; which, I confess, hath always been with me the strongest objection against any project, how well soever intended.

But in order to justify my friend, he confessed that this expedient was put into his head by the famous Psalmanazar, a native of the island Formosa, who came from thence to London above twenty years ago, and in conversation told my friend that in his country when any young person happened to be put to death, the executioner sold the carcass to persons of quality as a prime dainty; and that in his time the body of a plump girl of fifteen, who was crucified for an attempt to poison the emperor, was sold to his Imperial Majesty's prime minister of state, and other great mandarins of the court, in joints from the gibbet, at four hundred crowns. Neither indeed can I deny that if the same use were made of several plump young girls in this town, who without one single groat to their fortunes cannot stir abroad without a chair, and appear at the playhouse and assemblies in foreign fineries which they never will pay for, the kingdom would not be the worse.

Some persons of a desponding spirit are in great concern about that vast number of poor people who are aged, diseased, or maimed, and I have been desired to employ my thoughts what course may be taken to ease the nation of so grievous an encumbrance. But I am not in the least pain upon that matter, because it is very well known that they are every day dying and rotting by cold and famine, and filth and vermin, as fast as can be reasonably expected. And as to the younger laborers, they are now in almost as hopeful a condition. They cannot get work, and consequently pine away for want of nourishment to a degree that if any time they are accidentally hired to common labor, they have not strength to perform it; and thus the country and themselves are happily delivered from the evils to come.

I have too long distressed, and therefore shall return to my subject. I think the advantages by the proposal which I have made are obvious and many, as well as of the highest importance.

For first, as I have already observed, it would greatly lessen the number of Papists, with whom we are yearly overrun, being the principal breeders of the nation as well as our most dangerous enemies; and who stay at home on purpose to deliver the kingdom to the Pretender, hoping to take their advantage by the absence of so many good Protestants, who have chosen rather to leave their country than stay at home and pay tithes against their conscience to an Episcopal curate.

Secondly, the poorer tenants will have something valuable of their own, which by law may be made liable to distress, and help to pay their landlord's rent, their corn and cattle being already seized and money a thing unknown.

Thirdly, whereas the maintenance of an hundred thousand children, from two years old and upwards, cannot be computed at less than ten shillings a piece per annum, the nation's stock will be thereby increased fifty thousand pounds per annum, besides the profit of a new dish introduced to the tables of all gentlemen of fortune in the kingdom who have any refinement in taste. And the money will circulate among ourselves, the goods being entirely of our own growth and manufacture.

Fourthly, the constant breeders, besides the gain of eight shilling sterling per annum by the sale of their children, will be rid of the charge of maintaining them after the first year.

Fifthly, this food would likewise bring great custom to taverns, where the vintners will certainly be so prudent as to procure the best receipts for dressing it to perfection, and consequently have their houses frequented by all the fine gentlemen, who justly value themselves upon their knowledge in good eating; and a skillful cook, who understands how to oblige his guests, will contrive to make it as expensive as they please.

Sixthly, this would be a great inducement to marriage, which all wise nations have either encouraged by rewards or enforced by laws and penalties. It would increase the care and tenderness of mothers toward their children, when they were sure of a settlement for life to the poor babes, provided in some sort by the public, to their annual profit instead of expense. We should see an honest emulation among the married women, which of them could bring the fattest child to the market. Men would become as fond of their wives during the time of pregnancy as they are now of their mares in foal, their cows in calf, or sows when they are ready to farrow; nor offer to beat or kick them (as is too frequent a practice) for fear of a miscarriage.

Many other advantages might be enumerated. For instance, the addition of some thousand carcasses in our exportation of barreled beef, the propagation of swine's flesh, and improvements in the art of making good bacon, so much wanted among us by the great destruction of pigs, too frequent at our tables, which are no way comparable in taste or magnificence to a well-grown, fat, yearling child, which roasted whole will make a considerable figure at a lord mayor's feast or any other public entertainment. But this and many others I omit, being studious of brevity.

Supposing that one thousand families in this city would be constant customers for infants' flesh, besides others who might have it at merry meetings, particularly weddings and christenings, I compute that Dublin would take off annually about twenty thousand carcasses, and the rest of the kingdom (where probably they will be sold somewhat cheaper) the remaining eighty thousand.

I can think of no one objection that will possibly he raised against this proposal, unless it should be urged that the number of people will be thereby much lessened in the kingdom. This I freely own, and it was indeed one principal design in offering it to the world. I desire the reader will observe, that I calculate my remedy for this one individual kingdom of Ireland and for no other that ever was, is, or I think ever can be upon earth. Therefore, let no man talk to me of other expedients: of taxing our absentees at five shillings a pound; of using neither clothes nor household furniture except what is of our own growth and manufacture; of utterly rejecting the materials and instruments that promote foreign luxury; of curing the expensiveness of pride, vanity, idleness, and gaming in our women; of introducing a vein of parsimony, prudence, and temperance; of learning to love our country, in the want of which we differ even from Laplanders and the inhabitants of Topinamboo; of quitting our animosities and factions, nor acting any longer like the Jews, who were murdering one another at the very moment their city was taken; of being a little cautious not to sell our country and conscience for nothing; of teaching landlords to have at least one degree of mercy toward their tenants; lastly, of putting a spirit of honesty, industry, and skill into our shopkeepers; who, if a resolution could now be taken to buy only our native goods, would immediately unite to cheat and exact upon us in the price, the measure, and the goodness, nor could ever yet be brought to make one fair proposal of just dealing, though often and earnestly invited to it.

Therefore, I repeat, let no man talk to me of these and the like expedients, till he hath at least some glimpse of hope that there will ever be some hearty and sincere attempt to put them in practice.

But as to myself, having been wearied out for many years with offering vain, idle, visionary thoughts, and at length utterly despairing of success, I fortunately fell upon this proposal, which, as it is wholly new, so it hath something solid and real, of no expense and little trouble, full in our own power, and whereby we can incur no danger in disobliging England. For this kind of commodity will not bear exportation, the flesh being of too tender a consistence to admit a long continuance in salt, although perhaps I could name a country which would be glad to eat up our whole nation without it.

After all, I am not so violently bent upon my own opinions as to reject any offer proposed by wise men, which shall be found equally innocent, cheap, easy, and effectual. But before something of that kind shall be advanced in contradiction to my scheme, and offering a better, I desire the author or authors will be pleased maturely to consider two points. First, as things now stand, how they will be able to find food and raiment for an hundred thousand useless mouths and backs. And secondly, there being a round million of creatures in human figure throughout this kingdom, whose sole subsistence put into a common stock would leave them in debt two millions of pounds sterling, adding those who are beggars by profession to the bulk of farmers, cottagers, and laborers, with their wives and children who are beggars in effect; I desire those politicians who dislike my overture, and may perhaps be so bold to attempt an answer, that they will first ask the parents of these mortals whether they would not at this day think it a great happiness to have been sold for food at a year old in the manner I prescribe, and thereby have avoided such a perpetual scene of misfortunes as they have since gone through by the oppression of landlords, the impossibility of paying rent without money or trade, the want of common sustenance, with neither house nor clothes to cover them from the inclemencies of the weather, and the most inevitable prospect of entailing the like or greater miseries upon their breed forever.

I profess, in the sincerity of my heart, that I have not the least personal interest in endeavoring to promote this necessary work, having no other motive than the public good of my country, by advancing our trade, providing for infants, relieving the poor, and giving some pleasure to the rich. I have no children by which I can propose to get a single penny; the youngest being nine years old, and my wife past childbearing.

Organ Transplantation: A Modest Proposal

Warren J. Warwick

Pediatrician Warren J. Warwick (1928–) earned his M.D. in Minnesota in 1954 and became a professor of pediatrics at the University of Minnesota. He specializes in pulmonary diseases, experimental pathology, immunology, and cystic fibrosis. His research and skill have led him to numerous medical fellowships and serve as the basis for his articles.

The transplantation of organs to replace those worn out or injured by disease has captured the headlines and the imagination of the world. With great expectations people everywhere await more information. Organ transplantation seems natural to persons who have lived for generations with machines that are restored to function through replacement of malfunctioning parts. No one would consider discarding a good car because the the battery wore out; instead he would buy a new battery, replace the old, and drive on. Such is the expectation latent in the people today. They claim to realize that this new era may still be many years away, but they really think it will occur in only a few years.

We, as physicians, have a responsibility to individually and collectively prepare the public for the advances that will have to be made before today's research techniques can become the "cut out and replace" surgery of everyday life. We know, but we must teach the people that at present the researchers must almost destroy the body's ability to resist infections so that the body will not destroy the new organ. The people will have to be educated to support ever more research in this area through both private contributions and tax monies.

The people are reading of the large teams—fifteen to thirty persons in Dr. [Christiaan] Bernard's—that are required to transplant one heart. They will have to be educated to the need for the even larger sums of money needed to train sufficient technicians, physicians, nurses, and surgeons for these teams and at the same time for general health care to maintain the present level of health in our country. This may mean a doubling of the number of medical schools and perhaps the formation of postgraduate schools for organ transplantation. The people must actively support legislation to provide federal funds for this expansion because the medical manpower needs will be beyond the means of private and even state finances.

The people require also to know the magnitude of the problem. They are beginning to realize the fives and tens of patients receiving organ transplantation today represent a potential 50 to 100,000 or more every year. They are beginning to imagine that organ transplants can save annually the lives of thousands of patients who would otherwise die from diseases of the heart, kidney, liver, or lung, and this is without consideration of the transplantations of corneas to cure blindness, skin to heal burns, muscles to cure paralysis, glands to cure deficiencies, pancreas to cure diabetes, perhaps even arms and legs or fingers and toes to help people maimed in accidents or war.

The people can surely accept with ease the need for more money to solve rejection phenomena and accept with reservation the financial sacrifice that will be required to build the medical schools to train physicians and paramedical personnel, but we physicians must help them and perhaps condition them to accept new attitudes toward their bodies and the bodies of their fellowmen. Adiran Kantrowitz, performer of two heart transplants, says the number of donors for heart transplants cannot approach the need. Senator Walter Mondale questioned over one hundred transplants and how organs should be procured. In order to have enough organs to meet a gargantuan demand—we must teach, ourselves first and then the people, a new and better morality toward the body and soul (assuming a theistic dialectic) or toward the body and mankind (assuming an atheistic dialectic). A consideration of our present sources of organs should clarify the problem and suggest solutions.

Our first source is living persons who voluntarily donate organs when the body has reserves, i.e., a kidney or part of the skin. The second source is cadavers whose organs can be obtained through consent of the kin after the patient is dead, but before the organs are lifeless.

The first source is very limited and, as far as the people are concerned can be ignored. The second source is considerable—theoretically all organs from every body after death. This source, however, has two limitations. First, many fatal diseases are systemic and damage more than one organ. Thus, the number of each usable organ will be much smaller than the number of deaths. Moreover, persons dying of old age may have grossly normal but aged organs that, while capable of functioning for a few more years in another older person, would surely wear out too soon if transplanted into a younger person. For transplantation purposes the accidental death of an otherwise healthy young person is best. Automobile accidents alone would provide a good supply if it were not that many of the victims die before they reach a hospital and, thus, before their organs can be harvested. Nonetheless, accidents bode well to be important, for healthy accident victims of all ages could provide many of the needed organs. But all such sources are limited by convention and by law. Organs cannot be taken from bodies without the specific permission of the surviving kin who legally control disposition of the body.

Before we look further into these problems, let us make some assumptions about the research and medical progress that will be made in the future. Let us assume that biochemical methods will be developed to permit the safe transplantation of healthy organs from one person to another without the risk of organ rejection and that medical and surgical techniques will be perfected so that every major hospital in the country will have one or more teams trained to transplant all organs.

Then back to the source of supply. Based on our analysis, we have only one source to exploit—the surviving organs of the dead. Now we reason: if the person has a soul that is independent of his body, the normal processes of decay of his body after death will not hurt the soul anymore than the decay of his estate will hurt his soul. Therefore, the body should be considered no more sacred than the dead person's estate, which is taxed by the government. Since the person's use of his body is abetted by the government through laws, public health measures, and surely by that time a socialized medicine, we may reason that the body has been maintained by the state and that the state has material investment in the physical material of the body. We may reason further that the state thereby acquires a right to tax the body as well as the estate, and, therefore, the right to claim the useful organs of that body at the time of death. Through a system of socialized medicine the organs will be used to preserve the life and restore the usefulness of other citizens.

This concept may be hard for the public to accept at once, but, if given proper advance instruction of the over-all value to each and all, the people will most readily grant their understanding as approval. One example of potential great benefit to a large number of patients from the complete conservation of healthy organs from a single death should convince most of the people of the need for a new philosophy of the body. In our example we find a young man dead of a head injury received in a motorcycle accident. That body could provide a kidney apiece for two persons with diseased kidneys, a pancreas for a diabetic patient, a liver, a heart for a coronary patient, lungs for two persons with bronchitis or emphysema, or stomach for a cancer victim, a colon for a person with ulcerative colitis, a thyroid, two adrenals, and a thymus, bones for bone grafts, blood for transfusions, and over a square yard of skin for one or more patients with burns.Thus, the body of one healthy adult could save the lives of six to a dozen of his fellow men. A consummation devoutly to be wished, a far better use of no longer needed flesh than temporary preservation in formaldehyde and burial in a casket. An end that all persons should desire, a true chance to live on after death in the lives of others. And for those who cannot entirely loose themselves from the burial of the dead, we have the remnant, the untransplantable parts of the body, that can be assembled and committed to ashes or dust.

Having accomplished acceptance of the new philosophy of the body, we must lead the public to a new definition of death. Obviously, a dead body that is cold and stiff can provide few organs of value, save the cornea, heart valves, and bones. Therefore, we must redefine death so that the required organs will still be useful—if possible, while these organs are still red from fresh oxygen in the blood. A statistical point of view would best serve our needs. Assuming a cold and stiff body to be 100 percent dead, we must set a new standard such as "probable death" or "95 percent dead." Research into this problem should parallel research into the transplantation problem. Techniques will have to be devised to record all modalities of life and to establish criteria for the 95 percent death. There is a slight danger latent in calling a patient "statistically dead." We know, statistically speaking, that 5 percent of the time, there will be temporal advancement of the biological fact by a few hours. But these few hours are of no conceivable value to a body "statistically dead," especially when compared to the value of the years of function to be granted to the several persons who would receive the organs harvested from the body. The 95 percent dead body will still have function in most parts so that some organs may be removed without the taint of lifelessness in their cells. That the recipient of such organs will be able to recover and return to active and productive life will be our justification for the statistical definition of death. It must be clear to us physicians and to the public that the greater good of the greater number must rule.

These two hurdles past, all the other necessary steps will be easy. Mobile body-rescue teams will be activated. Surgeons trained at rescuing living organs from dead bodies will be assigned to operating rooms in large helicopters that will fly to accidents. Accident watching clubs, analogous to the airplane spotters of World War II, as well as television monitors will be located along busy highways and intersections to spot and report all accidents the instant they happen.

In fact, we can anticipate cars with built-in automatic systems to signal an accident, pinpoint the location, and record the heartbeat of the driver. This would be particularly valuable in remote areas of the country. It would also have a spinoff value—earlier treatment for accident-insured persons and much improved chances for recovery.

It seems probable that even the most careful husbanding of organs from present levels of auto accident deaths will not satisfy the demands of our growing population. If not, simple measures can be taken. Prohibition of seat belts and other safety devices, cancellation of speed limits, and removal of warning signs would make driving a greater risk and pleasure to our thrill-seeking youth and would increase the number of accidents. Some would accuse the government of killing off its citizens; again, the greater gain (six to twelve lives for the loss of one) for the greater number would be the guiding principle and would ultimately receive the public's support.

The cost of this program will be great, but the spinoff in restoration of healthy tax payers will defray some costs. Moreover, measures for cost cutting in other medical and welfare areas are available, and the money saved in these programs can be used to cut costs in organ transplantation. Every state has institutions filled with micro-cephalic and other monsters without human personalities, but with healthy organs. The state would charge for its humanitarian services to these bodies, even as the state would obtain the organs of the dead through a legislated death tax. A dollar value would be calculated for each transplantable organ, and when the state's services to the body equals the organs' worth, the state would collect for its services by transplanting the organs to deserving recipients. The approach would provide some of the small organs needed for children; most adult organs are too large and have too short a useful life expectancy to be good bets for young children.

Even this may not provide enough pediatric-sized organs to handle the large number of congenital malformations of the heart, liver, kidneys, or lungs that we see and care for. But new sources can be imagined. Could not congenital malformations of specific lethal nature be induced in the fetuses of women who do no want to have another living child, but who shy away from abortions? Some women could make a career of bearing these short-lived monsters and selling their organs. The anencephalic monster would seem most useful. Research will have to be done to determine the best time and the best drugs to induce such a disorder without impairing organs useful for transplantation. Since the organs would be used to restore infants with other congenital abnormalities to normal productive lives, the mothers performing this service would become revered members of society.

These are but a few of the many bright new advances in the ethics of humanity and the practice of medicine for which we must prepare if organ transplantation is to be developed as the ultimate treatment for the diseases of man.

In our efforts to bring these enlightened concepts to universal acceptance, we must be prepared to reply to a pair of recurrent reactionary rationalizations. First, that disease prevention is better than treatment. Second, that early—preferably presymptomatic—diagnosis will permit prompt treatment, prevent permanent damage, and arrest the progress of disease. These two approaches have been advocated by experts and societies for many years but the public has rejected them. They can best be countered by any of hundreds of relevant and specific examples. That the number of smokers increases yearly, despite knowledge of the dangers of smoking, and that physicians, as well as the people, fail to have annual physical examinations come readily to mind.

We as physicians must not back proved losers. Organ transplantation is clearly a predictable winner of the public's support. It will come sooner if we, as physicians, become leaders in forming the moral enlightenment required to bring about that golden age. Man, in his social awareness of humanity, will not withhold himself as a contribution to the greater good of the people.

Suggestions for Discussion or Writing

1. What is Swift's purpose in writing "A Modest Proposal?" What is Warwick's purpose in writing "Organ Transplantation: A Modest Proposal?" Are the authors serious about their proposals? How do you know? What words, phrases, or examples give you a clue?

2. What is the predominant tone in each essay? Does the tone enhance or detract form each author's intended meaning? In what way?

3. What strategies does each author use to support his argument? Do they enhance the arguments or not? Why?

4. Compare "A Modest Proposal" to "Organ Transplantation: A Modest Proposal." In what ways does Swift's essay provide a basic pattern for Warwick to follow? How are the two essays similar? How are they different?

5. How do you feel about each author's argument? Are you persuaded? Angered? Amused? Why?

Introduction to Figurative Language

Using Figurative Language

Literal versus Figurative

Being literal is describing things as they are. A writer is factual, restrained, and does not necessarily use language in an innovative or fanciful way. A writer is realistic. Many times realism is not expected, however.

When a writer is figurative (nonliteral), however, she often makes comparisons between things, trying to use language in unusual ways as she writes and talks. Many authors do this because it helps the audience to think and understand. They also use figurative language because of the pleasure it gives them and others (for the sheer fun of it).

Using Language Indirectly

Critical thinking also involves the interpretation of language used indirectly. Figurative language is also called metaphorical language, or language using figures of speech—like metaphors and similes (comparisons between two things—to be defined more fully and discussed later). To think figuratively, we need to make associations between things; that is, we need to compare something literal with something else in an imaginative way.

Although many people associate figurative language simply with poetry, nonliteral use of language can be found even in the most technical documents and in everyday speech. When we talk about the mouth of a river or the leg of the table, we are using a metaphor. Practical equipment makes liberal use of metaphors in the description of parts: butterfly valve, A-frame house, male coupling, sawhorse, and so on. A comment such as "it's hot as blazes out there" is a common use of a simile. Figurative language is not restricted to literature, by any means. But sometimes it is a reasonable way to begin looking at figurative language because literature is so rich in its use.

Advantages of Using Figurative Language

Figurative language makes us think deeply about language and the way we use language. It makes us see the world in a different way. For example, once we understand how symbols are used, we can see symbolism not only in written works, but also in the physical world. Other figures of speech, such as metaphors and similes, show connections that we might not otherwise have made between two objects or ideas. Critical thinking is stimulated as we see how rich or strange the comparison is. Figurative language gives us new ideas and new ways to approach both reading and writing, and new ideas are exciting.

There are quite a few different kinds of figurative language, but the basic figures, and the ones discussed here are metaphor, simile, personification, allusion, symbol, and a combination of these.

Types of Figurative Language

Metaphor

A metaphor compares two different things by implicitly asserting that they are alike in some way. Instead of using connective words (such as *like* or *as*) to draw the comparison, a metaphor states that something *is* something else. For instance, Sophocles wrote that "sons are the anchors of a mother's life." Sylvia Plath's poem "Stillborn" (page 534) contains the metaphor of wiring compared to giving birth, Mary Oliver speaks of being the fish in her poem "The Fish" (page 591), and many of the other poems in the text contain metaphors. In addition, metaphors are found in Martin Luther King, Jr.'s "I Have a Dream" (page 411), in which he compares the treatment of African-Americans to a default on a promissory note. In Garrison Keillor's "Protestant" (page 447) the metaphor "Mr. Cox smelled the burning rubber of Error" gives a delightful dimension to the essay. Other examples include

> *Facts alone are wanted in life. Plant nothing else, and root out everything else.* *(Charles Dickens)*

> *Time is but a stream I go a-fishing in. I drink at it; but while I drink I see the sandy bottom and detect how shallow it is. Its thin current slides away, but eternity remains. I would drink deeper; fish in the sky, whose bottom is pebbly with stars.* *(Thoreau)*

> *The Lord is my Shepherd.* (Psalm 23)

> *Television is the opiate of the white middle class. (John Hersey)*

> *California is the flashy blonde you like to take out once or twice. Minnesota is the girl you want to marry.* (Time)

Occasionally, metaphors are overdone, or too many conflicting metaphors are combined in writing. These are called mixed metaphors. Someone told to keep his eye on the ball and his shoulder to the wheel is being given conflicting (mixed metaphor) instructions. A humorous example of mixed metaphors is shown in the following cartoon.

"The clouds, throbbing little Volkswagens of trouble, rush hither and yon, churning like ill-bred butter; the seas, hopping mad, belch and groan, contempuously rolling carpets forever seeking pastoral vacuum cleaners."

from Worst Case Scenarios: A Collection of Cartoons by Jack Ziegler. Copyright © 1990 by Jack Ziegler. Reprinted by permission of Fireside Publishing.

Simile

A simile compares two different things by explicitly asserting that they are alike in some way. The words most frequently used to introduce the comparisons are *like* and *as*. A simile in Dylan Thomas' poem "Do Not Go Gentle Into That Good Night" (page 215) reads as follows: "Blind eyes could blaze like meteors . . ." Clinton Larson uses a simile in "Homestead in Idaho" (page 335) when he says, "The colors crept down like frost and the glory of God, intermingling in them night and day." In the essay, "Heaven and Earth in Jest" (page 455) by Annie Dillard, the simile, "I'd wake in daylight to find my body covered with paw prints in blood; I looked as though I'd been painted with roses," shows that similes are not restricted to fiction or poetry. A poem rich with similes, "Harlem," (page 436) by Langston Hughes, shows how the lost dream of a subculture can take many expressions. Other examples follow:

> *The track crossed a swampy part where the moss hung as white as lace from every limb.* (Eudora Welty)

> *We are not satisfied, and we will not be satisfied until justice rolls down like waters and righteousness like a mighty stream.* (Martin Luther King, Jr.)

> *It felt good to know the sky, and he'd wonder what it was like to know it as God does, galaxies and even clusters of galaxies flung like seeds to the far fences of the universe.* (Bruce Jorgensen)

The whites of his eyes were discoloured, like ancient billiard balls. (Aldous Huxley)

Personification

Personification, in its widest definition, is endowing lifeless things (ideas, objects, etc.) with the qualities of living things. In a narrower definition, personification is attributing to any nonhuman entity (including animals) human form or sensibilities. The essay by William Zinsser, "Shanghai Blues" (page 491), describes improvisation as "the lifeblood of jazz." Other examples include these:

Because I could not stop for Death,
He kindly stopped for me. (Emily Dickinson)

The ninth wave, slow gathering fold by fold
All its loose-flowing garments into one,
Plunges upon the shore, and floods the dun
Pale reach of sands, and changes them to gold.
(Henry Wadsworth Longfellow)

The heavens were perspiring a cold sweat that blanketed everything.
(William W. Watt)

A lone iris was panting, purple-tongued. (W. S. Merwin)

A humorous approach to personification can be found in the following cartoon:

Eric steps out of a biting wind.

Allusion

An allusion is an incomplete reference to some well-known event, person, place, or thing in history, mythology, literature, television, art, sports, or scripture, and so on. Since this reference is usually brief and highly connotative, it functions as a kind of shorthand for providing the knowing reader with a rich abundance of inferred comparisons and associations. For instance, to say that someone is like Job from the Bible might communicate as much in one sentence as we could otherwise communicate in several paragraphs.

Writers create interesting connotations by alluding to Don Quixote, the Golden Fleece, the Lotus Eaters, Midas, Achilles' heel, Hercules, Pandora's box, Oedipus, Cleopatra, Othello, Hiroshima, Uncle Tom, Catch–22, Waterloo, the Boston Tea Party, Watergate, the Good Samaritan, Superman, Marshal Dillon, "Mr. Rogers' Neighborhood," Pilate, Pollyanna, the 1961 New York Mets, crying wolf, and so on. The reference to Russia in Daphne Du Maurier's "The Birds" (page 573) makes the allusion to the Cold War tension before communism disintegrated. A scriptural allusion in Alistair Cooke's "The Huddled Masses" (page 400) describes the late nineteenth- and early twentieth-century immigrants as seeing "America as the Land of Canaan." Other examples include:

> *We need more Elijahs in the pulpit today—more men who will dare to upbraid an Ahab and defy a Jezebel.*   *(William Jennings Bryan)*

> *Below them seventy-five yards, one of the brown hawks had lit on a power pole. Allen watched, then slowly reached for the Browning. "Okay, you jokers, move aside," he said, "and we'll see who's the Daniel Boone around here."*   *(Douglas Thayer)*

> *Eichmann was not Iago or Macbeth, and nothing would have been farther from his mind than to determine with Richard III "to prove a villain."*
> *(Hannah Arendt)*

Symbol

A symbol is something (usually concrete) that not only has literal meaning, but stands for something else (usually abstract). Instead of being precise or absolute, symbols can be used to suggest many meanings. For example, the moon has been used as a symbol of peace, serenity, chastity, love, loneliness, and inconstancy. The symbols of Shakespeare's head and the map in Stephen Spender's "Elementary School Class Room in a Slum" (page 292) represent an education in the arts and broad knowledge of the world—neither of which the slum children will ever have. These symbols are thus called "wicked" for tempting what they cannot deliver. Alice Walker's eye in "Beauty: When the Other Dancer Is the Self" (page 356) becomes a symbol of her lost self-esteem.

In the following passage from *Moby Dick,* Herman Melville discusses how "white" is an ambiguous symbol:

Though in many natural objects, whiteness refiningly enhances beauty, as if imparting some special virtue of its own, . . . [and though whiteness has been associated] with whatever is sweet, and honorable, and sublime, there yet lurks an elusive something in the innermost idea of this hue, which strikes more of panic to the soul than the redness which affrights in blood. . . . Whiteness . . . is at once the most meaning symbol of spiritual things, nay, the very veil of the Christian's Deity; and yet [it is also] the intensifying agent in things the most appalling to mankind. Is it that by its indefiniteness it shadows forth the heartless voids and immensities of the universe, and thus stabs us from behind with the thought of annihilation, when beholding the white depths of the Milky Way? Or is it, that as in essence whiteness is not so much a color as the visible absence of color, and at the same time the concrete of all colors; is it for these reasons that there is such a dumb blankness, full of meaning, in a wide landscape of snows—a colorless, all-color of atheism from which we shrink?

Another example of a universal symbol is the rose. Depending on the color, a rose represents beauty of various kinds, love, purity, truth, or political leanings. This poem shows one interpretation of its symbolic colors:

> The red rose whispers of passion,
>   And the white rose breathes of love;
> Oh, the red rose is a falcon,
>   And the white rose is a dove.
> But I send you a cream-white rosebud,
>   With a flush on its petal tips;
> For the love that is purest and sweetest
>   Has a kiss of desire on the lips.
> (John Boyle O'Reilly)

Combinations

Authors often use figurative language in combinations. There is no set way of combining; they simply combine the figures as they see fit, as Sylvia Plath does in "Face Lift" (page 396) when she combines metaphor and simile, "He makes me feel something precious/ is leaking from the finger-vents. At the count of two/ Darkness wipes me out like chalk on a blackboard." In reading, we commonly see combinations, as shown in the examples below:

Metaphor/Personification: The bow of God's wrath is bent, and the arrow made ready on the string, and justice bends the arrow at your heart and strains the bow, and it is nothing more than the mere pleasure of God . . . that keeps the arrow one moment from being made drunk with your blood.
(Jonathan Edwards)

Metaphor/Simile: The blood seethes and boils in the veins, the brains are boiling in the skull, the heart in the breast glowing and bursting, the bowels

a redhot mass of burning pulp, the tender eyes flaming like molten balls.
(James Joyce)

Simile/Allusion: He walked as softly as the Ghost in Hamlet, and more
slowly. *(Charles Dickens)*

Simile/Personification: Big dead trees, like black men with one arm, were
standing in the purple stalks of the withered cotton field. *(Eudora Welty)*

Simile/Metaphor/Personification: By the outer margin of the pit was an oval
pond; and over it hung the attenuated skeleton of a chrome-yellow moon,
which had only a few days to last—the morning star dogging her on the right
hand. The pool glittered like a dead man's eye, and as the world awoke and
breeze blew, shaking and elongating the reflection of the moon without
breaking it, and turning the image of the star to a phosphoric streak upon
the water. *(Thomas Hardy)*

Student Example: Finding Figurative Language

Identifying figurative language can sharpen critical thinking skills, deepen an understanding of reading, and enrich our writing. Rachelle Williams writes of the symbolism of the cornfield as being the unexplored experience of sex in "Sex Education." The character in the story gets lost in a cornfield and panics, then acts foolishly when she sees someone she knows. The story implies that this behavior sometimes occurs when young people first encounter sexual experienc

The second telling of the story is to a group of young mothers. The emphasis is drifting from Aunt Minnie's own feelings to how to tell the young mothers' own daughters "about how not to get lost. Or how to act, if they did" (p. 286). She tries to point out that sex isn't that big of a deal and illustrate it with her analogy of "And anyhow that patch of corn wasn't as big as she let on" (p. 287).

Because of the analogy and the symbolism in the story, Rachelle Williams notes that "this time the story had more meaning and depth for the listener." She also comments that the third time the story is told, "Aunt Minnie is in the winter of her life," using metaphor to identify Aunt Minnie's age.

As we turn back to our own writing assignment, we can use literal or figurative writing to analyze our own work. Is the essay straightforward or subtle? If we are presenting the material straight, and without secondary meanings, then we need to watch out for language, tone, or hidden assumptions which will subvert our efforts. However, if we are trying to use some figurative language, then we need to make sure we are on target. We may also want to try some figurative language just for the fun of it. But remember, a light touch is best here. A little figurative language goes a long way. We should also consider what our audience would understand. Not all allusions are accessible to a general audience.

Student Exercises: Figurative Language

1. Tell how metaphors are used in science or in everyday communication.

2. Write your ideas on the potential symbolism of each of the following: serpent, fox, eagle, lamb, lion, wind, sea, river, sunset, garden, grave, autumn, gold, blood, darkness, light, circle, sun, or stars.

3. Identify the figurative language in Martin Luther King, Jr.'s "I Have a Dream" (page 411). Why does this language make the essay effective?

4. Find figurative language in other essays, stories and poetry in the text. How do they affect the meaning of the work?

Discussion Questions: Figurative Language

1. Is "To Dorothy" (page 214) a love poem? What are the hidden assumptions found in the poem? Why is the last line and a half metaphorical? Discuss the assumptions in the child's statement.

2. Robert Hayden is a noted African-American writer. Does this fact change your perception of his poem, "Those Winter Sundays" (page 214)? How is the experience Hayden describes universal? Does the metaphorical use of cold show it splintering and breaking? What does the author mean by this description? How does it enlarge your understanding of the experience?

3. Dylan Thomas's poem, "Do Not Go Gentle Into That Good Night," (page 215) describes his struggle to understand his father's approach to death. How do his metaphors of words "forking lightning" and "deeds dancing in a green bay" depict the healthy, young life? How is the stanza on wild men both literal and figurative?

4. Susan Elizabeth Howe's "To a Marathon Runner" (page 216) uses the figurative language that the "long miles are an old friend." What kind of figurative language is this? How is it appropriate to a runner? Discuss how two of the similes in the poem—"Training . . . like stars cross the sky" and "patient as seasons, as the way wind cuts, rivers work on canyon walls"— work to give additional depth to the poem.

5. William Stafford's poem, "Widow," (page 217) mixes the literal with the figurative when he describes the behavior of a grief-stricken widow trying to come to grips with life. How effective is the personification of a "surprised-looking bed"? What do you think the bed looked like? What does the poem mean when it says, "maybe this day the stillness begins"?

6. How many different allusions can you find in the e.e. cummings poem "next to of course god america i" (page 218)? Can you match the snatches of songs and clichés with its past?

7. The scar in Jane Hirshfield's poem, "For What Binds Us," (page 220) is a symbol. What is it a symbol of?

Readings in Figurative Language

Metaphor

The following poems give further examples of figurative language. Marvin Bell's poem for his wife shows how the metaphor of a weed sweeping away the day represents the mundane movement of time that moves toward death or "sleep."

To Dorothy
Marvin Bell (b. 1937)

You are not beautiful, exactly.
You are beautiful, inexactly.
You let a weed grow by the mulberry
and let a mulberry grow by the house.
So close, in the personal quiet
of a windy night, it brushes the wall
and sweeps away the day till we sleep.

A child said it, and it seemed true:
"Things that are lost are all equal."
But it isn't true. If I lost you,
the air wouldn't move, nor the tree grow.
Someone would pull the weed, my flower.
The quiet wouldn't be yours. If I lost you,
I'd have to ask the grass to let me sleep.

Robert Hayden's metaphor describes the "blueblack cold" of morning. The combination of colors makes the reader think of the darkness of early morning, but also gives the feeling of something so cold that it bruises.

Those Winter Sundays
Robert Hayden (b.1913)

Sundays too my father got up early
and put his clothes on in the blueblack cold,
then with cracked hands that ached
from labor in the weekday weather made
banked fires blaze. No one ever thanked him.

I'd wake and hear the cold splintering, breaking.
When the rooms were warm, he'd call,
and slowly I would rise and dress,
fearing the chronic angers of that house,

Speaking indifferently to him, who had driven out the cold
and polished my good shoes as well.
What did I know, what did I know
of love's austere and lonely offices?

Simile

Dylan Thomas's poem is written in a villanelle form with strong repeating lines
to provide emphasis. His simile, "blind eyes could blaze like meteors," stresses his
theme of not allowing old age to make us give up. Even though someone may be blind,
he or she still can have brightness and excitement.

Do Not Go Gentle Into That Good Night
Dylan Thomas (1914–1953)

Do not go gentle into that good night,
Old age should burn and rave at close of day;
Rage, rage against the dying of the light.

Though wise men at their end know dark is right,
Because their words had forked no lightning they
Do not go gentle into that good night.

Good men, the last wave by, crying how bright
Their frail deeds might have danced in a green bay,
Rage, rage against the dying of the light.

Wild men who caught and sang the sun in flight,
And learn, too late, they grieved it on its way,
Do not go gentle into that good night.

Grave men, near death, who see with blinding sight
Blind eyes could blaze like meteors and be gay,
Rage, rage against the dying of the light.

And you, my father, there on the sad height,
Curse, bless me now with your fierce tears, I pray.
Do not go gentle into that good night.
Rage, rage against the dying of the light.

Susan Howe's poem describes the sensory impressions of a long-distance
runner—the "cool air under trees" and the "warmth shimmering along the road," the
"breeze" and "fine mist," the "sun" on one's back. She also includes the simile of
training at night "like stars cross the sky," giving both the visual impression of the
movement of stars and the reliability of heavenly movement. Her simile, "patient as
seasons," is expanded to describe "the way winds cuts" and "rivers work on canyon
walls," giving additional images of the faithfulness of the runner's training.

To a Marathon Runner
Susan Elizabeth Howe (b. 1949)

for Dave

Training, you run at night, like stars
Cross the sky, their path a spiral
Vast as possibility. Your way
Is not distance but presence, the feel
Of every footfall across silence and time.
Days shadow you, cool air
Under trees, warmth shimmering
Along the road. Miles pass, and nights
Are never the same—breeze, a fine mist,
Or the echo of an Indian summer day.
You run through them all, patient
As seasons, as the way wind cuts,
Rivers work on canyon walls.
The balance shifts between knowing
And being known.

After enough miles
You finally come to the start.
This race isn't about limits but about the heart's
Illusions: immovable objects and irresistible
Force. Beginning early, you will run
Through wind and stars into morning, till sun
Warms your back and you take your place
Among elements you have come to know.
The long miles are as old friends;
You will wear each other down.
And you will find yourself ahead,
In the next stride, the next moment,
Until goal and effort become one and you
Have learned this road. At the finish
You will breathe deeply, and your heart will endure.

Personification

In William Stafford's description of the lonely widow's house, he gives the furniture human qualities to give the feeling of the utter loss the widow feels when the inanimate objects must become her companions. The bed is "surprised-looking," the table is "forgiving," and the calendar "had waited all year for this date." Even the dishes needed help. Through personification, Stafford increases the mood of loneliness.

Widow
William Stafford (b. 1914)

On the first day when light came through the curtain
a mosquito thought was bothering her—what if
I am important? She wandered the house—the forgiving
table, the surprised-looking bed. Dishes
in the rack needed putting away, and she helped
them. But afterward she regretted—maybe nothing
should move, maybe this day the stillness begins.

She looked out a front window and held every
neighborhood shadow exactly where it was. Then
she carefully X'd out the calendar that had waited
all year for this date. She held out her hand
in a shaft of sun and flexed her fingers, in case
time had passed, in case her body was already gone.

John Davies, a modern Welsh poet, describes the reactions of his young daughter upon seeing dandelions float down the stream. His personification describes the bridge sending a "long dark shadow after them" and mentions the "trees' fingers." The dandelions themselves seem alive as they "wriggle" and "risk the trees' fingers trailing." His personification makes nature come almost as alive as the child.

Dandelions
John Davies (b. 1944)

Now, they are fleeing downstream, those dandelions
my small daughter has not-quite-thrown;
she raised her arm and let them go, and
the bridge sent its long dark shadow after them.

They flutter around boulders, wriggle, risk
the trees' fingers trailing, as though to justify
not just her casual faith in them but, too,
momentum, what the casually hurrying river's for.

She stands, beckoning at water and dandelions
and the sunlit afternoon. And I cannot tell her why,
now that she wants them back, they are beyond us
both. Useless to explain the river runs one way.

Allusion

Although the greater number of poets from the past used classical mythology, biblical references, previous literature, and historical events for their allusions, e.e. cummings takes snatches of songs and short sayings that have become overused (clichés), as well as references to historical events. Some of the allusions may be more familiar ("oh say can you see by the dawn's early") than snatches from earlier popular melodies ("by jingo by gee by gosh"). The poem is meant to be ironic, showing how slogans are meant to promote patriotism, but in wartime people still are killed. The poem is in quotation marks to indicate that it has been spoken by someone and does not have punctuation or capitalization not only because that is cummings' style, but also to give a feeling of thoughtless rushing.

"next to of course god america i"
e.e. cummings (1894–1962)

"next to of course god america i
love you land of the pilgrims; and so forth oh
say can you see by the dawn's early my
country 'tis of centuries come and go
and are no more what of it we should worry
in every language even deafanddumb
thy sons acclaim your glorious name by gorry
by jingo by gee by gosh by gum
why talk of beauty what could be more beautiful than these heroic happy dead
who rushed like lions to the roaring slaughter
they did not stop to think they died instead
then shall the voice of liberty be mute?"
He spoke. And drank rapidly a glass of water

Marianne Moore, on the other hand, uses allusions to places and objects to give the feeling of a particular setting (place and time period). The rigidness and elaborate-ness of the objects described reflect the king who built Versailles. The multiplying of detail is abruptly cut short with the terse message, "the king is dead," just as these elaborate objects are. A careful look at the objects also yields symbolism in repre-senting the king and his reign.

No Swan So Fine
Marianne Moore (1887–1972)

"No water so still as the
    dead fountains of Versailles."[1] No swan,
with swart blind look askance
and gondoliering legs,[2] so fine
    as the chintz china one with fawn-
brown eyes and toothed gold
    collar on to show whose bird it was.

[1]Famous palace of French kings, built during the late seventeenth and early eighteenth centuries.
[2]Italian gondoliers in Venice steer their boats from the stern.

Lodged in the Louis Fifteenth
  candelabrum-tree[3] of cockscomb
tinted buttons, dahlias,
sea-urchins, and everlastings,[4]
  it perches on the branching foam
of polished sculptured
flowers—at ease and tall. The king is dead.

Symbol

Some of the symbols in Roethke's poem are the worm—meaning our mortality; that is, the worm is related to the fact that when creatures die, they are eaten by worms; the tree, which can mean among other things, either the tree of life or the tree of knowledge (allusions to the Garden of Eden), or the tree (the cross) upon which Christ was crucified. Light can be a symbol of Christ, but it also can symbolize knowledge or truth. Nature is a symbol of our sojourn in mortality or of the personification of natural phenomena. Sleep, in much literature, is a symbol of death—prefiguring the final sleep in the grave. In the same symbolism pattern, walking symbolizes birth.

As we read the poem, we should think of these symbols to give the poem deeper meaning. For example, we are born to die—birth has in it the seeds of death because everything that is born will die.

The Waking
Theodore Roethke (1908–1963)

I wake to sleep, and take my waking slow.
I feel my fate in what I cannot fear.
I learn by going where I have to go.

We think by feeling. What is there to know?
I hear my being dance from ear to ear.
I wake to sleep, and take my waking slow.

Of those so close beside me, which are you?
God bless the Ground! I shall walk softly there,
And learn by going where I have to go.

Light takes the Tree; but who can tell us how?
The lowly worm climbs up a winding stair;
I wake to sleep, and take my waking slow.

---

[3]"A pair of Louis XV candelabra with Dresden figures of swans belonging to Lord Balfour" [Moore's note].

[4]Plants whose flowers may be dried without losing their form or color; also, the flowers from such plants.

Great Nature has another thing to do
To you and me; so take the lively air,
And, lovely, learn by going where to go.

This shaking keeps me steady, I should know
What falls away is always. And is near.
I wake to sleep, and take my waking slow.
I learn by going where I have to go.

Jane Hirshfield has one major symbol in her poem—the scar made after an injury. She describes it on horses as "proud flesh" and notes that it is stronger than regular flesh. The scar is like an honor (she uses a simile in this description) and makes not only horses but also people stronger. She is making the assumption that when people are hurt or scarred (specifically in love relationships), they become stronger because of the experience.

For What Binds Us
Jane Hirshfield (b. 1953)

There are names for what binds us:
strong forces, weak forces.
Look around, you can see them:
the skin that forms in a half-empty cup,
nails rusting into the places they join,
joints dovetailed on their own weight.
The way things stay so solidly
wherever they've been set down—
and gravity, scientists say, is weak.

And see how the flesh grows back
across a wound, with a great vehemence,
more strong
than the simple, untested surface before.
There's a name for it on horses,
when it comes back darker and raised: proud flesh,

as all flesh
is proud of its wounds, wears them
as honors given out after battle,
small triumphs pinned to the chest—

And when two people have loved each other
see how it is like a
scar between their bodies,
stronger, darker, and proud;
how the black cord makes of them a single fabric
that nothing can tear or mend.

part

2

Readings

...ously
...nerever
...superiority
...social hierar-
...were at the top,
...ians, elements in a
...h its upper and lower
...as much snobbish anguish
...er immigrant families.

...ey were mostly the persecuted and
...rly young lady whose poetic dramas
...gotten in the thunder of five lines inscribed
...se unlettered millions were, for the most part,
...he eye, of a father or a cousin wearing a suit and shiny shoes, just
...doctor or a merchant in the old country.
...Long before they arrived at the ports of embarkation—Constantinople,
Piraeus, Antwerp, Bremen—emigrant trains had started deep inside Russia.
Most of them were linked box cars, sometimes with benches, the men in
one car, the women and children in another. Every few hundred miles the
train would be shunted on to a siding in order to pick up other new armies,
of Austrians, Hungarians, Lithuanians, and finally a troop of Germans,
before they came to, say, Hamburg. There they were corralled and checked
to see if they had the three essential passports to America: an exit paper,
twenty-five spare dollars to prevent their becoming a public charge, and the
price of the passage. By the 1890s lively rate wars between steamship lines
had halved the steerage fare about twenty dollars to ten. In an enclosure
outside Hamburg they would be bathed, de-loused, and fed, and their bag-

Perspectives on Schooling
Challenging Modern Education

Introduction

Modern American education has been under attack: scores on national tests are dropping, students do not seem to have the skills and knowledge they once had, no one knows how to "think" nowadays. Recent books by Bloom and Hirsch lament the decline of motivation. Yet America continues to lead the world in technological development, social reforms, medical innovations and ecological concerns. Notwithstanding the problems, somewhere, someone is doing something right.

The essay "Books" by Allan Bloom, which begins this section, introduces some of the concerns of education: lack of reading, literary criticism impeding the vitality of the texts, and lack of heroes or villains causing a dulling of the impact of education. Harold Stevenson's "Learning from Asian Schools" challenges the stereotypes of foreign education and suggests patterns of learning that American education would do well to consider. Richard Feynman examines rote learning—memorizing rather than understanding—a system that verifies some negative stereotypes of education.

From the teacher's perspective, Lionel Trilling's story shows the struggle to teach and deal with difficult students, but from the student's perspective, Walt Whitman gives a vignette of the learning situation outside a classroom. Samuel H. Scudder discusses the master teacher, Louis Agassiz, demonstrating the value of close looking. Stephen Jay Gould gives another look at this teacher as he is challenged by revolutionary views.

"Sex Education" by Dorothy Canfield shows an approach to learning by telling a story three different ways, and Stephen Spender challenges the readers to think of teaching middle-class values and aspirations to students without hope of reaching these goals in "An Elementary School Class Room in a Slum." Martha Collins's poem "The Story We Know" is a villanelle about the story of life—learning and knowing the commonplace things that make up our existence.

The selections ask questions not only of our educational system, but also of our individual learning styles. The answers are not always easily found, but some answers, perhaps, may come from a new generation of students who see the problems in education firsthand. Even if the questions do not lead to definitive answers, the questions coming from these selections should open new insights and perspectives on education.

Books

from *The Closing of the American Mind*

Allan Bloom

Allan Bloom (1930–) is Professor in the Committee on Social Thought and the College and codirector of the John M. Olin Center for Inquiry into the Theory and Practice of Democracy at the University of Chicago. He has taught at Yale, the University of Paris, the University of Toronto, Tel Aviv University, and Cornell University, where he was the recipient of the Clark Teaching Award in 1967. His book The Closing of the American Mind *has created much discussion and controversy.*

1   I have begun to wonder whether the experience of the greatest texts from early childhood is not a prerequisite for a concern throughout life for them and for lesser but important literature. The soul's longing, its intolerable irritation under the constraints of the conditional and limited, may very well require encouragement at the outset. At all events, whatever the cause, our students have lost the practice of and the taste for reading. They have not learned how to read, nor do they have the expectation of delight or improvement from reading. They are "authentic," as against the immediately preceding university generations, in having few cultural pretensions and in refusing hypocritical ritual bows to high culture.

2   When I first noticed the decline in reading during the late sixties, I began asking my large introductory classes, and any other group of younger students to which I spoke, what books really count for them. Most are silent, puzzled by the question. The notion of books as companions is foreign to them. Justice [Hugo] Black with his tattered copy of the Constitution in his pocket at all times is not an example that would mean much to them. There is no printed word to which they look for counsel, inspiration or joy. Sometimes one student will say "the Bible." (He learned it at home, and his Biblical studies are not usually continued at the university.) There is always a girl who mentions Ayn Rand's *The Fountainhead,* a book, although hardly literature, which, with its sub-Nietzschean assertiveness, excites somewhat eccentric youngsters to a new way of life. A few students mention recent books that struck them and supported their own self-interpretation, like *The Catcher in the Rye.* (Theirs is usually the most genuine response and also shows a felt need for help in self-interpretation. But it is an uneducated response. Teachers should take advantage of the need expressed in it to show such students that better writers can help them more.) After such sessions I am pursued by a student or two who wants to make it clear that he or she is really influenced by books, not just by one or two but by many. Then he recites a list of classics he may have grazed in high school.

3   Imagine such a young person walking through the Louvre or the Uffizi, and you can immediately grasp the condition of his soul. In his innocence of the stories of

Biblical and Greek or Roman antiquity, Raphael, Leonardo, Michelangelo, Rembrandt and all the others can say nothing to him. All he sees are colors and forms—modern art. In short, like almost everything else in his spiritual life, the paintings and statues are abstract. No matter what much of modern wisdom asserts, these artists counted on immediate recognition of their subjects and, what is more, on their having a powerful meaning to their viewers. The works were the fulfillment of those meanings, giving them a sensuous reality and hence completing them. Without those meanings, and without their being something essential to the viewer as a moral, political and religious being, the works lose their essence. It is not merely the tradition that is lost when the voice of civilization that elaborates over millennia has been stilled in this way. It is being itself that vanishes beyond the dissolving horizon. One of the most flattering things that ever happened to me as a teacher occurred when I received a postcard from a very good student on his first visit to Italy, who wrote, "You are not a professor of political philosophy but a travel agent." Nothing could have better expressed my intention as an educator. He thought I had prepared him to see. Then he could begin thinking for himself with something to think about. The real sensation of the Florence in which Machiavelli is believable is worth all the formulas of metaphysics ten times over. Education in our times must try to find whatever there is in students that might yearn for completion, and to reconstruct the learning that would enable them autonomously to seek that completion.

4   In a less grandiose vein, students today have nothing like the Dickens who gave so many of us the unforgettable Pecksniffs, Micawbers, Pips, with which we sharpened our vision, allowing us some subtlety in our distinction of human types. It is a complex set of experiences that enables one to say so simply, "He is a Scrooge." Without literature, no such observations are possible and the fine art of comparison is lost. The psychological obtuseness of our students is appalling, because they have only pop psychology to tell them what people are like, and the range of their motives. As the awareness that we owed almost exclusively to literary genius falters, people become more alike, for want of knowing they can be otherwise. What poor substitutes for real diversity are the wild rainbows of dyed hair and other external differences that tell the observer nothing about what is inside.

5   Lack of education simply results in students' seeking for enlightenment wherever it is available, without being able to distinguish between the sublime and trash, insight and propaganda. For the most part, students turn to the movies, ready prey to interested moralisms such as the depictions of Gandhi or Thomas More—largely designed to further passing political movements and to appeal to simplistic needs for greatness—or to insinuating flattery of their secret aspirations and vices, giving them a sense of significance. *Kramer vs. Kramer* may be up-to-date about divorces and sex roles, but anyone who does not have *Anna Karenina* or *The Red and the Black* as part of his viewing equipment cannot sense what might be lacking, or the difference between an honest presentation and an exercise in consciousness-raising, trashy sentimentality and elevated sentiment. As films have emancipated themselves from the literary tyranny under which they suffered and which gave them a bad conscience, the ones with serious pretensions have become intolerably ignorant and manipulative. The distance from the contemporary and its high seriousness that students most need in

order not to indulge their petty desires and to discover what is most serious about themselves cannot be found in the cinema, which now only knows the present. Thus, the failure to read good books both enfeebles the vision and strengthens our most fatal tendency—the belief that the here and now is all there is.

6   The only way to counteract this tendency is to intervene most vigorously in the education of those few who come to the university with a strong urge for *un je ne sai quoi,* who fear that they may fail to discover it, and that the cultivation of their minds is required for the success of their quest. We are long past the age when a whole tradition could be stored up in all students, to be fruitfully used later by some. Only those who are willing to take risks and are ready to believe the implausible are now fit for a bookish adventure. The desire must come from within. People do what they want, and now the most needful things appear so implausible to them that it is hopeless to attempt universal reform. Teachers of writing in state universities, among the noblest and most despised laborers in the academy, have told me that they cannot teach writing to students who do not read, and then it is practically impossible to get them to read, let alone like it. This is where high schools have failed most, filled with teachers who are products of the sixties and reflecting the pallor of university-level humanities. The old teachers who loved Shakespeare or Austen or Donne, and whose only reward for teaching was the perpetuation of their taste have all but disappeared.

7   The last enemy of the vitality of classic texts is feminism. The struggles against elitism and racism in the sixties and seventies had little direct effect on students' relations to books. The democratization of the university helped dismantle its structure and caused it to lose its focus. But the activists had no special quarrel with the classic texts, and they were even a bit infected by their Frankfurt School masters' habit of parading their intimacy with high culture. Radicals had at an earlier stage of egalitarianism already dealt with the monarchic, aristocratic and antidemocratic character of most literary classics by no longer paying attention to their manifest political content. Literary criticism concentrated on the private, the intimate, the feelings, thoughts and relations of individuals, while reducing to the status of a literary convention of the past the fact that the heroes of many classic works were soldiers and statesmen engaged in ruling and faced with political problems. Shakespeare, as he has been read for most of this century, does not constitute a threat to egalitarian right thinking. And as for racism, it just did not play a role in the classic literature, at least in the forms in which we are concerned about it today, and no great work of literature is ordinarily considered racist.

8   But *all* literature up to today is sexist. The Muses never sang to the poets about liberated women. It's the same old *chanson* from the Bible and Homer through Joyce and Proust. And this is particularly grave for literature, since the love interest was most of what remained in the classics after politics was purged in the academy, and was also what drew students to reading them. These books appealed to eros while educating it. So activism has been directed against the content of books. The latest translation of Biblical text—sponsored by the National Council of the Churches of Christ—suppresses gender references to God, so that future generations will not have to grapple with the fact that God was once a sexist. But this technique has only limited applicability. Another tactic is to expunge the most offensive authors—for example, Rousseau—from the education of the young or to include feminist responses in college

courses, pointing out the distorting prejudices, and using the books only as evidence of the misunderstanding of woman's nature and the history of injustice to it. Moreover, the great female characters can be used as examples of the various ways women have coped with the enslavement to the sexual role. But never, never, must a student be attracted to those old ways and take them as models for himself or herself. However, all this effort is wasted. Students cannot imagine that the old literature could teach them anything about the relations they want to have or will be permitted to have. So they are indifferent.

9   Having heard over a period of years the same kinds of responses to my question about favorite books, I began to ask students who their heroes are. Again, there is usually silence, and most frequently nothing follows. Why should anyone have heroes? One should be oneself and not form oneself in an alien mold. Here positive ideology supports them: their lack of hero-worship is a sign of maturity. They posit their own values. They have turned into a channel first established in the *Republic* by Socrates, who liberated himself from Achilles, and picked up in earnest by Rousseau in *Emile*. Following on Rousseau, Tolstoy depicts Prince Andrei in *War and Peace*, who was educated in Plutarch and is alienated from himself by his admiration for Napoleon. But we tend to forget that Andrei is a very noble man indeed and that his heroic longings give him a splendor of soul that dwarfs the petty, vain, self-regarding concerns of the bourgeoisie that surrounds him. Only a combination of natural sentiment and unity with the spirit of Russia and its history can, for Tolstoy, produce human beings superior to Andrei, and even they are only ambiguously superior. But in America we have only the bourgeoisie, and the love of the heroic is one of the few counterpoises available to us. In us the contempt for the heroic is only an extension of the perversion of the democratic principle that denies greatness and wants everyone to feel comfortable in his skin without having to suffer unpleasant comparison. Students have not the slightest notion of what an achievement it is to free oneself from public guidance and find resources for guidance within oneself. From what source within themselves would they draw the goals they think they set for themselves? Liberation from the heroic only means that they have no resources whatsoever against conformity to the current "role models." They are constantly thinking of themselves in terms of fixed standards that they did not make. Instead of being overwhelmed by Cyrus, Theseus, Moses, or Romulus, they unconsciously act out the roles of the doctors, lawyers, businessmen or TV personalities around them. One can only pity young people without admirations they can respect or avow, who are artificially restrained from the enthusiasms for great virtue.

10   In encouraging this deformity, democratic relativism joins a branch of conservatism that is impressed by the dangerous political consequences of idealism. These conservatives want young people to know that this tawdry old world cannot respond to their demands for perfection. In the choice between the somewhat arbitrarily distinguished realism and idealism, a sensible person would want to be both, or neither. But, momentarily accepting a distinction I reject, idealism as it is commonly conceived should have primacy in an education, for man is a being who must take his orientation by his possible perfection. To attempt to suppress this most natural of all inclinations because of possible abuses, is almost literally, to throw out the baby with the bath.

Utopianism is, as Plato taught us at the outset, the fire with which we must play because it is the only way we can find out what we are. We need to criticize false understandings of Utopia, but the easy way out provided by realism is deadly. As it now stands, students have powerful images of what a perfect body is and pursue it incessantly. But deprived of literary guidance, they no longer have any image of a perfect soul, and hence do not long to have one. They do not even imagine that there is such a thing.

11   Following on what I learned from this second question, I began asking a third: Who do you think is evil? To this one there is an immediate response: Hitler. (Stalin is hardly mentioned.) After him, who else? Up until a couple of years ago, a few students said Nixon, but he has been forgotten and at the same time is being rehabilitated. And there it stops. They have no idea of evil; they doubt its existence. Hitler is just another abstraction, an item to fill up an empty category. Although they live in a world in which the most terrible deeds are being performed and they see brutal crime in the streets, they turn aside. Perhaps they believe that evil deeds are performed by persons who, if they got the proper therapy, would not do them again—that there are evil deeds, not evil people. There is no *Inferno* in this comedy. Thus the most common student view lacks an awareness of the depths as well as the heights, and hence lacks gravity.

Suggestions for Discussion or Writing

1. Who is Allan Bloom's audience? Does he have more than one audience?

2. What is Bloom's purpose in the essay? What does he expect of students? Of teachers? Of the American school system?

3. Is Bloom correct in his assertion that students today have no heroes? Who are the heroes of the current era?

4. What books do you consider important for a basic education?

5. What is Bloom's view of evil? Do you agree with his suggestion that there are no evil persons, just evil deeds?

Learning from Asian Schools

Harold W. Stevenson

Harold W. Stevenson (1924–) received his Ph.D. from Stanford University and is currently a professor of psychology at the University of Michigan in Ann Arbor. His recent book, Learning Gap: Why Our Schools are Failing and What We Can Learn from Japanese and Chinese Education *(1992), reflects his extensive research in cross-national studies of children's academic achievement. He has received a Guggenheim fellowship and an award from the American Psychological Association for his work in developmental psychology.*

1   During the past decade, it has become a truism that American students are not being adequately prepared to compete in a global economy. The latest research shows that the deficiencies become apparent as early as kindergarten and persist throughout the school years. These deficiencies have been most evident when the students are compared with their peers in East Asia. Yet contrary to popular stereotypes the high levels of achievement in Asian schools are not the result of rote learning and repeated drilling by over-burdened, tense youngsters. Children are motivated to learn; teaching is innovative and interesting. Knowledge is not forced on children; instead the students are led to construct their own ways of representing this knowledge. The long school days in Asia are broken up by extensive amounts of recess. The recess in turn fosters a positive attitude toward academics.

2   My colleagues and I gained these insights in a series of five collaborative, large cross-national studies begun in 1980. We explored the children's experiences both at home and at school in the U.S., China, Taiwan and Japan. We found that there is nothing mysterious about the teaching styles and techniques used in Asian schools. Rather these societies embody many of the ideals Americans have for their own schools. They just happen to apply them in an interesting, productive way that makes learning enjoyable.

3   The vast cultural differences preclude direct translation of many of the practices and beliefs from those cultures to our own. But these comparative data have helped us realize how far Americans have strayed from the effective application of well-known teaching methods. The studies have revealed new perspectives about our own culture and fresh ideas about how our educational system might be improved. Indeed, simply increasing the length of school days would be meaningless if there were no change in the way American teachers are asked to perform their jobs.

4   Results from cross-national studies can be greatly distorted if the research procedures are not comparable in each area and if the test materials are not culturally appropriate. We avoided the first potential problem by selecting a full range of schools in five metropolitan areas: Minneapolis, Chicago, Sendai, Beijing and Taipei. These cities are similar in size and cultural status within their own countries. In each

metropolitan region, we selected from 10 to 20 elementary schools that represented a range of students from different socioeconomic backgrounds. (Because socio-economic status is not easy to define, we used the parents' educational level as the basis for selection.) We then randomly chose two first-grade and two fifth-grade classrooms in each school.

5 To avoid the difficulty in translating materials developed in one culture for use in another, we constructed our own tests. We began by compiling computer files of every concept and skill included in the students' mathematics textbooks and every word and grammatical structure in their reading material. With these files, we were able to create test items that were relevant to each culture and that were at the appropriate levels of difficulty.

6 Armed with these materials, we administered mathematics and reading tests to thousands of students in the first- and fifth-grade classrooms. Later we randomly selected samples of six boys and six girls from each classroom for more in-depth testing and interviews. In one of the studies, we visited a total of 204 classrooms in 11 schools in Beijing, 10 in Taipei, 10 in Sendai, and 20 in Chicago.

7 The test results confirmed what has become common knowledge: school-children in Asia perform better academically than do those in the U.S. In mathematics the average scores of the Asian first graders were above the American average, but scores of some of the American schools were as high as some of those in Sendai and Taipei. By fifth grade, however, the American students lost much ground: the average score of only one of the Chicago-area schools was as high as the worst of the Asian schools. On a computation test, for example, only 2.2 percent of the Beijing first graders and 1.4 percent of the fifth graders scored as low as the mean for their Chicago counterparts. On a test of word problems, only 2.6 percent of the Beijing first graders and 10 percent of the fifth graders scored at or below corresponding American means.

8 The deficiencies of American children appear to build throughout the school years. When we compared the scores of kindergarten children and of first, fifth and 11th graders in Minneapolis, Sendai and Taipei, we found a relative decline in the scores among the American students, improvement in Taiwan and steady high performance in Japan.

9 American students' shortcomings are not limited to mathematics. Although Americans performed the best on reading in the first grade, the Asian students had caught up by the fifth grade. The rise is remarkable when one considers the reading demands of Asian languages. Chinese students had to learn several thousand characters by the fifth grade, and Japanese students had to learn Chinese characters, two syllabaries (symbols for the syllables in Japanese) and the Roman alphabet.

10 Because of the early onset and pervasiveness of cross-cultural differences in academic achievement, it seemed obvious that we would have to investigate attitudes, beliefs and practices related to children's success. We spent hundreds of hours observing in the classrooms, interviewed the teachers, children and mothers and gave questionnaires to the fathers.

11 American parents show a surprisingly high level of satisfaction with their children's level of academic performance. From kindergarten through the 11th grade, more than three times as many Minneapolis mothers as Asian mothers said they were very satisfied with their child's current level of achievement.

12   The U.S. students were also very positive about their abilities. More than 30 percent of the Chicago fifth graders considered themselves to be "among the best" in mathematics, in reading, in sports and in getting along with other children. Such self-ratings were significantly higher than those made by Sendai and Taipei children for mathematics and by Sendai children for reading. Taipei children gave the highest self-ratings for reading. Except for social skills, many fewer Beijing children gave themselves such positive ratings.

13   In another set of questions, we asked the mothers how well the school was educating their own children. More than 80 percent of the American mothers expressed a high level of satisfaction. Except at kindergarten, when mothers in all four societies were quite satisfied, Minneapolis mothers felt much better about their children's schools than did mothers in Taipei and Sendai.

14   Why should American mothers be so positive? One likely explanation is that they lack clear standards to which they can refer. No national or state curricula define what children should learn at each grade, and few mothers receive more than vague reports about their children's performance. American mothers also seem to place a lesser emphasis on academic achievement. In the U.S., childhood is a time for many different types of accomplishment. Doing well in school is only one of them.

15   Asian mothers, on the other hand, have told us repeatedly that their children's primary task is to do well in school. The mothers' own job is to try to do everything possible to ensure that success. They regarded education as critical to their children's future. Thus, Asian mothers find it more difficult to be satisfied with moderate levels of performance.

16   The American mothers' contentment had clearly been transmitted to their children. Fifth graders were asked whether they agreed with the statement, "I am doing as well in school as my parents want me to." American children thought this statement was more true of them than did the Asian children. We obtained similar results when we asked the question in terms of their teachers' satisfaction.

17   The American mothers we interviewed apparently were not strongly impressed by recent criticisms of U.S. education. As far as they were concerned, the relatively poor academic showing of U.S. students did not reflect the abilities of their own children or their children's schools. For American mothers, problems existed at other schools and with other children. Our interviews revealed little evidence that American mothers were motivated to seek improvements in the quality of their children's education or that American children believed they were doing anything but a satisfactory job in school.

18   We explored academic motivation in another way by posing a hypothetical question to the children: "Let's say there is a wizard who will let you make a wish about anything you want. What would you wish?" The most frequent wishes fell into four categories: money; material objects, such as toys or pets; fantasy, such as wanting to be sent to the moon or to have more wishes; and educational aspirations, such as doing well in school or going to college. Almost 70 percent of the Chinese children focused their wishes on education. American children were more interested in receiving money and material objects. Fewer than 10 percent of the American children expressed wishes about education.

19   The enthusiasm Asian children express about school comes in part, of course, from the well-known societal emphasis on education. Several studies of immigrants have documented the willingness of Asian children to work hard. This attitude stems from Confucian beliefs about the role of effort and ability in achievement. The malleability of human behavior has long been emphasized in Chinese writings, and a similar theme is found in Japanese philosophy. Individual differences in potential are deemphasized, and great importance is placed on the role of effort and diligence in modifying the course of human development.

20   In contrast, Americans are much more likely to point to the limitations imposed by an assumed level of innate ability. This belief has potentially devastating effects. When parents believe success in school depends for the most part on ability rather than effort, they are less likely to foster participation in activities related to academic achievement. Such parents may question whether spending time in academic pursuits after school is useful for children of presumed low ability. They may readily accept poor performance. Furthermore, if the parents believe the child has high ability, they may question whether such activities are needed.

21   It is relatively easy to demonstrate the greater emphasis placed by Americans on innate ability. One approach is to ask children to rate the importance of certain factors for doing well in school. Beijing children emphasized effort rather than ability. Chicago children thought both to be of near-equal importance.

22   In another approach we asked Taipei, Sendai and Minneapolis children to indicate the degree to which they agreed with the statement that "everybody in the class has about the same amount of ability in math." American children expressed less strong agreement than did the Chinese or Japanese children. Mothers followed the same pattern of response. When asked about the degree to which they agreed that "any student can be good at math if he/she works hard enough," Minneapolis mothers expressed less agreement than did Sendai or Taipei mothers.

23   Children may work harder because they believe achievement depends on diligence. The idea that increased effort will lead to improved performance is an important factor in accounting for the willingness of Chinese and Japanese children, teachers and parents to spend so much time and effort on the children's academic work.

24   The enthusiasm for school also seems to come from the happy times that Asian children appear to have there. That these children regard school as pleasant—rather than as regimented, austere and demanding—surprises most Americans. Our stereotype is that the intense quest for academic excellence reduces the possibilities of making school a place that children enjoy. This clearly is not the case.

25   When we compare the daily routine in Asian and American schools, we realize how easy it is to overlook the constraints of American schools. Classes begin shortly after the students arrive, and the children leave just after their last class ends. Rarely is there more than a single recess. The lunch period—a potential time for play and social interaction—is usually limited to a half an hour or less. As a consequence, American children spend most of their time at school in the classroom.

26   In contrast, the daily routine in Asian schools offers many opportunities for social experience. There are frequent recesses, long lunch periods and afterschool activities

and clubs. Such opportunities make up about one fourth of the time spent during the eight hours at school. The school day is longer in Asia mainly because of the time devoted to these nonacademic periods. Play, social interaction and extracurricular activity may not contribute directly to academic success, but they make school an enjoyable place. The enjoyment likely creates cooperative attitudes.

27   The relative lack of nonacademic activities in American schools is reflected in greater amounts of time spent in play after school. American mothers estimated that their elementary school children spend nearly 25 hours a week playing. We found this surprisingly high until we considered how little time was available for play at school. Estimates for Chinese children were much lower—their social life at school is reflected in the shorter amounts of time they play after returning home.

28   Chicago children also spent nearly twice as much time as Beijing children watching television. But compared with Americans, Japanese students from kindergarten through high school spent even more time watching television. The difference in this case appears to be that Japanese children are more likely to watch television after they have completed their homework.

29   American children were reported to spend significantly less time than Asian children in doing homework and reading for pleasure—two pursuits that are likely to contribute to academic achievement. Mothers estimated that the Taipei children spent about four times as much time each doing homework as did American children and over twice as much as did Japanese children. American children were estimated to spend less time reading for pleasure than their Asian peers throughout their school years.

30   The enjoyment Asian students have at school may be the reason they appear to Western visitors as well behaved and well adjusted. These observations, however, have always been informal, and no data exist to support or refute them. So we decided to ask mothers and teachers in Beijing and Chicago about these matters. In particular, we questioned them about physical symptoms of tension, which we thought would be a good indicator of adjustment.

31   Chinese mothers reported fewer complaints by their children of stomachaches and headaches, as well as fewer requests to stay home from school than did American mothers. The Chinese mothers also more frequently described their children as happy and obedient. Only 4 percent of the Chinese mothers, but 20 percent of the American mothers, said their children encountered problems in getting along with other children.

32   The intense dedication of Chinese elementary school children to schoolwork did not appear to result in tension or maladjustment. Nor have we found patterns of psychological disturbance among several thousand Chinese and Japanese 11th graders in self-evaluations of stress, depression, academic anxiety or psychosomatic complaints. Our data do not support the Western assumption that Asian children must experience extraordinary stress from their more demanding curriculum. The clear academic goals and the enthusiastic support given by family, teachers and peers may reduce the strain from working so hard.

33   The achievement of Asian students is facilitated by the extensive amount of attention teachers can give the children. Indeed, one of the biggest differences we found was the amount of time the teachers had. Beijing teachers were incredulous after

we described a typical day in American schools. When, they asked, did the teachers prepare their lessons, consult with one another about teaching techniques, grade the students' papers and work with individual students who were having difficulties? Beijing teachers, they explained, are responsible for classes for no more than three hours a day; for those with homeroom duties, the total is four hours. The situation is similar in Japan and Taiwan, where, according to our estimates, teachers are in charge of classes only 60 percent of the time they are at school.

34   Teaching is more of a group endeavor in Asia than it is in the U.S. Teachers frequently consult with one another, because, in following the national curriculum, they are all teaching the same lesson at about the same time. More experienced teachers help newer ones. Head teachers in each grade organize meetings to discuss technique and to devise lesson plans and handouts. The group may spend hours designing a single lesson or discussing how to frame questions that will produce the greatest understanding from their pupils. They also have a teachers' room, where all the instructors have desks and where they keep their books and teaching materials. They spend most of the time there when not teaching.

35   American teachers have neither the time nor the incentive to share experiences with one another or to benefit from hearing about the successes and failures of other instructors. Each teacher's desk is in the classroom, and little space is allocated specifically for informal discussions and meetings. The teachers' room in American schools is typically a place to rest rather than to work. As a result, American teachers spend most of their time at school isolated in their own classrooms, with few opportunities for professional interaction or consultation.

36   With no national curriculum or guidelines, American schools typically develop their own agenda. In any year the curriculum may not be consistent within a city or even a single school. Adding further to the diversity in the curricula among American classrooms is the fact that teachers are free to proceed through textbooks at any rate they wish, skipping the parts they do not find especially interesting or useful.

37   The demanding daily schedule places serious constraints on the ability of American teachers to create exciting well-organized lessons. They usually must prepare for their classes at home during evenings and weekends. Furthermore, they must cover all elementary school subjects, because teachers for specific academic subjects typically do not appear until junior high school. Evenings are not the most appropriate time to begin such a difficult task, for teachers are tired from the demands of school and their own affairs. There are, of course, excellent American teachers. And there are individual differences among Asian teachers. But what has impressed us in our observations and in the data from our studies is how remarkably well most East Asian teachers do their jobs.

38   Asian teachers can be described best as well-informed, well-prepared guides. They do not see themselves primarily as dispensers of information and arbiters of what is correct but rather as persons responsible for guiding students skillfully through the material. Each lesson typically begins with a statement of its purpose and ends with a summary of its content. The lesson follows a well-planned script in which children are led through a series of productive interactions and discussions. Teachers regard

children as active participants in the learning process who must play an important role in producing, explaining and evaluating solutions to problems.

39   The skill shown by Asian teachers is not acquired in college. In fact, some teachers in China have only a high school education. The pattern for training teachers resembles that provided to other professionals: in-service training under the supervision of skilled models. Colleges are assumed to provide basic knowledge about subject matter, as well as about child development and theories of learning. But Asian instructors believe the art of teaching can be accomplished better in classrooms of elementary schools than in lecture halls of colleges. This approach stands in sharp contrast to that taken in the U.S. where teaching skill is generally thought to be best acquired through several specialized courses in teaching methods.

40   The skills employed by Asian teachers are also more effective in attracting and maintaining children's attention. We found Asian children listening to the teacher more frequently than American children—at least 80 percent of the time versus approximately 60 percent. This finding may also result from differences in the number of recesses in Asian and American schools. Attention is more likely to falter after several hours of classes than it is if opportunities for play and relaxation precede each class, as is the case in Asian schools.

41   Another likely reason for the American children's lack of attention lies in the manner in which U.S. teachers often structure the lessons. Because of the time spent on seatwork—exercises or assignments children are to complete at their desks—and the way in which seatwork is used, American children have fewer opportunities to interact with the teacher than do children in Asian classrooms. American teachers rely more heavily on seatwork than do Asian teachers, which is not surprising. Giving children such tasks is one of the few ways American teachers can gain some free time in their grueling daily schedule.

42   In the U.S., teachers usually explain the concepts during the early part of the lesson and then assign seatwork during the later part. Asian teachers, on the other hand, intersperse brief periods of seatwork throughout the class period. Seatwork is a means of getting children to practice what they have just learned and of quickly spotting difficulties the children might be encountering. American teachers are less likely to take advantage of the diagnostic value of seatwork.

43   Children's attention also increases when they receive feedback. If students do not receive some type of acknowledgment from the teacher or some indication of whether their work is correct, they are more likely to lose interest. In a surprisingly large number of classes, Chicago teachers failed to provide feedback to the children, especially when the children were doing seatwork. In nearly half of the 160 class periods we observed in the Chicago fifth grades, teachers failed to offer any type of evaluation as the children worked alone at their desks. In striking contrast, a lack of such acknowledgment was practically never observed in Sendai and only infrequently in Taipei.

44   In addition, Asian teachers make more frequent use of materials that can be manipulated. Jean Piaget and other psychologists (as well as most parents and teachers) have discovered that young children enjoy manipulating concrete objects, which is often a more effective way to learn than is listening to verbal instruction. Even so,

American teachers were much less likely than Asian teachers to provide concrete objects for manipulation in mathematics classes.

45   Finally, Asian teachers make the subjects interesting by giving them some meaningful relation in the children's everyday lives. In mathematics, word problems often serve this function. They can transform mathematics from a subject of dull computation to one requiring active problem solving. We found that American teachers were much less likely than Asian teachers to introduce word problems. Fifth-grade American teachers presented word problems in less than one out of five class periods; Sendai teachers included word problems in more than eight out of every 10 lessons. Similar differences emerged when we calculated how often children were asked to construct word problems themselves. This exercise rarely occurred in American classrooms.

46   Asian teachers are able to engage children's interest not because they have insights that are unknown in the U.S. but because they take well-known principles and have the time and energy to apply them with remarkable skill. They incorporate a variety of teaching techniques within each lesson, rely more frequently on discussion than on lectures, teach children how to make smooth transitions from one type of activity to another and seldom engage in irrelevant discussions—all approaches to teaching that American instructors would agree are reasonable and effective.

47   Perhaps the most pointed difference between the goals of Asian and American teachers emerged when we asked teachers in Beijing and Chicago what they considered to be the most important characteristics of a good instructor. "Clarity," said nearly half of the Beijing teachers. "Sensitivity to the needs of individuals," was the most common response of the Chicago teachers. Beijing teachers were also more likely to emphasize enthusiasm, and Chicago teachers were more likely to stress patience.

48   Have the goals of education diverged to such a degree in Eastern and Western cultures that American teachers see their main tasks as those of evaluating and meeting the needs of individuals, while Asian teachers can devote their attention to the process of teaching? If this is the case, the academic achievement of American children will not improve until conditions are as favorable as those provided in Asia. Clearly, a challenge in the U.S. is to create a greater cultural emphasis on education and academic success. But we must also make changes in the training of teachers and in their teaching schedules, so that they, too, will be able to incorporate sound teaching practices into their daily routines.

Suggestions for Discussion or Writing

1. In the first paragraph of this article, Stevenson gives several reasons that Asian schools are superior to American schools. Other observations and conclusions come later in the article. How does he support his first assumptions on Asian education?

2. What other factors influence the quality of Asian education?

3. How do patterns of television behavior differ between Asian and American students?

4. What is Stevenson's pattern of development in this article? Outline the major points of this article.

5. Does Stevenson use inductive or deductive reasoning to present the facts of his research? How effective is his argument?

"O Americano, Outra Vez!"

from *"Surely You're Joking, Mr. Feynman!"*:
Adventures of a Curious Character

Richard P. Feynman

Richard Phillips Feynman (1918–) shared the 1965 Nobel Prize in physics with Julian S. Schwinger and Sin-itiro Tomonaga for his improved theory of quantum electro-dynamics. Born in Far Rockaway on the outskirts of New York City near the sea, Feynman was a mischievous young man who seemed to have an almost compulsive need to solve puzzles. He entered MIT at the age of 17 to pursue his love of science and earned a Ph.D. from Princeton in 1942. He has worked as a theoretical physicist at Los Alamos National Laboratory in New Mexico, on the Manhattan Project, in Brazil, where he taught physics and math as a visiting professor, and at the California Institute of Technology. His essays and stories are based on many of his teaching experiences. This selection shows his impatience with hypocrisy and pretension as well as his dedication to science and teaching.

1   In regard to education in Brazil, I had a very interesting experience. I was teaching a group of students who would ultimately become teachers, since at that time there were not many opportunities in Brazil for a highly trained person in science. These students had already had many courses, and this was to be their most advanced course in electricity and magnetism—Maxwell's equations, and so on.

2   The university was located in various office buildings throughout the city, and the course I taught met in a building which overlooked the bay.

3   I discovered a very strange phenomenon: I could ask a question which the students would answer immediately. But the next time I would ask the question—the same subject, and the same question, as far as I could tell—they couldn't answer it at all! For instance, one time I was talking about polarized light, and I gave them all some strips of polaroid.

4   Polaroid passes only light whose electric vector is in a certain direction, so I explained how you could tell which way the light is polarized from whether the polaroid is dark or light.

5   We took first two strips of polaroid and rotated them until they let the most light through. From doing that we could tell that the two strips were admitting light polarized in the same direction—what passed through one piece of polaroid could also pass through the other. But then I asked them how one could tell the *absolute* direction of polarization, from a *single* piece of polaroid.

6   They hadn't any idea.

7   I knew this took a certain amount of ingenuity, so I gave them a hint: "Look at the light reflected from the bay outside."

8   Nobody said anything.

9   Then I said, "Have you ever heard of Brewster's Angle?"

10   "Yes, sir! Brewster's Angle is the angle at which light reflected from a medium with an index of refraction is completely polarized."

11   "And which way is the light polarized when it's reflected?"

12   "The light is polarized perpendicular to the plane of the reflection, sir." Even now, I have to think about it; they knew it cold! They even knew the tangent of the angle equals the index!

13   I said, "Well?"

14   Still nothing. They had just told me that light reflected from a medium with an index, such as the bay outside, was polarized; they had even told me which *way* it was polarized.

15   I said, "Look at the bay outside, through the polaroid. Now turn the polaroid."

16   "Ooh, it's polarized!" they said.

17   After a lot of investigation, I finally figured out that the students had memorized everything, but they didn't know what anything meant. When they heard "light that is reflected from a medium with an index," they didn't know that it meant a material *such as water*. They didn't know that the "direction of the light" is the direction in which you *see* something when you're looking at it, and so on. Everything was entirely memorized, yet nothing had been translated into meaningful words. So, if I asked, "What is Brewster's Angle?" I'm going to the computer with the right keywords. But if I say, "Look at the water," nothing happens—they don't have anything under "Look at the water!"

18   Later I attended a lecture at the engineering school. Their lecture went like this, translated into English: "Two bodies . . . are considered equivalent . . . if equal torques . . . will produce . . . equal acceleration." The students were all sitting there taking dictation, and when the professor repeated the sentence, they checked it to make sure they wrote it down right. Then they wrote down the next sentence, and on and on. I was the only one who knew the professor was talking about objects with the same moment of inertia, and it was hard to figure out.

19   I didn't see how they were going to learn anything from that. Here he was talking about moments of inertia, but there was no discussion about how hard it is to push a door open when you put heavy weights on the outside, compared to when you put them near the hinge—*nothing!*

20   After the lecture, I talked to a student: "You take all those notes—what do you do with them?"

21   "Oh, we study them," he says, "We'll have an exam."

22   "What will the exam be like?"

23   "Very easy. I can tell you now one of the questions." He looks at his notebook and says, " 'When are two bodies equivalent?' And the answer is 'Two bodies are considered equivalent if equal torques will produce equal acceleration.' " So, you see, they could pass the examinations, and "learn" all this stuff, and not know anything at all, except what they had memorized.

24   Then I went to an entrance exam for students coming into the engineering school. It was an oral exam, and I was allowed to listen to it. One of the students was absolutely super: He answered everything nifty! The examiners asked him what diamagnetism was, and he answered it perfectly. Then they asked, "When light comes at an angle through a sheet of material with a certain thickness, and a certain index N, what happens to the light?"

25   "It comes out parallel to itself, sir—displaced."

26   "And how much is it displaced?"

27   "I don't know, sir, but I can figure it out." So he figured it out. He was very good. But I had, by this time, my suspicions.

28   After the exam I went up to this bright young man, and explained to him that I was from the United States, and that I wanted to ask him some questions that would not affect the result of his examination in any way. The first question I ask is, "Can you give me some example of a diamagnetic substance?"

29   "No."

30   Then I asked, "If this book was made of glass, and I was looking at something on the table through it, what would happen to the image if I tilted the glass?"

31   "It would be deflected, sir, by twice the angle that you've turned the book."

32   I said, "You haven't got it mixed up with a mirror, have you?"

33   "No, sir!"

34   He had just told me in the examination that the light would be displaced, parallel to itself, and therefore the image would move to one side, but would not be turned by any angle. He had even figured out how *much* it would be displaced, but he didn't realize that a piece of glass is a material with an index, and that his calculation had applied to my question.

35   I taught a course at the engineering school on mathematical methods in physics, in which I tried to show how to solve problems by trial and error. It's something that people don't usually learn, so I began with some simple examples of arithmetic to illustrate the method. I was surprised that only about eight out of the eighty or so students turned in the first assignment. So I gave a strong lecture about having to actually try it, not just sit back and watch *me* do it.

36   After the lecture some students came up to me in a little delegation, and told me that I didn't understand the backgrounds that they have, that they can study without doing the problems, that they have already learned arithmetic, and that this stuff was beneath them.

37   So I kept going with the class, and no matter how complicated or obviously advanced the work was becoming, they were never handing a thing in. Of course I realized what it was: They couldn't *do* it!

38   One other thing I could never get them to do was to ask questions. Finally, a

student explained it to me: "If I ask you a question during the lecture, afterwards everybody will be telling me, 'What are you wasting our time for in the class? We're trying to *learn* something. And you're stopping it by asking him a question.' "

39   It was a kind of one-upmanship, where nobody knows what's going on, and they'd put the other one down as if they *did* know. They all fake that they know, and if one student admits for a moment that something is confusing by asking a question, the others take a high-handed attitude, acting as if it's not confusing at all, telling him that he's wasting their time.

40   I explained how useful it was to work together, to discuss the questions, to talk it over, but they wouldn't do that either, because they would be losing face if they had to ask someone else. It was pitiful! All the work they did, intelligent people, but they got themselves into this funny state of mind, this strange kind of self-propagating "education" which is meaningless, utterly meaningless!

41   At the end of the academic year, the students asked me to give a talk about my experiences of teaching in Brazil. At the talk there would be not only students, but professors and government officials, so I made them promise that I could say whatever I wanted. They said, "Sure. Of course. It's a free country."

42   So I came in, carrying the elementary physics textbook that they used in the first year of college. They thought this book was especially good because it had different kinds of typeface—bold black for the most important things to remember, lighter for less important things, and so on.

43   Right away somebody said, "You're not going to say anything bad about the textbook, are you? The man who wrote it is here, and everybody thinks it's a good textbook."

44   "You promised I could say whatever I wanted."

45   The lecture hall was full. I started out by defining science as an understanding of the behavior of nature. Then I asked "What is a good reason for teaching science? Of course, no country can consider itself civilized unless . . . yak, yak, yak." They were all sitting there nodding, because I know that's the way they think.

46   Then I say, "That, of course, is absurd, because why should we feel we have to keep up with another country? We need to do it for a *good* reason, a *sensible* reason; not just because other countries do." Then I talked about the utility of science, and its contributions to the improvement of the human condition, and all that—I really teased them a little bit.

47   Then I say, "The main purpose of my talk is to demonstrate to you that *no* science is being taught in Brazil!"

48   I can see them stir, thinking, "What? No science? This is absolutely crazy! We have all these classes."

49   So I tell them that one of the first things to strike me when I came to Brazil was to see elementary school kids in bookstores, buying physics books. There are so many kids learning physics in Brazil, beginning much earlier than kids do in the United States, that it's amazing you don't find many physicists in Brazil—why is that? So many kids working so hard, and nothing comes of it.

50   Then I gave the analogy of a Greek scholar who loves the Greek language, who knows that in his own country there aren't many children studying Greek. But he comes to another country, where he is delighted to find everybody studying Greek—

even the smaller kids in the elementary schools. He goes to the examination of a student who is coming to get his degree in Greek, and asks him "What were Socrates' ideas on the relationship between Truth and Beauty?"—and the student can't answer. Then he asks the student "What did Socrates say to Plato in the Third symposium?" the student lights up and goes, *"Brrrrrrrrrrr-up"*—he tells you everything, word for word, that Socrates said, in beautiful Greek.

51   But what Socrates was talking about in the Third Symposium was the relationship between Truth and Beauty!

52   What this Greek scholar discovers is, the students in another country learn Greek by first learning to pronounce the letters, then the words, and then the sentences and paragraphs. They can recite, word for word, what Socrates said, without realizing that those Greek words actually *mean* something. To the student they are all artificial sounds. Nobody has ever translated them into words the students can understand.

53   I said "That's how it looks to me, when I see you teaching the kids 'science' here in Brazil" (Big blast, right?)

54   Then I held up the elementary physics textbook they were using. "There are no experimental results mentioned anywhere in this book, except in one place where there is a ball, rolling down an inclined plane, in which it says how far the ball got after one second, two seconds, and so on. The numbers have 'errors' in them—that is, if you look at them, you think you're looking at experimental results, because the numbers are a little above, or a little below, the theoretical values. The book even talks about having to correct the experimental errors—very fine. The trouble is, when you calculate the value of the acceleration constant from these values, you get the right answer. But a ball rolling down an inclined plane, *if it is actually done,* has an inertia to get it to turn, and will, *if you do the experiment,* produce five-sevenths of the right answer, because of the extra energy needed to go into the rotation of the ball. Therefore this single example of experimental 'results' is obtained from a *fake* experiment. Nobody had rolled such a ball, or they would never have gotten those results!

55   "I have discovered something else," I continued. "By flipping the pages at random, and putting my finger in and reading the sentences on that page, I can show you what's the matter—how it's not science, but memorizing, in *every* circumstance. Therefore, I am brave enough to flip through the pages now, in front of this audience, to put my finger in, to read, and to show you."

56   So I did it. *Brrrrrrup*—I stuck my finger in, and I started to read: "Triboluminescence. Triboluminescence is the light emitted when crystals are crushed . . . "

57   I said, "And there, have you got science? No! You have only told what a word means in terms of other words. You haven't told anything about nature—*what* crystals produce light when you crush them, *why* they produce light. Did you see any student go home and *try* it? He can't.

58   "But if, instead, you were to write, 'When you take a lump of sugar and crush it with a pair of pliers in the dark, you can see a bluish flash. Some other crystals do that too. Nobody knows why. The phenomenon is called "triboluminescence." ' Then someone will go home and try it. Then there's an experience of nature." I used that example to show them, but it didn't make any difference where I would have put my finger in the book; it was like that everywhere.

59   Finally, I said that I couldn't see how anyone could be educated by this self-propa-gating system in which people pass exams, and teach others to pass exams, but nobody knows anything. "However," I said, "I must be wrong. There were two students in my class who did very well, and one of the physicists I know was educated entirely in Brazil. Thus, it must be possible for some people to work their way through the system, bad as it is."

60   Well, after I gave the talk, the head of the science education department got up and said, "Mr. Feynman has told us some things that are very hard for us to hear, but it appears to be that he really loves science, and is sincere in his criticism. Therefore, I think we should listen to him. I came here knowing we have some sickness in our system of education; what I have learned is that we have a *cancer!*"—and he sat down.

61   That gave other people the freedom to speak out, and there was a big excitement. Everybody was getting up and making some suggestions. The students got some committee together to mimeograph the lectures in advance, and they got other committees organized to do this and that.

62   Then something happened which was totally unexpected for me. One of the students got up and said, "I'm one of the two students who Mr. Feynman referred to at the end of his talk. I was not educated in Brazil; I was educated in Germany, and I've just come to Brazil this year."

63   The other student who had done well in class had a similar thing to say. And the professor I had mentioned got up and said, "I was educated here in Brazil during the war, when, fortunately, all of the professors had left the university, so I learned everything by reading alone. Therefore I was not really educated under the Brazilian system."

64   I didn't expect that. I knew the system was bad, but 100 percent—it was terrible!

65   Since I had gone to Brazil under a program sponsored by the United States Government, I was asked by the State Department to write about my experiences in Brazil, so I wrote out the essentials of the speech I had just given. I found out later through the grapevine that the reaction of somebody in the State Department was, "That shows you how dangerous it is to send somebody to Brazil who is so naive. Foolish fellow; he can only cause trouble. He didn't understand the problems." Quite the contrary! I think this person in the State Department was naive to think that because he saw a university with a list of courses and descriptions, that's what it was.

Suggestions for Discussion or Writing

1. What was Feynman's main criticism of the Brazilian school system—students, teachers, and administrators—he encountered? Why?

2. Have you ever been the kind of student Feynman describes? Why or how did you find yourself in that position?

3. What is Feynman's approach to education? How does his approach compare with Trilling's in "Of This Time, Of That Place"? With Scudder's in "Take This Fish and Look at It"?

4. How do you account for the positive reaction of his audience to Feynman's speech and the negative reaction of the State Department official to his report?

Take This Fish and Look at It

Samuel H. Scudder

The foremost orthopteralogist of his time, Samuel Hubbard Scudder (1837–1911) was born in Boston, Massachusetts, where, as a child, he first became fascinated by insects. As a branch of entomology, Orthoptera is the study of grasshoppers, crickets, cockroaches and mantises. Scudder pursued his study of insects at Williams College (1853–1877) and at Harvard (1857–1864) under Louis Agassiz, a prominent naturalist and geologist from Switzerland. In 1889 he published a three-volume work, The Butterflies of the Eastern United States and Canada, *after 30 years of study and preparation.*

1   It was more than fifteen years ago that I entered the laboratory of Professor Agassiz, and told him I had enrolled my name in the Scientific School as a student of natural history. He asked me a few questions about my object in coming, my antecedents generally, the mode in which I afterwards proposed to use the knowledge I might acquire, and, finally, whether I wished to study any special branch. To the latter I replied that, while I wished to be well grounded in all departments of zoology, I purposed to devote myself specially to insects.

2   "When do you wish to begin?" he asked.

3   "Now," I replied.

4   This seemed to please him, and with an energetic "Very well!" he reached from a shelf a huge jar of specimens in yellow alcohol. "Take this fish," he said, "and look at it; we will call it a haemulon; by and by I will ask what you have seen."

5   With that he left me, but in a moment returned with explicit instructions as to the care of the object entrusted to me.

6   "No man is fit to be a naturalist," said he, "who does not know how to take care of specimens."

7   I was to keep the fish before me in a tin tray, and occasionally moisten the surface with alcohol from the jar, always taking care to replace the stopper tightly. Those were not the days of ground-glass stoppers and elegantly shaped exhibition jars; all the old students will recall the huge necklace glass bottles with their leaky, wax-besmeared corks, half eaten by insects, and begrimed with cellar dust. Entomology was a cleaner science than ichthyology, but the example of the Professor, who had unhesitatingly

plunged to the bottom of the jar to produce the fish, was infectious; and though this alcohol had a "very ancient and fishlike smell," I really dared not show any aversion within these sacred precincts, and treated the alcohol as though it were pure water. Still I was conscious of a passing feeling of disappointment, for gazing at a fish did not commend itself to an ardent entomologist. My friends at home, too, were annoyed when they discovered that no amount of eau-de-Cologne would drown the perfume which haunted me like a shadow.

8   In ten minutes I had seen all that could be seen in that fish, and started in search of the Professor—who had, however, left the Museum; and when I returned, after lingering over some of the odd animals stored in the upper apartment, my specimen was dry all over. I dashed the fluid over the fish as if to resuscitate the beast from a fainting fit, and looked with anxiety for a return of the normal sloppy appearance. This little excitement over, nothing was to be done but to return to a steadfast gaze at my mute companion. Half an hour passed—an hour—another hour; the fish began to look loathsome. I turned it over and around; looked it in the face—ghastly; from behind, beneath, above, sideways, at three-quarters' view—just as ghastly. I was in despair; at an early hour I concluded that lunch was necessary; so, with infinite relief, the fish was carefully replaced in the jar, and for an hour I was free.

9   On my return, I learned that Professor Agassiz had been at the Museum, but had gone, and would not return for several hours. My fellows were too busy to be disturbed by continued conversation. Slowly I drew forth that hideous fish, and with a feeling of desperation again looked at it. I might not use a magnifying-glass; instruments of all kinds were interdicted. My two hands, my two eyes, and the fish: it seemed a most limited field. I pushed my finger down its throat to feel how sharp the teeth were. I began to count the scales in the different rows, until I was convinced that was nonsense. At last a happy thought struck me—I would draw the fish; and now with surprise I began to discover new features in the creature. Just then the Professor returned.

10   "That is right," said he; "a pencil is one of the best of eyes. I am glad to notice, too, that you keep your specimen wet, and your bottle corked."

11   With these encouraging words, he added:

12   "Well, what is it like?"

13   He listened attentively to my brief rehearsal of the structure of parts whose names were still unknown to me; the fringed gill-arches and movable operculum; the pores of the head, fleshy lips and lidless eyes; the lateral line, the spinous fins and forked tail; the compressed and arched body. When I finished, he waited as if expecting more, and then, with an air of disappointment:

14   "You have not looked very carefully; why," he continued more earnestly, "you haven't even seen one of the most conspicuous features of the animal, which is plainly before your eyes as the fish itself; look again, look again!" and he left me to my misery.

15   I was piqued; I was mortified. Still more of that wretched fish! But now I set myself to my task with a will, and discovered one new thing after another, until I saw how just the Professor's criticism had been. The afternoon passed quickly; and when, towards it close, the Professor inquired:

16   "Do you see it yet?"

17   "No," I replied, "I am certain I do not, but I see how little I saw before."

18   "That is next best," said he, earnestly, "but I won't hear you now; put away your fish and go home; perhaps you will be ready with a better answer in the morning. I will examine you before you look at the fish."

19   This was disconcerting. Not only must I think of my fish all night, studying, without the object before me, what this unknown but most visible feature might be; but also, without reviewing my discoveries, I must give an exact account of them the next day. I had a bad memory; so I walked home by Charles River in a distracted state, with my two perplexities.

20   The cordial greeting from the Professor the next morning was reassuring; here was a man who seemed to be quite as anxious as I that I should see for myself what he saw.

21   "Do you perhaps mean," I asked, "that the fish has symmetrical sides with paired organs?"

22   His thoroughly pleased "Of course! Of course!" repaid the wakeful hours of the previous night. After he had discoursed most happily and enthusiastically—as he always did—upon the importance of this point, I ventured to ask what I should do next.

23   "Oh, look at your fish!" he said, and left me again to my own devices. In a little more than an hour he returned, heard my new catalogue.

24   "That is good, that is good!" he repeated; "but that is not all; go on"; and so for three long days he placed that fish before my eyes, forbidding me to look at anything else, or to use any artificial aid. "Look, look, look," was his repeated injunction.

25   This was the best entomological lesson I ever had—a lesson whose influence has extended to the details of every subsequent study; a legacy the Professor had left to me, as he has to so many others, of inestimable value, which we could not buy, with which we cannot part.

26   A year afterward, some of us were amusing ourselves with chalking outlandish beasts on the Museum blackboard. We drew prancing starfishes; frogs in mortal combat; hydra-headed worms; stately crawfishes standing on their tails, bearing aloft umbrellas; and grotesque fishes with gaping mouths and staring eyes. The Professor came in shortly after, and was as amused as any at our experiments. He looked at the fishes.

27   "Haemulons, every one of them," he said; "Mr. _____ drew them."

28   True; and to this day, if I attempt to draw a fish, I can draw nothing but haemulons.

29   The fourth day, a second fish of the same group was placed beside the first, and I was bidden to point out the resemblances and differences between the two; another and another followed, until the entire family lay before me, and a whole legion of jars covered the table and surrounding shelves; the odor had become a pleasant perfume; and even now, the sight of an old six-inch, worm-eaten cork brings fragrant memories.

30   The whole group of haemulons was thus brought in review; and, whether engaged upon the dissection of the internal organs, the preparation and examination of the bony framework, or the description of the various parts, Agassiz's training method of observing facts and their orderly arrangement was ever accompanied by the urgent exhortation not to be content with them.

31   "Facts are stupid things," he would say, "until brought into connection with some general law."

32   At the end of eight months, it was almost with reluctance that I left these friends and turned to insects; but what I had gained by this outside experience has been of greater value than years of later investigation in my favorite groups.

Suggestions for Discussion or Writing

1. What was it that made Scudder examine the fish so closely? Curiosity? Boredom? Some other motivation?

2. When does Scudder's attitude toward the fish begin to change? Why does his attitude change?

3. What do you think Scudder's attitude toward education is?

4. What did Scudder learn from observation that he could not learn from a textbook? Are some things easier learned from a textbook? What is the difference between this type of observation and the type described in Whitman's poem?

5. Why does Agassiz say that "a pencil is one of the best of eyes"?

Agassiz in the Galápagos

Stephen Jay Gould

Born in New York City in 1941, Stephen Jay Gould received his Ph.D. at Columbia University in 1967. He has been Professor of Geology at Harvard since 1973 and has published widely in the natural science field. His book, Bully for Brontosaurus: Reflections in Natural History *(1991) by Norton Press, carries a whimsical title but contains solid, scholarly information, a trademark of many of Gould's books and articles. Some of his current essays are also found in* Between Home and Heaven *(1992), published by the National Museum of American Art in association with the University of New Mexico Press.*

1   I once had a gutsy English teacher who used a drugstore paperback called *Word Power Made Easy* instead of the insipid fare officially available. It contained some nifty words, and she would call upon us in turn for definitions. I will never forget the spectacle of five kids in a row denying that they knew what "nymphomania" meant— the single word, one may be confident, that everyone had learned with avidity. Sixth in line was the class innocent; she blushed and then gave a straightforward,

accurate definition in her sweet, level voice. Bless her for all of us and our cowardly discomfort; I trust that all has gone well for her since last we met on graduation day.

2   Nymphomania titillated me to my pubescent core, but two paired words from the same lesson—anachronism and incongruity—interested me more for the eerie feeling they inspired. Nothing elicits a greater mixture of fascination and distress in me than objects or people that seem to be in the wrong place or time. The *little* things that offend a sense of order are the most disturbing. Thus, I was stunned in 1965 to discover that Alexander Kerensky was alive, well, and living as a Russian émigré in New York. Kerensky, the man who preceded the Bolsheviks in 1917? Kerensky, so linked with Lenin and times long past my thoughts, still among us? (He died, in fact, in 1970, at age 89.)

3   In July 1981, on a ship headed for the Galápagos Islands, I encountered an incongruity that struck me just as forcefully. I was listening to a lecture when a throwaway line cut right into me. "Louis Agassiz," the man said, "visited the Galápagos and made scientific collections there in 1872." What? The primal creationist, the last great holdout against Darwin, in the Galápagos, the land that stands for evolution and prompted Darwin's own conversion? One might as well let a Christian into Mecca. It seems as incongruous as a president of the United States portraying an inebriated pitcher in the 1926 World Series.

4   Louis Agassiz was, without doubt, the greatest and most influential naturalist of nineteenth-century America. A Swiss by birth, he was the first great European theorist in biology to make America his home. He had charm, wit, and connections aplenty, and he took the Boston Brahmins by storm. He was an intimate of Emerson, Longfellow, anyone who really mattered in America's most patrician town. He published and raised money with equal zeal and virtually established natural history as a professional discipline in America; indeed, I am writing this article in the great museum that he built.

5   But Agassiz's summer of fame and fortune turned into a winter of doubt and befuddlement. He was Darwin's contemporary (two years older), but his mind was indentured to the creationist world view and the idealist philosophy that he had learned from Europe's great scientists. The erudition that had so charmed America's rustics became his undoing; Agassiz could not adjust to Darwin's world. All his students and colleagues became evolutionists. He fretted and struggled, for no one enjoys being an intellectual outcast. Agassiz died in 1873, sad and intellectually isolated but still arguing that the history of life reflects a preordained, divine plan and that species are the created incarnations of ideas in God's mind.

6   Agassiz did, however, visit the Galápagos a year before he died. My previous ignorance of this incongruity is at least partly excusable, for he never breathed a word about it in any speech or publication. Why this silence, when his last year is full of documents and pronouncements? Why was he there? What impact did those finches and tortoises have upon him? Did the land that so inspired Darwin, fueling his transition from prospective preacher to evolutionary agnostic, do nothing for Agassiz? Is not this silence as curious as the basic fact of Agassiz's visit? These questions bothered me throughout my stay in the Galápagos, but I could not learn the answers until I returned to the library that Agassiz himself had founded more than a century ago.

7   Agassiz's friend Benjamin Peirce had become superintendent of the Coast Survey. In February of 1871, he wrote to Agassiz offering him the use of the *Hassler,* a steamer fit for deep-sea dredging. I suspect that Peirce had a strong ulterior motive beyond the desire to collect some deep-sea fishes: he hoped that Agassiz's intellectual stagnation might be broken by a long voyage of direct exposure to nature. Agassiz had spent so much time raising money for his museum and politicking for natural history in America that his contact with organisms other than the human kind had virtually ceased. Agassiz's life now belied his famous motto: study nature, not books. Perhaps he could be shaken into modernity by renewed contact with the original source of his fame.

8   Agassiz understood only too well and readily accepted Peirce's offer. Agassiz's friends rejoiced, for all were saddened by the intellectual hardening of such a great mind. Darwin himself wrote to Agassiz's son: "Pray give my most sincere respects to your father. What a wonderful man he is to think of going round Cape Horn; if he does go, I wish he could go through the Strait of Magellan." The *Hassler* left Boston in December 1871, moved down the eastern coast of South America, fulfilled Darwin's hope by sailing through the Strait of Magellan, passed up the western coast of South America, reached the Galápagos (at the equator, 600 miles off the coast of Ecuador) on June 10, 1872, and finally docked at San Francisco on August 24.

9   A possible solution to the enigma of Agassiz's silence immediately suggests itself. The Galápagos are pretty much "on the way" along Agassiz's route. Perhaps the *Hassler* only stopped for provisions—just passing by. Perhaps the cruise was so devoted to deep-sea dredging and Agassiz's observations of glaciers in the southern Andes that the Galápagos provided no special interest or concern.

10   This easy explanation is clearly incorrect. In fact, Agassiz planned the *Hassler* voyage as a test of evolutionary theory. The dredging itself was not designed merely to collect unknown creatures but to gather evidence that Agassiz hoped would establish the continuing intellectual validity of his lingering creationism. In a remarkable letter to Peirce, written just two days before the *Hassler* set sail, Agassiz stated exactly what he expected to find in the deep dredges.

11   Agassiz believed that God had ordained a plan for the history of life and then proceeded to create species in the appropriate sequence throughout geological time. God matched environments to the preconceived plan of creation. The fit of life to environment does not record the evolutionary tracking of changing climates by organisms, but rather the construction of environments by God to fit the preconceived plan of creation: "the animal world designed from the beginning has been the motive for the physical changes which our globe has undergone," Agassiz wrote to Peirce. He then applied this curiously inverted argument to the belief, then widespread but now disproved, that the deep oceans formed a domain devoid of change or challenge—a cold, calm, and constant world. God could only have made such an environment for the most primitive creatures of any group. The deep oceans would therefore harbor living representatives of the simple organisms found as fossils in ancient rocks. Since evolution demands progressive change through time, the persistence of these simple and early forms will demonstrate the bankruptcy of Darwinian theory. (I

don't think Agassiz ever understood that the principle of natural selection does not predict global and inexorable progress but only adaptation to local environments. The persistence of simple forms in a constant deep sea would have satisfied Darwin's evolutionary theory as well as Agassiz's God. But the depths are not constant, and their life is not primitive.)

12   The letter to Peirce displays that mixture of psychological distress and intellectual pugnacity so characteristic of Agassiz's opposition to evolution in his later years. He knows that the world will scoff at his preconceptions, but he will pursue them to the point of specific predictions nonetheless—the discovery of "ancient" organisms alive in the deep sea:

13   *I am desirous to leave in your hands a document which may be very compromising for me, but which I nevertheless am determined to write in the hope of showing within what limits natural history has advanced toward that point of maturity when science may anticipate the discovery of facts. If there is, as I believe to be the case, a plan according to which the affinities among animals and the order of their succession in time were determined from the beginning . . . if this world of ours is the work of intelligence, not only merely the product of force and matter, the human mind, as a part of the whole, should so chime with it, that, from what is known, it may reach the unknown.*

14   But Agassiz did not sail only to test evolution in the abstract. He chose his route as a challenge to Darwin, for he virtually retraced—and by conscious choice—the primary part of the *Beagle*'s itinerary. The Galápagos were not a convenient way station but a central part of the plot. His later silence becomes more curious.

15   The *Beagle* did circumnavigate the globe, but Darwin's voyage was basically a surveying expedition of the South American coast. Agassiz's route therefore retraces the essence of Darwin's pathway—physically if not intellectually. One cannot read Elizabeth Agassiz's account of the *Hassler* expedition without recognizing the uncanny (and obviously not accidental) similarity with Darwin's famous account of the *Beagle*'s voyage. (Elizabeth accompanied Louis on his trip.) Darwin concentrated primarily upon geology and so did Agassiz. The trip may have been advertised as a dredging expedition, but Agassiz was most interested in reaching southern South America to test his theory of a global ice age. He had studied glacial striations and moraines in the Northern Hemisphere and had determined that a great ice sheet had once descended from the north. (Striations are scratches on bedrock made by pebbles frozen into the bases of glaciers. Moraines are hills of debris pushed by flowing ice to the fronts and sides of glaciers.) If the ice age had been global, striations and moraines in South America would indicate a spread from Antarctica at the same time. Agassiz's predictions were, in this case, upheld—and he exulted in copious print (faithfully transcribed by Elizabeth and published in the *Atlantic Monthly*).

16   Darwin was appalled by the rude life and appearance of the "savage" Fuegians and so was Agassiz. Elizabeth recorded their joint impressions: "Nothing could be more coarse and repulsive than their appearance, in which the brutality of the savage

was in no way redeemed by physical strength or manliness. . . . They scrambled and snatched fiercely, like wild animals, for whatever they could catch."

17   If there be any lingering doubt about Agassiz's conscious decision to evaluate Darwin by retracing his experiences, consider this passage, written at sea to his German colleague Carl Gegenbaur:

18   *I have sailed across the Atlantic Ocean through the Strait of Magellan, and along the western coast of South America to the northern latitudes. Marine animals were, naturally, my primary concern, but I also had a special purpose. I wanted to study the entire Darwinian theory, free from all external influences and former surroundings. Was it not on a similar voyage that Darwin developed his present opinions! I took few books with me . . . primarily Darwin's major works.*

19   I can find few details about Agassiz's stay in the Galápagos. We know that he arrived on June 10, 1872, spent a week or more, and visited five islands, one more than Darwin did. Elizabeth claims that Louis "enjoyed extremely his cruise among these islands of such rare geological and zoological interest." We know that he collected (or rather sat on the rocks while his assistants gathered) the famous iguanas that go swimming in the ocean to eat marine algae (some of his specimens are still in glass jars in our museum). We know that he crossed and greatly admired the bare fields of recently cooled ropy lava "full of the most singular and fantastic details." I walked across a similar field, one that Agassiz could not have seen since it formed during the 1890s. I was mesmerized by the frozen signs of former activity—the undulating, ropy patterns of flow, the burst bubbles, and lengthy cracks of contraction. And I saw Pele's tears, the most beautiful geological object, at small scale, that I have ever witnessed. When highly liquid lava is ejected from small vents, it may emerge as droplets of basalt that build drip castles of iridescent stone about their outlet—tears from Pele, the Hawaiian goddess of volcanoes (not from Martinique's Mount Pelée, which has an extra *e*).

20   Thus, I return to my original inquiry: if Agassiz went to the Galápagos as a central part of his plan to evaluate evolution by putting himself in Darwin's shoes, what effect did Darwin's most important spot have upon him? In response to this question we have only Agassiz's public silence (and one private communication, to which I will shortly return).

21   Two nonintellectual reasons may partly explain Agassiz's uncharacteristic reticence. First, despite his productive observations on South American glaciers, the *Hassler* expedition was basically a failure and a profound disappointment—and Agassiz may have chosen largely to forget about it. The dredging equipment never worked properly, and Agassiz recovered no specimens from the deepest oceans. The crew tried its best, but the ship was a misery. Jules Marcou, Agassiz's faithful biographer, wrote: "It was a great, almost a cruel, carelessness to embark a man so distinguished, so old [Agassiz was 64; perhaps concepts of age have changed], and so much an invalid as Agassiz was, in an unseaworthy craft, sailing under the United States flag."

22   Secondly, Agassiz was ill during much of the voyage, and his listlessness and discomfort increased as he left his beloved southern glaciers and moved into the sultry tropics. (The Galápagos, however, despite their equatorial location, lie in the path of a cool oceanic current and are generally temperate; the northernmost species of penguin inhabits its shores.) Shortly after his return to Harvard, Agassiz wrote to Pedro II, emperor of Brazil (and an old buddy from a previous voyage):

23   *When I traversed the Strait of Magellan . . . work again became easy for me. The beauty of its sites, the resemblance of the mountains to those of Switzerland, the interest that the glaciers awakened in me, the happiness in seeing my predictions affirmed beyond all my hopes—all these conspired to set me on the right course again, even to rejuvenate me. . . . Afterwards, I gradually declined as we advanced towards the tropical regions; the heat exhausted me greatly, and during the month that we spent in Panama I was quite incapable of the least effort.*

24   (For all citations from letters, I have relied upon the originals in Harvard's Houghton Library; none has been published in full before, although several have been excerpted in print. Agassiz wrote with equal facility in French [to Pedro II], German [to Gegenbaur], and English [to Peirce], and I have supplied the translations. I thank my secretary Agnes Pilot for transcribing the Gegenbaur letter into sensible Roman. Agassiz wrote it in the old German script that is all squiggles to me.)

25   So far as I can tell, Agassiz's only statement about the Galápagos occurs in a private letter to Benjamin Peirce, composed at sea on July 29, 1872, the day after he had written to Gegenbaur (and said nothing about the Galápagos). The letter begins with the lament of all landlubbers: "I fancy this note may reach you in Martha's Vineyard, and I heartily wish I could be there with you, and take some rest from this everlasting rocking." Agassiz continues with his only statement:

26   *Our visit to the Galápagos has been full of geological and zoological interest. It is most impressive to see an extensive archipelago, of most recent origin, inhabited by creatures so different from any known in other parts of the world. Here we have a positive limit to the length of time that may have been granted for the transformation of these animals, if indeed they are in any way derived from others dwelling in different parts of the world. The Galápagos are so recent that some of the islands are barely covered with the most scanty vegetation, itself peculiar to these islands. Some parts of their surface are entirely bare, and a great many of the craters and lava streams are so fresh, that the atmospheric agents have not yet made an impression on them. Their age does not, therefore, go back to earlier geological periods; they belong to our times, geologically speaking; Whence, then, do their inhabitants (animals as well as plants) come? If descended from some other type, belonging to any neighboring land, then it does not require such unspeakably long periods for the transformation of species as the modern advocates of transmutation*

claim; and the mystery of change, with such marked and characteristic differences between existing species, is only increased, and brought to level with that of creation. If they are autochthones, from what germs did they start into existence? I think that careful observers, in view of these facts, will have to acknowledge that our science is not yet ripe for a fair discussion of the origin of organized beings.

27   The quotation is long, but it is, so far as I know, exclusive. Its most remarkable aspect is an extreme weakness, almost speciousness, of argument. Agassiz makes but a single point: many animals of the Galápagos live nowhere else. Yet the islands are so young that a slow process of evolution could not have transformed them from related ancestors in the time available. Thus, they were created where we find them (the obvious bottom line, despite Agassiz's final disclaimer that we know too little to reach any firm conclusion).

28   Two problems: First, although the Galápagos are young (two to five million years for the oldest islands by current reckoning), they are not so pristine as Agassiz indicates. In the letter, Agassiz describes lava flows of the past hundred years or so, and these are virtually devoid of vegetation and so fresh that one can almost see the flow and feel the heat. But Agassiz surely knew that several of the islands (including some on his itinerary) are more densely vegetated and, although not ancient, were surely not formed in a geological yesterday.

29   Second, Agassiz leaves out the most important aspect of Darwin's argument. The point is not that so many species of the Galápagos are unique but rather that their nearest relatives are invariably found on the adjacent South American mainland. If God created the Galápagos species where we find them, why did he imbue them with signs of South American affinity (especially since the temperate climates and lava habitats of the Galápagos are so different from the tropical environments of the ancestral forms)? What sense can such a pattern make unless the species of the Galápagos are modified descendants of South American forms that managed to cross the oceanic barrier? Darwin wrote in *Voyage of the Beagle:*

30   *Why, on these small points of land, which within a late geological period must have been covered by the ocean, which are formed by basaltic lava, and therefore differ in geological character from the American continent, and which are placed under a peculiar climate,—why were their aboriginal inhabitants . . . created on American types of organization.*

31   And the famous, poetic statement earlier in the chapter: "We seem to be brought somewhat near to the great fact—that mystery of mysteries—the first appearance of new beings on this earth."

32   Agassiz could not have misunderstood, for, like Darwin, he was a professional biogeographer. He had also used arguments of geographical distribution as his primary defense for creationism. Why did he skirt Darwin's principal argument? Why did he say so little about the Galápagos and argue so poorly?

33   I think that we must consider two possibilities as resolutions to the conundrum of

Agassiz's silence (or failure to consider the critical points in his one private statement). Perhaps he knew that his argument to Peirce was hokey and inadequate. Perhaps the Galápagos, and the entire *Hassler* voyage, had produced the same change of heart that Darwin had experienced in similar circumstances and Agassiz simply couldn't muster the courage to admit it.

34   I cannot accept such a resolution. As I said earlier, we see abundant signs of psychological distress and deep sadness in Agassiz's last defenses of creationism. No one enjoys being an intellectual pariah, especially when cast in the role of a superannuated fuddy-duddy (the part of ignored but prophetic seer at least elicits moral courage). Yet, however weak his arguments (and they deteriorated as the evidence for evolution accumulated), I sense no failure of Agassiz's resolve. The letter to Peirce seems to represent still another of Agassiz's flawed, but perfectly sincere, defenses of an increasing indefensible, yet steadfastly maintained, view of life. (Agassiz's last article, posthumously published in the *Atlantic Monthly* in 1874, was a ringing apologia for creationism entitled "Evolution and Permanence of Type.")

35   I think that we must accept the second resolution: Agassiz said so little about the Galápagos because his visit made preciously little impact upon him. The message is familiar but profound nonetheless. Scientific discovery is not a one-way transfer from unambiguous nature to minds that are always open. It is a reciprocal interaction between a multifarious and confusing nature and minds sufficiently receptive (as many are not) to extract a weak but sensible pattern from the prevailing noise. There are no signs on the Galápagos that proclaim: Evolution at work. Open your eyes and ye shall see it. Evolution is an inescapable inference, not a raw datum. Darwin, young, restless, and searching, was receptive to the signal. Agassiz, committed and defensive, was not. Had he not already announced in the first letter to Peirce that he knew what he must find? I do not think he was free to reach Darwin's conclusions, and the Galápagos Islands, therefore, carried no important message for him. Science is a balanced interaction of mind and nature.

36   Agassiz lived for little more than a year after the *Hassler* docked. James Russell Lowell, traveling abroad, learned of his friend's death from a newspaper and wrote in poetic tribute (quoted from E. Lurie's fine biography of Agassiz, *Louis Agassiz: A Life in Science,* University of Chicago Press, 1960):

37   . . . with vague, mechanic eyes,
        I scanned the festering news we half despise
        When suddenly,
        As happens if the brain, from overweight
        Of blood, infect the eye,
        Three tiny words grew lurid as I read,
        And reeled commingling: Agassiz is dead!

38   I do not know. Perhaps a bit of his incorporeal self went up to a higher realm, as some religions assert. Perhaps he saw there old Adam Sedgwick, the great British geologist (and reverend), who at age 87 wrote to Agassiz a year before the *Hassler* sailed:

39   *It will never be my happiness to see your face again in this world. But let me, as a Christian man, hope that we may meet hereafter in heaven, and see such visions of God's glory in the moral and material universe, as shall reduce to a mere germ everything which has been elaborated by the skill of man.*

40   Be that as it may, Agassiz's ideas had suffered an intellectual death before he ever reached the Galápagos. Life is a series of trades. We have lost the comfort of Agassiz's belief that a superior intelligence directly regulates every stop of life's history according to a plan that places us above all other creatures. ("If it had been otherwise," Agassiz wrote to Pedro II in June 1873, "there would be nothing but despair.") We have found a message in the animals and plants of the Galápagos, and all other places, that enables us to appreciate them, not as disconnected bits of wonder, but as integrated products of a satisfactory and general theory of life's history. That, to me at least, is a good trade.

Suggestions for Discussion or Writing

1. Why was Louis Agassiz famous? How do you know that he was a pivotal figure in his field?

2. What is the conflict between Agassiz's views and Darwin's views? Describe each of the views. How much do you know about the differences between creationism and evolution?

3. Why is the area of the Galápagos significant?

4. Why does Gould think Agassiz was silent about his trip?

5. What assumptions does Gould make about Agassiz's reaction to his voyage? How does he support or reject each of his solutions (resolutions)?

Of This Time, Of That Place

Lionel Trilling

Lionel Trilling (1905–1975), an influential literary critic, supported the notion that literature is a way to study the moral responsibility of the individual to the society. Born in New York City, Trilling was educated at Columbia University, where he later taught literature from 1932 to 1975. He was the author of The Liberal Imagination *(1950),* The Opposing Self *(1955),* Beyond Culture *(1965), and* Sincerity and Authenticity *(1972), as well as one novel,* The Middle of the Journey *(1947), and several short stories.*

I

1   It was a fine September day. By noon it would be summer again but now it was a true autumn with a touch of chill in the air. As Joseph Howe stood on the porch of the house in which he lodged, ready to leave for his first class of the year, he thought with pleasure of the long indoor days that were coming. It was a moment when he could feel glad of his profession.

2   On the lawn the peach tree was still in fruit and young Hilda Aiken was taking a picture of it. She held the camera tight against her chest. She wanted the sun behind her but she did not want her own long morning shadow in the foreground. She raised the camera but that did not help, and she lowered it but that made things worse. She twisted her body to the left, then to the right. In the end she had to step out of the direct line of the sun. At last she snapped the shutter and wound the film with intense care.

3   Howe, watching her from the porch, waited for her to finish and called good morning. She turned, startled, and almost sullenly lowered her glance. In the year Howe had lived at the Aikens', Hilda had accepted him as one of her family, but since his absence of the summer she had grown shy. Then suddenly she lifted her head and smiled at him, and the humorous smile confirmed his pleasure in the day. She picked up her bookbag and set off for school.

4   The handsome houses on the streets to the college were not yet fully awake but they looked very friendly. Howe went by the Bradby house where he would be a guest this evening at the first dinner-party of the year. When he had gone the length of the picket fence, the whitest in town, he turned back. Along the path was a fine row of asters and he went through the gate and picked one for his buttonhole. The Bradbys would be pleased if they happened to see him invading their lawn and the knowledge of this made him even more comfortable.

5   He reached the campus as the hour was striking. The students were hurrying to their classes. He himself was in no hurry. He stopped at his dim cubicle of an office and lit a cigarette. The prospect of facing his class had suddenly presented itself to him and his hands were cold, the lawful seizure of power he was about to make seemed momentous. Waiting did not help. He put out his cigarette, picked up a pad of theme paper and went to his classroom.

6   As he entered, the rattle of voices ceased and the twenty-odd freshmen settled themselves and looked at him appraisingly. Their faces seemed gross, his heart sank at their mass impassivity, but he spoke briskly.

7   "My name is Howe," he said and turned and wrote it on the blackboard. The carelessness of the scrawl confirmed his authority. He went on: "My office is 412 Slemp Hall and my office hours are Monday, Wednesday, and Friday from eleven-thirty to twelve-thirty."

8   He wrote "M., W., F., 11:30–12:30." He said: "I'll be very glad to see any of you at that time. Or if you can't come then, you can arrange with me for some other time."

9   He turned again to the blackboard and spoke over his shoulder. "The text for the course is Jarman's *Modern Plays,* revised edition. The co-op has it in stock." He wrote that name, underlined "revised edition" and waited for it to be taken down in the note-books.

10   When the bent heads were raised again, he began his speech of prospectus. "It is hard to explain _____" he said, and paused as they composed themselves. "It is hard to explain what a course like this is intended to do. We are going to try to learn something about modern literature and something about prose composition."

11   As he spoke, his hands warmed and he was able to look directly at the class. Last year on the first day the faces had seemed just as cloddish, but as the term wore on they became gradually alive and quite likeable. It did not seem possible that the same thing could happen again.

12   "I shall not lecture in this course," he continued. "Our work will be carried on by discussion and we will try to learn by an exchange of opinion. But you will soon recognize that my opinion is worth more than anyone else's here."

13   He remained grave as he said it, but two boys understood and laughed. The rest took permission from them and laughed too. All Howe's private ironies protested the vulgarity of the joke but the laughter made him feel benign and powerful.

14   When the little speech was finished, Howe picked up the pad of paper he had brought. He announced that they would write an extemporaneous theme. Its subject was traditional: "Who I am and why I came to Dwight College." By now the class was more at ease and it gave a ritualistic groan of protest. Then there was a stir as fountain-pens were brought out and the writing arms of the chairs were cleared and the paper was passed about. At last all the heads bent to work and the room became still.

15   Howe sat idly at his desk. The sun shone through the tall clumsy windows. The cool of the morning was already passing. There was a scent of autumn and of varnish, and the stillness of the room was deep and oddly touching. Now and then a student's head was raised and scratched in the old elaborate student's pantomime that calls the teacher to witness honest intellectual effort.

16   Suddenly a tall boy stood within the frame of the open door. "Is this," he said, and thrust a large nose into a college catalogue, "is this the meeting place of English 1A? The section instructed by Dr. Joseph Howe?"

17   He stood on the very sill of the door, as if refusing to enter until he was perfectly sure of all his rights. The class looked up from work, found him absurd and gave a low mocking cheer.

18   The teacher and the new student, with equal pointedness, ignored the disturbance. Howe nodded to the boy, who pushed his head forward and then jerked it back in a wide elaborate arc to clear his brow of a heavy lock of hair. He advanced into the room and halted before Howe, almost at attention. In a loud clear voice he announced: "I am Tertan, Ferdinand R., reporting at the direction of Head of Department Vincent."

19   The heraldic formality of this statement brought forth another cheer. Howe looked at the class with a sternness he could not really feel, for there was indeed something ridiculous about this boy. Under his displeased regard the rows of heads dropped to work again. Then he touched Tertan's elbow, led him up to the desk and stood so as to shield their conversation from the class.

20   "We are writing an extemporaneous theme," he said. "The subject is: 'Who I am and why I came to Dwight College.'"

21   He stripped a few sheets from the pad and offered them to the boy. Tertan hesitated and then took the paper, but he held it only tentatively. As if with the effort of making

something clear, he gulped, and a low smile fixed itself on his face. It was at once knowing and shy.

22   "Professor," he said, "to be perfectly fair to my classmates"—he made a large gesture over the room—"and to you"—he inclined his head to Howe—"this would not be for me an extemporaneous subject."

23   Howe tried to understand. "You mean you've already thought about it—you've heard we always give the same subject? That doesn't matter."

24   Again the boy ducked his head and gulped. It was the gesture of one who wishes to make a difficult explanation with perfect candor. "Sir," he said, and made the distinction with great care, "the topic I did not expect but I have given much ratiocination to the subject."

25   Howe smiled and said: "I don't think there is an unfair advantage. Just go ahead and write."

26   Tertan narrowed his eyes and glanced sidewise at Howe. His strange mouth smiled. Then in quizzical acceptance, he ducked his head, threw back the heavy dank lock, dropped into a seat with a great loose noise and began to write rapidly.

27   The room fell silent again and Howe resumed his idleness. When the bell rang, the students who had groaned when the task had been set now groaned again because they had not finished. Howe took up the papers and held the class while he made the first assignment. When he dismissed it, Tertan bore down on him, his slack mouth ready for speech.

28   "Some professors," he said "are pedants. They are Dryasdusts. However, some professors are free souls and creative spirits. Kant, Hegel, and Nietzsche were all professors." With this pronouncement he paused. "It is my opinion," he continued, "that you would occupy the second category."

29   Howe looked at the boy in surprise and said with good-natured irony: "With Kant, Hegel, and Nietzsche?"

30   Not only Tertan's hand and head but his whole awkward body waved away the stupidity. "It is the kind and not the quantity of the kind," he said sternly.

31   Rebuked, Howe said as simply and seriously as he could: "It would be nice to think so." He added: "Of course, I am not a professor."

32   This was clearly a disappointment but Tertan met it. "In the French sense," he said with composure. "Generically, a teacher."

33   Suddenly he bowed. It was such a bow, Howe fancied, as a stage director might teach an actor playing a medieval student who takes leave of Abelard—stiff, solemn, with elbows close to the body and feet together. Then, quite as suddenly, he turned and left.

34   A queer fish, and as soon as Howe reached his office he sifted through the batch of themes and drew out Tertan's. The boy had filled many sheets with his unformed headlong scrawl. "Who am I?" he had begun. "Here, in a mundane, not to say commercialized academe, is asked the question which from time long immemorably out of mind has accreted doubts and thoughts in the psyche of man to pester him as a nuisance. Whether in St. Augustine (or Austin as sometimes called) of Miss Bashkirt-sieff or Frederic Amiel or Empedocles, or in less lights of the intellect than these, this posed question has been ineluctable."

35   Howe took out his pencil. He circled "academe" and wrote "vocab" in the margin. He underlined "time long immemorably out of mind" and wrote "Diction!" But this

seemed inadequate for what was wrong. He put down his pencil and read ahead to discover the principle of error in the theme. "To-day as ever, in spite of gloomy prophets of the dismal science (economics) the question is uninvalidated. Out of the starry depths of heaven hurtles this spear of query demanding to be caught on the shield of the mind ere it pierces the skull and the limbs be unstrung."

36   Baffled but quite caught, Howe read on. "Materialism, by which is meant the philosophic concept and not the moral idea, provides no aegis against the question which lies beyond the tangible (metaphysics). Existence without alloy is the question presented. Environment and heredity relegated aside, the rags and old clothes of practical life discarded, the name and the instrumentality of livelihood do not, as the prophets of the dismal science insist on in this connection, give solution to the interrogation which not from the professor merely but veritably from the cosmos is given. I think, therefore I am (cogito etc.) but who am I? Tertan I am, but what is Tertan? Of this time, of that place, of some parentage, what does it matter?"

37   Existence without alloy: the phrase establishes itself. Howe put aside Tertan's paper and at random picked up another. "I am Arthur J. Casebeer, Jr.," he read. "My father is Arthur J. Casebeer and my grandfather was Arthur J. Casebeer before him. My mother is Mina Wimble Casebeer. Both of them are college graduates and my father is in insurance. I was born in St. Louis eighteen years ago and we still make our residence there."

38   Arthur J. Casebeer, who knew who he was, was less interesting than Tertan, but more coherent. Howe picked up Tertan's paper again. It was clear that none of the routine marginal comments, no "sent. str." or "punct." or "vocab." could cope with this torrential rhetoric. He read ahead, contenting himself with underscoring the errors against the time when he should have the necessary "conference" with Tertan.

39   It was a busy and official day of cards and sheets, arrangements and small decisions, and it gave Howe pleasure. Even when it was time to attend the first of the weekly Convocations he felt the charm of the beginning of things when intention is still innocent and uncorrupted by effort. He sat among the young instructors on the platform and joined in their humorous complaints at having to assist at the ceremony, but actually he got a clear satisfaction from the ritual of prayer and prosy speech and even from wearing his academic gown. And when the Convocation was over the pleasure continued as he crossed the campus, exchanging greetings with many he had not seen since the spring. They were people who did not yet and perhaps never would, mean much to him, but in a year they had grown amiably to be part of his life. They were his fellow-townsmen.

40   The day had cooled again at sunset and there was a bright chill in the September twilight. Howe carried his voluminous gown over his arm, he swung his doctoral hood by its purple neckpiece and on his head he wore his mortarboard with its heavy gold tassel bobbing just over his eye. These were the weighty and absurd symbols of his new profession and they pleased him. At twenty-six Joseph Howe had discovered that he was neither so well off nor so bohemian as he had once thought. A small income, adequate when supplemented by a sizable cash legacy, was genteel poverty when the cash was all spent. And the literary life—the room at the Lafayette or the small apartment without a lease, the long summers on the Cape, the long afternoons and the social evenings—began to weary him. His writing filled his mornings and should

perhaps have filled his life, yet it did not. To the amusement of his friends and with a certain sense that he was betraying his own freedom, he had used the last of his legacy for a year at Harvard. The small but respectable reputation of his two volumes of verse had proved useful—he continued at Harvard on a fellowship and when he emerged as Dr. Howe he received an excellent appointment, with prospects, at Dwight.

41   He had his moments of fear when all that had ever been said of the dangers of the academic life had occurred to him. But after a year in which he had tested every possibility of corruption and seduction he was ready to rest easy. His third volume of verse, most of it written in his first year of teaching, was not only ampler, but, he thought, better than its predecessors.

42   There was a clear hour before the Bradby dinner-party and Howe looked forward to it. But he was not to enjoy it, for lying with his mail on the hall table was a copy of this quarter's issue of *Life and Letters,* to which his landlord subscribed. Its severe cover announced that its editor, Frederic Woolley, had this month contributed an essay called "Two Poets," and Howe, picking it up, curious to see who the two poets might be, felt his own name start out at him with cabalistic power—Joseph Howe. As he continued to turn the pages his hand trembled.

43   Standing in the dark hall, holding the neat little magazine, Howe knew that his literary contempt for Frederic Woolley meant nothing, for he suddenly understood how he respected Woolley in the way of the world. He knew this by the trembling of his hand. And of the little world as well as the great, for although the literary groups of New York might dismiss Woolley, his name carried high authority in the academic world. At Dwight it was even a revered name, for it had been here at the college that Frederic Woolley had made the distinguished scholarly career from which he had gone on to literary journalism. In middle life he had been induced to take the editorship of *Life and Letters,* a literary monthly not widely read but heavily endowed and in its pages he had carried on the defence of what he sometimes called the older values. He was not without wit, he had great knowledge and considerable taste and even in the full movement of the "new" literature he had won a certain respect for his refusal to accept it. In France, even in England, he would have been connected with a more robust tradition of conservatism, but America gave him an audience not much better than genteel. It was known in the college that to the subsidy of *Life and Letters* the Bradbys contributed a great part.

44   As Howe read, he saw that he was involved in nothing less than an event. When the Fifth Series of *Studies in Order and Value* came to be collected, this latest of Frederic Woolley's essays would not be merely another step in the old direction. Clearly and unmistakably, it was a turning point. All his literary life Woolley had been concerned with the relation of literature to morality, religion and the private and delicate pieties, and he had been unalterably opposed to all that he had called "inhuman humanitarianism." But here, suddenly, dramatically late, he had made an about-face, turning to the public life and to the humanitarian politics he had so long despised. This was the kind of incident the histories of literature made much of. Frederic Woolley was opening for himself a new career and winning a kingdom of new youth. He contrasted two poets, Thomas Wormser who was admirable, Joseph Howe who was almost dangerous. He spoke of the "precious subjectivism" of Howe's verse. "In times

like ours," he wrote, "with millions facing penury and want, one feels that the qualities of the *tour d'ivoire* are well-nigh inhuman, nearly insulting. The *tour d'ivoire* becomes the *tour d'ivresse* and it is not self-intoxicated poets that our people need." The essay said more: "the problem is one of meaning. I am not ignorant that the creed of the esoteric poets declares that a poem does not and should not *mean* anything, that it *is* something. But poetry is what the poet makes it, and if he is a true poet he makes what his society needs. And what is needed now is the tradition in which Mr. Wormser writes, the true tradition of poetry. The Howes do no harm, but they do no good when positive good is demanded of all responsible men. Or do the Howes indeed do no harm? Perhaps Plato would have said they do, that in some ways theirs is the Phrygian music that turns men's minds from the struggle. Certainly it is true that Thomas Wormser writes in the lucid Dorian mode which sends men into battle with evil."

45   It was easy to understand why Woolley had chosen to praise Thomas Wormser. The long, lilting lines of *Corn Under Willows* hymned, as Woolley put it, the struggle for wheat in the Iowa fields and expressed the real lives of real people. But why out of the dozen more notable examples he had chosen Howe's little volumes as the examples of "precious subjectivism" was hard to guess. In a way it was funny, this multiplication of himself into "the Howes." And yet his becoming the multiform political symbol by whose creation Frederic Woolley gave the sign of a sudden new life, this use of him as a sacrifice whose blood was necessary for the rites of rejuvenation, made him feel oddly unclean.

46   Nor could Howe get rid of a certain practical resentment. As a poet he had a special and respectable place in the college life. But it might be another thing to be marked as the poet of a wilful and selfish obscurity.

47   As he walked to the Bradbys Howe was a little tense and defensive. It seemed to him that all the world knew of the "attack" and agreed with it. And indeed the Bradbys had read the essay, but Professor Bradby, a kind and pretentious man said, "I see my old friend knocked you about a bit, my boy," and his wife Eugenia looked at Howe with her child-like blue eyes and said: "I shall *scold* Frederic for the untrue things he wrote about you. You aren't the least obscure." They beamed at him. In their genial snobbery they seemed to feel that he had distinguished himself. He was the leader of Howeism. He enjoyed the dinner-party as much as he had thought he would.

48   And in the following days, as he was more preoccupied with his duties, the incident was forgotten. His classes had ceased to be mere groups. Student after student detached himself from the mass and required or claimed a place in Howe's awareness. Of them all it was Tertan who first and most violently signalled his separate existence. A week after classes had begun Howe saw his silhouette on the frosted glass of his office door. It was motionless for a long time, perhaps stopped by the problem of whether or not to knock before entering. Howe called, "Come in!" and Tertan entered with his shambling stride.

49   He stood beside the desk, silent and at attention. When Howe asked him to sit down, he responded with a gesture of head and hand as if to say that such amenities were beside the point. Nevertheless he did take the chair. He put his ragged crammed brief-case between his legs. His face, which Howe now observed fully for the first time, was confusing, for it was made up of florid curves, the nose arched in the bone

and voluted in the nostril, the mouth loose and soft and rather moist. Yet the face was so thin and so narrow as to seem the very type of asceticism. Lashes of unusual length veiled the eyes and, indeed, it seemed as if there were a veil over the whole countenance. Before the words actually came, the face screwed itself into an attitude of preparation for them.

50   "You can confer with me now?" Tertan said.

51   "Yes, I'd be glad to. There are several things in your last two themes I want to talk to you about." Howe reached for the packet of themes on his desk and sought for Tertan's. But the boy was waving them away.

52   "These are done perforce," he said, "under the pressure of your requirement. They are not significant, mere duties." Again his great hand flapped vaguely to dismiss his themes. He leaned forward and gazed at his teacher.

53   "You are," he said, "a man of letters? You are a poet?" It was more declaration than question.

54   "I should like to think so," Howe said.

55   At first Tertan accepted the answer with a show of appreciation, as though the understatement made a secret between himself and Howe. Then he chose to misunderstand. With his shrewd and disconcerting control of expression, he presented to Howe a puzzled grimace. "What does that mean?" he said.

56   Howe retracted the irony. "Yes. I am a poet." It sounded strange to say.

57   "That," Tertan said, "is a wonder." He corrected himself with his ducking head. "I mean that is wonderful!"

58   Suddenly he dived at the miserable brief-case between his legs, put it on his knees and began to fumble with the catch, all intent on the difficulty it presented. Howe noted his suit was worn thin, his shirt almost un-clean. He became aware, even, of a vague and musty odor of garments worn too long in unaired rooms. Tertan conquered the lock and began to concentrate upon a search into the interior. At last he held in his hand what he was after, a torn and crumpled copy of *Life and Letters*.

59   "I learned it from here," he said, holding it out.

60   Howe looked at him sharply, his hackles a little up. But the boy's face was not only perfectly innocent, it even shone with a conscious admiration. Apparently nothing of the import of the essay had touched him except the wonderful fact that his teacher was a "man of letters." Yet this seemed too stupid and Howe, to test it, said: "The man who wrote that doesn't think it's wonderful."

61   Tertan made a moist hissing sound as he cleared his mouth of saliva. His head, oddly loose on his neck, wove a pattern of contempt in the air. "A critic," he said, "who admits *prima facie* that he does not understand." Then he said grandly: "It is the inevitable fate."

62   It was absurd, yet Howe was not only aware of the absurdity but of a tension suddenly and wonderfully relaxed. Now that the "attack" was on the table between himself and this strange boy and subject to the boy's funny and absolutely certain contempt, the hidden force of his feeling was revealed to him in the very moment that it vanished. All unsuspected, here had been a film over the world, a transparent but discoloring haze of danger. But he had no time to stop over the brightened aspect of things. Tertan was going on. "I also am a man of letters. Putative."

63   "You have written a good deal?" Howe meant to be no more than polite and he was surprised at the tenderness he heard in his words.

64   Solemnly the boy nodded, threw back the dank lock and sucked in a deep anticipatory breath. "First, a work of homiletics, which is a defence of the principles of religious optimism against the pessimism of Schopenhauer and the humanism of Nietzsche."

65   "Humanism? Why do you call it humanism?"

66   "It is my nomenclature for making a deity of man," Tertan replied diligently. "Then three fictional works, novels. And numerous essays in science, combating materialism. Is it your duty to read these if I bring them to you?"

67   Howe answered simply: "No, it isn't exactly my duty, but I shall be happy to read them."

68   Tertan stood up and remained silent. He rested his bag on the chair. With a certain compunction—for it did not seem entirely proper that, of two men of letters, one should have the right to blue-pencil the other, to grade him or to question the quality of his "sentence structure"—Howe reached for Tertan's papers. But before he could take them up, the boy suddenly made his bow-to-Abelard, the stiff inclination of the body with the hands seeming to emerge from the scholar's gown. Then he was gone.

69   But after his departure something was still left of him. The timbre of his curious sentence, the downright finality of so quaint a phrase as "It is the inevitable fate" still rang in the air. Howe gave the warmth of his feeling to the new visitor who stood at the door announcing himself with a genteel clearing of the throat.

70   "Dr. Howe, I believe?" the student said. A large hand advanced into the room and grasped Howe's hand. "Blackburn, sir, Theodore Blackburn, vice-president of the Student Council. A great pleasure, sir."

71   Out of a pair of ruddy cheeks a pair of small eyes twinkled good-naturedly. The large face, the large body were not so much fat as hefty and suggested something "typical," monk, politician, or innkeeper.

72   Blackburn took the seat beside Howe's desk. "I may have seemed to introduce myself in my public capacity, sir," he said. "But it is really as an individual that I came to see you. That is to say, as one of your students to be."

73   Blackburn spoke with an "English" intonation and went on: "I was once an English major, sir."

74   For a moment Howe was startled, for the roast-beef look of the boy and the manner of his speech gave a second's credibility to one sense of his statement. Then the collegiate meaning of the phrase asserted itself, but some perversity made Howe say what was not really in good taste even with so forward a student: "Indeed? What regiment?"

75   Blackburn stared and then gave a little pouf-pouf of laughter. He waved the misapprehension away. "*Very* good, sir. It certainly is an ambiguous term." He chuckled in appreciation of Howe's joke, then cleared his throat to put it aside. "I look forward to taking your course in the romantic poets, sir," he said earnestly. "To me the romantic poets are the very crown of English literature."

76   Howe made a dry sound, and the boy, catching some meaning in it, said: "Little as I know them, of course. But even Shakespeare who is so dear to us of the

Anglo-Saxon tradition is in a sense but the preparation for Shelley, Keats and Byron. And Wadsworth."

77   Almost sorry for him, Howe dropped his eyes. With some embarrassment, for the boy was not actually his student, he said softly: "Wordsworth."

78   "Sir?"

79   "Wordsworth, not Wadsworth. You said Wadsworth."

80   "Did I, sir?" Gravely he shook his head to rebuke himself for the error. "Words-worth, of course—slip of the tongue." Then quite in command again, he went on. "I have a favor to ask of you, Dr. Howe. You see, I began my college course as an English major"—he smiled—"as I said."

81   "Yes?"

82   "But after my first year I shifted. I shifted to the social sciences. Sociology and government—I find them stimulating and very *real*." He paused, out of respect for reality. "But now I find that perhaps I have neglected the other side."

83   "The other side?" Howe said.

84   "Imagination, fancy, culture. A well-rounded man." He trailed off as if there were perfect understanding between them. "And so, sir, I have decided to end my senior year with your course in the romantic poets."

85   His voice was filled with an indulgence which Howe ignored as he said flatly and gravely: "But that course isn't given until the spring term."

86   "Yes, sir, and that is where the favor comes in. Would you let me take your romantic prose course? I can't take it for credit, sir, my program is full, but just for background it seems to me that I ought to take it. I do hope," he concluded in a manly way, "that you will consent."

87   "Well, its no great favor, Mr. Blackburn. You can come if you wish, though there's not much point in it if you don't do the reading."

88   The bell rang for the hour and Howe got up.

89   "May I begin with this class, sir?" Blackburn's smile was candid and boyish.

90   Howe nodded carelessly and together, silently, they walked to the classroom down the hall. When they reached the door Howe stood back to let his student enter, but Blackburn moved adroitly behind him and grasped him by the arm to urge him over the threshold. They entered together with Blackburn's hand firmly on Howe's biceps, the student inducting the teacher into his own room. Howe felt a surge of temper rise in him and almost violently he disengaged his arm and walked to the desk, while Blackburn found a seat in the front row and smiled at him.

II

91   The question was: At whose door must the tragedy be laid?

92   All night the snow had fallen heavily and only now was abating in sparse little flurries. The windows were valanced high with white. It was very quiet, something of the quiet of the world had reached the class and Howe found that everyone was glad to talk or listen. In the room there was a comfortable sense of pleasure in being human.

93   Casebeer believed that the blame for the tragedy rested with heredity. Picking up the book he read: "The sins of the fathers are visited on their children." This opinion

was received with general favor. Nevertheless Johnson ventured to say that the fault was all Pastor Manders' because the Pastor had made Mrs. Alving go back to her husband and was always hiding the truth. To this Hibbard objected with logic enough: "Well, then, it was really all her husband's fault. He *did* all the bad things." De Witt, his face bright with an impatient idea, said that the fault was all society's. "By society I don't mean upper-crust society," he said. He looked around a little defiantly, taking in any members of the class who might be members of upper-crust society. "Not in that sense. I mean the social unit."

94   Howe nodded and said: "Yes, of course."

95   "If the society of the time had progressed far enough in science," De Witt went on, "then there would be no problem for Mr. Ibsen to write about. Captain Alving plays around a little, gives way to perfectly natural biological urges, and he gets a social disease, a venereal disease. If the disease is cured, no problem. The problem of heredity disappears and li'l Oswald just doesn't get paresis. No paresis, no problem—no problem, no play."

96   This was carrying the ark into battle and the class looked at De Witt with respectful curiosity. It was his usual way and on the whole they were sympathetic with his struggle to prove to Howe that science was better than literature. Still, there was something in his reckless manner that alienated them a little.

97   "Or take birth-control, for instance," De Witt went on. "If Mrs. Alving had had some knowledge of contraception, she wouldn't have had to have li'l Oswald at all. No li'l Oswald, no play."

98   The class was suddenly quieter. In the back row Stettenhover swung his great football shoulders in a righteous sulking gesture, first to the right, then to the left. He puckered his mouth ostentatiously. Intellect was always ending up by talking dirty.

99   Tertan's hand went up and Howe said: "Mr. Tertan." The boy shambled to his feet and began his long characteristic gulp. Howe made a motion with his fingers, as small as possible, and Tertan ducked his head and smiled in apology. He sat down. The class laughed. With more than half the term gone, Tertan had not been able to remember that one did not rise to speak. He seemed unable to carry on the life of the intellect without this mark of respect for it. To Howe the boy's habit of rising seemed to accord with the formal shabbiness of his dress. He never wore the casual sweaters and jackets of his classmates. Into the free and comfortable air of the college classroom he brought the stuffy sordid strictness of some crowded metropolitan high school.

100   "Speaking from one sense," Tertan began slowly, "there is no blame ascribable. From the sense of determinism, who can say where the blame lies? The preordained is the preordained and it cannot be said without rebellion against the universe, a palpable absurdity."

101   In the back row Stettenhover slumped suddenly in his seat, his heels held out before him, making a loud dry disgusted sound. His body sank until his neck rested on the back of his chair. He folded his hands across his belly and looked significantly out of the window, exasperated not only with Tertan but with Howe, with the class, with the whole system designed to encourage this kind of thing. There was a certain insolence in the movement and Howe flushed. As Tertan continued to speak, Howe walked casually towards the window and placed himself in the line of Stettenhover's vision. Howe stared at the great fellow, who pretended not to see him. There was so

much power in the big body, so much contempt in the Greek-athlete face under the crisp Greek-athlete curls, that Howe felt almost physical fear. But at last Stettenhover admitted him to focus and under his disapproving gaze sat up with slow indifference. His eyebrows raised high in resignation, he began to examine his hands. Howe relaxed and turned his attention back to Tertan.

102   "Flux of existence," Tertan was saying, "produces all things, so that judgment wavers. Beyond the phenomena, what? But phenomena are adumbrated and to them we are limited."

103   Howe saw it for a moment as perhaps it existed in the boy's mind—the world of shadows which are cast by a great light upon a hidden reality as in the old myth of the Cave. But the little brush with Stettenhover had tried him and he said irritably: "But come to the point, Mr. Tertan."

104   He said it so sharply that some of the class looked at him curiously. For three months he had gently carried Tertan through his verbosities, to the vaguely respectful surprise of the other students, who seemed to conceive that there existed between this strange classmate and their teacher some special understanding from which they were content to be excluded. Tertan looked at him mildly and at once came brilliantly to the point. "This is the summation of the play," he said and took up his book and read: " 'Your poor father never found any outlet for the overmastering joy of life that was in him. And I brought no holiday into his home, either. Everything seemed to turn upon duty and I am afraid I made your poor father's home unbearable to him, Oswald.' Spoken by Mrs. Alving."

105   Yes, that was surely the "summation" of the play and Tertan had hit it, as he hit, deviously and eventually, the literary point of almost everything. But now, as always, he was wrapping it away from sight. "For most mortals," he said, "there are only joys of biological urgings, gross and crass, such as the sensuous Captain Alving. For certain few there are the transmutations beyond these to a contemplation of the utter whole."

106   Oh, the boy was mad. And suddenly the word, used in hyperbole, intended almost for the expression of exasperated admiration, became literal. Now that the word was used, it became simply apparent to Howe that Tertan was mad.

107   It was a monstrous word and stood like a bestial thing in the room. Yet it so completely comprehended everything that had puzzled Howe, it so arranged and explained what for three months had been perplexing him that almost at once its horror became domesticated. With this word Howe was able to understand why he had never been able to communicate to Tertan the value of a single criticism of correction of his wild, verbose themes. Their conferences had been frequent and long but had done nothing to reduce to order the splendid confusion of the boy's ideas. Yet, impossible though its expression was, Tertan's incandescent mind could always strike for a moment into some dark corner of thought.

108   And now it was suddenly apparent that it was not a faulty rhetoric that Howe had to contend with. With his new knowledge he looked at Tertan's face and wondered how he could have so long deceived himself. Tertan was still talking and the class had lapsed into a kind of patient unconsciousness, a coma of respect for words which, for all that most of them knew, might be profound. Almost with a suffusion of shame, Howe believed that in some dim way the class had long ago had some intimation of

Tertan's madness. He reached out as decisively as he could to seize the thread of Tertan's discourse before it should be entangled farther.

109   "Mr. Tertan says that the blame must be put upon whoever kills the joy of living in another. We have been assuming that Captain Alving was a wholly bad man, but what if we assume that he became bad only because Mrs. Alving, when they were first married, acted towards him in the prudish way she says she did?"

110   It was a ticklish idea to advance to freshmen and perhaps not profitable. Not all of them were following.

111   "That would put the blame on Mrs. Alving herself, whom most of you admire. And she herself seems to think so." He glanced at his watch. The hour was nearly over. "What do you think, Mr. De Witt?"

112   De Witt rose to the idea, wanted to know if society couldn't be blamed for educating Mrs. Alving's temperament in the wrong way. Casebeer was puzzled. Stettenhover continued to look at his hands until the bell rang.

113   Tertan, his brows lowering in thought, was making as always for a private word. Howe gathered his books and papers to leave quickly. At this moment of his discovery and with the knowledge still raw, he could not engage himself with Tertan. Tertan sucked in his breath to prepare for speech and Howe made ready for the pain and confusion. But at that moment Casebeer detached himself from the group with which he had been conferring and which he seemed to represent. His constituency remained at a tactful distance. The mission involved the time of an assigned essay. Casebeer's presentation of the plea—it was based on the freshmen's heavy duties at the fraternities during Carnival Week—cut across Tertan's preparations for speech. "And so some of us fellows thought," Casebeer concluded with heavy solemnity, "that we could do a better job, give our minds to it more, if we had more time."

114   Tertan regarded Casebeer with mingled curiosity and revulsion. Howe not only said that he would not postpone the assignment but went on to talk about the Carnival and even drew the waiting constituency into the conversation. He was conscious of Tertan's stern and astonished stare, then of his sudden departure.

115   Now that the fact was clear, Howe knew that he must act on it. His course was simple enough. He must lay the case before the Dean. Yet he hesitated. His feeling for Tertan must now, certainly, be in some way invalidated. Yet could he, because of a word, hurry to assign to official and reasonable solicitude what had been, until this moment, so various and warm? He could at least delay and, by moving slowly, lend a poor grace to the necessary, ugly act of making his report.

116   It was with some notion of keeping the matter in his own hands that he went to the Dean's office to look up Tertan's records. In the outer office the Dean's secretary greeted him brightly and at his request brought him the manila folder with the small identifying photograph pasted in the corner. She laughed. "He was looking for the birdie in the wrong place," she said.

117   Howe leaned over her shoulder to look at the picture. It was as bad as all the Dean's office photographs were, but it differed from all that Howe had ever seen. Tertan, instead of looking into the camera, as no doubt he had been bidden, had, at the moment of exposure, turned his eyes upward. His mouth, as though conscious of the trick played on the photographer, had the sly superior look that Howe knew.

118   The secretary was fascinated by the picture. "What a funny boy," she said. "He looks like Tartuffe!"

119   And so he did, with the absurd piety of the eyes and the conscious slyness of the mouth and the whole face bloated by the bad lens.

120   "Is he *like* that?" the secretary said.

121   "Like Tartuffe? No."

122   From the photograph there was little enough comfort to be had. The records themselves gave no clue to madness, though they suggested sadness enough. Howe read of a father, Stanislaus Tertan, born in Budapest and trained in engineering in Berlin, once employed by the Hercules Chemical Corporation—this was one of the factories that dominated the south end of the town—but now without employment. He read of a mother Erminie (Youngfellow) Tertan, born in Manchester, educated at a Normal School at Leeds, now housewife by profession. The family lived on Greenbriar Street, which Howe knew as a row of once elegant homes near what was now the factory district. The old mansions had long ago been divided into small and primitive apartments. Of Tertan himself there was little to learn. He lived with his parents, had attended a Detroit high school and had transferred to the local school in his last year. His rating for intelligence, as expressed in numbers, was high, his scholastic record was remarkable, he held a college scholarship for his tuition.

123   Howe laid the folder on the secretary's desk. "Did you find what you wanted to know?" she asked.

124   The phrases from Tertan's momentous first theme came back to him. "Tertan I am, but who is Tertan? Of this place, of that place, of some parentage, what does it matter?"

125   "No, I didn't find it," he said.

126   Now that he had consulted the sad half-meaningless record he knew all the more firmly that he must not give the matter out of his own hands. He must not release Tertan to authority. Not that he anticipated from the Dean anything but the greatest kindness for Tertan. The Dean would have the experience and skill which he himself could not have. One way or another the Dean could answer the question: "What is Tertan?" Yet this was precisely what he feared. He alone could keep alive—not for ever but for a somehow important time—the question: "What is Tertan?" He alone could keep it still a question. Some sure instinct told him that he must not surrender the question to a clean official desk in a clear official light to be dealt with, settled and closed.

127   His request came thus unbidden, even forbidden, and it was one of the most surprising and startling incidents of his life. Later, when he reviewed the events, so disconnected in themselves or so merely odd, of the story that unfolded for him that year, it was over this moment, on its face the least notable, that he paused longest. It was frequently to be with fear and never without a certainty of its meaning in his own knowledge of himself that he would recall this simple, routine request and the feeling of shame and freedom it gave him as he sent everything down the official shute. In the end, of course, no matter what he did to "protect" Tertan, he would have had to make the same request and lay the matter on the Dean's clean desk. But it would always be a landmark of his life that, at the very moment when he was rejecting the official way, he had been, without will or intention, so gladly drawn to it.

128   After the storm's last delicate flurry, the sun had come out. Reflected by the new snow, it filled the office with a golden light which was almost musical in the way it made all the commonplace objects of efficiency shine with a sudden sad and noble significance. And the light, now that he noticed it, made the utterance of his perverse and unwanted request even more momentous.

129   The secretary consulted the engagement pad. "He'll be free any minute. Don't you want to wait in the parlor?"

130   She threw open the door of the large and pleasant room in which the Dean held his Committee meetings and in which his visitors waited. It was designed with a homely elegance on the masculine side of the eighteenth-century manner. There was a small coal fire in the grate and the handsome mahogany table was strewn with books and magazines. The large windows gave on the snowy lawn and there was such a fine width of window that the white casements and walls seemed at this moment but a continuation of the snow, the snow but an extension of casement and walls. The outdoors seemed taken in and made safe, the indoors seemed luxuriously freshened and expanded.

131   Howe sat down by the fire and lighted a cigarette. The room had its intended effect upon him. He felt comfortable and relaxed, yet nicely organized, some young diplomatic agent of the eighteenth century, the newly fledged Swift carrying out Sir William Temple's business. The rawness of Tertan's case quite vanished. He crossed his legs and reached for a magazine.

132   It was that famous issue of *Life and Letters* that his idle hand had found and his blood raced as he sifted through it and the shape of his own name, Joseph Howe, sprang out at him, still cabalistic in its power. He tossed the magazine back on the table as the door of the Dean's office opened and the Dean ushered out Theodore Blackburn.

133   "Ah, Joseph!" the Dean said.

134   Blackburn said: "Good morning, Doctor." Howe winced at the title and caught the flicker of amusement over the Dean's face. The Dean stood with his hand high on the door-jamb and Blackburn, still in the doorway, remained standing almost under his long arm.

135   Howe nodded briefly to Blackburn, snubbing his eager deference. "Can you give me a few minutes?" he said to the Dean.

136   "All the time you want. Come in." Before the two men could enter the office, Blackburn claimed their attention with a full "Er." As they turned to him, Blackburn said: "Can *you* give *me* a few minutes, Dr. Howe?" His eyes sparkled at the little audacity he had committed, the slightly impudent play with hierarchy. Of the three of them Blackburn kept himself the lowest, but he reminded Howe of his subaltern relation to the Dean.

137   "I mean, of course," Blackburn went on easily, "when you've finished with the Dean."

138   "I'll be in my office shortly," Howe said, turned his back on the ready "Thank you, sir," and followed the Dean into the inner room.

139   "Energetic boy," said the Dean. "A bit beyond himself but very energetic. Sit down."

140   The Dean lighted a cigarette, leaned back in his chair, sat easy and silent for a

moment, giving Howe no signal to go ahead with business. He was a young Dean, not much beyond forty, a tall handsome man with sad, ambitious eyes. He had been a Rhodes scholar. His friends looked for great things from him and it was generally said that he had notions of education which he was not yet ready to try to put into practice.

141   His relaxed silence was meant as a compliment to Howe. He smiled and said: "What's the business, Joseph?"

142   "Do you know Tertan—Ferdinand Tertan, a freshman?"

143   The Dean's cigarette was in his mouth and his hands were clasped behind his head. He did not seem to search his memory for the name. He said: "What about him?"

144   Clearly the Dean knew something and he was waiting for Howe to tell him more. Howe moved only tentatively. Now that he was doing what he had resolved not to do, he felt more guilty at having been so long deceived by Tertan and more need to be loyal to his error.

145   "He's a strange fellow." he ventured. He said stubbornly: "In a strange way he's very brilliant." He concluded: "But very strange."

146   The springs of the Dean's swivel chair creaked as he came out of his sprawl and leaned forward to Howe. "Do you mean he's so strange that it's something you could give a name to?"

147   Howe looked at him stupidly. "What do you mean?" he said.

148   "He's very brilliant, in a way. I looked him up and he had a top intelligence rating. But somehow, and it's hard to explain just how, what he says is always on the edge of sense and doesn't quite make it."

149   The Dean looked at him and Howe flushed up. The Dean had surely read Woolley on the subject of "the Howes" and the *tour d'ivresse*. Was that quick glance ironical?

150   The Dean picked up some papers from his desk and Howe could see that they were in Tertan's impatient scrawl. Perhaps the little gleam in the Dean's glance had come only from putting facts together.

151   "He sent me this yesterday," the Dean said. "After an interview I had with him. I haven't been able to do more than glance at it. When you said what you did, I realized there was something wrong."

152   Twisting his mouth, the Dean looked over the letter. "You seem to be involved," he said without looking up. "By the way, what did you give him at mid-term?"

153   Flushing, setting his shoulders, Howe said firmly: "I gave him an A-minus."

154   The Dean chuckled. "Might be a good idea if some of our nicer boys went crazy—just a little." He said, "Well," to conclude the matter and handed the papers to Howe. "See if this is the same thing you've been finding. Then we can go into the matter again."

155   Before the fire in the parlor, in the chair that Howe had been occupying, sat Blackburn. He sprang to his feet as Howe entered.

156   "I said my office, Mr. Blackburn." Howe's voice was sharp. Then he was almost sorry for the rebuke, so clearly and naively did Blackburn seem to relish his stay in the parlor, close to authority.

157   "I'm in a bit of a hurry, sir," he said, "and I did want to be sure to speak to you, sir."

158   He was really absurd, yet fifteen years from now he would have grown up to himself, to the assurance and mature beefiness. In banks, in consular offices, in

brokerage firms, on the bench, more seriously affable, a little sterner, he could make use of his ability to be administered by his job. It was almost reassuring. Now he was exercising his too-great skill on Howe. "I owe you an apology, sir," he said.

159   Howe knew that he did but showed surprise.

160   "I mean, Doctor, after your having been so kind about letting me attend your class, I stopped coming." He smiled in depreciation. "Extra-curricular activities take up so much of my time. I'm afraid I undertook more than I could perform."

161   Howe had noticed the absence and had been a little irritated by it after Blackburn's elaborate plea. It was an absence that might be interpreted as a comment on the teacher. But there was only one way for him to answer. "You've no need to apologize," he said. "It's wholly your affair."

162   Blackburn beamed. "I'm so glad you feel that way about it, sir. I was worried you might think I had stayed away because I was influenced by—" He stopped and lowered his eyes.

163   Astonished, Howe said: "Influenced by what?"

164   "Well, by—" Blackburn hesitated and for answer pointed to the table on which lay the copy of *Life and Letters*. Without looking at it, he knew where to direct his hand. "By the unfavorable publicity, sir." He hurried on. "And that brings me to another point, sir. I am secretary of Quill and Scroll, sir, the student literary society, and I wonder if you would address us. You could read your own poetry, sir, and defend your own point of view. It would be very interesting."

165   It was truly amazing. Howe looked long and cruelly into Blackburn's face, trying to catch the secret of the mind that could have conceived this way of manipulating him, this way so daring and inept—but not entirely inept—with its malice so without malignity. The face did not yield its secret. Howe smiled broadly and said: "Of course I don't think you were influenced by the unfavorable publicity."

166   "I'm still going to take—regularly, for credit—your romantic poets course next term," Blackburn said.

167   "Don't worry, my dear fellow, don't worry about it."

168   Howe started to leave and Blackburn stopped him with: "But about Quill, sir?"

169   "Suppose we wait until next term? I'll be less busy then."

170   And Blackburn said: "Very good, sir, and thank you."

171   In his office the little encounter seemed less funny to Howe, was even in some indeterminate way disturbing. He made an effort to put it from his mind by turning to what was sure to disturb him more, the Tertan letter read in the new interpretation. He found what he had always found, the same florid leaps beyond fact and meaning, the same headlong certainty. But as his eye passed over the familiar scrawl it caught his own name and for the second time that hour felt the race of his blood.

172   "The Paraclete," Tertan had written to the Dean, "from a Greek word meaning to stand in place of, but going beyond the primitive idea to mean traditionally the helper, the one who comforts and assists, cannot without fundamental loss be jettisoned. Even if taken no longer in the supernatural sense, the concept remains deeply in the human consciousness inevitably. Humanitarianism is no reply, for not every man stands in the place of every other man for this other's comrade comfort. But certain are chosen out of the human race to be the consoler of some other. Of these, for example, is Joseph Barker Howe, Ph.D. Of

intellects not the first yet of true intellect and lambent instructions, given to that which is intuitive and irrational, not to what is logical in the strict word, what is judged by him is of the heart and not of the head. Here is one chosen, in that he chooses himself to stand in the place of another for comfort and consolation. To him more than another I give my gratitude, with all respect to our Dean who reads this, a noble man, but merely dedicated, not consecrated. But not in the aspect of Paraclete only is Dr. Joseph Barker Howe established, for he must be the Paraclete to another aspect of himself, that which is driven and persecuted by the lack of understanding in the world at large, so that he in himself embodies the full history of man's tribulations and, overflowing upon others notably the present writer, is the ultimate end."

173   This was love. There was no escape from it. Try as Howe might to remember that Tertan was mad and all his emotions invalidated, he could not destroy the effect upon him of his student's stern, affectionate regard. He had betrayed not only a power of mind but a power of love. And however firmly he held before his attention the fact of Tertan's madness, he could do nothing to banish the physical sensation of gratitude he felt. He had never thought of himself as "driven and persecuted" and he did not now. But still he could not make meaningless his sensation of gratitude. The pitiable Tertan sternly pitied him, and comfort came from Tertan's never-to-be comforted mind.

III

174   In an academic community, even an efficient one, official matters move slowly. The term drew to a close with no action in the case of Tertan, and Joseph Howe had to confront a curious problem. How should he grade his strange student, Tertan?

175   Tertan's final examination had been no different from all his other writing, and what did one "give" such a student? De Witt must have his A, that was clear. Johnson would get a B. With Casebeer it was a question of a B-minus or a C-plus. And Stettenhover, who had been crammed by the team tutor to fill half a blue-book with his thin feminine scrawl, would have his C-minus which he would accept with mingled indifference and resentment. But with Tertan it was not so easy.

176   The boy was still in the college process and his name could not be omitted from the grade sheet. Yet what should a mind under suspicion of madness be graded? Until the medical verdict was given, it was for Howe to continue as Tertan's teacher and keep his judgment pedagogical. Impossible to give him an F: he had not failed. B was for Johnson's stolid mediocrity. He could not be put on the edge of passing with Stettenhover, for he exactly did not pass. In energy and richness of intellect he was perhaps even De Witt's superior, and Howe toyed grimly with the notion of giving him an A, but that would lower the value of the A De Witt had won with his beautiful and clear, if still arrogant, mind. There was a notation which the Registrar recognized—Inc. for incomplete and in the horrible comedy of the situation, Howe considered that. But really only a mark of M for Mad would serve.

177   In his perplexity, Howe sought the Dean, but the Dean was out of town. In the end, he decided to maintain the A-minus he had given Tertan at mid-term. After all,

there had been no falling away from that quality. He entered it on the grade sheet with something like bravado.

178   Academic time moves quickly. A college year is not really a year, lacking as it does three months. And it is endlessly divided into units which, at their beginning appear larger than they are—terms, half-terms, months, weeks. And the ultimate unit, the hour, is not really an hour, lacking as it does ten minutes. And so the new term advanced rapidly and one day the fields about town were all brown, cleared of even the few thin patches of snow which had lingered so long.

179   Howe, as he lectured on the romantic poets, became conscious of Blackburn emanating wrath. Blackburn did it well, did it with enormous dignity. He did not stir in his seat, he kept his eyes fixed on Howe in perfect attention, but he abstained from using his notebook, there was no mistaking what he proposed to himself as an attitude. His elbow on the writing-wing of the chair, his chin on the curled fingers of his hand, he was the embodiment of intellectual indignation. He was thinking his own thoughts, would give no public offence, yet would claim his due, was not to be intimidated. Howe knew that he would present himself at the end of the hour.

180   Blackburn entered the office without invitation. He did not smile, there was no cajolery about him. Without invitation he sat down beside Howe's desk. He did not speak until he had taken the blue-book from his pocket. He said: "What does this mean, sir?"

181   It was a sound and conservative student tactic. Said in the usual way it meant: "How could you have so misunderstood me?" or "What does this mean for my future in the course?" But there were none of the humbler tones in Blackburn's way of saying it.

182   Howe made the established reply: "I think that's for you to tell me."

183   Blackburn continued icy. "I'm sure I can't, sir."

184   There was silence between them. Both dropped their eyes to the blue-book on the desk. On its cover Howe had penciled: "F. This is very poor work."

185   Howe picked up the blue-book. There was always the possibility of injustice. The teacher may be bored by the mass of papers and not wholly attentive. A phrase, even the student's handwriting, may irritate him unreasonably. "Well," said Howe, "let's go through it." He had opened the first page. "Now here: you write: 'In *The Ancient Mariner,* Coleridge lives in and transports us to a honey-sweet world where all is rich and strange, a world of charm to which we can escape from the humdrum existence of our daily lives, the world of romance. Here, in this warm and honey-sweet land of charming dreams we can relax and enjoy ourselves.' "

186   Howe lowered the paper and waited with a neutral look for Blackburn to speak. Blackburn returned the look boldly, did not speak, sat stolid and lofty. At last Howe said, speaking gently: "Did you mean that, or were you just at a loss for something to say?"

187   "You imply that I was just 'bluffing'?" The quotation marks hung palpable in the air about the word.

188   "I'd like to know. I'd prefer believing that you were bluffing to believing that you really thought this."

189   Blackburn's eyebrows went up. From the height of a great and firm based idea he looked at his teacher. He clasped the crags for a moment and then pounced, craftily, suavely. "Do you mean, Dr. Howe, that there aren't two opinions possible?"

190   It was superbly done in its air of putting all of Howe's intellectual life into the balance. Howe remained patient and simple. "Yes, many opinions are possible, but not this one. Whatever anyone believes of *The Ancient Mariner,* no one can in reason believe that it represents a—a honey-sweet world in which we can relax."

191   "But that is what I *feel,* sir."

192   This was well done too. Howe said: "Look, Mr. Blackburn. Do you really relax with hunger and thirst, the heat and the sea-serpents, the dead men with staring eyes, Life in Death and the skeletons? Come now, Mr. Blackburn."

193   Blackburn made no answer and Howe pressed forward. "Now you say of Wordsworth: 'Of peasant stock himself, he turned from the effete life of the salons and found in the peasant the hope of a flaming revolution which would sweep away all the old ideas. This is the subject of his best poems.' "

194   Beaming at his teacher with youthful eagerness, Blackburn said: "Yes, sir, a rebel, a bringer of light to suffering mankind. I see him as a kind of Prothemeus."

195   "A kind of what?"

196   "Prothemeus, sir."

197   "Think, Mr. Blackburn. We were talking about him only today and I mentioned his name a dozen times. You don't mean Prothemeus. You mean—" Howe waited but there was no response.

198   "You mean Prometheus."

199   Blackburn gave no assent and Howe took the reins. "You've done a bad job here Mr. Blackburn, about as bad as could be done." He saw Blackburn stiffen and his genial face harden again. "It shows either a lack of preparation or a complete lack of understanding." He saw Blackburn's face begin to go to pieces and he stopped.

200   "Oh, sir," Blackburn burst out, "I've never had a mark like this before, never anything below a B, never. A thing like this has never happened to me before."

201   It must be true, it was a statement too easily verified. Could it be that other instructors accepted such flaunting nonsense? Howe wanted to end the interview. "I'll set it down to lack of preparation," he said. "I know you're busy. That's not an excuse but it's an explanation. Now suppose you really prepare and then take another quiz in two weeks. We'll forget this one and count the other."

202   Blackburn squirmed, with pleasure and gratitude. "Thank you, sir. You're really very kind, very kind."

203   Howe rose to conclude the visit. "All right then—in two weeks."

204   It was that day that the Dean imparted to Howe the conclusion of the case of Tertan. It was simple and a little anticlimactic. A physician had been called in, and had said the word, given the name.

205   "A classic case, he called it," the Dean said. "Not a doubt in the world," he said. His eyes were full of miserable pity and he clutched at a word. "A classic case, a classic case." To his aid and to Howe's there came the Parthenon and the form of the Greek drama, the Aristotelian logic, Racine and the Well-Tempered Clavichord, the blueness of the Aegean and its clear sky. Classic—that is to say, without a doubt, perfect in its way, a veritable model, and, as the Dean had been told, sure to take a perfectly predictable and inevitable course to a foreknown conclusion.

206　It was not only pity that stood in the Dean's eyes. For a moment there was fear too. "Terrible," he said, "it is simply terrible."

207　Then he went on briskly. "Naturally we've told the boy nothing. And naturally we won't. His tuition's paid by his scholarship and we'll continue him on the rolls until the end of the year. That will be the kindest. After that the matter will be out of our control. We'll see, of course, that he gets into the proper hands. I'm told there will be no change, he'll go on like this, be as good as this, for four to six months. And so we'll just go along as usual."

208　So Tertan continued to sit in Section 5 of English 1A, to his classmates still a figure of curiously dignified fun, symbol to most of them of the respectable but absurd intellectual life. But to his teacher he was now very different. He had not changed—he was still the greyhound casting for the scent of ideas and Howe could see that he was still the same Tertan, but he could not feel it. What he felt as he looked at the boy sitting in his accustomed place was the hard blank of a fact. The fact itself was formidable and depressing. But what Howe was chiefly aware of was that he had permitted the metamorphosis of Tertan from person to fact.

209　As much as possible he avoided seeing Tertan's upraised hand and eager eye. But the fact did not know of its mere actuality, it continued its existence as if it were Tertan, hand up and eye questioning, and one day it appeared in Howe's office with a document.

210　"Even the spirit who lives egregiously, above the herd, must have its relations with the fellow-man," Tertan declared. He laid the document on Howe's desk. It was headed "Quill and Scroll Society of Dwight College. Application for Membership."

211　"In most ways these are crass minds," Tertan said, touching the paper. "Yet as a whole, bound together in their common love of letters, they transcend their intellectual lacks, since it is not a paradox that the whole is greater than the sum of its parts."

212　"When are the elections?" Howe asked.

213　"They take place to-morrow."

214　"Thank you. Would you wish to implement that hope?" A rather dirty finger pointed to the bottom of the sheet. "A faculty recommender is necessary," Tertan said stiffly, and waited.

215　"And you wish me to recommend you?"

216　"It would be an honor."

217　"You may use my name."

218　Tertan's finger pointed again. "It must be a written sponsorship, signed by the sponsor." There was a large blank space on the form under the heading: "Opinion of Faculty Sponsor."

219　This was almost another thing and Howe hesitated. Yet there was nothing else to do and he took out his fountain-pen. He wrote: "Mr. Ferdinand Tertan is marked by his intense devotion to letters and by his exceptional love of all things of the mind." To this he signed his name which looked bold and assertive on the white page. It disturbed him, the strange affirming power of a name. With a business-like air, Tertan whipped up the paper, folded it with decision and put it into his pocket. He bowed and took his departure, leaving Howe with the sense of having done something oddly momentous.

220   And so much seemed odd and momentous to Howe that should not have seemed so. It was odd and momentous, he felt, when he sat with Blackburn's second quiz before him and wrote in an excessively firm hand the grade of C-minus. The paper was a clear, an indisputable failure. He was carefully and consciously committing a cowardice. Blackburn had told the truth when he had pleaded his past record. Howe had consulted it in the Dean's office. It showed no grade lower than a B-minus. A canvass to the adequate powers of a student imperfectly remembered and sometimes surprised that his abilities could be questioned at all.

221   As he wrote the grade, Howe told himself that this cowardice sprang from an unwillingness to have more dealings with a student he disliked. He knew it was simpler than that. He knew he feared Blackburn: that was the absurd truth. And cowardice did not solve the matter after all. Blackburn, flushed with a first success, attacked at once. The minimal passing grade had not assuaged his feelings, and he sat at Howe's desk and again the blue-book lay between them. Blackburn said nothing. With an enormous impudence, he was waiting for Howe to speak and explain himself.

222   At last Howe said sharply and rudely: "Well?" His throat was tense and the blood was hammering in his head. His mouth was tight with anger at himself at his disturbance.

223   Blackburn's glance was almost baleful. "This is impossible, sir."

224   "But there it is," Howe answered.

225   "Sir?" Blackburn had not caught the meaning but his tone was still haughty.

226   Impatiently Howe said: "There it is, plain as day. Are you here to complain again?"

227   "Indeed I am, sir." There was surprise in Blackburn's voice that Howe should ask the question.

228   "I shouldn't complain if I were you. You did a thoroughly bad job on your first quiz. This one is a little, only a very little, better." This was not true. If anything, it was worse.

229   "That might be a matter of opinion, sir."

230   "It is a matter of opinion. Of my opinion."

231   "Another opinion might be different, sir."

232   "You really believe that?" Howe said.

233   "Yes." The omission of the "sir" was monumental.

234   "Whose, for example?"

235   "The Dean's, for example." Then the fleshy jaw came forward a little. "Or a certain literary critic's, for example."

236   It was colossal and almost too much for Blackburn himself to handle. The solidity of his face almost crumpled under it. But he withstood his own audacity and went on. "And the Dean's opinion might be guided by the knowledge that the person who gave me this mark is the man whom a famous critic, the most eminent judge of literature in this country, called a drunken man. The Dean might think twice about whether such a man is fit to teach Dwight students."

237   Howe said in quiet admonition, "Blackburn, you're mad," meaning no more than to check the boy's extravagance.

238   But Blackburn paid no heed. He had another shot in the locker. "And the Dean might be guided by the information, of which I have evidence, documentary

evidence"—he slapped his breast-pocket twice—"that this same person personally recommended to the college literary society, the oldest in the country, that he personally recommended a student who is crazy, who threw the meeting into an uproar, a psychiatric case. The Dean might take that into account."

239   Howe was never to learn the details of that "uproar." He had always to content himself with the dim but passionate picture which at that moment sprang into his mind, of Tertan standing on some abstract height and madly denouncing the multitude of Quill and Scroll who howled him down.

240   He sat quiet a moment and looked at Blackburn. The ferocity had entirely gone from the student's face. He sat regarding his teacher almost benevolently. He had played a good card and now, scarcely at all unfriendly, he was waiting to see the effect. Howe took up the blue-book and negligently sifted through it. He read a page, closed the book, struck out the C-minus and wrote an F.

241   "Now you may take the paper to the Dean," he said. "You may tell him that after reconsidering it, I lowered the grade."

242   The gasp was audible. "Oh, sir!" Blackburn cried. "Please!" His face was agonized. "It means my graduation, my livelihood, my future. Don't do this to me!"

243   "It's done already."

244   Blackburn stood up. "I spoke rashly, sir, hastily. I had no intention, no real intention, of seeing the Dean. It rests with you—entirely, entirely. I *hope* you will restore the first mark."

245   "Take the matter to the Dean or not, just as you choose. The grade is what you deserve and it stands."

246   Blackburn's head dropped. "And will I be failed at mid-term, sir?"

247   "Of course."

248   From deep out of Blackburn's great chest rose a cry of anguish. "Oh, sir, if you want me to go down on my knees to you, I will, I will."

249   Howe looked at him in amazement.

250   "I will, I will. On my knees, sir. This mustn't, mustn't happen."

251   He spoke so literally, meaning so very truly that his knees and exactly his knees were involved and seeming to think that he was offering something of tangible value to his teacher, that Howe, whose head had become icy clear in the nonsensical drama, thought, "The boy is mad," and began to speculate fantastically whether something in himself attracted or developed aberration. He could see himself standing absurdly before the Dean and saying: "I've found another. This time it's the vice-president of the Council, the manager of the debating team, and secretary of Quill and Scroll."

252   One more such discovery, he thought, and he himself would be discovered! And there, suddenly, Blackburn was on his knees with a thump, his huge thighs straining his trousers, his hands outstretched in a great gesture of supplication.

253   With a cry, Howe shoved back his swivel chair and it rolled away on its casters half across the little room. Blackburn knelt for a moment to nothing at all, then got to his feet.

254   Howe rose abruptly. He said: "Blackburn, you will stop acting like an idiot. Dust your knees off, take your paper and get out. You've behaved like a fool and a malicious person. You have half a term to do a decent job. Keep your silly mouth shut and try to do it. Now get out."

255   Blackburn's head was low. He raised it and there was a pious light in his eyes. "Will you shake hands, sir?" he said. He thrust out his hand.

256   "I will not," Howe said.

257   Head and feet sank together. Blackburn picked up his blue-book and walked to the door. He turned and said: "Thank you, sir." His back, as he departed, was heavy with tragedy and stateliness.

IV

258   After years of bad luck with the weather, the College had a perfect day for Commencement. It was wonderfully bright, the air so transparent, the wind so brisk that no one could resist talking about it.

259   As Howe set out for the campus he heard Hilda calling from the back yard. She called, "Professor, professor," and came running to him.

260   Howe said: "What's this 'professor' business?"

261   "Mother told me," Hilda said. "You've been promoted. And I want to take your picture."

262   "Next year," said Howe. "I won't be professor until next year. And you know better than to call anybody 'professor'."

263   "It was just in fun," Hilda said. She seemed disappointed.

264   "But you can take my picture if you want. I won't look much different next year." Still, it was frightening. It might mean that he was to stay in this town all his life.

265   Hilda brightened. "Can I take it in this?" she said, and touched the gown he carried over his arm.

266   Howe laughed. "Yes, you can take it in this."

267   "I'll get my things and meet you in front of Otis," Hilda said. "I have the background all picked out."

268   On the campus the Commencement crowd was already large. It stood about in eager, nervous little family groups. As he crossed, Howe was greeted by a student, capped and gowned, glad of the chance to make an event for his parents by introducing one of his teachers. It was while Howe stood there chatting that he saw Tertan.

269   Three weeks had passed since Howe had last seen him, the weeks of examination, the lazy week before Commencement, and this was now a different Tertan. On his head he wore a panama hat, broad-brimmed and fine, of the shape associated with South American planters. He wore a suit of raw silk, luxurious but yellowed with age and much too tight, and he sported a whangee cane. He walked sedately, the hat tilted at a devastating angle, the stick coming up and down in time to his measured tread. He had, Howe guessed, outfitted himself to greet the day in the clothes of that ruined father whose existence was on the record in the Dean's office. Gravely and arrogantly he surveyed the scene—in it, his whole bearing seemed to say, but not of it. With his haughty step, with his flashing eye, Tertan was coming nearer. Howe did not wish to be seen. He shifted his position slightly. When he looked again, Tertan was not in sight.

270   The chapel clock struck the quarter hour. Howe detached himself from his chat and hurried to Otis Hall at the far end of the campus. Hilda had not yet come. He went

out into the high portico and, using the glass of the door for a mirror, put on his gown, adjusted the hood on his shoulders and set the mortar-board on his head. When he came down the steps Hilda had arrived.

271   Nothing could have told him more forcibly that a year had passed than the development of Hilda's photographic possessions from the box camera of the previous fall. By a strap about her neck was hung a leather case, so thick and strong, so carefully stitched and so molded to its contents that it could only hold a costly camera. The appearance was deceptive Howe knew, for he had been present at the Aiken's pre-Christmas conference about its purchase. It was only a fairly good domestic camera. Still, it looked very impressive. Hilda carried another leather case from which she drew a collapsible tripod. Decisively she extended each of its gleaming legs and set it up on the path. She removed the camera from its case and fixed it to the tripod. In its compact efficiency the camera almost had a life of its own, but Hilda treated it with easy familiarity, looked into its eye, glanced casually at its gauges. Then from a pocket she took still another leather case and drew from it a small instrument through which she looked first at Howe, who began to feel inanimate and lost, and then at the sky. She made some adjustment on the instrument, then some adjustment on the camera. She swept the scene with her eye, found a spot and pointed the camera in its direction. She walked to the spot, stood on it and beckoned to Howe. With each new leather case, with each new instrument and each new adjustment she had grown in ease and now she said: "Joe, will you stand here?"

272   Obediently Howe stood where he was bidden. She had yet another instrument. She took out a tape-measure on a mechanical spool. Kneeling down before Howe, she put the little metal ring of the tape under the tip of his shoe. At her request, Howe pressed it with the tip of his toe. When she had measured her distance, she nodded to Howe who released the tape. At a touch, it sprang back into the spool. "You have to be careful if you're going to get what you want." Hilda said. "I don't believe in all this snap-snap-snapping," she remarked loftily. Howe nodded in agreement, although he was beginning to think Hilda's care excessive.

273   Now at last the moment had come. Hilda squinted into the camera, moved the tripod slightly. She stood to the side, holding the plunger of the shutter-cable. "Ready," she said. "Will you relax, Joseph, please?" Howe realized that he was standing frozen. Hilda stood poised and precise as a setter, one hand holding the little cable, the other extended with curled dainty fingers like a dancer's, as if expressing to her subject the precarious delicacy of the moment. She pressed the plunger and there was the click. At once she stirred to action, got behind the camera, turned a new exposure. "Thank you," she said. "Would you stand under that tree and let me do a character study with light and shade?"

274   The childish absurdity of the remark restored Howe's ease. He went to the little tree. The pattern the leaves made on his gown was what Hilda was after. He had just taken a satisfactory position when he heard in the unmistakable voice: "Ah, Doctor! Having your picture taken?"

275   Blackburn beamed at Hilda. "And the little photographer," he said. Hilda fixed her eyes on the ground and stood closer to her brilliant and aggressive camera. Blackburn, teetering on his heels, his hands behind his back, wholly prelatical and

benignly patient, was not abashed at the silence. At last Howe said: "If you'll excuse us, Mr. Blackburn, we'll go on with the picture."

276   "Go right ahead, sir, I'm running along," But he only came closer. "Dr. Howe," he said fervently, "I want to tell you how glad I am that I was able to satisfy your standards at last."

277   Howe was surprised at the hard insulting brightness of his own voice and even Hilda looked up curiously as he said: "Nothing you have ever done has satisfied me and nothing you could ever do would satisfy me, Blackburn."

278   With a glance at Hilda, Blackburn made a gesture as if to hush Howe—as though all his former bold malice had taken for granted a kind of understanding between himself and his teacher, a secret which must not be betrayed to a third person. "I only meant, sir," he said, "that I was able to pass your course after all."

279   Howe said: "You didn't pass my course. I passed you out of my course. I passed you without even reading your paper. I wanted to be sure the college would be rid of you and when the grades were in and I read your paper, I saw I was right not to have read it first."

280   Blackburn presented a stricken face. "It was very bad, sir?"

281   But Howe had turned away. The paper had been fantastic. The paper had been, if he wished to see it so, mad. It was at this moment that the Dean came up behind Howe and caught his arm. "Hello, Joseph," he said. Leaning forward on Howe's arm and on Blackburn's, he said: "Hello, Hilda dear." Hilda replied quietly: "Hello, Uncle George."

282   Still clinging to their arms, still linking Howe and Blackburn, the Dean said: "Another year gone, Joe, and we've turned out another crop. After you've been here a few years, you'll find it reasonably upsetting—you wonder how there can be so many graduating classes while you stay the same. But, of course, you don't stay the same." Then he said, "Well," sharply to dismiss the thought. He pulled Blackburn's arm and swing him around to Howe. "Have you heard about Teddy Blackburn?" he asked. "He has a job already, before graduation, the first man of his class to be placed." Expectant of congratulations, Blackburn beamed at Howe. Howe remained silent.

283   "Isn't that good?" the Dean said. Still Howe did not answer and the Dean, puzzled and put out, turned to Hilda. "That's a very fine-looking camera, Hilda." She touched it with affectionate pride.

284   "Instruments of precision," said a voice. "Instruments of precision." Of the three with joined arms, Howe was the nearest to Tertan, whose gaze took in all the scene except the smile and the nod which Howe gave him. The boy leaned on his cane. The broad-brimmed hat, canting jauntily over his eye, confused the image of his face that Howe had established, suppressed the rigid lines of the ascetic and brought out the baroque curves. It made an effect of perverse majesty.

285   "Instruments of precision," said Tertan for the last time, addressing no one, making a casual comment to the universe. And it occurred to Howe that Tertan might not be referring to Hilda's equipment. The sense of the thrice-woven circle of the boy's loneliness smote him fiercely. Tertan stood in majestic jauntiness, superior to all the scene, but his isolation made Howe ache with a pity of which Tertan was more the cause than the object, so general and indiscriminate was it.

286   Whether in his sorrow he made some unintended movement towards Tertan which the Dean checked or whether the suddenly tightened grip on his arm was the Dean's own sorrow and fear, he did not know. Tertan watched them in the incurious way people watch a photograph being taken and suddenly the thought that, to the boy, it must seem that the three were posing for a picture together made Howe detach himself almost rudely from the Dean's grasp.

287   "I promised Hilda another picture," he announced—needlessly, for Tertan was no longer there, he had vanished in the last sudden flux of visitors who, now that the band had struck up, were rushing nervously to find seats.

288   "You'd better hurry," the Dean said. "I'll go along, it's getting late for me." He departed and Blackburn walked stately by his side.

289   Howe again took his position under the little tree which cast its shadow over his face and gown. "Just hurry, Hilda, won't you?" he said. Hilda held the cable at arm's length, her other arm crooked and her fingers crossed. She rose on her toes and said "Ready," and pressed the release. "Thank you," she said gravely and began to dismantle her camera as he hurried off to join the procession.

Suggestions for Discussion or Writing

1. How do Howe's attitudes about himself and the educational process change during the story? What specific incidents contribute to the change and how?

2. How accurate is Trilling's picture of a university classroom? Have you known students and teachers like those he describes? What do you think about these people?

3. Why does Trilling use so much detail in describing Hilda's camera equipment and the photo session in the first and final scenes? What connection might the camera have with the title of the story?

4. How do you think Blackburn will fare in the world outside the university? Why? How will Tertan fare? Why? What about the others: De Witt, Stettenhover, Casebeer?

5. Howe states that Tertan seems somehow heroic. In what way is Tertan a heroic figure? Is this a story about Howe or Tertan? Is Howe a heroic figure?

6. Study Tertan's character. Is he mad? Why is he so "strange" to Howe? What might Howe mean about the "thrice-woven circle of the boy's loneliness" in the last section? What connection does the title have with Tertan's life?

7. What part does the Dean play in the action? What is his attitude toward Blackburn? Toward Tertan? How do he and Joseph Howe differ?

Sex Education

Dorothy Canfield

Homemaker, educator, and writer, Dorothy Canfield Fisher (1879–1958) was born in Lawrence, Kansas. She received a degree in English from Ohio State in 1899 and a Ph.D. in French from Columbia University in 1905. She has written numerous essays and articles on education, including several about the Montessori method, which she helped introduce to the United States. She has also written novels, including The Squirrel Cage *(1912) and* The Deepening Stream *(1930), short stories, and children's stories. Her novels attack materialism, social discrimination, racial and religious intolerance, and brutality.*

1   It was three times—but at intervals of many years—that I heard my Aunt Minnie tell about an experience of her girlhood that had made a never-to-be forgotten impression on her. The first time was in her thirties, still young. But she had been married for ten years, so that to my group of friends all in the early teens, she seemed quite of another generation.

2   The day she told us the story, we had been idling on one end of her porch as we made casual plans for a picnic supper in the woods. Darning stockings at the other end, she paid no attention to us until one of the girls said, "Let's take blankets and sleep out there. It'd be fun."

3   "No," Aunt Minnie broke in sharply, "you mustn't do that."

4   "Oh, for goodness' sakes, why not!" said one of the younger girls, rebelliously, "the boys are always doing it. Why can't we, just once."

5   Aunt Minnie laid down her sewing. "Come here, girls," she said, "I want you should hear something that happened to me when I was your age."

6   Her voice had a special quality which, perhaps, young people of today would not recognize. But we did. We knew from experience that it was the dark voice grownups used when they were going to say something about sex.

7   Yet at first what she had to say was like any dull family anecdote; she had been ill when she was fifteen; and afterwards she was run down, thin, with no appetite. Her folks thought a change of air would do her good, and sent her from Vermont out to Ohio—or was it Illinois? I don't remember. Anyway, one of those places where the corn grows high. Her mother's Cousin Ella lived there, keeping house for her son-in-law.

8   The son-in-law was the minister of the village church. His wife had died some years before, leaving him a young widower with two little girls and a baby boy. He had been a normally personable man then, but the next summer, on the Fourth of July when he was trying to set off some fireworks to amuse his children, an imperfectly manufactured rocket has burst in his face. The explosion had left one side of his face badly scarred. Aunt Minnie made us see it, as she still saw it, in horrid detail: the

stiffened scarlet scar tissue distorting one cheek, the lower lip turned so far out at one corner that the moist red mucous-membrane lining always showed, one lower eyelid hanging loose, and watering.

9   After the accident, his face had been a long time healing. It was then that his wife's elderly mother had gone to keep house and take care of the children. When he was well enough to be about again, he found his position as pastor of the little church waiting for him. The farmers and village people in his congregation, moved by his misfortune, by his faithful service and by his unblemished character, said they would rather have Mr. Fairchild, even with his scarred face, than any other minister. He was a good preacher, Aunt Minnie told us, "and the way he prayed was kind of exciting. I'd never known a preacher, not to live in the same house with him, before. And when he was in the pulpit with everybody looking up at him, I felt the way his children did, kind of proud to think we had just eaten breakfast at the same table. I liked to call him 'Cousin Malcolm' before folks. One side of his face was all right, anyhow. You could see from that that he *had* been a good-looking man. In fact, probably one of these ministers that all the women—" Aunt Minnie paused, drew her lips together, and looked at us uncertainly.

10   Then she went back to the story as it happened—as it happened the first time I heard her tell it. "I thought he was a saint. Everybody out there did. That was all *they* knew. Of course, it made a person sick to look at that awful scar—the drooling corner of his mouth was the worst. He tried to keep that side of his face turned away from folks. But you always knew it was there. That was what kept him from marrying again, so Cousin Ella said. I heard her say lots of times that he knew no woman would touch any man who looked the way he did, not with a ten-foot pole.

11   "Well, the change of air did do me good. I got my appetite back, and ate a lot and played outdoors a lot with my cousins. They were younger than I (I had my sixteenth birthday there) but I still liked to play games. I got taller and laid on some weight. Cousin Ella used to say I grew as fast as the corn did. Their house stood at the edge of the village. Beyond it was one of those big cornfields they have out West. At the time when I first got there, the stalks were only up to a person's knee. You could see over their tops. But it grew like lightning, and before long, it was the way thick woods are here, way over your head, the stalks growing so close together it was dark under them.

12   "Cousin Ella told us youngsters that it was lots worse for getting lost in than woods, because there weren't any landmarks in it. One spot in a cornfield looked just like any other. 'You children keep out of it,' she used to tell us almost every day, '*especially you girls*. It's no place for a decent girl. You could easy get so far from the house nobody could hear you if you hollered. There are plenty of men in the town that wouldn't like anything better than—' she never said what.

13   "In spite of what she said, my little cousins and I figured out that if we went across one corner of the field, it would be a short cut to the village, and sometimes, without letting on to Cousin Ella, we'd go that way. After the corn got really tall, the farmer stopped cultivating, and we soon beat down a path in the loose dirt. The minute you were inside the field it was dark. You felt it as if you were miles from anywhere. It sort of scared you. But in no time the path turned and brought you out on the far end of Main Street. Your breath was coming fast, maybe, but that was what made you like to do it.

14   "One day I missed the turn. Maybe I didn't keep my mind on it. Maybe it had rained and blurred the tramped-down look of the path. I don't know what. All of a sudden, I knew I was lost. And the minute I knew that, I began to run, just as hard as I could run. I couldn't help it, any more than you can help snatching your hand off a hot stove. I didn't know what I was scared of, I didn't even know I was running, till my heart was pounding so hard I had to stop.

15   "The minute I stood still, I could hear Cousin Ella saying, 'There are plenty of men in this town that wouldn't like anything better than—' I didn't know, not really, what she meant. But I knew she meant something horrible. I opened my mouth to scream. But I put both my hands over my mouth to keep the scream in. If I made any noise, one of those men would hear me. I thought I heard one just behind me, and whirled around. And then I thought another one had tiptoed up behind me, the other way, and I spun around so fast I almost fell over. I stuffed my hands hard up against my mouth. And then—I couldn't help it—I ran again—but my legs were shaking so I soon had to stop. There I stood, scared to move for fear of rustling the corn and letting the men know where I was. My hair had come down, all over my face. I kept pushing it back and looking around, quick, to make sure one of the men hadn't found out where I was. Then I thought I saw a man coming towards me, and I ran away from him—and fell down, and burst some of the buttons off my dress, and was sick to my stomach—and thought I heard a man close to me and got up and staggered around, knocking into the corn because I couldn't even see where I was going.

16   "And then, off to one side, I saw Cousin Malcolm. Not a man. The minister. He was standing still, one hand up to his face thinking. He hadn't heard me.

17   "I was so *terrible* glad to see him, instead of one of those men, I ran as fast as I could and just flung myself on him, to make myself feel how safe I was."

18   Aunt Minnie had become strangely agitated. Her hands were shaking, her face was crimson. She frightened us. We could not look away from her. As we waited for her to go on, I felt little spasms twitch at the muscles inside my body. "And what do you think that *saint*, that holy minister of the Gospel, did to an innocent child who clung to him for safety? The most terrible look came into his eyes—you girls are too young to know what he looked like. But once you're married, you'll find out. He grabbed hold of me—that dreadful face of his was *right on mine*—and began clawing the clothes off my back."

19   She stopped for a moment, panting. We were too frightened to speak. She went on, "He had torn my dress right down to the waist before I—then I *did* scream—all I could—and pulled away from him so hard I almost fell down, and ran and all of a sudden I came out of the corn, right in the back yard of the Fairchild house. The children were staring at the corn, and Cousin Ella ran out of the kitchen door. They heard me screaming. Cousin Ella shrieked out, 'What is it? What happened? Did a man scare you?' and I said, 'Yes, yes, yes, a man—I ran—!' And then I fainted away. I must have. The next thing I knew I was on the sofa in the living room and Cousin Ella was slapping my face with a wet towel."

20   She had to wet her lips with her tongue before she could go on. Her face was gray now. "There! that's the kind of thing girls' folks ought to tell them about—so they'll know what men are like."

21   She finished her story as if she were dismissing us. We wanted to go away, but we were too horrified to stir. Finally one of the youngest girls asked in a low trembling voice, "Aunt Minnie, did you tell on him?"

22   "No, I was ashamed to," she said briefly. "They sent me home the next day anyhow. Nobody ever said a word to me about it and I never did either. Till now."

23   By what gets printed in some of the modern child-psychology books, you would think that girls to whom such a story had been told would never develop normally. Yet, as far as I can remember what happened to the girls in that group, we all grew up about like anybody else. Most of us married, some happily, some not so well. We kept house. We learned—more or less—how to live with our husbands, we had children and struggled to bring them up right—we went forward into life, just as if we had never been warned not to.

24   Perhaps, young as we were that day, we had already had enough experience of life so that we were not quite blank paper for Aunt Minnie's frightening story. Whether we thought of it then or not, we couldn't have failed to see that at this very time, Aunt Minnie had been married for ten years or more, comfortably and well married, too. Against what she had tried by that story to brand into our minds stood the cheerful home life in that house, the good-natured, kind, hard-working husband, and the children—three rough-and-tumble, nice little boys, so adored by their parents, and the sweet girl baby who died, of whom they could never speak without tears. It was such actual contact with adult life that probably kept generation after generation of girls from being scared by talks like Aunt Minnie's into a neurotic horror of living.

25   Of course, since Aunt Minnie was so much older than we, her boys grew up to be adolescents and young men while our children were still little enough so that our worries over them were nothing more serious than whooping cough and trying to get them to make their own beds. Two of our aunt's three boys followed, without losing their footing, the narrow path which leads across adolescence into normal adult life. But the middle one, Jake, repeatedly fell off into the morass. "Girl trouble," as the succinct family phrase put it. He was one of those boys who have "charm," whatever we mean by that, and was always being snatched at by girls who would be "all wrong" for him to marry. And once, at nineteen, he ran away from home, whether with one of these girls or not we never heard, for through all her ups and downs with this son, Aunt Minnie tried fiercely to protect him from scandal that might cloud his later life.

26   Her husband had to stay on his job to earn the family living. She was the one who went to find Jake. When it was gossiped around that Jake was in "bad company" his mother drew some money from the family savings-bank account, and silent, white-cheeked, took the train to the city where rumor said he had gone.

27   Some weeks later he came back with her. With no girl. She had cleared him of that entanglement. As of others, which followed, later. Her troubles seemed over when, at a "suitable" age, he fell in love with a "suitable" girl, married her and took her to live in our shire town, sixteen miles away, where he had a good position. Jake was always bright enough.

28   Sometimes, idly, people speculated as to what Aunt Minnie had seen that time

she went after her runaway son, wondering where her search for him had taken her—very queer places for Aunt Minnie to be in, we imagined. And how could such an ignorant, homekeeping woman ever have known what to say to an errant willful boy to set him straight?

29   Well, of course, we reflected, watching her later struggles with Jake's erratic ways, she certainly could not have remained ignorant, after seeing over and over what she probably had after talking with Jake about the things which, a good many times, must have come up with desperate openness between them.

30   She kept her own counsel. We never knew anything definite about the facts of those experiences of hers. But one day she told a group of us—all then married women—something which gave us a notion about what she had learned from them.

31   We were hastily making a layette for a not-especially welcome baby in a poor family. In those days, our town had no such thing as a district-nursing service. Aunt Minnie, a vigorous woman of fifty-five, had come in to help. As we sewed, we talked, of course; and because our daughters were near or in their teens, we were comparing notes about the bewildering responsibility of bringing up girls.

32   After a while, Aunt Minnie remarked, "Well, I hope you teach your girls some *sense*. From what I read, I know you're great on telling them 'the facts,' facts we never heard of when we were girls. Like as not, some facts I don't know, now. But knowing the facts isn't going to do them any more good than not knowing the facts ever did, unless they have some sense taught them, too."

33   "What do you mean, Aunt Minnie?" one of us asked her, uncertainly. She reflected, threading a needle, "Well, I don't know but what the best way to tell you what I mean is to tell you about something that happened to me, forty years ago. I've never said anything about it before. But I've thought about it a good deal. Maybe—"

34   She had hardly begun when I recognized the story—her visit to her Cousin Ella's Midwestern home, the widower with his scarred face and saintly reputation and, very vividly, her getting lost in the great cornfield. I knew every word she was going to say—to the very end, I thought.

35   But no, I did not. Not at all.

36   She broke off, suddenly to exclaim with impatience, "Wasn't I the big ninny? Not so big a ninny as that old cousin of mine. I could wring her neck for getting me in such a state. Only she didn't know any better, herself. That was the way they brought up young people in those days, scaring them out of their wits about the awfulness of getting lost, but not telling them a thing about how *not* to get lost. Or how to act, if they did.

37   "If I had had the sense I was born with, I'd have known that running my legs off in a zigzag was the worst thing I could do. I couldn't have been more than a few feet from the path when I noticed I wasn't on it. My tracks in the loose plow dirt might have been perfectly plain. If I'd a' stood still, and collected my wits, I could have looked down to see which way my footsteps went and just walked back over them to the path and gone on about my business.

38   "Now I ask you, if I'd been told how to do that, wouldn't it have been a lot better protection for me—if protection was what my aunt thought she wanted to give

me—than to scare me so at the idea of being lost that I turned deaf-dumb-and-blind when I thought I was?

39   "And anyhow that patch of corn wasn't as big as she let on. And she knew it wasn't. It was no more than a big field in a farming country. I was a well-grown girl of sixteen, as tall as I am now. If I couldn't have found the path, I could have just walked along one line of cornstalks—*straight*—and I'd have come out somewhere in ten minutes. Fifteen at the most. Maybe not just where I wanted to go. But all right, safe, where decent folks were living."

40   She paused, as if she had finished. But at the inquiring blankness in our faces, she went on, "Well, now, why isn't teaching girls—and boys, too, for the Lord's sake don't forget they need it as much as the girls—about the man-and-woman business, something like that? If you give them the idea—no matter whether it's *as* you tell them the facts, or as you *don't* tell them the facts, that it is such a terribly scary thing that if they take a step into it, something's likely to happen to them so awful that you're ashamed to tell them what—well, they'll lose their heads and run around like crazy things, first time they take one step away from the path.

41   "For they'll be trying out the paths, all right. You can't keep them from it. And a good thing, too. How else are they going to find what it's like? Boys' and girls' going together is a path across one corner of growing up. And when they go together, they're likely to get off the path some. Seems to me, it's up to their folks to bring them up so when they do, they don't start screaming and running in circles, but stand still, right where they are, and get their breath and figure out how to get back.

42   "And anyhow, you don't tell 'em the truth about sex" (I was astonished to hear her use the actual word, taboo to women of her generation) "if they get the idea from you that it's all there is to living. It's not. If you don't get to where you want to go in it, well, there's a lot of landscape all around it a person can have a good time in.

43   "D'you know, I believe one thing that gives girls and boys the wrong idea is the way folks *look!* My old cousin's face, I can see her now, it was red as a rooster's comb when she was telling me about men in that cornfield. I believe now she kind of *liked* to talk about it."

44   (Oh, Aunt Minnie—and yours! I thought.)

45   Someone asked "But how *did* you get out, Aunt Minnie?"

46   She shook her head, laid down her sewing. "More foolishness. That minister my mother's cousin was keeping house for—her son-in-law—I caught sight of him, down along one of the aisles of cornstalks, looking down at the ground, thinking, the way he often did. And I was so glad to see him I rushed right up to him, and flung my arms around his neck and hugged him. He hadn't heard me coming. He gave a great start, put one arm around me and turned his face full towards me—I suppose for just a second he had forgotten how awful one side of it was. His expression, his eyes—well, you're all married women, you know how he looked, the way any able-bodied man thirty-six or -seven, who'd been married and begotten children, would look—for a minute anyhow, if a full-blooded girl of sixteen, who ought to have known better, flung herself at him without any warning, her hair tumbling down, her dress half unbuttoned, and hugged him with all her might.

47   "I was what they called innocent in those days. That is, I knew just as little about what men are like as my folks could manage I should. But I was old enough to know all right what that look meant. And it gave me a start. But of course the real thing of it was that dreadful scar of his, so close to my face—that wet corner of his mouth, his eye drawn down with the red inside of the lower eyelid showing—

48   "It turned me so sick, I pulled away with all my might, so fast that I ripped one sleeve nearly loose, and let out a screech like a wildcat. And ran. Did I run? And in a minute, I was through the corn and had come out in the back yard of the house. I hadn't been more than a few feet from it, probably, any of the time. And then I fainted away. Girls were always fainting away; it was the way our corset strings were pulled tight, I suppose, and then—oh, a lot of fuss.

49   "But anyhow," she finished, picking up her work and going on setting, neat firm stitches with steady hands, "there's one thing, I never told anybody it was Cousin Malcolm I had met in the cornfield. I told my cousin that 'a man had scared me.' And nobody said anything more about it to me, not ever. That was the way they did it in those days. They thought if they didn't let on about something, maybe it wouldn't have happened. I was sent back to Vermont right away and Cousin Malcolm went on being minister of the church. I've always been," said Aunt Minnie moderately, "kind of proud that I didn't go and ruin a man's life for just one second's slip-up. If you could have called it that. For it *would* have ruined him. You know how hard as stone people are about other folks' letdowns. If I'd have told, not one person in that town would have had any charity. Not one would have tried to understand. One slip, *once,* and they'd have pushed him down in the mud. If I had told, I'd have felt pretty bad about it, later—when I came to have more sense. But I declare, I can't see how I came to have the decency, dumb as I was then, to know that it wouldn't be fair."

50   It was not long after this talk that Aunt Minnie's elderly husband died, mourned by her, by all of us. She lived alone then. It was peaceful October weather for her, in which she kept a firm roundness of face and figure, as quiet-living country-women often do, on into her sixties.

51   But then Jake, the boy who had girl trouble, had wife trouble. We heard he had taken to running after a young girl, or was it that she was running after him? It was something serious. For his nice wife left him and came back with the children to live with her mother in our town. Poor Aunt Minnie used to go see her for long talks which made them both cry. And she went to keep house for Jake, for months at a time.

52   She grew old, during those years. When finally she (or something) managed to get the marriage mended so that Jake's wife relented and went back to live with him, there was no trace left of her pleasant brisk freshness. She was stooped and slow-footed and shrunken. We, her kinspeople, although we would have given our lives for any one of our own children, wondered whether Jake was worth what it had cost his mother to—well, steady him, or reform him. Or perhaps just understand him. Whatever it took.

53   She came of a long-lived family and was able to go on keeping house for herself well into her eighties. Of course we and the other neighbors stepped in often to make sure she was all right. Mostly, during those brief calls, the talk turned on nothing more vital than her geraniums. But one midwinter afternoon, sitting with her in front of her cozy stove, I chanced to speak in rather hasty blame of someone who had, I thought,

acted badly. To my surprise this brought from her the story about the cornfield which she had evidently quite forgotten telling me, twice before.

54   This time she told it almost dreamily, swaying to and fro in her rocking chair, her eyes fixed on the long slope of snow outside her window. When she came to the encounter with the minister she said, looking away from the distance and back into my eyes, "I know now that I had been, all along, kind of *interested* in him, the way any girl as old as I was would be, in any youngish man living in the same house with her. And a minister, too. They have to have the gift of gab so much more than most men, women get to thinking they are more alive than men who can't talk so well. I *thought* the reason I threw my arms around him was because I had been so scared. And I certainly had been scared, by my old cousin's horrible talk about the cornfield being full of men waiting to grab girls. But that wasn't all the reason I flung myself at Malcolm Fairchild and hugged him. I know that now. Why in the world shouldn't I have been taught *some* notion of it then? 'Twould do girls good to know that they are just like everybody else—human nature *and* sex, all mixed up together. I didn't have to hug him. I wouldn't have, if he'd been dirty or fat and old, or chewed tobacco."

55   I stirred in my chair, ready to say, "But it's not so simple as all that to tell girls—" and she hastily answered my unspoken protest. "I know, I know, most of it can't be put into words. There just aren't any words to say something that's so both-ways-at-once all the time as this man-and-woman business. But look here, you know as well as I do that there are lots more ways than in words to teach young folks what you want 'em to know."

56   The old woman stopped her swaying rocker to peer far back into the past with honest eyes. "What was in my mind back there in the cornfield—partly anyhow—was what had been there all the time I was living in the same house with Cousin Malcolm—that he had long straight legs, and broad shoulders, and lots of curly brown hair, and was nice and flat in the front, and that one side of his face was good-looking. But most of all, that he and I were really alone, for the first time, without anybody to see us.

57   "I suppose, if it hadn't been for that dreadful scar, he'd have drawn me up, tight, and—most any man would—kissed me. I know how I must have looked, all red and hot and my hair down and my dress torn open. And, used as he was to big cornfields, he probably never dreamed that the reason I looked that way was because I was scared to be by myself in one. He may have thought—you know what he may have thought.

58   "Well—if his face had been like anybody's—when he looked at me the way he did, the way a man does look at a woman he wants to have, it would have scared me—some. But I'd have cried, maybe. And probably he'd have kissed me again. You know how such things go. I might have come out of the cornfield halfway engaged to marry him. Why not? I was old enough, as people thought then. That would have been nature. That was probably what he thought of, in that first instant.

59   "But what did I do? I had one look at his poor, horrible face, and started back as though I'd stepped on a snake. And screamed and ran.

60   "What do you suppose *he* felt, left there in the corn? He must have been sure that I would tell everybody he had attacked me. He probably thought that when he came out and went back to the village he'd already be in disgrace and put out of the pulpit.

61   "But the worst must have been to find out, so rough, so plain from the way I acted—as if somebody had hit him with an ax—the way he would look to any women he might try to get close to. That must have been—" she drew a long breath, "well, pretty hard on him."

62   After a silence, she murmured pityingly, "Poor man!"

Suggestions for Discussion or Writing

1. Why does Aunt Minnie's story change each time she tells it?

2. Why is this story called "Sex Education"?

3. According to Aunt Minnie, what should sex education really consist of? Do you think she is right?

4. How do you react to each of the three cornfield incidents Aunt Minnie describes? Which of her stories do you think is most accurate? Why?

5. How does the narrative preceding each version of Aunt Minnie's story affect her telling of the story?

When I Heard the Learn'd Astronomer

Walt Whitman

Walt Whitman (1819–1892) was born in West Hills, Long Island, New York, but grew up in Brooklyn. He worked as a schoolteacher, printer, journalist, government clerk, and volunteer at military hospitals during the Civil War. His journalistic experience is evident in the descriptive catalogs of his poetry. Whitman's first collection of poems, Leaves of Grass, *was published in 1855 at his own expense. He wrote poems in praise of America, democracy, and the individual. His poetry is noted for its symbolic and lyrical qualities and its emphasis on experience.*

When I heard the learn'd astronomer,
When the proofs, the figures, were ranged in columns before me,
When I was shown the charts and diagrams, to add, divide, and measure them,
When I sitting heard the astronomer where he lectured with much applause
    in the lecture-room,

5   How soon unaccountable I became tired and sick,
     Till rising and gliding out I wander'd off by myself,
     In the mystical moist night-air, and from time to time,
     Look'd up in perfect silence at the stars.

Suggestions for Discussion or Writing

1. What do you think Whitman means by "unaccountable"?

2. What effect does Whitman's use of the parallel structure of the "When" phrases have on the main theme of the poem?

3. What do you think this poem says about the value of "book learning" compared to personal experience? Does the poem call for a complete escape from our formal education system?

4. How do the references to sound ("heard") and "silence" contribute to the poem's theme?

The Story We Know

Martha Collins

A poet from the University of Massachusetts, Boston, Martha Collins (1940–) was educated at Stanford and at the University of Iowa. She was a Bunting Fellow at Radcliffe from 1982 to 1983. In 1985, she received the Pushcart Prize and the Mary Carolyn Davies Memorial Award of the Poetry Society of America. She is the author of The Catastrophe of Rainbows *(1985), a collection of poems; her new book,* The Arrangement of Space *(1992), was published by Gibb Smith Publishers.*

     The way to begin is always the same. Hello,
     Hello. Your hand, your name. So glad, Just fine,
     and Good-bye at the end. That's every story we know,

     and why pretend? But lunch tomorrow? No?
5   Yes? An omelette, salad, chilled white wine?
     The way to begin is simple, sane, Hello,

     and then it's Sunday, coffee, the *Times*, a slow
     day by the fire, dinner at eight or nine
     and Good-bye. In the end, this is a story we know

10   so well we don't turn the page, or look below

the picture, or follow the words to the next line:
The way to begin is always the same Hello.

But one night, through the latticed window, snow
begins to whiten the air, and the tall white pine.
15   Good-bye is the end of every story we know

that night, and when we close the curtains, oh,
we hold each other against that cold white sign
of the way we all begin and end. *Hello,*
Good-bye is the only story. We know, we know.

Suggestions for Discussion or Writing

1. What form does this poem take? Why is the form important to the poem?

2. What is "the story we know"? What is the significance of this story?

3. How is the "story" a metaphor? What does it represent?

4. What is the symbolism of the latticed window, the snow, and the tall white pine?

5. What is the "cold white sign" in the last stanza?

An Elementary School Class Room in a Slum

Stephen Spender

Stephen Harold Spender (1909–), an English poet, has written numerous poems, short stories, essays, criticism, and novels. His concern with poverty, suffering, and injustice stems in part from his association with a Marxist group during the 1930s. His poetry is lyrical and romantic, and often deals with his personal reaction to human problems. His Collected Poems: 1928–1985, *was published in 1986.*

Far far from gusty waves, these children's faces.
Like rootless weeds the torn hair round their paleness.
The tall girl with her weighed-down head. The paper-seeming boy
    with rat's eyes. The stunted unlucky heir
5   Of twisted bones, reciting a father's gnarled disease,
His lesson from his desk. At back of the dim class,

One unnoted, sweet and young; his eyes live in a dream
Of squirrels' game, in tree room, other than this.

On sour cream walls, donations. Shakespeare's head
10 Cloudless at dawn, civilized dome riding all cities.
Belled, flowery, Tyrolese valley. Open-handed map
Awarding the world its world. And yet, for these

Children, these windows, not this world, are world,
Where all their future's painted with a fog,
15 A narrow street sealed in with a lead sky,
Far far from rivers, capes, and stars of words.

Surely Shakespeare is wicked, the map a bad example
With ships and sun and love tempting them to steal—
For lives that slyly turn in their cramped holes
20 From fog to endless night? On their slag heap, these children

Wear skins peeped through by bones and spectacles of steel
With mended glass, like bottle bits on stones.
All of their time and space are foggy slum
So blot their maps with slums as big as doom.

25 Unless, governor, teacher, inspector, visitor,
This map becomes their window and these windows
That open on their lives like crouching tombs
Break, O break open, till they break the town
And show the children to the fields and all their world
30 Azure on their sands, to let their tongues
Run naked into books, the white and green leaves open
The history theirs whose language is the sun.

Suggestions for Discussion or Writing

1. How does Spender use nature imagery ("waves," "squirrels") in the first stanza to show the condition of the classroom?

2. How does Spender use weather and time imagery ("fog," "night") in stanzas two and three to show the state of the children's awareness?

3. The poem argues the children's case from a particular viewpoint. Is the argument mainly rational or emotional? How does the poem reflect the author's subjective or objective viewpoint?

4. What are some of the negative images ("twisted bones," "slag heap")? Why might these images be an important part of the poem?

5. What do you think the author wants you to do, after reading the poem? Does his argument convince you?

The American Home in Transition

Examining Family Relationships

Introduction

I n the last several decades, family patterns have been changing. Turmoil in the home, divorce, single-parent homes, and alternate lifestyles have become common. Sociologists and religious leaders lament the fall of the traditional family structure, but no one seems to be able to solve the problems. Is family life as America has traditionally viewed it permanently at risk?

The readings in this section have been chosen to illustrate some of the concerns and to examine some of the relationships in the family. H. L. Mencken, Katherine Anne Porter, and John S. Harris explore the long-term effects of marital problems. Is it marriage itself that is in crisis? Possibly, but any relationship between partners could come under scrutiny by looking at the questions raised here.

The other selections examine the relationships between parents and children. Arlene Skolnick addresses the problem of looking for the perfect family, and the dissatisfaction that comes with accepting less. George Gallup, Jr., and Marie Winn take a close look at the frightening changes in families. Tillie Olsen's story is an introspective analysis of how change affected the members of one family. Linda Weltner shows a family that makes monumental changes after the birth of a baby to simplify their needs and share a more satisfying life with their child.

"Shaving," the story by Leslie Norris, presents a gentle, rich relationship between father and son. Clinton Larson's "Homestead in Idaho," a narrative poem taken from historical documents, offers a tragic family story. Last of all, Judith Hemschmeyer's "I Remember the Room was Filled with Light" shows how a child mends the relationship between parents.

Every family is different, each with its own unique flavor, each with a mix of problems and joys. Although showing a full catalog of the diversity of relationships is impossible, these selections address some of the problems, but also show some of the possibilities of solving them.

The Necessary Enemy

Katherine Anne Porter

Katherine Anne Porter (1890–1980) was born in Indian Creek, Texas, and educated in convent schools in Louisiana. Her Catholic background and multicultural experiences are the basis for much of her writing. Her first collection of stories and poems, Flowering Judas, *was published in 1930 and was followed by* Pale Horse, Pale Rider *(1939) and* The Leaning Tower and Other Stories *(1944). She has published a collection of essays and articles,* The Days Before *(1952), as well as the novel* Ship of Fools *(1962), which was her first major popular success. She often uses seemingly insignificant events to show the truths of human nature, as in the short story "Rope" published in* Flowering Judas *(1930).*

1   She is a frank, charming, fresh-hearted young woman who married for love. She and her husband are one of those good-looking young pairs who ornament this modern scene rather more in profusion perhaps than ever before in our history. They are handsome, with a talent for finding their way in their world, they work at things that interest them, their tastes agree and their hopes. They intend in all good faith to spend their lives together, to have children and do well by them and each other—to be happy, in fact, which for them is the whole point of their marriage. And all in stride, keeping their wits about them. Nothing romantic, mind you; their feet are on the ground.

2   Unless they were this sort of person, there would be not much point to what I wish to say; for they would seem to be an example of the high-spirited, right-minded young whom the critics are always invoking to come forth and do their duty and practice all those sterling old-fashioned virtues which in every generation seem to be falling into disrepair. As for virtues, these young people are more or less on their own, like most of their kind; they get very little moral or other aid from their society; but after three years of marriage this very contemporary young woman finds herself facing the oldest and ugliest dilemma of marriage.

3   She is dismayed, horrified, full of guilt and forebodings because she is finding out little by little that she is capable of hating her husband, whom she loves faithfully. She can hate him at times as fiercely and mysteriously, indeed in terribly much the same way, as often she hated her parents, her brothers and sisters, whom she loves, when she was a child. Even then it had seemed to her a kind of black treacherousness in her, her private wickedness that, just the same, gave her her only private life. That was one thing her parents never knew about her, never seemed to suspect. For it was never given a name. They did and said hateful things to her and to each other as if by right, as if in them it was a kind of virtue. But when they said to her, "Control your feelings," it was never when she was amiable and obedient, only in the black times of her hate. So it was her secret, a shameful one. When they punished her, sometimes for

the strangest reasons, it was, they said, only because they loved her—it was for her good. She did not believe this, but she thought herself guilty of something worse than ever they had punished her for. None of this really frightened her: the real fright came when she discovered that at times her father and mother hated each other; this was like standing on the doorsill of a familiar room and seeing in a lightning flash that the floor was gone, you were on the edge of a bottomless pit. Sometimes she felt that both of them hated her, but that passed, it was simply not a thing to be thought of, much less believed. She thought she had outgrown all this, but here it was again, an element in her own nature she could not control, or feared she could not. She would have to hide from her husband, if she could, the same spot in her feelings she had hidden from her parents, and for the same no doubt disreputable, selfish reason: she wants to keep his love.

4   Above all, she wants him to be absolutely confident that she loves him, for that is the real truth, no matter how unreasonable it sounds, and no matter how her own feelings betray them both at times. She depends recklessly on his love; yet while she is hating him, he might very well be hating her as much or even more, and it would serve her right. But she does not want to be served right, she wants to be loved and forgiven—that is, to be sure he would forgive her anything, if he had any notion of what she had done. But best of all she would like not to have anything in her love that should ask for forgiveness. She doesn't mean about their quarrels—they are not so bad. Her feelings are out of proportion, perhaps. She knows it is perfectly natural for people to disagree, have fits of temper, fight it out; they learn quite a lot about each other that way, and not all of it disappointing either. When it passes, her hatred seems quite unreal. It always did.

5   Love. We are early taught to say it. I love you. We are trained to the thought of it as if there were nothing else, or nothing else worth having without it, or nothing worth having which it could not bring with it. Love is taught, always by precept, sometimes by example. Then hate, which no one meant to teach us, comes of itself. It is true that if we say I love you, it may be received with doubt, for there are times when it is hard to believe. Say I hate you, and the one spoken to believes it instantly, once for all.

6   Say I love you a thousand times to that person afterward and mean it every time, and still it does not change the fact that once we said I hate you, and meant that too. It leaves a mark on that surface love had worn so smooth with its eternal caresses. Love must be learned, and learned again and again; there is no end to it. Hate needs no instruction, but waits only to be provoked . . . hate, the unspoken word, the unacknowledged presence in the house, that faint smell of brimstone among the roses, that invisible tongue-tripper, that unkempt finger in every pie, that sudden oh-so-curiously *chilling* look—could it be boredom?—on your dear one's features, making them quite ugly. Be careful: love, perfect love, is in danger.

7   If it is not perfect, it is not love, and if it is not love, it is bound to be hate sooner or later. This is perhaps a not too exaggerated statement of the extreme position of Romantic Love, more especially in America, where we are all brought up on it, whether we know it or not. Romantic Love is changeless, faithful, passionate, and its sole end is to render the two lovers happy. It has no obstacles save those provided by the hazards of fate (that is to say, society), and such sufferings as the lovers may cause each other are only another word for delight: exciting jealousies, thrilling uncertainties, the ritual

dance of courtship within the charmed closed circle of their secret alliance; all *real* troubles come from without, they face them unitedly in perfect confidence. Marriage is not the end but only the beginning of true happiness, cloudless, changeless to the end. That the candidates for this blissful condition have never seen an example of it, nor ever knew anyone who had, makes no difference. That is the ideal and they will achieve it.

8   How did Romantic Love manage to get into marriage at last, where it was most certainly never intended to be? At its highest it was tragic; the love of Héloïse and Abélard. At its most graceful, it was the homage of the trouvère for his lady. In its most popular form, the adulterous strayings of solidly married couples who meant to stray for their own good reasons, but at the same time do nothing to upset the property settlements or the line of legitimacy; at its most trivial, the pretty trifling of shepherd and shepherdess.

9   This was generally condemned by church and state and a word of fear to honest wives whose mortal enemy it was. Love within the sober, sacred realities of marriage was a matter of personal luck, but in any case, private feelings were strictly a private affair having, at least in theory, no bearing whatever on the fixed practice of the rules of an institution never intended as a recreation ground for either sex. If the couple discharged their religious and social obligations, furnished forth a copious progeny, kept their troubles to themselves, maintained public civility and died under the same roof, even if not always on speaking terms, it was rightly regarded as a successful marriage. Apparently this testing ground was too severe for all but the stoutest spirits; it too was based on an ideal, as impossible in its way as the ideal Romantic Love. One good thing to be said for it is that society took responsibility for the conditions of marriage, and the sufferers within its bonds could always blame the system, not themselves. But Romantic Love crept into the marriage bed, very stealthily, by centuries, bringing its absurd notions about love as eternal springtime and marriage as a personal adventure meant to provide personal happiness. To a Western romantic such as I, though my views have been much modified by painful experience, it still seems to me a charming work of the human imagination, and it is a pity its central notion has been taken too literally and has hardened into a convention as cramping and enslaving as the older one. The refusal to acknowledge the evils in ourselves which therefore are implicit in any human situation is as extreme and unworkable a proposition as the doctrine of total depravity; but somewhere between them, or maybe beyond them, there does exist a possibility for reconciliation between our desires for impossible satisfactions and the simple unalterable fact that we also desire to be unhappy and that we create our own sufferings; and out of these sufferings we salvage our fragments of happiness.

10   Our young woman who has been taught that an important part of her human nature is not real because it makes trouble and interferes with her peace of mind and shakes her self-love, has been very badly taught; but she has arrived at a most important stage of her re-education. She is afraid her marriage is going to fail because she has not love enough to face its difficulties; and this because at times she feels a painful hostility toward her husband, and cannot admit its reality because such an admission would damage in her own eyes her view of what love should be, an absurd view, based on

her vanity of power. Her hatred is real as her love is real, but her hatred has the advantage at present because it works on a blind instinctual level, it is lawless; and her love is subjected to a code of ideal conditions, impossible by their very nature of fulfillment, which prevents its free growth and deprives it of its right to recognize its human limitations and come to grips with them. Hatred is natural in a sense that love, as she conceives it, a young person brought up in the tradition of Romantic Love, is not natural at all. Yet it did not come by hazard, it is the very imperfect expression of the need of the human imagination to create beauty and harmony out of chaos, no matter how mistaken its notion of these things may be, nor how clumsy its methods. It has conjured love out of the air, and seeks to preserve it by incantations; when she spoke a vow to love and honor her husband until death, she did a very reckless thing, for it is not possible by an act of the will to fulfill such an engagement. But it was the necessary act of faith performed in defense of a mode of feeling, the statement of honorable intention to practice as well as she is able the noble, acquired faculty of love, that very mysterious overtone to sex which is the best thing in it. Her hatred is part of it, the necessary enemy and ally.

Suggestions for Discussion or Writing

1. In what way, as Porter suggests, is hate the "necessary enemy" of love? What does she mean by calling it the "necessary enemy"? Do you agree with her? Why?

2. At one point Porter says, "Love must be learned, and learned again and again. . . ." What does she mean by this?

3. Porter asserts that we find it hard to believe when someone proclaims their love for us, but that when they declare hatred, we believe them instantly. In your experience, is this a true assessment? Why?

4. What, if any, are the differences between love and romantic love? Why does Porter object to romantic love in marriage? Do you agree with her? Why?

5. How does the female perspective affect the article's point of view? Would it be different if told from a male perspective? If so, how?

6. Who is the audience for this essay? What is the author's purpose?

The War Between Man and Woman

H. L. Mencken

Henry Louis Mencken (1880–1950) was born in Baltimore, Maryland, where at the age of 16 he graduated as valedictorian from the Baltimore Polytechnic Institute. His first two books, George Bernard Shaw: His Plays *(1905) and* The Philosophy of Friedrich Nietzsche *(1905), tried to explain European culture to the American public. During World War I he was forced to cease writing two of his columns because of their pro-German content. One of his earlier essays,* In Defense of Women *(1918), which tries to prove that women are more intelligent than men, was not well accepted. Other influential essays include* Prejudice *(1919–1927), a series of essays on American life, art, politics, and religion, and* The American Language *(1919), his most popular and influential book, which contrasted American English with British English.*

1   Not many men, worthy of the name, gain anything of net value by marriage, at least as the institution is now met with in Christendom. Even assessing its benefits at their most inflated worth, they are plainly overborne by crushing disadvantages. When a man marries it is no more than a sign that the feminine talent for persuasion and intimidation—i.e., the feminine talent for survival in a world of clashing concepts and desires, the feminine competence and intelligence—has forced him into a more or less abhorrent compromise with his own honest inclinations and best interests. Whether that compromise be a sign of his relative stupidity or of his relative cowardice it is all one: the two things, in their symptoms and effects, are almost identical. In the first case he marries because he has been clearly bowled over in a combat of wits; in the second he resigns himself to marriage as the safest form of liaison. In both cases his inherent sentimentality is the chief weapon in the hand of his opponent. It makes him cherish the fiction of his enterprise, and even of his daring, in the midst of the most crude and obvious operations against him. It makes him accept as real the bold play-acting that women always excel at, and at no time more than when stalking a man. It makes him, above all, see a glamor of romance in a transaction which, even at its best, contains almost as much gross trafficking, at bottom, as the sale of a mule.

2   A man in full possession of the modest faculties that nature commonly apportions to him is at least far enough above idiocy to realize that marriage is a bargain in which he seldom wants *all* that taking a wife offers and implies. He wants, at most, no more than certain parts. He may desire, let us say, a housekeeper to protect his goods and entertain his friends—but he may shrink from the thought of sharing his bathtub with any one, and home cooking may be downright poisonous to him. He may yearn for a son to pray at his tomb—and yet suffer acutely at the mere approach of relatives-in-law.

He may dream of a beautiful and complaisant mistress, less exigent and mercurial than any bachelor may hope to discover—and stand aghast at admitting her to his bank-book, his family-tree and his secret ambitions. He may want company and not intimacy, or intimacy and not company. He may want a cook and not a partner in his business, or a partner in his business and not a cook.

3   But in order to get the precise thing or things that he wants, he has to take a lot of other things that he doesn't want—that no sane man, in truth, could imaginably want—and it is to the enterprise of forcing him into this almost Armenian bargain that the woman of his "choice" addresses herself. Once the game is fairly set, she searches out his weaknesses with the utmost delicacy and accuracy, and plays upon them with all her superior resources. He carries a handicap from the start. His sentimental and unintelligent belief in theories that she knows quite well are not true—e.g., the theory that she shrinks from him, and is modestly appalled by the banal carnalities of marriage itself—give her a weapon against him which she drives home with instinctive and compelling art. The moment she discerns this sentimentality bubbling within him— that is, the moment his oafish smirks and eye-rolling signify that he had achieved the intellectual disaster that is called falling in love—he is hers to do with as she listeth. Save for acts of God, he is forthwith as good as married.

4   Men usually get their mates by this process of falling in love; save among the aristocracies of the North and Latin men, the marriage of convenience is relatively rare; a hundred men marry "beneath" them to every woman who perpetrates the same folly. And what is meant by falling in love? What is meant by it is a procedure whereby a man accounts for the fact of his marriage, after feminine initiative and generalship have made it inevitable, by enshrouding it in a purple maze of romance—in brief, by setting up the doctrine that an obviously self-possessed and mammalian woman, engaged deliberately in the most important adventure of her life, and with the keenest understanding of its utmost implications, is a naive, tender, moony and almost disembodied creature, enchanted and made perfect by emotions that have stolen upon her unawares, and which she could not acknowledge, even to herself, without blushing to death. By this preposterous doctrine, the defeat and enslavement of the man is made glorious, and even gifted with a touch of flattering naughtiness. The sheer horsepower of his wooing has assailed and overcome her maiden modesty; she trembles in his arms; he has been granted a free franchise to work his wicked will upon her. Thus do the ambulant images of God cloak their shackles proudly, and divert the judicious with their boastful shouts.

5   Women are much more cautious about embracing the conventional hocus-pocus of the situation. They seldom acknowledge that they have fallen in love, as the phrase is, until the man has revealed his delusion, and so cut off his retreat; to do otherwise would be to bring down upon their heads the mocking and contumely of all their sisters. With them, falling in love thus appears in the light of an afterthought, or, perhaps more accurately, in the light of a contagion. The theory, it would seem, is that the love of the man, laboriously avowed, has inspired it instantly, and by some unintelligible magic; that it was non-existent until the heat of his own flames set it off. This theory, it must be acknowledged, has a certain element of fact in it. A woman seldom allows herself to be swayed by emotion while the principal business is yet afoot and its issue still in

doubt; to do so would be to expose a degree of imbecility that is confined only to the half-wits of the sex. But once the man is definitely committed, she frequently unbends a bit, if only as a relief from the strain of a fixed purpose, and so, throwing off her customary inhibitions, indulges in the luxury of a more or less forced and mawkish sentiment. It is, however, almost unheard of for her to permit herself this relaxation before the sentimental intoxication of the man is assured. To do otherwise—that is, to confess, even *post facto,* to an anterior descent—would expose her to the scorn of all other women. Such a confession would be an admission that emotion had got the better of her at a critical intellectual moment, and in the eyes of women, as in the eyes of the small minority of genuinely intelligent men, no treason to the higher cerebral centers could be more disgraceful.

Suggestions for Discussion or Writing

1. Notice that Mencken's title includes the word "war." Describe the nature of this "war." Have you seen indications of the war in your own experience? What are they?

2. Who is responsible for the marriage of a couple—the man or the woman? How does the responsible party bring about the marriage? What compromises must the married man make, according to Mencken?

3. What tone dominates the essay? How does the tone of Mencken's essay compare to Gallup's?

4. What words, phrases, or arguments do you find particularly amusing? Why?

5. As explained in the last two paragraphs, how do men and women differ in their approach to getting a mate?

6. How accurate is the picture of men and women painted by Mencken?

The Faltering Family

George Gallup, Jr.

George Gallup, Jr. (1901– 1984) was born in Jefferson, Iowa. He earned a B.A., M.A., and Ph.D. from Iowa State University and began a long career in journalism, advertising, and public opinion when he became the head of the journalism department at Drake University in 1929. He is the founder of the Gallup Poll (1935) and developed the method of measuring the comparative interest of readers and radio audiences. He also established the Gallup International Research Institutes, Inc., and Quill and Scroll, the international honor society for high school journalists. He was inducted into the Advertising Hall of Fame in 1977 and supplied editorial surveys to newspapers as well as numerous articles on public opinion.

1   In a recent Sunday school class in a United Methodist Church in the Northeast, a group of eight- to ten-year olds were in a deep discussion with their two teachers. When asked to choose which of ten stated possibilities they most feared happening, their response was unanimous. All the children most dreaded a divorce between their parents.

2   Later, as the teachers, a man and a woman in their late thirties, reflected on the lesson, they both agreed they'd been shocked at the response. When they were the same age as their students, they said, the possibility of their parents' being divorced never entered their heads. Yet in just one generation, children seemed to feel much less security in their family ties.

3   Nor is the experience of these two Sunday school teachers an isolated one. Psychiatrists revealed in one recent newspaper investigation that the fears of children definitely do change in different periods; and in recent times, divorce has become one of the most frequently mentioned anxieties. In one case, for example, a four-year-old insisted that his father rather than his mother walk him to nursery school each day. The reason? He said many of his friends had "no daddy living at home, and I'm scared that will happen to me" (*The New York Times,* May 2, 1983).

4   In line with such reports, our opinion leaders expressed great concern about the present and future status of the American family. In the poll 33 percent of the responses listed decline in family structure, divorce, and other family-oriented concerns as one of the five major problems facing the nation today. And 26 percent of the responses included such family difficulties as one of the five major problems for the United States in the year 2000.

5   Historical and sociological trends add strong support to these expressions of concern. For example, today about one marriage in every two ends in divorce. Moreover, the situation seems to be getting worse, rather than better. In 1962, the number of divorces was 2.2 per 1,000 people, according to the National Center for Health Statistics. By 1982, the figure had jumped to 5.1 divorces per 1,000 people—a rate that had more than doubled in two decades.

6   One common concern expressed about the rise in divorces and decline in stability of the family is that the family unit has traditionally been a key factor in transmitting stable cultural and moral values from generation to generation. Various studies have shown that educational and religious institutions often can have only a limited impact on children without strong family support.

7   Even grandparents are contributing to the divorce statistics. One recent study revealed that about 100,000 people over the age of fifty-five get divorced in the United States each year. These divorces are usually initiated by men who face retirement, and the relationships being ended are those that have endured for thirty years or more (*The New York Times Magazine,* December 19, 1982).

8   What are the pressures that have emerged in the past twenty years that cause long-standing family bonds to be broken?

9   Many now agree that the sexual revolution of the 1960s worked a profound change on our society's family values and personal relationships. Certainly, the seeds of upheaval were present before that critical decade. But a major change that occurred in the mid-sixties was an explicit widespread rejection of the common values about sexual and family relationships that most Americans in the past had held up as an ideal.

10   We're just beginning to sort through all the changes in social standards that have occurred. Here are some of the major pressures that have contributed to those changes:

Pressure One: Alternative Lifestyles

11   Twenty years ago, the typical American family was depicted as a man and woman who were married to each other and who produced children (usually two) and lived happily ever after. This was the pattern that young people expected to follow in order to become "full" or "normal" members of society. Of course, some people have always chosen a different route—remaining single, taking many partners, or living with a member of their own sex. But they were always considered somewhat odd, and outside the social order of the traditional family.

12   In the last two decades, this picture has changed dramatically. In addition to the proliferation of single people through divorce, we also have these developments:

- Gay men and women have petitioned the courts for the right to marry each other and to adopt children. These demands are being given serious consideration, and there may even be a trend of sorts in this direction. For example, the National Association of Social Workers is increasingly supporting full adoption rights for gay people (*The New York Times,* January 10, 1983).

- Many heterosexual single adults have been permitted to adopt children and set up single-parent families. So being unattached no longer excludes people from the joys of parenthood.

- Some women have deliberately chosen to bear children out of wedlock and raise them alone. In the past, many of these children would have been given up for adoption, but no longer.

A most unusual case involved an unmarried psychologist, Dr. Afton Blake, who recently gave birth after being artificially inseminated with sperm from a sperm bank to which Nobel Prize winners had contributed (*The New York Times,* September 6, 1983).

- In a recent Gallup Youth Poll, 64 percent of the teenagers questioned said that they hoped their lives would be different from those of their parents. This included having more money, pursuing a different kind of profession, living in a different area, having more free time—and staying single longer.

  Most surveys show increasing numbers of unmarried couples living together. Also, there are periodic reports of experiments in communal living, "open marriages," and other such arrangements. Although the more radical approaches to relationships tend to come and go and never seem to attract large numbers of people, the practice of living together without getting married seems to be something that's here to stay. The law is beginning to respond to these arrangements with awards for "palimony"—compensation for long-term unmarried partners in a relationship. But the legal and social status of unmarried people who live together is still quite uncertain—especially as far as any children of the union are concerned.

- Increasing numbers of married couples are choosing to remain childless. Planned Parenthood has even established workshops for couples to assist them in making this decision (*Los Angeles Herald-Examiner,* November 27, 1979).

13   So clearly, a situation has arisen during the last twenty years in which traditional values are no longer as important. Also, a wide variety of alternatives to the traditional family have arisen. Individuals may feel that old-fashioned marriage is just one of many options.

Pressure Two: Sexual Morality

14   The changes in attitudes toward sexual morality have changed dramatically in the last two decades as the alternatives to traditional marriage. Hear what a widely used college textbook, published in 1953, said about premarital sex:

> *The arguments against premarital coitus outweigh those in its favor. Except for the matter of temporary physical pleasure, all arguments about gains tend to be highly theoretical, while the risks and unpleasant consequences tend to be in equal degree highly practical. . . .*
>
> *The promiscuity of young men is certainly poor preparation for marital fidelity and successful family life. For girls it is certainly no better and sometimes leads still further to the physical and psychological shock of abortion or the more prolonged suffering of bearing an illegitimate child*

and giving it up to others. From the viewpoint of ethical and religious leaders, the spread of disease through unrestrained sex activities is far more than a health problem. They see it as undermining the dependable standards of character and the spiritual values that raise life to the level of the "good society."

(This comes from *Marriage and the Family* by Professor Ray E. Baber of Pomona College, California, which was part of the McGraw-Hill Series in Sociology and Anthropology and required reading for some college courses.)

15   Clearly, attitudes have changed a great deal in just three decades. Teenagers have accepted the idea of premarital sex as the norm. In one recent national poll, 52 percent of girls and 66 percent of boys favored having sexual relations in their teens. Ironically, however, 46 percent of the teenagers thought that virginity in their future marital partner was fairly important. Youngsters, in other words, display some confusion about what they want to do sexually, and what they expect from a future mate.

16   But of course, only part of the problem of defining sexual standards lies with young people and premarital sex. The strong emphasis on achieving an active and rewarding sex life has probably played some role in encouraging many husbands and wives into rejecting monogamy. Here's some of the evidence that's been accumulating:

- Half of the men in a recent nationwide study admitted cheating on their wives (*Pensacola Journal,* May 30, 1978).

- Psychiatrists today say they see more patients who are thinking about having an extramarital affair and who wonder if it would harm their marriage (*New York Post,* November 18, 1976).

- A psychiatrist at the Albert Einstein College of Medicine says, "In my practice I have been particularly struck by how many women have been able to use an affair to raise their consciousness and their confidence."

17   So the desire for unrestrained sex now tends to take a place among other more traditional priorities, and this can be expected to continue to exert strong pressure on marriage relationships.

Pressure Three: The Economy

18   The number of married women working outside the home has been increasing steadily, and most of these women are working out of economic necessity. As a result, neither spouse may have time to concentrate on the nurturing of the children or of the marriage relationship.

19   One mother we interviewed in New Jersey told us about her feelings when she was forced to work full time in a library after her husband lost his job.

20   "It's the idea that I have no choice that really bothers me," she said. "I have to work, or we won't eat or have a roof over our heads. I didn't mind working part-time just to have extra money. I suppose that it's selfish, but I hate having to work every

day and then to come home, fix dinner, and have to start doing housework. Both my husband and I were raised in traditional families, where the father went to work and the mother stayed home and took care of the house and children. [My husband] would never think of cooking or doing housework. I've raised my boys the same way, and now I'm paying for it. Sometimes, I almost hate my husband, even though I know it's not his fault."

21   Unfortunately, such pressures probably won't ease in the future. Even if the economy improves and the number of unemployed workers decreases, few women are likely to give up their jobs. Economists agree that working-class women who have become breadwinners during a recession can be expected to remain in the work force. One reason is that many unemployed men aren't going to get their old jobs back, even when the economy improves.

22   "To the extent that [the men] may have to take lower-paying service jobs, their families will need a second income," says Michelle Brandman, associate economist at Chase Econometrics. "The trend to two paycheck families as a means of maintaining family income is going to continue" (*The Wall Street Journal,* December 8, 1982).

23   In addition to the pressures of unemployment, the cost of having, rearing, and educating children is steadily going up. Researchers have found that middle-class families with two children *think* they're spending only about 15 percent of their income on their children. Usually, though, they *actually* spend about 40 percent of their money on them. To put the cost in dollars and cents, if you had a baby in 1977, the estimated cost of raising that child to the age of eighteen will be $85,000, and that figure has of course been on the rise for babies born since then (*New York Daily News,* July 24, 1977).

24   Another important factor that promises to keep both spouses working full time in the future is the attitude of today's teenagers toward these issues. They're not so much concerned about global issues like overpopulation as they are about the high cost of living. Both boys and girls place a lot of emphasis on having enough money so that they can go out and do things. Consequently, most teenage girls surveyed say they expect to pursue careers, even after they get married.

25   So it would seem that by the year 2000 we can expect to see more working mothers in the United States. The woman who doesn't hold down any sort of outside job but stays at home to care for her children represents a small percentage of wives today. By the end of the century, with a few exceptions here and there, she may well have become a part of America's quaint past.

26   As women have joined the work force in response to economic needs, one result has been increased emotional strains on the marriage and family relationships. But there's another set of pressures that has encouraged women to pursue careers. That's the power of feminist philosophy to permeate attitudes in grassroots America during the past couple of decades.

Pressure Four: Grass-roots Feminist Philosophy

27   Many women may not agree with the most radical expressions of feminist philosophy that have arisen in the past decade or so. But most younger women—and

indeed, a majority of women in the United States—tend to agree with most of the objectives that even the radical feminist groups have been trying to achieve. The basic feminist philosophy has filtered down to the grass roots, and young boys and girls are growing up with feminist assumptions that may have been foreign to their parents and grandparents.

28   For example, child care and housework are no longer regarded strictly as "women's work" by the young people we've polled. Also, according to the Gallup Youth Poll, most teenage girls want to go to college and pursue a career. Moreover, they expect to marry later in life and to continue working after they're married. Another poll, conducted by *The New York Times* and CBS News, revealed that only 2 percent of the youngest age group interviewed—that is, those eighteen to twenty-nine years old—preferred "traditonal marriage." By this, they meant a marriage in which the husband is exclusively a provider and the wife is exclusively a homemaker and mother.

29   If these young people continue to hold views similar to these into later life, it's likely that the changes that are occurring today in the traditional family structure will continue. For one thing, more day-care centers for children will have to be established. Consequently, the rearing of children will no longer be regarded as solely the responsibility of the family, but will become a community or institutional responsibility.

30   But while such developments may lessen the strain on mothers and fathers, they may also weaken the bonds that hold families together. Among other things, it may become psychologically easier to get a divorce if a person is not getting along with a spouse, because the divorcing spouses will believe it's less likely that the lives of the children will be disrupted.

31   So the concept of broadening the rights of women vis-á-vis their husbands and families had certainly encouraged women to enter the working world in greater numbers. They're also more inclined to seek a personal identity that isn't tied up so much in their homelife.

32   These grass-roots feminist forces have brought greater benefits to many, but at the same time they've often worked against traditional family ties, and we remain uncertain about what is going to replace them. Feminists may argue that the traditional family caused its own demise—or else why would supposedly content wives and daughters have worked so hard to transform it? Whatever its theories, though, feminism is still a factor that, in its present form, appears to exert a destabilizing influence on many traditional familial relationships among husbands, wives, and children.

33   As things stand now, our family lives are in a state of flux and will probably continue to be out of balance until the year 2000. The pressures we've discussed will continue to have an impact on our family lives in future years. But at the same time, counterforces, which tend to drive families back together again, are also at work.

34   One of these factors is a traditionalist strain in the large majority of American women. The vast majority of women in this country—74 percent—continue to view marriage with children as the most interesting and satisfying life for them personally, according to a Gallup Poll for the White House Conference on Families released in June, 1980.

35   Another force supporting family life is the attitude of American teenagers toward divorce. According to a recent Gallup Youth Poll, 55 percent feel that divorces are too easy to get today. Also, they're concerned about the high rate of divorce, and they want to have enduring marriages themselves. But at the same time—in a response that reflects the confusion of many adult Americans on the subject—67 percent of the teens in this same poll say it's right to get a divorce if a couple doesn't get along together. In other words, they place little importance on trying to improve or salvage a relationship that has run into serious trouble.

36   There's a similar ambivalence in the experts we polled. As we've seen, 33 percent of them consider family problems as a top concern today, and 26 percent think these problems will be a big difficulty in the year 2000. But ironically, less than 3 percent suggest that strengthening family relationships is an important consideration in planning for the future! It's obvious, then, that we're confused and ambivalent in our feelings about marriage and the family. Most people know instinctively, without having to read a poll or a book, that happiness and satisfaction in life are rooted largely in the quality of our personal relationships. Furthermore, the most important of those relationships usually begin at home. So one of the greatest challenges we face before the year 2000, both as a nation and as individuals, is how to make our all-important family ties strong and healthy. It's only upon such a firm personal foundation that we can hope to venture forth and grapple effectively with more public problems.

Suggestions for Discussion or Writing

1. State the thesis of Gallup's essay in your own words. What kinds of evidence does he use to support his thesis?

2. In giving his evidence, what assumptions does Gallup make? Are his assumptions stated or implicit? How so?

3. According to Gallup, why are more women working outside the home? Why does he think this is a permanent change in the American lifestyle?

4. The author seems to maintain an atmosphere of objectivity in his essay. How does he accomplish this? Are there any words or phrases that reveal his true opinion on the subject?

5. In his conclusion Gallup states that "most people know instinctively . . . that happiness and satisfaction in life are rooted largely in the quality of our personal relationships." Do you agree with him? What other areas of life might offer similar satisfaction? In your experience is there anything satisfying enough to replace personal relationships? Why?

6. Do you plan to follow the same lifestyle as your parents? Why? What factors might lead you to choose another lifestyle?

The Paradox of Perfection

Arlene Skolnick

Arlene Skolnick (1933–   ) is a research psychologist at the Institute of Human Development at the University of California, Berkeley. She has been an editor or co-editor for the following books: Family in Transition, The Intimate Environment, Rethinking Childhood, *and* The Psychology of Human Development.

1   The American Family, as even readers of *Popular Mechanics* must know by now, is in what Sean O'Casey would have called "a terrible state of chassis." Yet, there are certain ironies about the much-publicized crisis that give one pause.

2   True, the statistics seem alarming. The U.S. divorce rate, though it has reached something of a plateau in recent years, remains the highest in American history. The number of births out-of-wedlock among all races and ethnic groups continues to climb. The plight of many elderly Americans subsisting on low fixed incomes is well known.

3   What puzzles me is an ambiguity, not in the facts, but in what we are asked to make of them. A series of opinion polls conducted in 1978 by Yankelovich, Skelley, and White, for example, found that 38 percent of those surveyed had recently witnessed one or more "destructive activities" (e.g., a divorce, a separation, a custody battle) within their own families or those of their parents or siblings. At the same time, 92 percent of the respondents said the family was highly important to them as a "personal value."

4   Can the family be at once a cherished "value" and a troubled institution? I am inclined to think, in fact, that they go hand in hand. A recent "Talk of the Town" report in *The New Yorker* illustrates what I mean:

> *A few months ago word was heard from Billy Gray, who used to play brother Bud in "Father Knows Best," the 1950s television show about the nice Anderson family who lived in the white frame house on a side street in some mythical Springfield—the house at which the father arrived each night swinging open the front door and singing out "Margaret, I'm home!" Gray said he felt "ashamed" that he had ever had anything to do with the show. It was all "totally false," he said, and had caused many Americans to feel inadequate, because they thought that was the way life was supposed to be and that their own lives failed to measure up.*

5   As Susan Sontag has noted in *On Photography,* mass-produced images have "extraordinary powers to determine our demands upon reality." The family is especially vulnerable to confusion between truth and illusion. What, after all, is "normal"? All of us have a backstairs view of our own families, but we know The Family, in the aggregate, only vicariously.

6   Like politics or athletics, the family has become a media event. Television offers nightly portrayals of lump-in-throat family "normalcy" *(The Waltons, Little House on the Prairie)* and even humorous "deviance" *(One Day at a Time, The Odd Couple).* Family advisers sally forth in syndicated newspaper columns to uphold standards, mend relationships, suggest counseling, and otherwise lead their readers back to the True Path. For commercial purposes, advertisers spend millions of dollars to create stirring vignettes of glamorous-but-ordinary families, the kind of family most 11-year-olds wish they had.

7   All Americans do not, of course, live in such a family, but most share an intuitive sense of what the "ideal" family should be—reflected in the precepts of religion, the conventions of etiquette, and the assumptions of law. And, characteristically, Americans tend to project the ideal back into the past, the time when virtues of all sorts are thought to have flourished.

8   We do not come off well by comparison with that golden age, nor could we, for it is as elusive and mythical as Brigadoon. If Billy Gray shames too easily, he has a valid point: While Americans view the family as the proper context for their own lives—9 out of 10 people live in one—they have no realistic context in which to view the family. Family history, until recently, was as neglected in academe as it still is in the press. [The Summer 1980] White House Conference on Families is "policy-oriented," which means present-minded. The familiar, depressing charts of "leading family indicators"—marriage, divorce, illegitimacy—in newspapers and newsmagazines rarely survey the trends before World War II. The discussion, in short, lacks ballast.

9   Let us go back to before the American Revolution.

10   Perhaps what distinguishes the modern family most from its colonial counterpart is its newfound privacy. Throughout the 17th and 18th centuries, well over 90 percent of the American population lived in small rural communities. Unusual behavior rarely went unnoticed, and neighbors often intervened directly in a family's affairs, to help or to chastise.

11   The most dramatic example was the rural "charivari," prevalent in both Europe and the United States until the early 19th century. The purpose of these noisy gatherings was to censure community members for familial transgressions—unusual sexual behavior, marriages between persons of grossly discrepant ages, or "household disor-der," to name a few. As historian Edward Shorter describes it in *The Making of the Modern Family*:

> *Sometimes the demonstration would consist of masked individuals circling somebody's house at night, screaming, beating on pans, and blowing cow horns. . . . (O)n other occasions, the offender would be seized and marched through the streets, seated perhaps backwards on a donkey or forced to wear a placard describing his sin.*

12   The state itself had no qualms about intruding into a family's affairs by statute, if necessary. Consider 17th-century New England's "stubborn child" laws that, though never actually enforced, sanctioned the death penalty for chronic disobedience to one's parents.

13   If the boundaries between home and society seem blurred during the colonial era, it is because they were. People were neither very emotional nor very self-conscious about family life, and, as historian John Demos points out, family and community were "joined in a relation of profound reciprocity." In his *Of Domestical Duties,* William Gouge, a 17th-century Puritan preacher, called the family "a little community." The home, like the larger community, was as much an economic as a social unit; all members of the family worked, be it on the farm, or in a shop, or in the home.

14   There was not much to idealize. Love was not considered the basis for marriage but one possible result of it. According to historian Carl Degler, it was easier to obtain a divorce in colonial New England than anywhere else in the Western world, and the divorce rate climbed steadily throughout the 18th century, though it remained low by contemporary standards. Romantic images to the contrary, it was rare for more than two generations (parents and children) to share a household, for the simple reason that very few people lived beyond the age of 60. It is ironic that our nostalgia for the extended family—including grandparents and grandchildren—comes at a time when, thanks to improvements in health care, its existence is less threatened than ever before.

15   Infant mortality was high in colonial days, though not as high as we are accustomed to believe, since food was plentiful and epidemics, owing to generally low population density, were few. In the mid-1700s, the average age of marriage was about 24 for men, 21 for women—not much different from what it is now. Households, on average, were larger, but not startlingly so: A typical household in 1790 included about 5.6 members, versus about 3.5 today. Illegitimacy was widespread. Premarital pregnancies reached a high in 18th-century America (10 percent of all first births) that was not equalled until the 1950s.

Form Follows Function

16   In simple demographic terms, then, the differences between the American family in colonial times and today are not all that stark; the similarities are sometimes striking.

17   The chief contrast is psychological. While Western societies have always idealized the family to some degree, the most vivid literary portrayals of family life before the 19th century were negative or, at best, ambivalent. In what might be called the "high tragic" tradition—including Sophocles, Shakespeare, and the Bible, as well as fairy tales and novels—the family was portrayed as a high-voltage emotional setting, laden with dark passion, sibling rivalries, and violence. There was also the "low comic" tradition—the world of henpecked husbands and tyrannical mothers-in-law.

18   It is unlikely that our 18th-century ancestors ever left the Book of Genesis or *Tom Jones* with the feeling that their own family lives were seriously flawed.

19   By the time of the Civil War, however, American attitudes toward the family had changed profoundly. The early decades of the 19th century marked the beginnings of America's gradual transformation into an urban, industrial society. In 1820, less than 8 percent of the U.S. population lived in cities; by 1860, the urban concentration approached 20 percent, and by 1900 that proportion had doubled.

20   Structurally, the American family did not immediately undergo a comparable transformation. Despite the large families of many immigrants and farmers, the size

of the average family declined—slowly but steadily—as it had been doing since the 17th century. Infant mortality remained about the same and may even have increased somewhat, owing to poor sanitation in crowded cities. Legal divorces were easier to obtain than they had been in colonial times. Indeed, the rise in the divorce rate was a matter of some concern during the 19th century, though death, not divorce, was the prime cause of one-parent families, as it was up to 1965.

21   Functionally, however, America's industrial revolution had a lasting effect on the family. No longer was the household typically a group of interdependent workers. Now, men went to offices and factories and became breadwinners; wives stayed home to mind the hearth; children went off to the new public schools. The home was set apart from the dog-eat-dog arena of economic life; it came to be viewed as a utopian retreat or, in historian Christopher Lasch's phrase, a "haven in a heartless world." Marriage was now valued primarily for its emotional attractions. Above all, the family became something to worry about.

22   The earliest and most saccharine "sentimental model" of the family appeared in the new mass media that proliferated during the second quarter of the 19th century. Novels, tracts, newspaper articles, and ladies' magazines—there were variations for each class of society—elaborated a "Cult of True Womanhood" in which piety, submissiveness, and domesticity dominated the pantheon of desirable feminine qualities. This quotation from *The Ladies Book* (1830) is typical:

> *See, she sits, she walks, she speaks, she looks—unutterable things! Inspiration springs up in her very paths—and illuminates her whole orbit. With her, man not only feels safe, but actually renovated.*

23   In the late 1800s, science came into the picture. The "professionalization" of the housewife took two different forms. One involved motherhood and childrearing, according to the latest scientific understanding of children's special physical and emotional needs. (It is no accident that the publishing of children's books became a major industry during this period.) The other was the domestic science movement— "home economics," basically—which focused on woman as full-time homemaker, applying "scientific" and "industrial" rationality to shopping, making meals, and housework.

24   The new ideal of the family prompted a cultural split that has endured, one that Tocqueville had glimpsed (and rather liked) in 1835. Society was divided more sharply into man's sphere and woman's sphere. Toughness, competition, and practicality were the masculine values that ruled the outside world. The softer values—affection, tranquility, piety—were worshipped in the home and the church. In contrast to the colonial view, the ideology of the "modern" family implied a critique of everything beyond the front door.

25   What is striking as one looks at the writings of the 19th-century "experts"—the physicians, clergymen, phrenologists, and "scribbling ladies"—is how little their essential message differs from that of the sociologists, psychiatrists, pediatricians, and women's magazine writers of the 20th century, particularly since World War II.

26   Instead of men's and women's spheres, of course, sociologists speak of "instrumental" and "expressive" roles. The notion of the family as a retreat from the harsh

realities of the outside world crops up as "functional differentiation." And, like the 19th-century utopians who believed society could be regenerated through the perfection of family life, 20th-century social scientists have looked at the failed family as the source of most American social problems.

27   None of these who promoted the sentimental model of the family—neither the popular writers nor the academics—considered the paradox of perfectionism: the ironic possibility that it would lead to trouble. Yet it has. The image of the perfect, happy family makes ordinary families seem like failures. Small problems loom as big problems if the "normal" family is thought to be one where there are no real problems at all.

28   One sees this phenomenon at work on the generation of Americans born and reared during the late 19th century, the first generation reared on the mother's milk of sentimental imagery. Between 1900 and 1920, the U.S. divorce rate doubled, from four to eight divorces annually per 1,000 married couples. The jump—comparable to the 100 percent increase in the divorce rate between 1960 and 1980—is not attributable to changes in divorce laws, which were not greatly liberalized. Rather, it would appear that, as historian Thomas O'Neill believes, Americans were simply more willing to dissolve marriages that did not conform to their idea of domestic bliss—and perhaps try again.

A "Fun" Morality

29   If anything, family standards became even more demanding as the 20th century progressed. The new fields of psychology and sociology opened up whole new definitions of familial perfection. "Feelings"—fun, love, warmth, good orgasm— acquired heightened popular significance as the invisible glue of successful families.

30   Psychologist Martha Wolfenstein, in an analysis of several decades of government-sponsored infant care manuals, has documented the emergence of a "fun morality." In former days, being a good parent meant carrying out certain tasks with punctilio [strictness or exactness]; if your child was clean and reasonably obedient, you had no cause to probe his psyche. Now, we are told, parents must commune with their own feelings and those of their children—an edict which has seeped into the ethos of education as well. The distinction is rather like that between religions of deed and religions of faith. It is one thing to make your child brush his teeth; it is quite another to transform the whole process into a joyous "learning experience."

31   The task of 20th-century parents has been further complicated by the advice offered them. The experts disagree with each other and often contradict themselves. The kindly Dr. Benjamin Spock, for example, is full of contradictions. In a detailed analysis of Baby and Child Care, historian Michael Zuckerman observes that Spock tells mothers to relax ("trust yourself") yet warns them that they have an "ominous power" to destroy their children's innocence and make them discontented "for years" or even "forever."

32   As we enter the 1980s, both family images and family realities are in a state of transition. After a century and a half, the web of attitudes and nostrums comprising the "sentimental model" is beginning to unravel. Since the mid-1960s, there has been

a youth rebellion of sorts, a new "sexual revolution," a revival of feminism, and the emergence of the two-worker family. The huge postwar Baby-Boom generation is pairing off, accounting in part for the upsurge in the divorce rate (half of all divorces occur within seven years of first marriage). Media images of the family have become more "realistic," reflecting new patterns of family life that are emerging (and old patterns that are re-emerging).

33   Among social scientists, "realism" is becoming something of an ideal in itself. For some of them, realism translates as pluralism: All forms of the family, by virtue of the fact that they happen to exist, are equally acceptable—from communes and cohabitation to one-parent households, homosexual marriages, and, come to think of it, the nuclear family. What was once labeled "deviant" is now merely "variant." In some college texts, "the family" has been replaced by "family systems." Yet, this new approach does not seem to have squelched perfectionist standards. Indeed, a palpable strain of perfectionism runs through the pop literature on "alternative" family life-styles.

34   For the majority of scholars, realism means a more down-to-earth view of the American household. Rather than seeing the family as a haven of peace and tranquility, they have begun to recognize that even "normal" families are less than ideal, that intimate relations of any sort inevitably involve antagonism as well as love. Conflict and change are inherent in social life. If the family is now in a state of flux, such is the nature of resilient institutions; if it is beset by problems, so is life. The family will survive.

Suggestions for Discussion or Writing

1. Why, according to Skolnick, has the ideal of a "perfect" family been harmful to the American public? Do you agree with her view? Why?

2. Skolnick discussed the "professionalization of the housewife" as being a cultural tradition linked to a specific historical period. Does her argument convince you? In what way may this image have reflected earlier attitudes? Is it an image that in uniquely American?

3. How has childrearing changed in recent centuries? Is Skolnick's view consistent with current theories? What is your own theory of childrearing?

4. After all the negative views Skolnick presents of the current family, why does she come to the conclusion that "the family will survive"?

5. Compare this essay with Gallup's essay on "The Faltering Family." How do the arguments differ?

The End of Play

Marie Winn

Marie Winn (1936–   ), born in Prague, Czechoslovakia, immigrated to the U.S. with her parents Joseph, a doctor, and Joan, a lawyer. She was educated at Radcliffe and Columbia and became a freelance writer contributing to the New York Times Magazine, *the* New York Book Review *and* Parade. *She and her husband have co-authored several children's books. Among her other writing is* Summer in Prague *(1973), which won the American Library Association award for "notable book,"* The Plug-In Drug: Television, Children, and the Family *(1977), and* Children Without Childhood *(1983). She lives in New York where she continues her freelance writing.*

1   Of all the changes that have altered the topography of childhood, the most dramatic has been the disappearance of childhood play. Whereas a decade or two ago children were easily distinguished from the adult world by the very nature of their play, today children's occupations do not differ greatly from adult diversions.

2   Infants and toddlers, to be sure, continue to follow certain timeless patterns of manipulation and exploration; adolescents, too, have not changed their free-time habits so very much, turning as they ever have towards adult pastimes and amusements in their drive for autonomy, self-mastery, and sexual discovery. It is among the ranks of school-age children, those six-to-twelve-year-olds who once avidly filled their free moments with childhood play, that the greatest change is evident. In the place of traditional, sometimes ancient childhood games that were still popular a generation ago, in the place of fantasy and make-believe play—"You be the mommy and I'll be the daddy"—doll play or toy-soldier play, jump-rope play, ball-bouncing play, today's children have substituted television viewing and, most recently, video games.

3   Many parents have misgivings about the influence of television. They sense that a steady and time-consuming exposure to passive entertainment might damage the ability to play imaginatively and resourcefully, or prevent this ability from developing in the first place. A mother of two school-age children recalls: "When I was growing up, we used to go out into the vacant lots and make up week-long dramas and sagas. This was during third, fourth, fifth grades. But my own kids have never done that sort of thing, and somehow it bothers me. I wish we had cut down on the TV years ago, and maybe the kids would have learned how to play."

4   The testimony of parents who eliminate television for periods of time strengthens the connection between children's television watching and changed play patterns. Many parents discover that when their children don't have television to fill their free time, they resort to the old kinds of imaginative, traditional "children's play." Moreover, these parents often observe that under such circumstances "they begin to seem more like children" or "they act more childlike." Clearly, a part of the definition of childhood, in adults' minds, resides in the nature of children's play.

5   Children themselves sometimes recognize the link between play and their own special definition as children. In an interview about children's books with four ten-year-old girls, one of them said: "I read this story about a girl my age growing up twenty years ago—you know, in 1960 or so—and she seemed so much younger than me in her behavior. Like she might be playing with dolls, or playing all sorts of children's games, or jump-roping or something." The other girls all agreed that they had noticed a similar discrepancy between themselves and fictional children in books of the past: those children seemed more like children. "So what do *you* do in your spare time, if you don't play with dolls or play make-believe games or jump rope or do things kids did twenty years ago?" they were asked. They laughed and answered, "We watch TV."

6   But perhaps other societal factors have caused children to give up play. Children's greater exposure to adult realities, their knowledge of adult sexuality, for instance, might make them more sophisticated, less likely to play like children. Evidence from the counterculture communes of the sixties and seventies adds weight to the argument that it is television above all that has eliminated children's play. Studies of children raised in a variety of such communes, all television-free, showed the little communards continuing to fill their time with those forms of play that have all but vanished from the lives of conventionally reared American children. And yet these counterculture kids were casually exposed to all sorts of adult matters—drug taking, sexual intercourse. Indeed, they sometimes incorporated these matters into their play: "We're mating," a pair of six-year-olds told a reporter to explain their curious bumps and grinds. Nevertheless, to all observers the commune children preserved a distinctly childlike and even innocent demeanor, an impression that was produced mainly by the fact that they spent most of their time playing. Their play defined them as belonging to a special world of childhood.

7   Not all children have lost the desire to engage in the old-style childhood play. But so long as the most popular, most dominant members of the peer group, who are often the most socially precocious, are "beyond" playing, then a common desire to conform makes it harder for those children who still have the drive to play to go ahead and do so. Parents often report that their children seem ashamed of previously common forms of play and hide their involvement with such play from their peers. "My fifth-grader still plays with dolls," a mother tells, "but she keeps them hidden in the basement where nobody will see them." This social check on the play instinct serves to hasten the end of childhood for even the least advanced children.

8   What seems to have replaced play in the lives of great numbers of preadolescents these days, starting as early as fourth grade, is a burgeoning interest in boy-girl interactions—"going out" or "going together." These activities do not necessarily involve going anywhere or doing anything sexual, but nevertheless are the first stage of a sexual process that used to commence at puberty or even later. Those more sophisticated children who are already involved in such manifestly unchildlike interests make plain their low opinion of their peers who still *play*. "Some of the kids in the class are real weird," a fifth-grade boy states. "They're not interested in going out, just in trucks and stuff, or games pretending they're monsters. Some of them don't even *try* to be cool."

Video Games versus Marbles

9   Is there really any great difference, one might ask, between that gang of kids playing video games by the hour at their local candy store these days and those small fry who used to hang around together spending equal amounts of time playing marbles? It is easy to see a similarity between the two activities: each requires a certain amount of manual dexterity, each is almost as much fun to watch as to play, each is simple and yet challenging enough for that middle-childhood age group for whom time can be so oppressive if unfilled.

10   One significant difference between the modern pre-teen fad of video games and the once popular but now almost extinct pastime of marbles is economic: playing video games costs twenty-five cents for approximately three minutes of play; playing marbles, after a small initial investment, is free. The children who frequent video-game machines require a considerable outlay of quarters to subsidize their fun; two, three, or four dollars is not an unusual expenditure for an eight- or nine-year-old spending an hour or two with his friends playing Asteroids or Pac-Man or Space Invaders. For most of the children the money comes from their weekly allowance. Some augment this amount by enterprising commercial ventures—trading and selling comic books, or doing chores around the house for extra money.

11   But what difference does it make where the money comes from? Why should that make video games any less satisfactory as an amusement for children? In fact, having to pay for the entertainment, whatever the source of the money, and having its duration limited by one's financial resources changes the nature of the game, in a subtle way diminishing the satisfactions it offers. Money and time become intertwined, as they so often are in the adult world and as, in the past, they almost never were in the child's world. For the child playing marbles, meanwhile, time has a far more carefree quality, bounded only by the requirements to be home by suppertime or by dark.

12   But the video-game-playing child has an additional burden—a burden of choice, of knowing that the money used for playing Pac-Man could have been saved for Christmas, could have been used to buy something tangible, perhaps something "worthwhile," as his parents might say, rather than being "wasted" on video games. There is a certain sense of adultness that spending money imparts, a feeling of being a consumer, which distinguishes a game with a price from its counterparts among the traditional childhood games children once played at no cost.

13   There are other differences as well. Unlike child-initiated and child-organized games such as marbles, video games are adult-created mechanisms not entirely within the child's control, and thus less likely to impart a sense of mastery and fulfillment: the coin may get jammed, the machine may go haywire, the little blobs may stop eating the funny little dots. Then the child must go to the storekeeper to complain, to get his money back. He may be "ripped off" and simply lose his quarter, much as his parents are when they buy a faulty appliance. This possibility of disaster gives the child's play a certain weight that marbles never imposed on its light-hearted players.

14   Even if a child has a video game at home requiring no coin outlay, the play it provides is less than optimal. The noise level of the machine is high—too high, usually, for the child to conduct a conversation easily with another child. And yet, according

to its enthusiasts, this very noisiness is a part of the game's attraction. The loud whizzes, crashes, and whirrs of the video-game machine "blow the mind" and create an excitement that is quite apart from the excitement generated simply by trying to win a game. A traditional childhood game such as marbles, on the other hand, has little built-in stimulation; the excitement of playing is generated entirely by the players' own actions. And while the pace of a game of marbles is close to the child's natural physiological rhythms, the frenzied activities of video games serve to "rev up" the child in an artificial way, almost in the way a stimulant or an amphetamine might. Meanwhile the perceptual impact of a video game is similar to that of watching television—the action, after all, takes place on a television screen—causing the eye to defocus slightly and creating a certain alteration in the child's natural state of consciousness.

15   Parents' instinctive reaction to their children's involvement with video games provides another clue to the difference between this contemporary form of play and the more traditional pastimes such as marbles. While parents, indeed most adults, derive open pleasure from watching children at play, most parents today are not delighted to watch their kids flicking away at the Pac-Man machine. This does not seem to them to be real play. As a mother of two school-age children anxiously explains, "We used to do real childhood sorts of things when I was a kid. We'd build forts and put on crazy plays and make up new languages, and just generally we *played*. But today my kids don't play that way at all. They like video games and of course they still go in for sports outdoors. They go roller skating and ice skating and skiing and all. But they don't seem to really *play*."

16   Some of this feeling may represent a certain nostalgia for the past and the old generation's resistance to the different ways of the new. But it is more likely that most adults have an instinctive understanding of the importance of play in their own childhood. This feeling stokes their fears that their children are being deprived of something irreplaceable when they flip the levers on the video machines to manipulate the electronic images rather than flick their fingers to send a marble shooting towards another marble.

Play Deprivation

17   In addition to television's influence, some parents and teachers ascribe children's diminished drive to play to recent changes in the school curriculum, especially in the early grades.

18   "Kindergarten, traditionally a playful port of entry into formal school, is becoming more academic, with children being taught specific skills, taking tests, and occasionally even having homework," begins a report on new directions in early childhood education. Since 1970, according to the United States census, the proportion of three- and four-year-olds enrolled in school has risen dramatically, from 20.5 percent to 36.7 percent towards academic acceleration in the early grades. Moreover, middle-class nursery schols in recent years have introduced substantial doses of academic material into their daily programs, often using those particular devices originally intended to help culturally deprived preschoolers in compensatory programs such as Headstart to

catch up with their middle-class peers. Indeed, some of the increased focus on academic skills in nursery schools and kindergartens is related to the widespread popularity among young children and their parents of *Sesame Street,* a program originally intended to help deprived children attain academic skills, but universally watched by middle-class toddlers as well.

19   Parents of the *Sesame Street* generation often demand a "serious," skill-centered program for their preschoolers in school, afraid that the old-fashioned, play-centered curriculum will bore their alphabet-spouting, number-chanting four- and five-year-olds. A few parents, especially those whose children have not attended television classes or nursery school, complain of the high-powered pace of kindergarten these days. A father whose five-year-old daughter attends a public kindergarten declares: "There's a lot more pressure put on little kids these days than when we were kids, that's for sure. My daughter never went to nursery school and never watched *Sesame,* and she had a lot of trouble when she entered kindergarten this fall. By October, just a month and a half into the program, she was already flunking. The teacher told us our daughter couldn't keep up with the other kids. And believe me, she's a bright kid! All the other kids were getting gold stars and smiley faces for their work, and every day Emily would come home in tears because she didn't get a gold star. Remember when we were in kindergarten? We were *children* then. We were allowed just to play!"

20   A kindergarten teacher confirms the trend towards early academic pressure. "We're expected by the dictates of the school system to push a lot of curriculum," she explains. "Kids in our kindergarten can't sit around playing with blocks any more. We've just managed to squeeze in one hour of free play a week, on Fridays."

21   The diminished emphasis on fantasy and play and imaginative activities in early childhood education and the increased focus on early academic-skill acquisition have helped to change childhood from a play-centered time of life to one more closely resembling the style of adulthood: purposeful, success-centered, competitive. The likelihood is that these preschool "workers" will not metamorphose back into players when they move on to grade school. This decline in play is surely one of the reasons why so many teachers today comment that their third- or fourth-grades act like tired businessmen instead of like children.

22   What might be the consequences of this change in children's play? Children's propensity to engage in that extraordinary series of behaviors characterized as "play" is perhaps the single great dividing line between childhood and adulthood, and has probably been so throughout history. The make-believe games anthropologists have recorded of children in primitive societies around the world attest to the universality of play and to the uniqueness of this activity to the immature members of each society. But in those societies, and probably in Western society before the middle or late eighteenth century, there was always a certain similarity between children's play and adult work. The child's imaginative play took the form of imitation of various aspects of adult life, culminating in the gradual transformation of the child's play from make-believe work to *real* work. At this point, in primitive societies or in our own society of the past, the child took her or his place in the adult work world and the distinctions between adulthood and childhood virtually vanished. But in today's technologically advanced society there is no place for the child in the adult work world.

There are not enough jobs, even of the most menial kind, to go around for adults, much less for children. The child must continue to be dependent on adults for many years while gaining the knowledge and skills necessary to become a working member of society.

23   This is not a new situation for children. For centuries children have endured a prolonged period of dependence long after the helplessness of early childhood is over. But until recent years children remained childlike and playful far longer than they do today. Kept isolated from the adult world as a result of deliberate secrecy and protectiveness, they continued to find pleasure in socially sanctioned childish activities until the imperatives of adolescence led them to strike out for independence and self-sufficiency.

24   Today, however, with children's inclusion in the adult world both through the instrument of televison and as a result of a deliberately preparatory, integrative style of child rearing, the old forms of play no longer seem to provide children with enough excitement and stimulation. What then are these so-called children to do for fulfillment if their desire to play has been vitiated and yet their entry into the working world of adulthood must be delayed for many years? The answer is precisely to get involved in those areas that cause contemporary parents so much distress: addictive television viewing during the school years followed, in adolescence or even before, by a search for similar oblivion via alcohol and drugs; exploration of the world of sensuality and sexuality before achieving the emotional maturity necessary for altruistic relationships.

25   Psychiatrists have observed among children in recent years a marked increase in the occurrence of depression, a state long considered antithetical to the nature of childhood. Perhaps this phenomenon is at least somewhat connected with the current sense of uselessness and alienation that children feel, a sense that play may once upon a time have kept in abeyance.

Suggestions for Discussion or Writing

1. What basic assumptions underlie Winn's argument? Do you agree with her assumptions?

2. What is Winn's thesis statement? What evidence does she use to support her thesis?

3. According to Winn, what are the causes for the loss of play among children these days? How does she define "play"? Are there factors other than those discussed by Winn that may account for the loss of play?

4. What might be Winn's purpose in writing the essay? Support your ideas with evidence from the text.

5. How would Winn's article differ if she had written it for an audience of junior or senior high school students rather than for a general audience? How would her arguments change? How would her tone change?

Stripping Down to Bare Happiness

Linda Weltner

Linda Weltner is a freelance writer who has published in various newspapers including the New York Times. *She is a regular columnist for the* Boston Globe. *She also writes children's books. This article was first published in her column with the* Globe *in 1982.*

1 "What we're talking about is simplification, not deprivation," explains a friend of mine. "It isn't that you can't do all the things you like, but you change. You don't like them anymore. Some of the old habits seem so wasteful and unsatisfying, you really lose your taste for them. So you still have everything you want—only on less money."

2 When I first met them, Sara and Michael were a two-career couple with a home of their own, and a large boat bought with a large loan. What interested them in a concept called voluntary simplicity was the birth of their daughter and a powerful desire to raise her themselves. Neither one of them, it turned out, was willing to restrict what they considered their "real life" into the brief time before work and the tired hours afterward.

3 "A lot of people think that as they have children and things get more expensive, the only answer is to work harder in order to earn more money. It's not the only answer," insists Michael.

4 The couple's decision was to trade two full-time careers for two half-time careers, and to curtail consumption. They decided to spend their money only on things that contributed to their major goal, the construction of a world where family and friendship, work and play, were all of a piece, a world, moreover, which did not make wasteful use of the earth's resources.

5 Today, they live in the same suburban community in a handsome, energy-efficient home they designed themselves. Small by most standards, it is easy to clean, furnish, maintain and heat. The first floor, one large room, has a kitchen area along one wall, a birch table and chairs for dining, a living area defined by a comfortable couch and a wood stove, and a corner work area. Upstairs is a child's bedroom, topped by a loft which is the master bedroom, an office that serves them both, and a bathroom. It is bright and light and in harmony with its surroundings. Soon there will be a solar greenhouse outside the front door.

6 How can a couple with two part-time freelance jobs afford to build their own home, own a car, and share a small boat with another couple—all without a loan? How can they maintain a high standard of living that provides "everything" they want? What is it they have given up that they do not miss?

7 Expensive clutter, for one thing—medicine cabinets full of cosmetics and over-the-counter drugs they will never use, kitchen cabinets crowded with items they would

eventually throw away. The one clothes closet Sara shares with Michael easily contains the basic items in their wardrobes, many of them well-made classic styles from L. L. Bean. "I'm constantly giving things away," Sara explains. By sifting and discarding, by keeping track of what they have, Sara and Michael have a clear idea of what they really need.

8   They do not have a dishwasher. The number of hand-thrown pottery dishes they own would not fill one. They do not own a clothes dryer; the wet clothes, drying indoors in winter, eliminate the need for a humidifier. Sara's dark hair is short. She does not need a hairdryer, electric curlers, or a curling iron. Their front yard is wooded. They do not need a power mower, grass spreader, or electric clippers. They do not own a TV, and so they and their child are not constantly saturated with images of new toys, new things, and new temptations.

9   They have exchanged the expenses of work in a commuter age—the extra car, the cost of gasoline, professional wardrobes, lunches and frequent dinners out, and babysitting fees—for the time to pay attention to the quality of their lives. They have given up paper products, processed foods, expensive hobbies, first-run movies, restaurants, and paying for the services of others in return for home cooking, mid-week family picnics, library books, participation in community arts programs, thrift shops, an active YMCA membership, and do-it-yourself projects.

10   "That yearning feeling that's so much a part of this culture goes on forever," says Sara. "But it doesn't matter if you're making $15,000 or $50,000. There'll always be things you wish you could afford. Money really wasn't the reason we changed. We did it for our own personal satisfaction, and for anyone thinking of simplifying life, there's only one basic rule: 'If it isn't satisfying, don't do it.'. . ."

11   Sara and Michael lent me their copy of "99 Ways to a Simple Lifestyle," an Anchor Press/Doubleday paperback compiled by the Center for Science in the Public Interest, a handbook of practical suggestions that can be applied to anyone's living situation. I read it carefully, giving myself high marks in some areas, surprised at my socially sanctioned irrational behavior in others.

12   That night, accompanying my daughter on a shopping trip, I came across an inexpensive hand towel that matched our kitchen wallpaper, and a pair of "bargain" sandals too handsome to resist. When I stood in the parking lot, $11 poorer, no happier on leaving the store than I had been entering it, I felt like a child, helpless in the face of my own impulses.

13   It is a world of illusion, this shopping merry-go-round we ride, but with all the action and excitement, it is sometimes hard to find the resolve and the courage to dismount.

Suggestions for Discussion or Writing

1. Why do Sara and Michael want to change their lives? How committed are they to that change?

2. What of the "luxuries" of life have they found they can do without? What are the results of this simplification?

3. What was their basic rule in simplifying their lives?

4. How is the essay structured? Who is the "I" of the first paragraph and when does that voice reappear?

5. What assumptions can be made about the consumer-driven lifestyle that is common in America? How are these assumptions false? How are they true?

Shaving

Leslie Norris

Leslie Norris (1921–   ), born in Merthyr Tydfil, Glamorganshire, Wales, attended the Training College at Coventry, England (1947–1949), and the University of Southampton Institute of Education (1955–1958). He served in the Royal Air Force during World War II and is a teacher, lecturer, visiting professor, and poet. He has won many awards for his short stories and poems and has published in the New Yorker, *the* Atlantic Monthly *and the* Missouri Review, *among others. His books include* The Tongue of Beauty *(1943),* Poems *(1946),* The Ballad of Billy Rose *(1964),* Finding Gold *(1967),* Walking the White Fields: Poems 1967–1980 *(1980),* Norris's Ark *(1988), and* The Girl from Cardigan *(1988), in which this story appears.*

1   Earlier, when Barry had left the house to go to the game, an overnight frost had still been thick on the roads. But the brisk April sun had soon dispersed it, and now he could feel the spring warmth on his back through the thick tweed of his coat. His left arm was beginning to stiffen up where he'd jarred it in a tackle, but it was nothing serious. He flexed his shoulders against the tightness of his jacket and was surprised again by the unexpected weight of his muscles, the thickening strength of his body. A few years back, he thought, he had been a small, unimportant boy, one of a swarming gang laughing and jostling to school, hardly aware that he possessed an identity. Time had transformed him. He walked solidly now, and often alone. He was tall, strongly made, his hands and feet were adult and heavy, the rooms in which all his life he'd moved had grown too small for him. Sometimes a devouring restlessness drove him from the house to walk long distances in the dark. He hardly understood how it had happened. Amused and quiet, he walked the High Street among the morning shoppers.

2   He saw Jackie Bevan across the road and remembered how, when they were both six years old, Jackie had swallowed a pin. The flustered teachers had clucked about Jackie as he stood there, bawling, cheeks awash with tears, his nose wet. But now Jackie was tall and suave, his thick, pale hair sleekly tailored, his gray suit enviable. He was talking to a girl as golden as a daffodil.

3   "Hey, hey!" called Jackie. "How's the athlete? How's Barry boy?"

4   He waved a graceful hand at Barry.

5   "Come and talk to Sue," he said.

6   Barry shifted his bag to his left hand and walked over, forming in his mind the answers he'd make to Jackie's questions.

7   "Did we win?" Jackie asked. "Was the old Barry Stanford magic in glittering evidence yet once more this morning? Were the invaders sent hunched and silent back to their hovels in the hills? What was the score? Give us an epic account, Barry, without modesty or delay. This is Sue, by the way."

8   "I've seen you about," the girl said.

9   "You could hardly miss him," said Jackie. "Four men, roped together, once spent a week climbing him—they thought he was Everest. He ought to carry a warning beacon, he's a danger to aircraft."

10   "Silly," said the girl, smiling at Jackie. "He's not much taller than you are."

11   She had a nice voice, too.

12   "We won," Barry said. "Seventeen points to three. It was a good game. The ground was hard, though."

13   He could think of nothing else to say.

14   "Let's all go for a frivolous cup of coffee," Jackie said. "Let's celebrate your safe return from the rough fields of victory. We could pour libations all over the floor for you."

15   "I don't think so," Barry said. "Thanks. I'll go straight home."

16   "Okay," said Jackie, rocking on his heels so that the sun could shine on his smile. "How's your father?"

17   "No better," Barry said. "He's not going to get better."

18   "Yes, well," said Jackie, serious and uncomfortable, "tell him my mother and father ask about him."

19   "I will," Barry said. "He'll be pleased."

20   Barry dropped the bag in the front hall and moved into the room which had been the dining room until his father's illness. His father lay in bed, his long body gaunt, his still head scarcely denting the pillow. He seemed asleep, thin blue lids covering his eyes, but when Barry turned away, he spoke.

21   "Hullo, son," he said. "Did you win?"

22   His voice was a dry, light rustling, hardly louder than the breath which carried it. Its sound moved Barry to a compassion that almost unmanned him, but he stepped close to the bed and looked down at the dying man.

23   "Yes," he said. "We won fairly easily. It was a good game."

24   His father lay with eyes closed, inert, his breath irregular and shallow.

25   "Did you score?" he asked.

26   "Twice," Barry said. "I had a try in each half."

27   He thought of the easy certainty with which he'd caught the ball before his second try; casually, almost arrogantly, he had taken it on the tips of his fingers, on his full burst for the line. Nobody could have stopped him. But watching his father's weakness he felt humble and ashamed, as if the morning's game, its urgency and effort, was not worth talking about. His father's face, fine-skinned and pallid, carried a dark stubble of beard, almost a week's growth, and his obstinate, strong hair stuck out over his brow.

28   "Good," said his father, after a long pause. "I'm glad it was a good game."

29   Barry's mother bustled about the kitchen, a tempest of orderly energy.

30   "Your father's not well," she said. "He's down today, feels depressed. He's a particular man, your father. He feels dirty with all that beard on him."

31   She slammed shut the stove door.

32   "Mr. Cleaver was supposed to come up and shave him," she said, "and that was three days ago. Little things have always worried your father, every detail must be perfect for him."

33   Barry filled a glass with milk from the refrigerator. He was very thirsty.

34   "I'll shave him," he said.

35   His mother stopped, her head on one side.

36   "Do you think you can?" she asked. "He'd like it if you can."

37   "I can do it," Barry said.

38   He washed his hands as carefully as a surgeon. His father's razor was in a blue leather case, hinged at the broad edge and with one hinge broken. Barry unfastened the clasp and took out the razor. It had not been properly cleaned after its last use and lather had stiffened into hard yellow rectangles between the teeth of the guard. There were water-shaped rust stains, brown as chocolate, on the surface of the blade. Barry removed it, throwing it in the waste bin. He washed the razor until it glistened, and dried it on a soft towel, polishing the thin handle, rubbing its metal head to a glittering shine. He took a new blade from its waxed envelope, the paper clinging to the thin metal. The blade was smooth and flexible to the touch, the little angles of its cutting clearly defined. Barry slotted it into the grip of the razor, making it snug and tight in the head.

39   The shaving soap, hard, white, richly aromatic, was kept in a wooden bowl. Its scent was immediately evocative and Barry could almost see his father in the days of his health, standing before his mirror, thick white lather on his face and neck. As a little boy Barry had loved the generous perfume of the soap, had waited for his father to lift the razor to his face, for one careful stroke to take away the white suds in a clean revelation of the skin. Then his father would renew the lather with a few sweeps of his brush, one with an ivory handle and the bristles worn, which he still used.

40   His father's shaving mug was a thick cup, plain and serviceable. A gold line ran outside the rim of the cup, another inside, just below the lip. Its handle was large and sturdy, and the face of the mug carried a portrait of the young Queen Elizabeth II, circled by a wreath of leaves, oak perhaps, or laurel. A lion and a unicorn balanced precariously on a scroll above her crowned head, and the Union Jack, the Royal Standard, and other flags were furled each side of the portrait. And beneath it all, in small black letters, ran the legend: "Coronation June 2nd 1953." The cup was much older than Barry. A pattern of faint translucent cracks, fine as a web, had worked itself haphazardly, invisibly almost, through the white glaze. Inside, on the bottom, a few dark bristles were lying, loose and dry. Barry shook them out, then held the cup in his hand, feeling its solidness. Then he washed it ferociously, until it was clinically clean.

41   Methodically he set everything on a tray, razor, soap, brush, towels. Testing the hot water with a finger, he filled the mug and put that, too, on the tray. His care was

absorbed, ritualistic. Satisfied that his preparations were complete, he went downstairs, carrying the tray with one hand.

42   His father was waiting for him. Barry set the tray on a bedside table and bent over his father, sliding an arm under the man's thin shoulders, lifting him without effort so that he sat against the high pillows.

43   "By God, you're strong," his father said. He was as breathless as if he'd been running.

44   "So are you," said Barry.

45   "I was," his father said. "I used to be strong once."

46   He sat exhausted against the pillows.

47   "We'll wait a bit," Barry said.

48   "You could have used your electric razor," his father said. "I expected that."

49   "You wouldn't like it," Barry said. "You'll get a closer shave this way."

50   He placed the large towel about his father's shoulders.

51   "Now," he said, smiling down.

52   The water was hot in the thick cup. Barry wet the brush and worked up the lather. Gently he built up a covering of soft foam on the man's chin, on his cheeks and stark cheekbones.

53   "You're using a lot of soap," his father said.

54   "Not too much," Barry said. "You've got a lot of beard."

55   His father lay there quietly, his wasted arms at his sides.

56   "It's comforting," he said. "You'd be surprised how comforting it is."

57   Barry took up the razor, weighing it in his hand, rehearsing the angle which he'd use it. He felt confident.

58   "If you have prayers to say . . . " he said.

59   "I've said a lot of prayers," his father answered.

60   Barry leaned over and placed the razor delicately against his father's face, setting the head accurately on the clean line near the ear where the long hair ended. He held the razor in the tips of his fingers and drew the blade sweetly through the lather. The new blade moved light as a touch over the hardness of the upper jaw and down to the angle of the chin, sliding away the bristles so easily that Barry could not feel their release. He sighed as he shook the razor in the hot water, washing away the soap.

61   "How's it going?" his father asked.

62   "No problem," Barry said. "You needn't worry."

63   It was as if he had never known what his father had really looked like. He was discovering under his hands the clear bones of the face and head, they became sharp and recognizable under his fingers. When he moved his father's face a gentle inch to one side, he touched with his fingers the frail temples, the blue veins of his father's life. With infinite and meticulous care he took away the hair from his father's face.

64   "Now for your neck," he said. "We might as well do the job properly."

65   "You've got good hands," his father said. "You can trust those hands, they won't let you down."

66   Barry cradled his father's head in the crook of his left arm, so that the man could tilt back his head, exposing the throat. He brushed fresh lather under the chin and into

the hollows alongside the stretched tendons. His father's throat was fleshless and vulnerable, his head was a hard weight on the boy's arm. Barry was filled with unreasoning protective love. He lifted the razor and began to shave.

67   "You don't have to worry," he said. "Not at all. Not about anything."

68   He held his father in the bend of his strong arm and they looked at each other. Their heads were very close.

69   "How old are you?" his father said.

70   "Seventeen," Barry said. "Near enough seventeen."

71   "You're young," his father said, "to have this happen."

72   "Not too young," Barry said. "I'm bigger than most men."

73   "I think you are," his father said.

74   He leaned his head tiredly against the boy's shoulder. He was without strength, his face was cold and smooth. He had let go all his authority, handed it over. He lay back on his pillow, knowing his weakness and mortality, and looked at his son with wonder, with a curious humble pride.

75   "I won't worry then," he said. "About anything."

76   "There's no need," Barry said. "Why should you worry?"

77   He wiped his father's face clean of all soap with a damp towel. The smell of illness was everywhere, overpowering even the perfumed lather. Barry settled his father down and took away the shaving tools, putting them by with the same ceremonial precision with which he'd prepared them: the cleaned and glittering razor in its broken case; the soap, its bowl wiped and dried, on the shelf between the brush and the coronation mug; all free of taint. He washed his hands and scrubbed his nails. His hands were firm and broad, pink after their scrubbing. The fingers were short and strong, the little fingers slightly crooked, and soft dark hair grew on the backs of his hands and his fingers just above the knuckles. Not long ago they had been small, bare hands, not very long ago.

78   Barry opened wide the bathroom window. Already, although it was not yet two o'clock, the sun was retreating and people were moving briskly, wrapped in their heavy coats against the cold that was to come. But now the window was full in the beam of the dying sunlight, and Barry stood there, illuminated in its golden warmth for a whole minute, knowing it would soon be gone.

Suggestions for Discussion or Writing

1. How are father and son alike? How are they different? Describe the relationship between father and son. How do they feel about each other? How do you know? Of what significance is Barry's athletic prowess? How does it help reveal his character?

2. Why is the shaving equipment described in such detail? Of what significance is the "large and sturdy" shaving mug, the ivory-handled razor, the coat of arms on the mug? Why does Barry wash his hands "like a surgeon," and make the tools "clinically clean"? How is the mug and shaving incident symbolic?

3. Why must Barry use the mug, brush and razor rather than the electric shaver?

4. During the shave, Barry tells his dad, "No problem. You needn't worry." What, besides shaving, is he talking about?

5. What does the beam of sunlight in the last paragraph symbolize? What is significant about Barry's last one-minute rest in the light?

I Stand Here Ironing

Tillie Olsen

Tillie Olsen (1913–   ) was born in Omaha, Nebraska. In her youth she joined the Young Communist League and was jailed for organizing packing-house workers into a union. She earned a Doctor of Arts and Letters from the University of Nebraska in 1979 and has been a lecturer and visiting professor at Amherst, Stanford, and M.I.T. In 1961 she won the O. Henry Award for the best short story of the year, "Tell Me a Riddle." Her other works include Silences *(1978) and* Yonnondio: From the Thirties *(1974), which describes the struggles of a family to survive social and economic despair and ruin. Her writing is deeply rooted in the belief that the will to live can never be snuffed out but will always survive.*

1   I stand here ironing, and what you asked me moves tormented back and forth with the iron.

2   "I wish you would manage the time to come in and talk with me about your daughter. I'm sure you can help me understand her. She's a youngster who needs help and whom I'm deeply interested in helping."

3   "Who needs help." . . . Even if I came, what good would it do? You think because I am her mother I have a key, or that in some way you could use me as a key? She has lived for nineteen years. There is all that life that has happened outside of me, beyond me.

4   And when is there time to remember, to sift, to weigh, to estimate, to total? I will start and there will be an interruption and I will have to gather it all together again. Or I will become engulfed with all I did or did not do, with what should have been and what cannot be helped.

5   She was a beautiful baby. The first and only one of our five that was beautiful at birth. You do not guess how new and uneasy her tenancy in her now-loveliness. You did not know her all those years she was thought homely, or see her poring over her baby pictures, making me tell her over and over how beautiful she had been—and

would be, I would tell her—and was now, to the seeing eye. But the seeing eyes were few or nonexistent. Including mine.

6   I nursed her. They feel that's important nowadays. I nursed all the children, but with her, with all the fierce rigidity of first motherhood, I did like the books then said. Though her cries battered me to trembling and my breasts ached with swollenness, I waited till the clock decreed.

7   Why do I put that first? I do not even know if it matters, or if it explains anything.

8   She was a beautiful baby. She blew shining bubbles of sound. She loved motion, loved light, loved color and music and textures. She would lie on the floor in her blue overalls patting the surface so hard in ecstasy her hands and feet would blur. She was a miracle to me, but when she was eight months old I had to leave her daytimes with the woman downstairs to whom she was no miracle at all, for I worked or looked for work and for Emily's father, who "could no longer endure" (he wrote in his good-bye note) "sharing want with us."

9   I was nineteen. It was the pre-relief, pre-WPA world of the depression. I would start running as soon as I got off the streetcar, running up the stairs, the place smelling sour, and awake or asleep to startle awake, when she saw me she would break into a clogged weeping that could not be comforted, a weeping I can hear yet.

10   After a while I found a job hashing at night so I could be with her days, and it was better. But it came to where I had to bring her to his family and leave her.

11   It took a long time to raise the money for her fare back. Then she got chicken pox and I had to wait longer. When she finally came, I hardly knew her, walking quick and nervous like her father, looking like her father, thin, and dressed in a shoddy red that yellowed her skin and glared at the pockmarks. All the baby loveliness gone.

12   She was two. Old enough for nursery school they said, and I did not know then what I know now—the fatigue of the long day, and the lacerations of group life in the kinds of nurseries that are only parking places for children.

13   Except that it would have made no difference if I had known. It was the only place there was. It was the only way we could be together, the only way I could hold a job.

14   And even without knowing, I knew. I knew the teacher that was evil because all these years it has curdled into my memory, the little boy hunched in the corner, her rasp, "why aren't you outside, because Alvin hits you? that's no reason, go out, scaredy." I knew Emily hated it even if she did not clutch and implore "don't go Mommy" like the other children, mornings.

15   She always had a reason why we should stay home. Momma, you look sick. Momma, I feel sick. Momma, the teachers aren't there today, they're sick. Momma, we can't go, there was fire there last night. Momma, it's a holiday today, no school, they told me.

16   But never a direct protest, never rebellion. I think of our others in their three-four-year oldness—the explosions, the tempers, the denunciations, the demands—and I feel suddenly ill. I put the iron down. What in me demanded that goodness in her? And what was the cost, the cost to her of such goodness?

17   The old man living in the back once said in his gentle way: "You should smile at Emily more when you look at her." What *was* in my face when I looked at her? I loved her. There were all the acts of love.

18   It was only with the others I remembered what he said, and it was the face of joy, and not of care or tightness or worry I turned to them—too late for Emily. She does not smile easily, let alone almost always as her brothers and sisters do. Her face is closed and somber, but when she wants, how fluid. You must have seen it in her pantomimes, you spoke of her rare gift for comedy on the stage that rouses a laughter out of the audience so dear they applaud and applaud and do not want to let her go.

19   Where does it come from, that comedy? There was none of it in her when she came back to me that second time, after I had had to send her away again. She had a new daddy now to learn to love, and I think perhaps it was a better time.

20   Except when we left her alone nights, telling ourselves she was old enough.

21   "Can't you go some other time, Mommy, like tomorrow?" she would ask. "Will it be just a little while you'll be gone? Do you promise?"

22   The time we came back, the front door open, the clock on the floor in the hall. She rigid awake. "It wasn't just a little while. I didn't cry. Three times I called you, just three times, and then I ran downstairs to open the door so you could come faster. The clock talked loud. I threw it away, it scared me what it talked."

23   She said the clock talked loud again that night I went to the hospital to have Susan. She was delirious with the fever that comes before red measles, but she was fully conscious all the week I was gone and the week after we were home when she could not come near the new baby or me.

24   She did not get well. She stayed skeleton thin, not wanting to eat, and night after night she had nightmares. She would call for me, and I would rouse from exhaustion to sleepily call back: "You're all right, darling, go to sleep it's just a dream," and if she still called, in a sterner voice, "now go to sleep, Emily, there's nothing to hurt you." Twice, only twice, when I had to get up for Susan anyhow, I went in to sit with her.

25   Now when it is too late (as if she would let me hold and comfort her like I do the others) I get up and go to her at once at her moan or restless stirring. "Are you awake, Emily? Can I get you something?" And the answers is always the same: "No, I'm all right, go back to sleep, Mother."

26   They persuaded me at the clinic to send her away to a convalescent home in the country where "she can have the kind of food and care you can't manage for her, and you'll be free to concentrate on the new baby." They still send children to that place. I see pictures on the society page of sleek young women planning affairs to raise money for it, or dancing at the affairs, or decorating Easter eggs or filling Christmas stockings for the children.

27   They never have a picture of the children so I do not know if the girls still wear those gigantic red bows and the ravaged looks on the every other Sunday when parents can come to visit "unless otherwise notified"—as we were notified the first six weeks.

28   Oh it is a handsome place, green lawns and tall trees and fluted flower beds. High up on the balconies of each cottage the children stand, the girls in their red bows and white dresses, the boys in white suits and giant red ties. The parents stand below shrieking up to be heard and the children shriek down to be heard, and between them the invisible wall "Not To Be Contaminated by Parental Germs of Physical Affection."

29   There was a tiny girl who always stood hand in hand with Emily. Her parents never came. One visit she was gone. "They moved her to Rose Cottage" Emily shouted in explanation. "They don't like you to love anybody here."

30   She wrote once a week, the labored writing of a seven-year-old. "I am fine. How is the baby. If I write my leter nicly I will have a star. Love." There never was a star. We wrote every other day, letters she could never hold or keep but only hear read—once. "We simply do not have room for children to keep any personal posses-sions," they patiently explained when we pieced one Sunday's shrieking together to plead how much it would mean to Emily, who loved so to keep things, to be allowed to keep her letters and cards.

31   Each visit she looked frailer. "She isn't eating," they told us.

32   (They had runny eggs for breakfast or mush with lumps, Emily said later. I'd hold it in my mouth and not swallow. Nothing ever tasted good, just when they had chicken.)

33   It took us eight months to get her released home, and only the fact that she gained back so little of her seven lost pounds convinced the social worker.

34   I used to try to hold and love her after she came back, but her body would stay stiff, and after a while she'd push away. She ate little. Food sickened her, and I think much of life too. Oh she had physical lightness and brightness, twinkling by on skates, bouncing like a ball up and down up and down over the jump rope, skimming over the hill; but these were momentary.

35   She fretted about her appearance, thin and dark and foreign-looking at a time when every little girl was supposed to look or thought she should look a chubby blonde replica of Shirley Temple. The doorbell sometimes rang for her, but no one seemed to come and play in the house or be a best friend. Maybe because we moved so much.

36   There was a boy she loved painfully through two school semesters. Months later she told me how she had taken pennies from my purse to buy him candy. "Licorice was his favorite and I brought him some every day, but he still liked Jennifer better'n me. Why, Mommy?" The kind of question for which there is no answer.

37   School was a worry to her. She was not glib or quick in a world where glibness and quickness were easily confused with ability to learn. To her overworked and exasperated teachers she was an overconscientious "slow learner" who kept trying to catch up and was absent entirely too often.

38   I let her be absent, though sometimes the illness was imaginary. How different from my now-strictness about attendance with the others. I wasn't working. We had a new baby, I was home anyhow. Sometimes, after Susan grew old enough, I would keep her home from school, too, to have them all together.

39   Mostly Emily had asthma, and her breathing, harsh and labored, would fill the house with a curiously tranquil sound. I would bring the two old dresser mirrors and her boxes of collections to her bed. She would select beads and single earrings, bottle tops and shells, dried flowers and pebbles, old postcards and scraps, all sorts of oddments; then she and Susan would play Kingdom, setting up landscapes and furniture, peopling them with action.

40   Those were the only times of peaceful companionship between her and Susan. I have edged away from it, that poisonous feeling between them, that terrible balancing of hurts and needs I had to do between the two, and did so badly, those earlier years.

41   Oh there are conflicts between the others too, each one human, needing, demand-ing, hurting, taking—but only between Emily and Susan, no, Emily toward Susan that corroding resentment. It seems so obvious on the surface, yet it is not obvious. Susan,

the second child, Susan, golden- and curly-haired and chubby, quick and articulate and assured, everything in appearance and manner Emily was not; Susan, not able to resist Emily's precious things, losing or sometimes clumsily breaking them; Susan telling jokes and riddles to company for applause while Emily sat silent (to say to me later: that was *my* riddle, Mother, I told it to Susan); Susan, who for all the five years' difference in age was just a year behind Emily in developing physically.

42   I am glad for that slow physical development that widened the difference between her and her contemporaries, though she suffered over it. She was too vulnerable for that terrible world of youthful competition, of preening and parading, of constant measuring of yourself against every other, of envy, "If I had that copper hair," "If I had that skin. . . ." She tormented herself enough about not looking like the others, there was enough of the unsureness, the having to be conscious of words before you speak, the constant caring—what are they thinking of me? without having it all magnified by the merciless physical drives.

43   Ronnie is calling. He is wet and I change him. It is rare there is such a cry now. That time of motherhood is almost behind me when the ear is not one's own but must always be racked and listening for the child cry, the child call. We sit for a while and I hold him, looking out over the city spread in charcoal with its soft aisles of light. *"Shoogily,"* he breathes and curls closer. I carry him back to bed, asleep. *Shoogily.* A funny word, a family word, inherited from Emily, invented by her to say: *comfort.*

44   In this and other ways she leaves her seal, I say aloud. And startle at my saying it. What do I mean? What did I start to gather together, to try and make coherent? I was at the terrible, growing years. War years. I do not remember them well. I was working, there were four smaller ones now, there was not time for her. She had to help be a mother, and housekeeper, and shopper. She had to set her seal. Mornings of crisis and near hysteria trying to get lunches packed, hair combed, coats and shoes found, everyone to school or Child Care on time, the baby ready for transportation. And always the paper scribbled on by a smaller one, the book looked at by Susan then mislaid, the homework not done. Running out to that huge school where she was one, she was lost, she was a drop; suffering over the unpreparedness, stammering and unsure in her classes.

45   There was so little time left at night after the kids were bedded down. She would struggle over books, always eating (it was in those years she developed her enormous appetite that is legendary in our family) and I would be ironing, or preparing food for the next day, or writing V-mail to Bill, or tending the baby. Sometimes, to make me laugh, or out of her despair, she would imitate happenings or types at school.

46   I think I said once: "Why don't you do something like this in the school amateur show?" One morning she phoned me at work, hardly understandable through the weeping: "Mother, I did it. I won, I won; they gave me first prize; they clapped and clapped and wouldn't let me go."

47   Now suddenly she was Somebody, and as imprisoned in her difference as she had been in anonymity.

48   She began to be asked to perform at other high schools, even in colleges, then at city and statewide affairs. The first one we went to, I only recognized her that first

moment when thin, shy, she almost drowned herself into the curtains. Then: Was this Emily? The control, the command, the convulsing and deadly clowning, the spell, then the roaring, stamping audience, unwilling to let this rare and precious laughter out of their lives.

49   Afterwards: You ought to do something about her with a gift like that—but without money or knowing how, what does one do? We have left it all to her, and the gift has as often eddied inside, clogged and clotted, as been used and growing.

50   She is coming. She runs up the stairs two at a time with her light graceful step, and I know she is happy tonight. Whatever it was that occasioned your call did not happen today.

51   "Aren't you ever going to finish the ironing, Mother? Whistler painted his mother in a rocker. I'd have to paint mine standing over an ironing board." This is one of her communicative nights and she tells me everything and nothing as she fixes herself a plate of food out of the icebox.

52   She is so lovely. Why did you want me to come in at all? Why were you concerned? She will find her way.

53   She starts up the stairs to bed. "Don't get me up with the rest in the morning." "But I thought you were having midterms." "Oh, those," she comes back in, kisses me, and says quite lightly, "in a couple of years when we'll all be atom-dead they won't matter a bit."

54   She has said it before. She *believes* it. But because I have been dredging the past, and all that compounds a human being is so heavy and meaningful in me, I cannot endure it tonight.

55   I will never total it all. I will never come in to say: She was a child seldom smiled at. Her father left me before she was a year old. I had to work her first six years when there was work, or I sent her home and to his relatives. There were years she had care she hated. She was dark and thin and foreign-looking in a world where the prestige went to blondeness and curly hair and dimples, she was slow where glibness was prized. She was a child of anxious, not proud, love. We were poor and could not afford for her the soil of easy growth. I was a young mother, I was a distracted mother. There were the other children pushing up, demanding. Her younger sister seemed all that she was not. There were years she did not want me to touch her. She kept too much in herself, her life was such she had to keep too much in herself. My wisdom came too late. She has much to her and probably little will come of it. She is a child of her age, of depression, of war, of fear.

56   Let her be. So all that is in her will not bloom—but in how many does it? There is still enough left to live by. Only help her to know—help make it so there is cause for her to know—that she is more than this dress on the ironing board, helpless before the iron.

Suggestions for Discussion or Writing

1. How does the narrator view her role as a mother? How do the changes in her life affect her view? Support your conclusions with evidence from the text.

2. Describe Emily's personality. How do you know she is as you describe? What turning points does Emily experience and how do they affect her personality?

3. How is the iron symbolic in the story? What is the significance of the title?

4. How does Olsen's word choice ("the pre-relief, pre-WPA world of the depression") indicate the time and setting of the story? How does the era affect the narrator's and Emily's lives?

5. The narrator periodically asks herself questions throughout the story. What do you think is the purpose of these questions? What indications are there that the narrator is not only talking to herself? Who is her audience?

I Remember the Room Was Filled with Light

Judith Hemschemeyer

Born in Sheboygan, Wisconsin in 1935, Judith Hemschemeyer received her B.A. from the University of Wisconsin and her M.A. from the University of Grenoble. She is the author of several books of poetry including I Remember the Room Was Filled with Light, *in which this poem appears.* Very Close and Very Slow *was published in 1975 and* Give What You Can *in 1978. She has worked at several universities as a visiting poet, including the University of Utah. She now lives in Orlando, Florida.*

They were still young, younger than I am now.
I remember the room was filled with light
And moving air. I was watching him
Pick brass slivers from his hands as he did each night
5   After work. Bits of brass gleamed on his brow.
She was making supper. I stood on the rim
Of a wound just healing; so when he looked up
And asked me when we were going to eat
I ran to her, though she could hear. She smiled
10   And said 'Tell him . . . ' Then 'Tell her . . . ' On winged feet
I danced between them, forgiveness in my cup,
Wise messenger of the gods, their child.

Suggestions for Discussion or Writing

1. How does the title relate to the subject of the poem?

2. What assumptions can we make about the occupation of the father in this poem?

3. What is the rhyme scheme of this poem? How noticeable is the pattern? Does it add to or detract from the poem? Why?

4. What are the metaphors of the poem? Why are they effective?

5. What is the child's perception of her family?

Homestead in Idaho

Clinton F. Larson

Clinton F. Larson (1919–   ) was reared in American Fork, Utah, the home of Wayne C. Booth, his high school chum. He earned his B.A. from the University of Utah, then joined the armed forces. On his return from service in World War II, he joined the faculty of Brigham Young University (1947). His collection of 73 poems, Centennial Portraits, *was published by BYU during the national bicentennial celebration of 1975–76. He was the co-editor of* Modern Poetry of Western America *(1975) and has written several poetic dramas, such as* Mary of Nazareth.

I

"Solomon? Since I talked with him I've thought
Again about trying to make a go of it
In Idaho. As I say, this rainy weather
In Oregon is looking better and better to me.
5   The first time I met him, it was in Al's Bar,
Down the street. Five years ago, I think.
Well, you know, Al keeps a friendly place,
One where you don't mind stepping in
And acting neighborly. Well, there he was,
10   Down at the end of the bar. I noticed him
Because he was shaking, folding and unfolding a clipping.
'You from these parts?' I said. With all this space
In the West, it doesn't hurt to close it up
Whenever you can. He said, 'Well, no, not really,'
15   And kept folding and unfolding the clipping and looking

Down at his hands. When he stopped, I could hardly
See it, his hands were so square and big,
Like the farm work of his time. Besides, he took
His hat off, and you could see the white skin
20   Of his head, particularly near the part,
Where his hat took a settled, permanent place.
But his face had lightened to a buckskin color.
He had the look of a farmer who had seen a lot
Of land that needed working. Then it rose
25   From him, 'I suppose you would say from Idaho.
I wanted to homestead there,' he said. 'I tried it
Last year, or was it then? Not much money
To start with, but my wife Geneva and I and our children
Found a place. But it seemed a thousand miles
30   From nowhere, at least two weeks east from here.
I built a cabin from the boards I had brought
Along. Geneva said, 'Solomon, we can make it,
But we need money for spring. Go back to Tamarack
And leave us here.' Then I told her how I felt.
35   But she said, 'We can make it with the provisions we brought.
Go back, Solomon. By spring, we'll have a start,
Then a barn by those trees, cows grazing there,
And a house like we've wanted, beside a stream.'
Well, the way she looked, her eyes imploring,
40   And her soft brown hair, and her hope, how could I
Say no? So off I went, Geneva waving to me
Until I was out of sight. It was the hardest thing
I have ever done to look around and see
Where I was going. I worked at Tamarack
45   Autumn and winter, numb from wondering
How they were, all alone out there, and wanting
To get back to them. April finally came,
And I loaded the wagon with everything we needed,
Dresses and dry goods, shoes and ribbons besides.
50   I travelled as hard as I could, considering the horses,
And kept looking and looking for the smoke far off
In front of me, coming from the chimney,
To tell me I was near. But I never saw it.'
He looked at the clipping in his hands,
55   Smudged and yellow, and said, 'When I got there,
It looked like autumn and winter had never left,
The snow still hanging on the roof, the door
Open, nothing planted, nothing done,
And then I went inside, to see the dusty cribs
60   And Geneva, still against them . . . and the floor

Red and dusted with shadows. And I was here,
Trying for money so we could get started . . .
I couldn't stay out there.' And he looked at me
As if pleading for help, then down into his hands,
65   Unfolding and folding the clipping as if by doing it
He could wear out his sorrow."

II

The colors of the sun against the hills
In the evensong of life, and yet another
Year had gone. The colors crept down
70   Like frost and the glory of God, intermingling
In them night and day. All was over
When the family saw them, over like the evening
Wind. In the meadows and clusters of pines
It whispered to the edge of the sullen earth,
75   In the seethe of knowing, under the shaken plume
Of knowledge. Solomon and Geneva saw
The land cut, as it were, for them, a place
For them between the great divide and the sea.
There, he said in the voice of conscience, there
80   Is our home, or the hope of it. Geneva,
Can it be that home if we settle here?
A half of a year will make it ours if we stay,
She replied in the moment of seeing him
As she wished him to be. And then in resolve,
85   Let me stay the winter with the children
While you work in Tamarack, and so
It was out, the only way of keeping
The land. Where in the flicker of grey is death,
The wandering light, release? I want this home,
90   She said, in the tolerance of a breath, and I
Shall stay. Where is the imperious will but fast
Against the land that holds them? To Tamarack,
He said, bright as possession, like the coin of having
Mastery. There is my knoll where home
95   Shall be, not this cabin of our duration
As we should not be, itinerants in hope of more.
A winter more, she said, and it is ours,
The gaze of meadows, the water and soil
Urgent for grain, the quiet sky, and the light
100   Lazy as spring. Our home! And I shall keep it,
Winter through, she said, as if it were no winter,
But a day of rest. And then beside him, their children,

Or in his arms, awake to happiness. The future
Declined from that day and would not rest.
105   But as a bole of pain grew into that tower
Of resolve and broke it easily, sacred
As a sacrifice. He said, then think of me
In Tamarack, and turned to what he needed
Away from home. Geneva? The subtle portrait
110   On a stand beside a bed. The wisps
Of hair she flicked to clear her face, brown
As the veil of earth, eyes quizzical as worry,
But light as a soft morning, her body lithe
And restless, supple to the rule of God.
115   And Solomon? A name like a fetish he tried
To honor, but not as a patriarch, but more
Like a seer: angular as a fence or cross,
Bending as he seemed to fit, concern
Like an agony to please, a burden
120   To his clothes that could not shape themselves,
And although like the square largeness
Of his hands. Together, they kept the cabin
Like a tidy loom where they would weave
The colors through their bright fidelity.
125   Their children? Hard to presuppose or know,
But theirs. Such small alliances, wont
To shimmer with translucent light, a guess
Of women that might have been, of course like her,
Or him, as others might suppose, not they.
130   She whispered what he might take, advice
Hanging from her words like surety.
And he, the slight concerns of food and health
Like the hundreds of miles that would intervene,
And for safety the gun and knife in a drawer,
135   Nearby. Then the wood for winter near the door,
Neatly stacked, and provisions in the loft
And ready. What else? What else but land
Beyond their vision, the canyons, and peaks like clouds
In the thin blue haze, and time. He turned, ready,
140   Holding her with one arm, as he pulled
His horse from grazing to the suggestion of the miles
Ahead, and leaned to kiss his children, and then
Away, easily in the saddle, gazing back at her,
The children, cabin, everything diminishing
145   As he moved, and he waved, and they, in the slow
Desperation of goodbye. He could not turn forward
For seeing them there, until they were taken from view

By a vale beyond their meadow sinking into darkness,
And they were gone. From that time on he pieced
150   The events of time together like fragments he could not
Understand, though the evidence impaled the past
Like needles dropping suddenly through his inquiry.
There must have been a disturbance beyond the door,
And she left the cabin with the gun on her arm,
155   The sharp wind of October against her frailty
Where she shivered in the grey dusk. The rising
Wind, then the thunder over the plain that shook her.
She went into the darkness of a shed, wildly
Gazing. Then the severe and immediate rattle
160   Behind her, and the strike behind her knee, the prongs
Of venom there that made her scream. Now
The whirling thoughts for Solomon or help
From anywhere. Bleed the poison out.
Go slowly, she told herself, and bleed the poison
165   Out. Stumbling to the cabin, she opened the door
In the glaze of fright and found the drawer that held
The knife. She sat, livid against the lightning,
To find the place to cut. Nowhere to see,
Behind and under, but she felt the red periods there.
170   A piece of kindling for a brace, a cloth
For tourniquet. She took the knife and swept it
With her hand. But the chickens in the shed.
They must not starve. A few steps back
To the shed, and she emptied a pail of grain
175   And opened the door. As she moved, she held
The stick of the tourniquet numbly against her leg.
Slowly, slowly to the cabin, then wildly in
To seize the knife. She held it against her leg
And with a gasp twisted it in. But too deep!
180   The blood pulsed against her hand, again,
Again, no matter how tightly she twisted the stick
To keep it in. It spread on the rough floor
As she felt herself weaken, the waves of blackness
Before her eyes. The children! What will happen
185   To them? she cried to herself. The lamp flickered
At the sill. What good is the need and planning now?
Tears for dust. The girls will starve to death
In the clatter of the wind, and the light of afternoon
Will carve through their sallow loneliness.
190   They will lie and cry for food, and no one will hear.
The waning fire, the gusts at the filming window.
Solomon! Forgive me! What can I do?

What else can I do? She took the gun again
And turned it to the crib, propping its weight.
195   She looked at them as they slept, arms lightly
Across each other. You will be with me,
She whispered to them. The trigger once, then again,
The flat sounds walling her against the error
That they would live beyond her careful dying.
200   The gun fell from her. She crawled to the bed
In the corner and, taking her finger, traced
In blood on the white sheet, "Rattlesnake bit,
Babies would starve—" and the land fell away
Beyond her sight, and all that she was collapsed
205   In an artifice of death that he afterwards saw.
Solomon!

Suggestions for Discussion or Writing

1. Of what significance is the name Solomon? Of what significance is the clipping?

2. What is the effect of dividing the story into two parts? How does each part relate to the other? How does the telling of the event differ in Parts I and II? What role do the questions play in Part II?

3. Why does Geneva let the chickens out, even though it means using precious time? What does this act reveal about her character?

4. What words, phrases, or images foreshadow the tragedy?

5. Do you think Geneva did the right thing? What would you have done?

6. What is the effect of the very last line of the poem? What word begins the poem? How does the difference in punctuation reveal the narrator's emotions?

Incident in the Ice Cream Parlor

John Sterling Harris

John Sterling Harris (1929–   ) was raised in Tooele, Utah, attended the University of Utah and later received a B.A. in Spanish from Brigham Young University. After graduation, he served in the Army as a small-weapons instructor, an area of expertise which is the basis for a number of critical and technical articles he has written. After earning an M.A. from BYU in American literature, he went to the University of Texas, where he discovered and pursued his interest in technical writing. He has been teaching technical writing and American literature at BYU since 1962. He has written three books on technical writing and is currently working on a second book of poetry. The following selection from his first book of poetry, Barbed Wire *(1974), is noted for its conciseness and clarity, frequently associated with technical writing.*

They sat there,
Both past fifty and heavy—
She more than he
Opposite each other
5   But looking elsewhere.

While we at the next table
Tried our dialogue
Amid juvenile questions,
Signs of siblings rivaling
10   And you'll get no ice cream if—

They ate methodically
With small spoons,
Until the chocolate and
The marshmallow ran together
15   In the bottom of the dish.

Then they left without a word,
While we quelled debate
Over the relative merits
Of apple cobbler
20   And tutti frutti.

Suggestions for Discussion or Writing

1. Contrast the tone of stanzas 1 and 3 with 2 and 4. What does the tone reveal about the first couple and their relationship? What does the tone reveal about the second couple?

2. Does the second couple have children? How do you know?

3. Why does the couple eat "methodically" with "small spoons"? What is the significance of the lines "The marshmallow ran together / In the bottom of the dish" in stanza 3?

4. What do the couples' choices of ice cream reveal about their lives, both as couples and as individuals?

5. What do you think will happen to the young couple when their children grow up? Do you suppose the older couple had children? Do you think the poem describes family relationships or stages of life?

Human Minds and Bodies
Understanding Ourselves

Introduction

Our physical and mental processes sometimes seem inscrutable. Why do we think or feel as we do? Specialists probe, frauds exploit, researchers study, and the common lay person ponders the secrets of mind and body. Just when medicine or procedures are found to cure one ailment, the human body develops new and unexplainable problems. Everyone struggles with health at some time of life or another.

Several of the essays in this section look at physical health—Richard Selzer's "The Surgeon As Priest" from the physician's point of view, and the rest of the articles or poems from the patient's point of view. Randy Shilts begins his book on AIDS, *And the Band Played On,* with the first documented AIDS case, a health worker from Africa. Lori Oliwenstein discusses experimentation with the AIDS virus on different kinds of primates. Charles Wright describes cancer in his poem, and Sylvia Plath a surgery. Alice Walker looks at the mental trauma and attitude change that stems from disfigurement. Tess Gallagher's poem "Candle, Lamp & Firefly" takes us to the end of illness, to death.

Katherine Griffin, on the other hand, examines mental problems in her essay on depression, "The Unbearable Darkness of Being." Conrad Aiken and Charlotte Perkins Gilman look at mental problems and the serious ramification of minds in turmoil in their stories "Silent Snow, Secret Snow" and "The Yellow Wallpaper."

Our minds and our bodies are the sum of what we are. Within our own small spheres, we listen to the signs that tell us how we are like or unlike others. We hear the beat of our own hearts and think thoughts utterly our own. Yet together we comprise the human race. Our questions about ourselves are therefore both personal and universal.

The Surgeon As Priest

Richard Selzer

Richard Selzer (1928–) was born in Troy, New York, became fascinated with the world of medicine, and received his M.D. at Albany Medical College in 1953. In 1960, after post-doctoral study at Yale and three years of service in the U.S. Army, he began his private practice in general surgery. He has since been an associate professor of surgery at Yale Medical School and has contributed articles with detailed descriptions of the human anatomy, operating techniques, and patient reaction to sickness and surgery to Harper's, Esquire, Redbook, Mademoiselle, American Review, *and* Antaeus. *His other writing includes a collection of short stories,* Rituals of Surgery *(1974); two collections of essays,* Mortal Lessons *(1977) and* Confessions of a Knife *(1979); and a collection of essays and fiction,* Letters to a Young Doctor *(1982).*

1   In the foyer of a great medical school there hangs a painting of Vesalius. Lean, ascetic, possessed, the anatomist stands before a dissecting table upon which lies the naked body of a man. The flesh of the two is silvery. A concentration of moonlight, like a strange rain of virus, washes them. The cadaver has dignity and reserve; it is distanced by its death. Vesalius reaches for his dissecting knife. As he does so, he glances over his shoulder at a crucifix on the wall. His face wears an expression of guilt and melancholy and fear. He knows that there is something wrong, forbidden in what he is about to do, but he cannot help himself, for he is a fanatic. He is driven by a dark desire. To see, to feel, to discover is all. His is a passion, not a romance.

2   I understand you, Vesalius. Even now, after so many voyages within, so much exploration, I feel the same sense that one must not gaze into the body, the same irrational fear that it is an evil deed for which punishment awaits. Consider. The sight of our internal organs is denied us. To how many men is it given to look upon their own spleens, their hearts, and live? The hidden geography of the body is a Medusa's head one glimpse of which would render blind the presumptuous eye. Still, rigid rules are broken by the smallest inadvertencies: I pause in the midst of an operation being performed under spinal anesthesia to observe the face of my patient, to speak a word or two of reassurance. I peer above the screen separating his head from his abdomen, in which I am most deeply employed. He is not asleep, but rather stares straight upward, his attention riveted, a look of terrible discovery, of wonder upon his face. Watch him. This man is violating a taboo. I follow his gaze upward, and see in the great operating lamp suspended above his belly the reflection of his viscera. There is the liver, dark and turgid above, there the loops of his bowel winding slow, there his blood runs extravagantly. It is that which he sees and studies with so much horror and fascination. Something primordial in him has been aroused—a fright, a longing. I feel it, too, and quickly bend above his open body to shield it from his view. How dare he look within the Ark! Cover his eyes! But it is too late; he has already *seen,* that which no man should;

he has trespassed. And I am no longer a surgeon, but a hierophant who must do magic to ward off the punishment of the angry gods.

3   I feel some hesitation to invite you to come with me into the body. It seems a reckless, defiant act. Yet there is more than dread reflected from these rosy coasts, these restless estuaries of pearl. And it is time to share it, the way the catbird shares the song which must be a joy to him and is a living truth to those who hear it. So shall I make of my fingers, words; of my scalpel, a sentence; of the body of my patient, a story.

4   One enters the body in surgery, as in love, as though one were an exile returning at last to his hearth, daring uncharted darkness in order to reach home. Turn sideways, if you will, and slip with me into the cleft I have made. Do not fear the yellow meadows of fat, the red that sweats and trickles where you step. Here, give me your hand. Lower between the beefy cliffs. Now rest a bit upon the peritoneum. All at once, gleaming, the membrane parts . . . and you are *in*.

5   It is the stillest place that ever was. As though suddenly you are struck deaf. Why, when the blood sluices fierce as Niagara, when the brain teems with electricity, and the numberless cells exchange their goods in ceaseless commerce—why is it so quiet? Has some priest in charge of these rites uttered the command "Silence"? This is no silence of the vacant stratosphere, but the awful quiet of ruins, of rainbows, full of expectation and holy dread. Soon you shall know surgery as a Mass served with Body and Blood, wherein disease is assailed as though it were sin.

6   Touch the great artery. Feel it bound like a deer in the might of its lightness, and know the thunderless boil of the blood. Lean for a bit against this bone. It is the only memento you will leave to the earth. Its tacitness is everlasting. In the hush of the tissue wait with me for the shaft of pronouncement. Press your ear against this body, the way you did as a child holding a seashell and heard faintly the half-remembered, longed-for sea. Now strain to listen *past* the silence. In the canals, cilia paddle quiet as an Iroquois canoe. Somewhere nearby a white whipslide of tendon bows across a joint. Fire burns here but does not crackle. Again, listen. Now there *is* sound—small splashings, tunneled currents of air, slow gaseous bubbles ascend through dark, unlit lakes. Across the diaphragm and into the chest . . . here at last it is all noise; the whisper of the lungs, the *lubdup, lubdup* of the garrulous heart.

7   But it is good you do not hear the machinery of your marrow lest it madden like the buzzing of a thousand coppery bees. It is frightening to lie with your ear in the pillow, and hear the beating of your heart. Not that it beats . . . but that it might stop, even as you listen. For anything that moves must come to rest; no rhythm is endless but must one day lurch . . . then halt. Not that it is a disservice to a man to be made mindful of his death, but—at three o'clock in the morning it is less than philosophy. It is Fantasy, replete with dreadful images forming in the smoke of alabaster crematoria. It is then that one thinks of the bristlecone pines, and envies them for having lasted. It is their slowness, I think. Slow down, heart, and drub on.

8   What is to one man a coincidence is to another a miracle. It was one or the other of these that I saw last spring. While the rest of nature was in flux, Joe Riker remained obstinate through the change of the seasons. "No operation," said Joe. "I don't want no operation."

9   Joe Riker is a short-order cook in a diner where I sometimes drink coffee. Each week for six months he had paid a visit to my office, carrying his affliction like a pet mouse under his hat. Every Thursday at four o'clock he would sit on my examining table, lift the fedora from his head, and bend forward to show me the hole. Joe Riker's hole was as big as his mouth. You could have dropped a plum in it. Gouged from the tonsured top of his head was a mucky puddle whose meaty heaped edge rose above the normal scalp about it. There was no mistaking the announcement from this rampart.

10   The cancer had chewed through Joe's scalp, munched his skull, then opened the membranes underneath—the dura mater, the pia mater, the arachnoid—until it had laid bare this short-order cook's brain, pink and gray, and pulsating so that with each beat a little pool of cerebral fluid quivered. Now and then a drop would manage the rim to run across his balding head, and Joe would reach one furry hand up to wipe it away, with the heel of his thumb, the way such a man would wipe away a tear.

11   I would gaze then upon Joe Riker and marvel. How dignified he was, as though that tumor, gnawing him, denuding his very brain, had given him a grace that a lifetime of good health had not bestowed.

12   "Joe," I say, "let's get rid of it. Cut out the bad part, put in a metal plate, and you're cured." And I wait.

13   "No operation," says Joe. I try again.

14   "What do you mean, 'no operation'? You're going to get meningitis. Any day now. And die. That thing is going to get to your brain."

15   I think of it devouring the man's dreams and memories. I wonder what they are. The surgeon knows all the parts of the brain, but he does not know his patient's dreams and memories. And for a moment I am tempted . . . to take the man's head in my hands, hold it to my ear, and listen. But his dreams are none of my business. It is his flesh that matters.

16   "No operation," says Joe.

17   "You give me a headache," I say. And we smile, not because the joke is funny anymore, but because we've got something between us, like a secret.

18   "Same time next week?" Joe asks. I wash out the wound with peroxide, and apply a dressing. He lowers the fedora over it.

19   "Yes," I say, "same time." And the next week he comes again.

20   There came the week when Joe Riker did not show up; nor did he the week after that, nor for a whole month. I drive over to his diner. He is behind the counter, shuffling back and forth between the grill and the sink. He is wearing the fedora. He sets a cup of coffee in front of me.

21   "I want to see your hole," I say.

22   "Which one?" he asks, and winks.

23   "Never mind that," I say. "I want to see it." I am all business.

24   "Not here," says Joe. He looks around, checking the counter, as though I have made an indecent suggestion.

25   "My office at four o'clock," I say.

26   "Yeah," says Joe, and turns away.

27   He is late. Everyone else has gone for the day. Joe is beginning to make me angry. At last he arrives.

28   "Take off your hat," I say, and he knows by my voice that I am not happy. He does, though, raise it straight up with both hands the way he always does, and I see . . . that the wound has healed. Where once there had been a bitten-out excavation, moist and shaggy, there is now a fragile bridge of shiny new skin.

29   "What happened?" I manage.

30   "You mean that?" He points to the top of his head. "Oh well," he says, "the wife's sister, she went to France, and brought me a bottle of water from Lourdes. I've been washing it out with that for a month."

31   "Holy water?" I say.

32   "Yeah," says Joe. "Holy water."

33   I see Joe now and then at the diner. He looks like anything but a fleshly garden of miracles. Rather, he has taken on a terrible ordinariness—Eden after the Fall, and minus its most beautiful creatures. There is a certain slovenliness, a dishevelment of the tissues. Did the disease ennoble him, and now that it is gone, is he somehow diminished? Perhaps I am wrong. Perhaps the only change is just the sly wink with which he greets me, as though to signal that we have shared something furtive. Could such a man, I think as I sip my coffee, could such a man have felt the brush of wings? How often it seems that the glory leaves as soon as the wound is healed. But then it is only saints who bloom in martyrdom, becoming less and less the flesh that pains, more and more ghost-colored weightlessness.

34   It was many years between my first sight of the living human brain and Joe Riker's windowing. I had thought then, long ago: Could this one-pound loaf of sourdough be the pelting brain? *This,* along whose busy circuitry run Reason and Madness in perpetual race—a race that most often ends in a tie? But the look deceives. What seems a fattish snail drowsing in its shell, in fact lives in quickness, where all is dart and stir and rapids of electricity.

35   Once again to the operating room . . .

36   How to cut a paste that is less solid than a cheese—Brie, perhaps? And not waste any of it? For that would be a decade of remembrances and wishes lost there, wiped from the knife. Mostly it is done with cautery, burning the margins of the piece to be removed, coagulating with the fine electric current these blood vessels that course everywhere. First a spot is burned, then another alongside the first, and the cut is made between. One does not stitch—one cannot sew custard. Blood is blotted with little squares of absorbent gauze. These are called patties. Through each of these a long black thread has been sewn, lest a blood-soaked patty slip into some remote fissure, or flatten against a gyrus like a starfish against a coral reef, and go unnoticed come time to close the incision. A patty abandoned brainside does not benefit the health, or improve the climate of the intelligence. Like the bodies of slain warriors, they must be retrieved from the field, and carried home, so they do not bloat and mortify, poisoning forever the plain upon which the battle was fought. One pulls them out by their black thread and counts them.

37   Listen to the neurosurgeon: "Patty, buzz, suck, cut," he says. Then "Suck, cut, patty, buzz." It is as simple as a nursery rhyme.

38   The surgeon knows the landscape of the brain, yet does not know how a thought is made. Man has grown envious of this mystery. He would master and subdue it

electronically. He would construct a computer to rival or surpass the brain. He would harness Europa's bull to a plow. There are men who implant electrodes into the brain, that part where anger is kept—the rage center, they call it. They press a button, and a furious bull halts in mid-charge, and lopes amiably to nuzzle his matador. Anger has turned to sweet compliance. Others sever whole tracts of brain cells with their knives, to mollify the insane. Here is surgery grown violent as rape. These men cannot know the brain. They have not the heart for it.

39   I last saw the brain in the emergency room. I wiped it from the shoulder of a young girl to make her smashed body more presentable to her father. Now I stand with him by the stretcher. We are arm in arm, like brothers. All at once there is that terrible silence of discovery. I glance at him, follow his gaze and see that there is more brain upon her shoulder, newly slipped from the cracked skull. He bends forward a bit. He must make certain. It *is* her brain! I watch the knowledge expand upon his face, so like hers. I, too, stare at the fragment flung wetly, now drying beneath the bright lights of the emergency room, its cargo of thoughts evaportaing from it, mingling for this little time with his, with mine, before dispersing in the air.

40   On the east coast of the Argolid, in the northern part of the Peloponesus, lies Epidaurus. O bury my heart there, in that place I have never seen, but that I love as a farmer loves his home soil. In a valley nearby, in the fourth century B.C., there was built the temple of Aesculapius, the god of medicine. To a great open colonnaded room, the abaton, came the sick from all over Greece. Here they lay down on pallets. As night fell, the priests, bearing fire for the lamps, walked among them, commanding them to sleep. They were told to dream of the god, and that he would come to them in their sleep in the form of a serpent, and that he would heal them. In the morning they arose cured. . . .

41   Walk the length of the abaton; the sick are in their places, each upon his pallet. Here is one that cannot sleep. See how his breath rises and falls against some burden that presses upon it. At last, he dozes, only to awaken minutes later, unrefreshed. It is toward dawn. The night lamps flicker low, casting snaky patterns across the colonnade. Already the chattering swallows swoop in and out among the pillars. All at once the fitful eyes of the man cease their roving, for he sees between the candle-lamp and the wall the shadow of an upraised serpent, a great yellow snake with topaz eyes. It slides closer. It is arched and godlike. It bends above him, swaying, the tongue and the lamplight flickering as one. Exultant, he raises himself upon one arm, and with the other, reaches out for the touch that heals.

42   On the bulletin board in the front hall of the hospital where I work, there appeared an announcement. "Yeshi Dhonden," it read, "will make rounds at six o'clock on the morning of June 10." The particulars were then given, followed by a notation: "Yeshi Dhonden is Personal Physician to the Dalai Lama." I am not so leathery a skeptic that I would knowingly ignore an emissary from the gods. Not only might such sangfroid be inimical to one's earthly well-being, it could take care of eternity as well. Thus, on the morning of June 10, I join the clutch of whitecoats waiting in the small conference room adjacent to the ward selected for the rounds. The air in the room is heavy with ill-concealed dubiety and suspicion of bamboozlement. At precisely six o'clock, he materializes, a short, golden, barrelly man dressed in a sleeveless robe of saffron and maroon. His scalp is shaven, and the only visible hair is a scanty black line above each hooded eye.

43   He bows in greeting while his young interpreter makes the introduction. Yeshi Dhonden, we are told, will examine a patient selected by a member of the staff. The diagnosis is as unknown to Yeshi Dhonden as it is to us. The examination of the patient will take place in our presence, after which we will reconvene in the conference room where Yeshi Dhonden will discuss the case. We are further informed that for the past two hours Yeshi Dhonden has purified himself by bathing, fasting, and prayer. I, having breakfasted well, performed only the most desultory of ablutions, and given no thought at all to my soul, glance furtively at my fellows. Suddenly, we seem a soiled, uncouth lot.

44   The patient had been awakened early and told that she was to be examined by a foreign doctor, and had been asked to produce a fresh specimen of urine, so when we enter her room, the woman shows no surprise. She has long ago taken on that mixture of compliance and resignation that is the facies of chronic illness. This was to be but another in an endless series of tests and examinations. Yeshi Dhonden steps to the bedside while the rest stand apart, watching. For a long time he gazes at the woman, favoring no part of her body with his eyes, but seeming to fix his glance at a place just above her supine form. I, too, study her. No physical sign nor obvious symptom gives a clue to the nature of the disease.

45   At last he takes her hand, raising it in both of his own. Now he bends over the bed in a kind of crouching stance, his head drawn down into the collar of his robe. His eyes are closed as he feels for her pulse. In a moment he has found the spot, and for the next half hour he remains thus, suspended above the patient like some exotic golden bird with folded wings, holding the pulse of the woman beneath his fingers, cradling her hand in his. All the power of the man seems to have been drawn down into this one purpose. It is palpation of the pulse raised to the state of ritual. From the foot of the bed, where I stand, it is as though he and the patient have entered a special place of isolation, of apartness, about which a vacancy hovers, and across which no violation is possible. After a moment the woman rests back upon her pillow. From time to time, she raises her head to look at the strange figure above her, then sinks back once more. I cannot see their hands joined in a correspondence that is exclusive, intimate, his fingertips receiving the voice of her sick body through the rhythm and throb she offers at her wrist. All at once I am envious—not of him, not of Yeshi Dhonden for his gift of beauty and holiness, but of her. I want to be held like that, touched so, *received*. And I know that I, who have palpated a hundred thousand pulses, have not felt a single one.

46   At last Yeshi Dhonden straightens, gently places the woman's hand upon the bed, and steps back. The interpreter produces a small wooden bowl and two sticks. Yeshi Dhonden pours a portion of the urine specimen into the bowl, and proceeds to whip the liquid with the two sticks. This he does for several minutes until a foam is raised. Then, bowing above the bowl, he inhales the odor three times. He sets down the bowl and turns to leave. All this while, he has not uttered a single word. As he nears the door, the woman raises her head and calls out to him in a voice at once urgent and serene. "Thank you, doctor," she says, and touches with her other hand the place he had held on her wrist, as though to recapture something that had visited there. Yeshi Dhonden turns back for a moment to gaze at her, then steps into the corridor. Rounds are at an end.

47   We are seated once more in the conference room. Yeshi Dhonden speaks now for the first time, in soft Tibetan sounds that I have never heard before. He has barely begun when the young interpreter begins to translate, the two voices continuing in tandem—a bilingual fugue, the one chasing the other. It is like the chanting of monks. He speaks of winds coursing through the body of the woman, currents that break against barriers, eddying. These vortices are in her blood, he says. The last spendings of an imperfect heart. Between the chambers of her heart, long, long before she was born, a wind had come and blown open a deep gate that must never be opened. Through it charge the full waters of her river, as the mountain stream cascades in the springtime, battering, knocking loose the land, and flooding her breath. Thus he speaks, and is silent.

48   "May we now have the diagnosis?" a professor asks.

49   The host of these rounds, the man who knows, answers.

50   "Congenital heart disease," he says. "Interventricular septal defect, with resultant heart failure."

51   A gateway in the heart, I think. That must not be opened. Through it charge the full waters that flood her breath. So! Here then is the doctor listening to the sounds of the body to which the rest of us are deaf. He is more than doctor. He is priest.

52   I know . . . I know . . . the doctor to the gods is pure knowledge, pure healing. The doctor to man stumbles, must often wound; his patient must die, as must he.

53   Now and then it happens, as I make my own rounds, that I hear the sounds of his voice, like an ancient Buddhist prayer, its meaning long since forgotten, only the music remaining. Then a jubilation possesses me, and I feel myself touched by something divine.

Suggestions for Discussion or Writing

1. Who was Vesalius? What conflict does he represent? How does the author overcome (or participate in) this conflict?

2. What part do sound images and references to sound play in the author's description of the human anatomy, surgery, and doctor/patient relationships? Why might a surgeon be preoccupied with sounds?

3. Notice that the author includes several incidents of almost mystical healing. What part do the Joe Riker story, the temple of Aesculapius, and the examination by Yeshi Dhonden play in the essay? What is the significance of the title?

4. What is the author's attitude toward the body? What specific phrases or incidents let you know? According to the author, what relationship does the body have with divinity and nature?

The First Documented AIDS Case

from *"Prologue," And the Band Played On: Politics, People and the AIDS Epidemic*

Randy Shilts

Randy Shilts graduated at the top of his class in journalism school and has worked as a freelance journalist for public television, and for publications such as The Village Voice, The Washington Post, The Boston Globe, *and, since 1982,* The San Francisco Chronicle. *He broke ground as one of the first successful openly gay reporters on a major publication. He received an EMMY for his program on children of Holocaust survivors. His book from which this article was taken,* And the Band Played On: Politics, People and the AIDS Epidemic, *was nominated for the National Book Critics Circle Award for the best nonfiction of 1987. His first book (1982) was entitled* The Mayor of Castro Street: The Life and Times of Harvey Milk.

1   By October 2, 1985, the morning Rock Hudson died, the word was familiar to almost every household in the Western world.

AIDS.

2   Acquired Immune Deficiency Syndrome had seemed a comfortably distant threat to most of those who had heard of it before, the misfortune of people who fit into rather distinct classes of outcasts and social pariahs. But suddenly, in the summer of 1985, when a movie star was diagnosed with the disease and the newspapers couldn't stop talking about it, the AIDS epidemic became palpable and the threat loomed everywhere.

3   Suddenly there were children with AIDS who wanted to go to school, laborers with AIDS who wanted to work, and researchers who wanted funding, and there was a threat to the nation's public health that could no longer be ignored. Most significantly, there were the first glimmers of awareness that the future would always contain this strange new word. AIDS would become a part of American culture and indelibly change the course of our lives.

4   The implications would not be fleshed out for another few years, but on that October day in 1985 the first awareness existed just the same. Rock Hudson riveted America's attention upon this deadly new threat for the first time, and his diagnosis became a demarcation that would separate the history of America before AIDS from the history that came after.

5   The timing of this awareness, however, reflected the unalterable tragedy at the heart of the AIDS epidemic: By the time America paid attention to the disease, it was too late to do anything about it. The virus was already pandemic in the nation, having

spread to every corner of the North American continent. The tide of death that would later sweep America could, perhaps, be slowed, but it could not be stopped.

6   The AIDS epidemic, of course, did not arise full grown from the biological landscape; the problem had been festering throughout the decade. The death tolls of the late 1980s are not startling new developments but an unfolding of events predicted for many years. There had been a time when much of this suffering could have been prevented, but by 1985 that time had passed. Indeed, on the day the world learned that Rock Hudson was stricken, some 12,000 Americans were already dead or dying of AIDS and hundreds of thousands more were infected with the virus that caused the disease. But few had paid any attention to this; nobody, it seemed, had cared about them.

7   The bitter truth was that AIDS did not just happen to America—it was allowed to happen by an array of institutions, all of which failed to perform their appropriate tasks to safeguard the public health. This failure of the system leaves a legacy of unnecessary suffering that will haunt the Western world for decades to come.

8   There was no excuse, in this country and in this time, for the spread of a deadly new epidemic. For this was a time in which the United States boasted the world's most sophisticated medicine and the world's most extensive public health system, geared to eliminate such pestilence from our national life. When the virus appeared, the world's richest nation housed the most lavishly financed scientific research establishments—both inside the vast governmental health bureaucracy and in other institutions—to investigate new diseases and quickly bring them under control. And making sure that government researchers and public health agencies did their jobs were the world's most unfettered and aggressive media, the public's watchdogs. Beyond that, the group most affected by the epidemic, the gay community, had by then built a substantial political infrastructure, particularly in cities where the disease struck first and most virulently. Leaders were in place to monitor the gay community's health and survival interests.

9   But from 1980, when the first isolated gay men began falling ill from strange and exotic ailments, nearly five years passed before all these institutions—medicine, public health, the federal and private scientific research establishments, the mass media, and the gay community's leadership—mobilized the way they should in a time of threat. The story of these first five years of AIDS in America is a drama of national failure, played out against a backdrop of needless death.

10   People died while Reagan administration officials ignored pleas from government sicentists and did not allocate adequate funding for AIDS research until the epidemic had already spread throughout the country.

11   People died while scientists did not at first devote appropriate attention to the epidemic because they perceived little prestige to be gained in studying a homosexual affliction. Even after this denial fades, people died while some scientists, most notably those in the employ of the United States government, competed rather than collaborated in international research efforts, and so diverted attention and energy away from the central struggle against the disease itself.

12   People died while public health authorities and the political leaders who guided them refused to take the tough measures necessary to curb the epidemic's spread, opting for political expediency over the public health.

13   And people died while gay community leaders played politics with the disease, putting political dogma ahead of the preservation of human life.

14   People died and nobody paid attention because the mass media did not like covering stories about homosexuals and was especially skittish about stories that involved gay sexuality. Newspapers and television largely avoided discussion of the disease until the death toll was too high to ignore and the casualties were no longer just the outcasts. Without the media to fulfill its role as public guardian, everyone else was left to deal—and not deal—with AIDS as they saw fit.

15   In those early years, the federal government viewed AIDS as a budget problem, local public health officials saw it as a political problem, gay leaders considered AIDS a public relations problem, and the news media regarded it as a homosexual problem that wouldn't interest anybody else. Consequently, few confronted AIDS for what it was, a profoundly threatening medical crisis.

16   Fighting against this institutional indifference were a handful of heroes from disparate callings. Isolated teams of scientists in research centers in America and Europe risked their reputation and often their jobs to pioneer early research on AIDS. There were doctors and nurses who went far beyond the call of duty to care for its victims. Some public health officials struggled valiantly to have the epidemic addressed in earnest. A handful of gay leaders withstood vilification to argue forcefully for a sane community response to the epidemic and to lobby for the funds that provided the first breakthroughs in research. And there were many victims of the epidemic who fought rejection, fear, isolation, and their own deadly prognoses to make people understand and to make people care.

17   Because of their efforts, the story of politics, people, and the AIDS epidemic is, ultimately, a tale of courage as well as cowardice, compassion as well as bigotry, inspiration as well as venality, and redemption as well as despair.

18   It is a tale that bears telling, so that it will never happen again, to any people, anywhere.

Christmas Eve, 1976

Kinshasa, Zaire

19   The hot African sky turned black and sultry; it wasn't like Christmas at all.

20   The unrelenting mugginess of the equatorial capital made Dr. Ib Bygbjerg even lonelier for Denmark. In the kitchen, Dr. Grethe Rask, determined to assuage her young colleague's homesickness, began preparing an approximation of the dinner with which Danes traditionally begin their Christmas observance, the celebration known through centuries of custom as the Feast of the Hearts.

21   The preparations brought back memories of the woman's childhood in Thisted, the ancient Jutland port nestled on the Lim Fjord not far from the North Sea. As the main course, Grethe Rask knew, there needed to be something that flies. In Jutland that would mean goose or duck; in Zaire, chicken would have to suffice. As she began preparing the fowl, Grethe again felt the familiar fatigue wash over her. She had spent the last two years haunted by weariness, and by now, she knew she couldn't fight it.

22   Grethe collapsed on her bed. She had been among the Danish doctors who came to replace the Belgian physicians who were no longer welcome in this new nation eager to forget its recent colonial incarnation as the Belgian Congo. Grethe had first gone there in 1964, returning to Europe for training in stomach surgery and tropical diseases. She had spent the last four years in Zaire but, despite all this time in Africa, she remained unmistakably from the Danish stock who proudly announce themselves as north of the fjord. To be north of the Lim Fjord was to be direct and decisive, independent and plainspoken. The Jutlanders born south of the stretch of water that divides the Danish peninsula tend toward weakness, as anyone north of the fjord might explain. Far from the kings in Copenhagen, these hardy northern people had nurtured their collective heritage for centuries. Grethe Rask from Thisted mirrored this.

23   It explained why she was here in Zaire, 5,000 miles from where she might forge a lucrative career as a surgeon in the sprawling modern hospitals of Copenhagen. Such a cosmopolitan career meant people looking over her shoulder, giving orders. Grethe preferred the work she had done at a primitive hospital in the remote village of Abumombazi in the north of Zaire. She alone was in charge there.

24   The hospital conditions in Abumombazi were not as deplorable as in other parts of the country. A prominent Zairian general came from the region. He had had the clout to attract a white doctor to the village, and there, with Belgian nuns, Grethe worked with what she could beg and borrow. This was Central Africa, after all, and even a favored clinic would never have such basics as sterile rubber gloves or disposable needles. You just used needles again and again until they wore out; once gloves had worn through, you risked dipping your hands in your patient's blood because that was what needed to be done. The lack of rudimentary supplies meant that a surgeon's work had risks that doctors in the developed world could not imagine, particularly because the undeveloped part, specifically Central Africa, seemed to sire new diseases with nightmarish regularity. Earlier that year, not far from Abumombazi, in a village along the Ebola River on the Zaire-Sudan border, a virulent outbreak of a horrifying new disease had demonstrated the dangers of primitive medicine and new viruses. A trader from the village of Enzara, suffering from fevers and profuse, uncontrollable bleeding, had come to the teaching hospital for nurses in Maridi. The man apparently had picked up the disease sexually. Within days, however, 40 percent of the student nurses in Maridi were stricken with the fever, transmitted by contact with the patient's infected blood either through standard care procedures or through accidental needle-sticks.

25   Frightened African health officials swallowed their pride and called the World Health Organization, who came with a staff from the American Centers for Disease Control. By the time the young American doctors arrived, thirty-nine nurses and two doctors were dead. The CDC doctors worked quickly, isolating all patients with fevers. Natives were infuriated when the Americans banned the traditional burials of the victims since the ritual bathing of the bodies was clearly spreading the disease further. Within weeks, however, the epidemic was under control. In the end, the Ebola Fever virus, as it came to be known, killed 53 percent of the people it infected, seizing 153 lives before it disappeared as suddenly and mysteriously as it had arisen. Sex and blood were two horribly efficient ways to spread a new virus, and years later, a tenuous relief would fill the voices of doctors who talked of how fortunate it was for humankind that

this new killer had awakened in this most remote corner of the world and had been stamped out so quickly. A site just a bit closer to regional crossroads could have unleashed a horrible plague. With modern roads and jet travel, no corner of the earth was very remote anymore; never again could diseases linger undetected for centuries among a distant people without finding some route to fan out across the planet.

26   The battle between humans and disease was nowhere more bitterly fought than here in the fetid equatorial climate, where heat and humidity fuel the generation of new life forms. One historian has suggested that humans, who first evolved in Africa eons ago, migrated north to Asia and Europe simply to get to climates that were less hospitable to the deadly microbes the tropics so efficiently bred.

27   Here, on the frontiers of the world's harshest medical realities, Grethe Rask tended the sick. In her three years in Abumombazi, she had bullied and cajoled people for the resources to build her jungle hospital, and she was loved to the point of idolization by the local people. Then, she returned to the Danish Red Cross Hospital, the largest medical institution in the bustling city of Kinshasa, where she assumed the duties of chief surgeon. Here she met Ib Bygbjerg, who had returned from another rural outpost in the south. Bygbjerg's thick dark hair and small compact frame belied his Danish ancestry, the legacy, he figured, of some Spanish sailor who made his way to Denmark centuries ago. Grethe Rask had the features one would expect of a woman from Thisted, high cheekbones and blond hair worn short in a cut that some delicately called mannish.

28   To Bygbjerg's eye, on that Christmas Eve, there were troubling things to note about Grethe's appearance. She was thin, losing weight from a mysterious diarrhea. She had been suffering from the vague yet persistent malaise for two years now, since her time in the impoverished northern villages. In 1975, the problem had receded briefly after drug treatments, but for the past year, nothing had seemed to help. The surgeon's weight dropped further, draining and weakening her with each passing day.

29   Even more alarming was the disarray in the forty-six-year-old woman's lymphatic system, the glands that play the central role in the body's never-ending fight to make itself immune from disease. All of Grethe's lymph glands were swollen and had been for nearly two years. Normally, a lymph node might swell here or there to fight this or that infection, revealing a small lump on the neck, under an arm, or perhaps, in the groin. There didn't seem to be any reason for her glands to swell; there was no precise infection anywhere, much less anything that would cause such a universal enlargement of the lymph nodes all over her body.

30   And the fatigue. It was the most disconcerting aspect of the surgeon's malaise. Of course, in the best of times, this no-nonsense woman from north of the fjord did not grasp the concept of relaxation. Just that day, for example, she had not been scheduled to work, but she put in a full shift, anyway; she was always working, and in this part of the world nobody could argue because there was always so much to be done. But the weariness, Bygbjerg could tell, was not bred by overwork. Grethe had always been remarkably healthy, throughout her arduous career. No, the fatigue was something darker; it had become a constant companion that weighted her every move, mocking the doctor's industry like the ubiquitous cackling of the hyena on the savannah.

31   Though she was neither sentimental nor particularly Christian, Grethe Rask had wanted to cheer her young colleague; instead, she lay motionless, paralyzed again. Two hours later, Grethe stirred and began, halfheartedly, to finish dinner. Bygbjerg was surprised that she was so sick then that she could not muster the strength to stay awake for something as special as the Feast of the Hearts.

Suggestions for Discussion or Writing

1. Why was Rock Hudson's death significant in the problem of AIDS awareness?

2. What is Shilts's attitude toward government response to AIDS? What facts does he bring to bear on the problem?

3. When does Grethe Rask first show AIDS-related illnesses? What does that say about the spread of AIDS?

4. What assumptions does Shilts make about the infectious nature of AIDS?

5. What figurative language is found in this article? How does the figurative language help to make the descriptions more vivid?

Beauty: When the Other Dancer Is the Self

Alice Walker

Alice Walker (1944–) was born in Eatonton, Georgia, the eighth child of black sharecroppers. She earned a B.A. from Sarah Lawrence College in 1965 and joined the civil rights movement. She taught at Jackson State University (1968–1969) and Tougaloo College (1969–1970). She has lived in Kenya, Uganda, and the Soviet Union and now lives in New York. Her first volume of poetry, Once *(1968), was followed by an autobiographical volume of poetry,* Revolutionary Petunia *(1973). She also has written novels, including* The Third Life of Grange Copeland *(1970) and the Pulitzer Prize-winning* The Color Purple *(1982), which was a motion picture success in 1985. Among her other works are* You Can't Keep a Good Woman Down *(1981) and a collection of feminist writings called* In Search of Our Mother's Gardens *(1983). Her writing explores personal and family relationships and the strengths of black women amidst racial oppression.*

1   It is a bright summer day in 1947. My father, a fat, funny man with beautiful eyes and a subversive wit, is trying to decide which of his eight children he will take with him to the county fair. My mother, of course, will not go. She is knocked out from getting most of us ready: I hold my neck stiff against the pressure of her knuckles as she hastily completes the braiding and then beribboning of my hair.

2   My father is the driver for the rich old white lady up the road. Her name is Miss Mey. She owns all the land for miles around, as well as the house in which we live. All I remember about her is that she once offered to pay my mother thirty-five cents for cleaning her house, raking up piles of her magnolia leaves, and washing her family's clothes, and that my mother—she of no money, eight children, and a chronic earache—refused it. But I do not think of this in 1947. I am two and a half years old. I want to go everywhere my daddy goes. I am excited at the prospect of riding in a car. Someone has told me fairs are fun. That there is room in the car for only three of us doesn't faze me at all. Whirling happily in my starchy frock, showing off my biscuit-polished patent-leather shoes and lavender socks, tossing my head in a way that makes my ribbons bounce, I stand, hands on hips, before my father. "Take me, Daddy," I say with assurance; "I'm the prettiest!"

3   Later, it does not surprise me to find myself in Miss Mey's shiny black car, sharing the back seat with the other lucky ones. Does not surprise me that I thoroughly enjoy the fair. At home that night I tell the unlucky ones all I can remember about the merry-go-round, the man who eats live chickens, and the teddy bears, until they say: that's enough baby Alice. Shut up now, and go to sleep.

4   It is Easter Sunday, 1950. I am dressed in a green, flocked, scalloped-hem dress (handmade by my adoring sister, Ruth) that has its own smooth satin petticoat and tiny hot-pink roses tucked into each scallop. My shoes, new T-strap patent leather, again highly biscuit-polished. I am six years old and have learned one of the longest Easter speeches to be heard that day, totally unlike the speech I said when I was two: "Easter lilies / pure and white / blossom in / the morning light." When I rise to give my speech I do so on a great wave of love and pride, and expectation. People in the church stop rustling their new crinolines. They seem to hold their breath. I can tell they admire my dress, but it is my spirit, bordering on sassiness (womanishness), they secretly applaud.

5   "That girl's a little *mess*," they whisper to each other, pleased.

6   Naturally I say my speech without stammer or pause, unlike those who stutter, stammer, or, worst of all, forget. This is before the word "beautiful" exists in people's vocabulary, but "Oh, isn't she the *cutest* thing?" frequently floats my way. "And got so much sense!" they gratefully add . . . for which thoughtful addition I thank them to this day.

7   *It was great fun being cute. But then, one day, it ended.*

8   I am eight years old and a tomboy. I have a cowboy hat, cowboy boots, checkered shirt and pants, all red. My playmates are my brothers, two and four years older than I. Their colors are black and green, the only difference in the way we are dressed. On Saturday nights we all go to the picture show, even my mother; Westerns are her favorite kind of movie. Back home, "on the ranch," we pretend we are Tom Mix, Hopalong Cassidy, Lash LaRue (we've even named one of our dogs Lash LaRue); we chase each other for hours rustling cattle, being outlaws, delivering damsels from

distress. Then my parents decide to buy my brothers guns. These are not "real" guns. They shoot "BBs," copper pellets my brothers say will kill birds. Because I am a girl, I do not get a gun. Instantly I am relegated to the position of Indian. Now there appears a great distance between us. They shoot and shoot at everything with their new guns. I try to keep up with my bow and arrows.

9   One day while I am standing on top of our makeshift "garage"—pieces of tin nailed across some poles—holding my bow and arrow and looking out toward the fields, I feel an incredible blow in my right eye. I look down just in time to see my brother lower his gun.

10   Both brothers rush to my side. My eye stings, and I cover it with my hand. "If you tell," they say, "we will get a whipping. You don't want that to happen, do you?" I do not. "Here is a piece of wire," says the older brother, picking it up from the roof; "say you stepped on one end of it and the other flew up and hit you." The pain is beginning to start. "Yes," I say. "Yes, I will say that is what happened." If I do not say this is what happened, I know my brothers will find ways to make me wish I had. But now I will say anything that gets me to my mother.

11   Confronted by our parents we stick to the lie agreed upon. They place me on a bench on the porch and I close my left eye while they examine the right. There is a tree growing from underneath the porch that climbs past the railing to the roof. It is the last thing my right eye sees. I watch as its trunk, its branches, and then its leaves are blotted out by the rising blood.

12   I am in shock. First there is intense fever, which my father tries to break using lily leaves bound around my head. Then there are chills: my mother tries to get me to eat soup. Eventually, I do not know how, my parents learn what has happened. A week after the "accident" they take me to see a doctor. "Why did you wait so long to come?" he asks, looking into my eye and shaking his head. "Eyes are sympathetic," he says. "If one is blind, the other will likely become blind too."

13   This comment of the doctor's terrifies me. But it is really how I look that bothers me most. Where the BB pellet struck there is a glob of whitish scar tissue, a hideous cataract, on my eye. Now when I stare at people—a favorite pastime, up to now—they will stare back. Not at the "cute" little girl, but at her scar. For six years I do not stare at anyone, because I do not raise my head.

14   Years later, in the throes of a mid-life crisis, I ask my mother and sister whether I changed after the "accident." "No," they say, puzzled. "What do you mean?"

15   *What do I mean?*

16   I am eight, and for the first time, doing poorly in school, where I have been something of a whiz since I was four. We have just moved to the place where the "accident" occurred. We do not know any of the people around us because this is a different county. The only time I see the friends I knew is when we go back to our old church. The new school is the former state penitentiary. It is a large stone building, cold and drafty, crammed to overflowing with boisterous, ill-disciplined children. On the third floor there is a huge circular imprint of some partition that has been torn out.

17   "What used to be here?" I ask a sullen girl next to me on our way past it to lunch.

18   "The electric chair," says she.

19   At night I have nightmares about the electric chair; and about all the people reputedly "fried" in it. I am afraid of the school, where all the students seem to be budding criminals.

20   "What's the matter with your eye?" they ask, critically.

21   When I don't answer (I cannot decide whether it was an "accident" or not), they shove me, insist on a fight.

22   My brother, the one who created the story about the wire, comes to my rescue. But then brags so much about "protecting" me, I become sick.

23   After months of torture at the school, my parents decide to send me back to our old community, to my old school. I live with my grandparents and the teacher they board. But there is no room for Phoebe, my cat. By the time my grandparents decide there *is* room, and I ask for my cat, she cannot be found. Miss Yarborough, the boarding teacher, takes me under her wing, and begins to teach me to play the piano. But soon she marries an African—a "prince," she says—and is whisked away to his continent.

24   At my old school there is at least one teacher who loves me. She is the teacher who "knew me before I was born" and bought my first baby clothes. It is she who makes life bearable. It is her presence that finally helps me turn on the one child at the school who continually calls me "one-eyed bitch." One day I simply grab him by his coat and beat him until I am satisfied. It is my teacher who tells me my mother is ill.

25   My mother is lying in bed in the middle of the day, something I have never seen. She is in too much pain to speak. She has an abscess in her ear. I stand looking down on her, knowing that if she dies, I cannot live. She is being treated with warm oils and hot bricks held against her cheeks. Finally a doctor comes. But I must go back to my grandparents' house. The weeks pass but I am hardly aware of it. All I know is that my mother might die, my father is not so jolly, my brothers still have their guns, and I am the one sent away from home.

26   "You did not change," they say.

27   *Did I imagine the anguish of never looking up?*

28   I am twelve. When relatives come to visit I hide in my room. My cousin Brenda, just my age, whose father works in the post office and whose mother is a nurse, comes to find me. "Hello," she says. And then she asks, looking at my recent school picture, which I did not want taken, and on which the "glob," as I think of it, is clearly visible, "You still can't see out of that eye?"

29   "No," I say, and flop back on the bed over my book.

30   That night, as I do almost every night, I abuse my eye. I rant and rave at it, in front of the mirror. I plead with it to clear up before morning. I tell it I hate and despise it. I do not pray for sight. I pray for beauty.

31   "You did not change," they say.

32   I am fourteen and baby-sitting for my brother Bill, who lives in Boston. He is my favorite brother and there is a strong bond between us. Understanding my feelings of shame and ugliness he and his wife take me to a local hospital, where the "glob" is removed by a doctor named O. Henry. There is still a small bluish crater where the scar tissue was, but the ugly white stuff is gone. Almost immediately I become a different person from the girl who does not raise her head. Or so I think. Now that I've raised my head I win the boyfriend of my dreams. Now that I've raised my head I have

plenty of friends. Now that I've raised my head classwork comes from my lips as faultlessly as Easter speeches did, and I leave high school as valedictorian, most popular student, and *queen,* hardly believing my luck. Ironically, the girl who was voted most beautiful in our class (and was) was later shot twice through the chest by a male companion, using a "real" gun, while she was pregnant. But that's another story in itself. Or is it?

33   "You did not change," they say.

34   It is now thirty years since the "accident." A beautiful journalist comes to visit and to interview me. She is going to write a cover story for her magazine that focuses on my latest book. "Decide how you want to look on the cover," she says. "Glamorous, or whatever."

35   Never mind "glamorous," it is the "whatever" that I hear. Suddenly all I can think of is whether I will get enough sleep the night before the photography session: if I don't, my eye will be tired and wander, as blind eyes will . . . I think up reasons why I should not appear on the cover of a magazine. "My meanest critics will say I've sold out," I say. "My family will now realize I write scandalous books."

36   "But what's the real reason you don't want to do this?" he asks.

37   "Because in all probability," I say in a rush, "my eye won't be straight."

38   "It will be straight enough," he says. Then, "Besides, I thought you'd made your peace with that."

39   And I suddenly remember that I have.

40   *I remember:*

41   I am talking to my brother Jimmy, asking if he remembers anything unusual about the day I was shot. He does not know I consider that day the last time my father, with his sweet home remedy of cool lily leaves, chose me, and that I suffered and raged inside because of this. "Well," he says, "all I remember is standing by the side of the highway with Daddy, trying to flag down a car. A white man stopped, but when Daddy said he needed somebody to take his little girl to the doctor, he drove off."

42   *I remember:*

43   I am in the desert for the first time. I fall totally in love with it. I am so overwhelmed by its beauty, I confront for the first time, consciously, the meaning of the doctor's words years ago: "Eyes are sympathetic. If one is blind, the other will likely become blind too." I realize I have dashed about the world madly, looking at this, looking at that, storing up images against the fading of the light. *But I might have missed seeing the desert!* The shock of that possibility—and gratitude for over twenty-five years of sight—sends me literally to my knees. Poem after poem comes—which is perhaps how poets pray.

On Sight
I am so thankful I have seen
The Desert
And the creatures in the desert
And the desert itself.

The desert has its own moon
Which I have seen

With my own eye.
There is no flag on it.

Trees of the desert have arms
All of which are always up
That is because the moon is up
The sun is up
Also the sky
The stars
Clouds
None with flags.

If there were flags, I doubt
The trees would point.
Would you?

44   *But mostly, I remember this:*

45   I am twenty-seven, and my baby daughter is almost three. Since her birth I have worried about her discovery that her mother's eyes are different from other people's. Will she be embarrassed? I think. What will she say? Every day she watches a televison program called "Big Blue Marble." It begins with a picture of the earth as it appears from the moon. It is bluish, a little battered-looking, but full of light, with whitish clouds swirling around it. Every time I see it I weep with love, as if it is a picture of Grandma's house. One day when I am putting Rebecca down for her nap, she suddenly focuses on my eye. Something inside me cringes, gets ready to try to protect myself. All children are cruel about physical differences, I know from experience, and that they don't always mean to be is another matter. I assume Rebecca will be the same.

46   But no-o-o-o. She studies my face intently as we stand, her inside and me outside the crib. She even holds my face maternally between her dimpled little hands. Then, looking every bit as serious and lawyer-like as her father, she says, as if it may just possibly have slipped my attention: "Mommy, there's a *world* in your eye." (As in, "Don't be alarmed, or do anything crazy.") And then, gently, but with great interest: "Mommy, where did you *get* that world in your eye?"

47   For the most part, the pain left then. (So what, if my brothers grew up to buy even more powerful pellet guns for their sons and to carry real guns themselves. So what, if a young "Morehouse man" once nearly fell off the steps of Trevor Arnett Library because he thought my eyes were blue.) Crying and laughing I ran to the bathroom, while Rebecca mumbled and sang herself off to sleep. Yes indeed, I realized, looking into the mirror. There *was* a world in my eye. And I saw that it was possible to love it: that in fact, for all it had taught me of shame and anger and inner vision, I *did* love it. Even to see it drifting out of orbit in boredom, or rolling up out of fatigue, not to mention floating back at attention in excitement (bearing witness, a friend has called it), deeply suitable to my personality, and even characteristic of me.

48   That night I dream I am dancing to Stevie Wonder's song "Always" (the name of the song is really "As," but I hear it as "Always"). As I dance, whirling and joyous, happier than I've ever been in my life, another bright-faced dancer joins me. We dance

and kiss each other and hold each other through the night. The other dancer has obviously come through all right, as I have done. She is beautiful, whole and free. And she is also me.

Suggestions for Discussion or Writing

1. Contrast Walker's early years with those immediately following the "accident." How did physical appearance affect her self-esteem?

2. Walker seems embittered more by her disfigurement than by her loss of sight. How might you explain this?

3. How do her brothers and parents react immediately following the "accident"? How does she react to her family both immediately and many years after the accident?

4. What people most affect her self-esteem, for better or for worse, and how?

5. Would Walker's reactions have been different if she were male?

6. How is the author affected by her desert experience? How is her experience and change reflected by the poem "On Sight"?

7. What is the significance of the title? How does it reflect Walker's final acceptance of her physical disfigurement?

Modeling the Plague

Lori Oliwenstein

Lori Oliwenstein has been a researcher and reporter and an editorial assistant for Discover *magazine. She is currently an associate news editor for the magazine. She has written articles on such diverse topics as the volcano-climate connection, "Hot Air" (May 1990); a condor born in captivity, "Nine Months of the Condor" (January 1989); and the golden-crowned sifaka (a newly discovered lemur species), "Our New Cousin" (January 1990), as well as many other articles.*

1   There are hundreds of AIDS researchers out there trying to figure out how the virus vanquishes humans, or looking for drugs or a vaccine that will vanquish the disease. In either case they're up against a problem. Obviously they can't do much experimentation on humans. And while cells in a lab dish can reveal a lot, they behave differently than they do in living creatures. What researchers really want to do is try

their vaccines (or test their hypotheses) on some sort of primate model. Primates are our closest living relatives, and thus they would be most likely to respond to a vaccine or drug or to infection by a virus the way we would.

2 But by and large primates have proved impervious to the most common AIDS-causing virus, HIV-1, falling prey instead to a similar, but not identical, simian virus called SIV. And those few that can be infected with HIV (like gibbons and chimpanzees) are endangered species that science doesn't want to endanger any further. That's why researchers' hopes were buoyed by the announcement this summer of two other potential models.

3 The pigtail macaque, *Macaca nemestrina,* is not an endangered species. Yet its vulnerability to HIV wasn't detected until recently because primate research centers in this country don't have a tradition of using it. "Most centers concentrate on long-tailed and rhesus macaques," says microbiologist Michael Agy of the Regional Primate Research Center at the University of Washington in Seattle. "But at the University of Washington, the pigtail macaque is our main primate."

4 Researchers at the center were using pigtails to study SIV and a less common form of the AIDS virus, HIV-2. (Some scientists now think that certain strains of HIV-2 and SIV are identical viruses, but that's a whole other story.) "We had noticed that the pigtail macaques were getting sicker faster than the long-tails," says Agy. So the researchers decided to see what would happen when the animals were exposed to HIV-1.

5 Two macaques were injected with the virus; shortly afterward they developed swollen glands and a rash on the abdomen. More important, the virus continued to multiply in their immune cells, a clear sign of ongoing infection. So, concludes Agy, pigtail macaques look like a promising model for studying the early infection process and how to stop it with vaccines.

6 Joseph Sodroski's group at Harvard Medical School, and their colleagues at the New England Regional Primate Research Center, had a trickier time with their model. Their primate—the common long-tailed macaque, *Macaca fascicularis*—was susceptible only to SIV. To get around the problem they built a chimeric virus, taking the core of the monkey virus SIV and wrapping it in the coat, or envelope, of HIV. The ruse worked: all four long-tailed macaques injected with the chimera, dubbed SHIV, became infected. That should make them useful for most types of vaccine testing, contends Sodroski. "The majority of vaccines being tested today," he explains, "are directed specifically against the outer part of the virus."

7 Both models, however, have their limitations. To study drugs that treat AIDS, or to learn how the virus makes us so overwhelmingly sick, we need a model that gets sick as well. Yet despite their initial symptoms, pigtail macaques don't go on to suffer the catastrophic immune collapse we call AIDS. Neither the first pair of infected monkeys, nor any of the approximately 40 animals infected since, has developed the full-blown disease. It's been a similar tale with the long-tailed macaques: five months after infection, none showed signs of illness. "That's why we're now working to make our chimera more virulent and pathogenic," says Sodroski.

8 Agy points out that his pigtail macaque model has the advantage of using whole HIV-1 virus, not just its envelope, so it more closely mimics what's going on in

humans. Still, he concedes, it falls short of ideal. "An ideal model would not only succumb to the virus that is responsible for the disease in man but go on to develop the disease." And such a model remains to be found—or created.

Suggestions for Discussion or Writing

1. The pigtail macaque primate initially was not used to test the AIDS virus. Why?

2. Is animal testing of a virus important? Why?

3. What symptoms of HIV-1 are similar both to humans and pigtail macaques? How are the diseases different?

4. What assumptions can be made about testing or "modeling" experimental treatments for AIDS?

The Unbearable Darkness of Being

Katherine Griffin

Katherine Griffin is a staff writer for Health *magazine, formerly* In Health. *Her articles have included such information as the effect of smell on work environments, "A Whiff of Things to Come" (Nov/Dec 1992); the fitness of American children, "Kids Gone Soft" (Mar/Apr 1990); and many other articles on health.*

I am Job.
Events conspire to snatch
The illusion of control from my grasp and I slide,
fingernails scratching into metal walls into depth unknown.

1 Twenty-seven-year-old Melissa Roberts [the name has been changed] seems an unlikely author of these troubled words. With her intelligent blue eyes, shy, dimpled smile, and curly blond hair, she looks every inch the wholesome Mid-western college girl, someone who has lived a life dappled in sunlight.

2 In fact, Roberts is intimately acquainted with darkness. When she began graduate school in Washington, D.C., four years ago, she was a bright, motivated, straight-A student. By the start of her second semester she hardly knew herself. The smallest upsets—a pop quiz, a critical glance—triggered floods of tears. Her grades dropped

to a C average. "I just couldn't concentrate," she says. "I couldn't sleep. I didn't have the energy to reach out to anybody. Nothing had any meaning to it at all."

3   When 42-year-old Baltimore high school counselor Lissa Falk entered her twenties, she became constantly tired in a way that doctors couldn't explain. She often felt there was little point to her life. By the time she hit 30, it was all she could do to drag herself home from work every day and climb into bed, where she cried for hours. "I was in constant psychic pain," she recalls. "It's like the feeling when somebody very dear to you dies. But it goes on and on and doesn't end."

4   Both women felt isolated and ashamed, as though they were the only people in the world who had ever sunk to such depths. Neither had any idea what was happening to her. In fact, both were seriously depressed, and they were far from alone. Depression has been called the common cold of psychiatric disorders: Over the next six months alone, some 10 million people in this country will suffer from it, twice as many of them women as men. If current trends continue, one in nine American women and one in 18 men will be stricken at some time in their lives.

5   For members of the baby boom generation, born from 1945 to 1964, the risk is even higher. Some studies have found older baby boomers like Falk two to four times as likely as their parents to become depressed by age 30. The younger boomers like Roberts, born from the early 1960s on, appear to be following a similar pattern. And both groups are falling ill with depression at a much earlier age than did their parents and grandparents: around their late teens and twenties rather than in middle age.

6   Being depressed means much more than feeling down in the dumps for a few days. The unrelenting lassitude and hopelessness that Falk felt in her twenties are typical of the chronic, less severe form of depression called dysthymia; it lasts for at least two years. Major depression brings similar symptoms, but they're concentrated into a few months or less, and are much more intense and painful. Thoughts of suicide tantalize, offering what seems the only escape from the torment that life has become. About 15 percent of severe depressives who are not properly treated do kill themselves; many more attempt it.

7   Fortunately, depression is eminently treatable. Eighty percent of people suffering from major depression—the most common form—can be treated successfully with drugs, therapy, or both; the success rate for dysthymia is thought to be similar.

8   And yet only a third of depressed people ever seek treatment. For one thing, they often feel the depression is their own fault, and that they should be able to pull themselves out of it. For another, many depressives come to believe the world truly is as dim and featureless as they perceive it to be. "I studied existentialist philosophers in college," Falk says. "I just thought, 'Well, I'm smarter than other people. Life really is worthless.'" The feelings add up to a paralyzing conviction that there is no name and no solution for the affliction destroying their lives.

9   As Roberts wrote in one of the poems giving voice to her nightmare:

I am despairing
That I have been abandoned;
Exiled behind walls of glass,
An exhibit lacking even a classification.

10   Melissa Roberts's sojourn into the shadows began when she left behind a boyfriend in Boulder, Colorado, to start graduate school in international relations.

11   "School was extremely competitive," she says, cradling a mug of tea in a Washington, D.C., delicatessen one dark afternoon. "I couldn't tell whether my boyfriend missed me. I started feeling more and more isolated. I tried to go to all kinds of things where you'd meet people, but nothing was working."

12   Desperate to break out of her numbness, she let herself be talked into a one-night stand—and got pregnant. Twelve weeks later, she miscarried.

13   "My first reaction was relief," she says. "A month later, it just hit me. All I wanted to do was sit and stare at the wall. Underlying everything was this . . . sea of pain."

14   The simple conclusion to draw would be that Roberts's miscarriage caused her depression. In fact, she was at risk from the day she was born.

15   For one thing, depression runs in her family. Several cousins have attempted suicide, and one has been diagnosed as manic-depressive, a condition that swings moods from intense highs to deep, dark lows. In the past ten years, study after study has shown that immediate family members of depressed people are two to three times more likely to become depressed than the general population.

16   Though there's no clear evidence of a gene for depression, severely depressed people have an unusual biochemical profile that researchers suspect is inherited and can influence mood. They sometimes have high levels of the hormone cortisol in their blood, and are thought to have too little of the nerve transmitters serotonin, dopamine, and norepinephrine circulating in their brains.

17   But depression may also run in families because children simply absorb their parents' way of looking at the world and make it their own. Tiffany Field, a psychologist at the University of Miami, has found that infants as young as three months old react to their depressed mothers' behavior with depressive responses of their own. "They don't coo and smile like other babies," she says.

18   Melissa Roberts was spared growing up with a depressed mother, but her relationship with her father probably heightened her vulnerability. Somewhere between Roberts's third and sixth birthdays, her mother became jealous of the affection Roberts's father showed toward his daughter. Rather than stand up to his wife's objections, Roberts's father turned away from his daughter.

19   "He just withdrew," Roberts says. "There was always this feeling that he totally abandoned me."

20   Some therapists believe that the loss of a parent early in childhood, whether by death, divorce, or some other separation, causes a kind of grief that manifests itself later in life as depression. This is particularly true if the grief is not fully expressed at the time of the loss. Not only does the child later set up situations to relive that loss, but other losses can then trigger a depression far out of proportion to the triggering event.

21   Roberts's generation is the first whose parents were as likely to divorce as to stay married. Similarly, both older and younger baby boomers are likely to see *their* marriages end in divorce, which then doubles their chances of depression. The boomers also came of age at a time when moving frequently had become the norm. All these things lead to what psychologists call loss of attachment bonds: family members living

thousands of miles apart, close friends scattered across the country, communities not as strong as they used to be. Fewer intimate bonds—a lack Roberts felt acutely in her first months of graduate school—mean greater risk of depression.

22   In addition, the boomers were born into a crowded generation. The older ones, in particular, grew up at a time when the economy seemed infinitely expansive; the social upheavals of the 1960s raised expectations of an unfettered future. But entering adulthood, they ran up against fierce competition for schools, jobs, houses, and just about everything else. Beginning in 1973 the economy began to contract, and real wages have not increased since then.

23   "My theory is, people feel depressed when there's a gap between expectation and fulfillment," says Gerald L. Klerman, a psychiatrist at Cornell Medical Center in New York City. "If you have high expectations that are not being fulfilled, you feel frustrated, disappointed, maybe even powerless."

24   Even for boomers who have attained economic or professional success, there is often a lingering sense that the cost to the rest of their lives has been too high.

25   Carey Mills [the name has been changed] is a case in point. By the time she was in her early thirties, she had earned a Ph.D. in clinical psychology and become the only woman on the psychiatry faculty of a major California medical school. "But I didn't have the other pieces of what I needed," she says. "I was very deficient in relationship skills." She slipped in and out of depression during her twenties, and found her symptoms worsening in her mid-thirties, after her marriage ended in divorce.

26   Now in her early forties, Mills is remarried and the mother of two young children, with a thriving clinical practice in New York City. But it took several years of therapy for her to bring her life into balance.

27   She now recognizes that she became depressed partly because she was abused as a child. Reported abuse has risen 147 percent in the past ten years, and is emerging as an important predictor of depression. It's one of several social ills—poverty and economic discrimination are others—that afflict women more often than men, and may help explain why women are more susceptible to depression.

28   And yet, for all that's now known about the triggers for depression, they are sometimes conspicuously absent from the lives of those who become depressed. For example, while high school counselor Lissa Falk is divorced, she wasn't abused as a child, didn't lose a parent when she was young, still lives near longtime friends in the city where she grew up, and isn't disappointed in her career. And one of her worst depressions came just after a period that was one of her happiest in years.

29   It was the fall of her 35th year. She had recently bought a house and was enjoying her job at a new school. But in the dark days of November—a time that had always been difficult for her, as it is for many depressives—she began feeling irritable, moody, apathetic. She counted the days until Christmas vacation, thinking she just needed some rest. Christmas came and went, and her mood only worsened.

30   Finally, on a cold, rainy February day, she dragged herself out to see a specialist she'd heard of at Johns Hopkins Hospital.

31   "I thought, 'I have done everything I can do,' " Falk recalls. " 'If I go to this guy, and there's nothing he can do, then there's nothing left. I will have to kill myself because I cannot stand this any more.' "

32   For Falk, it was a drug called nortriptyline that finally brought her out of depression's dark thicket. Just three weeks after the specialist correctly diagnosed her and prescribed the drug, Falk began feeling better. That was eight years ago. She's had occasional low spells since then, but nothing like before. "Everyday life is richer," she says. "I'm not distracted by these terrible thoughts. I don't get yanked down under the waves."

33   The tricyclics are among several classes of antidepressant drugs that, while not panaceas, work remarkably well. Several forms of psychotherapy, both short- and long-term, can also help.

34   Falk expects to continue taking the drug for the rest of her life, an idea that bothered her at first. "But it's just what I've got to do to keep myself healthy," she says. What she does regret is that none of her doctors diagnosed her earlier. "That essentially wasted ten years of my life."

35   Melissa Roberts was luckier. Shortly after her miscarriage, she began seeing a therapist, who diagnosed her with dysthymia. Things started looking up about nine months later, when she began connecting her childhood with the things in her adult life that plunged her into despair. "I think what I've been doing throughout a lot of my depressive cycles was re-creating that rejection I experienced with my father," she says.

36   Roberts realized that with the men she was attracted to—her former boyfriend, for instance, and her one-night stand—she usually had to carry both sides of the emotional relationship, as she did with her father. Now she's trying to minimize her involvement with withdrawn men; in effect, to eliminate that depressive trigger from her life. She's also working hard to create a strong network of friends to keep herself from getting isolated.

37   Roberts is doing better in school now, too. She's not so susceptible to crying spells. And perhaps most important, she is learning to live with her tendency toward depression, knowing there is a way out.

38   "Information takes a lot of the fear away," she says. "I'm not a zoo exhibit without a name any more."

Suggestions for Discussion or Writing

1. What is the "darkness" spoken of in this article? How is this metaphor appropriate for the condition described?

2. Why don't people usually seek treatment for this problem? What assumptions do people make about their own behavior that would hinder proper treatment?

3. What assumptions does Griffin make on the causes of the increasing prevalence of depression?

4. What treatments are successful for depression, according to Griffin?

5. Compare the case studies of Melissa Roberts, Carey Mills, and Lissa Falk. How are they similar? How are they different?

6. How is the depression in this article compared to the illnesses described in either "Silent Snow, Secret Snow" or "The Yellow Wallpaper"? What are the similarities and differences?

Silent Snow, Secret Snow

Conrad Aiken

Conrad Aiken (1889–1973), born in Savanna, Georgia, was a poet, essayist, novelist, and short-story writer. In 1911 and again in 1916–1922 he traveled to Europe, where he met Ezra Pound, T. S. Eliot, and Amy Lowell. During his lifetime he tutored English at Harvard University, was a reviewer for New Republic, Poetry, Chicago Daily News, Poetry Journal, *and* Dial, *and wrote as a London correspondent for the* New Yorker *under the pseudonym Samual Jeake, Jr. He was appointed the Poet Laureate of Georgia in 1973 and has won numerous poetry and writing awards, including the Pulitzer Prize for* Selected Poems *(1930) and the National Book Award for* Collected Poems *(1954). Among the large body of his writings are poetry collections, children's poems, short-story collections, novels, and many essays, plays, and criticism. By volume alone he is one of America's most prolific writers.*

1   Just why it should have happened, or why it should have happened just when it did, he could not, of course, possibly have said; nor perhaps would it even have occurred to him to ask. The thing was above all a secret, something to be preciously concealed from Mother and Father; and to that very fact it owed an enormous part of its deliciousness. It was like a peculiarly beautiful trinket to be carried unmentioned in one's trouser pocket—a rare stamp, an old coin, a few tiny gold links found trodden out of shape on the path in the park, a pebble of carnelian, a seashell distinguishable from all others by an unsual spot or stripe—and, as if it were any one of these, he carried around with him everywhere a warm and persistent and increasingly beautiful sense of possession. Nor was it only a sense of possession—it was also a sense of protection. It was as if, in some delightful way, his secret gave him a fortress, a wall behind which he could retreat into heavenly seclusion. This was almost the first thing he had noticed about it—apart from the oddness of the thing itself—and it was this that now again, for the fiftieth time, occurred to him, as he sat in the little schoolroom. It was the half hour for geography. Miss Buell was revolving with one finger, slowly, a huge terrestrial globe which had been placed on her desk. The green and yellow continents passed and repassed, questions were asked and answered, and now the little girl in front of him, Deirdre, who had a funny little constellation of freckles on the back of her neck, exactly

like the Big Dipper, was standing up and telling Miss Buell that the equator was the line that ran round the middle.

2 Miss Buell's face, which was old and grayish and kindly, with gray stiff curls beside the cheeks, and eyes that swam very brightly, like little minnows, behind thick glasses, wrinkled itself into a complication of amusements.

3 "Ah! I see. The earth is wearing a belt, or a sash. Or someone drew a line round it!"

4 "Oh no—not that—I mean—"

5 In the general laughter, he did not share, or only a very little. He was thinking about the Arctic and Antarctic regions, which of course, on the globe, were white. Miss Buell was now telling them about the tropics, the jungles, the steamy heat of equatorial swamps, where the birds and butterflies, and even the snakes, were like living jewels. As he listened to these things, he was already, with a pleasant sense of half-effort, putting his secret between himself and the words. Was it really an effort at all? For effort implied something voluntary, and perhaps even something one did not especially want; whereas this was distinctly pleasant, and came almost of its own accord. All he needed to do was to think of that morning, the first one, and then of all the others—

6 But it was all so absurdly simple! It had amounted to so little. It was nothing, just an idea—and just why it should have become so wonderful, so permanent, was a mystery—a very pleasant one, to be sure, but also, in an amusing way, foolish. However, without ceasing to listen to Miss Buell, who had now moved up to the north temperate zones, he deliberately invited his memory of the first morning. It was only a moment or two after he had waked up—or perhaps the moment itself. But was there, to be exact, an exact moment? Was one awake all at once? or was it gradual? Anyway, it was after he had stretched a lazy hand up toward the headrail, and yawned, and then relaxed again among his warm covers, all the more grateful on a December morning, that the thing had happened. Suddenly, for no reason, he had thought of the postman, he remembered the postman. Perhaps there was nothing so odd in that. After all, he heard the postman almost every morning in his life—his heavy boots could be heard clumping round the corner at the top of the little cobbled hill-street, and then, progressively nearer, progressively louder, the double knock at each door, the crossings and recrossings of the street, till finally the clumsy steps came stumbling across to the very door, and the tremendous knock came which shook the house itself.

7 (Miss Buell was saying, "Vast wheat-growing areas in North America and Siberia."

8 Deirdre had for the moment placed her left hand across the back of her neck.)

9 But on this particular morning, the first morning, as he lay there with his eyes closed, he had for some reason *waited* for the postman. He wanted to hear him come round the corner. And that was precisely the joke—he never did. He never came. He never had come—*round the corner*—again. For when at last the steps *were* heard, they had already, he was quite sure, come a little down the hill, to the first house; and even so, the steps were curiously different—they were softer, they had a new secrecy about them, they were muffled and indistinct; and while the rhythm of them was the same, it now said a new thing—it said peace, it said remoteness, it said cold, it said sleep. And he had understood the situation at once—nothing could have seemed simpler— there had been snow in the night, such as all winter he had been longing for; and it

was this which had rendered the postman's first footsteps inaudible, and the later ones faint. Of course! How lovely! And even now it must be snowing—it was going to be a snow street, across the faces of the old houses, whispering and hushing, making little triangles of white in the corners between cobblestones, seething a little when the wind blew them over the ground to a drifted corner; and so it would be all day, getting deeper and deeper and silenter and silenter.

10   (Miss Buell was saying, "Land of perpetual snow.")

11   All this time, of course (while he lay in bed), he had kept his eyes closed, listening to the nearer progress of the postman, the muffled footsteps thumping and slipping on the snow-sheathed cobbles; and all the other sounds—the double knocks, a frosty far-off voice or two, a bell ringing thinly and softly as if under a sheet of ice—had the same slightly abstracted quality, as if removed by one degree from actuality—as if everything in the world had been insulated by snow. But when at last, pleased, he opened his eyes, and turned them toward the window, to see for himself this long-desired and now so clearly imagined miracle—what he saw instead was brilliant sunlight on a roof; and when, astonished, he jumped out of bed and stared down into the street, expecting to see the cobbles obliterated by the snow, he saw nothing but the bare bright cobbles themselves.

12   Queer, the effect this extraordinary surprise had had upon him—all the following morning he had kept with him a sense as of snow falling about him, a secret screen of new snow between himself and the world. If he had not dreamed such a thing—and how could he have dreamed it while awake?—how else could one explain it! In any case, the delusion had been so vivid as to affect his entire behavior. He could not now remember whether it was on the first or the second morning—or was it even the third?—that his mother had drawn attention to some oddness in his manner.

13   "But my darling"—she had said at the breakfast table—"what has come over you? You don't seem to be listening. . . ."

14   And how often that very thing had happened since!

15   (Miss Buell was now asking if anyone knew the difference between the North Pole and the Magnetic Pole. Deirdre was holding up her flickering brown hand, and he could see the four white dimples that marked the knuckles.)

16   Perhaps it hadn't been either the second or third morning—or even the fourth or fifth. How could he be sure? How could he be sure just when the delicious *progress* had become clear? Just when it had really *begun*? The intervals weren't very precise. . . . All he now knew was, that at some point or other—perhaps the second day, perhaps the sixth—he had noticed that the presence of the snow was a little more insistent, the sound of it clearer; and, conversely, the sound of the postman's footsteps more indistinct. Not only could he not hear the steps come round the corner, he could not even hear them at the first house. It was below the first house that he heard them; and then, a few days later, it was below the second house that he heard them; and then, a few days later again, below the third. Gradually, gradually, the snow was becoming heavier, the sound of its seething louder, the cobblestones more and more muffled. When he found, each morning, on going to the window, after the ritual of listening, that the roofs and cobbles were as bare as ever, it made no difference. This was, after all, only what he had expected. It was even what pleased him, what rewarded him: the

thing was his own, belonged to no one else. No one else knew about it, not even his mother and father. There, outside, were the bare cobbles; and here, inside, was the snow. Snow growing heavier each day, muffling the world, hiding the ugly, and deadening increasingly—above all—the steps of the postman.

17   "But, my darling"—she had said at the luncheon table—"what has come over you? You don't seem to listen when people speak to you. That's the third time I've asked you to pass your plate. . . ."

18   How was one to explain this to Mother? or to Father? There was, of course, nothing to be done about it: nothing. All one could do was to laugh embarrassedly, pretend to be a little ashamed, apologize, and take a sudden and somewhat disingenuous interest in what was being done or said. The cat had stayed out all night. He had a curious swelling on his left cheek—perhaps somebody had kicked him, or a stone had struck him. Mrs. Kempton was or was not coming to tea. The house was going to be housecleaned, or "turned out," on Wednesday instead of Friday. A new lamp was provided for his evening work—perhaps it was eyestrain which accounted for this new and so peculiar vagueness of his—Mother was looking at him with amusement as she said this, but with something else as well. A new lamp? A new lamp. Yes, Mother, No, Mother, Yes, Mother. School is going very well. The geometry is very easy. The history is very dull. The geography is very interesting—particularly when it takes one to the North Pole. Why the North Pole? Oh, well, it would be fun to be an explorer. Another Peary or Scott or Shackleton. And then abruptly he found his interest in the talk at an end, stared at the pudding on his plate, listened, waited, and began once more—ah, how heavenly, too, the first beginnings—to hear or feel—for could he actually hear it?—the silent snow, the secret snow.

19   (Miss Buell was telling them about the search for the Northwest Passage, about Hendrik Hudson, the *Half Moon*.)

20   This had been, indeed, the only distressing feature of the new experience; the fact that it so increasingly had brought him into a kind of mute misunderstanding, or even conflict, with his father and mother. It was as if he were trying to lead a double life. On the one hand, he had to be Paul Hasleman, and keep up the appearance of being that person—dress, wash, and answer intelligently when spoken to—; on the other, he had to explore this new world which had been opened to him. Nor could there be the slightest doubt—not the slightest—that the new world was the profounder and more wonderful of the two. It was irresistible. It was miraculous. Its beauty was simply beyond anything—beyond speech as beyond thought—utterly incommunicable. But how then, between the two worlds, of which he was thus constantly aware, was he to keep a balance? One must get up, one must go to breakfast, one must talk with Mother, go to school, do one's lessons—and, in all this, try not to appear too much of a fool. But if all the while one was also trying to extract the full deliciousness of another and quite separate existence, one which could not easily (if at all) be spoken of—how was one to manage? How was one to explain? Would it be safe to explain? Would it be absurd? Would it merely mean that he would get into some obscure kind of trouble?

21   These thoughts came and went, came and went, as softly and secretly as the snow; they were not precisely a disturbance, perhaps they were even a pleasure; he liked to have them; their presence was something almost palpable, something he could stroke

with his hand, without closing his eyes, and without ceasing to see Miss Buell and the schoolroom and the globe and the freckles on Deirdre's neck; nevertheless he did in a sense cease to see, or to see the obvious external world, and substituted for this vision the vision of snow, the sound of snow, and the slow, almost soundless, approach of the postman. Yesterday, it had been only at the sixth house that the postman had become audible; the snow was much deeper now, it was falling more swiftly and heavily, the sound of its seething was more distinct, more soothing, more persistent. And this morning, it had been—as nearly as he could figure—just above the seventh house—perhaps only a step or two above; at most, he had heard two or three footsteps before the knock had sounded. . . . And with each such narrowing of the sphere, each nearer approach of the limit at which the postman was first audible, it was odd how sharply was increased the amount of illusion which had to be carried into the ordinary business of daily life. Each day, it was harder to get out of bed, to go to the window, to look out at the—as always—perfectly empty and snowless street. Each day it was more difficult to go through the perfunctory motions of greeting Mother and Father at breakfast, to reply to their questions, to put his books together and go to school. And at school, how extraordinarily hard to conduct with success simultaneously the public life and the life that was secret! There were times when he longed—positively ached— to tell everyone about it—to burst out with it—only to be checked almost at once by a far-off feeling as of some faint absurdity which was inherent in it—but *was* it absurd?—and more importantly by a sense of mysterious power in his very secrecy. Yes; it must be kept secret. That, more and more, became clear. At whatever cost to himself, whatever pain to others—

22   (Miss Buell looked straight at him, smiling, and said, "Perhaps we'll ask Paul. I'm sure Paul will come out of his daydream long enough to be able to tell us. Won't you, Paul?" He rose slowly from his chair, resting one hand on the brightly varnished desk, and deliberately stared through the snow toward the blackboard. It was an effort, but it was amusing to make it. "Yes," he said slowly, "it was what we now call the Hudson River. This he thought to be the Northwest Passage. He was disappointed." He sat down again, and as he did so Deirdre half turned in her chair and gave him a shy smile, of approval and admiration.)

23   At whatever pain to others.

24   This part of it was very puzzling, very puzzling. Mother was very nice, and so was Father. Yes, that was all true enough. He wanted to be nice to them, to tell them everything—and yet, was it really wrong of him to want to have a secret place of his own?

25   At bedtime, the night before, Mother had said, "If this goes on, my lad, we'll have to see a doctor, we will! We can't have our boy—" But what was it she had said: "Live in another world"? "Live so far away"? The word "far" had been in it, he was sure, and then Mother had taken up a magazine again and laughed a little, but with an expression which wasn't mirthful. He had felt sorry for her . . .

26   The bell rang for dismissal. The sound came to him through long curved parallels of falling snow. He saw Deirdre rise, and had himself risen almost as soon—but not quite as soon—as she.

27   On the walk homeward, which was timeless, it pleased him to see through the accompaniment, or counterpoint, of snow, the items of mere externality on his way. There were many kinds of brick in the sidewalks, and laid in many kinds of pattern. The garden walls, too, were various, some of wooden palings, some of plaster, some of stone. Twigs of bushes leaned over the walls: the little hard green winterbuds of lilac, on gray stems, sheathed and fat; other branches very thin and fine and black and desiccated. Dirty sparrows huddled in the bushes, as dull in color as dead fruit left in leafless trees. A single starling creaked on a weather vane. In the gutter, beside a drain, was a scrap of torn and dirty newspaper, caught in a little delta of filth; the word ECZEMA appeared in large capitals, and below it was a letter from Mrs. Amelia D. Cravath, 2100 Pine Street, Fort Worth, Texas, to the effect that after being a sufferer for years she had been cured by Caley's Ointment. In the little delta, beside the fanshaped and deeply runneled continent of brown mud, were lost twigs, descended from their parent trees, dead matches, a rusty horse chestnut burr, a small concentration of eggshell, a streak of yellow sawdust which had been wet and now was dry and congealed, a brown pebble, and a broken feather. Farther on was a cement sidewalk, ruled into geometrical parallelograms, with a brass inlay at one end commemorating the contractors who had laid it, and, halfway across, an irregular and random series of dog tracks, immortalized in synthetic stone. He knew these well, and always stepped on them; to cover the little hollows with his own foot had always been a queer pleasure; today he did it once more, but perfunctorily and detachedly, all the while thinking of something else. That was a dog, a long time ago, who had made a mistake and walked on the cement while it was still wet. He had probably wagged his tail, but that hadn't been recorded. Now, Paul Hasleman, aged twelve, on his way home from school, crossed the same river, which in the meantime had frozen into rock. Homeward through the snow, the snow falling in bright sunshine. Homeward?

28   Then came the gateway with the two posts surmounted by egg-shaped stones which had been cunningly balanced on their ends, as if by Columbus, and mortared in the very act of balance; a source of perpetual wonder. On the brick wall just beyond, the letter H had been stenciled, presumably for some purpose. H? H.

29   The green hydrant, with a little green-painted chain attached to the brass screw-cap.

30   The elm tree, with the great gray wound in the bark, kidneyshaped, into which he always put his hand—to feel the cold but living wood. The injury, he had been sure, was due to the gnawings of a tethered horse. But now it deserved only a passing palm, a merely tolerant eye. There were more important things. Miracles. Beyond the thoughts of trees, mere elms. Beyond the thoughts of sidewalks, mere stone, mere brick, mere cement. Beyond the thoughts even of his own shoes, which trod these sidewalks obediently, bearing a burden—far above—of elaborate mystery. He watched them. They were not very well polished; he had neglected them, for a very good reason: they were one of the many parts of the increasing difficulty of the daily return to daily life, the morning struggle. To get up, having at last opened one's eyes, to go to the window, and discover no snow, to wash, to dress, to descend the curving stairs to breakfast—

31   At whatever pain to others, nevertheless, one must persevere in severance, since the incommunicability of the experience demanded it. It was desirable, of course, to

be kind to Mother and Father, especially as they seemed to be worried, but it was also desirable to be resolute. If they should decide—as appeared likely—to consult the doctor, Doctor Howells, and have Paul inspected, his heart listened to through a kind of dictaphone, his lungs, his stomach—well, that was all right. He would go through with it. He would give them answer for question, too—perhaps such answers as they hadn't expected? No. That would never do. For the secret world must, at all costs, be preserved.

32   The birdhouse in the apple tree was empty—it was the wrong time of year for wrens. The little round black door had lost its pleasure. The wrens were enjoying other houses, other nests, remoter trees. But this too was a notion which he only vaguely and grazingly entertained—as if, for the moment, he merely touched an edge of it; there was something further on, which was already assuming a sharper importance; something which already teased at the corners of his eyes, teasing also at the corner of his mind. It was funny to think that he so wanted this, so awaited it—and yet found himself enjoying this momentary dalliance with the birdhouse, as if for a quite deliberate postponement and enhancement of the approaching pleasure. He was aware of his delay, of his smiling and detached and now almost uncomprehending gaze at the little birdhouse; he knew what he was going to look at next: it was his own little cobbled hill-street, his own house, the little river at the bottom of the hill, the grocer's shop with the cardboard man in the window—and now, thinking of all this, he turned his head, still smiling, and looking quickly right and left through the snowladen sunlight.

33   And the mist of snow, as he had foreseen, was still on it—a ghost of snow falling in the bright sunlight, softly and steadily floating and turning and pausing, soundlessly meeting the snow that covered, as with a transparent mirage, the bare bright cobbles. He loved it—he stood still and loved it. Its beauty was paralyzing—beyond all words, all experience, all dream. No fairy story he had ever read could be compared with it—none had ever given him this extraordinary combination of ethereal loveliness with a something else, unnameable, which was just faintly and deliciously terrifying. What was this thing? As he thought of it, he looked upward toward his own bedroom window, which was open—and it was as if he looked straight into the room and saw himself lying half awake in his bed. There he was—at this very instant he was still perhaps actually there—more truly there than standing here at the edge of the cobbled hill-street, with one hand lifted to shade his eyes against the snow-sun. Had he indeed ever left his room, in all this time? since that very first morning? Was the whole progress still being enacted there, was it still the same morning, and himself not yet wholly awake? And even now, had the postman not yet come round the corner? . . .

34   This idea amused him, and automatically, as he thought of it, he turned his head and looked toward the top of the hill. There was, of course, nothing there—nothing and no one. The street was empty and quiet. And all the more because of its emptiness it occurred to him to count the houses—a thing which, oddly enough, he hadn't before thought of doing. Of course, he had known there weren't many—many, that is, on his own side of the street, which were the ones that figured in the postman's progress—but nevertheless it came as something of a shock to find that there were precisely *six,* above his own house—his house was the seventh.

35   Six!

36   Astonished, he looked at his own house—looked at the door, on which was the number thirteen—and then realized that the whole thing was exactly and logically and absurdly what he ought to have known. Just the same, realization gave him abruptly, and even a little frighteningly, a sense of hurry. He was being hurried—he was being rushed. For—he knit his brow—he couldn't be mistaken—it was just above the *seventh* house, his *own* house, that the postman had first been audible this very morning. But in that case—in that case—did it mean that tomorrow he would hear nothing? The knock he had heard must have been the knock of their own door. Did it mean—and this was an idea which gave him a really extraordinary feeling of surprise—that he would never hear the postman again?—that tomorrow morning the postman would already have passed the house, in a snow so deep as to render his footsteps completely inaudible? That he would have made his approach down the snow-filled street so soundlessly, so secretly, that he, Paul Hasleman, there lying in bed, would not have waked in time, or waking, would have heard nothing?

37   But how could that be? Unless even the knocker should be muffled in the snow—frozen tight, perhaps? . . . But in that case—

38   A vague feeling of disappointment came over him; a vague sadness as if he felt himself deprived of something which he had long looked forward to, something much prized. After all this, all this beautiful progress, the slow delicious advance of the postman through the silent and secret snow, the knock creeping closer each day, and the footsteps nearer, the audible compass of the world thus daily narrowed, narrowed, narrowed, as the snow soothingly and beautifully encroached and deepened, after all this, was he to be defrauded of the one thing he had so wanted—to be able to count, as it were, the last two or three solemn footsteps, as they finally approached his own door? Was it all going to happen, at the end, so suddenly? or indeed, had it already happened? with no slow and subtle gradations of menace, in which he could luxuriate?

39   He gazed upward again, toward his own window which flashed in the sun; and this time almost with a feeling that it would be better if he *were* still in bed, in that room; for in that case this must still be the first morning, and there would be six more mornings to come—or, for that matter, seven or eight or nine—how could he be sure?—or even more.

40   After the inquisition began, he stood before the doctor, under the lamp, and submitted silently to the usual thumpings and tappings.

41   "Now will you please say 'Ah!'?"

42   "Ah!"

43   "Now again, please, if you don't mind."

44   "Ah."

45   "Say it slowly, and hold it if you can—"

46   "Ah-h-h-h-h-h—"

47   "Good."

48   How silly all this was. As if it had anything to do with his throat! Or his heart, or lungs!

49   Relaxing his mouth, of which the corners, after all this absurd stretching, felt uncomfortable, he avoided the doctor's eyes, and stared toward the fireplace, past his

mother's feet (in gray slippers) which projected from the green chair, and his father's feet (in brown slippers) which stood neatly side by side on the hearth rug.

50   "Hm. There is certainly nothing wrong there . . . ?"

51   He felt the doctor's eyes fixed upon him, and, as if merely to be polite, returned the look, but with a feeling of justifiable evasiveness.

52   "Now, young man, tell me—do you feel all right?"

53   "Yes, sir, quite all right."

54   "No headaches? no dizziness?"

55   "No, I don't think so."

56   "Let me see. Let's get a book, if you don't mind—yes, thank you, that will do splendidly—and now, Paul, if you'll just read it, holding it as you would normally hold it—"

57   He took the book and read:

58   "And another praise have I to tell for this the city our mother, the gift of a great god, a glory of the land most high; the might of horses, the might of young horses, the might of the sea. . . . For thou, son of Cronus, our lord Poseidon, hath throned herein this pride, since in these roads first thou didst show forth the curb that cures the rage of steeds. And the shapely oar, apt to men's hands, hath a wondrous speed on the brine, following the hundred-footed Nereids. . . . O land that art praised above all lands, now is it for thee to make those bright praises seen in deeds."

59   He stopped, tentatively, and lowered the heavy book.

60   "No—as I thought—there is certainly no superficial sign of eyestrain."

61   Silence thronged the room, and he was aware of the focused scrutiny of the three people who confronted him . . . .

62   "We could have his eyes examined—but I believe it is something else."

63   "What could it be?" That was his father's voice.

64   "It's only this curious absent mindedness—" This was his mother's voice.

65   In the presence of the doctor, they both seemed irritatingly apologetic.

66   "I believe it is something else. Now Paul—I would like very much to ask you a question or two. You will answer them, won't you—you know I'm an old, old friend of yours, eh? That's right! . . . "

67   His back was thumped twice by the doctor's fat fist—then the doctor was grinning at him with false amiability, while with one fingernail he was scratching the top button of his waistcoat. Beyond the doctor's shoulder was the fire, the fingers of flame making light prestidigitation against the sooty fireback, the soft sound of their random flutter the only sound.

68   "I would like to know—is there anything that worries you?"

69   The doctor was again smiling, his eyelids low against the little black pupils, in each of which was a tiny white bead of light. Why answer him? why answer him at all? "At whatever pain to others"—but it was all a nuisance, this necessity for resistance, this necessity for attention; it was as if one had been stood up on a brilliantly lighted stage, under a great round blaze of spotlight; as if one were merely to bark or growl. And meanwhile, to miss these last few precious hours, these hours of which each minute was more beautiful than the last, more menacing—! He still looked, as if from a great distance, at the beads of light in the doctor's eyes, at the fixed false smile,

and then, beyond, once more at his mother's slippers, his father's slippers, the soft flutter of the fire. Even here, even amongst these hostile presences, and in this arranged light, he could see the snow, he could hear it—it was in the corners of the room, where the shadow was deepest, under the sofa, behind the half-opened door which led to the dining room. It was gentler here, softer, its seethe the quietest of whispers, as if, in deference to a drawing room, it had quite deliberately put on its "manners"; it kept itself out of sight, obliterated itself, but distinctly with an air of saying, "Ah, but just wait! Wait till we are alone together! Then I will begin to tell you something new! Something white! something cold! something sleepy! something of cease, and peace, and the long bright curve of space! Tell them to go away. Banish them. Refuse to speak. Leave them, go upstairs to your room turn out the light and get into bed—I will go with you, I will be waiting for you, I will tell you a better story than Little Day of the Skates, or The Snow Ghost—I will surround your bed, I will close the windows, pile a deep drift against the door, so that none will ever again be able to enter. Speak to them! . . . " It seemed as if the little hissing voice came from a slow white spiral of falling flakes in the corner by the front window—but he could not be sure. He felt himself smiling, then, and said to the doctor, but without looking at him, looking beyond him still—

70   "Oh no, I think not—"

71   "But are you sure, my boy?"

72   His father's voice came softly and coldly then—the familiar voice of silken warning.

73   "You needn't answer at once, Paul—remember we're trying to help you—think it over and be quite sure, won't you?"

74   He felt himself smiling again, at the notion of being quite sure. What a joke! As if he weren't so sure that reassurance was no longer necessary, and all this cross-examination a ridiculous farce, a grotesque parody! What could they know about it? these gross intelligences, these humdrum minds so bound to the usual, the ordinary? Impossible to tell them about it! Why, even now, even now, with the proof so abundant, so formidable, so imminent, so appallingly present here in this very room, could they believe it?—could even his mother believe it? No—it was only too plain that if anything were said about it, the merest hint given, they would be incredulous—they would laugh—they would say "Absurd!"—think things about him which weren't true. . . .

75   "Why no, I'm not worried—why should I be?"

76   He looked then straight at the doctor's low-lidded eyes, looked from one of them to the other, from one bead of light to the other, and gave a little laugh.

77   The doctor seemed to be disconcerted by this. He drew back in his chair, resting a fat white hand on either knee. The smile faded slowly from his face.

78   "Well, Paul!" he said, and paused gravely, "I'm afraid you don't take this quite seriously enough. I think you perhaps don't quite realize—don't quite realize—" He took a deep quick breath and turned, as if helplessly, at a loss for words, to the others. But Mother and Father were both silent—no help was forthcoming.

79   "You must surely know, be aware, that you have not been quite yourself, of late? Don't you know that? . . . "

80   It was amusing to watch the doctor's renewed attempt at a smile, a queer disorganized look, as of confidential embarrassment.

81   "I feel all right, sir," he said, and again gave the little laugh.

82   "And we're trying to help you." The doctor's tone sharpened.

83   "Yes, sir, I know. But why? I'm all right. I'm just *thinking,* that's all."

84   His mother made a quick movement forward, resting a hand on the back of the doctor's chair.

85   "Thinking?" she said. "But my dear, about what?"

86   This was a direct challenge—and would have to be directly met. But before he met it, he looked again into the corner by the door, as if for reassurance. He smiled again at what he saw, at what he heard. The little spiral was still there, still softly whirling, like the ghost of a white kitten chasing the ghost of a white tail, and making as it did so the faintest of whispers. It was all right! If only he could remain firm, everything was going to be all right.

87   "Oh, about anything, about nothing—*you* know the way you do!"

88   "You mean—daydreaming?"

89   "Oh, no—thinking!"

90   "But thinking about *what?*"

91   "Anything."

92   He laughed a third time—but this time, happening to glance upward toward his mother's face, he was appalled at the effect his laughter seemed to have upon her. Her mouth had opened in an expression of horror. . . . This was too bad! Unfortunate! He had known it would cause pain, of course—but he hadn't expected it to be quite so bad as this. Perhaps—perhaps if he just gave them a tiny gleaming hint—?

93   "About the snow," he said.

94   "What on earth?" This was his father's voice. The brown slippers came a step nearer on the hearthrug.

95   "But my dear, what do you mean?" This was his mother's voice.

96   The doctor merely stared.

97   "Just *snow,* that's all. I like to think about it."

98   "Tell us about it, my boy."

99   "But that's all it is. There's nothing to tell. *You* know what snow is?"

100   This he said almost angrily, for he felt that they were trying to corner him. He turned sideways so as no longer to face the doctor, and the better to see the inch of blackness between the windowsill and the lowered curtain—the cold inch of beckoning and delicious night. At once he felt better, more assured.

101   "Mother—can I go to bed, now, please? I've got a headache."

102   "But I thought you said—"

103   "It's just come. It's all these questions—! Can I, mother?"

104   "You can go as soon as the doctor has finished."

105   "Don't you think this thing ought to be gone into thoroughly, and *now?*" This was Father's voice. The brown slippers again came a step nearer, the voice was the well-known "punishment" voice, resonant and cruel.

106   "Oh, what's the use, Norman—"

107   Quite suddenly, everyone was silent. And without precisely facing them, nevertheless he was aware that all three of them were watching him with an extraordinary intensity—staring hard at him—as if he had done something monstrous, or was himself some kind of monster. He could hear the soft irregular flutter of the flames; the cluck-click-cluck-click of the clock; far and faint, two sudden spurts of laughter from the kitchen, as quickly cut off as begun; a murmur of water in the pipes; and then, the silence seemed to deepen, to spread out, to become world-long and world-wide, to become timeless and shapeless, and to center inevitably and rightly, with a slow and sleepy but enormous concentration of all power, on the beginning of a new sound. What this new sound was going to be, he knew perfectly well. It might begin with a hiss, but it would end with a roar—there was no time to lose—he must escape. It mustn't happen here—

108   Without another word, he turned and ran up the stairs.

109   Not a moment too soon. The darkness was coming in long white waves. A prolonged sibilance filled the night—a great seamless seethe of wild influence went abruptly across it—a cold low humming shook the windows. He shut the door and flung off his clothes in the dark. The bare black floor was like a little raft tossed in waves of snow, almost overwhelmed, washed under whitely, up again, smothered in curled billows of feather. The snow was laughing; it spoke from all sides at once; it pressed closer to him as he ran and jumped exulting into this bed.

110   "Listen to us!" it said. "Listen! We have come to tell you the story we told you about. You remember? Lie down. Shut your eyes, now—you will no longer see much—in this white darkness who could see, or want to see? We will take the place of everything. . . . Listen—"

111   A beautiful varying dance of snow began at the front of the room from the opening door—the snow drew back hissing—something alien had come into the room—something hostile. This thing rushed at him, clutched at him, shook him—and he was not merely horrified, he was filled with such a loathing as he had never known. What was this? this cruel disturbance? this act of anger and hate? It was as if he had to reach up a hand toward another world for any understanding of it—an effort of which he was only barely capable. But of that other world he still remembered just enough to know the exorcising words. They tore themselves from his other life suddenly—

112   "Mother! Mother! Go away! I hate you!"

113   And with that effort, everything was solved, everything became all right: the seamless hiss advanced once more, the long white wavering lines rose and fell like enormous whispering sea-waves, the whisper becoming louder, the laughter more numerous.

114   "Listen!" it said. "We'll tell you the last, the most beautiful and secret story—shut your eyes—it is a very small story—a story that gets smaller and smaller—it comes inward instead of opening like a flower—it is a flower becoming a seed—a little cold seed—do you hear? we are leaning closer to you—"

115   The hiss was now becoming a roar—the whole world was a vast moving screen of snow—but even now it said peace, it said remoteness, it said cold, it said sleep.

Suggestions for Discussion or Writing

1. What kind of mental disorder is Paul suffering from? What are the usual manifestations of the disorder? Which of these does Paul display?

2. How do Paul's parents and doctor react to Paul's disorder? Is their reaction understandable? Why? In what ways does Paul manipulate his parents and the doctor? Is Paul manipulated in any way? How and by what?

3. How do Paul's perceptions of his parents, especially of his mother, change as his illness worsens? Why does Paul think his last statement makes everything "all right"?

4. What particular qualities does Paul see in the snow? Are any of these unusual in relation to snow? How might you explain these discrepancies?

5. What part do the mailman's footsteps play in Paul's illness? How do they indicate the progression of his illness?

6. Why does Aiken put some information in parentheses? How does this strategy indicate what is happening inside Paul's mind?

The Yellow Wallpaper

Charlotte Perkins Gilman

Charlotte Perkins Gilman (1860–1935) was born in Hartford, Connecticut. She was an early advocate for women's rights and wrote an influential study examining women's roles in society entitled Women and Economics *(1898). Her fiction reflects the issues facing women of that period, both in domestic and social realms. A collection of her fiction,* The Charlotte Perkins Gilman Reader, *was published in 1979.*

1 It is very seldom that mere ordinary people like John and myself secure ancestral halls for the summer.

2 A colonial mansion, a hereditary estate, I would say a haunted house and reach the height of romantic felicity—but that would be asking too much of fate!

3 Still I will proudly declare that there is something queer about it.

4 Else, why should it be let so cheaply? And why have stood so long untenanted?

5 John laughs at me, of course, but one expects that.

6 John is practical in the extreme. He has no patience with faith, an intense horror of superstition, and he scoffs openly at any talk of things not to be felt and seen and put down in figures.

7   John is a physician, and *perhaps*—(I would not say it to a living soul, of course, but this is dead paper and a great relief to my mind)—*perhaps* that is one reason I do not get well faster.

8   You see, he does not believe I am sick! And what can one do?

9   If a physician of high standing, and one's own husband, assures friends and relatives that there is really nothing the matter with one but temporary nervous depression—a slight hysterical tendency—what is one to do?

10   My brother is also a physician, and also of high standing, and he says the same thing.

11   So I take phosphates or phosphites—whichever it is—and tonics, and air and exercise, and journeys, and am absolutely forbidden to "work" until I am well again.

12   Personally, I disagree with their ideas.

13   Personally, I believe that congenial work, with excitement and change, would do me good.

14   But what is one to do?

15   I did write for a while in spite of them; but it *does* exhaust me a good deal—having to be so sly about it, or else meet with heavy opposition.

16   I sometimes fancy that in my condition, if I had less opposition and more society and stimulus—but John says the very worst thing I can do is to think about my condition, and I confess it always makes me feel bad.

17   So l will let it alone and talk about the house.

18   The most beautiful place! It is quite alone, standing well back from the road, quite three miles from the village. It makes me think of English places that you read about, for there are hedges and walls and gates that lock, and lots of separate little houses for the gardeners and people.

19   There is a *delicious* garden! I never saw such a garden—large and shady, full of box-bordered paths, and lined with long grape-covered arbors with seats under them.

20   There were greenhouses, but they are all broken now.

21   There was some legal trouble, I believe, something about the heirs and co-heirs; anyhow, the place has been empty for years.

22   That spoils my ghostliness, I am afraid, but I don't care—there is something strange about the house—I can feel it.

23   I even said so to John one moonlight evening, but he said what I felt was a draught, and shut the window.

24   I get unreasonably angry with John sometimes. I'm sure I never used to be so sensitive. I think it is due to this nervous condition.

25   But John says if I feel so I shall neglect proper self-control; so I take pains to control myself—before him, at least, and that makes me very tired.

26   I don't like our room a bit. I wanted one downstairs that opened onto the piazza and had roses all over the window, and such pretty old-fashioned chintz hangings! But John would not hear of it.

27   He said there was only one window and not room for two beds, and no near room for him if he took another.

28   He is very careful and loving, and hardly lets me stir without special direction.

29   I have a schedule prescription for each hour in the day; he takes all care from me, and so I feel basely ungrateful not to value it more.

30   He said he came here solely on my account, that I was to have perfect rest and all the air I could get. "Your exercise depends on your strength, my dear," said he, "and your food somewhat on your appetite; but air you can absorb all the time." So we took the nursery at the top of the house.

31   It is a big, airy room, the whole floor nearly, with windows that look all ways, and air and sunshine galore. It was nursery first, and then playroom and gymnasium, I should judge, for the windows are barred for little children, and there are rings and things in the walls.

32   The paint and paper look as if a boys' school had used it. It is stripped off—the paper—in great patches all around the head of my bed, about as far as I can reach, and in a great place on the other side of the room low down. I never saw a worse paper in my life. One of those sprawling, flamboyant patterns committing every artistic sin.

33   It is dull enough to confuse the eye in following, pronounced enough constantly to irritate and provoke study, and when you follow the lame uncertain curves for a little distance they suddenly commit suicide—plunge off at outrageous angles, destroy themselves in unheard-of contradictions.

34   The color is repellent, almost revolting: a smouldering unclear yellow, strangely faded by the slow-turning sunlight. It is a dull yet lurid orange in some places, a sickly sulphur tint in others.

35   No wonder the children hated it! I should hate it myself if I had to live in this room long.

36   There comes John, and I must put this away—he hates to have me write a word.

37   We have been here two weeks, and I haven't felt like writing before, since that first day.

38   I am sitting by the window now, up in this atrocious nursery, and there is nothing to hinder my writing as much as I please, save lack of strength.

39   John is away all day, and even some nights when his cases are serious.

40   I am glad my case is not serious!

41   But these nervous troubles are dreadfully depressing.

42   John does not know how much I really suffer. He knows there is no reason to suffer, and that satisfies him.

43   Of course it is only nervousness. It does weigh on me so not to do my duty in any way!

44   I meant to be such a help to John, such a real rest and comfort, and here I am a comparative burden already!

45   Nobody would believe what an effort it is to do what little I am able—to dress and entertain, and order things.

46   It is fortunate Mary is so good with the baby. Such a dear baby!

47   And yet I *cannot* be with him, it makes me so nervous.

48   I suppose John never was nervous in his life. He laughs at me so about this wallpaper!

49   At first he meant to repaper the room, but afterward he said that I was letting it get the better of me, and that nothing was worse for a nervous patient than to give way to such fancies.

50   He said that after the wallpaper was changed it would be the heavy bedstead, and then the barred windows, and then that gate at the head of the stairs, and so on.

51   "You know the place is doing you good," he said, "and really, dear, I don't care to renovate the house just for a three month's rental."

52   "Then do let us go downstairs," I said. "There are such pretty rooms there."

53   Then he took me in his arms and called me a blessed little goose, and said he would go down to the cellar, if I wished, and have it whitewashed into the bargain.

54   But he is right enough about the beds and windows and things.

55   It is as airy and comfortable a room as anyone need wish, and, of course, I would not be so silly as to make him uncomfortale just for a whim.

56   I'm really getting quite fond of the big room, all but that horrid paper.

57   Out of one window I can see the garden—those mysterious deep-shaded arbors, the riotous old-fashioned flowers, and bushes and gnarly trees.

58   Out of another I get a lovely view of the bay and a little private wharf belonging to the estate. There is a beautiful shaded lane that runs down there from the house. I always fancy I see people walking in these numerous paths and arbors, but John has cautioned me not to give way to fancy in the least. He says that with my imaginative power and habit of story-making, a nervous weakness like mine is sure to lead to all manner of excited fancies, and that I ought to use my will and good sense to check the tendency. So I try.

59   I think sometimes that if I were only well enough to write a little it would relieve the press of ideas and rest me.

60   But I find I get pretty tired when I try.

61   It is so discouraging not to have any advice and companionship about my work. When I get really well, John says we will ask Cousin Henry and Julia down for a long visit; but he says he would as soon put fireworks in my pillow-case as to let me have those stimulating people about now.

62   I wish I could get well faster.

63   But I must not think about that. This paper looks to me as if it *knew* what a vicious influence it had!

64   There is a recurrent spot where the pattern lolls like a broken neck and two bulbous eyes stare at you upside down.

65   I get positively angry with the impertinence of it and the everlastingness. Up and down and sideways they crawl, and those absurb unblinking eyes are everywhere. There is one place where two breadths didn't match, and the eyes go all up and down the line, one a little higher than the other.

66   I never saw so much expression in an inanimate thing before, and we all know how much expression they have! I used to lie awake as a child and get more entertainment and terror out of blank walls and plain furniture than most children could find in a toy-store.

67   I remember what a kindly wink the knobs of our big old bureau used to have, and there was one chair that always seemed like a strong friend.

68   I used to feel that if any of the other things looked too fierce I could always hop into that chair and be safe.

69   The furniture in this room is no worse than inharmonious, however, for we had to bring it all from downstairs. I suppose when this was used as a playroom they had

to take the nursery things out, and no wonder! I never saw such ravages as the children have made here.

70 The wallpaper, as I said before, is torn off in spots, and it sticketh closer than a brother—they must have had perseverance as well as hatred.

71 Then the floor is scratched and gouged and splintered, the plaster itself is dug out here and there, and this great heavy bed, which is all we found in the room, looks as if it had been through the wars.

72 But I don't mind it a bit—only the paper.

73 There comes John's sister. Such a dear girl as she is, and so careful of me! I must not let her find me writing.

74 She is a perfect and enthusiastic housekeeper, and hopes for no better profession. I verily believe she thinks it is the writing which made me sick!

75 But I can write when she is out, and see her a long way off from these windows.

76 There is one that commands the road, a lovely shaded winding road, and one that just looks off over the country. A lovely country, too, full of great elms and velvet meadows.

77 This wallpaper has a kind of sub-pattern in a different shade, a particularly irritating one, for you can only see it in certain lights and not clearly then.

78 But in the places where it isn't faded and where the sun is just so—I can see a strange, provoking, formless sort of figure that seems to skulk about behind that silly and conspicuous front design.

79 There's sister on the stairs!

80 Well, the Fourth of July is over! The people are all gone, and I am tired out. John thought it might do me good to see a little company, so we just had Mother and Nellie and the children down for a week.

81 Of course I didn't do a thing. Jennie sees to everything now.

82 But it tired me all the same.

83 John says if I don't pick up faster he shall send me to Weir Mitchell* in the fall.

84 But I don't want to go there at all. I had a friend who was in his hands once, and she says he is just like John and my brother, only more so!

85 Besides, it is such an undertaking to go so far.

86 I don't feel as if it was worthwhile to turn my hand over for anything, and I'm getting dreadfully fretful and querulous.

87 I cry at nothing, and cry most of the time.

88 Of course I don't when John is here, or anybody else, but when I am alone.

89 And I am alone a good deal just now. John is kept in town very often by serious cases, and Jennie is good and lets me alone when I want her to.

90 So I walk a little in the garden or down that lovely lane, sit on the porch under the roses, and lie down up here a good deal.

91 I'm getting really fond of the room in spite of the wallpaper. Perhaps *because* of the wallpaper.

92 It dwells in my mind so!

*Silas Weir Mitchell (1829–1914), neurologist who introduced the "rest cure" for psychoneurotics.

93   I lie here on this great immovable bed—it is nailed down, I believe—and follow that pattern about by the hour. It is as good as gymnastics, I assure you. I start, we'll say, at the bottom, down in the corner over there where it has not been touched, and I determine for the thousandth time that I *will* follow that pointless pattern to some sort of a conclusion.

94   I know a little of the principle of design, and I know this thing was not arranged on any laws of radiation, or alternation, or repetition, or symmetry, or anything else that I ever heard of.

95   It is repeated, of course, by the breadths, but not otherwise.

96   Looked at in one way, each breadth stands alone; the bloated curves and flourishes—a kind of "debased Romanesque" with delirium tremens go waddling up and down in isolated columns of fatuity.

97   But, on the other hand, they connect diagonally, and the sprawling outlines run off in great slanting waves of optic horror, like a lot of wallowing sea-weeds in full chase.

98   The whole thing goes horizontally, too, at least it seems so, and I exhaust myself trying to distinguish the order of its going in that direction.

99   They have used a horizontal breadth for a frieze, and that adds wonderfully to the confusion.

100   There is one end of the room where it is almost intact, and there, when the crosslights fade and the low sun shines directly upon it, I can almost fancy radiation after all—the interminable grotesque seems to form around a common center and rush off in headlong plunges of equal distraction.

101   It makes me tired to follow it. I will take a nap, I guess.

102   I don't know why I should write this.

103   I don't want to.

104   I don't feel able.

105   And I know John would think it absurd. But I *must* say what I feel and think in some way—it is such a relief!

106   But the effort is getting to be greater than the relief.

107   Half the time now I am awfully lazy, and lie down ever so much. John says I mustn't lose my strength, and has me take cod liver oil and lots of tonics and things, to say nothing of ale and wine and rare meat.

108   Dear John! He loves me very dearly, and hates to have me sick. I tried to have a real earnest reasonable talk with him the other day, and tell him how I wish he would let me go and make a visit to Cousin Henry and Julia.

109   But he said I wasn't able to go, nor able to stand it after I got there; and I did not make out a very good case for myself, for I was crying before I had finished.

110   It is getting to be a great effort for me to think straight. Just this nervous weakness, I suppose.

111   And dear John gathered me up in his arms, and just carried me upstairs and laid me on the bed, and sat by me and read to me till it tired my head.

112   He said I was his darling and his comfort and all he had, and that I must take care of myself for his sake, and keep well.

113   He says no one but myself can help me out of it, that I must use my will and self-control and not let any silly fancies run away with me.

114   There's one comfort—the baby is well and happy, and does not have to occupy this nursery with the horrid wallpaper.

115   If we had not used it, that blessed child would have! What a fortunate escape! Why, I wouldn't have a child of mine, an impressionable little thing, live in such a room for worlds.

116   I never thought of it before, but it is lucky that John kept me here after all; I can stand it so much easier than a baby, you see.

117   Of course I never mention it to them any more—I am too wise—but I keep watch for it all the same.

118   There are things in that wallpaper that nobody knows about but me, or ever will.

119   Behind that outside pattern the dim shapes get clearer every day.

120   It is always the same shape, only very numerous.

121   And it is like a woman stooping down and creeping about behind that pattern. I don't like it a bit. I wonder—I begin to think—I wish John would take me away from here!

122   It is so hard to talk with John about my case, because he is so wise, and because he loves me so.

123   But I tried it last night.

124   It was moonlight. The moon shines in all around just as the sun does.

125   I hate to see it sometimes, it creeps so slowly, and always comes in by one window or another.

126   John was asleep and I hated to waken him, so I kept still and watched the moonlight on that undulating wallpaper till I felt creepy.

127   The faint figure behind seemed to shake the pattern, just as if she wanted to get out.

128   I got up softly and went to feel and see if the paper *did* move, and when I came back John was awake.

129   "What is it, little girl?" he said. "Don't go walking about like that—you'll get cold."

130   I thought it was a good time to talk, so I told him that I really was not gaining here, and that I wished he would take me away.

131   "Why, darling!" said he. "Our lease will be up in three weeks, and I can't see how to leave before.

132   "The repairs are not done at home, and I cannot possibly leave town just now. Of course, if you were in any danger, I could and would, but you really are better, dear, whether you can see it or not. I am a doctor, dear, and I know. You are gaining flesh and color, your appetite is better, I feel really much easier about you."

133   "I don't weigh a bit more," said I, "nor as much; and my appetite may be better in the evening when you are here but it is worse in the morning when you are away!"

134   "Bless her little heart!" said he with a big hug. "She shall be as sick as she pleases! But now let's improve the shining hours by going to sleep, and talk about it in the morning!"

135   "And you won't go away?" I asked gloomily.

136   "Why, how can I, dear? It is only three weeks more and then we will take a nice little trip of a few days while Jennie is getting the house ready. Really, dear, you are better!"

137   "Better in body perhaps—" I began, and stopped short, for he sat up straight and looked at me with such a stern, reproachful look that I could not say another word.

138   "My darling," said he, "I beg of you, for my sake and for our child's sake, as well as for your own, that you will never for one instant let that idea enter your mind! There is nothing so dangerous, so fascinating, to a temperament like yours. It is a false and foolish fancy. Can you not trust me as a physician when I tell you so?"

139   So of course I said no more on that score, and we went to sleep before long. He thought I was asleep first, but I wasn't, and lay there for hours trying to decide whether that front pattern and the back pattern really did move together or separately.

140   On a pattern like this, by daylight, there is a lack of sequence, a defiance of law, that is a constant irritant to a normal mind.

141   The color is hideous enough, and unreliable enough, and infuriating enough, but the pattern is torturing.

142   You think you have mastered it, but just as you get well under way in following, it turns a back-somersault and there you are. It slaps you in the face, knocks you down, and tramples upon you. It is like a bad dream.

143   The outside pattern is a florid arabesque, reminding one of a fungus. If you can imagine a toadstool in joints, an interminable string of toadstools, budding and sprouting in endless convolutions—why, that is something like it.

144   That is, sometimes!

145   There is one marked peculiarity about this paper, a thing nobody seems to notice but myself, and that is that it changes as the light changes.

146   When the sun shoots in through the east window—I always watch for that first long, straight ray—it changes so quickly that I never can quite believe it.

147   That is why I watch it always.

148   By moonlight—the moon shines in all night when there is a moon—I wouldn't know it was the same paper.

149   At night in any kind of light, in twilight, candlelight, lamplight, and worst of all by moonlight, it becomes bars! The outside pattern, I mean, and the woman behind it is as plain as can be.

150   I didn't realize for a long time what the thing was that showed behind, that dim sub-pattern, but now I am quite sure it is a woman.

151   By daylight she is subdued, quiet. I fancy it is the pattern that keeps her so still. It is so puzzling. It keeps me quiet by the hour.

152   I lie down ever so much now. John says it is good for me, and to sleep all I can.

153   Indeed he started the habit by making me lie down for an hour after each meal.

154   It is a very bad habit, I am convinced, for you see, I don't sleep.

155   And that cultivates deceit, for I don't tell them I'm awake—oh, no!

156   The fact is I am getting a little afraid of John.

157   He seems very queer sometimes, and even Jennie has an inexplicable look.

158   It strikes me occasionally, just as a scientific hypothesis, that perhaps it is the paper!

159   I have watched John when he did not know I was looking, and come into the room suddenly on the most innocent excuses, and I've caught him several times *looking at the paper*! And Jennie too. I caught Jennie with her hand on it once.

160   She didn't know I was in the room, and when I asked her in a quiet, a very quiet voice, with the most restrained manner possible, what she was doing with the paper, she turned around as if she had been caught stealing, and looked quite angry—asked me why I should frighten her so!

161   Then she said that the paper stained everything it touched, that she had found yellow smooches on all my clothes and John's and she wished we would be more careful!

162   Did not that sound innocent? But I know she was studying that pattern, and I am determined that nobody shall find it out but myself?

163   Life is very much more exciting now than it used to be. You see, I have something more to expect, to look forward to, to watch. I really do eat better, and am more quiet than I was.

164   John is so pleased to see me improve! He laughed a little the other day, and said I seemed to be flourishing in spite of my wallpaper.

165   I turned it off with a laugh. I had no intention of telling him it was *because* of the wallpaper—he would make fun of me. He might even want to take me away.

166   I don't want to leave now until I have found it out. There is a week more, and I think that will be enough.

167   I'm feeling so much better!

168   I don't sleep much at night, for it is so interesting to watch developments; but I sleep a good deal during the daytime.

169   In the daytime it is tiresome and perplexing.

170   There are always new shoots on the fungus, and new shades of yellow all over it. I cannot keep count of them, though I have tried conscientiously.

171   It is the strangest yellow, that wallpaper! It makes me think of all the yellow things I ever saw—not beautiful ones like buttercups, but old, foul, bad yellow things.

172   But there is something else about that paper—the smell! I noticed it the moment we came into the room, but with so much air and sun it was not bad. Now we have had a week of fog and rain, and whether the windows are open or not, the smell is here.

173   It creeps all over the house.

174   I find it hovering in the dining-room, skulking in the parlor, hiding in the hall, lying in wait for me on the stairs.

175   It gets into my hair.

176   Even when I go to ride, if I turn my head suddenly and surprise it—there is that smell!

177   Such a peculiar odor, too! I have spent hours in trying to analyze it, to find what it smelled like.

178   It is not bad—at first—and very gentle, but quite the subtlest, most enduring odor I ever met.

179   In this damp weather it is awful. I wake up in the night and find it hanging over me.

180   It used to disturb me at first. I thought seriously of burning the house—to reach the smell.

181   But now I am used to it. The only think I can think of that it is like is the *color* of the paper! A yellow smell.

182   There is a very funny mark on this wall, low down, near the mopboard. A streak that runs round the room. It goes behind every piece of futniture, except the bed, a long, straight, even *smooch,* as if it had been rubbed over and over.

183   I wonder how it was done and who did it, and what they did it for. Round and round and round—round and round and round—it makes me dizzy!

184   I really have discovered something at last.

185   Through watching so much at night, when it changes so, I have finally found out.

186   The front pattern *does* move—and no wonder! The woman behind shakes it!

187   Sometimes I think there are a great many women behind, and sometimes only one, and she crawls around fast, and her crawling shakes it all over.

188   Then in the very bright spots she keeps still, and in the very shady spots she just takes hold of the bars and shakes them hard.

189   And she is all the time trying to climb through. But nobody could climb through that pattern—it strangles so; I think that is why it has so many heads.

190   They get through and then the pattern strangles them off and turns them upside down, and makes their eyes white!

191   If those heads were covered or taken off it would not be half so bad.

192   I think that woman gets out in the daytime!

193   And I'll tell you why—privately—I've seen her!

194   I can see her out of every one of my windows!

195   It is the same woman, I know, for she is always creeping, and most women do not creep by daylight.

196   I see her in that long shaded lane, creeping up and down. I see her in those dark grape arbors, creeping all around the garden.

197   I see her on that long road under the trees, creeping along, and when a carriage comes she hides under the blackberry vines.

198   I don't blame her a bit. It must be very humiliating to be caught creeping by daylight!

199   I always lock the door when I creep by daylight. I can't do it at night, for I know John would suspect something at once.

200   And John is so queer now that I don't want to irritate him. I wish he would take another room! Besides, I don't want anybody to get that woman out at night but myself.

201   I often wonder if I could see her out of all the windows at once.

202   But, turn as fast as I can, I can only see out of one at one time.

203   And though I always see her, she may be able to creep faster than I can turn! I have watched her sometimes away off in the open country, creeping as fast as a cloud shadow in a wind.

204   If only that top pattern could be gotten off from the under one! I mean to try it, little by little.

205   I have found out another funny thing, but I shan't tell it this time! It does not do to trust people too much.

206   There are only two more days to get this paper off, and I believe John is beginning to notice. I don't like the look in his eyes.

207   And I heard him ask Jennie a lot of professional questions about me. She had a very good report to give.

208   She said I slept a good deal in the daytime.

209   John knows I don't sleep very well at night, for all I'm so quiet!

210   He asked me all sorts of questions, too, and pretended to be very loving and kind.

211   As if I couldn't see through him!

212   Still, I don't wonder he acts so, sleeping under this paper for three months.

213   It only interests me, but I feel sure John and Jennie are affected by it.

214   Hurrah! This is the last day, but it is enough. John is to stay in town over night, and won't be out until this evening.

215   Jennie wanted to sleep with me—the sly thing; but I told her I should undoubtedly rest better for a night all alone.

216   That was clever, for really I wasn't alone a bit! As soon as it was moonlight and that poor thing began to crawl and shake the pattern, I got up and ran to help her.

217   I pulled and she shook. I shook and she pulled, and before morning we had peeled off yards of that paper.

218   A strip about as high as my head and half around the room.

219   And then when the sun came and that awful pattern began to laugh at me, I declared I would finish it today!

220   We go away tomorrow, and they are moving all my furniture down again to leave things as they were before.

221   Jennie looked at the wall in amazement, but I told her merrily that I did it out of pure spite at the vicious thing.

222   She laughed and said she wouldn't mind doing it herself, but I must not get tired.

223   How she betrayed herself that time!

224   But I am here, and no person touches this paper but Me—not *alive*!

225   She tried to get me out of the room—it was too patent! But I said it was so quiet and empty and clean now that I believed I would lie down again and sleep all I could, and not to wake me even for dinner—I would call when I woke.

226   So now she is gone, and the servants are gone, and the things are gone, and there is nothing left but that great bedstead nailed down, with the canvas mattress we found on it.

227   We shall sleep downstairs tonight, and take the boat home tomorrow.

228   I quite enjoy the room, now it is bare again.

229   How those children did tear about here!

230   This bedstead is fairly gnawed!

231   But I must get to work.

232   I have locked the door and thrown the key down into the front path.

233   I don't want to go out, and I don't want to have anybody come in, till John comes.

234   I want to astonish him.

235   I've got a rope up here that even Jennie did not find. If that woman does get out, and tries to get away, I can tie her!

236   But I forgot I could not reach far without anything to stand on!

237   This bed will *not* move!

238   I tried to lift and push it until I was lame, and then I got so angry I bit off a little piece at one corner—but it hurt my teeth.

239   Then I peeled off all the paper I could reach standing on the floor. It sticks horribly and the pattern just enjoys it! All those strangled heads and bulbous eyes and waddling fungus growths just shriek with derision!

240   I am getting angry enough to do something desperate. To jump out of the window would be admirable exercise, but the bars are too strong even to try.

241   Besides I wouldn't do it. Of course not. I know well enough that a step like that is improper and might be misconstrued.

242   I don't like to *look* out of the windows even—there are so many of those creeping women, and they creep so fast.

243   I wonder if they all come out of that wallpaper as I did?

244   But I am securely fastened now by my well-hidden rope—you don't get *me* out in the road there!

245   I suppose I shall have to get back behind the pattern when it comes night, and that is hard!

246   It is so pleasant to be out in this great room and creep around as I please!

247   I don't want to go outside. I won't, even if Jennie asks me to.

248   For outside you have to creep on the ground, and everything is green instead of yellow.

249   But here I can creep smoothly on the floor, and my shoulder just fits in that long smooch around the wall, so I cannot lose my way.

250   Why, there's John at the door!

251   It is no use, young man, you can't open it!

252   How he does call and pound!

253   Now he's crying to Jennie for an axe.

254   It would be a shame to break down that beautiful door!

255   "John, dear!" said I in the gentlest voice. "The key is down by the front steps, under a plantain leaf!"

256   That silenced him for a few moments.

257   Then he said, very quietly indeed, "Open the door, my darling!"

258   "I can't," said I. "The key is down by the front door under a plantain leaf!" And then I said it again, several times, very gently and slowly, and said it so often that he had to go and see, and he got it of course, and came in. He stopped short by the door.

259   "What is the matter?" he cried. "For God's sake, what are you doing!"

260   I kept on creeping just the same, but I looked at him over my shoulder.

261   "I've got out at last," said I, "in spite of you and Jane. And I've pulled off most of the paper, so you can't put me back!"

262   Now why should that man have fainted? But he did, and right across my path by the wall, so that I had to creep over him every time!

Suggestions for Discussion or Writing

1. How does the first-person narration of this story change the reader's perception of the events? What is the woman in the story like?

2. Why does the husband in the story insist on doing what he does? What is his character like?

3. When do you realize that the story may not be exactly as the woman perceives? How ill is she?

4. What is the significance of the details she gives about the setting of the story?

5. What does the wallpaper symbolize?

Candle, Lamp & Firefly

Tess Gallagher

Born in Port Angeles, Washington, in 1932, Tess Gallagher received an M.F.A. at the University of Iowa in 1974. She has received the Elliston Award (1976), two NEA Grants (1977, 1981), a Guggenheim Fellowship (1978), and the APR Award (1981), as well as other honors and awards. The poem in this text comes from her collection Willingly. *Other works by Gallagher are* Amplitude: New and Selected Poems *(1987),* Concert of Tenses: Essays on Poetry *(1986),* Lover of Horses and Other Stories *(1992), and* Portable Kisses: Love Poems *(1992).*

How can I think what thoughts
to have of you with a mind so unready?
What I remember most: you did not want
to go. Then choice slipped from you
5 like snow from the mountain, so death
could graze you over with the sweet
muzzles of the deer moving up from
the valleys, pausing to stare
down and back toward the town. But you
10 did not gaze back. Like a cut rose
on the fifth day, you bowed
into yourself and we watched the shell-
shaped petals drop in clumps, then,
like wine, deepen into the white cloth.

15 What have you written here on my sleep
with flesh so sure I have no choice
but to stare back when your face and

gestures follow me into daylight?
Your arms, too weak at your death
20   for embracing, closed around me and held,
and such a tenderness was mixed there
with longing that I asked, "Is it good
where you are?"

We echoed a long time in the kiss
25   that was drinking me—*daughter, daughter,*
daughter—until I was gone as when a sun
drops over the rim of an ocean, gone
yet still there. Then the dampness,
The chill of your body pulled from me
30   into that space the condemned
look back to after parting.
Between sleep and death
I carry no proof that we met, no proof
but to tell what even I must call dream
35   and gently dismiss. So does
a bird dismiss one tree for another
and carries each time the flight between
like a thing never done.
And what is proof then, but some trance
40   to kill the birds? And what are dreams
when the eyes open on similar worlds
and you are dead in my living?

Suggestions for Discussion or Writing

1. What metaphors and similes does Gallagher use in the poem?

2. What assumptions can you make about the incident which inspired this poem?

3. How is sleep like death? How do they link in this poem?

4. What physical details of the poem add to its impact?

5. What words in the poem indicate the mood or tone? How do they affect the poem?

Cancer Rising

Charles Wright

Charles Penzel Wright, Jr. (1935–), born in Pickwick Dam, Tennessee, received his M.F.A. from the University of Iowa in 1963 and did graduate work at the University of Rome. He joined the faculty at the University of California at Irvine, where he taught from 1966 to 1983. He has been a Fulbright Scholar at the University of Rome and a Fulbright Professor at the University of Padua. Wright teaches at the University of Virginia at Charlottesville. Among his works are The Dream Animal *(1968),* The Grave of the Right Hand *(1970),* Bloodlines *(1975), from which the following selection comes,* Wright: A Profile *(1979), and* The Southern Cross *(1981). He received the 1976 Edgar Allan Poe Award for his poetry and the American Book Award for* Country Music: Early Selected Poems *(1983).*

It starts with a bump, a tiny bump, deep in the throat.
The mockingbird knows: she spreads it around
Like music, like something she's heard, a gossip to be
Repeated, but not believed.
5   And the bump grows, and the song grows, the song
Ascendant and self-reflective, its notes
Obscuring the quarter-tone, the slick flesh and the burning.
And the bump drops off and disappears, but
Its roots do not disappear—they dig on through the moist meat.

10   The roots are worms, worms in a cheese.
And what they leave, in their blind passage,
Filtered, reorganized, is a new cheese, a cheese
For one palate and one tongue.
But this takes time, and comes later,
15   The small mounds, heaps of a requisite sorrow,
Choked and grown in the beds,
The channels no longer channels, but flesh of a kind
Themselves, the same flesh and the song . . .

Midnight again, the mockingbird, high
20   In the liquidambar, runs through her scales. What burdens
Down-shift and fall, their weights sprung:
The start, the rise, the notes
Oil for the ear of death, oil for the wind, the corpse
Sailing into the universe, the geranium . . .
25   The music, like high water, rises inexorably . . .

Toward heaven, that intergalactic queasiness
Where all fall to the same riff.

Tallow, tallow and ash. The fire winds
Like a breath through the bone, a common tune,
30   Hummable, hard to extrapolate:
That song again, the song of burnt notes.
The blue it rises into, the cobalt,
Proves an enduring flame: Persian death bowl,
The bead, crystal
35   And drowned delta, Ephesian reed.
Blue of the twice-bitten rose, blue of the dove . . .

Suggestions for Discussion or Writing

1. What relationship does the mockingbird and its song have with the growing bump? Why and in what way is music associated with the rising cancer?

2. In the third stanza how do the following words or phrases contribute to the tone and theme: "liquidambar," "oil for the ear of death," and "the geranium." Why is heaven "intergalactic queasiness"? What is "the same riff"? What other words, phrases, or images seem unusual and how do they contribute to the poem? How do these images relate to cancer?

3. In the fourth stanza what is represented by "tallow" and "ash"? What are the "fire winds"? What is the significance of "blue it rises into," "the cobalt," "Persian death bowl," "Ephesian reed," "twice-bitten rose," and "dove"? Of what significance is the color blue? How do these images relate to cancer?

4. Of what significance is the title "Cancer Rising"?

Face Lift

Sylvia Plath

Sylvia Plath (1932–1963), born in Boston, Massachusetts, was educated at Smith College and earned a Fulbright Scholarship to Cambridge for graduate work. She had begun a promising writing career as early as age 18 when some drawings, poems, and stories were published in Seventeen. *She later*

won Mademoiselle's *College Fiction Contest. Her autobiographical novel*
The Bell Jar *(1963), first published under the pseudonym Victoria Lucas,*
recounts the experiences of an isolated individual who suffers a mental and
emotional crisis. Though the last pages of the novel are optimistic, she
committed suicide in London at age 31. Among her other works are The
Colossus *(1960),* Ariel *(1965),* Crossing the Water *(1971),* Lyonesse *(1971),*
and Johnny Panic and the Bible of Dreams, and Other Prose Writings *(1978).*
Much of her work has been published by her husband after her death.

You bring me good news from the clinic.
Whipping off your silk scarf, exhibiting the tight white
Mummy-cloths, smiling: I'm all right.
When I was nine, a lime-green anesthetist
5   Fed me banana gas through a frog-mask. The nauseous vault
Boomed with bad dreams and the Jovian voices of surgeons.
Then mother swam up, holding a tin basin.
 O I was sick.

They've changed all that. Traveling.
10   Nude as Cleopatra in my well-boiled hospital shift,
Fizzy with sedatives and unusually humorous,
I roll to an anteroom where a kind man
Fists my fingers for me. He makes me feel something precious
Is leaking from the finger-vents. At the count of two
15   Darkness wipes me out like chalk on a blackboard . . .
I don't know a thing.

For five days I lie in secret,
Tapped like a cask, the years draining into my pillow.
Even my best friend thinks I'm in the country.
20   Skin doesn't have roots, it peels away easy as paper.
When I grin, the stitches tauten. I grow backward. I'm twenty,
Broody and in long skirts on my first husband's sofa, my fingers
Buried in the lambswool of the dead poodle;
I hadn't a cat yet.

25   Now She's done for, the dewlapped lady
I watched settle, line by line, in my mirror—
Old sock-face, sagged on a darning egg.
They've trapped her in some laboratory jar.
Let her die there, or wither incessantly for the next fifty years,
30   Nodding and rocking and fingering her thin hair.
Mother to myself, I wake swaddled in gauze,
Pink and smooth as a baby.

Suggestions for Discussion or Writing

1. Of what significance are the following phrases in the first stanza: "lime-green anesthetist," "banana gas," "Jovian voices," and "well-boiled hospital shift"?

2. How do the flashbacks to earlier years (nine years old), to the first husband, and to the dead poodle contribute to the phenomena of anesthesia?

3. What relationship might there be between the phrase "The years draining into my pillow" and "something precious . . . leaking from the finger-vents"?

4. What is the predominant tone of the poem? What words, phrases and images indicate that tone?

5. Is the character glad to have gotten a face lift? How do you know? Has anything besides her face changed?

6. Of what significance are the sensory images of touch, such as "fingers / Buried in the lambswool," and "fingering her thin hair"? Do you notice any other touch images?

7. Have you ever experienced surgery or something similar? How does your experience compare to that described in the poem?

Different Faces in the Crowd
Developing Cultural Awareness

nine

Introduction

I n a nation begun with diversity, Americans have become one people. Still, separateness receives a mixed review. Sometimes being one people is easier to accept in a small group setting. On the other hand, blending with one's peers can seem absolutely vital. Historically, many ethnic groups have had periods of inequity and prejudice. Some of those inequities have ameliorated; other problems continue.

Alistair Cooke's essay, "The Huddled Masses" introduces this section with an overview of the mass immigration which made America the "melting pot" of the world. The struggle to blend is illustrated by Martin Luther King, Jr.'s "I Have a Dream" for African Americans; by Jose Antonio Villarreal's "Pocho" for Hispanic Americans; by Chief Dan George's "My People, the Indians" for Native Americans, and by Jeanne Wakatsuki Houston's "Living in Two Cultures" for Japanese Americans. The struggles are vivid and poignant. Even more important, the struggles are representative of many people at many times of our history.

But history is not always kind. Several readings discuss different approaches to prejudice from the black culture: Andrea Lee's "Black and Well-To-Do," and Langston Hughes's "Harlem." Similar difficulties are shown in the Native American culture by Leslie Marmon Silko's "Lullaby," a tragic story of cultural misunderstanding and sorrow, and N. Scott Momaday's poem "Comparatives," which contains metaphors reflecting culture. Ana Castillo's poem "Napa, California" describes the difficulties of immigrant labor.

A joining of cultures, of ethnic groups, of races, and of traditions with full equality under the law has been the dream of America. At the same time, the uniqueness of separate traditions cries out to be preserved. Not all problems are solved by government-imposed integration, by immigration quotas, by busing, by deporting illegal aliens, or by preferential treatment of ethnic minorities. But the questions need to be asked continually.

The Huddled Masses

Alistair Cooke

Alistair Cooke (1908–) was an immigrant from England in 1937. He has worked as a broadcaster, commentator, and journalist interpreting and describing American life. This chapter comes from his book America, *which was first given as part of a television series on the immigrant experience and American culture.*

1 "We call England the Mother country," Robert Benchley, once remarked, "because most of us come from Poland or Italy." It's not quite as drastic as that, but today the chances of an American being of wholly English stock are, outside the South, no more than one in four. Only the English visitor is still surprised by this palpable fact. When a German makes his first trip across the Atlantic, he can go into almost any large city between southern Pennsylvania and the Great Lakes, and on across the prairie into the small towns of Kansas, and he will find himself among people whose physique is familiar, who share many of his values and his tastes in food and drink. The Scandinavian will be very much at home with the landscape and the farming of Minnesota, and he will not be surprised to hear that the state is represented in Congress by men named Langen and Olson and Nelsen. A Polish Catholic would easily pass as a native among the sandy potato fields, the lumbering wooden churches, and the Doroskis and Stepnoskis of eastern Long Island.

2 For three quarters of the population that hears itself so often hailed as "the American people" are the descendants of immigrants from Asia and Africa and, most of all, from the continent of Europe. They brought over with them their religions and folkways and their national foods, not least their national prejudices, which for a long time in the new country turned the cities of the Northeast and the Midwest into adjoining compounds of chauvinists, distrustful not only of immigrants from other nations everywhere but too often of their neighbors three or four blocks away.

3 But even the most clannish of them sooner or later had to mix with the peoples already there and learn among other things a new kind of politics, in which the dominant power went to men who knew how to balance the needs of one national group against another. The American delicatessen became an international store for the staples that the old immigrant could not do without. Few American children, certainly in the cities, need to be told that goulash comes from Hungary, liverwurst from Germany, borscht from Russia, and lasagna from Italy. And even Gentiles who never tasted the combination probably know that lox—smoked salmon—and the doughnut-shaped rolls called bagels are as inseparable, in Jewish households of any nationality, as an Englishman's—and an Anglo-Saxon American's—bacon and eggs.

4 Why did they come? Why do they still come? For a mesh of reasons and impulses that condition any crucial decision in life. But the most powerful was one common to most of the immigrants from the 1840s on—hard times in the homeland. They chose

America because, by the early nineteenth century, Europeans, especially if they were poor, had heard that the Americans had had a revolution that successfully overthrew the old orders of society. Madame de Stael could tell a Boston scholar, in 1817, "You are the advance guard of the human race." And Goethe, ten years later, wrote for anybody to read: "Amerika, du hast es besser als unser Kontinent" (which may be loosely translated as: "America, you have things better over there"). He was thinking of the freedom from the binding force of "useless traditions." But people who had never heard of Madame de Stael and Goethe picked up the new belief that there was a green land far away preserved "from robbers, knights and ghosts afrighting." Whenever life could hardly be worse at home, they came to believe that life was better in America.

5   In Ireland in the middle 1840s human life had touched bottom. Ironically, two causes of the Irish plight came from America. The rising competition of American agriculture made thousands of very small farmers (300,000 of Ireland's 685,000 farms had less then three acres) shift from tillage to grazing, on barren ground. And the potato blight, which was to putrefy vast harvests in a few weeks, had crossed the Atlantic from America in 1845. Within five years the potato famine had claimed almost a million Irish lives, over twenty thousand of them dropping in the fields from starvation.

6   The young Queen Victoria was informed that the state of Ireland was "alarming" and that the country was so full of "inflammable matter" that it could explode into rebellion. So she paid a royal visit, serenely admired the beauty of the scenery, and was relieved that the people "received us with the greatest enthusiasm." Nevertheless, at Kingston and at Cork she noted: "You see more ragged and wretched people here than I ever saw anywhere else." One of those ragged people could well have been a bankrupt farmer from Wexford County who had gone to Cork. Most such, with any energy left over after the famine, retreated to the towns and either joined sedition societies or headed for America. This one destination was chosen for him by the simple fact that Boston was the end of the Cunard line. His name was Patrick Kennedy, great-grandfather of the thirty-fifth President of the United States. He was one of the 1,700,000 Irish—a little less than one quarter of the whole population when the famine began—who left for America in the 1840s and 1850s.

7   Hunger, then, was the spur in Ireland. There were other, equally fearful incentives. In the single year of 1848 political storms swept across Europe—in Austria, an abdication, arrests, and executions; in Italy, a revolution and a declaration of war by the Pope against Austria; in Sicily, an uprising against the King of Naples; in Germany, a liberal revolution that failed. Both then and throughout the rest of the century and on into our own, in any troubled country, whether or not its mischief could be laid to known culprits, there was always the ancient scapegoat of the Jew. In eastern and central Europe the ghettos had long been routine targets for the recruiting sergeant and the secret police, and their inhabitants were acquainted from childhood with what one of them called "the stoniest sound in the world: the midnight knock on the door." It would be hard to calculate but easy to guess at the millions of American Jews whose forefathers were harried and haunted by these persecutors. It is something hardly thought of by most of us who came here by free choice, or who were born here without ever having to make a choice.

8   In some cities of Europe, Jews were permitted to practice their religion in compounds. But in many more places, where the Jews had been systematically vilified for fifteen hundred years, authorities considered their rituals to be as sinister as black magic, and the more daring or devout worshipped in stealth. In America, they had heard, they could worship openly in their own fashion. Orthodox, Reform, Conservative—or, as radical Reconstructionists, they could look to the United States as a permitted rallying ground on which to muster the faithful for the return to Palestine. I dwell on the Jews because, in the great tidal wave of the late nineteenth- and early twentieth-century immigration, they were the most numerous of those who saw America as the Land of Canaan; because their story offers the most dramatic and arduous exercise in the struggle to assimilate; and because, as much or more than other peoples, they created the American polyglot metropolis against which, in 1924, the Congress protested with restrictive legislation that tried, too late, to restore the United States to its northern European origins.

9   So late as 1880, there were only a quarter of a million Jews in the United States. By 1924 there were four and a half million, the product of a westward movement that started in the early nineteenth century with their exodus from the ghettos of eastern Europe into the new factories of western Europe. They had moved in that direction earlier throughout the Thirty Years War and then after the later Cossack massacres and peasant revolts. But the factory system provided them with a legal right to flee from their inferior citizenship in Germany and from pogroms in Russia, Poland, and Romania. In the last quarter of the nineteenth century, both city and rural Jews were the willing quarry of emigration agents from America carrying glowing broadsides from house to house about high wages, good clothes, abundant food, and civil liberties available in the New World. The sweet talk of these promoters might be sensibly discounted, but not the bags of mail containing "America letters" from relatives who had made the voyage and whose more practical accounts of an attainable decent life were read aloud in cottages, markets, and factories.

10   The word spread beyond the factories and ghettos to the farmers of southern and central Europe. And whereas before 1890 the immigrant stream had flowed out of Scandinavia, Germany, Ireland, England, and Canada, in the next thirty years the mass of immigrants came from Italy, Austria-Hungary, Russia, and again and always, Ireland.

11   The Germans formed a strong and special current in the mainstream of immigration. There were already a quarter of a million of them in the United States at the time of the Declaration of Independence, and in the thirty years between 1860 and 1890 they contributed more refugees than any other nation, among them more varied social types, more professionals, and more scholars than the others. They also settled far and wide. The German Jews, beginning as small merchants, prospered more conspicuously and founded many of the great banking families of New York. Wherever the Germans went, they tended to establish themselves, both by superiority of talent and a marked gift of clannishness, at the head of the social hierarchy of Jewry. The Sephardic Jews and the German Jews were at the top, and at the bottom were the Lithuanians and the Hungarians, elements in a social system that discouraged intermarriage between its upper and lower strata the defiance of which has probably caused as much snobbish anguish as the love matches of Jews and Gentiles in other immigrant families.

12   All told, in the first two decades of this century, an unbelievable fourteen and a half million immigrants arrived. They were mostly the persecuted and the poor, "the wretched refuse of your teeming shore" apostrophized by Emma Lazarus, a wealthy and scholarly young lady whose poetic dramas and translations of Heine are forgotten in the thunder of five lines inscribed on the Statue of Liberty. These unlettered millions were, for the most part, to become the "huddled masses" who, in the tenements of the American cities, would have quite a time of it "yearning to breathe free." They had never heard of Thomas Jefferson or George Washington. But they were the easy victims of the absurd myth that the streets of America were paved with gold—not much, perhaps, but enough to offer striking proof, in sepia photographs sent back to Poland or Hungary, of well-fed families who looked you in the eye, of a father or cousin wearing a suit and shiny shoes, just like a doctor or a merchant in the old country.

13   Long before they had arrived at the ports of embarkation—Constantinople, Piraeus, Antwerp, Bremen—emigrant trains had started deep inside Russia. Most of them were linked box cars, sometimes with benches, the men in one car, the women and children in another. Every few hundred miles the train would be shunted to a siding in order to pick up other new armies, of Austrians, Hungarians, Lithuanians, and finally a troop of Germans, before they came to, say, Hamburg. There they were corralled and checked to see if they had the three essential passports to America: an exit paper, twenty-five spare dollars to prevent their becoming a public charge, and the price of the passage. By the 1890s lively rate wars between steamship lines had halved the steerage fare from about twenty dollars to ten. In an enclosure outside Hamburg they would be bathed, de-loused, and fed, and their baggage and clothes fumigated. Then they were ferried out to the big ship and stowed aboard, as many as nine hundred in steerage.

14   In the floating commune of the emigrant ship, the status symbols were few but well defined. A suitcase, however battered, was most likely the mark of a city man. To a poor peasant, a wicker basket was elegance enough. Most people tied everything up in a blanket or a sheet. They had brought with them what they thought would be indispensable to a decent life afloat. First, the necessity of a pillow, goose-feather, if they were lucky—a point of pride, a relic, and a symbol that some families kept throughout their lives. Village girls took along their only certain dowry, a special extra petticoat and, for formal occasions, a corset. Many of the young women were engaged to men from the home town on the other side of the Atlantic. It was well understood that the ambitious male, engaged or already married, went on ahead to stake out the fortune, which was more often the bare living that could sustain a family. Many of these engagements were broken once for all on the way over by the rude proximity of males in steerage.

15   Like all travelers, both simple and sophisticated, they were deeply suspicious of the other nation's food. It was a common thing to take along a cooking pot, a few raw vegetables, and a hunk of sausage or some other final reminder of the favorite snack. The religious invariably took with them the tokens of their faith, a cross or a prayer book or phylacteries; and a member of closely-knit family would cherish an heirloom yielded up in the moment of parting. It could be nothing more pretentious than a brass candlestick or a lock of hair.

16   For two weeks or eight days, depending on the size of the ship, they sewed, played cards, sang to harmonicas or tin whistles, counted their savings, continually checked their exit papers, complained about the atrocious food and the ubiquity of the rats. The ones who could read, probably less than half the flock, recited the cheering promise of the emigrant agents' broadsides and pamphlets. The young women nursed the elders and the chronically seasick and resisted, or succumbed to, the advances of spry bachelors. There was no possibility of privacy in the swarm of steerage.

17   But as America came nearer, some of them suffered from nervous recall of the stratagems that had got them this far. Bright youngsters who had carefully failed their high school examinations in order to prove their unfitness for military service. Oldsters who began to mask a fever with massive doses of medicine. Embezzlers, petty criminals, and betrothed men skipping breach-of-promise suits who had obviously had the wit to fake an exit pass or steal the passage money. A lot of people had a lot to hide.

18   Far down in the lower bay of New York City, they crowded to the rail to eye their first Americans in the persons of the immigration inspectors, two men and a woman in uniform clambering up a ladder from a cutter that had nosed alongside. The captain was required to note on the ship's manifest the more flagrant cases of contagious disease, for only seventy years ago they were still on the lookout for yellow fever and leprosy. The unlucky victims of such ailments were taken off in a quarantine boat to a special island to be deported as soon as possible.

19   The harbor was sometimes choked with ships at anchor. In the early 1900s there could be as many as fifteen thousand immigrants arriving in one day, and the ships had to drop anchor and wait. But eventually the engines would rumble again, and there, like a battleship on the horizon, stood what the song calls "Manhattan, an isle of joy." Closer, it grew into a cluster of pinnacles known as skyscrapers. And then the midtown skyscrapers topped the ones first seen. It was unlike any other city, and to the European it always seemed audacious and magical, and threatening.

20   Soon the newcomers would be on the docks sorting their bundles and baggage in a babble of languages, and when that was done they were tagged with numbers. Until 1892 they were cleared for entry at Castle Garden, once a fort, then a theater and a public amusement place down at the Battery. However, the volume of immigrants grew so great, and so many of them managed to disappear into Manhattan before being "processed," that a larger and more isolated sorting point had to be found. So, from 1892 on, once the immigrants had been tagged with numbers they were shipped aboard a ferry or a barge to what was to be known in several languages as "the isle of tears," the clearing station, Ellis Island.

21   It had been used by the early Dutch as a picnic ground. Much later its three acres were increased by landfill into twenty-seven, and it became a government arsenal. Today, it looks like a rather imposing college recently gutted by fire. It is totally derelict, a frowzy monument to the American habit of junking and forgetting whatever wears out. But wandering through its great central hall and tattered corridors, seeing the offices with their rusting files, the broken lavatories, and upturned dining tables, one can imagine the bedlam of its heyday, when the milling swarm of strangers was served and interrogated by hundreds of inspectors, wardens, interpreters, doctors,

nurses, waiters, cooks, and agents of immigrant aid societies; and all the while a guerrilla army of con men, land swindlers, and hackmen passed out fresh broadsides boosting the heavenly prospects of the inland towns and unheard-of settlements on the prairie.

22   The newcomers crowded into the main building and the first thing they heard over the general bedlam were the clarion voices of inspectors bellowing out numbers in Italian, German, Polish, Hungarian, Russian, and Yiddish. According to assigned numbers they were herded into groups of thirty and led through long tiled corridors up a wide staircase into the biggest hall most of them had ever seen. Its dimensions, its pillars, its great soaring windows still suggest the grand ballroom of some abdicated monarch. Once they were assembled there in their thousands, the clearance procedure began. I recently pressed an aged immigrant to describe it. "Procedure?" he squealed incredulously. "Din, confusion, bewilderment, madness!"

23   They moved in single file through a stockyard maze of passageways and under the eye of a doctor in a blue uniform who had in his hand a piece of chalk. He was a tough instant diagnostician. He would look at the hands, the hair, the faces and rap out a few questions. He might spot a panting old man with purple lips, and he would chalk on his back a capital "H" for suspected heart disease. Any facial blotches, a hint of gross eczema brought forth a chalked "F" for facial rash. Children in arms were made to stand down to see if they rated an "L" for the limp of rickets or some other deficiency disease. There was one chalk that every family dreaded, for it guaranteed certain deportation. It was a circle with a cross in the middle, and it indicated "feeble-minded."

24   Next they moved on to two doctors dipping into bowls of disinfectant and snapping back the eyelids of suspects, usually with a buttonhook. They were looking for a disease very common then in southern and eastern Europe, trachoma. If you had it, an "E" was chalked on your back, and your first days in the New World were surely your last.

25   About eight in ten survived this scrutiny and passed to the final ordeal, the examination before an immigration inspector standing with an interpreter. Not noticeably gracious types, for they worked ten hours a day, seven days a week, they droned out an unchanging catechism: Who paid your passage? How many dependents? Ever been in prison? Can you read and write? (There was for a long time no legal obligation to be able to do either.) Is there a job waiting for you? (This was a famous catch, since a law called the Contract Labor Law forbade immigrants from signing up abroad for any work at all.) Finally, your name was checked against the ship's manifest. Many people were lucky to emerge into the new life with their old name. An Irish inspector glancing down at what to him was the gobbledygook of "Ouspenska" wrote on the landing card "Spensky." A Norwegian with an unpronounceable name was asked for the name of the town he had left. It was Drobak. The inspector promptly wrote down what he thought he'd heard. Another Norwegian standing nearby philosophically realized that his own name was just as unmanageable and decided that what was good enough for his friend was good enough for him. To this day the progeny of both families rejoice in the name of Robeck.

26   But a new identity was better than none, and it gave you a landing card. With it you were now ready to pay a visit to a currency booth to change your lire or drachmas,

or whatever, into dollars. This exchange could entail prolonged haggling and not a few fist fights with the cashiers, who for many years were short-change artists. But at last you were handed over to the travel agent or the railroad men, if you were going far afield, or you sought the help of an aid society or a beckoning politician, if New York was to be the end of the line. Most immigrants could hardly speak a word of English except the one they had memorized as the town of their destination. A man would unfold a scrap of paper and point to a blockprinted word: "Pringvilliams." Maybe he eventually arrived in Springfield, Massachusetts, and maybe he didn't. But at this point the immigrant's only concern was to get off Ellis Island. All of them looked in relief for the door that was marked "Push to New York." And they pushed.

27   Now, after another ferry ride, they set foot on the earth of the land that was paved with gold. I once asked a successful but unfailingly cynical immigrant if the reality hadn't meant a shattering disillusion. "But there was gold," he said, "to us. There were markets groaning with food and clothes. There were streetcars all over town. You could watch the automobiles. There was no military on horseback and no whips. The neighbors were out in the open, trading and shouting, enjoying free fights. And to a boy like me it was a ball, a friendship club. The streets were an open road." Admittedly, here was a man who had always been able to cope.

28   There were probably many more who came to feel that, at best, they had traded a fearful time in the homeland for a baffling or brutal time in the slums of the cities. Such people went for help to the immigrant aid societies, which proliferated for the needy and the puzzled of the separate nations. The Jews of any nation gravitated to a newspaper office, that of the *Jewish Daily Forward*. It still survives, as the last Yiddish daily left in the United States. Starting in 1897 it attained a high circulation of two hundred and fifty thousand. Today, only seventy-five thousand New Yorkers need or choose to read the daily news in Yiddish. But the desperate immigrants didn't buy it for the daily news alone. Some went to its office clutching painfully written letters for publication in a daily feature that for nearly eighty years has served as a first-aid station to the immigrant. It is called the "Bintel Brief," and from the beginning the column advertised the various plights of the stranded and helped parted relatives to come together again. It was a blessing to many a wife yearning to find her husband. And, of course, it was a curse to many a husband yearning not to find his wife. But in the main it listened to and advised immigrant Jews who were exploited or bewildered by the polyglot society they had moved into.

29   *DEAR EDITOR: I was born in a small town in Russia, and until I was sixteen I studied in Talmud Torahs and yeshivas, but when I came to America I changed quickly. I . . . became a free-thinker . . . When I go past a synagogue during these days and hear a cantor chanting the melodies of the prayers, I become very gloomy and my depression is so great that I cannot endure it . . . what is your opinion of this?*

30   *DEAR EDITOR: For a long time I worked in a shop with a Gentile girl, and we began to go out together and fell in love. We agreed that I would*

remain a Jew and she a Christian. But after we had been married a year, I realized it would not work . . . Advise me what to do now. I could never convert and there's no hope for me to keep her from going to church.

31   *DEAR EDITOR: In the name of all the workers of our shop, I write these words to you . . . we make raincoats. With us is a thirteen-year-old boy who works hard for the two and half dollars a week he earns. Just lately it happened that the boy came to work ten minutes late. This was a "crime" which the bosses couldn't overlook and for the lost ten minutes they docked him two cents.*

32   *DEAR EDITOR: I am a girl from Galicia and in the shop where I work I sit near a Russian Jew . . . once, in a short debate, he stated that all Galicians were no good . . . According to him the Galitzianer are inhuman savages . . . Dear Editor, does he really have a right to say this? I hope you will print my letter and give your opinion.*

33   The files of the "Bintel Brief" ache with troubles: of parents grieved that the American-born son refuses to keep kosher, of students who quit chemistry or law books because they were told no Jew could graduate; of a son in a torment of conscience because he feels he must go back and defend his mother and sisters from a new pogrom; of the ignorance and brutality of sweatshop bosses; of the hopelessness of escaping the bigotry of the neighborhood and the slights of the Gentile shopkeepers. Very many of these Jews found out what the Irish in New York had found out before them—that however much they felt imprisoned with their own kind, they were unwanted on the outside. After the first wave of Jews from southern and eastern Europe, the newspaper advertisements were dotted with new variations on the old warning, "No Irish need apply."

34   In the early years of this century, you could have gone down to New York's Lower East Side, and to similar parts of Pittsburgh and Chicago, and looked on the roaring maelstroms of any street scene as proof positive that the immigrants of many nations were already bubbling together in the melting pot. Yet, if you went closer and listened, you would know that they were all bustling within the confines of Little Italy or Little Russia. Mike Royko has pointed out that until as late as the 1950s Chicago

> *was a place where people stayed put for a while, creating tightly knit neighborhoods as small-townish as any village in the wheat fields. The neighborhood towns were part of larger ethnic states. To the north of the Loop was Germany. To the northwest Poland. To the west were Italy and Israel. To the southwest were Bohemia and Lithuania. And to the south was Ireland.*

35   Officially, you changed from a foreigner into an American citizen after filing naturalization papers, painfully boning up on a few elementary facts of American government, taking an indulgent verbal examination in these mysteries, and finally

appearing before a judge to take the oath. But becoming an American was more complicated and for most more painful. It entailed at first the enormous obstacle of the language, and there are countless thousands of aged immigrants today who have managed with American life with the barest pidgin English.

36   On young families raising first-generation Americans, the pressure to learn the language was intense as the children grew and went through the public school, which, in immigrant neighborhoods, had the dual purpose of teaching the rudiments of mathematics and geography and also of Americanizing the small stranger within the gates. Then the children went home and saw their parents reading an Italian or Russian or Yiddish paper and they began to notice thick accents. They felt uncomfortable and then they felt ashamed. This slow but sure discovery that the parents were odd, and to the extent of their oddity figures of fun, is a great and tragic theme in American life and literature. And the parents' shameful awareness of it sent them off in droves to night school, to make the final capitulation to the new land by learning the language of their sons and daughters.

37   I mentioned earlier that all you needed to get to America was an exit pass, twenty-five dollars, and reasonable health, but that what you were forbidden to have was a contract for a job in the new country. Toward the end of the Civil War, labor was so scarce that Congress made labor contracts signed abroad valid and protected by the courts. The subsequent rush into Europe of factory and railroad agents to sign up intending immigrants threatened a flood of cheap labor bound to industrial serfdom, and within four years the act was repealed.

38   In 1885 Congress decided to discourage unskilled immigrants by enacting a Contract Labor Law that prohibited the signing of foreigners to contract jobs, unless those jobs were professional or otherwise skilled. But the flood of the unskilled was not stopped, and the effect of the act was exactly the reverse of its intention. It meant that the really welcome immigrant was jobless, and in the high tide of immigration southern and central Europe was a bottomless pool of cheap labor. In the Midwest, they poured into the steel and coke factories and the railroad shops; in New York, into the garment factories. Among them were not only city people but peasants and poor farmers who had found themselves transplanted to a city block and were terrified of venturing further into the unknown Siberia of the countryside. Many thousands of them arrived just after the invention of such labor-saving devices as the sewing machine, which had been touted as a boon to the housewife, but was a curse to the seamstress. The labor that she had done for forty cents an hour was now being done by machines, and she had no choice but to stay on and work them for eight cents an hour.

39   The industrialists, the steel men, the iron and tin and railroad barons, came very easily to make the same large assumption about the inexhaustibility of cheap labor. But . . . the immigrant did not stay cowed forever. Henry Frick, (Andrew) Carnegie's bosom partner in his steel enterprises, was a fanatical opponent of labor unions, but he was quick to see that the latest wave of immigrants could be employed as strike-breakers. One year he employed Hungarians to break a strike. But within a year or two he had to hire Italians to break a strike of Hungarians, who by then were beginning to learn a specialty. In an irritable moment Frick got off a profound remark.

"The immigrant," he complained, "however illiterate or ignorant he may be, always learns too soon." Not soon enough, however, to deny these industrial tycoons their imperial hold on the raw materials of industry and, in the person of John Pierpont Morgan, on the national economy itself.

40   . . . For forty years after the Civil War the true national power lay with the oil monopoly, the steel trust, the railroad combines. They had all voted enthusiastically to elect (Theodore) Roosevelt Vice President. But when he got to the White House after McKinley's assassination, he looked at the ways, beginning with the standby stratagems of the holding companies, in which the Barons preserved their immunity from the law. He determined, if not to break them, to bring them under the control of Congress.

41   He had started, as Police Commissioner of New York, going after all the petty grafters who made life hell for the immigrants, and had achieved the feat of making Ellis Island decent and its inspectors able and courteous. As Governor of New York he went after the sweatshop owners and the tenement landlords. As President he charged up and down the social scale, flagellating everybody from food packagers to bankers, challenging them in the name of the federal government. The men who ran the trusts he called, in his squeaky but blazing fashion, "malefactors of great wealth." The trust he saw as an octopus whose longest tentacles bound the immigrants "as dwellers in a polyglot boarding house." His bravest mission was to try and see, through social legislation and new resources of education, that the immigrants should no longer be looked on as nationally identifiable pools of cheap labor. The country must stop talking about German-Americans and Italian-Americans and Polish-Americans: "We have room for but one language here, and that is the English language, for we intend to see that the crucible turns our people out as Americans." There must be no more "hyphenated Americans."

42   Roosevelt's aim was a double one: to liberate the immigrant from his daily grind in a polyglot compound, and to set him free from the hampering liabilities of his native tongue. The first aim did not begin to be achieved until 1911, when there was an appalling fire in New York's Triangle Shirtwaist Factory. It took a hundred and forty lives, roused the needle workers to go on strike and wakened the public conscience. And at the end of it, the airless sweatshop, with its two exits leading to one rickety staircase, was abolished by New York State law. So was the peddling out of piecework to the immigrant's home. It took this trauma to start the Jewish garment workers organizing in unions for decent hours and tolerable wages, and it marked the fiery beginning of their emergence into New York politics. Within a year William Howard Taft would confide to reporters that "Jews make the best Republicans." (Forty years later, Adlai Stevenson, with equal conviction, confided that "Jews make the best Democrats.")

43   The liberation of the immigrant from his mother tongue was something that only time and two generations of American schoolchildren would achieve. By, say, the Second World War, it had been done. But in the past ten years or so there has appeared a new strain of ethnic pride, almost an insistence on reverting to hyphenated Americanism. The blacks who, arguing that "black is beautiful," refused to be assimilated in the white man's world may have led the way, but a similar pride in national origin

is now being flaunted by immigrants old and new. As early as the first decade of the century, there were protests and small riots outside burlesque and vaudeville theaters against the caricaturing of German and Italian and Jewish traits. In the 1930s the motion picture industry devised a code to eliminate the representation of Greeks as conniving merchants, Italians as gangsters, Negroes as shiftless clowns. This new pride springs, I think, partly from a desperate desire of the underdog in the faceless cities to claim an identity, partly from the pragmatic aim of new immigrants—the Puerto Ricans after the Second World War, the Cubans after Castro's coup, the Hungarians after the Soviet invasion—to arrest at once their automatic consignment to the bottom of the labor market. They do not necessarily succeed, but at least they organize and agitate for the rights of equal pay and first-class citizenship.

44   Today the tenements are seventy years older than when the Poles and Italians and Lithuanians and Russians climbed into them, and they were old then. They are the crumbling homes of the newer refugees, and most of all of the native blacks who began sixty years ago to be refugees from the South and from the countryside everywhere. Today, in the cities, the masses are as huddled as ever, and they no longer come expecting El Dorado. More often than not they exchange a rural slum for a city hovel. They know it—and they hate it. And the threat of "the fire next time" is an ever-present one wherever the comfortable whites and the impoverished blacks grow farther apart.

45   But in the wake of the immigrant flood that we have been talking about, paupers become shopkeepers, and the sons and daughters of peasants bound for centuries to slivers of poor soil turned into clerks and nurses and accountants and schoolteachers and druggists and cab drivers and lawyers and doctors. Looking back on those sheepish legions, we should not pretend that they were ever rollicking characters in a musical comedy. But we should not forget, either, the millions who struggled for a decent and tidy life, and made it, and still do.

Suggestions for Discussion or Writing

1. Who is Cooke's audience for this essay? Could he have more than one audience? What is his purpose in writing the essay? Does he persuade you to any point of view?

2. How does Cooke use detail to express his thesis? What is his thesis in this essay? What is the tone of the essay?

3. Cook describes the integration of first-generation Americans into schools and into the American life. How does that description compare with Jose Antonio Villarreal's view of education in *Pocho*? Compare the two essays.

4. How does Jeanne Wakatsuki Houston's experience in the essay "Living in Two Cultures" verify the information given by Cooke?

I Have a Dream

Martin Luther King, Jr.

The well-known civil rights leader, Martin Luther King, Jr. (1929–1968), was born in Atlanta, Georgia, where he was ordained into the ministry at his father's Ebenezer Baptist Church in 1947 at the age of 18. The next year he graduated from Morehouse College and later received his divinity degree from Crozer Theological Seminary in Chester, Pennsylvania. He earned his Ph.D. in theology from Boston University in 1955. He entered the civil rights scene when he became the spokesman for the Montgomery Improvement Association, which was developed to protest the arrest of Rosa Parks, who had refused to give up her bus seat to a white man. The ensuing bus boycott lasted 382 days and eventually resulted in revised segregation laws. King published the story of the Montgomery protest in Stride toward Freedom *in 1958. A mass march on Washington led to King's "I Have a Dream" speech to 250,000 people. In the fall of 1964 he returned from a lecture tour in Europe to receive the Nobel Peace Prize. Four years later, in April 1968, he went to Memphis to support a sanitation workers' strike and was shot by James Earl Ray. He died almost instantly. His tombstone echoes the last words of his famous speech, "Free at last! free at last! thank God almighty, we are free at last!"*

1   Five score years ago, a great American, in whose symbolic shadow we stand, signed the Emancipation Proclamation. This momentous decree came as a great beacon light of hope to millions of Negro slaves who had been seared in the flames of withering injustice. It came as a joyous daybreak to end the long night of captivity.

2   But one hundred years later, we must fact the tragic fact that the Negro is still not free. One hundred years later, the life of the Negro is still sadly crippled by the manacles of segregation and the chains of discrimination. One hundred years later, the Negro lives on a lonely island of poverty in the midst of a vast ocean of material prosperity. One hundred years later, the Negro is still languishing in the corners of American society and finds himself an exile in his own land. So we have come here today to dramatize an appalling condition.

3   In a sense we have come to our nation's Capital to cash a check. When the architects of our republic wrote the magnificent words of the Constitution and the Declaration of Independence, they were signing a promissory note to which every American fell heir. This note was a promise that all men would be guaranteed the unalienable rights of life, liberty, and the pursuit of happiness.

4   It is obvious today that America has defaulted on this promissory note insofar as her citizens of color are concerned. Instead of honoring this sacred obligation, America has given the Negro people a bad check; a check which has come back marked "insufficient funds." But we refuse to believe that the bank of justice is bankrupt. We

refuse to believe that there are insufficient funds in the great vaults of opportunity of this nation. So we have come to cash this check—a check that will give us upon demand the riches of freedom and the security of justice. We have also come to this hallowed spot to remind America of the fierce urgency of *now*. This is no time to engage in the luxury of cooling off or to take the tranquilizing drugs of gradualism. *Now* is the time to make real the promises of Democracy. *Now* is the time to rise from the dark and desolate valley of segregation to the sunlit path of racial justice. *Now* is the time to open the doors of opportunity to all of God's children. *Now* is the time to lift our nation from the quicksands of racial injustice to the solid rock of brotherhood.

5   It would be fatal for the nation to overlook the urgency of the moment and to underestimate the determination of the Negro. This sweltering summer of the Negro's legitimate discontent will not pass until there is an invigorating autumn of freedom and equality. 1963 is not an end, but a beginning. Those who hope that the Negro needed to blow off steam and will now be content will have a rude awakening if the nation returns to business as usual. There will be neither rest nor tranquility in America until the Negro is granted his citizenship rights. The whirlwinds of revolt will continue to shake the foundation of our nation until the bright day of justice emerges.

6   But there is something that I must say to my people who stand on the warm threshold which leads into the palace of justice. In the process of gaining our rightful place we must not be guilty of wrongful deeds. Let us not seek to satisfy our thirst for freedom by drinking from the cup of bitterness and hatred. We must forever conduct our struggle on the high plane of dignity and discipline. We must not allow our creative protest to degenerate into physical violence. Again and again we must rise to the majestic heights of meeting physical force with soul force. The marvelous new militancy which has engulfed the Negro community must not lead us to a distrust of all white people, for many of our white brothers, as evidenced by their presence here today, have come to realize that their destiny is tied up with our destiny and their freedom is inextricably bound to our freedom. We cannot walk alone.

7   And as we walk, we must take the pledge that we shall march ahead. We cannot turn back. There are those who are asking the devotees of civil rights, "When will you be satisfied?" We can never be satisfied as long as the Negro is the victim of the unspeakable horrors of police brutality. We can never be satisfied as long as our bodies, heavy with the fatigue of travel, cannot gain lodging in the motels of the highways and the hotels of the cities. We cannot be satisfied as long as the Negro's basic mobility is from a smaller ghetto to a larger one. We can never be satisfied as long as a Negro in Mississippi cannot vote and a Negro in New York believes he has nothing for which to vote. No, no, we are not satisfied, and we will not be satisfied until justice rolls down like waters and righteousness like a mighty stream.

8   I am not unmindful that some of you come here out of great trials and tribulations. Some of you have come fresh from narrow jail cells. Some of you have come from areas where your quest for freedom left you battered by the storms of persecution and staggered by the winds of police brutality. You have been the veterans of creative suffering. Continue to work with the faith that unearned suffering is redemptive.

9   Go back to Mississippi, go back to Alabama, go back to South Carolina, go back to Georgia, go back to Louisiana, go back to the slums and ghettos of our northern

cities, knowing that somehow this situation can and will be changed. Let us not wallow in the valley of despair.

10   I say to you today, my friends, that in spite of the difficulties and frustrations of the moment I still have a dream. It is a dream deeply rooted in the American dream.

11   I have a dream that one day this nation will rise up and live out the true meaning of its creed: "We hold these truths to be self-evident; that all men are created equal."

12   I have a dream that one day in the red hills of Georgia the sons of former slaves and the sons of former slaveowners will be able to sit down together at the table of brotherhood.

13   I have a dream that one day even the state of Mississippi, a desert state sweltering with the heat of injustice and oppression, will be transformed into an oasis of freedom and justice.

14   I have a dream that my four little children will one day live in a nation where they will not be judged by the color of their skin but by the content of their character.

15   I have a dream today.

16   I have a dream that one day the state of Alabama, whose governor's lips are presently dripping with the words of interposition and nullification, will be transformed into a situation where little black boys and black girls will be able to join hands with little white boys and white girls and walk together as brothers and sisters.

17   I have a dream today.

18   I have a dream that one day every valley shall be exalted, every hill and mountain shall be made low, the rough places will be made plain, and the crooked places will be made straight, and the glory of the Lord shall be revealed, and all flesh shall see it together.

19   This is our hope. This is the faith with which I return to the South. With this faith we will be able to hew out of the mountain of despair a stone of hope. With this faith we will be able to transform the jangling discords of our nation into a beautiful symphony of brotherhood. With this faith we will be able to work together, to pray together, to struggle together, to go to jail together, to stand up for freedom together, knowing that we will be free one day.

20   This will be the day when all of God's children will be able to sing with a new meaning

> My country, 'tis of thee,
> Sweet land of liberty,
>   Of thee I sing:
> Land where my fathers died,
> Land of the pilgrims' pride,
> From every mountain-side
>   Let freedom ring.

21   And if America is to be a great nation this must become true. So let freedom ring from the prodigious hilltops of New Hampshire. Let freedom ring from the mighty mountains of New York. Let freedom ring from the heightening Alleghenies of Pennsylvania!

22   Let freedom ring from the snowcapped Rockies of Colorado!

23   Let freedom ring from the curvaceous peaks of California!

24   But not only that; let freedom ring from Stone Mountain of Georgia!

25   Let freedom ring from Lookout Mountain of Tennessee!

26   Let freedom ring from every hill and molehill of Mississippi. From every mountainside, let freedom ring.

27   When we let freedom ring, when we let it ring from every village and every hamlet, from every state and every city, we will be able to speed up that day when all of God's children, black men and white men, Jews and Gentiles, Protestants and Catholics, will be able to join hands and sing in the words of the old Negro spiritual, "Free at last! free at last! thank God almighty, we are free at last!"

Suggestions for Discussion or Writing

1. How does King use repetition to make his speech effective?

2. What part do biblical allusions, spiritual songs, and references to the Declaration of Independence play in the speech? How does each interact with and enhance the others?

3. "I Have a Dream" was originally presented as a speech. What was King's relationship with his audience? What words or phrases show that relationship?

4. What kinds of figurative language does the speech contain? How do these things enhance the speech?

5. What is the ultimate purpose of the speech? What does King want for the blacks of America? Do you think his dream has been fulfilled?

from *Pocho*

José Antonio Villarreal

Born in 1924 in Los Angeles, José Antonio Villarreal comes from parents who emigrated from Zacatecas, Mexico. His writing skills developed early, and by the third grade he had already produced short stories and poems. He joined the Navy during World War II and served in the Pacific. His college and graduate work has been at the University of California at Berkeley and at Los Angeles. He has worked as a college teacher, an editor, a translator, a technical writer, and a novelist. His first book, Pocho, *is especially notable because it was the first nationally published Chicano novel in the United States.*

1   He had been asking her questions again, and she was a little angry. She always became quiet when he asked her things. Suddenly she sat down and pulled him onto her lap. She held his head against her breasts, and her heart was beating through her dress loudly. She talked but she would not let him move his head to see her face.

2   "Look, little son," she said. "Many times I do not answer you when you ask me things, and other times I simply talk about something else. Sometimes this is because you ask things that you and I should not be talking about, but most of the time it is because I am ashamed that I do know what you ask. You see, we are simple people, your father and I. We did not have the education, because we came from the poorest class of people in México. Because I was raised by the Spanish people, I was taught to read and write. I even went to school for a time, but your father did not, and it was only because, from the time he was a small boy, he decided he would never be a peón, that he taught himself to read and write. But that is all we can do, read and write. We cannot teach the things that you want us to teach you. And I am deeply ashamed that we are going to fail in a great responsibility—that we cannot guide you, we cannot select your reading for you, we cannot even talk to you in your own language.

3   "No, let me finish telling you. Already I can see that books are your life. We cannot help you, and soon we will not even be able to encourage you, because you will be obliged to work. We could not afford to spare you to go to school even if there was a way for you to do it, and there is a great sadness in our hearts."

4   "But my father wants me to go to school. Always he tells me that, and he never takes me out of school to work, the way the other men do with their children," said Richard.

5   "I know. But he talks aloud to drown out the thoughts in his head and the knowledge in his heart. Inside, he knows that it is inevitable that you will have to go to work soon, for you are the only boy in the family, and when you are in secondary school, maybe it will be the end of your education."

6   Her words frightened him, because she was so sure of what she was saying, and he knew that she was telling him this to save him from heartbreak at some later time; then he thought of a thing that gave him hope. "I will finish the secondary, Mamá. Of that I am sure—as long as we live in town. My father cannot take me out of school until I become of age, and I will be too young. Then, after that, things might be different and I can continue on. Anyway, the girls can help out."

7   "What you say is true about the secondary school, but we cannot expect help from the girls much longer. They are growing up, and soon they will begin to marry. Their business and their responsibility will be with their husbands and their husbands' families."

8   "But they are young girls yet." He refused to be discouraged. "They will not possibly marry soon."

9   "Young? I was carrying our sister Concha when I was younger than she is now. No, my son, I know what I am telling you is true. Your father talks about you being a lawyer or a doctor when we return to México, but he knows that you will be neither and that we will never leave this place."

10   "But that was in México," he said. "In México, women marry young, but here we

are Americans and it is different. Take the case of my teachers who are twenty-five or almost thirty years old and they have not married!"

11   "That is different," she explained patiently, "for they are cotorronas and will never marry. Here in your country, teachers are all cotorronas. They are not allowed to marry."

12   "Why?"

13   "I do not know. Maybe it is because parents do not want married women to have such intimate relationships with their children. I do not know."

14   How silly! he thought. *Mothers* are married, and what is more intimate than a child and its mother? But he did not say this to her, because his thoughts suddenly switched into English, and it occurred to him that his mother always followed rules and never asked the why of them. He had known this but had never honestly accepted it, because it seemed such a loss to him to accept the fact that his mother was not infallible. And yet in a sense she was right, for Miss Crane and Miss Broughton and two or three others were close to seventy and were still called "Miss."

15   Back in Spanish, he remembered what she had just said about the professions, and knew that she wanted that for him and the family more than any other thing, with the possible exception of the priesthood, and, of course, that was impossible, because he was the only son and his father would undoubtedly shoot himself if his only son became a priest. He could almost hear his father say, when she timidly sought his reaction to such a possibility, "Make nuns of all the females if that will make you happy—let the boy be, for he is on earth for other things!" And Richard smiled that he would be spared that, at least. Then he suddenly felt a responsibility so heavy as to be a physical pressure, and first he became sad that his lot was a dictate and that his parents believed so strongly in the destiny, and then he was angry that traditions could take a body and a soul—for he had a soul; of that he was certain—and mold it to fit a pattern. He spoke out then, but not in anger, saying things he sensed but did not really understand, an uncomprehending child with the strong desire to have a say in his destiny, with the willful words of a child but with the knowledge and fear that his thoughts could not possibly come true.

16   "Then perhaps it is just as well that I cannot go on to school," he said. "For I do not intend to be a doctor or a lawyer or anything like that. If I were to go to school only to learn to work at something, then I would not do it. I would just work in the fields or in the cannery or something like that. My father would be disappointed in me if I did get an education, so it does not matter. When the time comes, I will do what I have to do."

17   She was surprised at his words, and she knew then that though she could understand him better than most people, she would never really get to know him.

18   "But all this reading, my son," she asked. "All this studying—surely it is for something? If you could go to the university, it would be to learn how you could make more money than you would make in the fields or the cannery. So you can change our way of living somewhat, and people could see what a good son we had, and it would make us all something to respect. Then, when you married and began your family, you would have a nice home and could be assured that you would be able to afford an education for your children."

19   He was disappointed and tried to keep the bitterness from his voice, but could not quite succeed. "And I am supposed to educate my children so that they can change my way of living and they theirs, and so on? Ah, Mamá! Try to understand me. I want to learn, and that is all. I do not want to be something—I *am*. I do not care about making a lot of money and what people think and about the family in the way you speak. I have to learn as much as I can, so that *I* can live . . . learn for *me*, for *myself*—Ah, but I cannot explain to you, and you would not understand me if I could!"

20   Whatever bond they had shared for a while was now gone. The magic of her moment was broken, and she talked to him once again as his superior, and her voice had that old trace of impersonal anger. "But that is wrong, Richard," she said. "That kind of thinking is wrong and unnatural—to have that kind of feeling against the family and the custom. It is as if you were speaking against the Church."

21   They were standing now, and she moved to the table where the *masa* was, and began to roll out tortillas. He tried to make her see him in his way. "Mamá, do you know what happens to me when I read? All those hours that I sit, as you sometimes say, 'ruining my eyes'? If I do ruin them, it would be worth it, for I do not need eyes where I go then. I travel, Mamá. I travel all over the world, and sometimes out of this whole universe, and I go back in time and again forward. I do not know I am here, and I do not care. I am always thinking of you and my father except when I read. Nothing is important to me then, and I even forget that I am going to die sometime. I know that I have so much to learn and so much to see that I cannot possibly have enough time to do it all, for the Mexican people are right when they say that life is only a breath. I do not know that I will find time to make a family, for the important thing is that I must learn, Mamá! Cannot you understand that?"

22   "I have told you I understand very little. I know only that you are blasphemous and you want to learn more in order to be more blasphemous still—if that is possible. I know that we cannot live in a dream, because everything around us is real."

23   "But that is exactly what I mean, Mamá. Everything does not necessarily have to be real. Who said that everything has to be real, anyway?"

24   She was perplexed, because she had got into a discussion in spite of her ignorance, yet she was intelligent enough to find her only answer. "I do not know, but I would say God said so. Yes, God must have said so, because He says everything. When you think of Him in the way you should, you will find the answers to any question you might have."

25   "It is too late for that, because I cannot believe everything that He says or said." He was deeply sorry that he must hurt her. He tried to ease her feelings, but was certain that in the end he would hurt her more. "You know, Mamá, it is partly because of that that I need to learn. I believe in God, Mamá—I believe in the Father, the Son, and the Holy Ghost, but I do not believe everything I am told about Him. Last year I tried to reach Him, to talk to Him about it. I used to go out into the orchard or the meadows and concentrate, but I never saw Him or heard His voice or that of one of His angels. And I was scared, because if He willed it so, I knew that the earth would open and it would swallow me up because I dared to demand explanations from Him. And yet I wanted so desperately to know that I found courage to do it. Then, after a long time that I did this, I stopped and tried to find Him in church, because I would be safer there;

He would not destroy a churchful of people just because of me. But I never saw Him or heard Him. Then, one day, I knew that indeed He *could* destroy the church, because if He could do the best thing in the world, He could also do the most evil thing in the world. Who am I, I thought, to dare bring out that which is cruel in Him? He *is* cruel, you know Mamá, but I believe in Him just the same. If I learn enough, I may sometime learn how to talk to Him. Some people do. You yourself have told me of miracles."

26   His mother looked at him as if he were not her son. She was frightened, and he thought she wanted to send him away, but she was his mother and loved him, and therefore she conquered her fear and held him and cried, "I have really lost you, my son! You are the light of my life and I have already lost you," she said. In spite of himself, his mother's tears always made him cry, and they rocked in each other's arms. "For a moment, I thought that I had given birth to the Devil in a little angel's body, and I knew that I could not bear the child I carry now in my womb. It will be born dead, I thought to myself—but only for a moment did I think that, my son. Forgive me, little one! Forgive me!"

27   His fear made him half believe that he was the Devil incarnate. Later, when his new sister was delivered stillborn and his mother almost died, he was griefstricken with the knowledge that he was to blame.

28   So now I have added murder and almost matricide to my evilness, he thought in his heart, but his mind knew that the tragedy had in no way been his fault. The senile midwife who worked the neighborhood was as much to blame as his mother, who obstinately refused to go to the hospital because of a certainty the doctor would be a man and would look at her private parts.

Suggestions for Discussion or Writing

1. Why is Richard's mother so sure that he will never be a doctor or a lawyer? What is there about his environment that would make her have this view?

2. What false assumptions does his mother have about the educational system in America?

3. Why doesn't Richard's father want him to be a priest? What inferences can be made about this issue?

4. What is the significance of Richard's statement, "I do not want to be something—I am." Why does it make his mother angry? How does she interpret that statement?

5. Why does the communication between mother and son break down at the end of the story? What two perspectives are they bringing to the encounter?

6. Why does Richard feel the intense guilt?

Black and Well-To-Do

Andrea Lee

Andrea Lee was born in Philadelphia. She received her bachelor's and master's degrees in English from Harvard. She and her husband spent ten months in Russia in 1978–79, where she began writing Russian Journal. *Lee is a staff writer for* The New Yorker.

1   I grew up in the kind of town few people believe exists: a black upper-middle-class suburb full of colonial-style houses and Volkswagen Rabbits. Yes, Virginia, there is a black bourgeoisie, and it has existed for years, and it summers on Martha's Vineyard.

2   The Philadelphia suburb of Yeadon, my home through childhood and adolescence, is one of many black enclaves that someday will make a very interesting study for a sociologist.

3   After World War II, housing speculators found it profitable to scare off white residents and sell whole streets of Yeadon to black professionals who were as eager as anyone else at that time to pursue the romantic suburban dream of fieldstone patios and eye-level ovens. In the 1950's, half the black doctors and lawyers in Philadelphia crowded into this rather small town, which was one of the few integrated suburbs, and we Yeadon kids grew up with tree houses and two-car garages and fathers who commuted into the city.

4   Our parents had a vision of pastoral normalcy for their children that was little different from the white ideal laid out in the Dick and Jane readers. Their attempts to provide this and to protect us from the slightest contact with race prejudice left us extraordinarily, perhaps unhealthily, sheltered: We were sent to Quaker schools and camps where race and class were discounted with eager innocence. When the Yeadon Civic Association (my father was president) discovered that a local swimming club was discriminating against blacks, the parents in my neighborhood simply built another club, which they christened "The Nile Swim Club." When we asked about the name, my father explained gravely: "This is a club only for Egyptians."

5   Childhood in Yeadon was a suburban idyll of shady streets and bicycles and ice cream from a drugstore called Doc's. This was the early 1960's, and as my friends and I grew older, we became dimly aware that the rest of the world was not necessarily Yeadon. Most of our parents were active in the civil rights movement, and at gatherings we listened avidly to their campaign references: Birmingham, Selma, Greensboro.

6   Occasionally, we kids would travel into the city and stare in horrified fascination at slums. When my generation of Yeadon preppies was graduated from high school in the late 1960's and early 1970's, however, we quickly realized that our vague concern was not enough, and many of us became radicalized. (Most of us were attending Ivy League colleges, and this increased our sense of guilt.)

7   During college holidays, Yeadon's driveways were colorful with dashikis and other, more complicated African garments, and a great deal of talk went on about the

brothers and sisters of the urban community. Yeadon parents were edgy and alienated from their children at this time, and a common conversation between mothers began: "Yes, she used to look so sweet, and now she's gone and gotten one of those . . . Afros."

8   In the 1970's, our guilt evaporated, and Yeadon became a place where parents vied with one another to produce tidbits about surgeon daughters and M.B.A. sons. Now, early in the 1980's, I find that in some circles, Yeadon is a synonym for conservatism and complacency, a place famed as being the hunting-ground of the AAP (Afro-American Prince or Princess) but I don't care.

9   Yeadon was a great town to grow up in, was as solid a repository of American virtues and American flaws as any other close-knit suburban community; moreover, it had, and still has, its own peculiar flavor—a lively mixture of materialism, idealism, and ironic humor that prevents the minds of its children from stagnating. I feel a surge of well-being when I return there in the summer to hear the symphony of lawn mowers and to find that the Nile Swim Club remains "for Egyptians only."

Suggestions for Discussion or Writing

1. Who is the audience for this essay? What is its purpose? Does it have a thesis statement? What facts support the thesis?

2. Andrea Lee deliberately breaks the stereotype of the American black culture. In what ways do you find her description convincing?

3. Why does her father give the name "The Nile Swim Club" to their local swimming club? Why does he say it is a club "only for Egyptians"?

4. Why does Lee feel guilty about Yeadon? Do you feel guilty about the place where you were reared? Why?

My People, the Indians

Chief Dan George

Chief Dan George (1899–1981), a Native American, has written several beautifully illustrated books containing essays and poetic prayers, including My Heart Soars *(1974) and* My Spirit Soars *(1982). His classic features became well known when, in his early sixties, he appeared in motion picture and television films. He received an Academy Award nomination for his performance in* Little Big Man.

1   Was it only yesterday that men first sailed around the moon? You and I marvel that men should travel so far and so fast. Yet if they have traveled far, then I

have traveled farther; and if they have traveled fast, then I faster, for I was born as if it were a thousand years ago, born in a culture of bows and arrows. But within the span of half a life, I was flung across the ages to the culture of the atom bomb, and from the bows and arrows to atom bombs is a distance far beyond a flight to the moon.

2   I was born in an age that loved the things of nature and gave them beautiful names like Tes-wall-u-wit, instead of dried-up names like Stanley Park.

3   I was born when people loved all nature and spoke to it as though it had a soul. I can remember going up Indian River with my father when I was very young. I can remember his watching the sun light fires of brilliance on Mount Pay-nay-ray as it rose above its peak. I can remember his singing thanks to it, as he often did, singing the Indian word "thanks" so very, very softly.

4   And then the people came. More and more people came. Like a crushing, rushing wave they came, hurling the years aside. And suddenly I found myself a young man in the midst of the twentieth century. I found myself and my people adrift in this new age, not part of it.

5   We were engulfed by its rushing tide, but only as a captive eddy, going round and round. On little reservations, on plots of land, we floated in a kind of gray unreality, ashamed of our culture that you ridiculed, unsure of who we were or where we were going, uncertain of our grip on the present, weak in our hope of the future. And that is where we pretty well stand today.

6   I had a glimpse of something better than this. For a few brief years, I knew my people when we lived the old life. I knew them when there was an unspoken confidence in the home and certain knowledge of the path we walked upon. But we were living in a dying culture that was slowly losing its forward thrust.

7   I think it was the suddenness of it all that hurt us so. We did not have time to adjust to the startling upheaval around us. We seemed to have lost what we had without a replacement for it. We did not have the time to take your twentieth-century progress and eat it little by little and digest it. It was forced feeding from the start, and our stomachs turned sick, and we vomited.

8   Do you know what it is like to be without mooring? Do you know what it is like to live in surroundings that are ugly and everywhere you look you see strange and ugly things? It depresses man, for man must be surrounded by the beautiful if his soul is to grow.

9   What did we see in the new surroundings you brought us? Laughing faces, pitying faces, sneering faces, conniving faces. Faces that ridiculed. Faces that stole from us. It is no wonder we turned to the only people who did not steal and who did not sneer, who came with love. They were the Christian missionaries; they came with love, and I, for one, will ever return that love.

10   Do you know what it is like to feel that you are of no value to society and to those around you? To know that people came to help you but not to work with you, for you knew that they knew you had nothing to offer?

11   Do you know what it is like to have your race belittled and to come to learn that you are only a burden to the country? Maybe we did not have the skills to make a meaningful contribution, but no one would wait for us to catch up. We were shoved aside as if we were dumb and could never learn.

12   Do you know what it is like to be without pride in your race, pride in your family, pride and confidence in yourself? Do you know what it is like? You don't know, for you have never tasted its bitterness.

13   I shall tell you what it is. It is not caring about tomorrow, for what does tomorrow matter? It is having a reserve that looks like a junkyard because the beauty in the soul is dead, and why should the soul express an external beauty that does not match it? It is getting drunk and, for a few brief moments, escaping from ugly reality and feeling a sense of importance. It is, most of all, awaking next morning to the guilt of betrayal. For the alcohol did not fill the emptiness, but only dug it deeper.

14   And now you hold out your hand and you beckon to me to come across the street. Come and integrate, you say. But how can I come? I am naked and ashamed. How can I come in dignity? I have no presents. I have no gifts. What is there in my culture you value? My poor treasures you only scorn.

15   Am I then to come as a beggar and receive all from your omnipotent hand? Somehow I must wait. I must delay. I must find myself. I must find my treasure. I must wait until you want something of me, until you need something that is me. Then I can raise my head and say to my wife and family, "Listen, they are calling. They need me. I must go."

16   Then I can walk across the street and hold my head high, for I will meet you as an equal. I will not scorn you for your seeming gifts, and you will not receive me in pity. Pity I can do without; my manhood I cannot.

17   I can only come as Chief Slaholt came to Captain Vancouver—as one sure of his authority, certain of his worth, master of his house, leader of his people. I shall not come as a cringing object of your pity. I shall come in dignity or I shall not come at all.

18   Society today talks big words of integration. Does it really exist? Can we talk of integration until there is integration of hearts and minds? Unless you have this, you have only a physical presence, and the walls are as high as the mountain range.

19   I know you must be saying, "Tell us what you want." What do we want? We want first of all to be respected and to feel we are people of worth. We want an equal opportunity to succeed in life, but we cannot succeed on your terms; we cannot raise ourselves on your norms. We need specialized help in education, specialized help in the formative years, special courses in English. We need counseling, we need equal job opportunities for our graduates; otherwise our students will lose courage and ask, what is the use of it all?

20   Let no one forget it—we are a people with special rights guaranteed by promises and treaties. We do not beg for these rights nor do we thank you; we do not thank you for them because we paid for them, and the great God knows that the price we paid was exorbitant. We paid with our culture, our dignity, and with our self-respect. We paid and paid and paid, until we became a beaten race, poverty-stricken and conquered.

21   But you have been kind to listen to me. I know that in your heart you wish you could help. I wonder if there is much you can do, and yet there is a lot you can do. When you meet my children, respect each one for what he is: a child of our Father in heaven and your brother. I think it all boils down to just that.

22 I would like to say a prayer that once was spoken, with little differences in wording, all across North America by the tribes of our people. This was long before the white men came.

23 *Oh, Great Spirit, whose voice I hear in the Winds, whose breath gives life to the world, hear me. I come to you as one of your many children. I am small and weak; I need your strength and wisdom. May I walk in beauty. Make my eyes ever behold the red and purple sunset. Make my hands respect the things that you have made and my ears sharp to hear your voice. Make me wise so that I may know the things you have taught your children, the lessons you have hidden in every leaf and rock. Make me strong, not to be superior to my brothers but to be able to fight my greatest enemy, myself. Make me ever ready to come to you with straight eyes, so that when life fades as the fading sunset, my spirit will come to you without shame.*

Questions for Discussion or Writing

1. Why does Chief Dan George feel that his people had such a difficult time adjusting to the drastic changes in their environment?

2. How does he characterize the prejudice and problems his people encounter?

3. What does George feel his people lack when encountering the white culture?

4. What does he feel his people want?

5. How is his view of the Native American culture echoed in Silko's "Lullaby"?

6. What can we learn from his prayer?

Living in Two Cultures

Jeanne Wakatsuki Houston

Jeanne Wakatsuki Houston (1934–) is American of Japanese descent. During World War II she, like other Japanese-Americans, was relocated from her home in California to an internment camp near Death Valley. Her experience there is recounted in a book Farewell to Manzanar. *She was educated at the University of San Jose and also attended the Sorbonne. The screenplay for* Farewell to Manzanar *received the Humanitas Prize and the Christopher Award.*

1   The memories surrounding my awareness of being female fall into two categories: those of the period before World War II, when my family made up my life, and those after the war, when I entered puberty and my world expanded to include the ways and values of my Caucasian peers. I did not think about my Asian-ness and how it influenced my self-image as a female until I married.

2   In remembering myself as a small child, I find it hard to separate myself from the entity of the family. I was too young to be given "duties" according to my sex, and I was unaware that this was the organizational basis for operating the family. I took it for granted that everyone just did what had to be done to keep things running smoothly. My five older sisters helped my mother with domestic duties. My four older brothers helped my father in the fishing business. What I vaguely recall about the sensibility surrounding our sex differences was that my sisters and I all liked to please our brothers. More so, we tried to attract positive attention from Papa. A smile or affectionate pat from him was like a gift from heaven. Somehow we never felt this way about Mama. We took her love for granted. But there was something special about Papa.

3   I never identified this specialness as being one of the blessings of maleness. After all, I played with my brother Kiyo, two years older than myself, and I never felt there was anything special about him. I could even make him cry. My older brothers were fun-loving, boisterous and very kind to me, especially when I made them laugh with my imitations of Carmen Miranda dancing or of Bonnie Baker singing "Oh, Johnny." But Papa was different. His specialness came not from being male, but from being the authority.

4   After the war and the closing of the camps, my world drastically changed. The family had disintegrated; my father was not longer godlike, despite my mother's attempt to sustain that pre-war image of him. I was spending most of my time with my new Caucasian friends and learning new values that clashed with those of my parents. It was also time that I assumed the duties girls were supposed to do, like cooking, cleaning the house, washing and ironing clothes. I remember washing and ironing my brother's shirts, being careful to press the collars correctly, trying not to displease them. I cannot even remember my brothers performing domestic chores while I lived at home. Yet, even though they may not have been working "out there," as the men were supposed to do, I did not resent it. It would have embarrassed me to see my brothers doing the dishes. Their reciprocation came in a different way. They were very protective of me and made me feel good and important for being a female. If my brother Ray had extra money, he would sometimes buy me a sexy sweater like my Caucasian friends wore, which Mama wouldn't buy for me. My brothers taught me to ride a bicycle and to drive a car, took me to my first dance, and proudly introduced me to their friends.

5   Although the family had changed, my identity as a female within it did not differ much from my older sisters who grew up before the war. The males and females supported each other but for different reasons. No longer was the survival of the family as a group our primary objective; we cooperated to help each other survive "out there" in the complicated world that had weakened Papa.

6   We were living in Long Beach then. My brothers encouraged me to run for school office, to try out for majorette and song leader, and to run for queen of various

festivities. They were proud that I was breaking social barriers still closed to them. It was acceptable for an Oriental male to excel academically and in sports. But to gain recognition socially in a society that had been fed the stereotyped model of the Asian male as cook, houseboy or crazed kamikaze pilot was almost impossible. The more alluring myth of mystery and exotica that surrounds the Oriental female made it easier, though no less inwardly painful, for me.

7   Whenever I succeeded in the *Hakujin* world, my brothers were supportive, whereas Papa would be disdainful, undermined by my obvious capitulation to the ways of the West. I wanted to be like my Caucasian friends. Not only did I want to look like them, I wanted to act like them. I tried hard to be outgoing and socially aggressive and to act confidently, like my girlfriends. At home I was careful not to show these personality traits to my father. For him it was bad enough that I did not even look very Japanese: I was too big, and I walked too assertively. My breasts were large, and besides that I showed them off in those sweaters the *Hakujin* girls wore! My behavior at home was never calm and serene, but around my father I still tried to be as Japanese as I could.

8   As I passed puberty and grew more interested in boys, I soon became aware that an Oriental female evoked a certain kind of interest from males. I was still too young to understand how or why an Oriental female fascinated Caucasian men, and of course, far too young to see then that it was a form of "not seeing." My brothers would warn me, "Don't trust the *Hakujin* boys. They only want one thing. They'll treat you like a servant and expect you to wait on them hand and foot. They don't know how to be nice to you." My brothers never dated Caucasian girls. In fact, I never really dated Caucasian boys until I went to college. In high school, I used to sneak out to dances and parties where I would meet them. I wouldn't even dare to think what Papa would do if he knew.

9   What my brothers were saying was that I should not act toward Caucasian males as I did toward them. I must not "wait on them" or allow them to think I would, because they wouldn't understand. In other words, be a Japanese female around Japanese men and act *Hakujin* around Caucasian men. This double identity within a "double standard" resulted not only in a confusion for me of my role or roles as female, but also in who or what I was racially. With the admonitions of my brothers lurking deep in my consciousness, I would try to be aggressive, assertive and "come on strong" toward Caucasian men. I mustn't let them think I was submissive, passive and all-giving like Madame Butterfly. With Asian males I would tone down my natural enthusiasm and settle into patterns instilled in me through the models of my mother and my sisters. I was not comfortable in either role.

10   Although I was attracted to males who looked like someone in a Coca-Cola ad, I yearned for the expressions of their potency to be like that of Japanese men, like that of my father: unpredictable, dominant, and brilliant—yet sensitive and poetic. I wanted a blond samurai.

11   When I met my blond samurai, during those college years in San Jose, I was surprised to see how readily my mother accepted the idea of our getting married. My father had passed away, but I was still concerned about her reaction. All of my married brothers and sisters had married Japanese-American mates. I would be the first to

marry a Caucasian. "He's a strong man and will protect you. I'm all for it," she said. Her main concern for me was survival. Knowing that my world was the world of the *Hakujin,* she wanted me to be protected, even if it meant marriage to one of them. It was 1957, and interracial couples were a rare sight to see. She felt that my husband-to-be was strong because he was acting against the norms of his culture, perhaps even against his parents' wishes. From her vantage point, where family and group opinions outweighed the individual's, this willingness to oppose them was truly a show of strength.

12   When we first married I wondered if I should lay out his socks and underwear every morning like my mother used to do for my father. But my brothers' warning would float up from the past: don't be subservient to Caucasian men or they will take advantage. So I compromised and laid them out sporadically, whenever I thought to do it . . . which grew less and less often as the years passed. (Now my husband is lucky if he can even find a clean pair of socks in the house!) His first reaction to this wifely gesture was to be uncomfortably pleased. Then he was puzzled by its sporadic occurrence, which did not seem to coincide as an act of apology or because I wanted something. On the days when I felt I should be a good Japanese wife, I did it. On other days, when I felt American and assertive, I did not.

13   When my mother visited us, as she often did when she was alive, I had to be on good behavior, much to my husband's pleasure and surprise. I would jump up from the table to fill his empty water glass (if she hadn't beat me to it) or butter his roll. If I didn't notice that his plate needed refilling, she would kick me under the table and reprimand me with a disapproving look. Needless to say, we never had mother-in-law problems. He would often ask, with hope in his voice, "When is your mother coming to visit?"

14   My mother had dutifully served my father throughout their marriage, but I never felt she resented it. I served my brothers and father and did not resent it. I was made to feel not only important for performing duties of my role, but absolutely integral for the functioning of the family. I realized a very basic difference in attitude between Japanese and American cultures toward serving another. In my family, to serve another could be uplifting, a gracious gesture that elevated oneself. For many white Americans, it seems that serving another is degrading, an indication of dependency or weakness in character, or a low place in the social ladder. To be ardently considerate is to be "self-effacing" or apologetic.

15   My father used to say, "Serving humanity is the greatest virtue. Giving service of yourself is more worthy than selling the service or goods of another." He would prefer that we be maids in someone's home, serving someone well, than be salesgirls where our function would be to exchange someone else's goods, handling money. Perhaps it was his way of rationalizing and giving pride to the occupations open to us as Orientals. Nevertheless, his words have stayed with me, giving me spiritual sustenance at times when I perceived that my willingness to give was misconstrued as a need to be liked or an act of manipulation to get something.

16   My husband and I often joke that the reason we have stayed married for so long is that we continually mystify each other with responses and attitudes that are plainly due to our different backgrounds. For years I frustrated him with unpredictable silences

and accusing looks. I felt a great reluctance to tell him what I wanted or what needed to be done in the home. I was inwardly furious that I was being put into the position of having to tell him what to do. I felt my femaleness, in the Japanese sense, was being degraded. I did not want to be the authority. That would be humiliating for him and for me. He, on the other hand, considering the home to be under my dominion, in the American sense, did not dare to impose on me what he thought I wanted. He wanted me to tell him or make a list, like his parents did in his home.

17   Entertaining socially was also confusing. Up to recent times, I still hesitated to sit at the head of our rectangular dining table when my husband sat at the other end. It seemed right to be seated next to him, helping him serve the food. Sometimes I did it anyway, but only with our close friends who didn't read my physical placement as psychological subservience.

18   At dinner parties I always served the men first, until I noticed the women glaring at me. I became self-conscious about it and would try to remember to serve the women first. Sometime I would forget and automatically turn to a man. I would catch myself abruptly, dropping a bowl of soup all over him. Then I would have to serve him first anyway, as a gesture of apology. My unconscious Japanese instinct still managed to get what it wanted.

19   Now I just entertain according to how I feel that day. If my Japanese sensibility is stronger, I act accordingly and feel comfortable. I have come to accept the cultural hybridness of my personality, to recognize it as a strength and not weakness. Because I am culturally neither pure Japanese nor pure American does not mean I am less of a person. It means I have been enriched by the heritage of both.

20   How my present attitudes will affect my children in later years remains to be seen. My world is radically different from my mother's world, and all indications point to an even wider difference between our world and our children's. Whereas my family's and part of my struggle was racially based, I do not foresee a similar struggle for our children. Their biracialism is, indeed, a factor in their identity and self-image, but I feel their struggle will be more to sustain human dignity in a world rapidly dehumanizing itself with mechanization and technology. My hope is they have inherited a strong will to survive, that essential trait ethnic minorities in this country have so sharply honed.

Suggestions for Discussion or Writing

1. What is Jeanne Wakatsuki Houston's thesis in her essay? Does she make a value judgment on her experience as a Japanese-American? How has she adjusted to the experience?

2. Why were the Japanese in internment camps during World War II? Why did that experience change her family?

3. How is Houston's experience different from José Antonio Villarreal's? How does each feel about his or her native culture? Compare each with Chief Dan George's attitudes.

4. How does Houston's attitude toward the men of her native culture compare to Silko's attitude toward the men of her native culture? How have they changed their attitudes because of the contact with the American culture?

5. Compare Houston's experience with her native Asian culture with the experience of the character in Hisaye Yamamoto's "Seventeen Syllables" (Chapter 11).

Lullaby

Leslie Marmon Silko

Leslie Marmon Silko, a Native American Navajo, was born in 1948 and raised in Arizona. Her writing includes the award-winning books Ceremony *(1977) and* Storyteller *(1981). After visiting a writer's conference, she became acquainted with James Wright and carried on a lengthy correspondence with him. A recent book,* Delicacy and Strength of Lace: Letters between Leslie Marmon Silko and James Wright *(1986), captures some of the beauty of that correspondence.*

1   The sun had gone down but the snow in the wind gave off its own light. It came in thick tufts like new wool—washed before the weaver spins it. Ayah reached out for it like her own babies had, and she smiled when she remembered how she had laughed at them. She was an old woman now, and her life had become memories. She sat down with her back against the wide cottonwood tree, feeling the rough bark on her back bones; she faced east and listened to the wind and snow sing a high-pitched Yeibechei song. Out of the wind she felt warmer, and she could watch the wide fluffy snow fill in her tracks, steadily, until the direction she had come from was gone. By the light of the snow she could see the dark outline of the big arroyo a few feet away. She was sitting on the edge of Cebolleta Creek, where in the springtime the thin cows would graze on grass already chewed flat to the ground. In the wide deep creek bed where only a trickle of water flowed in the summer, the skinny cows would wander, looking for new grass along winding paths splashed with manure.

2   Ayah pulled the old Army blanket over her head like a shawl. Jimmie's blanket—the one he had sent to her. That was a long time ago and the green wool was faded, and it was unraveling on the edges. She did not want to think about Jimmie. So she thought about the weaving and the way her mother had done it. On the tall wooden loom set into the sand under a tamarack tree for shade. She could see it clearly. She had been only a little girl when her grandma gave her the wooden combs to pull the

twigs and burrs from the raw, freshly washed wool. And while she combed the wool, her grandma sat beside her, spinning a silvery strand of yarn around the smooth cedar spindle. Her mother worked at the loom with yarns dyed bright yellow and red and gold. She watched them dye the yarn in boiling black pots full of beeweed petals, juniper berries, and sage. The blankets her mother made were soft and woven so tight that rain rolled off them like birds' feathers. Ayah remembered sleeping warm on cold windy nights, wrapped in her mother's blankets on the hogan's sandy floor.

3   The snow drifted now, with the northwest wind hurling it in gusts. It drifted up around her black overshoes—old ones with metal buckles. She smiled at the snow which was trying to cover her little by little. She could remember when they had no black rubber overshoes; only the high buckskin leggings that they wrapped over their elkhide moccasins. If the snow was dry or frozen, a person could walk all day and not get wet; and in the evenings the beams of the ceiling would hang with lengths of pale buckskin leggings, drying out slowly.

4   She felt peaceful remembering. She didn't feel cold any more. Jimmie's blanket seemed warmer than it had ever been. And she could remember the morning he was born. She could remember whispering to her mother, who was sleeping on the other side of the hogan, to tell her it was time now. She did not want to wake the others. The second time she called to her, her mother stood up and pulled on her shoes; she knew. They walked to the old stone hogan together, Ayah walking a step behind her mother. She waited alone, learning the rhythms of the pains while her mother went to call the old woman to help them. The morning was already warm even before dawn and Ayah smelled the bee flowers blooming and the young willow growing at the springs. She could remember that so clearly, but his birth merged into the births of the other children and to her it became all the same birth. They named him for the summer morning and in English they called him Jimmie.

5   It wasn't like Jimmie died. He just never came back, and one day a dark blue sedan with white writing on its doors pulled up in front of the boxcar shack where the rancher let the Indians live. A man in a khaki uniform trimmed in gold gave them a yellow piece of paper and told them that Jimmie was dead. He said the Army would try to get the body back and then it would be shipped to them; but it wasn't likely because the helicopter had burned after it crashed. All of this was told to Chato because he could understand English. She stood inside the doorway holding the baby while Chato listened. Chato spoke English like a white man and he spoke Spanish too. He was taller than the white man and he stood straighter too. Chato didn't explain why; he just told the military man they could keep the body if they found it. The white man looked bewildered; he nodded his head and he left. Then Chato looked at her and shook his head, and then he told her, "Jimmie isn't coming home anymore," and when he spoke, he used the words to speak of the dead. She didn't cry then, but she hurt inside with anger. And she mourned him as the years passed, when a horse fell with Chato and broke his leg, and the white rancher told them he wouldn't pay Chato until he could work again. She mourned Jimmie because he would have worked for his father then; he would have saddled the big bay horse and ridden the fence lines each day, with wire cutters and heavy gloves, fixing the breaks in the barbed wire and putting the stray cattle back inside again.

6   She mourned him after the doctors came to take Danny and Ella away. She was at the shack alone that day they came. It was back in the days before they hired Navajo women to go with them as interpreters. She recognized one of the doctors. She had seen him at the children's clinic at Cañoncito about a month ago. They were wearing khaki uniforms and they waved papers at her and a black ball-point pen, trying to make her understand their English words. She was frightened by the way they looked at the children, like the lizard watches the fly. Danny was swinging on the tire swing on the elm tree behind the rancher's house, and Ella was toddling around the front door, dragging the broomstick horse Chato made for her. Ayah could see they wanted her to sign the papers, and Chato had taught her to sign her name. It was something she was proud of. She only wanted them to go, and to take their eyes away from her children.

7   She took the pen from the man without looking at his face and she signed the papers in three different places he pointed to. She stared at the ground by their feet and waited for them to leave. But they stood there and began to point and gesture at the children. Danny stopped swinging. Ayah could see his fear. She moved suddenly and grabbed Ella into her arms; the child squirmed, trying to get back to her toys. Ayah ran with the baby toward Danny; she screamed for him to run and then she grabbed him around his chest and carried him too. She ran south into the foothills of juniper trees and black lava rock. Behind her she heard the doctors running, but they had been taken by surprise, and as the hills became steeper and the cholla cactus were thicker, they stopped. When she reached the top of the hill, she stopped to listen in case they were circling around her. But in a few minutes she heard a car engine start and they drove away. The children had been too surprised to cry while she ran with them. Danny was shaking and Ella's little fingers were gripping Ayah's blouse.

8   She stayed up in the hills for the rest of the day, sitting on a black lava boulder in the sunshine where she could see for miles all around her. The sky was light and blue and cloudless, and it was warm for late April. The sun warmth relaxed her and took the fear and anger away. She lay back on the rock and watched the sky. It seemed to her that she could walk into the sky, stepping through clouds endlessly. Danny played with little pebbles and stones, pretending they were bird's eggs and then little rabbits. Ella sat at her feet and dropped fistfuls of dirt into the breeze, watching the dust and particles of sand intently. Ayah watched a hawk soar high above them, dark wings gliding; hunting or only watching, she did not know. The hawk was patient and he circled all afternoon before he disappeared around the high volcanic peak the Mexicans called Guadalupe.

9   Late in the afternoon, Ayah looked down at the gray boxcar shack with the paint all peeled from the wood; the stove pipe in the roof was rusted and crooked. The fire she had built that morning in the oil drum stove had burned out. Ella was asleep in her lap now and Danny sat close to her, complaining that he was hungry; he asked when they would go to the house. "We will stay up here until your father comes," she told him, "because those white men were chasing us." The boy remembered then and he nodded at her silently.

10   If Jimmie had been there he could have read those papers and explained to her what they said. Ayah would have known then, never to sign them. The doctors came

back the next day and they brought a BIA [Bureau of Indian Affairs] policeman with them. They told Chato they had her signature and that was all they needed. Except for the kids. She listened to Chato sullenly; she hated him when he told her it was the old woman who died in the winter, spitting blood; it was her old grandma who had given the children this disease. "They don't spit blood," she said coldly. "The whites lie." She held Ella and Danny close to her, ready to run to the hills again. "I want a medicine man first," she said to Chato, not looking at him. He shook his head. "It's too late now. The policeman is with them. You signed the paper." His voice was gentle.

11   It was worse than if they had died: to lose the children and to know that somewhere, in a place called Colorado, in a place full of sick and dying strangers, her children were without her. There had been babies that died soon after they were born, and one that died before he could walk. She had carried them herself, up to the boulders and great pieces in the cliff that long ago crashed down from Long Mesa; she laid them in the crevices of sandstone and buried them in fine brown sand with round quartz pebbles that washed down the hills in the rain. She had endured it because they had been with her. But she could not bear this pain. She did not sleep for a long time after they took her children. She stayed on the hill where they had fled the first time, and she slept rolled up in the blanket Jimmie had sent. She carried the pain in her belly and it was fed by everything she saw: the blue sky of their last day together and the dust and pebbles they played with; the swing in the elm tree and the broomstick horse choked life from her. The pain filled her stomach and there was no room for food or for her lungs to fill with air. The air and the food would have been theirs.

12   She hated Chato, not because he let the policeman and doctors put the screaming children in the government car, but because he taught her to sign her name. Because it was like the old ones always told her about learning their language or any of their ways: it endangered you. She slept alone on the hill until the middle of November when the first snows came. Then she made a bed for herself where the children slept. She did not lie down beside Chato again until many years later, when he was sick and shivering and only her body could keep him warm. The illness came after the white rancher told Chato he was too old to work for him anymore, and Chato and his old woman should be out of the shack by the next afternoon because the rancher had hired new people to work there. That had satisfied her. To see how the white man repaid Chato's years of loyalty and work. All of Chato's fine-sounding English talk didn't change things.

13   It snowed steadily and the luminous light from the snow gradually diminished into the darkness. Somewhere in Cebolleta a dog barked and other village dogs joined with it. Ayah looked in the direction she had come, from the bar where Chato was buying the wine. Sometimes he told her to go on ahead and wait; and then he never came. And when she finally went back looking for him, she would find him passed out at the bottom of the wooden steps to Azzie's Bar. All the wine would be gone and most of the money too, from the pale blue check that came once a month in a government envelope. It was then that she would look at his face and his hands, scarred by ropes and the barbed wire of all those years, and she would think, this man is a stranger; for forty years she had smiled at him and cooked his food, but he remained

a stranger. She stood up again, with the snow almost to her knees, and she walked back to find Chato.

14   It was hard to walk in the deep snow and she felt the air burn in her lungs. She stopped a short distance from the bar to rest and readjust the blanket. But this time he wasn't waiting for her on the bottom step with his old Stetson hat pulled down and his shoulders hunched up in his long wool overcoat.

15   She was careful not to slip on the wooden steps. When she pushed the door open, warm air and cigarette smoke hit her face. She looked around slowly and deliberately, in every corner, in every dark place that the old man might find to sleep. The bar owner didn't like Indians in there, especially Navajos, but he let Chato come in because he could talk Spanish like he was one of them. The men at the bar stared at her, and the bartender saw that she left the door open wide. Snowflakes were flying inside like moths and melting into a puddle on the oiled wood floor. He motioned to her to close the door, but she did not see him. She held herself straight and walked across the room slowly, searching the room with every step. The snow in her hair melted and she could feel it on her forehead. At the far corner of the room, she saw red flames at the mica window of the old stove door; she looked behind the stove just to make sure. The bar got quiet except for the Spanish polka music playing on the jukebox. She stood by the stove and shook the snow from her blanket and held it near the stove to dry. The wet wool reminded her of new-born goats in early March, brought inside to warm near the fire. She felt calm.

16   In past years they would have told her to get out. But her hair was white and her face was wrinkled. They looked at her like she was a spider crawling slowly across the room. They were afraid; she could feel the fear. She looked at their faces steadily. They reminded her of the first time the white people brought her children back to her that winter. Danny had been shy and hid behind the thin white woman who brought them. And the baby had not known her until Ayah took her into her arms, and then Ella had nuzzled close to her as she had when she was nursing. The blonde woman was nervous and kept looking at a dainty gold watch on her wrist. She sat on the bench near the small window and watched the dark snow clouds gather around the mountains; she was worrying about the unpaved road. She was frightened by what she saw inside too: the strips of venison drying on a rope across the ceiling and the children jabbering excitedly in a language she did not know. So they stayed for only a few hours. Ayah watched the government car disappear down the road and she knew they were already being weaned from these lava hills and from this sky. They last time they came was in early June, and Ella stared at her the way the men in the bar were now staring. Ayah did not try to pick her up; she smiled at her instead and spoke cheerfully to Danny. When he tried to answer her, he could not seem to remember and he spoke English words with the Navajo. But he gave her a scrap of paper that he had found somewhere and carried in his pocket; it was folded in half, and he shyly looked up at her and said it was a bird. She asked Chato if they were home for good this time. He spoke to the white woman and she shook her head. "How much longer?" he asked, and she said she didn't know; but Chato saw how she stared at the boxcar shack. Ayah turned away then. She did not say good-bye.

17   She felt satisfied that the men in the bar feared her. Maybe it was her face and the way she held her mouth with teeth clenched tight, like there was nothing anyone could do to her now. She walked north down the road, searching for the old man. She did this because she had the blanket, and there would be no place for him except with her and the blanket in the old adobe barn near the arroyo. They always slept there when they came to Cebolleta. If the money and the wine were gone, she would be relieved because then they could go home again; back to the old hogan with a dirt roof and rock walls where she herself had been born. And the next day the old man could go back to the few sheep they still had, to follow along behind them, guiding them, into dry sandy arroyos where sparse grass grew. She knew he did not like walking behind old ewes when for so many years he rode big quarter-horses and worked with cattle. But she wasn't sorry for him; he should have known all long what would happen.

18   There had not been enough rain for their garden in five years; and that was when Chato finally hitched a ride into the town and brought back brown boxes of rice and sugar and big tins of welfare peaches. After that, at the first of the month they went to Cebolleta to ask the postmaster for the check; and then Chato would go to the bar and cash it. They did this as they planted the garden every May, not because anything would survive the summer dust, but because it was time to do this. The journey passed the days that smelled silent and dry like the caves above the canyon with yellow painted buffaloes on their walls.

19   He was walking along the pavement when she found him. He did not stop or turn around when he heard her behind him. She walked beside him and she noticed how slowly he moved now. He smelled strong of woodsmoke and urine. Lately he had been forgetting. Sometimes he called her by his sister's name and she had been gone for a long time. Once she had found him wandering on the road to the white man's ranch, and she asked him why he was going that way; he laughed at her and said, "You know they can't run that ranch without me," and he walked on determined, limping on the leg that had been crushed many years before. Now he looked at her curiously, as if for the first time, but he kept shuffling along, moving slowly along the side of the highway. His gray hair had grown long and spread out on the shoulders of the long overcoat. He wore the old hat pulled down over his ears. His boots were worn out at the toes and he had stuffed pieces of an old red shirt in the holes. The rags made his feet look like little animals up to their ears in the snow. She laughed at his feet; the snow muffled the sound of her laugh. He stopped and looked at her again. The wind had quit blowing and the snow was falling straight down; the southeast sky was beginning to clear and Ayah could see a star.

20   "Let's rest awhile," she said to him. They walked away from the road and up the slope to the giant boulders that had tumbled down from the red sandrock mesa throughout the centuries of rainstorms and earth tremors. In a place where the boulders shut out the wind, they sat down with their backs against the rock. She offered half of the blanket to him and they sat wrapped together.

21   The storm passed swiftly. The clouds moved east. They were massive and full, crowding together across the sky. She watched them with the feeling of horses—steely blue-gray horses startled across the sky. The powerful haunches pushed into the distances and the tail hairs streamed white mist behind them. The sky cleared. Ayah

saw that there was nothing between her and the stars. The light was crystalline. There was no shimmer, no distortion through earth haze. She breathed the clarity of the night sky; she smelled the purity of the half moon and the stars. He was lying on his side with his knees pulled up near his belly for warmth. His eyes were closed now, and in the light from the stars and the moon, he looked young again.

22   She could see it descend out of the night sky: an icy stillness from the edge of the thin moon. She recognized the freezing. It came gradually, sinking snowflake by snowflake until the crust was heavy and deep. It had the strength of the stars in Orion, and its journey was endless. Ayah knew that with the wine he would sleep. He would not feel it. She tucked the blanket around him, remembering how it was when Ella had been with her; and she felt the rush so big inside her heart for the babies. And she sang the only song she knew to sing for babies. She could not remember if she had ever sung it to her children, but she knew that her grandmother had sung it and her mother had sung it:

> The earth is your mother,
>> she holds you.
> The sky is your father,
>> he protects you.
> Sleep,
> sleep.
> Rainbow is your sister,
>> she loves you.
> The winds are your brothers,
>> they sing to you.
> Sleep,
> sleep.
> We are together always
> We are together always
> There never was a time
> when this
> was not so.

Suggestions for Discussion or Writing

1. How do the memories of the narrator and the details of the present show the differences between the old culture and the new?

2. Where do you see the conflicts between the traditions of the Native American culture and the white culture? Can you see the motives and beliefs in each culture?

3. What is the paper Ayah signs? Why does she sign it? What do the white doctors want?

4. Why is Chato fired? Is his dismissal culture or age related—or both? How do you know?

5. How does the title of the story relate to the events? How is it a metaphor
    for a large view of the culture?

Napa, California
Dedicado al Sr. Chávez, Sept. '75

Ana Castillo

*Born in 1953, Ana Castillo is rapidly becoming one of the more prominent
Hispanic writers and poets in America. She writes beautifully both in Spanish
and in English. Her books include* Otro Canto *(1977),* Women Are Not Roses
(1984), Mixquianhuala Letters *(1986) and* Sapogonia an Anti Romance in
3/8 Meter *(1990).*

We pick
    the bittersweet grapes
    at harvest
    one
5   by
    one
with leather worn hands
            as they pick
            at our dignity
10   and wipe our pride
            away
            like the sweat we wipe
            from our sun-beaten brows
            at midday

15 In fields
    so vast
    that our youth seems
    to pass before us
    and we have grown
20 very
      very
        old
            by dusk ...
            (bueno pues, ¿qué vamos a hacer, Ambrosio?
25   *¡bueno pues, seguirle, compadre, seguirle!*
            ¡Ay, Mama!

Sí pues, ¿qué vamos a hacer, compadre?
¡Seguirle, Ambrosio, seguirle!)[1]

We pick
30 with a desire
    that only survival
    inspires
While the end
    of each day only brings
35 a tired night
    that waits for the sun
    and the land
    that in turn waits
    for us . . .

Questions for Discussion or Writing

1. How do the following words and phrases reflect the culture from which this poem was taken: bittersweet, leather worn hands, pick at our dignity, and wipe our pride away, we have grown very old by dusk, a tired night?

2. What is the effect of the Spanish section of the poem? What does it say?

3. How does the poem reflect the plight of the immigrant worker?

4. Why does Castillo say that the land is waiting for them?

5. How is the name "Ambrosio" symbolic? How is the title symbolic?

Harlem

Langston Hughes

Called the "poet laureate of Harlem," James Langston Hughes (1902–1967) was born in Joplin, Missouri. He earned his B.A. from Lincoln University (1929) and received a Guggenheim fellowship for creative work in 1935. His first collection of poetry, The Weary Blues, *was published in 1926. The Best*

[1] Well then, what are we going to do Ambrosio?
Well then, follow him, my good friend, follow him!
Mama!
Yes, well, what are we going to do, friend?
Follow him, Ambrosio, follow him!

of Simple *(1961) is a series of humorous sketches of black life based on the experiences of the fictional character Jesse B. Semple. Hughes' other writing includes novels, short stories, autobiographies, and juvenile books. He is also the author of several nonfiction works including* A Pictorial History of the Negro in America *(1956),* Fight for Freedom: The Story of the NAACP *(1962), and* Black Misery *(1969). He received the 1960 Spingam Medal, which is awarded yearly to the African American who has achieved the most in his or her field.*

What happens to a dream deferred?

Does it dry up
like a raisin in the sun?

Or fester like a sore—
5 and then run?
Does it stink like rotten meat?
Or crust and sugar over—
like a syrupy sweet?

Maybe it just sags
10 like a heavy load.

Or does it explode?

Suggestions for Discussion or Writing

1. What expectations about the content of the poem does the title give you? How does the poem fill those expectations?

2. Why does the poem only ask questions and give tentative answers? What is the poem talking about?

3. How do the similes in lines two through nine work in the poem? What is being compared to a "raisin in the sun," "a sore," "rotten meat," etc.? What or who is the "dream deferred"?

4. What is the effect of the opposing images such as "rotten meat" and "syrupy sweet?"

Comparatives

N. Scott Momaday

A Kiowa American Indian from Lawton, Oklahoma, N. Scott Momaday was born in 1934 and received his education at Stanford (M.A. 1960, Ph.D. 1963). He has been a Professor of English at Stanford since 1973. His book House Made of Dawn *(1968) received a Pulitzer prize for fiction in 1969. He has also published* Way to a Rainy Mountain *(1969),* In the Presence of the Sun: Stories and Poems (1961–1991), *and a novel,* Ancient Child *(1989).*

Sunlit sea,
the drift of fronds,
and banners
of bobbing boats—
5   the seaside
of any day—
except: this
cold, bright body
of the fish
10   upon the planks,
the coil and
crescent of flesh
extending
just into death.

15   Even so,
in the distant,
inland sea,
a shadow runs,
radiant,
20   rude in the rock:
fossil fish,
fissure of bone
forever.
It is perhaps
25   the same thing,
an agony
twice perceived.

It is most like
wind on waves—
30   mere commotion,

mute and mean,
perceptible—
that is all.

Suggestions for Discussion or Writing

1. What do the first few lines of the poem describe? How is it different from the description in the middle of the poem?

2. Why is the inland sea symbolic?

3. What kind of sound patterns are found in the poem?

4. What metaphors are found in the poem?

5. How does the poem reflect the Native American culture?

The Unexplored Realm
Becoming Aware of the Spiritual Life

Introduction

I ndividual religious belief occupies a sheltered place in our lives, but attitudes toward the spiritual life differ widely. Organized religion is particularly vulnerable to attack, yet America is noted for its diversity of churches. Tolerance and hostility are seen side by side in communities. And even the most devout may at times question principles and practices.

Paul Tillich's essay "The Lost Dimension in Religion" is concerned with the shifting of belief to another level; any religion could be examined by the questions in his article. Garrison Keillor's essay "Protestant" focuses on the beliefs and practices he observed in his childhood religion, while Dan Wakefield's essay "Returning to Church" takes a look at a rediscovery of religious values. Richard Eberhart's poem "Attitudes" contrasts two different religious attitudes and practices surrounding death.

The two stories by Langston Hughes and Nathaniel Hawthorne take sharper views of religious beliefs. They examine the motive and behavior of people who seem to be deceived by faith. They see insincerity and falseness in their traditions.

On the other hand, Leo Tolstoy's sensitive story "The Three Hermits" shows the possibilities of the sublime and the beauty of religious faith. Gerard Manley Hopkins also shows an affirmation of faith, despite the carelessness of humanity, in "God's Grandeur." The spiritual realm is viewed with questions and new dimensions in Annie Dillard's "Heaven and Earth in Jest." Finally, Emily Dickinson's poem "Prayer is the little implement" very briefly touches on aspects of prayer.

Without faith in something, the world can look bleak. But each person must find the realm of faith alone. Unlike the appearance of scientific certainty, the spiritual realm seems ephemeral and elusive. Questions of faith must be answered by a different voice. Although the bloodiest battles have been caused by struggles over faith, the true battle must take place in the individual heart.

The Lost Dimension in Religion

Paul Tillich

Philosopher and theologian Paul Tillich (1866–1965) was born in Star-zeddel, Prussia, and educated in Berlin. He received his Ph.D. from Breslau in 1911. An outspoken critic of the Nazi party, Tillich was removed from his teaching position and immigrated to the U.S., where he taught at Harvard and the University of Chicago. Tillich's writing re-flects the religious and cultural dilemmas of his time and includes the following works: Religious Realization *and* The Religious Situation, *both published before he left Germany,* The Protestant Era *(1948),* The Shak-ing of the Foundations *(sermons, 1948),* Biblical Religion and the Search for Ultimate Realities *(1955), and* Systemic Theology *(1951–1963) in three volumes. These writings illustrate his concern about the tension between faith and skepticism, tradition and modernism, and deal with such subjects as psychology, culture, and existentialism.*

1   Every observer of our Western civilization is aware of the fact that something has happened to religion. It especially strikes the observer of the American scene. Everywhere he finds symptoms of what one has called religious revival, or more modestly, the revival of interest in religion. He finds them in churches with their rapidly increasing membership. He finds them in the mushroomlike growth of sects. He finds them on college campuses and in the theological faculties of universities. Most conspicuously, he finds them in the tremendous success of men like Billy Graham and Norman Vincent Peale, who attract masses of people Sunday after Sunday, meeting after meeting. The facts cannot be denied, but how should they be interpreted? It is my intention to show that these facts must be seen as expressions of the predicament of Western man in the second half of the twentieth century. But I would even go a step further. I believe that the predicament of man in our period gives us also an important insight into the predicament of man generally—at all times and in all parts of the earth.

2   There are many analyses of man and society in our time. Most of them show important traits in the picture, but few of them succeed in giving a general key to our present situation. Although it is not easy to find such a key, I shall attempt it and, in so doing, will make an assertion which may be somewhat mystifying at first hearing. The decisive element in the predicament of Western man in our period is his loss of the dimension of depth. Of course, "dimension of depth" is a metaphor. It is taken from the spatial realm and applied to man's spiritual life. What does it mean?

3   It means that man has lost an answer to the question: What is the meaning of life? Where do we come from, where do we go to? What shall we do, what should we become in the short stretch between birth and death? Such questions are not answered or even asked if the "dimension of depth" is lost. And this is precisely what has

happened to man in our period of history. He has lost the courage to ask such questions with an infinite seriousness—as former generations did—and he has lost the courage to receive answers to these questions, wherever they may come from.

4   I suggest that we call the dimension of depth the religious dimension in man's nature. Being religious means asking passionately the question of the meaning of our existence and being willing to receive answers, even if the answers hurt. Such an idea is usually called religion. It does not describe religion as the belief in the existence of gods or one God, and as a set of activities and institutions for the sake of relating oneself to these beings in thought, devotion and obedience. No one can deny that the religions which have appeared in history are religions in this sense. Nevertheless, religion in its innermost nature is more than religion in this narrower sense. It is the state of being concerned about one's own being and being universally.

5   There are many people who are ultimately concerned in this way who feel far removed, however, from religion in the narrower sense, and therefore from every historical religion. It often happens that such people take the question of the meaning of their life infinitely seriously and reject any historical religion just for this reason. They feel that the concrete religions fail to express their profound concern adequately. They are religious while rejecting the religions. It is this experience which forces us to distinguish the meaning of religion as living in the dimension of depth from particular expressions of one's ultimate concern in the symbols and institutions of a concrete religion. If we now turn to the concrete analysis of the religious situation of our time, it is obvious that our key must be the basic meaning of religion and not any particular religion, not even Christianity. What does this key disclose about the predicament of man in our period?

6   If we define religion as the state of being grasped by an infinite concern we must say: Man in our time has lost such infinite concern. And the resurgence of religion is nothing but a desperate and mostly futile attempt to regain what has been lost.

7   How did the dimension of depth become lost? Like any important event, it has many causes, but certainly not the one which one hears often mentioned from ministers' pulpits and evangelists' platforms, namely that a widespread impiety of modern man is responsible. Modern man is neither more pious nor more impious than man in any other period. The loss of the dimension of depth is caused by the relation of man to his world and to himself in our period, the period in which nature is being subjected scientifically and technically to the control of man. In this period, life in the dimension of depth is replaced by life in the horizontal dimension. The driving forces of the industrial society of which we are a part go ahead horizontally and not vertically. In popular terms this is expressed in phrases like "better and better," "bigger and bigger," "more and more." One should not disparage the feeling which lies behind such speech. Man is right in feeling that he is able to know and transform the world he encounters without a foreseeable limit. He can go ahead in all directions without a definite boundary.

8   A most expressive symbol of this attitude of going ahead in the horizontal dimension is the breaking through of the space which is controlled by the gravitational power of the earth into the world-space. It is interesting that one calls this world-space simply "space" and speaks, for instance, of space travel, as if every trip were not travel

into space. Perhaps one feels that the true nature of space has been discovered through our entering into indefinite world-space. In any case, the predominance of the horizontal dimension over the dimension of depth has been immensely increased by the opening up of the space beyond the space of the earth.

9   If we now ask what does man do and seek if he goes ahead in the horizontal dimension, the answer is difficult. Sometimes one is inclined to say that the mere movement ahead without an end, the intoxication with speeding forward without limits, is what satisfies him. But this answer is by no means sufficient. For on his way into space and time man changes the world he encounters. And the changes made by him change himself. He transforms everything he encounters into a tool; and in doing so he himself becomes a tool. But if he asks, a tool for what, there is no answer. One does not need to look far beyond everyone's daily experience in order to find examples to describe this predicament. Indeed our daily life in office and home, in cars and airplanes, at parties and conferences, while reading magazines and watching television, while looking at advertisements and hearing radio, are in themselves continuous examples of a life which has lost the dimension of depth. It runs ahead, every moment is filled with something which must be done or seen or said or planned. But no one can experience depth without stopping and becoming aware of himself. Only if he has moments in which he does not care about what comes next can he experience the meaning of this moment here and now and ask himself about the meaning of his life. As long as the preliminary, transitory concerns are not silenced, no matter how interesting and valuable and important they may be, the voice of the ultimate concern cannot be heard. This is the deepest root of the loss of the dimension of depth in our period—the loss of religion in its basic and universal meaning.

10   If the dimension of depth is lost, the symbols in which life in this dimension has expressed itself must also disappear. I am speaking of the great symbols of the historical religions in our Western world, of Judaism and Christianity. The reason that the religious symbols became lost is not primarily scientific criticism, but it is a complete misunderstanding of their meaning; and only because of this misunderstanding was scientific critique able, and even justified, in attacking them. The first step toward the non-religion of the Western world was made by religion itself. When it defended its great symbols, not as symbols, but as literal stories, it had already lost the battle. In doing so the theologians (and today many religious laymen) helped to transfer the powerful expressions of the dimension of depth into objects or happenings on the horizontal plane. There the symbols lose their power and meaning, and become an easy prey to physical, biological and historical attack.

11   If the symbol of creation which points to the divine ground of everything is transferred to the horizontal plane, it becomes a story of events in a removed past for which there is no evidence, but which contradicts every piece of scientific evidence. If the symbol of the Fall of Man, which points to the tragic estrangement of man and his world from their true being is transferred to the horizontal plane, it becomes a story of a human couple a few thousand years ago in what is now present-day Iraq. One of the most profound psychological descriptions of the general human predicament becomes an absurdity on the horizontal plane. If the symbols of the Savior and the salvation through Him which point to the healing power in history and personal life

are transferred to the horizontal plane, they become stories of a half-divine being coming from a heavenly place and returning to it. Obviously, in this form, they have no meaning whatsoever for people whose view of the universe is determined by scientific astronomy.

12   If the idea of God (and the symbols applied to Him) which expresses man's ultimate concern is transferred to the horizontal plane, God becomes a being among others whose existence or non-existence is a matter of inquiry. Nothing, perhaps is more symptomatic of the loss of dimension of depth than the permanent discussion about the existence or nonexistence of God—a discussion in which both sides are equally wrong, because the discussion itself is wrong and possible only after the loss of the dimension of depth.

13   When in this way man has deprived himself of the dimension of depth and the symbols expressing it, he then becomes a part of the horizontal plane. He loses his self and becomes a thing among things. He becomes an element in the process of manipulated production and manipulated consumption. This is now a matter of public knowledge. We have become aware of the degree to which everyone in our social structure is managed, even if one knows it and even if one belongs himself to the managing group. The influence of the gang mentality on adolescents, of the corporation's demands on the executives, of the conditioning of everyone by public communication, by propaganda and advertising under the guidance of motivation research, et cetera, have all been described in many books and articles.

14   Under these pressures, man can hardly escape the fate of becoming a thing among the things he produces, a bundle of conditioned reflexes without a free, deciding and responsible self. The immense mechanism, set up by man to produce objects for his use, transforms man himself into an object used by the same mechanism of production and consumption.

15   But man has not ceased to be man. He resists this fate anxiously, desperately, courageously. He asks the question, for what? And he realizes that there is no answer. He becomes aware of the emptiness which is covered by the continuous movement ahead and the production of means for ends which become means again without an ultimate end. Without knowing what has happened to him, he feels that he has lost the meaning of life, the dimension of depth.

16   Out of this awareness the religious question arises and religious answers are received or rejected. Therefore, in order to describe the contemporary attitude toward religion, we must first point to the places where the awareness of the predicament of Western man in our period is most sharply expressed. These places are the great art, literature and partly, at least, the philosophy of our time. It is both the subject matter and the style of these creations which show the passionate and often tragic struggle about the meaning of life in a period in which man has lost the dimension of depth. This art, literature, philosophy is not religious in the narrower sense of the word; but it asks the religious question more radically and more profoundly than most directly religious expressions of our time.

17   It is the religious question which is asked when the novelist describes a man who tries in vain to reach the only place which could solve the problem of his life, or a man who disintegrates under the memory of a guilt which persecutes him, or a man who

never had a real self and is pushed by his fate without resistance to death, or a man who experiences a profound disgust of everything he encounters.

18   It is the religious question which is asked when the poet opens up the horror and the fascination of the demonic regions of his soul, or if he leads us into the deserts and empty places of our being, or if he shows the physical and moral mud under the surface of life, or if he sings the song of transitoriness, giving words to the ever-present anxiety of our hearts.

19   It is the religious question which is asked when the playwright shows the illusion of life in a ridiculous symbol, or if he lets the emptiness of a life's work end in self-destruction, or if he confronts us with the inescapable bondage to mutual hate and guilt, or if he leads into the dark cellar of lost hopes and slow disintegration.

20   It is the religious question which is asked when the painter breaks the visible surface into pieces, then reunites them into a great picture which has little similarity with the world at which we normally look, but which expresses our anxiety and our courage to face reality.

21   It is the religious question which is asked when the architect, in creating office buildings or churches, removes the trimmings taken over from past styles because they cannot be considered an honest expression of our own period. He prefers the seeming poverty of a purpose-determined style to the deceptive richness of imitated styles of the past. He knows that he gives no final answer, but he does give an honest answer.

22   The philosophy of our time shows the same hiddenly religious traits. It is divided into two main schools of thought, the analytic and existentialist. The former tries to analyze logical and linguistic forms which are always used and which underlie all scientific research. One may compare them with the painters who dissolve the natural forms of bodies into cubes, planes and lines; or with those architects who want the structural "bones" of their buildings to be conspicuously visible and not hidden by covering features. This self-restriction produces the almost monastic poverty and seriousness of this philosophy. It is religious—without any contact with religion in its method—by exercising the humility of "learned ignorance."

23   In contrast to this school the existentialist philosophers have much to say about the problems of human existence. They bring into rational concepts what the writers and poets, the painters and architects, are expressing in their particular material. What they express is the human predicament in time and space, in anxiety and guilt and the feeling of meaninglessness. From Pascal in the seventeenth century to Heidegger and Sartre in our time, philosophers have emphasized the contrast between human dignity and human misery. And by doing so, they have raised the religious question. Some have tried to answer the question they have asked. But if they did so, they turned back to past traditions and offered to our time that which does not fit our time. Is it possible for our time to receive answers which are born out of our time?

24   Answers given today are in danger of strengthening the present situation and with it the questions to which they are supposed to be the answers. This refers to some of the previously mentioned major representatives of the so-called resurgence of religion, as for instance the evangelist Billy Graham and the counseling and healing minister, Norman Vincent Peale. Against the validity of the answers given by the former, one

must say, that in spite of his personal integrity, his propagandistic methods and his primitive theological fundamentalism fall short of what is needed to give an answer to the religious question of our period. In spite of all his seriousness, he does not take the radical questions of our period seriously.

25   The effect that Norman Peale has on large groups of people is rooted in the fact that he confirms the situation which he is supposed to help overcome. He heals people with the purpose of making them fit again for the demands of the competitive and conformist society in which we are living. He helps them to become adapted to the situation which is characterized by the loss of the dimension of depth. Therefore, his advice is valid on this level; but it is the validity of this level that is the true religious question of our time. And this question he neither raises nor answers.

26   In many cases the increase of church membership and interest in religious activities does not mean much more than the religious consecration of a state of things in which the religious dimension has been lost. It is the desire to participate in activities which are socially strongly approved and give internal and a certain amount of external security. This is not necessarily bad, but it certainly is not an answer to the religious question of our period. Is there an answer? There is always an answer, but the answer may not be available to us. We may be too deeply steeped in the predicament out of which the question arises to answer it. To acknowledge this is certainly a better way toward a real answer than to bar the way to it by deceptive answers. And it may be that in this attitude the real answer (within available limits) is given. The real answer to the question of how to regain the dimension of depth is not given by increased church membership or church attendance, nor by conversion or healing experiences. But it is given by the awareness that we have lost the decisive dimension of life, the dimension of depth, and that there is no easy way of getting it back. Such awareness is in itself a state of being grasped by that which is symbolized in the term, dimension of depth. He who realizes that he is separated from the ultimate source of meaning shows by this realization that he is not only separated but also reunited. And this is just our situation. What we need above all—and partly have—is the radical realization of our predicament, without trying to cover it up by secular or religious ideologies. The revival of religious interest would be a creative power in our culture if it would develop into a movement of search for the lost dimension of depth.

27   This does not mean that the traditional religious symbols should be dismissed. They certainly have lost their meaning in the literalistic form into which they have been distorted, thus producing the critical reaction against them. But they have not lost their genuine meaning, namely, of answering the question which is implied in man's very existence in powerful, revealing and saving symbols. If the resurgence of religion would produce a new understanding of the symbols of the past and their relevance for our situation, instead of premature and deceptive answers, it would become a creative factor in our culture and a saving factor for many who live in estrangement, anxiety and despair. The religious answer has always been the character of "in spite of." In spite of the loss of dimension of depth, its power is present, and most present in those who are aware of the loss and are striving to regain it with ultimate seriousness.

Suggestions for Discussion or Writing

1. What is Tillich's purpose in writing this essay? What is the "predicament of man generally"?

2. According to Tillich, what is the "dimension of depth"? How did this dimension of depth become lost?

3. Tillich defines two kinds of religion: religion in its "innermost nature": and in its "narrower sense." What are these two religions? How do they differ?

4. Tillich explains several "symbols" (space travel, creation) to advance his argument. What do these symbolize? How are the symbols interrelated?

5. Tillich says that people's awareness of their religious predicament is most "sharply expressed" in the art, literature, and "philosophy of our time." Do you agree? How do modern art, literature, and philosophy reflect people's attitudes toward all aspects of life? Give examples from your own experience with the arts including music, sculpture, painting, literature.

6. What solution does Tillich offer to the problem of the lost dimension in religion? Is his solution adequate? What solution do you offer?

7. How does this article relate to your own views about the state of religion and the current "predicament" of humanity?

Protestant

from *Lake Wobegon Days*

Garrison Keillor

Garrison Keillor (1942–) was born in Anoka, Minnesota. He has become well known for his radio program, "The Prairie Home Companion." His book Lake Wobegon Days *captures some of the humor, nostalgia, and delight of the program. The following selection is taken from his book.*

1   Our family was dirt poor, which I figured out as a child from the fact we had such a bad vacuum. When you vacuumed the living room, it would groan and stop and you had to sit and wait for it to groan and start up, then vacuum like mad before it quit again, but it didn't have good suction either. You had to stuff the hairballs into it. I also knew it because Donald Hoglund told me. He asked me how much my dad earned, and I said a thousand dollars, the most money I could imagine, and he shrieked,

"You're poor! You're poor!" So we were. And, in a town where everyone was either Lutheran or Catholic, we were neither one. We were Sanctified Brethren, a sect so tiny that nobody but us and God knew about it, so when kids asked what I was, I just said Protestant. It was too much to explain, like having six toes. You would rather keep your shoes on.

2   Grandpa Cotten was once tempted toward Lutheranism by a preacher who gave a rousing sermon on grace that Grandpa heard as a young man while taking Aunt Esther's dog home who had chased a Model T across town. He sat down on the church steps and listened to the voice boom out the open windows until he made up his mind to go in and unite with the truth, but he took one look from the vestibule and left. "He was dressed up like the pope of Rome," said Grandpa, "and the altar and the paintings and the gold candlesticks—my gosh, it was just a big show. And he was reading the whole darn thing off a page, like an actor."

3   Jesus said, "Where two or three are gathered together in my name, there am I in the midst of them," and the Brethren believed that was enough. We met in Uncle Al's and Aunt Flo's bare living room with plain folding chairs arranged facing in toward the middle. No clergyman in a black smock. No organ or piano, for that would make one person too prominent. No upholstery, it would lead to complacency. No picture of Jesus, He was in our hearts. The faithful sat down at the appointed hour and waited for the Spirit to move one of them to speak or to pray or to give out a hymn from our Little Flock Hymnal. No musical notation, for music must come from the heart and not off a page. We sang the texts to a tune that fit the meter, of the many tunes that we knew. The idea of reading a prayer was sacrilege to us—"If a man can't remember what he wants to say to God, let him sit down and think a little harder," Grandpa said.

4   "There's the Lord's Prayer," said Aunt Esther meekly. We were sitting on the porch after Sunday dinner. Esther and Harvey were visiting from Minneapolis and had attended Lake Wobegon Lutheran, she having turned Lutheran when she married him, a subject that was never brought up in our family.

5   "You call that prayer? Sitting and reciting like a bunch of school children?"

6   Harvey cleared his throat and turned to me with a weak smile. "Speaking of school, how are you doing?" he asked.

7   There was a lovely silence in the Brethren assembled on Sunday morning as we waited for the Spirit. Either the Spirit was moving someone to speak who was taking his sweet time or else the Spirit was playing a wonderful joke on us and letting us sit, or perhaps silence was the point of it. We sat listening to the rain on the roof, distant traffic, a radio playing from across the street, kids whizzing by on bikes, dogs barking, as we waited for the Spirit to inspire us. It was like sitting on the porch with your family, when nobody feels they have to make talk. So quiet in church. Minutes drifted by in silence that was sweet to us. The old Regulator clock ticked, the rain stopped and the room changed light as the sun broke through—shafts of brilliant sun through the windows and motes of dust falling through it—the smell of clean clothes and floor wax and wine and the fresh bread of Aunt Flo which was Christ's body given for us. Jesus in our midst, who loves us. So peaceful, and we loved each other too. I thought perhaps the Spirit was leading me to say that, but I was just a boy, and children were supposed to keep still. And my affections were not pure. They were tainted with a

sneaking admiration of Catholics—Catholic Christmas, Easter, and Living Rosary, and the Blessing of the Animals, all magnificent. Everything we did was plain, but they were regal and gorgeous—especially the Feast Day of St. Francis, which they did right out in the open, a feast for the eyes. Cows, horses, some pigs, right on the church lawn. The turmoil, animals bellowing and barking and clucking and cats scheming how to escape and suddenly leaping out of the girl's arms who was holding on tight, the cat dashing through the crowd, dogs straining at the leash, and the ocarina band of third-graders playing Catholic dirges, and the great calm of the sisters, and the flags, and the Knights of Columbus decked out in their handsome black suits—I stared at it until my eyes almost fell out, and then I wished it would go on much longer.

8   "Christians," my uncle Al used to say, "do not go in for show," referring to the Catholics. We were sanctified by the blood of the Lord, therefore we were saints, like St. Francis, but we didn't go in for feasts or ceremonies, involving animals or not. We went in for sitting, all nineteen of us, in Uncle Al's and Aunt Flo's living room on Sunday morning and having a plain meeting and singing hymns in our poor thin voices while not far away the Catholics were whooping it up. I wasn't allowed inside Our Lady, of course, but if the Blessing of the Animals on the Feast Day of St. Francis was any indication, I didn't know but what they had elephants in there and acrobats. I sat in our little group and envied them for the splendor and gorgeousness, as we tried to sing without even a harmonica to give us the pitch. Hymns, Uncle Al said, didn't have to be sung perfect, because God looks on the heart, and if you are In The Spirit, then all praise is good.

9   The Brethren, also known as the Saints Gathered in the Name of Christ Jesus, who met in the living room were all related to each other and raised in the Faith from infancy except Brother Mel who was rescued from a life of drunkenness, saved as a brand from the burning, a drowning sailor, a sheep on the hillside, whose immense red nose testified to his previous condition. I envied his amazing story of how he came to be with us. Born to godly parents, Mel left home at fifteen and joined the Navy. He sailed to distant lands in a submarine and had exciting experiences while traveling the downward path, which led him finally to the Union Gospel Mission in Minneapolis where he heard God's voice "as clear as my voice speaking to you." He was twenty-six, he slept under bridges and in abandoned buildings, he drank two quarts of white muscatel every day, and then God told him that he must be born again, and so he was, and he became the new Mel, except for his nose.

10   Except for his nose, Mel Burgess looked like any forty-year-old Brethren man: sober, preferring dark suits, soft-spoken, tending toward girth. His nose was what made you look twice: battered, swollen, very red with tiny purplish lines, it looked ancient and very dead on his otherwise fairly handsome face, the souvenir of what he had been saved from, the "Before" of his "Before . . . and After" advertisement for being born again.

11   For me, there was nothing before. I was born among the born-again. This living room so hushed, the Brethren in their customary places on folding chairs (the comfortable ones were put away on Sunday morning) around the end-table draped with a white cloth and the glass of wine and loaf of bread (unsliced) was as familiar to me as my mother and father, the founders of my life. I had always been here.

12   Our family sat in one row against the picture window. Al and Florence and their three, Janet and Paul and Johnny, sat opposite us, I saw the sky and the maple tree reflected in my uncle's glasses. To our left, Great-Aunt Mary sat next to Aunt Becky and Uncle Louie, and to our right were Grandma and Grandpa and Aunt Faith, and behind them was Mel, sitting on the piano bench. His wife, Rita, was a Lutheran. She only came occasionally and when she did, she stood out like a brass band. She used lipstick and had plucked eyebrows and wore bright hats. Brethren women showed only a faint smudge of powder on their cheeks and their hats were small and either black or navy blue. Once Rita spoke up in the meeting—Al had stood up to read from the Lord's Word, and she said, "Pardon me, which chapter did you say?"—and we all shuddered as if she had dropped a plate on the floor: *women did not speak in meeting.* Another time, Sunday morning, she made as if to partake of the bread as it was passed, and Grandpa snatched it away from her. It had to be explained to Rita later that she could not join in the Lord's Supper with us because she was not in fellowship.

13   We were "exclusive" Brethren, a branch that believed in keeping itself pure of false doctrine by avoiding association with the impure. Some Brethren assemblies, mostly in larger cities, were not so strict and broke bread with strangers—we referred to them as "the so-called Open Brethren," the "so-called" implying the shakiness of their position—whereas we made sure that any who fellowshipped with us were straight on all the details of the Faith, as set forth by the first Brethren who left the Anglican Church in 1865 to worship on the basis of correct principles. In the same year, they posed for a photograph: twenty-one bearded gentlemen in black frock coats, twelve sitting on a stone wall, nine standing behind, gazing solemnly into a sunny day in Plymouth, England, united in their opposition to the pomp and corruption of the Christian aristocracy.

14   Unfortunately, once free of the worldly Anglicans, these firebrands were not content to worship in peace but turned their guns on each other. Scholarly to the core and perfect literalists every one, they set to arguing over points that, to any outsider, would have seemed very minor indeed but which to them were crucial to the Faith, including the question: if Believer A is associated with Believer B who has somehow associated himself with C who holds a False Doctrine, must D break off association with A, even though A does not hold the Doctrine, to avoid the taint?

15   The correct answer is: Yes. Some Brethren, however, felt that D should only speak with A and urge him to break off with B. The brethren who felt otherwise promptly broke off with them. This was the Bedford Question, one of several controversies that, inside of two years, split the Brethren into three branches.

16   Once having tasted the pleasure of being Correct and defending True Doctrine, they kept right on and broke up at every opportunity, until, by the time I came along, there were dozens of tiny Brethren groups, none of which were speaking to any of the others.

17   Our Lake Wobegon bunch was part of a Sanctified Brethren branch known as the Cox Brethren, which was one of a number of "exclusive" Brethren branches—that is, to *non*-Coxians, we were known as "Cox Brethren"; to ourselves, we were simply *The* Brethren, the last remnant of the true Church. Our name came from Brother Cox in South Dakota who was kicked out of the Johnson Brethren in 1932—for preaching

the truth! So naturally my grandpa and most of our family went with Mr. Cox and formed the new fellowship.

18   The split with the Johnsons was triggered by Mr. Johnson's belief that what was abominable to God in the Old Testament must be abominable still, which he put forward at the Grace & Truth Bible Conference in Rapid City in 1932. Mr. Cox stood up and walked out, followed by others. The abomination doctrine not only went against the New Covenant of Grace principle, it opened up rich new areas of controversy in the vast annals of Jewish law. Should Brethren then refrain from pork, meat that God had labeled "Unclean"? Were we to be thrown into the maze of commandments laid out in Leviticus and Deuteronomy, where we are told to smite our enemies with the sword and stone to death rebellious children?

19   Mr. Johnson's sermon was against women's slacks, and he had quoted Deuteronomy 22:5, "The woman shall not wear that which pertaineth unto a man, neither shall a man put on a woman's garment: for all that do so are an abomination unto the Lord thy God," but Mr. Cox, though he was hardly pro-slacks, felt Mr. Johnson failed to emphasize grace as having superseded the law, and when Mr. Johnson said, "An abomination to God under the law is still an abomination to God under grace," Mr. Cox smelled the burning rubber of Error and stood up and marched. He and the other walkouts proceeded to a grove of trees and prayed for Mr. Johnson's soul, and Mr. Johnson and those seated inside did the same for them. The split was never repaired, though as a result of being thought in favor of slacks, the Cox Brethren became death on the subject. My mother never wore slacks, though she did dress my sister in winter leggins, which troubled Grandpa. "It's not the leggins so much as what they represent and what they could lead to," he told her. He thought that baby boys should not wear sleepers unless they were the kind with snaps up the legs. Mother pointed out that the infant Jesus was wrapped in swaddling clothes. "That doesn't mean he wore a dress," Grandpa said. "They probably wrapped his legs separately."[1]

20   Intense scholarship was the heart of the problem. We had no ordained clergy, believing in the priesthood of all believers, and all were exhorted to devote themselves to Bible study. Some did, Brother Louie and Brother Mel in particular. In Wednesday-night Bible reading, they carried the ball, and some nights you could see that the Coxes of Lake Wobegon might soon divide into the Louies and Mels.

[1]Brethren history is confusing, even to those of us who have heard a lot on the subject at a young age—the Dennis Brethren, for example: I have no idea whether they left us or we left them. Ditto the Reformed Sanctified, and the Bird Brethren, though I think that Sabbath observance was involved in our (i.e., the *Beale* Brethren, what we were called before 1932 when we Coxes left the Johnson wing) dispute with the Birds, who tended to be lax about such things as listening to the radio on Sunday and who went in for hot baths to an extent the Beales considered sensual. The Beale, or Cold Water, Brethren felt that the body was a shell or a husk that the spirit rode around in and that it needed to be kept in line with cold baths. But by the time I came along, we listened to the radio on Sunday and ran the bath hot, and yet we never went back and patched things up with the Birds. Patching up was not a Brethren talent. As my grandpa once said of the Johnson Brethren, "Anytime they want to come to us and admit their mistake, we're perfectly happy to sit and listen to them and then come to a decision about accepting them back." [Author's note]

21   One summer night, they set out to cover the issue of speaking in tongues, Louie arguing that the manifestation of the Spirit was to be sought earnestly, Mel holding that it was a miraculous gift given to the early Church but not given by God today. I forgot the Scripture verses each of them brought forward to defend his position, but I remember the pale faces, the throat-clearing, the anguished looks, as those two voices went back and forth, straining at the bit, giving no ground—the poisoned courtesy ("I think my brother is overlooking Paul's very *clear* message to the Corinthians. . . ," "Perhaps my brother needs to take a closer look, a *prayerful* look, at this verse in Hebrews . . . ") as the sun went down, neighbor children were called indoors, the neighbors turned out their lights, eleven o'clock came—they wouldn't stop!

22   "Perhaps," Grandpa offered, "it would be meet for us to pray for the Spirit to lead us," hoping to adjourn, but both Louis and Mel felt that the Spirit *had* led, that the Spirit had written the truth in big black letters—if only some people could see it.

23   The thought of Uncle Louie speaking in tongues was fascinating to me. Uncle Louie worked at the bank, he spoke to me mostly about thrift and hard work. What tongue would he speak? Spanish? French? Or would it sound like gibberish? Louie said that speaking in tongues was the true sign, that those who believed *heard* and to those who didn't it was only gabble—what if he stood up and said, "Feemalator, jasperator, hoo ha ha, Wamalamagamanama, zis boom bah!" and everyone else said, "Amen! That's right, brother! Praise God!" and *I was the only one who said, "Huh?"*

24   Bible reading finally ended when Flo went up to bed. We heard her crying in the bathroom. Al went up to comfort her. Grandpa took Louie aside in the kitchen. Mel went straight home. We all felt shaky.

25   It was soon after the tongues controversy that the Lake Wobegon Brethren folded their tent and merged with another Cox Assembly in St. Cloud, thirty-two miles away. Twenty-eight Brethren worshiped there, in a large bare rented room on the second floor of the bus depot. We had gone there for special meetings, revivals, and now we made the long drive every Sunday and every Wednesday night. Grandpa fought for this. "It is right for Brethren to join together," he said. Louie agreed. Mel didn't. He felt God had put us in Lake Wobegon to be a witness. But finally he gave in. "Think of the children," Grandpa said. One fear of Grandpa's was that we children would grow up and marry outside the Faith if only because we knew nobody in the Faith except for relatives. Faced with the lonely alternative, we'd marry a Lutheran, and then, dazzled by the splendid music and vestments and stained glass, we'd forsake the truth for that carnival down the street. Grandpa knew us pretty well. He could see us perk up on Sunday morning when the Lutheran organ pealed out at ten-thirty. The contrast between the church of Aunt Flo's living room and the power and glory of Lutheranism was not lost on him. Among other Brethren boys and girls, nature would take its course, and in due time, we'd find someone and make a Brethren family. Grandpa was looking to the future.

26   The shift to St. Cloud changed things, all right, but not all for the better.

27   My mother hated the move from the start. She had no Scripture to quote, only a feeling that we had taken a step away from the family, from ourselves. We had walked to Flo's house, we had sat in Sunday school class in her kitchen and celebrated the Lord's death in the living room. The bread we broke was bread Flo baked, and she

also made the wine, in a pickle crock in the basement. Flo's two cats, Ralph and Pumpkin, walked in and out of the service, and along toward the end, having confessed our unworthiness and accepted our redemption by Christ, the smell of Flo's pot roast, baking at low heat, arose to greet us. Before it was Flo's and Al's, the house had been Grandpa's and Grandma's—Mother had known this room since she was tiny, and though she bowed to Grandpa's wishes, she felt in her heart that she was leaving home. Sunday in St. Cloud meant a long drive, and she was a nervous rider who saw death at every turn. She arrived at the St. Cloud Assembly in a frazzled state. The second-floor room was huge and bare and held no associations for her. The long silences were often broken by the roar of bus engines and rumble of bus announcements downstairs. Waiting for the Spirit to guide us to a hymn, a prayer, a passage from Scripture, we heard, *"Now boarding at Gate One . . . Greyhound Bus service to Waite Park . . . St. Joseph . . . Collegeville . . . Avon . . . Albany . . . Freeport . . . Melrose . . . and Sauk Center. All aboard, please!"*

28   Whenever a special Bible study meeting was scheduled for Sunday afternoon at three, we couldn't drive home after morning meeting, have dinner, and get back to St. Cloud in time, so one Sunday our family traipsed over to a restaurant that a friend of Dad's had recommended, Phil's House of Good Food. The waitress pushed two tables together and we sat down and studied the menus. My mother blanched at the prices. A chicken dinner went for $2.50, the roast beef for $2.75. "It's a nice place," Dad said, multiplying the five of us times $2.50. "I'm not so hungry, I guess," he said, "Maybe I'll just have soup." We weren't restaurant goers—"Why pay good money for food you could make better at home?" was Mother's philosophy—so we weren't at all sure about restaurant custom: could, for example, a person who had been seated in a restaurant simply get up and walk out? Would it be proper? Would it be *legal?*

29   The waitress came and stood by Dad. "Can I get you something from the bar?" she said. Dad blushed a deep red. The question seemed to imply that he looked like a drinker. "No," he whispered, as if she had offered to take off her clothes and dance on the table. Then another waitress brought a tray of glasses to the table for four couples next to us. "Martini," she said, setting the drinks down, "whiskey sour, whiskey sour, Manhattan, whiskey sour, gin and tonic, martini, whiskey sour."

30   "Ma'am? Something from the bar?" Mother looked at her in disbelief.

31   Suddenly the room changed for us. Our waitress looked hardened, rough, cheap—across the room, a woman laughed obscenely, "Haw, haw, haw"—the man with her lit a cigarette and blew a cloud of smoke—a swear word drifted from the kitchen like a whiff of urine—even the soft lighting seemed suggestive, diabolical. To be seen in such a place on the Lord's Day—*what had we done?*

32   My mother rose from her chair. "We can't stay. I'm sorry," Dad told the waitress. We all got up and put on our coats. Everyone in the restaurant had a good look at us. A bald little man in a filthy white shirt emerged from the kitchen, wiping his hands. "Folks? Something wrong?" he said. "We're in the wrong place," Mother told him. Mother always told the truth, or something close to it.

33   "This is *humiliating,*" I said out on the sidewalk. "I feel like a *leper* or something. Why do we always have to make a big production out of everything? Why can't we be like regular people?"

34   She put her hand on my shoulder. "Be not conformed to this world," she said. I knew the rest by heart: " . . . but be ye transformed by the renewing of your mind, that ye may prove what is that good and acceptable and perfect will of God."

35   "Where we gonna eat?" Phyllis asked. "We'll find someplace reasonable," said Mother, and we walked six blocks across the river and found a lunch counter and ate sloppy joes (called Maid-Rites) for fifteen cents apiece. They did not agree with us, and we were aware of them all afternoon through prayer meeting and Young People's.

36   The Cox Brethren of St. Cloud held to the same doctrines as we did, but they were not so exclusive, more trusting of the world—for example, several families owned television sets. They kept them in their living rooms, out in the open, and on Sunday, after meeting and before dinner, the dad might say, "Well, I wonder what's on," knowing perfectly well what was on, and turn it on—a Green Bay Packers game—and watch it. On Sunday.

37   I ate a few Sunday dinners at their houses, and the first time I saw a television set in a Brethren house, I was dumbfounded. None of the Wobegonian Brethren had one; we were told that watching television was the same as going to the movies—*no,* in other words. I wondered why the St. Cloud people were unaware of the danger. You start getting entangled in the things of the world, and one thing leads to another. First it's television, then it's worldly books, and the next thing you know, God's people are sitting around drinking whiskey sours in dim smoky bars with waitresses in skimpy black outfits and their bosoms displayed like grapefruit.[2]

38   That was not my view but my parents'. "Beer is the drunkard's kindergarten," said Dad. Small things led to bigger ones. One road leads up, the other down. A man cannot serve two masters. Dancing was out, even the Virginia reel: it led to carnal desires. Card-playing was out, which led to gambling, though we did have Rook and Flinch—why those and not pinochle? "Because. They're different." No novels, which tended to glamorize iniquity. "How do you know if you don't read them?" I asked, but they *knew*. "You only have to touch a stove once to know it's hot," Mother said. (Which novel had she read? She wasn't saying.) Rock 'n' roll, jazz, swing, dance music, nightclub singing: all worldly. "How about Beethoven?" I asked, having heard something of his in school. "That depends," she said. "Was he a Christian?" I wasn't sure. I doubted he was.

39   On the long Sunday-night drive home, leaning forward from the back seat, I pressed them on inconsistencies like a little prosecutor: if dancing leads to carnal desire, how about holding hands? Is it wrong to put your arm around a girl? People

---

[2] Clarence Bunsen: "Most Brethren I knew were death on card-playing, and frowned on hand-holding, and of course they wouldn't go near a dance. They thought it brought out carnal desires. Well, maybe theirs lay closer to the surface, I don't know. Some were not only opposed to dancing but felt that marching in formation was wrong, so we called them the Left-Footed Brethren. Some others were more liberal, Mr. Bell for example, he thought cards were okay so long as you didn't play with a full deck. The Bijou used to show good movies but the Brethren and some Lutherans ganged up on Art and made him stop, so now you have to drive to St. Cloud if you want to see unmarried people together in one room with the door closed. It's a shame. I think if the church put in half the time on covetousness that it does on lust, this would be a better world for all of us." [Author's note]

gamble on football: is football wrong? Can you say "darn"? What if your teacher told you to read a novel? Or a short story? What if you were hitchhiking in a blizzard and were picked up by a guy who was listening to rock 'n' roll on the radio, should you get out of the car even though you would freeze to death? "I guess the smart thing would be to dress warmly in the first place," offered Dad. "And wait until a Ford comes along." All Brethren drove Fords.

Suggestions for Discussion or Writing

1. Who is Keillor's audience—members of the Brethren or nonmembers? Does it make a difference? Why?

2. What is the tone of the essay? Persuasive? Humorous? Ironic? Scholarly? How does Keillor achieve his tone?

3. Religious topics are somewhat sensitive to approach. How does Keillor avoid being sacrilegious? Does he succeed?

4. Does Keillor's religious heritage seem to have found the "lost dimension" mentioned in Tillich's article? Why or why not?

5. How does Keillor's religious view compare or contrast with your own?

Heaven and Earth in Jest

from *Pilgrim at Tinker Creek*

Annie Dillard

Poet and teacher Annie Dillard (1945–) earned her M.A. at Hollins College in 1968 and became a columnist and editor for Harper's *magazine. She taught poetry and creative writing before becoming a member of the U.S. Cultural Delegation to China and a member of the National Committee on U.S.–China Relations in 1982. She has written* Encounters with Chinese Writers *(1984) based on her experience with the Chinese. Some of her other writings include a poetry collection* Tickets for a Prayer Wheel *(1974), a nonfiction narrative* Holy the Firm *(1978), and* Memoirs: An American Childhood *(1987), and* The Writing Life *(1989). The essay "Heaven and Earth in Jest" is the first chapter of her Pulitzer Prize-winning* Pilgrim at Tinker Creek *(1974), a narrative on nature and life, after the manner of Henry David Thoreau's* Walden.

1   I used to have a cat, an old fighting tom, who would jump through the open window by my bed in the middle of the night and land on my chest. I'd half-awaken. He'd stick his skull under my nose and purr, stinking of urine and blood. Some nights he kneaded my bare chest with his front paws, powerfully, arching his back, as if sharpening his claws, or pummeling a mother for milk. And some mornings I'd wake in the daylight to find my body covered with paw prints in blood; I looked as though I'd been painted with roses.

2   It was hot, so hot the mirror felt warm. I washed before the mirror in a daze, my twisted summer sleep still hung about me like sea kelp. What blood was this, and what roses? It could have been the rose of union, the blood of murder, or the rose of beauty bare and the blood of some unspeakable sacrifice or birth. The sign on my body could have been an emblem or a stain, the keys to the kingdom or the mark of Cain. I never knew. I never knew as I washed, and the blood streaked, faded, and finally disappeared, whether I'd purified myself or ruined the blood sign of the passover. We wake, if we ever wake at all, to mystery, rumors of death, beauty, violence. . . . "Seem like we're just set down here," a woman said to me recently, "and don't nobody know why."

3   These are morning matters, pictures you dream as the final wave heaves you up on the sand to the bright light and drying air. You remember pressure, and a curved sleep you rested against, soft, like a scallop in its shell. But the air hardens your skin; you stand; you leave the lighted shore to explore some dim headland, and soon you're lost in the leafy interior, intent, remembering nothing.

4   I still think of that old tomcat, mornings, when I wake. Things are tamer now; I sleep with the window shut. The cat and our rites are gone and my life is changed, but the memory remains of something powerful playing over me. I wake expectant, hoping to see a new thing. If I'm lucky I might be jogged awake by a strange birdcall. I dress in a hurry, imagining the yard flapping with auks, or flamingos. This morning it was a wood duck, down at the creek. It flew away.

5   I live by a creek, Tinker Creek, in a valley in Virginia's Blue Ridge. An anchorite's hermitage is called an anchor-hold; some anchor-holds were simple sheds clamped to the side of a church like a barnacle to a rock. I think of this house clamped to the side of Tinker Creek as an anchor-hold. It holds me at anchor to the rock bottom of the creek itself and it keeps me steadied in the current, as a sea anchor does, facing the stream of light pouring down. It's a good place to live; there's a lot to think about. The creeks—Tinker and Carvin's—are an active mystery, fresh every minute. Theirs is the mystery of the continuous creation and all that providence implies: the uncertainty of vision, the horror of the fixed, the dissolution of the present, the intricacy of beauty, the pressure of fecundity, the elusiveness of the free, and the flawed nature of perfection. The mountains— Tinker and Brushy, McAfee's Knob and Dead Man—are a passive mystery, the oldest of all. Theirs is the one simple mystery of creation from nothing, of matter itself, anything at all, the given. Mountains are giant, restful, absorbent. You can heave your spirit into a mountain and the mountain will keep it, folded, and not throw it back as some creeks will. The creeks are the world with all its stimulus and beauty; I live there. But the mountains are home.

6   The wood duck flew away. I caught only a glimpse of something like a bright torpedo that blasted the leaves where it flew. Back at the house I ate a bowl of oatmeal; much later in the day came the long slant of light that means good walking.

7   If the day is fine, any walk will do; it all looks good. Water in particular looks its best, reflecting blue sky in the flat, and chopping it into graveled shallows and white chute and foam in the riffles. On a dark day, or a hazy one, everything's washed-out and lack-luster but the water. It carries its own lights. I set out for the railroad tracks, for the hill the flocks fly over, for the woods where the white mare lives. But I go to the water.

8   Today is one of those excellent January partly cloudies in which light chooses an unexpected part of the landscape to trick out in gilt, and then shadow sweeps it away. You know you're alive. You take huge steps, trying to feel the planet's roundness arc between your feet. Kazantzakis says that when he was young he had a canary and a globe. When he freed the canary, it would perch on the globe and sing. All his life, wandering the earth, he felt as though he had a canary on top of his mind, singing.

9   West of the house, Tinker Creek makes a sharp loop, so that the creek is both in back of the house, south of me, and also on the other side of the road, north of me. I like to go north. There the afternoon sun hits the creek just right, deepening the reflected blue and lighting the sides of trees on the banks. Steers from the pasture across the creek come down to drink; I always flush a rabbit or two there; I sit on a fallen trunk in the shade and watch the squirrels in the sun. There are two separated wooden fences suspended from cables that cross the creek just upstream from my tree-trunk bench. They keep the steers from escaping up or down the creek when they come down to drink. Squirrels, the neighborhood children, and I use the downstream fence as a swaying bridge across the creek. But the steers are there today.

10   I sit on the downed tree and watch the black steers slip on the creek bottom. They are all bred beef: beef heart, beef hide, beef hocks. They're a human product like rayon. They're like a field of shoes. They have cast-iron shanks and tongues like foam insoles. You can't see through to their brains as you can with other animals; they have beef fat behind their eyes, beef stew.

11   I cross the fence six feet above the water, walking my hands down the rusty cable and tightroping my feet along the narrow edge of the planks. When I hit the other bank and terra firma, some steers are bunched in a knot between me and the barbed-wire fence I want to cross. So I suddenly rush at them in an enthusiastic spirit, flailing my arms and hollering, "Lightning! Copperhead! Swedish meatballs!" They flee, still in a knot, stumbling across the flat pasture. I stand with the wind on my face.

12   When I slide under a barbed-wire fence, cross a field, and run over a sycamore trunk felled across the water, I'm on a little island shaped like a tear in the middle of Tinker Creek. On one side of the creek is a steep forested bank; the water is swift and deep on that side of the island. On the other side is the level field I walked through next to the steers' pasture; the water between the field and the island is shallow and sluggish. In summer's low water, flags and bulrushes grow along a series of shallow pools cooled by the lazy current. Water striders patrol the surface film, crayfish hump along the silt bottom eating filth, frogs shout and glare, and shiners and small bream hide among roots from the sulky green heron's eye. I come to this island every month

of the year. I walk around it, stopping and staring, or I straddle the sycamore log over the creek, curling my legs out of the water in winter, trying to read. Today I sit on dry grass at the end of the island by the lower side of the creek. I'm drawn to this spot. I come to it as an oracle; I return to it as a man years later will seek out the battlefield where he lost a leg or an arm.

13   A couple of summers ago I was walking along the edge of the island to see what I could see in the water, and mainly to scare frogs. Frogs have an inelegant way of taking off from invisible positions on the bank just ahead of your feet, in dire panic, emitting a froggy "Yike!" and splashing into the water. Incredibly, this amused me, and, incredibly, it amuses me still. As I walked along the grassy edge of the island, I got better and better at seeing frogs both in and out of the water. I learned to recognize, slowing down, the difference in texture of the light reflected from mudbank, water, grass, or frog. Frogs were flying all around me. At the end of the island I noticed a small green frog. He was exactly half in and half out of the water, looking like a schematic diagram of an amphibian, and he didn't jump.

14   He didn't jump; I crept closer. At last I knelt on the island's winterkilled grass, lost, dumbstruck, staring at the frog in the creek just four feet away. He was a very small frog with wide, dull eyes. And just as I looked at him, he slowly crumpled and began to sag. The spirit vanished from his eyes as if snuffed. His skin emptied and dropped; his very skull seemed to collapse and settle like a kicked tent. He was shrinking before my eyes like a deflating football. I watched the taut, glistening skin on his shoulders ruck, and rumple, and fall. Soon, part of his skin, formless as a pricked balloon, lay floating folds like bright scum on top of the water: it was a monstrous and terrifying thing. I gaped bewildered, appalled. An oval shadow hung in the water behind the drained frog; then the shadow glided way. The frog skin bag started to sink.

15   I had read about the giant water bug, but never had seen one. "Giant water bug" is really the name of the creature, which is an enormous, heavy-bodied brown beetle. It eats insects, tadpoles, fish and frogs. Its grasping forelegs are mighty and hooked inward. It seizes a victim with these legs, hugs it tight, and paralyzes it with enzymes injected during a vicious bite. That one bite is the only bite it ever takes. Through the puncture shoot the poisons that dissolve the victim's muscles and bones and organs— all but the skin—and through it the giant water bug sucks out the victim's body, reduced to a juice. This event is quite common in warm fresh water. The frog I saw was being sucked by a giant water bug. I had been kneeling on the island grass; when the unrecognizable flap of frog skin settled on the creek bottom, swaying, I stood up and brushed the knees of my pants. I couldn't catch my breath.

16   Of course, many carnivorous animals devour their prey alive. The usual method seems to be to subdue the victim by downing or grasping it so it can't flee, then eating it whole or in a series of bloody bites. Frogs eat everything whole, stuffing prey into their mouths with their thumbs. People have seen frogs with their wide jaws so full of live dragonflies they couldn't close them. Ants don't even have to catch their prey: in the spring they swarm over newly hatched, featherless birds in the nest and eat them tiny bite by bite.

17   That it's rough out there and chancy is no surprise. Every live thing is a survivor on a kind of extended emergency bivouac. But at the same time we are also created.

In the Koran, Allah asks, "The heaven and the earth and all in between, thinkest thou I made them *in jest?*" It's a good question. What do we think of the created universe, spanning an unthinkable void with an unthinkable profusion of forms? Or what do we think of nothingness, those sickening reaches of time in either direction? If the giant water bug was not made in jest, was it then made in earnest? Pascal uses a nice term to describe the notion of the creator's, once having called forth the universe, turning his back to it: *Deus Absconditus.* Is this what we think happened? Was the sense of it there, and God absconded with it, ate it, like a wolf who disappears round the edge of the house with the Thanksgiving turkey? "God is subtle," Einstein said, "but not malicious." Again, Einstein said that "nature conceals her mystery by means of her essential grandeur, not by her cunning." It could be that God has not absconded but spread, as our vision and understanding of the universe has spread, to a fabric of spirit and sense so grand and subtle, so powerful in a new way, that we can only feel blindly of its hem. In making the thick darkness a swaddling band for the sea, God "set bars and doors" and said, "Hitherto shalt thou come, but no further." But have we come even that far? Have we rowed out to the thick darkness, or are we all playing pinochle in the bottom of the boat?

18   Cruelty is a mystery, and the waste of pain. But if we describe a world to compass these things, a world that is a long, brute game, then we bump against another mystery: the inrush of power and light, the canary that sings on the skull. Unless all ages and races of men have been deluded by the same mass hypnotist (who?), there seems to be such a thing as beauty, a grace wholly gratuitous. About five years ago I saw a mockingbird make a straight vertical descent from the roof gutter of a four-story building. It was an act as careless and spontaneous as the curl of a stem or the kindling of a star.

19   The mockingbird took a single step into the air and dropped. His wings were still folded against his sides as though he were singing from a limb and not falling, accelerating thirty-two feet per second, through empty air. Just a breath before he would have been dashed to the ground, he unfurled his wings with exact, deliberate care, revealing the broad bars of white, spread his elegant white-banded tail, and so floated onto the grass. I had just rounded a corner when his insouciant step caught my eye; there was no one else in sight. The fact of his free fall was like the old philosophical conundrum about the tree that falls in the forest. The answer must be, I think, that beauty and grace are performed whether or not we will or sense them. The least we can do is try to be there.

20   Another time I saw another wonder: sharks off the Atlantic coast of Florida. There is a way a wave rises above the ocean horizon, a triangular wedge against the sky. If you stand where the ocean breaks on a shallow beach, you see the raised water in a wave is translucent, shot with lights. One late afternoon at low tide a hundred big sharks passed the beach near the mouth of a tidal river in a feeding frenzy. As each green wave rose from the churning water, it illuminated within itself the six- or eight-foot-long bodies of twisting sharks. The sharks disappeared as each wave rolled toward me; then a new wave would swell above the horizon, containing in it, like scorpions in amber, sharks that roiled and heaved. The sight held awesome wonders; power and beauty, grace tangled in a rapture with violence.

21   We don't know what's going on here. If these tremendous events are random combinations of matter run amok, the yield of millions of monkeys at millions of typewriters, then what is it in us, hammered out of those same typewriters, that they ignite? We don't know. Our life is a faint tracing on the surface of mystery, like the idle, curved tunnels of leaf miners on the face of a leaf. We must somehow take a wider view, look at the whole landscape, really see it, and describe what's going on here. Then we can at least wail the right question into the swaddling band of darkness, or, if it comes to that, choir the proper praise.

22   At the time of Lewis and Clark, setting the prairies on fire was a well-known signal that meant, "Come down to the water." It was an extravagant gesture, but we can't do less. If the landscape reveals one certainty, it is that the extravagant gesture is the very stuff of creation. After the one extravagant gesture of creation in the first place, the universe has continued to deal exclusively in extravagances, flinging intricacies and colossi down aeons of emptiness, heaping profusions of profilgacies with ever-fresh vigor. The whole show has been on fire from the word go. I come down to the water to cool my eyes. But everywhere I look I see fire; that which isn't flint is tinder, and the whole world sparks and flames.

23   I have come to the grassy island late in the day. The creek is up; icy water sweeps under the sycamore log bridge. The frog skin, of course, is utterly gone. I have stared at that one spot on the creek bottom for so long, focusing past the rush of water, that when I stand, the opposite bank seems to stretch before my eyes and flow grassily upstream. When the bank settles down I cross the sycamore log and enter again the big plowed field next to the steers' pasture.

24   The wind is terrific out of the west; the sun comes and goes. I can see the shadow on the field before me deepen uniformly and spread like a plague. Everything seems so dull I am amazed I can even distinguish objects. And suddenly the light runs across the land like a comber, and up the trees, and goes again in a wink: I think I've gone blind or died. When it comes again, the light, you hold your breath, and if it stays you almost forget about it until it goes again.

25   It's the most beautiful day of the year. At four o'clock the eastern sky is a dead stratus black flecked with low white clouds. The sun in the west illuminates the ground, the mountains, and especially the bare branches of trees, so that everywhere silver trees cut into the black sky like a photographer's negative of a landscape. The air and the ground are dry; the mountains are going on and off like neon signs. Clouds slide east as if pulled from the horizon, like a tablecloth whipped off a table. The hemlocks by the barbed-wire fence are flinging themselves east as though their backs would break. Purple shadows are racing east; the wind makes me face east, and again I feel the dizzying, drawn sensation I felt when the creek bank reeled.

26   At four-thirty the sky in the east is clear; how could that big blackness be blown? Fifteen minutes later another darkness is coming overhead from the northwest; and it's here. Everything is drained of its light as if sucked. Only at the horizon do inky black mountains give way to distant, lighted mountains—lighted not by direct illumination but rather paled by glowing sheets of mist hung before them. Now the blackness is in the east; everything is half in shadow, half in sun, every clod, tree, mountain, and hedge. I can't see Tinker Mountain through the line of hemlock, till it comes on like

a streetlight, ping, *ex nihilo*. Its sandstone cliffs pink and swell. Suddenly the light goes; the cliffs recede as if pushed. The sun hits a clump of sycamores between me and the mountains; the sycamore arms light up, and *I can't see the cliffs*. They're gone. The pale network of sycamore arms, which a second ago was transparent as a screen, is suddenly opaque, glowing with light. Now the sycamore arms snuff out, the mountains come on, and there are the cliffs again.

27   I walk home. By five-thirty the show has pulled out. Nothing is left but an unreal blue and a few banked clouds low in the north. Some sort of carnival magician has been here, some fast-talking worker of wonders who has the act backwards. "Something in this hand," he says, "something in this hand, something up my sleeve, something behind my back . . ." and abracadabra, he snaps his fingers, and it's all gone. Only the bland, blank-faced magician remains, in his unruffled coat, barehanded, acknowledging a smattering of baffled applause. When you look again the whole show has pulled up stakes and moved on down the road. It never stops. New shows roll in from over the mountains and the magician reappears unannounced from a fold in the curtain you never dreamed was an opening. Scarves of clouds, rabbits in plain view, disappear into the black hat forever. Presto chango. The audience, if there is an audience at all, is dizzy from head-turning, dazed.

28   Like the bear who went over the mountain, I went out to see what I could see. And, I might as well warn you, like the bear, all that I could see was the other side of the mountain: more of the same. On a good day I might catch a glimpse of another wooded ridge rolling under the sun like water, another bivouac. I propose to keep here what Thoreau called "a meteorological journal of the mind," telling some tales and describing some of the sights of this rather tamed valley, and exploring, in fear and trembling, some of the unmapped dim reaches and unholy fastnesses to which those tales and sights so dizzyingly lead.

29   I am no scientist. I explore the neighborhood. An infant who has just learned to hold his head up has a frank and forthright way of gazing about in bewilderment. He hasn't the faintest clue where he is, and he aims to learn. In a couple of years, what he will have learned instead is how to fake it: he'll have the cocksure air of a squatter who has come to feel he owns the place. Some unwonted, taught pride diverts us from our original intent, which is to explore the neighborhood, view the landscape, to discover at least *where* it is that we have been so startlingly set down, if we can't learn why.

30   So I think about the valley. It is my leisure as well as my work, a game. It is a fierce game I have joined because it is being played anyway, a game of both skill and chance, played against an unseen adversary—the conditions of time—in which the payoffs, which may suddenly arrive in a blast of light at any moment, might as well come to me as anyone else. I stake the time I'm grateful to have, the energies I'm glad to direct. I risk getting stuck on the board, so to speak, unable to move in any direction, which happens enough, God knows; and I risk the searing, exhausting nightmares that plunder rest and force me face down all night long in some muddy ditch seething with hatching insects and crustaceans.

31   But if I can bear the nights, the days are a pleasure. I walk out; I see something, some event that would otherwise have been utterly missed or lost; or something sees me, some enormous power brushes me with its clean wing, and I resound like a beaten bell.

32   I am an explorer, then, and I am also a stalker, or the instrument of the hunt itself. Certain Indians used to carve long grooves along the wooden shafts of their arrows. They called the grooves "lightning marks," because they resembled the curved fissure lightning slices down the trunks of trees. The function of lightning marks is this: if the arrow fails to kill the game, blood from a deep wound will channel along the lightning mark, streak down the arrow shaft and spatter to the ground, laying a trail dripped on broadleaves, on stones, that the barefoot and trembling archer can follow into whatever deep or rare wilderness it leads. I am the arrow shaft, carved along my length by unexpected lights and gashes from the very sky, and this book is the straying trial of blood.

33   Something pummels us, something barely sheathed. Power broods and lights. We're played on like a pipe; our breath is not our own. James Houston describes two young Eskimo girls sitting cross-legged on the ground, mouth on mouth, blowing by turns on each other's throat cords, making a low, unearthly music. When I cross again the bridge that is really the steers' fence, the wind has thinned to the delicate air of twilight; it crumples the water's skin. I watch the running sheets of light raised on the creek's surface. The sight has the appeal of the purely passive, like the racing of light under clouds on a field, the beautiful dream at the moment of being dreamed. The breeze is the merest puff, but you yourself sail headlong and breathless under the gale force of the spirit.

Suggestions for Discussion or Writing

1. Why has Dillard gone to Tinker Creek? What is her purpose in writing the book *Pilgrim at Tinker Creek*? Why might she choose the world "pilgrim" for her title?

2. Who is Dillard writing to? Does she have a specific audience in mind? What clues reveal her audience to you?

3. The first chapter, a kind of introduction to her book, contains many contrasting images such as the tom's bloody paw prints compared both to the "rose of union" and the "blood of murder" or the "rose of beauty bare" and the "blood of some unspeakable sacrifice or birth." What might be the significance of these contrasts between rose beauty and bloody sacrifice? What other opposites or contrasts do you notice? In what way do they reflect Dillard's purpose or main question?

4. Why does Dillard call her first chapter "Heaven and Earth in Jest"? How does this title reflect her fundamental concern about humankind or about life? How is Dillard's concern similar to Paul Tillich's in "The Lost Dimension in Religion"?

5. What view of the world and the people and things in it does Dillard take? Is she pessimistic? Optimistic? Awed? Some combination of these?

6. Notice that the essay is full of images of light and water. How does she use these images to build her main theme? Trace her use of water or light images.

Returning to Church

Dan Wakefield

Dan Wakefield was born in 1932 in Indianapolis. He graduated from Columbia University, becoming a journalist and freelance writer. He has been a contributing editor at Atlantic Monthly *since 1969. Wakefield has written* Between the Lines: A Reporter's Personal Journey through Public Events *(1966). His book* Starting Over *(1972) was made into a motion picture. He received a National Book Award nomination for* Going All the Way *(1970). Two more recent books,* Selling Out *(1986) and especially* Returning: A Spiritual Journey *(1988) are autobiographical.*

1   Just before Christmas of 1980, I was sitting in the Sevens, a neighborhood bar on Beacon Hill (don't all these stories of revelation begin in bars?), when a housepainter named Tony remarked out of the blue that he wanted to find a place to go to mass on Christmas Eve. I didn't say anything, but a thought came into my mind, as swift and unexpected as it was unfamiliar: *I'd like to do that, too.*

2   I had not gone to church since leaving my boyhood Protestant faith as a rebellious Columbia College intellectual more than a quarter-century before, yet I found myself that Christmas Eve in King's Chapel, which I finally selected from the ads on *The Boston Globe* religion page because it seemed least threatening. It was Unitarian, I knew the minister slightly as a neighbor, and I assumed "Candlelight Service" meant nothing more religiously challenging than carol singing.

3   As it happened, the Rev. Carl Scovel gave a sermon about "the latecomers" to the church on a text from an Evelyn Waugh novel called "Helena." I slunk down in my pew, literally beginning to shiver from what I thought was only embarrassment at feeling singled out for personal attention, and discomfort at being in alien surroundings. It turned out that I had a temperature of 102 that kept me in bed for three days with a violent case of the flu and a fearful suspicion that church was a very dangerous place, at least if you weren't used to it.

4   Perhaps my flesh was rebelling against this unaccustomed intrusion of spirit. Certainly going to church was out of character for me. My chosen public image was the jacket photo of "Starting Over," my novel about a divorced man seeking salvation through drugs, alcohol and promiscuity. I proudly posed for the picture in 1973 at my new living room bar, flanked by bottles of favorite vodkas, bourbons and burgundies. It did not look like the picture of a man who was headed to church.

5   In the year that led to my going to the Christmas Eve service, I felt I was headed for the edge of a cliff. I could have scored at the top of those magazine tests that list the greatest stresses in life, for that year saw the dissolution of a seven-year relationship with the woman I had fully expected to live with the rest of my life, I ran out of money, left the work I was doing, the house I owned, and the city I was living in, and attended the funeral of my father in May and my mother in November.

6   In the midst of this chaos, I one day grabbed an old Bible from among my books, and with a desperate instinct turned to the 23rd Psalm. It brought a sense of relief, and sometimes I recited it in my mind in the months that followed, but it did not give me any sense that I suddenly believed in God. It simply seemed an isolated source of solace and calm, such as any great poem might be. It certainly did not give rise to the notion of anything as radical as going to church.

7   After my Christmas Eve experience at King's Chapel, I didn't get up the nerve to go back again until Easter. I did not have any attacks of shivering or chills in the spring sunshine of that service, so it seemed that even as a "latecomer" and former avowed atheist, I could safely enter a place regarded as a house of God. Still, the prospect was discomforting. My two initial trips of return had been on major holidays, occasions when "regular" people went to church, simply in observance of tradition. To go back again meant crossing the Boston Common on a non-holiday Sunday morning wearing a suit and tie, a giveaway sign of churchgoing. I did it furtively, as if I were engaged in something that would not be approved of by my peers. I hoped they would all be home doing brunch and the Sunday papers, so I would not be "caught in the act." I recalled the remark of William F. Buckley Jr. in a television interview that if you mentioned God more than once at New York dinner parties, you aren't invited back.

8   To my surprise, I recognized neighbors and even some people I considered friends at church, on a "regular" Sunday. I had simply assumed I did not know people who went to church, yet here they were, with intellects intact, worshipping God. Once inside the church myself, I understood the appeal. No doubt my friends and neighbors found, as I did, relief and refreshment in connecting with age-old rituals, reciting psalms and singing hymns. There was a calm reassurance in the stately language of the litanies and chants of the Book of Common Prayer. (King's Chapel is "Unitarian in theology, Anglican in worship, and congregational in governance," a historical Boston amalgam that will be three centuries old next June.) I was grateful for the sense of shared reverence, of reaching beyond one's flimsy physical presence, while praying with a whole congregation.

9   I began to appreciate what was meant by the church as "sanctuary." The word itself took on new resonance for me; when I later heard of the "sanctuary" movement of New England churches offering shelter to Central American political refugees, I thought of the kind of private refuge that fortunate citizens like myself find in church from the daily assaults of business and personal pressures and worries, the psychic guerrilla warfare of everyday life.

10   Caught in an escalation of that kind of battle in my own professional campaigns (more painful because so clearly brought on by my own blundering), I joined the church in May 1982, not wanting to wait until the second Christmas Eve anniversary of my entry, as I had planned. I wanted the immediate sense of safety and refuge implied in belonging, being a member—perhaps like getting a passport and fleeing to a powerful embassy in the midst of some chaotic revolution.

11   Going to church, even belonging to it, did not solve life's problems—if anything, they seemed to intensify around this time—but it gave me a sense of living in a larger context, of being part of something greater than what I could see through the tunnel vision of my personal concerns. I now looked forward to Sunday because it *meant*

going to church; what once was strange now felt not only natural but essential. Even more remarkably, the practice of regular attendance at Sunday services, which such a short time ago seemed religiously "excessive," no longer seemed enough. Whatever it was I was getting from church on Sunday morning, I wanted—needed, it felt like—more of it.

12   I experienced what is a common phenomena for people who in some way or another begin a journey of the kind I so unexpectedly found myself on—a feeling simply and best described as a "thirst" for spiritual understanding and contact; to put it bluntly, I guess, *for God.* I noticed in the church bulletin an announcement of a Bible-study class in the parish house, and I went one stormy autumn evening to find myself with only the church's young seminarian on hand and one other parishioner. Rather than being disappointed by the tiny turnout, as I ordinarily would have been, I thought of the words "Where two or three are gathered together in My name, there am I in the midst of them," and I felt an interior glow that the pouring rain outside and occasional claps of thunder only made seem more vital and precious. I don't remember what text we studied that evening, but I can still smell the rain and the coffee and feel the aura of light and warmth.

13   Later in the season, I attended a Bible-study session the minister led for a gathering of about 20 people on the story of Abraham and Isaac, and I came away with a sense of the awesomeness and power of faith, a quality that loomed above me as tremendous and hard and challenging and tangibly real as mountains. The Bible-study classes, which I later, with other parishioners, learned to lead on occasion myself, became a source of power, like tapping into a rich vein.

14   Bible study was not like examining history, but holding up a mirror to my own life, a mirror in which I sometimes saw things I was trying to keep hidden, even from myself. The first scripture passage I was assigned to lead was from Luke, about the man who cleans his house of demons, and seven worse come. I did not have any trouble relating this to "contemporary life." It sounded unnervingly like an allegory about a man who had stopped drinking and was enjoying much better health, but took up smoking marijuana to "relax," all the while feeling good and even self-righteous about giving up the booze. It was my own story. I realized, with a shock, how I'd been deceiving myself, how much more "housecleaning" I had to do.

15   I was not only going to church and devoting time to Bible study and prayer during this period, I was actively engaged in purely secular programs of physical and mental therapy and "personal growth" to try to pull myself out of the pit I found myself in when I fled home to Boston in the spring of 1980. I got into an Exercycle and diet program that in six months cut my pulse rate from a dangerously stress-induced 120 to a healthy 60, and shed 20 pounds. I gave up the alcohol that I had used as regularly and purposely as daily medicine for 25 years, then gave up the marijuana that replaced it, and even threw away the faithful briar pipe I had clenched and puffed for a quarter of a century.

16   I used to worry about which of these addictions I kicked through "church" and which through secular programs, as if I had to assign proper "credit," and as if it were possible to compartmentalize and isolate the influence of God, like some kind of vitamin. The one thing I know about the deepest feeling connected with all my

assortment of life-numbing addictions is that at some point or other they felt as if they were "lifted," taken away, and instead of having to exercise iron control to resist them, it simply felt better not to have to do them anymore. The only concept I know to describe such experience is that of "grace," and the accompanying adjective "amazing" comes to mind along with it.

17   I do not for a moment suggest that giving up booze or even drugs, or losing weight or reducing the heart rate is necessarily—or even desirably—a byproduct of religious experience. For many people, such effects may not have anything to do with religion. Each person's quest is his own, with its own imperatives and directions.

18   I became fascinated by other people's spiritual experiences and, 30 years after it was first recommended to me, I read Thomas Merton's "The Seven Storey Mountain." I had avoided it even when the late poet Mark Van Doren, my favorite professor and Merton's former mentor at Columbia, had spoken of it with high regard, but now I devoured it, and went on to read everything else of Merton's I could get my hands on, from the sociopolitical "Conjectures of a Guilty Bystander" to the mystical "The Ascent to Truth." Most meaningful of all was a slim "meditation" by Merton, called "He Is Risen," which I found by chance in a New York bookstore; it says in matter-of-fact prose that Christ "is in history with us, walking ahead of us to where we are going. . . ."

19   I thought of these words walking the brick sidewalks of Beacon Hill, thinking for the first time of my life as a "journey" rather than a battle I was winning or losing that moment, on whose immediate crashing outcome the fate of the universe (i.e., the turbulent one in my own head) depended. I remembered years ago reading Dorothy Day's column in *The Catholic Worker* when I lived in Greenwich Village, and I appreciated now for the first time the sense of the title: "On Pilgrimage."

20   I cannot pinpoint any particular time when I suddenly believed in God again while all this was going on. I only know that such belief seemed as natural as for 25 or more years before it had been inconceivable. I realized this while looking at fish.

21   I had gone with my girlfriend of the last several years to the New England Aquarium, and as we gazed at the astonishingly brilliant colors of some of the small tropical fish—reds and yellows and oranges and blues that seemed to be splashed on by some innovative artistic genius—and watched the amazing lights of the flashlight fish that blinked on like the beacons of some creature of a sci-fi epic, I wondered how anyone could think that all this was the result of some chain of accidental explosions! Yet I realized in frustration that to try to convince me otherwise five years before would have been hopeless. Was this what they called "conversion"?

22   The term bothered me because it suggested being "born again," and like many of my contemporaries, I have been put off by what seems the melodramatic nature of that label, as well as the current political beliefs that seem to go along with it. Besides, I don't *feel* "reborn." No voice came out of the sky nor did a thunderclap strike me on the path through the Boston Common on the way to King's Chapel. I was relieved when our minister explained that the literal translation of "conversion" in both the Hebrew and Greek is not "rebirth" but "turning." That's what this has felt like—as if I were walking on one direction and then, in response to some inner pull, I turned—not even all the way around, but only at what seemed a slightly different angle.

23   I wish I could say that this turning has put me on a straight, solid path with blue skies above and a warm, benevolent sun shining down. I certainly enjoy better health than when I began to "turn" five years ago, but the path I am on now often seems as dangerous and as difficult as the one I was following before. Sometimes it doesn't even seem like a path at all. Sometimes I feel like a hapless passenger in the sort of small airplane they used to show in black and white movies of the 1930's, caught in a thunderstorm, bobbing through the night sky over jagged mountains without a compass.

24   I find strength in the hard wisdom of those who have delved much deeper into the spiritual realm than I, like Henri Nouwen, the Dutch Roman Catholic theologian who wrote in a book our minister recommended, called "Reaching Out," that ". . . it would be just another illusion to believe that reaching out to God will free us from pain and suffering. Often, indeed, it will take us where we would rather not go. But we know that without going there we will not find our life."

25   I was thrilled to meet Nouwen at lunch a few years ago, through the consideration of my friend and neighbor James Carroll, the former priest, now novelist. I told Father Nouwen I had read and appreciated his work, but that it dismayed me to read of his anguish in "Cry for Mercy: Prayers from the Genessee"; it made me wonder with discouragement what a chance a neophyte had in pursuit of the spiritual, when someone as advanced as Father Nouwen experienced anguish and confusion in his relation to God (I was neglecting numerous other, even more powerful examples, such as Jesus Christ calling out from the cross). Father Nouwen answered sharply that contrary to what many people may think, "Christianity is not for getting your life together!"

26   About a year ago, I felt as if finally, with God's help, I was on the right track in my own journey. Then I had an experience that was like running head-on into a wall. First, shock, then a kind of psychic pain as unrelenting as a dentist's drill. And in a torment I prayed, and there was no relief, and twice I turned back to my old way of dealing with things, by trying to numb the pain with drugs. Throughout all this, I never lost faith in God, never imagined He was not there, but only that His presence was obscured. Then the storm broke, like a fever, and I felt in touch again, and in the light. I was grateful, but I also knew such storms would come again, perhaps even more violently.

27   I learned that belief in God does not depend on how well things are going, that faith and good works do not necessarily have any correlation to earthly reward or even tranquility, no matter how much we wish they would and think they should. I believe in God because the gift of faith (if not the gift of understanding) has been given to me, and I go to church and pray and meditate to try to be closer to His presence, and, most difficult of all, to discern His will. I know, as it says in the Book of Common Prayer, that His "service is perfect freedom," and my great frustration and anxiety is in the constant choices of how best to serve, with the particular gifts as well as limitations I've been given.

28   A month or so ago, I went to Glastonbury Abbey, a Benedictine monastery in Hingham, only 40 minutes or so from Boston, to spend a day and night in private retreat. I went with about 17 questions in my head about following God or the path He

wills us to take. In the chapel bookstore, I saw a thin paperback volume, "Abandonment to Divine Providence," which I picked up, took to my room and devoured. It was written by an 18th-century Jesuit named Jean-Pierre de Caussade, and it sounds (at least in this new translation) as if it had been written yesterday, specifically to answer my questions. I continue to read in it almost every day, and I always find some new passage that seems to speak to the urgency of that moment. This is what I read today, when I felt again jarred and confused about what to choose and where to turn:

29   "So we follow our wandering paths, and the very darkness acts as our guide and our doubts serve to reassure us. The more puzzled Isaac was at not finding a lamb for the sacrifice, the more confidently did Abraham leave all to providence."

Suggestions for Discussion or Writing

1. Why does Wakefield find his desire to attend church puzzling?

2. What surprised him at his first positive experience at church?

3. What does he mean when he calls church a "sanctuary"?

4. What changes in his life style does Wakefield experience due to his interest in church?

5. Wakefield learned "that a belief in God does not depend on how well things are going." Why does he conclude that he believes in God?

The Three Hermits

translated by Louise and Aylmer Maude

Leo Tolstoy

Born in Yasnaya Polyand, Russia, Leo Tolstoy (1828–1910) was a Russian author and moral philosopher whose work treats moralistic themes. Tolstoy experienced a religious conversion in 1880 and became a great supporter of nonviolence. He is perhaps most famous for his chronicle of two families during the Napoleonic wars, War and Peace *(1869). His* Anna Karenina *(1877) tells of a woman destroyed by passions and society's hypocrisy. Among his other works are* The Death of Ivan Ilyitch *(1886) and* Resurrection *(1899), as well as a number of fine short stories.*

And in praying use not vain repetitions as the Gentiles do: for they think that
they shall be heard for their much speaking. Be not therefore like them, for
your Father knoweth what things ye have need of, before ye ask him.

Matthew 6:7, 8

1   A bishop was sailing from Archangel to the Solovétsk Monastery, and on the same
vessel were a number of pilgrims on their way to visit the shrines at that place.
The voyage was a smooth one. The wind favorable and the weather fair. The pilgrims
lay on deck, eating, or sat in groups talking to one another. The Bishop, too, came on
deck, and as he was pacing up and down he noticed a group of men standing near the
prow and listening to a fisherman, who was pointing to the sea and telling them
something. The Bishop stopped, and looked into the direction in which the man was
pointing. He could see nothing, however, but the sea glistening in the sunshine. He
drew nearer to listen, but when the man saw him, he took off his cap and was silent.
The rest of the people also took off their caps and bowed.

2   "Do not let me disturb you, friends," said the Bishop. "I came to hear what this
good man was saying."

3   "This fisherman was telling us about the hermits," replied one, a tradesman, rather
bolder than the rest.

4   "What hermits?" asked the Bishop, going to the side of the vessel and seating
himself on a box. "Tell me about them. I should like to hear. What were you pointing at?"

5   "Why, that little island you can just see over there," answered the man, pointing
to a spot ahead and a little to the right. "That is the island where the hermits live for
the salvation of their souls."

6   "Where is the island?" asked the Bishop. "I see nothing."

7   "There, in the distance, if you please look along my hand. Do you see that little
cloud? Below it, and a bit to the left, there is just a faint streak. That is the island."

8   The Bishop looked carefully, but his unaccustomed eyes could make out nothing
but the water shimmering in the sun.

9   "I cannot see it," he said, "But who are the hermits that live there?"

10   "They are holy men," answered the fisherman. "I had long heard tell of them, but
never chanced to see them myself till the year before last."

11   And the fisherman related how once, when he was out fishing he had been stranded
at night upon that island, not knowing where he was. In the morning, as he wandered
about the island, he came across an earth hut, and met an old man standing near it.
Presently two others came out, and after having fed him and dried his things, they
helped him mend his boat.

12   "And what are they like?" asked the Bishop.

13   "One is a small man and his back is bent. He wears a priest's cassock and is very
old; he must be more than a hundred, I should say. He is so old that the white of his
beard is taking a greenish tinge, but he is always smiling, and his face is as bright as
an angel's from heaven. The second is taller, but he also is very old. He wears a tattered
peasant coat. His beard is broad, and of a yellowish grey color. He is a strong man.
Before I had time to help him, he turned my boat over as if it were only a pail. He too
is kindly and cheerful. The third is tall, and has a beard as white as snow and reaching

to his knees. He is stern, with overhanging eyebrows; and he wears nothing but a piece of matting tied around his waist."

14   "And did they speak to you?" asked the Bishop.

15   "For the most part they did everything in silence, and spoke but little even to one another. One of them would just give a glance, and the other would understand him. I asked the tallest whether they had lived there long. He frowned, and muttered something as if he were angry, but the oldest one took his hand and smiled, and then the tall one was quiet. The oldest one only said: 'Have mercy upon us,' and smiled."

16   While the fisherman was talking, the ship had drawn nearer to the island.

17   "There, now you can see it plainly, if your Lordship will please to look," said the tradesman, pointing with his hand.

18   The Bishop looked, and now he really saw a dark streak—which was the island. Having looked at it a while, he left the prow of the vessel, and going to the stern, asked the helmsman:

19   "What island is that?"

20   "That one," replied the man, "has no name. There are many such in this sea."

21   "Is it true that there are hermits who live there for the salvation of their souls?"

22   "So it is said, your Lordship, but I don't know if it's true. Fishermen say they have seen them; but of course they may only be spinning yarns."

23   "I should like to land on the island and see those men," said the Bishop. "How could I manage it?"

24   "The ship cannot get close to the island," replied the helmsman, "but you might be rowed there in a boat. You had better speak to the captain."

25   The captain was sent for and came.

26   "I should like to see these hermits," said the Bishop. "Could I not be rowed ashore?"

27   The captain tried to dissuade him.

28   "Of course it could be done," said he, "but we should lose much time. And if I may venture to say so to your Lordship, the old men are not worth your pains. I have heard say that they are foolish old fellows, who understand nothing, and never speak a word, any more than the fish in the sea."

29   "I wish to see them," said the Bishop, "and I will pay you for your trouble and loss of time. Please let me have a boat."

30   There was no help for it, so the order was given. The sailors trimmed the sails, the steersman put up the helm, and the ship's course was set for the island. A chair was placed at the prow for the Bishop, and he sat there, looking ahead. The passengers all collected at the prow, and gazed at the island. Those who had the sharpest eyes could presently make out the rocks on it, and then a mud hut was seen. At last one man saw the hermits themselves. The captain brought a telescope and, after looking through it, handed it to the Bishop.

31   "It's right enough. There are three men standing on the shore. There, a little to the right of that big rock."

32   The Bishop took the telescope, got it into position, and saw the three men: a tall one, a shorter one, and one very small and bent, standing on the shore and holding each other by the hand.

33   The captain turned to the Bishop.

34   "The vessel can get no nearer than this, your Lordship. If you wish to go ashore, we must ask you to go in the boat, while we anchor here."

35   The cable was quickly let out; the anchor cast, and the sails furled. There was a jerk, and the vessel shook. Then, a boat having been lowered, the oarsmen jumped in, and the Bishop descended the ladder and took his seat. The men pulled at their oars and the boat moved rapidly towards the island. When they came within a stone's throw, they saw three old men: a tall one with only a piece of matting tied round his waist, a shorter one in a tattered peasant coat, and a very old one bent with age and wearing an old cassock—all three standing hand in hand.

36   The oarsmen pulled in to the shore, and held on with the boathook while the Bishop got out.

37   The old men bowed to him, and he gave them his blessing, at which they bowed still lower. Then the Bishop began to speak to them.

38   "I have heard," he said, "that you, godly men, live here saving your own souls and praying to our Lord Christ for your fellow men. I, an unworthy servant of Christ, am called, by God's mercy, to keep and teach His flock. I wished to see you, servants of God, and to do what I can to teach you, also."

39   The old men looked at each other smiling, but remained silent.

40   "Tell me," said the Bishop, "what you are doing to save your souls, and how you serve God on this island."

41   The second hermit sighed, and looked at the oldest, the very ancient one. The latter smiled, and said:

42   "We do not know how to serve God. We only serve and support ourselves, servant of God."

43   "But how do you pray to God?" asked the Bishop.

44   "We pray in this way," replied the hermit, "Three are ye, three are we, have mercy on us."

45   And when the old man said this, all three raised their eyes to heaven, and repeated:

46   "Three are ye, three are we, have mercy on us!"

47   The Bishop smiled.

48   "You have evidently heard something about the Holy Trinity," said he. "But you do not pray aright. You have won my affection, godly men. I see you wish to please the Lord, but you do not know how to serve Him. That is not the way to pray; but listen to me, and I will teach you. I will teach you, not a way of my own, but the way in which God in the Holy Scriptures has commanded all men to pray to Him."

49   And the Bishop began explaining to the hermits how God had revealed Himself to men; telling them of God the Father, and God the Son, and God the Holy Ghost.

50   "God the Son came down on earth," said he, "to save men, and this is how He taught us all to pray. Listen, and repeat after me: 'Our Father.'"

51   And the first old man repeated after him, "Our Father," and the second said, "Our Father," and the third said, "Our Father."

52   "Which art in heaven," continued the Bishop.

53   The first hermit repeated, "Which art in heaven," but the second blundered over the words, and the tall hermit could not say them properly. His hair had grown over

his mouth so that he could not speak plainly. The very old hermit, having no teeth, also mumbled indistinctly.

54   The Bishop repeated the words again, and the old men repeated them after him. The Bishop sat down on a stone, and the old men stood before him, watching his mouth, and repeating the words as he uttered them. And all day long the Bishop labored, saying a word twenty, thirty, a hundred times over, and the old men repeated it after him. They blundered, and he corrected them, and made them begin again.

55   The Bishop did not leave off till he had taught them the whole of the Lord's Prayer so that they could not only repeat it after him, but could say it by themselves. The middle one was the first to know it, and to repeat the whole of it alone. The Bishop made him say it again and again, and at last the others could say it too.

56   It was getting dark and the moon was appearing over the water, before the Bishop rose to return to the vessel. When he took leave of the old men they all bowed down to the ground before him. He raised them, and kissed each one of them, telling them to pray as he had taught them. Then he got into the boat and returned to the ship.

57   And as he sat in the boat and was rowed to the ship he could hear the three voices of the hermits loudly repeating the Lord's Prayer. As the boat drew near the vessel their voices could no longer be heard, but they could still be seen in the moonlight, standing as he had left them on the shore, the shortest in the middle, the tallest on the right, the middle one on the left. As soon as the Bishop had reached the vessel and got on board, the anchor was weighed and the sails unfurled. The wind filled them and the ship sailed away, and the Bishop took a seat in the stern and watched the island they had left. For a time he could still see the hermits, but presently they disappeared from sight, though the island was still visible. At last it too vanished, and only the sea was to be seen, rippling in the moonlight.

58   The pilgrims lay down to sleep, and all was quiet on deck. The Bishop did not wish to sleep, but sat alone at the stern, gazing at the sea where the island was no longer visible, and thinking of the good old men. He thought how pleased they had been to learn the Lord's Prayer; and he thanked God for having sent him to teach and help such godly men.

59   So the Bishop sat, thinking, and gazing at the sea where the island had disappeared. And the moonlight flickered before his eyes, sparkling, now here, now there, upon the waves. Suddenly he saw something white and shining, on the bright path which the moon cast across the sea. Was it a seagull, or the little gleaming sail of some small boat? The Bishop fixed his eyes on it, wondering.

60   "It must be a boat sailing after us," thought he, "but it is overtaking us very rapidly. It was far, far away a minute ago, but now it is much nearer. It cannot be a boat, for I can see no sail; but whatever it may be, it is following us and catching us up."

61   And he could not make out what it was. Not a boat, nor a bird, nor a fish! It was too large for a man, and besides a man could not be out there in the midst of the sea. The Bishop rose, and said to the helmsman:

62   "Look there, what is that, my friend? What is it?" the Bishop repeated, though he could now see plainly what it was—the three hermits running upon the water, all gleaming white, their grey beards shining, and approaching the ship as quickly as though it were not moving.

63   The steersman looked, and let go the helm in terror.

64   "Oh, Lord! The hermits are running after us on the water as though it were dry land!"

65   The passengers, hearing him, jumped up and crowded to the stern. They saw the hermits coming along hand in hand, and the two outer ones beckoning the ship to stop. All three were gliding along upon the water without moving their feet. Before the ship could be stopped, the hermits had reached it, and raising their heads, all three as with one voice, began to say:

66   "We have forgotten your teaching, servant of God. As long as we kept repeating it we remembered, but when we stopped saying it for a time, a word dropped out, and now it has all gone to pieces. We can remember nothing of it. Teach us again."

67   The Bishop crossed himself, and leaning over the ship's side, said:

68   "Your own prayer will reach the Lord, men of God. It is not for me to teach you. Pray for us sinners."

69   And the Bishop bowed low before the old men; and they turned and went back across the sea. And a light shone until daybreak on the spot where they were lost to sight.

Suggestions for Discussion or Writing

1. Tolstoy quotes Matthew 6:7, 8 before he begins his story. What relationship does this scripture have to the theme of the story?

2. The fisherman describes each of the three hermits' physical natures to the Bishop. Later, when the Bishop is rowed ashore to see the hermits, their basic descriptions are repeated. What is the significance of each description? Why do the three hermits stand hand in hand? Do you think it is significant that there are three hermits? Why?

3. Why does the Bishop teach the hermits the Lord's Prayer? How does this prayer differ from the one the hermits always used?

4. As the hermits come gliding over the ocean toward the ship, the steersman cries out, "Oh, Lord! The hermits are running after us on the water as though it were dry land!" What biblical incident do these lines allude to?

5. Why, when the three hermits ask the Bishop to reteach them the Lord's Prayer, does the Bishop reply, "Your own prayer will reach the Lord, men of God. It is not for me to teach you. Pray for us sinners"? Why does the Bishop treat the hermits differently now? What does the Bishop learn from the three hermits?

Salvation

Langston Hughes

Called the "poet laureate of Harlem," James Langston Hughes (1902–1967)
was born in Joplin, Missouri. He earned his B.A. from Lincoln University
(1929) and received a Guggenheim fellowship for creative work in 1935. His
first collection of poetry, The Weary Blues, *was published in 1926.* The Best
of Simple *(1961) is a series of humorous sketches of black life based on the*
experiences of the fictional character Jesse B. Semple. Hughes' other writing
includes novels, short stories, autobiographies, and juvenile books. He is
also the author of several nonfiction works including A Pictorial History of
the Negro in America *(1956),* Fight for Freedom: The Story of the NAACP
(1962) and Black Misery *(1969). He received the 1960 Spingam Medal which*
is awarded yearly to the African American who has achieved the most in his or
her field.

1   I was saved from sin when I was going on thirteen. But not really saved. It happened like this. There was a big revival at my Auntie Reed's church. Every night for weeks there had been much preaching, singing, praying, and shouting, and some very hardened sinners had been brought to Christ, and the membership of the church had grown by leaps and bounds. Then just before the revival ended, they held a special meeting for children, "to bring the young lambs to the fold." My aunt spoke of it for days ahead. That night I was escorted to the front row and placed on the mourners' bench with all the other young sinners, who had not yet been brought to Jesus.

2   My aunt told me that when you were saved you saw a light, and something happened to you inside! And Jesus came into your life! And God was with you from then on! She said you could see and hear and feel Jesus in your soul. I believed her. I had heard a great many old people say the same thing and it seemed to me they ought to know. So I sat there calmly in the hot, crowded church, waiting for Jesus to come to me.

3   The preacher preached a wonderful rhythmical sermon, all moans and shouts and lonely cries and dire pictures of hell, and then he sang a song about the ninety and nine safe in the fold, but one little lamb was left out in the cold. Then he said, "Won't you come? Won't you come to Jesus? Young lambs, won't you come?" And he held out his arms to all us young sinners there on the mourners' bench. And the little girls cried. And some of them jumped up and went to Jesus right away. But most of us just sat there.

4   A great many old people came and knelt around us and prayed, old women with jet-black faces and braided hair, old men with work-gnarled hands. And the church sang a song about the lower lights are burning, some poor sinners to be saved. And the whole building rocked with prayer and song.

5   Still I kept waiting to *see* Jesus.

6   Finally all the young had gone to the altar and were saved, but one boy and me.

He was a rounder's son named Westley. Westley and I were surrounded by sisters and deacons praying. It was very hot in the church, and getting late now. Finally Westley said to me in a whisper: "God damn! I'm tired o' sitting here. Let's get up and be saved." So he got up and was saved.

7   Then I was left all alone on the mourners' bench. My aunt came and knelt at my knees and cried, while prayers and songs swirled all around me in the little church. The whole congregation prayed for me alone, in a mighty wail of moans and voices. And I kept waiting serenely for Jesus, waiting, waiting—but he didn't come. I wanted to see him, but nothing happened to me. Nothing! I wanted something to happen to me, but nothing happened.

8   I heard the songs and the minister saying: "Why don't you come? My dear child, why don't you come to Jesus? Jesus is waiting for you. He wants you. Why don't you come? Sister Reed, what is this child's name?"

9   "Langston," my aunt sobbed.

10   "Langston, why don't you come? Why don't you come and be saved? Oh, Lamb of God! Why don't you come?"

11   Now it was really getting late. I began to be ashamed of myself, holding up everything for so long. I began to wonder what God thought about Westley, who certainly hadn't seen Jesus either, but who was now sitting proudly on the platform, swinging his knickerbockered legs and grinning down at me, surrounded by deacons and old women on their knees praying. God had not struck Westley dead for taking his name in vain or for lying in the temple. So I decided that maybe to save further trouble, I'd better lie, too, and say that Jesus had come, and get up and be saved.

12   So I got up.

13   Suddenly the whole room broke into a sea of shouting, as they saw me rise. Waves of rejoicing swept the place. Women leaped in the air. My aunt threw her arms around me. The minister took me by the hand and led me to the platform.

14   When things quieted down, in a hushed silence, punctuated by a few ecstatic "Amens," all the new young lambs were blessed in the name of God. Then joyous singing filled the room.

15   That night, for the last time in my life but one—for I was a big boy twelve years old—I cried. I cried, in bed alone, and couldn't stop. I buried my head under the quilts, but my aunt heard me. She woke up and told my uncle I was crying because the Holy Ghost had come into my life, and because I had seen Jesus. But I was really crying because I couldn't bear to tell her that I had lied, that I had deceived everybody in the church, and I hadn't seen Jesus, and that now I didn't believe there was a Jesus any more, since he didn't come to help me.

Suggestions for Discussion or Writing

1. Why are pressures to stand up and be saved put on Hughes during the revival meeting? What did young Hughes expect to happen when he was "saved"? Were his expectations unrealistic? Why? How did he develop his expectations? What evidence have you seen to show that children often understand religious experiences differently from adults?

2. How do Westley's and Aunt Reed's attitudes toward the religious "conversion" differ from Hughes' attitude? What do their attitudes reveal about their personalities? What does Hughes' attitude reveal about his personality?

3. What is the basic conflict experienced by the narrator? Does his conflict raise any questions or conflicts in your own mind? If so, what are they?

4. Hughes uses the metaphor of an ocean in the thirteenth paragraph to describe the church and the people within. What words help develop this metaphor? What does the metaphor tell you about the feelings of the people within the church, particularly Hughes' feelings?

5. Have you ever been pressured by parents or friends to accept certain values or beliefs? How did you react?

6. As a result of his "conversion" experience, Hughes becomes disillusioned with religion, saying "I didn't believe there was a Jesus any more." Have you ever become disillusioned with something you'd previously accepted? What part does disillusionment with adults and society play in the growth from child to adult?

Young Goodman Brown

Nathaniel Hawthorne

Early American author Nathaniel Hawthorne (1804–1863) came from a long line of Puritan ancestors, including a judge at the Salem witchcraft trials. Born in Salem himself, he was educated at Bowdoin College, where he became friends with Henry Wadsworth Longfellow and Franklin Pierce who, as a U.S. president, later appointed him to the U.S. Consulate in Liverpool. As a result of his appointment, Hawthorne traveled extensively in England and Italy. His last major work, Our Old Home *(1863), is based on these European travels. He is well known for a number of his early works including* Twice-Told Tales *(1837),* The Scarlet Letter *(1850), and* The House of the Seven Gables *(1852). Hawthorne's preoccupation with the tension between good and evil is the focus of many of his novels and short stories, including "Young Goodman Brown."*

1   Young Goodman Brown came forth at sunset into the street at Salem village; but put his head back, after crossing the threshold, to exchange a parting kiss with his young wife. And Faith, as the wife was aptly named, thrust her own pretty head into the street, letting the wind play with the pink ribbons of her cap while she called to Goodman Brown.

2   "Dearest heart," whispered she, softly and rather sadly, when her lips were close to his ear, "prithee put off your journey until sunrise and sleep in your own bed to-night. A lone woman is troubled by such dreams and such thoughts that she's afeared of herself sometimes. Pray tarry with me this night, dear husband, of all nights in the year."

3   "My love and my Faith," replied young Goodman Brown, "of all nights in the year, this one must I tarry away from thee. My journey, as thou callest it, forth and back again, must needs be done 'twixt now and sunrise. What, my sweet, pretty wife, dost thou doubt me already, and we have but three months married?"

4   "Then God bless you!" said Faith, with the pink ribbons; "and may you find all well when you come back."

5   "Amen!" cried Goodman Brown. "Say thy prayers, dear Faith, and go to bed at dusk, and no harm will come to thee."

6   So they parted; and the young man pursued his way until, being about to turn the corner by the meeting-house, he looked back and saw the head of Faith still peeping after him with a melancholy air, in spite of her pink ribbons.

7   "Poor little Faith!" thought he, for his heart smote him. "What a wretch am I to leave her on such an errand! She talks of dreams, too. Methought as she spoke there was trouble in her face, as if a dream had warned her what work is to be done to-night. But no, no; 'twould kill her to think it. Well, she's a blessed angel on earth; and after this one night I'll cling to her skirts and follow her to heaven."

8   With this excellent resolve for the future, Goodman Brown felt himself justified in making more haste on his present evil purpose. He had taken a dreary road, darkened by all the gloomiest trees of the forest, which barely stood aside to let the narrow path creep through, and closed immediately behind. It was all as lonely as could be; and there is this peculiarity in such a solitude, that the traveller knows not who may be concealed by the innumerable trunks and thick boughs overhead; so that with only footsteps he may yet be passing through an unseen multitude.

9   "There may be a devilish Indian behind every tree," said Goodman Brown to himself; and he glanced fearfully behind him as he added, "What if the devil himself should be at my very elbow!"

10   His head being turned back, he passed a crook of the road, and, looking forward again, beheld the figure of a man, in grave and decent attire, seated at the foot of an old tree. He arose at Goodman Brown's approach and walked onward side by side with him.

11   "You are late, Goodman Brown," said he. "The clock of the Old South was striking as I came through Boston, and that is full fifteen minutes agone."

12   "Faith kept me back a while," replied the young man, with a tremor in his voice, caused by the sudden appearance of his companion, though it was not wholly unexpected.

13   It was now deep dusk in the forest, and deepest in that part of it where these two were journeying. As nearly as could be discerned, the second traveller was about fifty years old, apparently in the same rank of life as Goodman Brown, and bearing a considerable resemblance to him, though perhaps more in expression than features. Still, they might have been taken for father and son. And yet, though the elder person was as simply clad as the younger, and as simple in manner, too, he had an indescribable air of one who knew the world, and who would not have felt abashed at the

governor's dinner table or in King William's court, were it possible that his affairs should call him thither. But the only thing about him that could be fixed upon as remarkable was his staff, which bore the likeness of a great black snake, so curiously wrought that it might almost be seen to twist and wriggle itself like a living serpent. This, of course, must have been an ocular deception, assisted by the uncertain light.

14   "Come, Goodman Brown," cried his fellow-traveller, "this is a dull place for the beginning of a journey. Take my staff if you are so soon weary."

15   "Friend," said the other, exchanging his slow pace for a full stop, "having kept covenant by meeting thee here, it is my purpose now to return whence I came. I have scruples touching the matter thou wot'st of."

16   "Sayest thou so?" replied he of the serpent, smiling apart. "Let us walk on, nevertheless, reasoning as we go; and if I convince thee not thou shalt turn back. We are but a little way in the forest yet."

17   "Too far! too far!" exclaimed the goodman, unconsciously resuming his walk. "My father never went into the woods on such an errand, nor his father before him. We have been a race of honest men and good Christians since the days of the martyrs; and shall I be the first of the name of Brown that ever took this path and kept"—

18   "Such company, thou wouldst say," observed the elder person, interpreting his pause. "Well said, Goodman Brown! I have been as well acquainted with your family as with ever a one among the Puritans; and that's no trifle to say. I helped your grandfather, the constable, when he lashed the Quaker woman so smartly through the streets of Salem; and it was I that brought your father a pitch-pine knot, kindled at my own hearth, to set fire to an Indian village, in King Philip's war. They were my good friends, both; and many a pleasant walk have we had along this path, and returned merrily after midnight. I would fain be friends with you for their sake."

19   "If it be as thou sayest," replied Goodman Brown, "I marvel they never spoke of these matters; or, verily, I marvel not, seeing that the least rumor of the sort would have driven them from New England. We are a people of prayer, and good works to boot, and abide no such wickedness."

20   "Wickedness or not," said the traveller with the twisted staff, "I have a very general acquaintance here in New England. The deacons of many a church have drunk the communion wine with me; the selectmen of divers towns make me their chairman; and a majority of the Great and General Court are firm supporters of my interest. The governor and I, too—But those are state secrets."

21   "Can this be so?" cried Goodman Brown, with a stare of amazement at his undisturbed companion. "Howbeit, I have nothing to do with the governor and council; they have their own ways, and are no rule for a simple husbandman like me. But, were I to go on with thee, how should I meet the eye of that good old man, our minister, at Salem village? Oh, his voice would make me tremble both Sabbath day and lecture day."

22   Thus far the elder traveller had listened with due gravity; but now burst into a fit of irrepressible mirth, shaking himself so violently that his snake-like staff actually seemed to wriggle in sympathy.

23   "Ha! ha! ha!" shouted he again and again; then composing himself, "Well, go on, Goodman Brown, go on; but, prithee, don't kill me with laughing."

24   "Well, then, to end the matter at once," said Goodman Brown, considerably nettled, "there is my wife Faith. It would break her dear little heart; and I'd rather break my own."

25   "Nay, if that be the case," answered the other, "e'en go thy ways, Goodman Brown. I would not for twenty old women like the one hobbling before us that Faith should come to any harm."

26   As he spoke he pointed his staff at a female figure on the path, in whom Goodman Brown recognized a very pious and exemplary dame, who had taught him his catechism in youth, and was still his moral and spiritual adviser, jointly with the minister and Deacon Gookin.

27   "A marvel, truly, that Goody Cloyse should be so far in the wilderness at nightfall," said he. "But with your leave, friend, I shall take a cut through the woods until we have left this Christian woman behind. Being a stranger to you, she might ask whom I was consorting with and whither I was going."

28   "Be it so," said his fellow-traveller. "Betake you to the woods, and let me keep the path."

29   Accordingly the young man turned aside, but took care to watch his companion, who advanced softly along the road until he had come within a staff's length of the old dame. She, meanwhile, was making the best of her way, with singular speed for so aged a woman, and mumbling some indistinct words—a prayer, doubtless—as she went. The traveller put forth his staff and touched her withered neck with what seemed the serpent's tail.

30   "The devil!" screamed the pious old lady.

31   "Then Goody Cloyse knows her old friend?" observed the traveller, confronting her and leaning on his writhing stick.

32   "Ah, forsooth, and is it your worship indeed?" cried the good dame. "Yea, truly it is, and in the very image of my old gossip, Goodman Brown, the grandfather of the silly fellow that now is. But—would your worship believe it?—my broomstick hath strangely disappeared, stolen, as I suspect by that unhanged witch, Goody Cory, and that, too, when I was all anointed with the juice of smallage, and cinquefoil and wolf's bane—"

33   "Mingled with fine wheat and the fat of a new-born babe," said the shape of old Goodman Brown.

34   "Ah, your worship knows the recipe," cried the old lady, cackling aloud. "So, as I was saying, being all ready for the meeting, and no horse to ride on, I made up my mind to foot it; for they tell me there is a nice young man to be taken into communion to-night. But now your good worship will lend me your arm, and we shall be there in a twinkling."

35   "That can hardly be," answered her friend. "I may not spare you my arm Goody Cloyse; but here is my staff, if you will."

36   So saying, he threw it down at her feet, where, perhaps, it assumed life, being one of the rods which its owner had formerly lent to the Egyptian magi. Of this fact, however, Goodman Brown could not take cognizance. He cast up his eyes in astonishment, and, looking down again, beheld neither Goody Cloyse nor the serpentine staff, but his fellow-traveller alone, who waited for him as calmly as if nothing had happened.

37   "That old woman taught me my catechism," said the young man; and there was a world of meaning in this simple comment.

38   They continued to walk onward, while the elder traveller exhorted his companion to make good speed and persevere in the path, discoursing so aptly that his arguments seemed rather to spring up in the bosom of his auditor than to be suggested by himself. As they went, he plucked a branch of maple to serve for a walking stick, and began to strip it of the twigs and little boughs, which were wet with evening dew. The moment his fingers touched them they became strangely withered and dried up as with a week's sunshine. Thus the pair proceeded, at a good free pace, until suddenly, in a gloomy hollow of the road, Goodman Brown sat himself down on the stump of a tree and refused to go any farther.

39   "Friend," said he, stubbornly, "my mind is made up. Not another step will I budge on this errand. What if a wretched old woman do choose to go to the devil when I thought she was going to heaven: is that any reason why I should quit my dear Faith and go after her?"

40   "You will think better of this by and by," said his acquaintance, composedly. "Sit here and rest yourself a while; and when you feel like moving again, there is my staff to help you along."

41   Without more words, he threw his companion the maple stick, and was speedily out of sight as if he had vanished into the deepening gloom. The young man sat a few moments by the roadside, applauding himself greatly, and thinking with how clear a conscience he should meet the minister in his morning walk, nor shrink from the eye of good old Deacon Gookin. And what calm sleep would be his that very night, which was to have been spent so wickedly, but so purely and sweetly now, in the arms of Faith! Amidst these pleasant and praiseworthy meditations, Goodman Brown heard the tramp of horses along the road, and deemed it advisable to conceal himself within the verge of the forest, conscious of the guilty purpose that had brought him thither, though now so happily turned from it.

42   On came the hoof tramps and the voices of the riders, two grave old voices, conversing soberly as they drew near. These mingled sounds appeared to pass along the road, within a few yards of the young man's hiding-place; but, owing doubtless to the depth of the gloom at that particular spot, neither the travellers nor their steeds were visible. Though their figures brushed the small boughs by the wayside, it could not be seen that they intercepted, even for a moment, the faint gleam from the strip of bright light athwart which they must have passed. Goodman Brown alternately crouched and stood on tiptoe, pulling aside the branches and thrusting forth his head as far he durst without discerning so much as a shadow. It vexed him the more, because he could have sworn, were such a thing possible, that he recognized the voices of the minister and Deacon Gookin, jogging along quietly, as they were wont to do, when bound to some ordination or ecclesiastical council. While yet within hearing, one of the riders stopped to pluck a switch.

43   "Of the two, reverend sir," said the voice like the deacon's, "I had rather miss an ordination dinner than to-night's meeting. They tell me some of our community are to be here from Falmouth and beyond, and others from Connecticut and Rhode Island, besides several of the Indian powwows, who, after their fashion, know almost as much

deviltry as the best of us. Moreover, there is a goodly young woman to be taken into communion."

44   "Mighty well, Deacon Gookin!" replied the solemn old tones of the minister. "Spur up, or we shall be late. Nothing can be done, you know, until I get on the ground."

45   The hoofs clattered again; and the voices, talking so strangely in the empty air, passed on through the forest, where no church had ever been gathered or solitary Christian prayed. Whither, then, could these holy men be journeying so deep into the heathen wilderness? Young Goodman Brown caught hold of a tree for support, being ready to sink down on the ground, faint and overburdened with the heavy sickness of his heart. He looked up to the sky, doubting whether there really was a heaven above him. Yet there was the blue arch, and the stars brightening in it.

46   "With heaven above and Faith below, I will yet stand firm against the devil!" cried Goodman Brown.

47   While he still gazed upward into the deep arch of the firmament and had lifted his hands to pray, a cloud, though no wind was stirring, hurried across the zenith and hid the brightening stars. The blue sky was still visible, except directly overhead, where this mass of clouds was sweeping directly northward. Aloft in the air, as if from the depths of the cloud, came a confused and doubtful sound of voices. Once the listener fancied that he could distinguish the accents of towns-people of his own, men and women, both pious and ungodly, many of whom he had met at the communion table, and had seen others rioting at the tavern. The next moment, so indistinct were the sounds, he doubted whether he had heard aught but the murmur of the old forest, whispering without a wind. Then came a stronger swell of those familiar tones, heard daily in the sunshine at Salem village, but never until now from a cloud of night. There was one voice, of a young woman, uttering lamentation, yet with an uncertain sorrow, and entreating for some favor, which, perhaps, it would grieve her to obtain; and all the unseen multitude, both saints and sinners, seemed to encourage her onward.

48   "Faith!" shouted Goodman Brown, in a voice of agony and desperation; and the echoes of the forest mocked him, crying "Faith! Faith!" as if bewildered wretches were seeking her all through the wilderness.

49   The cry of grief, rage, and terror was yet piercing the night, when the unhappy husband held his breath for a response. There was a scream, drowned immediately in a louder murmur of voices, fading into far-off laughter, as the dark cloud swept away, leaving the clear and silent sky above Goodman Brown. But something fluttered lightly down through the air and caught on the branch of a tree. The young man seized it, and beheld a pink ribbon.

50   "My Faith is gone!" cried he, after one stupefied moment. "There is no good on earth; and sin is but a name. Come, devil; for to thee is this world given."

51   And, maddened with despair, so that he laughed loud and long, did Goodman Brown grasp his staff and set forth again, at such a rate that he seemed to fly along the forest path rather than to walk or run. The road grew wilder and drearier and more faintly traced, and vanished at length, leaving him in the heart of the dark wilderness, still rushing onward with the instinct that guides mortal men to evil. The whole forest was peopled with frightful sounds—the creaking of the trees, the howling of wild beasts, and the yell of Indians; while sometimes the wind toiled like a distant church

bell, and sometimes gave a broad roar around the traveller, as if all Nature were laughing him to scorn. But he was himself the chief horror of the scene, and shrank not from its other horrors.

52   "Ha! ha! ha!" roared Goodman Brown when the wind laughed at him. "Let us hear which will laugh loudest. Think not to frighten me with your deviltry. Come witch, come wizard, come Indian powwow, come devil himself, and here comes Goodman Brown. You may as well fear him as he fears you."

53   In truth, all through the haunted forest there could be nothing more frightful than the figure of Goodman Brown. On he flew among the black pines, brandishing his staff with frenzied gestures, now giving vent to an inspiration of horrid blasphemy, and now shouting forth such laughter as set all the echoes of the forest laughing like demons around him. The fiend in his own shape is less hideous than when he rages in the breast of man. Thus sped the demoniac on his course, until, quivering among the trees, he saw a red light before him, as when the felled trunks and branches of a clearing have been set on fire, and throw up their lurid blaze against the sky, at the hour of midnight. He paused, in a lull of the tempest that had driven him onward, and heard the swell of what seemed a hymn, rolling solemnly from a distance with the weight of many voices. He knew the tune; it was a familiar one in the choir of the village meeting-house. The verse died heavily away, and was lengthened by a chorus, not of human voices, but of all the sounds of the benighted wilderness pealing in awful harmony together. Goodman Brown cried out, and his cry was lost to his own ears by its unison with the cry of the desert.

54   In the interval of silence he stole forward until the light glared full upon his eyes. At one extremity of an open space, hemmed in by the dark wall of the forest, arose a rock, bearing some rude, natural resemblance either to an altar or a pulpit, and surrounded by four blazing pines, their tops aflame, their stems untouched, like candles at an evening meeting. The mass of foliage that had overgrown the summit of the rock was all on fire, blazing high into the night and fitfully illuminating the whole field. Each pendent twig and leafy festoon was in a blaze. As the red light arose and fell, a numerous congregation alternately shone forth, then disappeared in shadow, and again grew, as it were, out of the darkness, peopling the heart of the solitary woods at once.

55   "A grave and dark-clad company," quoth Goodman Brown.

56   In truth they were such. Among them, quivering to and fro between gloom and splendor, appeared faces that would be seen next day at the council board of the province, and others which, Sabbath after Sabbath, looked devoutly heavenward, and benignantly over the crowded pews, from the holiest pulpits in the land. Some affirm that the lady of the governor was there. At least there were high dames well known to her, and wives of honored husbands, and widows, a great multitude, and ancient maidens, all of excellent repute, and fair young girls, who trembled lest their mothers should espy them. Either the sudden gleams of light flashing over the obscure field bedazzled Goodman Brown, or he recognized a score of the church members of Salem village famous for their especial sanctity. Good old Deacon Gookin had arrived, but waited at the skirts of that venerable saint, his reverend pastor. But, irreverently consorting with these grave, reputable, and pious people, these elders of the church, these chaste dames and dewy virgins, there were men of dissolute lives and women of

spoiled fame, wretches given over to all mean and filthy vice, and suspected even of horrid crimes. It was strange to see that the good shrank not from the wicked, nor were the sinners abashed by the saints. Scattered also among their pale-faced enemies were the Indian priests, or powwows, who had often scared their native forest with more hideous incantations than any known to English witchcraft.

57   "But where is Faith?" thought Goodman Brown; and, as hope came into his heart, he trembled.

58   Another verse of the hymn arose, a slow and mournful strain, such as the pious love, but joined to words which expressed all that our nature can conceive of sin, and darkly hinted at far more. Unfathomable to mere mortals is the lore of fiends. Verse after verse was sung; and still the chorus of the desert swelled between like the deepest tone of a mighty organ; and with the final peal of that dreadful anthem there came a sound, as if the roaring wind, the rushing streams, the howling beasts, and every other voice in the unconcerted wilderness were mingling and according with the voice of guilty man in homage to the prince of all. The four blazing pines threw up a loftier flame, and obscurely discovered shapes and visages of horror on the smoke wreaths above the impious assembly. At the same moment the fire on the rock shot redly forth and formed a glowing arch above its base, where now appeared a figure. With reverence be it spoken, the figure bore no slight similitude, both in garb and manner, to some grave divine of the New England churches.

59   "Bring forth the converts!" cried a voice that echoed through the field and rolled into the forest.

60   At the word, Goodman Brown stepped forth from the shadow of the trees and approached the congregation, with whom he felt a loathful brotherhood by the sympathy of all that was wicked in his heart. He could have well-nigh sworn that the shape of his own dead father beckoned him to advance, looking downward from a smoke wreath, while a woman, with dim features of despair, threw out her hand to warn him back. Was this mother? But he had no power to retreat one step, nor to resist, even in thought, when the minister and good old Deacon Gookin seized his arms and led him to the blazing rock. Thither came also the slender form of a veiled female, led between Goody Cloyse, that pious teacher of the catechism and Martha Carrier, who had received the devil's promise to be queen of hell. A rampant hag was she. And there stood the proselytes beneath the canopy of fire.

61   "Welcome, my children" said the dark figure, "lo the communion of your race. Ye have found thus young your nature and your destiny. My children, look behind you!"

62   They turned; and flashing forth, as it were, in a sheet of flame, the fiend worshippers were seen; the smile of welcome gleamed darkly on every visage.

63   "There," resumed the sable form, "are all whom ye have reverenced from youth. Ye deemed them holier than yourselves and shrank from your own sin, contrasting it with their lives of righteousness and prayerful aspirations heavenward. Yet here are they all in my worshipping assembly. This night it shall be granted you to know their secret deeds: how hoary-bearded elders of the church have whispered wanton words to the young maids of their households; how many a woman, eager for widow's weeds, has given her husband a drink at bedtime and let him sleep his last sleep in her bosom;

how beardless youths have made haste to inherit their fathers' wealth; and how fair damsels—blush not, sweet ones—have dug little graves in the garden, and bidden me, the sole guest, to an infant's funeral. By the sympathy of your human hearts for sin ye shall scent out all the places—whether in church, bedchamber, street, field, or forest—where crime has been committed, and shall exult to behold the whole earth one stain of guilt, one mighty blood spat. Far more than this. It shall be yours to penetrate, in every bosom, the deep mystery of sin, the fountain of all wicked arts, and which inexhaustibly supplies more evil impulses than human power—than my power at its utmost—can make manifest in deeds. And now, my children, look upon each other."

64   They did so; and, by the blaze of the hell-kindled torches, the wretched man beheld his Faith, and the wife her husband, trembling before that unhallowed altar.

65   "Lo, there ye stand, my children," said the figure, in a deep and solemn tone, almost sad with its despairing awfulness, as if his once angelic nature could yet mourn for our miserable race. "Depending upon one another's hearts, ye had still hoped that virtue were not all a dream. Now are ye undeceived. Evil is the nature of mankind. Evil must be your only happiness. Welcome again, my children, to the communion of your race."

66   "Welcome," repeated the fiend worshippers, in one cry of despair and triumph.

67   And there they stood, the only pair, as it seemed, who were yet hesitating on the verge of wickedness in this dark world. A basin was hollowed naturally, in the rock. Did it contain water, reddened by the lurid light? or was it blood? or, perchance, a liquid flame? Herein did the shape of evil dip his hand and prepare to lay the mark of baptism upon their foreheads, that they might be partakers of the mystery of sin, more conscious of the secret guilt of others, both in deed and thought, than they could now be of their own. The husband cast one look at his pale wife, and Faith at him. What polluted wretches would the next glance show them to each other, shuddering alike at what they disclosed and what they saw!

68   "Faith! Faith!" cried the husband, "look up to heaven, and resist the wicked one."

69   Whether Faith obeyed he knew not. Hardly had he spoken when he found himself amid calm night and solitude, listening to a roar of the wind which died heavily away through the forest. He staggered against the rock, and felt it chill and damp; while a hanging twig, that had been all on fire, besprinkled his cheek with the coldest dew.

70   The next morning young Goodman Brown came slowly into the street of Salem village, staring around him alike a bewildered man. The good old minister was taking a walk along the graveyard to get an appetite for breakfast and meditate his sermon, and bestowed a blessing, as he passed, on Goodman Brown. He shrank from the venerable saint as if to avoid an anathema. Old Deacon Gookin was at domestic worship, and the holy words of his prayer were heard through the open window. "What God doth the wizard pray to?" quoth Goodman Brown. Goody Cloyse, that excellent old Christian, stood in the early sunshine at her own lattice, catechizing a little girl who had brought her a pint of morning's milk. Goodman Brown snatched away the child as from the grasp of the fiend himself. Turning the corner by the meeting-house, he spied the head of Faith, with the pink ribbons, gazing anxiously forth, and bursting into such joy at the sight of him that she skipped along the street and almost kissed

her husband before the whole village. But Goodman Brown looked sternly and sadly into her face, and passed on without a greeting.

71   Had Goodman Brown fallen asleep in the forest and only dreamed a wild dream of a witch-meeting?

72   Be it so if you will; but, alas! it was a dream of evil omen for young Goodman Brown. A stern, a sad, a darkly meditative, a distrustful, if not a desperate man did he become from the night of that fearful dream. On the Sabbath day, when the congregation were singing the holy psalm, he could not listen because an anthem of sin rushed loudly upon his ear and drowned all the blessed strain. When the minister spoke from the pulpit with power and fervid eloquence, and, with his hand on the open Bible, of the sacred truths of our religion, and of saint-like lives and triumphant deaths, and of future bliss or misery unutterable, then did Goodman Brown turn pale, dreading lest the roof should thunder down upon the gray blasphemer and his hearers. Often, awaking suddenly at midnight, he shrank from the bosom of Faith; and at morning or eventide, when the family knelt down at prayer, he scowled and muttered to himself, and gazed sternly at his wife, and turned away. And when he had lived long, and was borne to his grave a hoary corpse, followed by Faith, an aged woman, and children and grandchildren, a goodly procession, besides neighbors not a few, they carved no hopeful verse upon his tombstone, for his dying hour was gloom.

Suggestions for Discussion or Writing

1. Hawthorne's writing characteristically uses a great deal of symbolism. What might the following characters or images in "Young Goodman Brown" symbolize: the forest, the dark night, the old man traveler, the pink ribbon?

2. What is the significance of Brown's wife's name, Faith?

3. What does the following description of the old traveler reveal about young Goodman Brown: " . . . the second traveller was about fifty years old, apparently in the same rank of life as Goodman Brown, and bearing a considerable resemblance to him, though perhaps more in expression than features. Still they might have been taken for father and son"?

4. Did Goodman Brown really have the experience in the forest or was it all a dream? How do you know? How does Goodman Brown change as a result of his experience, whether real or imagined?

5. What is Hawthorne trying to teach by making the story symbolic? Is the story a parable? How so? What is the theme of the story? Is the use of symbolism effective? Why or why not?

6. Compare young Goodman Brown's experience with Langston Hughes' in "Salvation." To what degree does each experience disillusionment? Does one "survive" the experience better than the other? How are their experiences different?

God's Grandeur

Gerard Manley Hopkins

English poet and Jesuit priest Gerard Manley Hopkins (1844-1889) is known for his poetic innovations and intricate rhymes. As a young man Hopkins attended Oxford University and became a convert to Roman Catholicism in 1866. His early poems were lush and sensuous but at the time of his conversion he dedicated his poetic talents to the praise of God and nature. Some of his best-known and celebrated poems are "The Windhover," "Pied Beauty," "The Caged Skylark," "Spring and Fall," and this selection "God's Grandeur."

The world is charged with the grandeur of God.
    It will flame out, like shining from shook foil;
    It gathers to a greatness, like the ooze of oil
Crushed. Why do men then now not reck his rod?
5   Generations have trod, have trod, have trod;
    And all is seared with trade; bleared, smeared with toil;
    And wears man's smudge and shares man's smell: the soil
Is bare now, nor can foot feel, being shod.
And for all this, nature is never spent;
10   There lives the dearest freshness deep down things;
And though the last lights off the black West went
    Oh, morning, at the brown brink eastward, springs—
Because the Holy Ghost over the bent
  World broods with warm breast and ah! bright wings.

Suggestions for Discussion or Writing

1. What are the denotations and connotations of the following words: "charged," "shining," "reck," "rod," "seared," "bleared," "smeared," "smudge," "shod," "spent," "brink," "bent," "broods"?

2. What is "the grandeur of God"? the "ooze of oil / crushed"? "his rod"? "the last lights off the black west"? the "brown brink eastward"?

3. How does the repetition of "have trod, have trod, have trod" affect the meaning of the poem?

4. Why does Hopkins use the sonnet form to praise God and nature?

5. What seems to be the tone of the poem? What view of the world does it present?

Prayer is the little implement

Emily Dickinson

*Emily Dickinson (1830–1886) was born in and spent most of her life as a
recluse in Amherst, Massachusetts. She attended Amherst Academy and
spent a year at Mary Lyon's Female Seminary at South Hadley. Although
she did not publish her poems during her lifetime, she was published by her
sister in 1890 and in 1914 by her niece, but subsequently almost forgotten.
In 1924, a volume called* Life and Letters *was published which started her
popularity. She is now considered one of the greatest American poets of the
nineteenth century.*

Prayer is the little implement
Through which Men reach
Where Presence—is denied them.
They fling their Speech

5   By means of it—in God's Ear—
If then He hear—
This sums the Apparatus
Comprised in Prayer—

Suggestions for Discussion or Writing

1. What metaphors does Emily Dickinson use in her poem?

2. What is the "apparatus" she describes?

3. What does the "it" in the second stanza refer to?

4. What connotation do the words "implement" and "apparatus" have? How
   do these connotations affect the poem?

Attitudes

Richard Eberhart

The poet and educator Richard Eberhart (1904–) earned his bachelor's degree at Dartmouth, an M.A. in lyrical poetry from Cambridge in 1933, and went to graduate work at Harvard. He served as the private tutor for the son of King Prajadhipok of Siam, was the master of English at St. Mark's School in Massachusetts, and worked as a professor of English at Dartmouth for 28 years. Eberhart won the Bollinger Prize in Poetry from Yale University in 1962 and has since won the Pulitzer Prize for his Selected Poems: 1930–1965 *(1966) and the National Book Award for* Collected Poems: 1930–1976. *Eberhart, named the Poet Laureate of Dartmouth College (an honor also bestowed on Robert Frost), as well as the Poet Laureate of New Hampshire, has written several other poetry collections, including* Fields of Grace *(1972) and* Ways of Light *(1980), and several plays, including "The Apparition" (1951) and "The Bride from Mantua" (1964).*

Irish Catholic

After the long wake, when many were drunk,
Pat struggled out to the tracks, seething
Blinded, was struck by a train,
Died too. The funeral was for the mother and son.

The Catholic music soared to the high stones,
Hundreds swayed to the long, compulsive ritual.
As the mourners followed the caskets out
Wave followed wave of misery, of pure release.

New England Protestant

When Aunt Emily died, her husband would not look at her.
Uncle Peter, inarticulate in his cold intelligence,
Conceded few flowers, arranged the simplest service.
Only the intimate members of the family came.

Then the small procession went to the family grave.
No word was spoken but the parson's solemn few.
Silence, order, a prim dryness, not a tear.
We left the old man standing alone there.

Suggestions for Discussion or Writing

1. What seems to be the poet's attitude toward the two reactions to death? What descriptive details of the families' mourning does he use to express his attitude?

2. What is the traditional method of Catholic mourning? How does this tradition affect those who mourn for Pat and his mother?

3. How are New England Protestants traditionally characterized? How do their religious traditions affect their mourning for Aunt Emily?

4. Compare the two approaches to mourning displayed in the poem. Is one form more appropriate or effective than the other in your opinion? Why?

5. How do these traditions of mourning compare or contrast with your own?

Rings and Beautiful Things

Creating New Perceptions Through the Arts

Introduction

I n Robert M. Pirsig's *Zen and the Art of Motorcycle Maintenance*, the narrator investigates the meaning of "quality." Other questions of definition come to us from the Greeks and from philosophers throughout the ages: What is truth? What is beauty? Today we hear the question from cynical tourists at museums and galleries: Is this art? The search for beauty through the arts is ongoing. Often the old saying, "Beauty is in the eye of the beholder" justifies what may seem to another, abominable taste. Other times, an appreciation for certain artistic skills must be acquired through study.

"Kitsch," by Gilbert Highet, explores a taste for poor art or craftsmanship with tongue-in-cheek seriousness. What is beautiful to one person is worthless to another. Katherine Kuh explores a controversial topic—modern art. As an authority in the field, she helps the reader appreciate some of the values to be found in modern art.

Three selections center around the beauty in physical movement and dance: "The Ring of Time," "Pavlova," and "Ballet Blanc." They describe the excitement of viewing beauty in the grace and skill of the performer. The power of music is shown in "Shanghai Blues" and "Music Lessons."

Art in the written form is shown in Virginia Woolf's "What If Shakespeare Had Had a Sister?" in the touching story by Hisaye Yamamoto, "Seventeen Syllables," and in the metaphorical poem by Sylvia Plath, "Stillborn."

Refinement of the arts is often thought to be a factor which separates more advanced civilizations from less developed ones. As we grow in understanding and love for the beautiful, we make our lives richer, and as we learn to appreciate artistic excellence, we grow in knowledge and love of the gifts of the arts.

Shanghai Blues

William Zinsser

*William Zinsser (1922–) received his B.A. at Princeton University in 1944
and went on to become a writer, editor, and educator. He worked as a feature
writer, drama editor, film critic, and editorial writer for the New York* Herald
Tribune. *He has also been a columnist for* Look *magazine,* Life *magazine,
and the* New York Times. *In 1971 Zinsser joined the faculty at Yale
University where he taught for nine years. In addition to his journalism and
teaching careers, Zinsser also has written a number of books among which
are* Any Old Place With You *(1957),* Seen Any Good Movies Lately? *(1958),*
Pop Goes America *(1966), and* Writing with a Word Processor *(1983).*

1   Jazz came to China for the first time on the afternoon of June 2nd, when the American
bassist and French-horn player Willie Ruff introduced himself and his partner, the
pianist Dwike Mitchell, to several hundred students and professors who were crowded
into a large room at the Shanghai Conservatory of Music. The professors and the
students were all expectant, without knowing quite what to expect. They knew only
that they were about to hear the first American jazz concert ever presented to the
Chinese. Probably they were not surprised to find that the two musicians were black,
though black Americans are a rarity in the People's Republic. What they undoubtedly
didn't expect was that Ruff would talk to them in Chinese, and when he began they
murmured with delight.

2   Ruff is a lithe, dapper man of fifty who takes visible pleasure in sharing his
enthusiasms, and it was obvious that there was no place he would rather have been
than in China's oldest conservatory, bringing the music of his people to still another
country deprived of that commodity. In 1959, he and Mitchell—who have played
together as the Mitchell-Ruff Duo for twenty-six years—introduced jazz to the Soviet
Union, and for that occasion Ruff taught himself Russian, his seventh language. In
1979, he hit on the idea of making a similar trip to China, and he began taking intensive
courses in Chinese at Yale, where he is a professor of both music and Afro-American
studies. By last winter, he felt he was fluent enough in Mandarin to make the trip.

3   Now Ruff stood at the front of the room, holding several sheets of paper on which
he had written, in Chinese characters, what he wanted to tell his listeners about the
origins of Jazz. He looked somewhat like an Oriental sage himself. "In the last three
hundred and fifty years, black people in America have created a music that is a rich
contribution to Western culture," he began. "Of course, three hundred and fifty years,
compared to the long and distinguished history of Chinese music seems like only a
moment. But please remember that the music of American black people is an amalgam
whose roots are deep in African history, and that it has also taken many characteristics
from the music of Europe." Ruff has an amiable voice, and as he spoke the men and
women in the room were attentive but relaxed—not an audience straining to decipher

a foreigner's accent. "In Africa, the drum is the most important musical instrument," Ruff went on. "But to me the fascinating thing is that the people also use their drums to talk. Please imagine that the drum method of speech is so exquisite that Africans can, without recourse to words, recite proverbs, record history, and send long messages. The drum is to West African society what the book is to literate society."

4   I wondered what the audience would make of that. Not only was China the oldest of literate societies; we were in the one Asian city that was encrusted with Western thought as transmitted in books, in journals, and in musical notation. Even the architecture of Shanghai was a patchwork of Western shapes—a residue of the days when the city had a huge foreign population and was divided into districts that were controlled by different European countries. At the conservatory, we were in the former French concession, and its main building was in a red brick French Provincial style, with a sloping red tile roof and a porte cochère. Another French-style building housed the conservatory's library of a hundred thousand books about music. Newer buildings served as classrooms and practice rooms, and the music that eddied out of the windows was the dreary fare of Western academic rigor: vocal scales endlessly rising, piano arpeggios repeated until they were mastered, chamber groups, starting and stopping and starting again. We could have been in Vienna of the nineties or Paris of the twenties. In any case, we were a long way from Africa. And we were farther still from music created spontaneously.

5   "In the seventeenth century, when West Africans were captured and brought to America as slaves, they brought their drums with them," Ruff continued. "But the slave-owners were afraid of the drum because it was so potent; it could be used to incite the slaves to revolt. So they outlawed the drum. This very shrewd law had a tremendous effect on the development of black people's music. Our ancestors had to develop a variety of drum substitutes. One of them, for example, was tap dancing—I'm sure you've all heard of that. Now I'd like to show you another drum substitute that you probably don't know about—one that uses the hands and the body to make rhythm. It's called hambone." There was no translating "hambone" into Mandarin, but Ruff quickly had an intricate rhythm going to demonstrate, slapping himself with the palms of his hands and smacking his open mouth to create a series of resonating pops. Applause greeted this proof that the body could be its own drum.

6   "By the time jazz started to develop, all African instruments in America had disappeared," Ruff went on. "So jazz borrowed the instruments of Western music, like the ones that we're playing here today." He went over to his bass and showed how he used it as a percussion instrument by picking the strings with his fingers instead of playing them with a bow. "Only this morning," he said, "I gave a lesson to your distinguished professor of bass, and he is already *very good*."

7   Moving on from rhythm to terrain more familiar to his listeners, Ruff pointed out that jazz took its structural elements from European harmony. "Mr. Mitchell will give you an example of the music that American slaves found in the Christian churches— Protestant hymns that had been brought from Europe," he said. "Slaves were encouraged to embrace Christianity and to use its music. Please listen." Mitchell played an old Protestant hymn. "The slaves adopted these harmonized melodies and transformed them into their own, very emotional spirituals," Ruff said when Mitchell had finished.

"Mr. Mitchell and I will sing you a famous Negro spiritual from the days of slavery. It's called 'My Lord, What a Morning.' " With Mitchell playing a joyful accompaniment, the two men sang five or six choruses of the lovely old song, Mitchell carrying the melody in his deep voice, Ruff taking the higher, second part. The moment, musically beautiful, had an edge of faraway sadness. I couldn't help thinking of another alien culture onto which the Protestant hymns of Europe had once been strenuously grafted. It was just beyond the conservatory gates.

8   "Mr. Mitchell will now show you how the piano can be used as a substitute for the instruments of the orchestra," Ruff said. "Please notice that he uses his left hand to play the bass and also to make his rhythm section. Later, he will use his right hand to play the main melody and to fill in the harmony. This style is called ragtime." Mitchell struck up a jaunty rag. The students perked up at the playful pattern of notes. Ruff looked out at his class and beamed. The teacher in him was beginning to slip away; the musician in him was telling him to start the concert.

9   Mitchell and Ruff met in 1947, when they were servicemen at Lockbourne Air Force Base, outside Columbus, Ohio. Mitchell, then seventeen and a pianist in the unit band, needed an accompanist, and he gave the newly arrived Ruff, a sixteen-year-old French-horn player, a crash course in playing the bass. Thus the duo was unofficially born. When they were discharged, they followed separate paths and lost contact. Mitchell went to the Philadelphia Musical Academy. Ruff went to the Yale School of Music, where he studied with Paul Hindemith. Venturing out with his master's degree in 1954, he was told that no American symphony orchestra would hire a black musician, and he accepted an offer to join the Tel Aviv Symphony as first French horn. Shortly before he was to leave, he happened to turn his television set on to "The Ed Sullivan Show." Lionel Hampton's orchestra was playing, and as the camera panned over to the piano Ruff saw a familiar figure at the keyboard. Mitchell, it turned out, had been Hampton's pianist for the past two years. Ruff telephoned him backstage at the CBS studio. Mitchell hinted of imminent vacancies in the brass section. A few days later, Israel lost—and Hampton got—a superb French horn.

10   The Mitchell-Ruff Duo—"The oldest continuous group in jazz without personnel changes," Ruff says—was formed in 1955, when the two men left Hampton and struck out on their own. They were booked regularly by the major night clubs as the second act with the great bands of the day: Louis Armstrong, Duke Ellington, Dizzy Gillispie, Miles Davis. "They were our mentors," Ruff recalls. "They'd play a set and then we'd play a set and they'd hang around and tell us what we could be doing better. We learned everything from those men. Count Basie's band raised us. In 1956, they were the hottest band in the country—they were the most expensive band and we were the cheapest—and we sold out Birdland every night. One evening, Miles Davis brought Billie Holiday in to hear us, and we just about fell through the floor. We were still just kids."

11   Meanwhile, they caught the attention of another set of patrons—a group of older women in New York who had formed an organization called Young Audiences to introduce elementary- and high-school students to chamber music. For teachers, the women chose young professionals who could communicate with words as well as with music, and Mitchell and Ruff were the first people they selected to teach jazz. Ruff

recalls, "It was done under the supervision of the founders—Mrs. Lionello Perera, a great patron of music, and Mrs. Edgar Leventritt, who started the Leventritt Competition—and Nina Collier and several other ladies who sat on the board. They taught us definite techniques, such as how to catch the attention of children, and they also gave us lessons in grooming and enunciation and conduct. They were very stern and really quite unpleasant, but instructive. Everything they told us turned out to be true."

12   Armed with these graces, Mitchell and Ruff hit the road for Young Audiences, often giving seven or eight performances a day, going from school to school, first in New York and later in Boston, Baltimore, and San Francisco. They did a tour of Indian schools in New Mexico. The duo alternated these forays with its stands in Manhattan clubs. Then, in 1959, it went to Russia. Ruff himself arranged the trip with Soviet officials after the State Department, which had been trying for two years to get Louis Armstrong into the Soviet Union, declined to help. In Russia, the two Americans found a thirst for jazz that surprised even them; when they left Moscow, nine hundred people came to the station to see them off. Mitchell, in turn, still remembers being moved by Russian songs that resembled spirituals he had heard in the black churches of his boyhood. Whether a scholar could find any such link doesn't matter to him; in music, he operates on an emotional level that has no need for evidence. "I felt a mysterious bond between their people and my people," he says. "I think I connected with their suffering."

13   Not long after that trip, the house of jazz began to crumble. Television was the new medium and rock the new musical message. "Night clubs started closing in the very early sixties," Ruff recalls. "The number of jazz performers who quit, died, or just disappeared was astounding. Many of them moved to Europe. Three of the greatest rhythm players—Oscar Pettiford, Bud Powell, and Kenny Clarke—had been living in Paris and playing for peanuts because they couldn't find any work in the United States. How devastating it was for us to play in Europe—as we did quite a bit then—and so many of these great men so reduced!"

14   Mitchell and Ruff survived because of their teaching bent. They caught the attention of two venerable booking agencies, Pryor-Menz and Alkahest, that wanted a young act to give concerts for college audiences and also explain the music, and thereby found the format—sixty or seventy concerts a year, mainly at colleges—that has been their principal source of income to this day.

15   A new tool came their way in 1967, when CBS Television sent them to Brazil to make a one-hour film tracing the African roots of Brazilian music. Ruff recognized the value of film as a teaching device, went back to college to study film, and has since visited Bali, Senegal, and the pygmies of the Central African Republic to make films about the drum music and language of those societies. He always came back to Yale (where he and I lived in the same college) elated by new rhythmical affinities that he had found among diverse cultures and among seemingly unrelated forms of life. His seminars on rhythm began to make startling connections as he brought Yale professors into them from such disciplines as neurology, limnology, geology, art, English, astronomy, physiology, and physics. The professors, in fact, became almost as elated as Ruff.

16   We flew to Shanghai on a Chinese 747—Ruff walked up and down the aisles trying out his Chinese on the passengers—and the next day we called on Professor Tan Shu-chen, deputy director of the Shanghai Conservatory of Music, who was, so far, our only contact. Two years ago, Ruff had sought the sponsorship of the Center for United States–China Arts Exchange, the group that has been sending American musicians to China, but he got no response. Ruff felt that no matter how many great American artists went to China—Isaac Stern, the Boston Symphony Orchestra, Roberta Peters—the music that they played and sang would be European music. The indigenous music of America was jazz, and the Chinese had never heard it in a live performance. (When Ruff asked a Chinese man on the plane whether his people were familiar with jazz, he said, "Oh, yes, we know Stephen Foster very well.") Lacking official support, Ruff decided to go anyway. He booked himself and Mitchell on a two-week tour to Shanghai and Peking, the two cities that had major conservatories, and then went looking for money. He got a grant from Coca-Cola that would cover their expenses and costs of filming their visit.

17   To have Professor Tan as our host was all that we could have asked. He had come to New York last winter in connection with the film "From Mao to Mozart—Isaac Stern in China," in which he describes his imprisonment during China's Cultural Revolution. Ruff invited him to visit the Yale School of Music, in the long-range hope of fostering some kind of collaboration that would help both institutions—an exchange of teachers or students or manuscripts between Yale and the Shanghai Conservatory, for instance. While Professor Tan was at Yale, he attended a class in which Ruff and Mitchell were playing, and he invited them in turn, to give a concert at the conservatory. That was all that a born improviser needed to hear. Now we were at the conservatory, and Professor Tan was showing us around. He had arranged the jazz concert for the next afternoon.

18   The Shanghai Conservatory of Music, which was founded in 1927, and which prides itself on being part of the cultural conscience of China, has six hundred and fifty students—the youngest are eight years old—and three hundred teachers. Most of the students live on campus. Quite a few are from Shanghai, but a large number are recruited from all over China by faculty members, who hold regional auditions.

19   The conservatory has five departments of instruction—piano; voice; strings and winds; composing and conducting; and traditional Chinese instruments—and two of musicology. One of these is a musical-research institute. The other, devoted to Chinese traditional and folk music, was recently formed to broaden the conservatory's involvement with the heritage of its own country. But the tilt is definitely Westward. Most of the conservatory's original teachers were Europeans, and many of its graduates have lived in the West and won recognition there. The curriculum, from what I could hear of it, was rooted in Europe: Bach, Scarlatti, Mozart, Beethoven, Brahms, Schubert, Chopin, Verdi. The biggest class that we saw consisted of a forty-piece student orchestra, led by a student conductor, playing Dvorak's Cello Concerto.

20   Professor Tan was a product of this tradition—and one of its first casualties when the Cultural Revolution struck. He was born in 1907, and as a boy he studied violin privately with Dutch and Italian teachers who were living in China. When he joined the Shanghai Municipal Orchestra, in 1927, he was its first Chinese member. He recalls

the conductor, an Italian named Mario Paci, as a man of such fierce temper that he constantly broke his baton. Thus he learned at an early age that one of the liveliest currents running through Western music is high emotion among its practitioners.

21   Professor Tan turned to teaching in 1929—at one point, he was teaching violin at six different colleges in Shanghai—and rejoined the symphony in 1937. By that time, it had four Chinese members; obviously, Shanghai was still a creature of the West. But that era would soon come to an end. During the Second World War, the Japanese occupied Shanghai, foreigners were interned in concentration camps, and the colonizing grip of the West was finally broken.

22   It was no time or place for a musician to make a living—"One month's salary would buy one shoe," Professor Tan recalled—and, seeking a more practical trade, he went to architecture school and earned his degree. He returned to music after the war, however, joining the Shanghai Conservatory in 1947, and becoming its deputy director in 1949, when the Communists came to power in China. The school then began its biggest era of growth. The student body and the faculty were greatly expanded, and European music regained its hold. But the older students were also required to go away and work for three months every year on farms and in factories. "The peasants and workers disliked Western music because it belonged to the rich people," Professor Tan recalled. "And our students couldn't practice much, because they met so much criticism. At the conservatory, we never knew where we stood. Periods of criticism would alternate with periods of relaxation. It was an uneasy time. In fact, just before the Cultural Revolution I was thinking of retiring from teaching. I had a sense of a coming storm. We are like animals—we can feel that."

23   The storm broke on June 5, 1966. The first winds of the Cultural Revolution hit the conservatory from within. "On the first day, posters were put up and meetings were held denouncing the director, Professor Ho Lu-ting," Professor Tan said. "The next day, the attack was aimed at me. I was accused of poisoning the minds of students. My crime was that I was teaching Mozart. I happen to be a blind admirer of European and American people and music and culture, so everything I had been teaching was poison. Bach and Beethoven were poison. And Brahms. And Paganini.

24   "At first, it was only posters and meetings. Then the conservatory was closed, and much of our music was destroyed. We were beaten every day by students and by young people who came in from outside. Boys of ten or eleven would throw stones at us. They really believed we were bad people—especially any professor who was over forty. The older you were, the worse you were. For a year, more than a hundred of us older teachers were beaten and forced to spend every day shut up together in a closed shed. Then there was a year when we had to do hard labor. Ten professors died from the strain; one of them had a heart attack when a young guard made him run after him for a mile. He just dropped at the end. Then came the solitary confinement. Our director was kept in prison, in chains, for five years. I was put in the worst room they could find here—a very small room in the basement, hardly any bigger than my bed. It had no light and no windows, and it was smelly because it was next to a septic tank, and there was nothing to do to pass the time. I was kept there for fourteen months."

25   In 1971, Professor Tan was allowed to go home to live with his family pending the verdict on his "crimes," but he still had to do physical labor at the conservatory

during the day. Needless to say, no Western music was played there. Finally, in 1976, the Gang of Four was overthrown, the professors were declared innocent, and the conservatory was reopened. Professor Tan told me that among the students he readmitted were some who had beaten and tormented him. I said that I could hardly imagine such forbearance. "I didn't think about that," he said. "The past is the past."

26   Professor Tan is a small, gentle man with white hair and a modest manner. He dresses in the informal work clothes that everybody wears in Shanghai; nobody would take him for one of the city's cultural eminences. He moves somewhat slowly and wears fairly strong glasses—marks, perhaps, of his long captivity. "The students have made astonishing progress since 1976, because now they can play wholeheartedly," he told me. "I love being able to teach the violin again. It's such an enjoyment to hear people who are truly talented. Yesterday, a girl played the 'Scottish Fantasy' of Max Bruch, and although I was supposed to be teaching her, I only sat and listened and never said a word. It was just right." He was equally pleased by the thought of bringing jazz to his students. "I've never seen any jazz musicians in China," he said. "Nobody here knows anything about jazz. When I heard Mr. Ruff and Mr. Mitchell play at Yale, I realized that it was very important music. I wanted my teachers and students to hear it. I wanted them to know what real American jazz is like."

27   When Mitchell finished his ragtime tune, the audience clapped—apparently glad to hear some of the converging elements that Ruff had talked about earlier. "Now we're going to give you an example of blues," Ruff said. "Blues" was another word that didn't lend itself to Mandarin, and it sounded unusually strung out: "blooooooze." Ruff continued, "One of the fundamental principles of jazz is form, and blues are a perfect illustration. Blues almost always have a twelve-bar form. This twelve-bar form never changes. It wouldn't change even if we stayed here and played it all night." He paused to let this sink in. "But you don't have to worry—we aren't going to play it that long." It was his first joke in Chinese, and it went over well. Mitchell then played an easygoing blues—a classic sample of what came up the river from New Orleans, with a strong left hand ornamented by graceful runs in the right hand. Ruff joined in on bass, and they played several twelve-bar choruses.

28   After that number, Ruff brought up the matter of improvisation, which he called "the lifeblood of jazz." He said that when he was young he had worried because his people hadn't developed from their experience in America a written tradition of opera, like Chinese opera, that chronicled great or romantic events. "But later I stopped worrying, because I saw that the master performers of our musical story—Louis Armstrong, Ella Fitzgerald, and so many others—have enriched our culture with the beauty of what they have created spontaneously. Now please listen one more time to the blues form, and count the measures along with me." He wanted his listeners to count, he said, because the rules of jazz require the improviser, however wild his melodic journeys, to repeat the harmonic changes that went into the first statement of the theme. "After you count with me a few times through, Mr. Mitchell will begin one of his famous improvisations," Ruff said.

29   Mitchell played a simple blues theme, emphasizing the chord changes, and Ruff counted the twelve bars aloud in English. Mitchell then restated the theme, embroidering it slightly, and this time Ruff counted in Chinese: *"Yi, cr, san, si, wu, liu, qi,*

ba . . . " This so delighted the students that they forgot to join him. "I can't hear you," Ruff said, teacher-fashion, but they kept quiet and enjoyed his climb up the numerical ladder. Afterward, Mitchell embarked on a series of dazzling improvisations, some constructed of runs like those played by Art Tatum, some built on strong progressions (he can move immense chord clusters up and down the keyboard with incredible speed); next, Ruff took a chorus on the bass; then they alternated their improvised flights, moving in twelve-bar segments to an ending that seemed inevitable—as if they had played it a hundred times before.

30   Changing the mood, Ruff announced that Mitchell would play "Yesterdays." Jerome Kern's plaintive melody is hardly the stuff of traditional jazz, nor was Mitchell's rendition of it—a treatment of classical intricacy, closer to Rachmaninoff (one of his heroes) than to any jazz pianist. The students applauded with fervor. Staying in a relatively classical vein, Ruff switched to the French horn, and the two men played Billy Strayhorn's "Lush Life" in a vein that was slow and lyrical, almost like a German lied, and that perhaps surprised the students with its lack of an obvious rhythm.

31   The next number was one that I didn't recognize. It moved at a bright tempo and had several engaging themes that were brought back by the piano or the French horn—the usual jazzmen's game of statement and response. Twice, Mitchell briefly introduced a contrapuntal motif that was a deliberate imitation of Bach, and each time it drew a ripple of amusement from the professors and the students. It was the first time they had heard a kind of music that they recognized from their own studies.

31   "That number is called 'Shanghai Blues,'" Ruff said at the end. "We just made it up." The audience buzzed with amazement and pleasure.

33   I had been watching the professors and students closely during the concert. Their faces had the look of people watching the slow approach of some great natural force—a tornado or a tidal wave. They had been listening to music that their experience had not prepared them to understand. Two black men were playing long stretches of music without resorting to any printed notes. Yet they obviously hadn't memorized what they were playing; their music took unexpected turns, seemingly at the whim of the musicians, straying all over the keyboard and all over the landscape of Western tonality. Nevertheless, there was order. Themes that had been abandoned came back in different clothes. If the key changed, as it frequently did, the two men were always in the same key. Often there was a playfulness between the two instruments, and always there was rapport. But if the two players were exchanging any signals, the message was too quick for the untrained eye.

34   I could tell that the music was holding the Chinese listeners in a strong grip. Their minds seemed to be fully engaged. Their bodies, however, were not. Only three pairs of feet in the whole room were tapping—Ruff's, Mitchell's and mine. Perhaps this was a Chinese characteristic, this stillness of listening. Moreover, the music wasn't easy. It never again approached the overt syncopation of the ragtime that Mitchell had played early in the program; that was where the essential gaiety of jazz had been most accessible. Nor did it have the flat-out gusto that an earlier generation of black musicians might have brought to China—the thumping rhythms and simpler harmonies of a James P. Johnson or a Fats Waller. It was not that Mitchell and Ruff were playing jazz that was pedantic or sedate. On the contrary, I have seldom heard Mitchell

play with more exuberant shifts of energy and mood. But the music was full of subtleties; even a Westerner accustomed to jazz would have been charmed by its intelligence and wit. I had to remind myself that the Chinese had heard no Western music of any kind from 1966 to 1976. A twenty-one-year-old student in the audience, for instance, would have begun to listen to composers like Mozart and Brahms only within the past five years. The jazz that he was hearing now was not so different as to be a whole new branch of music. Mitchell was clearly grounded in Bach and Chopin; Ruff's French horn had echoes of all the classical works—Debussy's "Reverie," Ravel's "Pavane"—in which that instrument has such uncanny power to move us.

35   After "Shanghai Blues," Ruff asked for questions.

36   "Where do people go to study jazz in America?" a student wanted to know. "What kind of courses do they take?"

37   Ruff explained the jazz courses, where they existed at all, would be part of a broad college curriculum that included, say, languages and history and physics. "But, really, jazz isn't learned in universities or conservatories," he said. "It's music that is passed on by older musicians to those of us who are younger."

38   It was not a helpful answer. What kind of subject didn't have its own academy? A shyness settled over the room, though the students seemed full of curiosity. Professor Tan got up and stood next to Ruff. "I urge you to ask questions," he said. "I can assure you that jazz has many principles that apply to your studies here. In fact, I have many questions myself."

39   An old professor stood up and asked, "When you created the 'Shanghai Blues' just now, did you have a form for it, or a logical plan?"

40   "I just started tapping my foot," Ruff replied, tapping his foot to reconstruct the moment. "And then I started to play the first thought that came into my mind with the horn. And Mitchell heard it. And he answered. And after that we heard and answered, heard and answered, heard and answered."

41   The old professor said, "But how can you ever play it again?"

42   "We never can," Ruff replied.

43   "That is beyond our imagination," the professor said. "Our students here play a piece a hundred times, or two hundred times, to get it exactly right. You play something once—something very beautiful—and then you just throw it away."

44   Now the questions tumbled out. What was most on the students' minds quickly became clear: it was the mystery of improvisation. (The Chinese don't even have a word for improvisation of this kind; Ruff translated it as "something created during the process of delivery.") All the questions poked at this central riddle—"Could a Chinese person improvise?" and "Could two strangers improvise together?" and "How can you compose at such speed?"—and during this period Ruff took one question and turned it into a moment that stood us all on our ear.

45   Was it really possible, a student wanted to know, to improvise on any tune at all—even one that the musicians had never heard before?

46   Ruff's reply was casual. "I would like to invite one of the pianists here to play a short traditional Chinese melody that I'm sure we would not know, and we will make a new piece based on that," he said.

47   The room erupted in oohs and cheers. I caught a look on Mitchell's face that said, "This time you've gone too far." The students began to call the name of the young man they wanted to have play. When they found him in the crowd, he was so diffident that he got down on the floor to keep from being dragged out. But his friends dragged him anyway, and, regaining his aplomb, he walked to the piano and sat down with the formality of a concert artist. He was about twenty-two. Mitchell stood to one side, looking grave.

48   The young man played his melody beautifully and with great feeling. It seemed to be his own composition, unknown to the other people. It began with four chords of distinctively Chinese structure, moved down the scale in a stately progression, paused, turned itself around with a transitional figure of lighter weight, and then started back up, never repeating itself and finally resolving the theme with a suspended chord that was satisfying because it was so unexpected. It was a perfect small piece, about fourteen bars long. The student walked back to his seat, and Mitchell went back to the piano. The room grew quiet.

49   Mitchell's huge hands hovered briefly over the keys, and then the young man's melody came back to him. It was in the same key; it had the same chords, slightly embellished near the end; and, best of all, it had the same mood. Having stated the theme, Mitchell broadened it the second time, giving it a certain majesty, coloring the student's chords with dissonances that were entirely apt. He gave the Chinese chords a jazz texture but still preserved their mood. Then Ruff joined him on his bass, and they took the melody through a number of variations, Mitchell giving it a whole series of new lives but never losing its integrity. I listened to his feat with growing excitement. For me, it was the climax of years of marvelling at his ear and at his sensitivity to the material at hand. The students were equally elated and astonished. For them, it was the ultimate proof—because it touched their own heritage—that for a jazz improvisor no point of departure is alien.

50   After that number, a few more questions were asked, and Mitchell and Ruff concluded with a Gershwin medley from "Porgy and Bess" and a genial rendition of "My Old Flame." Professor Tan thanked the two men and formally ended the concert. Then he went over to Mitchell and took his hands in his own. "You are an artist," he said.

51   Later, I told Mitchell that I thought Ruff had given him an unduly nervous moment when he invited the student to supply a melody.

52   "Well, naturally, I was nervous, because I didn't have any idea what to expect," he said. "But, you know, that boy phrased his piece *perfectly*. The minute he started to play, I got his emotions. I understood exactly what he was feeling, and the rest was easy. The notes and the chords just fell into place."

Suggestions for Discussion or Writing

1. According to Ruff, why did the jazz culture flourish in America? Could it have blossomed in any other nation? Why?

2. Who is narrating the incident and background information? What effect does this point of view have on the article? Who is the audience?

3. What was the "Cultural Revolution" Zinsser speaks of? Would it be possible to have such a revolution in America? Why?

4. How is Zinsser's piece structured? What are the benefits of combining a description of the events on stage with a narration of background and historical information?

5. What was it about the idea of "jazz" that most intrigued the Chinese students? Why were they fascinated with the notion?

6. What might be the author's reasons for relating the experiences of Ruff and Mitchell?

7. Do you think improvisation is a human characteristic? In what other ways do people improvise?

Kitsch

Gilbert Highet

Scholar and educator Gilbert Arthur Highet (1906–1978) was born in Glasgow, Scotland, immigrated to the United States in 1937, and became a naturalized citizen in 1951. He earned an M.A. at Glasgow University in 1929 and an M.A. at Oxford University in 1936, specializing in Greek and Latin. Highet became a professor of Greek and Latin languages and literature at Columbia University and received several honorary doctoral degrees for his teaching and scholarship. Besides being a radio commentator for the popular program "People, Places, and Books," he also was a judge for the Book of the Month Club for a number of years. Highet is known for his intellectual but entertaining approach to scholarship, literature, culture, and education. Among his written works are The Classical Tradition: Greek and Roman Influences on Western Literature *(1949),* Man's Unconquerable Mind *(1954),* The Powers of Poetry *(1960),* The Anatomy of Satire *(1962), which won a merit award from the American Philological Association, and* The Immortal Profession: The Joy of Teaching and Learning *(1976).*

1   If you have ever passed an hour wandering through an antique shop (not looking for anything exactly, but simply looking), you must have noticed how your taste gradually grows numb, and then—if you stay—becomes perverted. You begin to see unsuspected charm in those hideous pictures of plump girls fondling pigeons, you develop a psychopathic desire for spinning wheels and cobblers' benches, you are apt to pay out good money for a bronze statuette of Otto von Bismarck, with a metal hand

inside a metal frock coat and metal pouches under his metallic eyes. As soon as you take the things home, you realize that they are revolting. And yet they have a sort of horrible authority; you don't like them; you know how awful they are; but it is a tremendous effort to drop them in the garbage, where they belong.

2   To walk along a whole street of antique shops—that is an experience which shakes the very soul. Here is a window full of bulbous Chinese deities; here is another littered with Zulu assagais, Indian canoe paddles, and horse pistols which won't fire; the next shopfront is stuffed with Gaudy Italian majolica vases, and the next, even worse, with Austrian pottery—tiny ladies and gentlemen sitting on lace cushions and wearing lace ruffles, with every frill, every wrinkle and reticulation translated into porcelain: pink; stiff; but fortunately not unbreakable. The nineteenth century produced an appalling amount of junky art like this, and sometimes I imagine that clandestine underground factories are continuing to pour it out like illicit drugs.

3   There is a name for such stuff in the trade, a word apparently of Russian origin, kitsch: it means vulgar showoff, and it is applied to anything that took a lot of trouble to make and is quite hideous.

4   It is paradoxical stuff, kitsch. It is obviously bad: so bad that you can scarcely understand how any human being would spend days and weeks making it, and how anybody else would buy it and take it home and keep it and dust it and leave it to her heirs. It is terribly ingenious, and terribly ugly, and utterly useless; and yet it has one of the qualities of good art—which is that, once seen, it is not easily forgotten. Of course it is found in all the arts: think of the Milan Cathedral, or the statues in Westminster Abbey, or Liszt's setting of Schubert songs. There is a lot of it in the United States—for instance, the architecture of Miami, Florida, and Forest Lawn Cemetery in Los Angeles. Many of Hollywood's most ambitious historical films are superb kitsch. Most of Tin Pan Alley love songs are perfect 100 percent kitsch.

5   There is kitsch in the world of books also. I collect it. It is horrible, but I enjoy it.

6   The gem of my collection is the work of the Irish novelist Mrs. Amanda McKittrick Ros, whose masterpiece, *Delina Delaney*, was published about 1900. It is a strangely romantic tale, telling how Delina, a fisherman's daughter from Erin Cottage, was beloved by Lord Gifford, the heir of Columbia Castle, and—after many trials and even imprison-ment—married him. The story is dramatic, not to say impossible; but it is almost lost to view under the luxuriant style. Here, for example, is a sentence in which Mrs. Ros explains that her heroine used to earn extra cash by doing needlework.

> *She tried hard to assist in keeping herself a stranger to her poor old father's slight income by the use of the finest production of steel, whose blunt edge eyed the reely covering with marked greed, and offered its sharp dart to faultless fabrics of flaxen fineness.*

Revolting, but distinctive: what Mr. Polly called 'rockockyo' in manner. For the baroque vein, here is Lord Gifford saying goodbye to his sweetheart:

> *My darling virgin! my queen! my Delina! I am just in time to hear the toll of a parting bell strike its heavy weight of appalling softness against the*

weakest fibers of a heart of love, arousing and tickling its dormant action,
thrusting the dart of evident separation deeper into its tubes of tenderness,
and fanning the flame, already unextinguishable, into volumes of blaze.

Mrs. Ros had a remarkable command of rhetoric, and could coin an unforgettable phrase. She described her hero's black eyes as 'glittering jet revolvers.' When he became ill, she said he fell 'into a state of lofty fever'—doubtless because commoners have high fever, but lords have lofty fever. And her reflections on the moral degeneracy of society have rarely been equaled, in power and penetration:

> *Days of humanity, whither hast thou fled? When bows of compulsion,*
> *smiles for the deceitful, handshakes for the dogmatic, and welcome for*
> *the tool of power live under your objectionable, unambitious beat, not*
> *daring to be checked by the tongue of candour because the selfish world*
> *refuses to dispense with her rotten policies. The legacy of your forefa-*
> *thers, which involved equity, charity, reason, and godliness, is beyond*
> *the reach of their frivolous, mushroom offspring—deceit, injustice, mal-*
> *ice and unkindness—and is not likely to be codiciled with traits of*
> *harmony so long as these degrading vices of mock ambition fester the*
> *human heart.*

Perhaps one reason I enjoy this stuff is because it so closely resembles a typical undergraduate translation of one of Cicero's finest perorations: sound and fury, signifying nothing. I regret only that I have never seen Mrs. Ros's poetry. One volume was called *Poems of Puncture* and another *Bayonets of Bastard Sheen:* alas, jewels now almost unprocurable. But at least I know the opening of her lyric written on first visiting St. Paul's Cathedral:

> Holy Moses, take a look,
> Brain and brawn in every nook!

7   Such genius is indestructible. Soon, soon now, some earnest researcher will be writing a Ph.D. thesis on Mrs. Amanda McKittrick Ros, and thus (as she herself might put it) conferring upon her dewy brow the laurels of concrete immortality.

8   Next to Mrs. Ros in my collection of kitsch is the work of the Scottish poet William McGonagall. This genius was born in 1830, but did not find his vocation until 1877. Poor and inadequate poets pullulate in every tongue, but (as the *Times Literary Supplement* observes), McGonagall 'is the only truly memorable bad poet in our language.' In his command of platitude and his disregard of melody, he was the true heir of William Wordsworth as a descriptive poet.

9   In one way his talents, or at least his aspirations, exceeded those of Wordsworth. He was at his best in describing events he had never witnessed, such as train disasters, shipwrecks, and sanguinary battles, and in picturing magnificent scenery he had never beheld except with the eye of the imagination. Here is his unforgettable Arctic landscape:

> Greenland's icy mountains are fascinating and grand.
> And wondrously created by the Almighty's command;
> And the works of the Almighty there's few can understand;
> Who knows but it might be a part of Fairyland?
>
> Because there are churches of ice, and houses glittering like glass,
> And for scenic grandeur there's nothing can it surpass,
> Besides there's monuments and spires, also ruins,
> Which serve for a safe retreat from the wild bruins.
>
> The icy mountains they're higher than a brig's topmast.
> And the stranger in amazement stands aghast
> As he beholds the water flowing off the melted ice
> Adown the mountain sides, that he cries out, Oh! how nice!

10   McGonagall also had a strong dramatic sense. He loved to tell of agonizing adventures, more drastic perhaps but not less moving than that related in Wordsworth's 'Vaudracour an Julia.' The happy ending of one of his 'Gothic' ballads is surely unforgettable:

> So thus ends the story of Hanchen, a heroine brave,
> That tried hard her master's gold to save.
> And for her bravery she got married to the miller's eldest son,
> And Hanchen on her marriage night cried Heaven's will be done.

11   These scanty selections do not do justice to McGonagall's ingenuity as a rhymester. His sound effects show unusual talent. Most poets would be baffled by the problem of producing rhymes for the proper names *General Graham* and *Osman Digna*, but McGonagall gets them into a single stanza, with dazzling effect:

> Ye sons of Great Britain, I think no shame
> To write in praise of brave General Graham!
> Whose name will be handed down to posterity without any stigma,
> Because, at the Battle of El-Tab, he defeated Osman Digna.

12   One of McGonagall's most intense personal experiences was his visit to New York. Financially, it was not a success. In one of his vivid autobiographical sketches, he says, 'I tried occasionally to get an engagement from theatrical proprietors and music-hall proprietors, but alas! 'twas all in vain, for they all told me they didn't encourage rivalry.' However, he was deeply impressed by the architecture of Manhattan. In eloquent verses he expressed what many others have felt, although without adequate words to voice their emotion:

> Oh! Mighty City of New York, you are wonderful to behold.
> Your buildings are magnificent, the truth be it told;
> They were the only thing that seemed to arrest my eye,
> Because many of them are thirteen stories high.

And the tops of the houses are all flat,
And in the warm weather the people gather to chat;
Besides on the house-tops they dry their clothes,
And also many people all night on the house-tops repose.

13   Yet McGonagall felt himself a stranger in the United States. And here again his
close kinship with Wordsworth appears. The Poet Laureate, in a powerful sonnet
written at Calais, once reproached the English Channel for delaying his return by one
of those too frequent storms in which (reckless tyrant!) it will indulge itself:

Why cast ye back upon the Gallic shore,
Ye furious waves! a patriotic Son
Of England?

14   In the same vein McGonagall sings with rapture of his return to his 'ain countree':

And with regard to New York, and the sights I did see,
One street in Dundee is more worth to me,
And, believe me, the morning I sailed from New York
For bonnie Dundee—my heart it felt as light as a cork.

15   Indeed, New York is a challenging subject for ambitious poets. Here, from the
same shelf, is a delicious poem on the same theme, by Ezra Pound:

My City, my beloved
Thou art a maid with no breasts
Thou art slender as a silver reed.
Listen to me, attend me!
And I will breathe into thee a soul,
And thou shalt live for ever.

16   The essence of this kind of trash is incongruity. The kitsch writer is always sincere.
He really means to say something important. He feels he has a lofty spiritual message to
bring to an unawakened world, or else he has had a powerful experience which he must
communicate to the public. But either his message turns out to be a majestic platitude, or
else he chooses the wrong form in which to convey it—or, most delightful of all, there is
a fundamental discrepancy between the writer and his subject, as when Ezra Pound, born
in Idaho, addresses the largest city in the world as a maid with no breasts, and enjoins it
to achieve inspiration and immortality by listening to him. This is like climbing Mount
Everest in order to carve a head of Mickey Mouse in the east face.

17   Bad love poetry, bad religious poetry, bad mystical prose, bad novels both
autobiographical and historical—one can form a superb collection of kitsch simply
by reading with a lively and awakened eye. College songs bristle with it. The
works of Father Divine are full of it—all the more delightful because in him it
is usually incomprehensible. One of the Indian mystics, Sri Ramakrishna,

charmed connoisseurs by describing the Indian scriptures (in a phrase which almost sets itself to kitsch-music) as

> fried in the butter of knowledge and steeped in the honey of love.

Bad funeral poetry is a rich mine of the stuff. Here, for example, is the opening of a jolly little lament. 'The Funeral' by Stephen Spender, apparently written during his pink period:

> Death is another milestone on their way,
> With laughter on their lips and winds blowing round them
> They record simply
> How this one excelled all others in making driving belts.

Observe the change from humanism to communism. Spender simply took Browning's 'Grammarian's Funeral,' threw away the humor and the marching rhythm, and substituted wind and the Stakhanovist speed-up. Such also is a delicious couplet from Archibald MacLeish's elegy on the late Harry Crosby:

> He walks with Ernest in the streets of Sargossa
> They are drunk their mouths are hard they saw *que cosa.*

18 From an earlier romantic period, here is a splendid specimen. Coleridge attempted to express the profound truth that men and animals are neighbors in a hard world; but he made the fundamental mistake of putting it into a monologue address to a donkey:

> Poor Ass! Thy master should have learnt to show
> Pity—best taught by fellowship of Woe!
> Innocent foal! thou poor despised forlorn!
> I hail thee brother . . . .

19 Once you get the taste for this kind of thing it is possible to find pleasure in hundreds of experiences which you might otherwise have thought either anesthetic or tedious: bad translations, abstract painting, grand opera . . . Dr. Johnson, with his strong sense of humor, had a fancy for kitsch, and used to repeat a poem in celebration of the marriage of the Duke of Leeds, composed by 'an inferiour domestick . . . in such homely rhimes as he could make':

> When the Duke of Leeds shall married be
> To a fine young lady of high quality,
> How happy will that gentlewoman be
> In his Grace of Leed's good company.

> She shall have all that's fine and fair.
> And the best of silk and sattin shall wear;

And ride in a coach to take the air,
And have a house in St. James's Square.

20   Folk poetry is full of such jewels. Here is the epitaph on an old gentleman from Vermont who died in a sawmill accident:

How shocking to the human mind
The log did him to powder grind.
God did command his soul away
His summings we must all obey.

21   Kitsch is well known in drama, although, (except for motion pictures) it does not usually last long. One palmary instance was a play extolling the virtues of the Boy Scout movement, called *Young England*. It ran for a matter of years during the 1930's, to audiences almost wholly composed of kitsch-fanciers, who eventually came to know the text quite as well as the unfortunate actors. I can still remember the opening of one magnificent episode. Scene: a woodland glade. Enter the hero, a Scoutmaster, riding a bicycle, and followed by the youthful members of his troop. They pile bicycles in silence. Then the Scoutmaster raises his finger, and says (accompanied fortissimo by most of the members of the audience):

Fresh water must be our first consideration.

22   In the decorative arts kitsch flourishes, and is particularly widespread in sculpture. One of my favorite pieces of bad art is a statue in Rockefeller Center, New York. It is supposed to represent Atlas, the titan condemned to carry the sky on his shoulders. That is an ideal of somber, massive tragedy: greatness and suffering combined as in Hercules or Prometheus. But this version displays Atlas as a powerful moron, with a tiny head, rather like the pan-fried young men who appear in health magazines. Instead of supporting the heavens, he is lifting a spherical metal balloon: it is transparent, and quite empty; and yet he is balancing insecurely on one foot like a furniture mover walking upstairs with a beach ball; and he is scowling like a mad baboon. If he ever gets the thing up, he will drop it; or else heave it onto a Fifth Avenue bus. It is a supremely ridiculous statue, and delights me every time I see it.

23   Perhaps you think this is a depraved taste. But really it is an extension of experience. At one end, Homer. At the other, Amanda McKittrick Ros. At one end, *Hamlet*. At the other, McGonagall, who is best praised in his own inimitable words:

The poetry is moral and sublime
And in my opinion nothing could be more fine.
True genius there does shine so bright
Like unto the stars of night.

Suggestions for Discussion or Writing

1. What is the tone of Highet's essay? What words or phrases develop that tone? How does the tone enhance the main idea?

2. What *is* kitsch? What are the sources of kitsch? What is paradoxical about kitsch according to Highet?

3. Based on Highet's article how would you describe the predominant style of kitsch, whether it be written or visual "art"?

4. How does figurative language such as simile, metaphor, and allusion contribute to Highet's essay?

5. What might be the purpose of Highet's essay? Do you think he is poking fun at great literature? What purpose might Highet have in contrasting McGonagall's kitsch with Wordsworth's poetry?

6. What does Highet mean when he calls his love of kitsch a "depraved taste," an "extension of experience"? What are some things you consider kitsch? What qualifies as kitsch in your experience? Why?

The Ring of Time

E. B. White

Elwyn Brooks White (1899–1985) was born in Mt. Vernon, New York, and earned his B.A. at Cornell University in 1921. He was a newspaper reporter in both New York City and Seattle, and later worked for an advertising agency. His contributions first appeared in the New Yorker *in 1925 and he accepted a job on that publication's staff a year later. White is perhaps best known for his story of a pig and a spider,* Charlotte's Web *(1953), which was named a Newbery Honor Book and was later made into an animated film.* Stuart Little *and* The Trumpet of the Swan *(1971) are two more of his books written for children. White also coauthored, with James Thurber,* Is Sex Necessary? *(1929) and with K. S. White,* A Subtreasury of American Humor. The Elements of Style, *by Strunk and White, was developed from Cornell professor William Strunk's "Little Book" on grammar. White's books of essays include* The Second Tree from the Corner, Points of My Compass, One Man's Meat, *and* Essays of E. B. White. *His books of poetry are* The Fox of Peapack, The Lady Is Cold, *and* Poems and Sketches of E. B. White.

1   FIDDLER BAYOU, March 22, 1956—After the lions had returned to their cages, creeping angrily through the chutes, a little bunch of us drifted away and into an open doorway nearby, where we stood for a while in semidarkness, watching a big brown circus horse go harumphing around the practice ring. His trainer was a woman of about forty, and the two of them, horse and woman, seemed caught up on one of those desultory treadmills of afternoon from which there is no apparent escape. The day was hot, and we kibitzers were grateful to be briefly out of the sun's glare. The long rein, or tape, by which the woman guided her charge counterclockwise in his dull career formed the radius of their private circle, of which she was the revolving center; and she, too, stepped a tiny circumference of her own, in order to accommodate the horse and allow him his maximum scope. She had on a short-skirted costume and a conical straw hat. Her legs were bare and she wore high heels, which probed deep into the loose tanbark and kept her ankles in a state of constant turmoil. The great size and meekness of the horse, the repetitious exercise, the heat of the afternoon, all exerted a hypnotic charm that invited boredom; we spectators were experiencing a languor—we neither expected relief nor felt entitled to any. We had paid a dollar to get into the grounds, to be sure, but we had got our dollar's worth a few minutes before, when the lion trainer's whiplash had caught around a toe of one of the lions. What more did we want for a dollar?

2   Behind me I heard someone say, "Excuse me, please," in a low voice. She was halfway into the building when I turned and saw her—a girl of sixteen or seventeen, politely threading her way through us onlookers who blocked the entrance. As she emerged in front of us, I saw that she was barefoot, her dirty little feet fighting the uneven ground. In most respects she was like any of two or three dozen showgirls you encounter if you wander about the winter quarters of Mr. John Ringling North's circus, in Sarasota—cleverly proportioned, deeply browned by the sun, dusty, eager, and almost naked. But her grave face and the naturalness of her manner gave her a sort of quick distinction and brought a new note into the gloomy octagonal building where we had all cast our lot for a few moments. As soon as she had squeezed through the crowd, she spoke a word or two to the older woman, whom I took to be her mother, stepped to the ring, and waited until the horse coasted to a stop in front of her. She gave the animal a couple of affectionate swipes on his enormous neck and then swung herself aboard. The horse immediately resumed his rocking canter, the woman goading him on, chanting something that sounded like "Hop! Hop!"

3   In attempting to recapture this mild spectacle, I am merely acting as recording secretary for one of the oldest of societies—the society to those who, at one time or another, have surrendered, without even a show of resistance, to the bedazzlement of a circus rider. As a writing man, or secretary, I have always felt charged with the safekeeping of all unexpected items of worldly or unworldly enchantment, as though I might be held personally responsible if even a small one were to be lost. But it is not easy to communicate anything of this nature. The circus comes as close to being the world in microcosm as anything I know; in a way, it puts all the rest of show business in the shade. Its magic is universal and complex. Out of its wild disorder comes order; from its rank smell rises the good aroma of courage and daring; out of its preliminary shabbiness comes the final splendor. And buried in the familiar boasts of its advance

agents lies the modesty of most of its people. For me the circus is at its best before it has been put together. It is at its best at certain moments when it comes to a point, as through a burning glass, in the activity and destiny of a single performer out of so many. One ring is always bigger than three. One rider, one aerialist, is always greater than six. In short, a man has to catch the circus unawares to experience its full impact and share its gaudy dream.

4   The ten-minute ride the girl took achieved—as far as I was concerned, who wasn't looking for it, and unbeknownst to her, who wasn't even striving for it—the thing that is sought by performers everywhere, on whatever stage, whether struggling in the tidal currents of Shakespeare or bucking the difficult motion of a horse. I somehow got the idea she was just cadging a ride, improving a shining ten minutes in the diligent way all serious artists seize free moments to hone the blade of their talent and keep themselves in trim. Her brief tour included only elementary postures and tricks, perhaps because they were all she was capable of, perhaps because her warmup at this hour was unscheduled and the ring was not rigged for a real practice session. She swung herself off and on the horse several times, gripping his mane. She did a few kneestands—or whatever they are called—dropping to her knees and quickly bouncing back up on her feet again. Most of the time she simply rode in a standing position, well aft on the beast, her hands hanging easily at her sides, her head erect, her straw-colored ponytail lightly brushing her shoulders, the blood of exertion showing faintly through the tan of her skin. Twice she managed a one-foot stance—a sort of ballet pose, with arms outstretched. At one point the neck strap of her bathing suit broke and she went twice around the ring in the classic attitude of a woman making minor repairs to a garment. The fact that she was standing on the back of a moving horse while doing this invested the matter with a clownish significance that perfectly fitted the spirit of the circus—jocund, yet charming. She just rolled the strap into a neat ball and stowed it inside her bodice while the horse rocked and rolled beneath her in dutiful innocence. The bathing suit proved as self-reliant as its owner and stood up well enough without benefit of strap.

5   The richness of the scene was in its plainness, its natural condition—of horse, of ring, of girl, even to the girl's bare feet that gripped the bare back of her proud and ridiculous mount. The enchantment grew not out of anything that happened or was performed but out of something that seemed to go round and around and around with the girl, attending her, a steady gleam in the shape of a circle—a ring of ambition, of happiness, of youth. (And the positive pleasures of equilibrium under difficulties.) In a week or two, all would be changed, all (or almost all) lost: the girl would wear makeup, the horse would wear gold, the ring would be painted, the bark would be clean for the feet of the horse, the girl's feet would be clean for the slippers that she'd wear. All, all would be lost.

6   As I watched with the others, our jaws adroop, our eyes alight, I became painfully conscious of the element of time. Everything in the hideous old building seemed to take the shape of a circle, conforming to the course of the horse. The rider's gaze, as she peered straight ahead, seemed to be circular, as though bent by force of circumstance; then time itself began running in circles, and so the beginning was where the end was, and the two were the same, and one thing ran into the next and time went

round and around and got nowhere. The girl wasn't so young that she did not know the delicious satisfaction of having a perfectly behaved body and the fun of using it to do a trick most people can't do, but she was too young to know that time does not really move in a circle at all. I thought: "She will never be as beautiful as this again"—a thought that made me acutely unhappy—and in a flash my mind (which is too much of a busybody to suit me) had projected her twenty-five years ahead, and she was now in the center of the ring, on foot, wearing a conical hat and high-heeled shoes, the image of the older woman, holding the long rein, caught in the treadmill of an afternoon long in the future. "She is at that enviable moment in life [I thought] when she believes she can go once around the ring, make one complete circuit, and at the end be exactly the same age as at the start." Everything in her movements, her expression, told you that for her the ring of time was perfectly formed, changeless, predictable, without beginning or end, like the ring in which she was traveling at this moment with the horse that wallowed under her. And then I slipped back into my trance, and time was circular again—time, pausing quietly with the rest of us, so as not to disturb the balance of a performer.

7   Her ride ended as casually as it had begun. The older woman stopped the horse, and the girl slid to the ground. As she walked toward us to leave, there was a quick, small burst of applause. She smiled broadly, in surprise and pleasure; then her face suddenly regained its gravity and she disappeared through the door.

8   It has been ambitious and plucky of me to attempt to describe what is indescribable, and I have failed, as I knew I would. But I have discharged my duty to my society; and besides, a writer, like an acrobat, must occasionally try a stunt that is too much for him. At any rate, it is worth reporting that long before the circus comes to town, its most notable performances have already been given. Under the bright lights of the finished show, a performer need only reflect the electric candle power that is directed upon him; but in the dark and dirty old training rings and the makeshift cages, whatever light is generated, whatever excitement, whatever beauty, must come from original sources—from internal fires of professional hunger and delight, from the exuberance and gravity of youth. It is the difference between planetary light and the combustion of stars.

Suggestions for Discussion or Writing

1. According to White, why does he write the essay? Is there more than one purpose?

2. What audiences does White's essay appeal to? What words and phrases reveal these audiences?

3. Early in the essay, White states that he is "merely acting as a recording secretary" of the incident. What sensory details does he record? How do these details affect the reader? Does he merely record, or does he do more with the details?

4. How many different ways does White use the metaphor of the circle? What levels of meaning does he express by using the circle metaphor several ways? How are circles used in art, music, and dance?

5. How does White's role as a recorder relate to your own role in journalkeeping? What kinds of incidents and details do you record? Why is this recordkeeping valuable? How does recording the details of an incident help you interpret the significance of an incident?

What If Shakespeare Had Had a Sister?

Virginia Woolf

English novelist, essayist, and critic Virginia Woolf (1882–1941) associated with many well-known writers of her time. She founded the Hogarth Press in 1917 and published many upcoming writers such as E. M. Forster, Gertrude Stein, T. S. Eliot, and Katherine Mansfield. Her most successful novel, To the Lighthouse *(1927), is filled with characters based on people in her own life. Her other work includes* Voyage Out *(1915),* Night and Day *(1919),* A Room of One's Own *(1929), and* The Waves *(1931.) Woolf is known for her fine use of stream-of-consciousness and the interior monologue.*

1   It is a perennial puzzle why no woman wrote a word of that extraordinary literature [of the time of Elizabeth I] when every man, it seemed, was capable of song or sonnet. What were the conditions in which women lived, I asked myself; for fiction, imaginative work, that is, is not dropped like a pebble upon the ground, as science may be; fiction is like a spider's web, attached ever so lightly perhaps, but still attached to life at all four corners. Often the attachment is scarcely perceptible: Shakespeare's plays, for instance, seem to hang there complete by themselves. But when the web is pulled askew, hooked up at the edge, torn in the middle, one remembers that those webs are not spun in midair by incorporeal creatures, but are the work of suffering human beings, and are attached to grossly material things, like health and money and the houses we live in.

2   I went, therefore, to the shelf where the histories stand and took down one of the latest, Professor Trevelyan's *History of England.* Once more I looked up women, found "position of," and turned to the pages indicated. "Wife-beating," I read, "was a recognized right of man, and was practised without shame by high as well as low. . . . Similarly," the historian goes on, "the daughter who refused to marry the gentleman of her parents' choice was liable to be locked up, beaten and flung about the room, without any shock being inflicted on public opinion. Marriage was not an affair of personal affection, but of family avarice, particularly in the 'chivalrous' upper classes. . . . Betrothal often took place while one or both of the parties was in the cradle, and

marriage when they were scarcely out of the nurses' charge." That was about 1470, soon after Chaucer's time. The next reference to the position of women is some two hundred years later, in the time of the Stuarts. "It was still the exception for women of the upper and middle class to choose their own husbands, and when the husband had been assigned, he was lord and master, so far at least as law and custom could make him. Yet even so," Professor Trevelyan concludes, "neither Shakespeare's women nor those of authentic seventeenth-century memoirs, like the Verneys and the Hutchinsons, seem wanting in personality and character." Certainly, if we consider it, Cleopatra must have had a way with her; Lady Macbeth, one would suppose, had a will of her own; Rosalind, one might conclude, was an attractive girl. Professor Trevelyan is speaking no more than the truth when he remarks that Shakespeare's women do not seem wanting in personality and character. Not being a historian, one might go even further and say that women have burnt like beacons in all the works of all the poets from the beginning of time—Clytemnestra, Antigone, Cleopatra, Lady Macbeth, Phedre, Cressida, Rosalind, Desdemona, the Duchess of Malfi, among the dramatists; then among the prose writers: Millamant, Clarissa, Becky Sharp, Anna Karenina, Emma Bovary, Madame de Guermantes—the names flock to mind, nor do they recall women "lacking in personality and character." Indeed, if woman had no existence save in the fiction written by men, one would imagine her a person of the utmost importance; very various; heroic and mean; splendid and sordid; infinitely beautiful and hideous in the extreme; as great as a man, some think even greater. But this is woman in fiction. In fact, as Professor Trevelyan points out, she was locked up, beaten and flung about the room.

3   A very queer, composite being thus emerges. Imaginatively she is of the highest importance; practically she is completely insignificant. She pervades poetry from cover to cover; she is all but absent from history. She dominates the lives of kings and conquerors in fiction; in fact she was the slave of any boy whose parents forced a ring upon her finger. Some of the most inspired words, some of the most profound thoughts in literature fall from her lips; in real life she could hardly read, could scarcely spell, and was the property of her husband.

4   It was certainly an odd monster that one made up by reading the historians first and the poets afterwards—a worm winged like an eagle; the spirit of life and beauty in a kitchen chopping up suet. But these monsters, however amusing to the imagination, have no existence in fact. What one must do to bring her to life was to think poetically and prosaically at one and the same moment, thus keeping in touch with the fact—that she is Mrs. Martin, aged thirty-six, dressed in blue, wearing a black hat and brown shoes; but not losing sight of fiction either—that she is a vessel in which all sorts of spirits and forces are coursing and flashing perpetually. The moment, however, that one tries this method with the Elizabethan woman, one branch of illumination fails; one is held up by the scarcity of facts. One knows nothing detailed, nothing perfectly true and substantial about her. History scarcely mentions her. . . .

5   Here I am asking why women did not write poetry in the Elizabethan age, and I am not sure how they were educated; whether they were taught to write; whether they had sitting-rooms to themselves; how many women had children before they were twenty-one; what, in short, they did from eight in the morning till eight at night. They had no money evidently; according to Professor Trevelyan they were married whether

they liked it or not before they were out of the nursery, at fifteen or sixteen very likely. It would have been extremely odd, even upon this showing, had one of them suddenly written the plays of Shakespeare, I concluded, and I thought of that old gentleman, who is dead now, but was a bishop, I think, who declared that it was impossible for any woman, past, present, or to come, to have the genius of Shakespeare. He wrote to the papers about it. He also told a lady who applied to him for information that cats do not as a matter of fact go to heaven, though they have, he added, souls of a sort. How much thinking those old gentlemen used to save one! How the borders of ignorance shrank back at their approach! Cats do not go to heaven. Women cannot write the plays of Shakespeare.

6   Be that as it may, I could not help thinking, as I looked at the works of Shakespeare on the shelf, that the bishop was right at least in this; it would have been impossible, completely and entirely, for any woman to have written the plays of Shakespeare in the age of Shakespeare. Let me imagine, since facts are so hard to come by, what would have happened had Shakespeare had a wonderfully gifted sister, called Judith, let us say. Shakespeare himself went, very probably—his mother was an heiress—to the grammar school, where he may have learnt Latin—Ovid, Virgil and Horace—and the elements of grammar and logic. He was, it is well known, a wild boy who poached rabbits, perhaps shot a deer, and had, rather sooner than he should have done, to marry a woman in the neighborhood, who bore him a child rather quicker than was right. That escapade sent him to seek his fortune in London. He had, it seemed, a taste for the theatre; he began by holding horses at the stage door. Very soon he got work in the theatre, becoming a successful actor, and lived at the hub of the universe, meeting everybody, knowing everybody, practicing his art on the boards, exercising his wits in the streets, and even getting access to the palace of the queen. Meanwhile his extraordinarily gifted sister, let us suppose, remained at home. She was as adventurous, as imaginative, as agog to see the world as he was. But she was not sent to school. She had no chance of learning grammar and logic, let alone of reading Horace and Virgil. She picked up a book now and then, one of her brother's perhaps, and read a few pages. But then her parents came in and told her to mend the stockings or mind the stew. They would have spoken sharply but kindly, for they were substantial people who knew the conditions of life for a woman and loved their daughter—indeed, more likely than not she was the apple of her father's eye. Perhaps she scribbled some pages up in an apple loft on the sly, but was careful to hide them or set fire to them. Soon, however, before she was out of her teens, she was to be betrothed to the son of a neighboring wool-stapler. She cried out that marriage was hateful to her, and for that she was severely beaten by her father. Then he ceased to scold her. He begged her instead not to hurt him, not to shame him in this matter of her marriage. He would give her a chain of beads or a fine petticoat, he said; and there were tears in his eyes. How could she disobey him? How could she break his heart? The force of her own gift alone drove her to it. She made up a small parcel of her belongings, let herself down by a rope one summer's night and took the road to London. She was not seventeen. The birds that sang in the hedge were not more musical than she was. She had the quickest fancy, a gift like her brother's for the tune of words. Like him, she had a taste for the theatre. She stood at the stage door; she wanted to act, she said. Men laughed in her face. The

manager—a fat, loose-lipped man—guffawed. He bellowed something about poodles dancing and women acting—no woman, he said, could possibly be an actress. He hinted—you can imagine what. She could get no training in her craft. Could she even seek her dinner in a tavern or roam the streets at midnight? Yet her genius was for fiction and lusted to feed abundantly upon the lives of men and women and the study of their ways. At last—for she was very young—oddly, like Shakespeare the poet in her face, with the same grey eyes and rounded brows—at last Nick Greene the actor-manager took pity on her; she found herself with child by that gentleman and so—who shall measure the heat and violence of the poet's heart when caught and tangled in a woman's body?—killed herself one winter's night and lies buried at some crossroads where the omnibuses now stop outside the Elephant and Castle.

7   That, more or less, is how the story would run, I think, if a woman in Shakespeare's day had had Shakespeare's genius. But for my part, I agree with the deceased bishop, if such he was—it is unthinkable that any woman in Shakespeare's day should have had Shakespeare's genius. For genius like Shakespeare's is not born among laboring, uneducated, servile people. It was not born in England among the Saxons and the Britons. It is not born today among the working classes. How, then, could it have been born among women whose work began, according to Professor Trevelyan, almost before they were out of the nursery, who were forced to it by their parents and held to it by all the power of law and custom? Yet genius of a sort must have existed among women as it must have existed among the working classes. Now and again an Emily Bronte or a Robert Burns blazes out and proves its presence. But certainly it never got itself on to paper. When, however, one reads of a witch being ducked, of a woman possessed by devils, of a wise woman selling herbs, or even of a very remarkable man who had a mother, then I think we are on the track of a lost novelist, a suppressed poet, of some mute and inglorious Jane Austen, some Emily Bronte who dashed her brains out on the moor or mopped and mowed about the highways crazed with the torture that her gift had put her to. Indeed, I would venture to guess that Anon, who wrote so many poems without signing them, was often a woman. It was a woman Edward Fitzgerald, I think, suggested who made the ballads and the folk-songs crooning them to her children, beguiling her spinning with them, on the length of the winter's night.

8   This may be true or it may be false—who can say?—but what is true in it, so it seemed to me, reviewing the story of Shakespeare's sister as I had made it, is that any woman born with a great gift in the sixteenth century would certainly have gone crazed, shot herself, or ended her days in some lonely cottage outside the village, half witch, half wizard, feared and mocked at. For it needs little skill in psychology to be sure that a highly gifted girl who had tried to use her gift for poetry would have been so thwarted and hindered by other people, so tortured and pulled asunder by her own contrary instincts, that she must have lost her health and sanity to a certainty. No girl could have walked to London and stood at a stage door and forced her way into the presence of actor-managers without doing herself a violence and suffering an anguish which may have been irrational—for chastity may be a fetish invented by certain societies for unknown reasons—but were none the less inevitable. Chastity had then, it has even now, a religious importance in a woman's life, and so wrapped itself round with nerves and instincts that to cut it free and bring it to the light of day demands courage of the

rarest. To have lived a free life in London in the sixteenth century would have meant for a woman who was poet and playwright a nervous stress and dilemma which might well have killed her. Had she survived, whatever she had written would be twisted and deformed, issuing from a strained and morbid imagination. And undoubtedly, I thought, looking at the shelf where there are no plays by women, her work would have gone unsigned. That refuge she would have sought certainly. It was the relic of the sense of chastity that dictated anonymity to women even so late as the nineteenth century. Currer Bell, George Eliot, George Sand, all the victims of inner strife as their writings prove, sought ineffectively to veil themselves by using the name of a man. Thus they did homage to the convention, which if not implanted by the other sex was liberally encouraged by them (the chief glory of a woman is not to be talked of, said Pericles, himself a much-talked-of man), that publicity in women is detestable. Anonymity runs in their blood. . . .

9   I told you in the course of this paper that Shakespeare had a sister; but do not look for her in Sir Sidney Lee's life of the poet. She died young—alas, she never wrote a word. She lies buried where the omnibuses now stop, opposite the Elephant and Castle. Now my belief is that this poet who never wrote a word and was buried at the crossroads still lives. She lives in you and in me, and in many other women who are not here tonight, for they are washing up the dishes and putting the children to bed. But she lives; for great poets do not die; they are continuing presences; they need only the opportunity to walk among us in the flesh. This opportunity, as I think, it is now coming within your power to give her. For my belief is that if we live another century or so—I am talking of the common life which is the real life and not of the little separate lives which we live as individuals—and have five hundred a year each of us and rooms of our own; if we have the habit of freedom and the courage to write exactly what we think; if we escape a little from the common sitting-room and see human beings not always in their relation to each other but in relation to reality; and the sky, too, and the trees or whatever it may be in themselves; if we look past Milton's bogey, for no human being should cast out the view; if we face the fact, for it is a fact, that there is no arm to cling to, but that we go alone and that our relation is to the world of reality and not only to the world of men and women, then the opportunity will come and the dead poet who was Shakespeare's sister will put on the body which she has so often laid down. Drawing her life from the lives of the unknown who were her forerunners, as her brother did before her, she will be born. As for her coming without that preparation, without that effort on our part, without that determination that when she is born again she shall find it possible to live and write her poetry, that we cannot expect, for that would be impossible. But I maintain that she would come if we worked for her, and that so to work, even in poverty and obscurity, is worthwhile.

Suggestions for Discussion or Writing

1. By using Shakespeare's fictional sister as an example, what issue is Woolf exploring in this piece? What possibilities does she give as answers to the questions involved in this issue?

2. At one point Woolf speaks of an old bishop known to have "declared that it was impossible for any woman, past, present, or to come, to have the genius of Shakespeare." In what ways does Woolf agree with this statement? In what ways does she disagree?

3. According to Woolf, to what end would a woman of genius in the sixteenth century have come? Why? What happens to a woman of genius today? How are her circumstances the same as a sixteenth-century woman? How are her circumstances different?

4. What seems to be Woolf's purpose in writing the essay? What action does she call for?

Pavlova

Agnes De Mille

Agnes De Mille, also known as Agnes George Prude, was born in 1905 in New York and began a career of dance at an early age. She studied under Koslov, Marie Rambert, Antony Tudor, and Tamara Karsavina in London (1922–1938). Dancer, director, choreographer, and finally author, she choreographed for the Ballet Russe de Monte Carlo (1943), then choreographed in Hollywood, working for over fourteen musical films including Oklahoma *(1943),* Carousel *(1945), and* Brigadoon *(1947). Her autobiography,* Dance to the Piper: Memoirs of the Ballet, *appeared in 1951. In 1972 she choreographed for the Royal Winnipeg Ballet and then published* Speak to Me, Dance with Me *in 1973.*

1   Anna Pavlova! My life stops as I write that name. Across the daily preoccupation of lessons, lunch boxes, tooth brushings and quarrelings with Margaret flashed this bright, unworldly experience and burned in a single afternoon a path over which I could never retrace my steps. I had witnessed the power of beauty, and in some chamber of my heart I lost forever my irresponsibility. I was as clearly marked as though she had looked me in the face and called my name. For generations my father's family had loved and served the theater. All my life I had seen actors and actresses and had heard theater jargon at the dinner table and business talk of box-office grosses. I had thrilled at Father's projects and watched fascinated his picturesque occupations. I took a proprietary pride in the profitable and hasty growth of "The Industry." But nothing in his world or my uncle's prepared me for theater as I saw it that Saturday afternoon.

2   Since that day I have gained some knowledge in my trade and I recognize that her technique was limited; that her arabesques were not as pure or classically correct as Markova's, that her jumps and batterie were paltry, her turns not to be compared in strength and number with the strenuous durability of Baronova or Toumanova. I know that her scenery was designed by second-rate artists, her music was on a level with restaurant orchestrations, her company definitely inferior to all the standards we insist on today, and her choreography mostly hack. And yet I say that she was in her person the quintessence of theatrical excitement.

3   As her little bird body revealed itself on the scene, either immobile in trembling mystery or tense in the incredible arc which was her lift, her instep stretched ahead in an arch never before seen, the tiny bones of her hands in ceaseless vibration, her face radiant, diamonds glittering under her dark hair, her little waist encased in silk, the great tutu balancing, quickening and flashing over her beating, flashing, quivering legs, every man and woman sat forward, every pulse quickened. She never appeared to rest static, some part of her trembled, vibrated, beat like a heart. Before our dazzled eyes, she flashed with the sudden sweetness of a hummingbird in action too quick for our understanding by our gross utilitarian standards, in action sensed rather than seen. The movie cameras of her day could not record her allegro. Her feet and hands photographed as a blur.

4   Bright little bird bones, delicate bird sinews! She was all fire and steel wire. There was not an ounce of spare flesh on her skeleton, and the life force used and used her body until she died of the fever of moving, gasping for breath, much too young.

5   She was small, about five feet. She wore a size one and a half slipper, but her feet and hands were large in proportion to her height. Her hand could cover her whole face. Her trunk was small and stripped of all anatomy but the ciphers of adolescence, her arms and legs relatively long, the neck extraordinarily long and mobile. All her gestures were liquid and possessed of an inner rhythm that flowed to inevitable completion with the finality of architecture or music. Her arms seemed to lift not from the elbow or the arm socket, but from the base of the spine. Her legs seemed to function from the waist. When she bent her head her whole spine moved and the motion was completed the length of the arm through the elongation of her slender hand and the quivering reaching fingers. I believe there has never been a foot like hers, slender, delicate and of such astonishing aggressiveness when arched as to suggest the ultimate in human vitality. Without in any way being sensual, being, in fact, almost sexless, she suggested all exhilaration, gaiety and delight. She jumped, and we broke bonds with reality. We flew. We hung over the earth, spread in the air as we do in dreams, our hands turning in the air as in water—the strong forthright taut plunging leg balanced on the posed arc of the foot, the other leg stretched to the horizon like the wing of a bird. We lay balancing, quivering, turning, and all things were possible, even to us, the ordinary people.

6   I have seen two dancers as great or greater since, Alicia Markova and Margot Fonteyn, and many other women who have kicked higher, balanced longer or turned faster. These are poor substitutes for passion. In spite of her flimsy dances, the bald and blatant virtuosity, there was an intoxicated rapture, a focus of energy, Dionysian in its physical intensity, that I have never seen equaled by a performer in any theater of the world. Also she was the *first* of the truly great in our experience.

7   I sat with the blood beating in my throat. As I walked into the bright glare of the afternoon, my head ached and I could scarcely swallow. I didn't wish to cry. I certainly couldn't speak. I sat in a daze in the car oblivious to the grownup's ceaseless prattle. At home I climbed the stairs slowly to my bedroom and, shutting myself in, placed both hands on the brass rail at the foot of my bed, then rising laboriously to the tips of my white buttoned shoes I stumped the width of the bed and back again. My toes throbbed with pain, my knees shook, my legs quivered with weakness. I repeated the exercise. The blessed, relieving tears stuck at last on my lashes. Only by hurting my feet could I ease the pain in my throat.

8   Death came to Anna Pavlova in 1931, when she was fifty. She had not stopped touring for a single season. Her knees had sustained some damage, but she would not rest, and she was in a state of exhaustion when the train that was carrying her to Holland was wrecked. She ran out into the snow in her nightgown and insisted on helping the wounded. When she reached The Hague she had double pneumonia. Her last spoken words were, "Get the *Swan* dress ready."[1]

9   Standing on Ninth Avenue under the El, I saw the headlines on the front page of the *New York Times*. It did not seem possible. She was in essence the denial of death. My own life was rooted to her in a deep spiritual sense and had been during the whole of my growing up. It mattered not that I had only spoken to her once and that my work lay in a different direction. She was the vision and the impulse and the goal.

Suggestions for Discussion or Writing

1. Why is Agnes De Mille's assessment of Anna Pavlova especially valid?

2. How does her description of Pavlova border on the poetic? What metaphors does she use?

3. Why does De Mille find Pavlova to be one of the great dancers of history even though she was not as good in some techniques as other dancers?

4. Compare De Mille's description of a dancer with Pollitt's description.

[1]One of Pavlova's most celebrated dances was as a dying swan, in a ballet created especially for her.

Modern Art

Katherine Kuh

Born in 1904 in St. Louis, Missouri, Katherine W. Kuh received an M.A. at the University of Chicago. A specialist in modern art, she was director of the Art Institute of Chicago from 1936–1943 and the Curator of Modern Painting and Sculpture from 1953–1957. She has been the Art Editor of the Saturday Review *and an art consultant at Southern Illinois University (1964–1968). Her books include* Break-up: The Core of Modern Art *(1965),* Art Has Many Faces *(1951),* The Artist's Voice *(1962), and* The Open Eye *(1971).*

1   The art of our century has been characterized by shattered surfaces, broken color, segmented compositions, dissolving forms and shredded images. Curiously insistent is this consistent emphasis on break-up. However, dissolution today does not necessarily mean lack of discipline. It can also mean a new kind of discipline, for disintegration is often followed by reconstruction, the artist deliberately smashing his material only to reassemble it in new and unexpected relationships. Moreover, the process of breaking up is quite different from the process of breaking down. And during the last hundred years, every aspect of art has been broken up—color, light, pigment, form, line, content, space, surface and design.

2   In the nineteenth century, easels were moved out-of-doors and color was broken into relatively minute areas in order to approximate the reality of sunlight and to preserve on canvas nature's own fleeting atmospheric effects. Known as Impressionism, this movement was the first step in a long sequence of experiments that finally banished the Renaissance emphasis on humanism, on three-dimensional form and on a traditional center of interest. Here was the beginning of a gradual but steady tendency toward diffusion in art. A few years later, Vincent Van Gogh transformed broken color into broken pigment. Less interested in realistic light than in his own highly charged emotions, he allowed smashing rhythmic brushstrokes to mirror his personal turbulence. In doing so he foretold twentieth-century Expressionism, that aptly named movement which relied on pitted surfaces, broken outlines, unpredictable color and scarred textures to intensify emotional expression. As the Impressionists were bent on freeing nature from sham, so the Expressionists hope to liberate their own feelings from all trace of artificiality.

3   Perhaps the most revolutionary break-up in modern art took place a little more than fifty years ago with the advent of Cubism. It was the Cubists, Picasso, Braque, Duchamp, Picabia, Léger, Delaunay and Juan Gris, who responded to the inordinate multiplicity of present-day life by breaking up and arbitrarily rearranging transparent planes and surfaces so that all sides of an object could be seen at once. As the Cubists broke through the boundaries of conventional form to show multiple aspects simultaneously, their Italian colleagues, the Futurists, hoped to encompass the uninterrupted

motion of an object at one time. This they tried to do by a series of overlapping transparent forms illustrating the path of an object as it moved through space.

4 With Surrealism came another kind of break-up, the break-up of chronology. Frankly influenced by Freudian discoveries, this movement splintered time sequence with an abandon borrowed from the world of fragmented dreams. Content was purposely unhinged in denial of all rational expression, allowing disconnected episodes to recreate the disturbing life of our unconscious. At the same time, perspective and distance often became severely dislocated. Denying the orderly naturalism of the Renaissance, painters today project space and distance from innumerable eye levels, intentionally segmenting their compositions into conflicting perspectives. We look from above, from below, from diverse angles, from near, from far—all at one and the same time (not an unfamiliar experience for eyes accustomed to air travel). Here again is the Cubist idea of simultaneity, the twentieth-century urge to approach a scene from many different directions with a single condensed encounter.

5 Finally we come to the total break-up of Abstract Expressionism, a technique that celebrates the specific act of painting (sometimes appropriately called Action Painting). Now everything is shattered—line, light, color, form, pigment, surface and design. These canvases defy all the old rules as they reveal the immediate spontaneous feelings of the artist in the processs of painting. There is no one central idea, no beginning, no end—only an incessant flow and flux where lightning brushstrokes report the artist's impulsive and compulsive reactions. The pigment actually develops a life of its own, almost strong enough to hypnotize the painter. Here break-up turns into both content and form, with the impetuous paint itself telling the full story. No naturalistic image is needed to describe these artists' volatile feelings.

6 As one looks back over the last hundred years, the history of break-up becomes a key to the history of art. Why painters and sculptors of this period have been so involved with problems of dissolution is a question only partly answered by the obvious impact of modern scientific methods of destruction. One cannot deny that the last two devastating wars and the possibility of a still more devastating one to come do affect our daily thinking. Since the discovery of the atom bomb, science has become almost synonymous with destruction. The influence of contemporary warfare with its colossal explosions and upheavals has unquestionably had much to do with the tendency toward fragmentation in art, but there have been other and earlier causes.

7 From the beginning, it was science in one form or another that affected modern painting and sculpture. In nineteenth-century Europe the interest in atmospheric phenomena was not an isolated expression limited to the Impressionists. At that time, numerous scientists were experimenting with all manner of optical color laws, writing widely on the subject as they investigated the relationship of color to the human eye. Artists like Monet and Seurat were familiar with these findings and not unnaturally applied them to their paintings. It would be a grave mistake to underestimate the influence of contemporary scientific research on the development of Impressionism. The wonders of natural light became a focus for nineteenth-century artists exactly as the magic of artificial light stimulated painters of the precentury. If the earlier men were more interested in rural landscapes seen out-of-doors in the sunlight, the later

artists quite reasonably concentrated on city scenes, preferably at night when man-made luminosity tends to puncture both form and space.

8   Other scientific investigations also exerted considerable influence on present-day painters and sculptors. Inventions like the microscope and telescope, with their capacity to enlarge, isolate and probe, offer the artist provocative new worlds to explore. These instruments, which break up structures only to examine them more fully, demonstrate how details can be magnified and separated from the whole and operate as new experiences. Repeatedly artists in recent years have exploited this idea, allowing one isolated symbol to represent an entire complex organism. Miró often needs merely part of a woman's body to describe all women, or Léger, one magnified letter of the alphabet to conjure up the numberless printed words that daily bombard us.

9   As scientists smash the atom, so likewise artists smash traditional forms. For how, indeed, can anyone remain immune to the new mushroom shape that haunts us day and night? The American painter, Morris Graves, put it well recently, "You simply can't keep the world out any longer. Like everyone else, I've been caught in our scientific culture." This is not to say that painters are interested in reproducing realistic scenes of atomic explosions, but rather that they are concerned with the reactions accompanying these disasters. It is just possible that, with their extra-sensitized intuition, artists may have unconsciously predicted the discovery of atomic energy long before "the bomb" became a familiar household word, for the history of break-up in art antedates the history of nuclear break-up.

10   Even the invention of the X-ray machine has brought us closer to penetrating form. We no longer think of outer coverings as solid or final; we know they can be visually pierced merely by rendering them transparent. We have also learned from science that space penetrates everything.

11   The sculptor Gabo claims, "Space is a reality in all of our experiences and it is present in every object. . . . That's what I've tried to show in certain of my stone carvings. When they turn, observe how their curved forms seem interpenetrated by space." For the artist today, nothing is static or permanent. The new popular dances are no more potently kinetic than the new staccato art forms that everywhere confront us.

12   With the dramatic development of speedier transportation and swifter communication comes a visual overlapping responsible for much of contemporary art. In modern life one is simultaneously subjected to countless experiences that become fragmented, superimposed, and finally rebuilt into new experiences. Speed is a cogent part of our daily life.

13   How natural, then, that artists reflect this pressure by showing all sides of an object, its entire motion, its total psychological content in one concerted impact. It is almost as if the pressures of time had necessitated a visual speed-up not unlike the industrial one associated with the assembly line and mass production. Speed with its multiple overlays transforms our surroundings into jazzed, interrupted images.

14   Modern technology and science have produced a wealth of new materials and new ways of using old materials. For the artist this means wider opportunities. There is no doubt that the limitations of materials and nature of tools both restrict and shape a

man's work. Observe how the development of plastics and light metals along with new methods of welding and brazing have changed the direction of sculpture. Transparent plastic materials allow one to look through an object, to see its various sides superimposed on each other (as in Cubism or in an X ray). Today, welding is as prevalent as casting was in the past. This new method encourages open designs, often of great linear agility, where surrounding and intervening space becomes as important as form itself. In fact, it becomes a kind of negative form. While bronze casting and stone carving are techniques more readily adapted to solid volumes, welding permits perforated metal designs of extreme versatility that free sculpture from the static restrictions which for centuries have moored it to the floor.

15   More ambiguous than other scientific inventions familiar to modern artists, but no less influential, are the psychoanalytic studies of Freud and his followers, discoveries that have infiltrated recent art, especially Surrealism. The Surrealists, in the struggle to escape the monotony and frustrations of everyday life, claimed that dreams were the only hope. Turning to the irrational world of their unconscious, they banished all time barriers and moral judgments to combine disconnected dream experiences from the past, present and intervening psychological states. The Surrealists were concerned with overlapping emotions more than with overlapping forms. Their paintings often become segmented capsules of associative experiences. For them, obsessive and often unrelated images replaced the direct emotional messages of Expressionism. They did not need to smash pigment and texture; they went beyond this to smash the whole continuity of logical thought.

16   There is little doubt that contemporary art has taken much from contemporary life. In a period when science has made revolutionary strides, artists in their studios have not been unaware of scientists in their laboratories. But this has rarely been a one-way street. Painters and sculptors, though admittedly influenced by modern science, have also molded and changed our world. If break-up has been a vital part of their expression, it has not always been a symbol of destruction. Quite the contrary: it has been used to examine more fully, to penetrate more deeply, to analyze more thoroughly, to enlarge, isolate and make more familiar certain aspects of life that earlier we were apt to neglect. In addition, it sometimes provides rich multiple experiences so organized as not merely to reflect our world, but in fact to interpret it.

Suggestions for Discussion or Writing

1. How does Kuh say that art has changed through the past two centuries?

2. What are some of the movements in art that she describes?

3. What have been some of the major influences on modern art?

4. What is the thesis of Kuh's essay? What are the major points she makes to prove her thesis?

5. How does modern art interpret reality?

Seventeen Syllables

from Seventeen Syllables and Other Stories

Hisaye Yamamoto

Hisaye Yamamoto was born in 1921 in Redondo Beach, California, of immigrant parents from Japan. She attended Compton Junior College, majoring in French, Spanish, German, and Latin. For twelve years, she also attended a Japanese school. During World War II, she and her family were sent to Poston, Arizona, for relocation, and then to Massachusetts. After the war, she and her family returned to California. She has worked as a journalist with the Los Angeles Tribune *and* The Catholic Worker. *Her writing has brought a John Hay Whitney Foundation Opportunity Fellowship and the 1986 American Book Award for Lifetime Achievement from the Before Columbus Foundation.*

1   The first Rosie knew that her mother had taken to writing poems was one evening when she finished one and read it aloud for her daughter's approval. It was about cats, and Rosie pretended to understand it thoroughly and appreciate it no end, partly because she hesitated to disillusion her mother about the quantity and quality of Japanese she had learned in all the years now that she had been going to Japanese school every Saturday (and Wednesday, too, in the summer). Even so, her mother must have been skeptical about the depth of Rosie's understanding, because she explained afterwards about the kind of poem she was trying to write.

2   See, Rosie, she said, it was a *haiku*, a poem in which she must pack all her meaning into seventeen syllables only which were divided into three lines of five, seven, and five syllables. In the one she had just read, she had tried to capture the charm of a kitten, as well as comment on the superstition that owning a cat of three colors meant good luck.

3   "Yes, yes, I understand. How utterly lovely," Rosie said, and her mother, either satisfied or seeing through the deception and resigned, went back to composing.

4   The truth was that Rosie was lazy; English lay ready on the tongue but Japanese had to be searched for and examined, and even then put forth tentatively (probably to meet with laughter). It was so much easier to say yes, yes, even when one meant no, no. Besides, this was what was in her mind to say: I was looking through one of your magazines from Japan last night, Mother, and toward the back I found some *haiku* in English that delighted me. There was one that made me giggle off and on until I fell asleep—

5   It is morning, and lo!
I lie awake, comme il faut,
sighing for some dough.

6   Now, how to reach her mother, how to communicate the melancholy song? Rosie knew formal Japanese by fits and starts, her mother had even less English, no French. It was much more possible to say yes, yes.

7   It developed that her mother was writing the *haiku* for a daily newspaper, the *Mainichi Shimbun*, that was published in San Francisco. Los Angeles, to be sure, was closer to the farming community in which the Hayashi family lived and several Japanese vernaculars were printed there, but Rosie's parents said they preferred the tone of the northern paper. Once a week, the *Mainichi* would have a section devoted to *haiku*, and her mother became an extravagant contributor, taking for herself the blossoming pen name, Ume Hanazono.

8   So Rosie and her father lived for a while with two women, her mother and Ume Hanazono. Her mother (Tome Hayashi by name) kept house, cooked, washed, and, along with her husband and the Carrascos, the Mexican family hired for the harvest, did her ample share of picking tomatoes out in the sweltering fields and boxing them in tidy strata in the cool packing shed. Ume Hanazono, who came to life after the dinner dishes were done, as an earnest, muttering stranger who often neglected speaking when spoken to and stayed busy at the parlor table as late as midnight scribbling with pencil on scratch paper or carefully copying characters on good paper with her fat, pale green Parker.

9   The new interest had some repercussions on the household routine. Before, Rosie had been accustomed to her parents and herself taking their hot baths early and going to bed almost immediately afterwards, unless her parents challenged each other to a game of flower cards or unless company dropped in. Now if her father wanted to play cards, he had to resort to solitaire (at which he always cheated fearlessly), and if a group of friends came over, it was bound to contain someone who was also writing *haiku*, and the small assemblage would be split in two, her father entertaining the non-literary members and her mother comparing ecstatic notes with the visiting poet.

10   If they went out, it was more of the same thing. But Ume Hanazono's life span, even for a poet's, was very brief—perhaps three months at most.

11   One night they went over to see the Hayano family in the neighboring town to the west, an adventure both painful and attractive to Rosie. It was attractive because there were four Hayano girls, all lovely and each one named after a season of the year (Haru, Natsu, Aki, Fuyu), painful because something had been wrong with Mrs. Hayano ever since the birth of her first child. Rosie would sometimes watch Mrs. Hayano, reputed to have been the belle of her native village, making her way about a room, stooped, slowly shuffling, violently trembling (*always* trembling), and she would be reminded that this woman, in the same condition, had carried and given issue to three babies. She would look wonderingly at Mr. Hayano, handsome, tall, and strong, and she would look at her four pretty friends. But it was not a matter she could come to any decision about.

12   On this visit, however, Mrs. Hayano sat all evening in the rocker, as motionless and unobtrusive as it was possible for her to be, and Rosie found the greater part of the evening practically anaesthetic. Too, Rosie spent most of it in the girls' room,

because Haru, the garrulous one, said almost as soon as the bows and other greetings were over, "Oh, you must see my new coat!"

13   It was a pale plaid of grey, sand, and blue, with an enormous collar, and Rosie, seeing nothing special in it, said, "Gee, how nice."

14   "Nice?" said Haru, indignantly. "Is that all you can say about it? It's gorgeous! And so cheap, too. Only seventeen-ninety-eight, because it was a sale. The saleslady said it was twenty-five dollars regular."

15   "Gee," said Rosie. Natsu, who never said much and when she said anything said it shyly, fingered the coat covetously and Haru pulled it away.

16   "Mine," she said, putting it on. She minced in the aisle between the two large beds and smiled happily. "Let's see how your mother likes it."

17   She broke into the front room and the adult conversation and went to stand in front of Rosie's mother, while the rest watched from the door. Rosie's mother was properly envious. "May I inherit it when you're through with it?"

18   Haru, pleased, giggled and said yes, she could, but Natsu reminded gravely from the door, "You promised me, Haru."

19   Everyone laughed but Natsu, who shamefacedly retreated into the bedroom. Haru came in laughing, taking off the coat. "We were only kidding, Natsu," she said. "Here, you try it on now."

20   After Natsu buttoned herself into the coat, inspected herself solemnly in the bureau mirror, and reluctantly shed it, Rosie, Aki, and Fuyu got their turns, and Fuyu, who was eight, drowned in it while her sisters and Rosie doubled up in amusement. They all went into the front room later, because Haru's mother quaveringly called to her to fix the tea and rice cakes and open a can of sliced peaches for everybody. Rosie noticed that her mother and Mr. Hayano were talking together at the little table—they were discussing a *haiku* that Mr. Hayano was planning to send to the *Mainichi*, while her father was sitting at one end of the sofa looking through a copy of *Life*, the new picture magazine. Occasionally, her father would comment on a photograph, holding it toward Mrs. Hayano and speaking to her as he always did—loudly, as though he thought someone such as she must surely be at least a trifle deaf also.

21   The five girls had their refreshments at the kitchen table, and it was while Rosie was showing the sisters her trick of swallowing peach slices without chewing (she chased each slippery crescent down with a swig of tea) that her father brought his empty teacup and untouched saucer to the sink and said, "Come on, Rosie, we're going home now."

22   "Already?" asked Rosie.

23   "Work tomorrow," he said.

24   He sounded irritated, and Rosie, puzzled, gulped one last yellow slice and stood up to go, while the sisters began protesting, as was their wont.

25   "We have to get up at five-thirty," he told them, going into the front room quickly, so that they did not have their usual chance to hang onto his hands and plead for an extension of time.

26   Rosie, following, saw that her mother and Mr. Hayano were sipping tea and still talking together, while Mrs. Hayano concentrated, quivering, on raising the handleless Japanese cup to her lips with both her hands and lowering it back to her lap. Her father,

saying nothing, went out the door, onto the bright porch, and down the steps. Her mother looked up and asked, "Where is he going?"

27   "Where is he going?" Rosie said. "He said we were going home now."

28   "Going home?" Her mother looked with embarrassment at Mr. Hayano and his absorbed wife and then forced a smile. "He must be tired," she said.

29   Haru was not giving up yet. "May Rosie stay overnight?" she asked, and Natsu, Aki, and Fuyu came to reinforce their sister's plea by helping her make a circle around Rosie's mother. Rosie, for once having no desire to stay, was relieved when her mother, apologizing to the perturbed Mr. and Mrs. Hayano for her father's abruptness at the same time, managed to shake her head no at the quartet, kindly but adamant, so that they broke their circle and let her go.

30   Rosie's father looked ahead into the windshield as the two joined him. "I'm sorry," her mother said. "You must be tired." Her father, stepping on the starter, said nothing. "You know how I get when it's *haiku*," she continued. "I forget what time it is." He only grunted.

31   As they rode homeward silently, Rosie, sitting between, felt a rush of hate for both—for her mother for begging, for her father for denying her mother. I wish this old Ford would crash, right now, she thought, then immediately, no, no, I wish my father would laugh, but it was too late; already the vision had passed through her mind of the green pick-up crumpled in the dark against one of the mighty eucalyptus trees they were just riding past, of the three contorted, bleeding bodies, one of them hers.

32   Rose ran between two patches of tomatoes, her heart working more rambunctiously than she had ever known it to. How lucky it was that Aunt Taka and Uncle Gimpachi had come tonight, though, how very lucky. Otherwise she might not have really kept her half-promise to meet Jesus Carrasco. Jesus was going to be a senior in September at the same school she went to, and his parents were the ones helping with the tomatoes this year. She and Jesus, who hardly remembered seeing each other at Cleveland High where there were so many other people and two whole grades between them, had become great friends this summer—he always had a joke for her when he periodically drove the loaded pick-up up from the fields to the shed where she was usually sorting while her mother and father did the packing, and they laughed a great deal together over infinitesimal repartee during the afternoon break for chilled watermelon or ice cream in the shade of the shed.

33   What she enjoyed most was racing him to see which could finish picking a double row first. He, who could work faster, would tease her by slowing down until she thought she would surely pass him this time, then speeding up furiously to leave her several sprawling vines behind. Once he had made her screech hideously by crossing over, while her back was turned, to place atop the tomatoes in her green-stained bucket a truly monstrous, pale green worm (it had looked more like an infant snake). And it was when they had finished a contest this morning, after she had pantingly pointed a green finger at the immature tomatoes evident in the lugs at the end of his row and he had returned the accusation (with justice), that he had startlingly brought up the matter of their possibly meeting outside the range of both their parents' dubious eyes.

34   "What for?" she had asked.

35   "I've got a secret I want to tell you," he said.

36   "Tell me now," she demanded.

37   "It won't be ready till tonight," he said.

38   She laughed. "Tell me tomorrow then."

39   "It'll be gone tomorrow," he threatened.

40   "Well, for seven hakes, what is it?" she had asked, more than twice, and when he had suggested that the packing shed would be an appropriate place to find out, she had cautiously answered maybe. She had not been certain she was going to keep the appointment until the arrival of mother's sister and her husband. Their coming seemed a sort of signal of permission, of grace, and she had definitely made up her mind to lie and leave as she was bowing them welcome.

41   So as soon as everyone appeared settled back for the evening, she announced loudly that she was going to the privy outside, "I'm going to the benjo!" and slipped out the door. And now that she was actually on her way, her heart pumped in such an undisciplined way that she could hear it with her ears. It's because I'm running, she told herself, slowing to a walk. The shed was up ahead, one more patch away, in the middle of the fields. Its bulk, looming in the dimness, took on a sinisterness that was funny when Rosie reminded herself that it was only a wooden frame with a canvas roof and three canvas walls that made a slapping noise on breezy days.

42   Jesus was sitting on the narrow plank that was the sorting platform and she went around to the other side and jumped backwards to seat herself on the rim of a packing stand. "Well, tell me," she said without greeting, thinking her voice sounded reassuringly familiar.

43   "I saw you coming out the door," Jesus said. "I heard you running part of the way, too."

44   "Uh-huh," Rosie said. "Now tell me the secret."

45   "I was afraid you wouldn't come," he said.

46   Rosie delved around on the chicken-wire bottom of the stall for number two tomatoes ripe, which she was sitting beside, and came up with a left-over that felt edible. She bit into it and began sucking out the pulp and seeds. "I'm here," she pointed out.

47   "Rosie, are you sorry you came?"

48   "Sorry? What for?" she said. "You said you were going to tell me something."

49   "I will, I will," Jesus said, but his voice contained disappointment, and Rosie fleetingly felt the older of the two, realizing a brand-new power which vanished without category under her recognition.

50   "I have to go back in a minute," she said. "My aunt and uncle are here from Wintersburg. I told them I was going to the privy."

51   Jesus laughed. "You funny thing," he said. "You slay me!"

52   "Just because you have a bathroom *inside*," Rosie said. "Come, tell me."

53   Chuckling, Jesus came around to lean on the stand facing her. They still could not see each other very clearly, but Rosie noticed that Jesus became very sober again as he took the hollow tomato from her hand and dropped it back into the stall.

When he took hold of her empty hand, she could find no words to protest; her vocabulary had become distressingly constricted and she thought desperately that all that remained intact now was yes and no and oh, and even these few sounds would not easily come out. Thus, kissed by Jesus, Rosie fell for the first time entirely victim to a helplessness delectable beyond speech. But the terrible, beautiful sensation lasted no more than a second, and the reality of Jesus' lips and tongue and teeth and hands made her pull away with such strength that she nearly tumbled.

54   Rosie stopped running as she approached the lights from the windows of home. How long since she had left? She could not guess, but gasping yet, she went to the privy in back and locked herself in. Her own breathing deafened her in the dark, close space, and she sat and waited until she could hear at last the nightly calling of the frogs and crickets. Even then, all she could think to say was oh, my, and the pressure of Jesus' face against her face would not leave.

55   No one had missed her in the parlor, however, and Rosie walked in and through quickly, announcing that she was next going to take a bath. "Your father's in the bathhouse," her mother said, and Rosie, in her room, recalled that she had not seen him when she entered. There had been only Aunt Taka and Uncle Gimpachi with her mother at the table, drinking tea. She got her robe and straw sandals and crossed the parlor again to go outside. Her mother was telling them about the *haiku* competition in the *Mainichi* and the poem she had entered.

56   Rosie met her father coming out of the bathhouse. "Are you through, Father?" she asked. "I was going to ask you to scrub my back."

57   "Scrub your own back," "he said shortly, going toward the main house.

58   "What have I done now?" "she yelled after him. She suddenly felt like doing a lot of yelling. But he did not answer, and she went into the bathhouse. Turning on the dangling light, she removed her denims and T-shirt and threw them in the big carton for dirty clothes standing next to the washing machine. Her other things she took with her into the bath compartment to wash after her bath. After she had scooped a basin of hot water from the square wooden tub, she sat on the grey cement of the floor and soaped herself at exaggerated leisure, singing "Red Sails in the Sunset" at the top of her voice and using da-da-da where she suspected her words. Then, standing up, still singing, for she was possessed by the notion that any attempt now to analyze would result in spoilage and she believed that the larger her volume the less she would be able to hear herself think, she obtained more hot water and poured it on until she was free of lather. Only then did she allow herself to step into the steaming vat, one leg first, then the remainder of her body inch by inch until the water no longer stung and she could move around at will.

59   She took a long time soaking, afterwards remembering to go around outside to stoke the embers of the tin-lined fireplace beneath the tub and to throw on a few more sticks so that the water might keep its heat for her mother, and when she finally returned to the parlor, she found her mother still talking *haiku* with her aunt and uncle, the three of them on another round of tea. Her father was nowhere in sight.

60   At Japanese school the next day (Wednesday, it was), Rosie was grave and giddy by turns. Preoccupied at her desk in the row for students on Book Eight, she made up for it

at recess by performing wild mimicry for the benefit of her friend Chizuko. She held her nose and whined a witticism or two in what she considered was the manner of Fred Allen; she assumed intoxication and a British accent to go over the climax of the Rudy Vallee recording of the pub conversation about William Ewart Gladstone; she was the child Shirley Temple piping, "On the Good Ship Lollipop"; she was the gentleman soprano of the Four Inkspots trilling, "If I Didn't Care." And she felt reasonably satisfied when Chizuko wept and gasped, "Oh, Rosie, you ought to be in the movies!"

61   Her father came after her at noon, bringing her sandwiches of minced ham and two nectarines to eat while she rode, so that she could pitch right into the sorting when they got home. The lugs were piling up, he said, and the ripe tomatoes in them would probably have to be taken to the cannery tomorrow if they were not ready for the produce haulers tonight. "This heat's not doing them any good. And we've got no time for a break today."

62   It *was* hot, probably the hottest day of the year, and Rosie's blouse stuck damply to her back even under the protection of the canvas. But she worked as efficiently as a flawless machine and kept the stalls heaped, with one part of her mind listening in to the parental murmuring about the heat and the tomatoes and with another part planning the exact words she would say to Jesus when he drove up with the first load of the afternoon. But when at last she saw that the pick-up was coming, her hands went berserk and the tomatoes started falling in the wrong stalls, and her father said, "Hey, Hey! Rosie, watch what you're doing!"

63   "Well, I have to go to the *benjo*," she said, hiding panic.

64   "Go in the weeds over there," he said, only half-joking.

65   "Oh, Father!" she protested.

66   "Oh, go on home," her mother said. "We'll make out for a while."

67   In the privy Rosie peered through a knothole toward the fields, watching as much as she could of Jesus. Happily she thought she saw him look in the direction of the house from time to time before he finished unloading and went back toward the patch where his mother and father worked. As she was heading for the shed, a very presentable black car purred up the dirt driveway to the house and its driver motioned to her. Was this the Hayashi home, he wanted to know. She nodded. Was she a Hayashi? Yes, she said, thinking that he was a good-looking man. He got out of the car with a huge, flat package and she saw that he warmly wore a business suit. "I have something here for your mother then," he said, in a more elegant Japanese than she was used to.

68   She told him where her mother was and he came along with her, patting his face with an immaculate white handkerchief and saying something about the coolness of San Francisco. To her surprised mother and father, he bowed and introduced himself as, among other things, the *haiku* editor of the *Mainichi Shimbun*, saying that since he had been coming as far as Los Angeles anyway, he had decided to bring her the first prize she had won in the recent contest.

69   "First prize?" her mother echoed, believing and not believing, pleased and overwhelmed. Handed the package with a bow, she bobbed her head up and down numerous times to express her utter gratitude.

70   "It is nothing much," he added, "but I hope it will serve as a token of our great appreciation for your contributions and our great admiration of your considerable talent."

71   "I am not worthy," she said, falling easily into his style. "It is I who should make some sign of my humble thanks for being permitted to contribute."

72   "No, no, to the contrary," he said, bowing again.

73   But Rosie's mother insisted, and then saying that she knew she was being unorthodox, she asked if she might open the package because her curiosity was so great. Certainly she might. In fact, he would like her reaction to it, for personally, it was one of his favorite *Hiroshiges*.

74   Rosie thought it was a pleasant picture, which looked to have been sketched with delicate quickness. There were pink clouds, containing some graceful calligraphy, and a sea that was a pale blue except at the edges, containing four sampans with indications of people in them. Pines edged the water and on the far-off beach there was a cluster of thatched huts towered over by pine-dotted mountains of grey and blue. The frame was scalloped and gilt.

75   After Rosie's mother pronounced it without peer and somewhat prodded her father into nodding agreement, she said Mr. Kuroda must at least have a cup of tea after coming all this way, and although Mr. Kuroda did not want to impose, he soon agreed that a cup of tea would be refreshing and went along with her to the house, carrying the picture for her.

76   "Ha, your mother's crazy!" Rosie's father said, and Rosie laughed uneasily as she resumed judgment on the tomatoes. She had emptied six lugs when he broke into an imaginary conversation with Jesus to tell her to go and remind her mother of the tomatoes, and she went slowly.

77   Mr. Kuroda was in his shirtsleeves expounding some *haiku* theory as he munched a rice cake, and her mother was rapt. Abashed in the great man's presence, Rosie stood next to her mother's chair until her mother looked up inquiringly, and then she started to whisper the message, but her mother pushed her gently away and reproached, "You are not being very polite to our guest."

78   "Father says the tomatoes . . ." Rosie said aloud, smiling foolishly.

79   "Tell him I shall only be a minute," her mother said, speaking the language of Mr. Kuroda.

80   When Rosie carried the reply to her father, he did not seem to hear and she said again, "Mother says she'll be back in a minute."

81   "All right, all right," he nodded, and they worked again in silence. But suddenly, her father uttered an incredible noise, exactly like the cork of a bottle popping, and the next Rosie knew, he was stalking angrily toward the house, almost running in fact, and she chased after him crying, "Father! Father! What are you going to do?"

82   He stopped long enough to order her back to the shed. "Never mind!" he shouted. "Get on with the sorting!"

83   And from the place in the fields where she stood, frightened and vacillating, Rosie saw her father enter the house. Soon Mr. Kuroda came out alone, putting on his coat. Mr. Kuroda got into his car and backed out down the driveway onto the highway. Next

her father emerged, also alone, something in his arms (it was the picture, she realized), and, going over to the bathhouse woodpile, he threw the picture on the ground and picked up the axe. Smashing the picture, glass and all (she heard the explosion faintly), he reached over for the kerosene that was used to encourage the bath fire and poured it over the wreckage. I am dreaming, Rosie said to herself, I am dreaming, but her father, having made sure that his act of cremation was irrevocable, was even then returning to the fields.

84   Rosie ran past him and toward the house. What had become of her mother? She burst into the parlor and found her mother at the back window watching the dying fire. They watched together until there remained only a feeble smoke under the blazing sun Her mother was very calm.

85   "Do you know why I married your father?" she said without turning.

86   "No," said Rosie. It was the most frightening question she had ever been called upon to answer. Don't tell me now, she wanted to say, tell me tomorrow, tell me next week, don't tell me today. But she knew she would be told now, that the telling would combine with the other violence of the hot afternoon to level her life, her world to the very ground.

87   It was like a story of the magazines illustrated in sepia, which she had consumed so greedily for a period until the information had somehow reached her that those wretchedly unhappy autobiographies, offered to her as the testimonials of living men and women, were largely inventions: Her mother, at nineteen, had come to America and married her father as an alternative to suicide.

88   At eighteen she had been in love with the first son of one of the well-to-do families in her village. The two had met whenever and wherever they could, secretly, because it would not have done for his family to see him favor her—her father had no money; he was a drunkard and a gambler besides. She had learned she was with child; an excellent match had already been arranged for her lover. Despised by her family, she had given premature birth to a stillborn son, who would be seventeen now. Her family did not turn her out, but she could no longer project herself in any direction without refreshing in them the memory of her indiscretion. She wrote to Aunt Taka, her favorite sister in America, threatening to kill herself if Aunt Taka would not send for her. Aunt Taka hastily arranged a marriage with a young man of whom she knew, but lately arrived from Japan, a young man of simple mind, it was said, but of kindly heart. The young man was never told why his unseen betrothed was so eager to hasten the day of meeting.

89   The story was told perfectly, with neither groping for words nor untoward passion. It was as though her mother had memorized it by heart, reciting it to herself so many times over that its nagging vileness had long since gone.

90   "I had a brother then?" Rosie asked, for this was what seemed to matter now; she would think about the other later, she assured herself, pushing back the illumination which threatened all that darkness that had hitherto been merely mysterious or even glamorous. "A half-brother?"

91   "Yes."

92   "I would have liked a brother," she said.

93   Suddenly, her mother knelt on the floor and took her by the wrists. "Rosie," she

said urgently, "Promise me you will never marry!" Shocked more by the request than the revelation, Rosie stared at her mother's face. Jesus, Jesus, she called silently, not certain whether she was invoking the help of the son of the Carrascos or of God, until there returned sweetly the memory of Jesus' hand, how it had touched her and where. Still her mother waited for an answer, holding her wrists so tightly that her hands were going numb. She tried to pull free. "Promise," her mother whispered fiercely, "promise." "Yes, yes I promise," Rosie said. But for an instant she turned away, and her mother, hearing the familiar glib agreement, released her. Oh, you, you, you, her eyes and twisted mouth said, you fool. Rosie, covering her face, began at last to cry, and the embrace and consoling hand came much later than she expected.

(1949)

Suggestions for Discussion or Writing

1. How does Rosie's experience with life mirror her mother's experience?

2. Why is the story more effective being told through Rosie's eyes than through her mother's eyes?

3. Why is the mother's gift for writing so important to her?

4. Why does Rosie's father destroy the picture?

5. What is the significance of the last paragraph of the story? What can you infer about the relationships in the family from it?

Music Lessons

Mary Oliver

Born in Cleveland, Ohio, Mary Oliver (1935–) attended Ohio State and Vassar College. She has been the chairwoman of the Writing Department of the Fine Arts Work Center in Massachusetts and a visiting professor at Case Western Reserve University. She has won numerous poetry awards including the Poetry Society of America first prize for "No Voyage" (1962) and the Devil's Advocate Award for "Christmas, 1966" (1968). Her other work includes The River Styx, Ohio, and Other Poems *(1972),* The Night Traveler *(1978),* Sleeping in the Forest *(1979), and* The American Primitive *(1983) for which she won the 1984 Pulitzer Prize for poetry. "Music Lessons" is taken from her book* Twelve Moons *(1979) but appeared originally in* The Ohio Review.

Sometimes, in the middle of the lesson,
we exchanged places. She would gaze a moment at her hands
spread over the keys; then the small house with its knick-knacks,
its shut windows

5   its photographs of her sons and the serious husband,
vanished as new shapes formed. Sound
became music, and music a white
scarp for the listener to climb

alone. I leaped rock over rock to the top
10   and found myself waiting, transformed,
and still she played, her eyes luminous and willful,
her pinned hair falling down—

forgetting me, the house, the neat green yard,
she fled in that lick of flame all tedious bonds:
15   supper, the duties of flesh and home,
the knife at the throat, the death in the metronome.

Suggestions for Discussion or Writing

1. Who is the speaker of the poem? Who is the poem about? How are these two alike? Different? What is the effect of the music on each person in the poem?

2. What is the "scarp" in the poem? How does the listener climb it?

3. What is the significance of the description "her eyes luminous and willful, her pinned hair falling down"?

4. What is the "knife at the throat" and "the death in the metronome?"

5. What do the descriptions of the house add to the poem?

Stillborn

Sylvia Plath

Sylvia Plath (1932–1963), born in Boston, was educated at Smith College and earned a Fulbright Scholarship to Cambridge for graduate work. She had begun a promising writing career as early as age 18 when some of her drawings, poems and stories were published in Seventeen. *She later won* Mademoiselle's *College Fiction Contest. Her autobiographical novel* The

Bell Jar *(1963), first published under the pseudonym Victoria Lucas, recounts the experiences of an isolated individual who suffers a mental and emotional crisis. Though the last pages of the novel are optimistic, she committed suicide in London at age 31. Among her other works are* The Colossus *(1960),* Ariel *(1965),* Crossing the Water *(1971),* Lyonesse *(1971), and* Johnny Panic and the Bible of Dreams, and Other Prose Writings *(1978). Much of her work has been published by her husband after her death.*

These poems do not live: it's a sad diagnosis.
They grew their toes and fingers well enough,
Their little foreheads bulged with concentration.
If they missed out on walking about like people
It wasn't for any lack of mother love.

5

O, I cannot understand what happened to them!
They are proper in shape and number and every part.
They sit so nicely in the pickling fluid!
They smile and smile and smile and smile at me.
And still the lungs won't fill and the heart won't start.

10

They are not pigs, they are not even fish,
Though they have a piggy and a fishy air—
It would be better if they were alive, and that's what they were.
But they are dead, and their mother near dead with distraction,
And they stupidly stare, and do not speak of her.

15

Suggestions for Discussion or Writing

1. What is being personified in the poem? What are they being compared to? What words or phrases support your answer?

2. In what way is the title significant? In what way does the title indicate the metaphor in the poem?

3. What might Plath mean by saying "the lungs won't fill and the heart won't start?" What is the "pickling fluid" for?

4. How are poems ever "piggy" or "fishy"?

5. The poet says of the poems, "It would be better if they were alive, and that's what they were. / But they are dead. . . . " What is dead? Why?

6. What does Plath's poem tell you about the creative process?

Ballet Blanc

Katha Pollitt

Katha Pollitt was born in New York City in 1949 and received her education at Radcliffe and Columbia. She is currently teaching at Princeton University. Her book, Antarctic Traveller *(1982) received the National Book Critics Circle Award. She has also received the Discovery/The Nation Award, the Robert Frost Award, and grants from the Ingram Merrill Foundation and the National Endowment for the Arts.*

Baryshnikov leaps higher than your heart
in the moonlit forest, center stage, and pleads
with the ghostly corps, who pirouette gauzed white
and powdered blue, like pearls, the star Sylphides

5   of Paris, 1841. You swoon
back in red plush. Oboes, adagio,
sing *love is death*—but death's this lustrous queen
who twirls forever on one famous toe

while hushed in shadows, tier on golden tier
10 swirls to apotheosis in the ceiling.
Miles away, through clouds, one chandelier
swings dizzily. What feeling

sweeps you? Dinner's roses and tall candles,
a certain wine-flushed face, your new blue dress
15 merge with the scented crush of silks and sables—
through which, you're more and more aware, two eyes

stroke, meltingly, your neck. You glow, you sway,
it's as though the audience were dancing too
and with a last, stupendous tour jeté
20 turned for a solo suddenly to *you*

and you become the Duke, the Queen, Giselle,
and waltz in a whirl of white through the painted grove,
your gestures as extravagant as tulle,
as wild as nineteenth-century hopeless love,

25 as grand as bravo! and brava! On wings,
you splurge and take a taxi home instead.
The park looms rich and magical. It's spring,
almost. You float upstairs and into bed

and into dreams so deep you never hear
30   how all night long that witch, your evil fairy,
crows her knowing cackle in your ear:
Tomorrow you will wake up ordinary.

Suggestions for Discussion or Writing

1. What metaphors are used in the poem? Are they effective? Why?

2. What do the "dinner's roses," "tall candles," and "the new blue dress" represent?

3. What experience does Pollitt suggest when she tells you to "become the Duke, the Queen"?

4. What is the evil fairy of the last stanza?

5. How does the description of Anna Pavlova in De Mille's essay reflect this poem?

Outside the Four Walls
Exploring the Natural World

Introduction

N ature in its fierceness or its gentleness has always been a fascinating study for the naturalist and the artist. Lessons of our own mortality are dramatically revealed by the unforgiving nature of the elements. Animals, insects, and growing things in all their varieties teach us of the myriad cycles that occur, often unnoticed, all around us.

Rachel Carson's essay "The Changing Year" shows us the sea in its seasonal variations. Life in its depths and the movement toward survival—feeding, growing, reproducing, dying—mirror our own most basic concerns.

A careful look at the lifestyles of insects in "The Brown Wasps," "The Spider and the Wasp," and "The Death of the Moth" gives us further insights into our own behavior. Eiseley compares the lives of the homeless to the brown wasps. Woolf's essay looks at the struggle and death of a simple moth, which puts our own lives in perspective.

The selections on birds also give different views of life. "Hook," the story by Walter Van Tilburg Clark, helps us sympathize with the struggles of a hawk and demonstrates how nature can be at odds with humans—with sympathy on the side of the bird. Edna St. Vincent Millay's "Wild Swans" is also sympathetic to the birds. Daphne du Maurier's "The Birds" again shows nature and humans in conflict, but this time it is nature which threatens human life. Mary Oliver's "The Fish" shows nature being destroyed—only to become part of the destroyer.

"My Wood" by E. M. Forster shows the futility and consequences of trying to control nature. To own a piece of land is to corrupt the free enjoyment of earth's bounties.

Finally, Richard Eberhart's poem "The Groundhog" is a fine study in the natural processes. Existence is fragile. The disintegration of the groundhog points to the pattern that every living thing must follow.

Nature in its beauty, its complexity, its fearsomeness, its patterns, and its interdependence can be seen through our windows. But only by experiencing its awesomeness outside the four walls can we truly appreciate the richness around us.

The Brown Wasps

Loren Eiseley

Born in Lincoln, Nebraska, Loren Eiseley (1907–1977) received his Ph.D. in sociology and anthropology from the University of Pennsylvania in 1937. He taught the history of science at the University of Kansas, became the curator of early man at the University of Pennsylvania Museum, was appointed a member of the presidential task force on the preservation of natural beauty, and worked on the advisory board for the National Parks Division of the Department of the Interior. A contributor to numerous anthologies and magazines, Eiseley is best known for his Firmament of Time *(1960), which won several awards. He is also known for his writings about Darwin,* Darwin's Century, *which won the 1958 Athenaeum of Philadelphia Award for nonfiction.*

1   There is a corner in the waiting room of one of the great Eastern stations where women never sit. It is always in the shadow and overhung by rows of lockers. It is, however, always frequented—not so much by genuine travelers as by the dying. It is here that a certain element of the abandoned poor seeks a refuge out of the weather, clinging for a few hours longer to the city that has fathered them. In a precisely similar manner I have seen, on a sunny day in midwinter, a few old brown wasps creep slowly over an abandoned wasp nest in a thicket. Numbed and forgetful and frost blackened, the hum of the spring hive still resounded faintly in their sodden tissues. Then the temperature would fall and they would drop away into the white oblivion of the snow. Here in the station it is in no way different save that the city is busy in its snows. But the old ones cling to their seats as though these were symbolic and could not be given up. Now and then they sleep, their gray old heads resting with painful awkwardness on the backs of the benches.

2   Also they are not at rest. For an hour they may sleep in the gasping exhaustion of the ill-nourished and aged who have to walk in the night. Then a policeman comes by on his round and nudges them upright.

3   "You can't sleep here," he growls.

4   A strange ritual then begins. An old man is difficult to waken. After a muttered conversation the policeman presses a coin into his hand and passes fiercely along the benches prodding and gesturing toward the door. In his wake, like birds rising and settling behind the passage of a farmer through a cornfield, the men totter up, move a few paces, and subside once more upon the benches.

5   One man, after a slight, apologetic lurch, does not move at all. Tubercularly thin, he sleeps on steadily. The policeman does not look back. To him, too, this has become a ritual. He will not have to notice it again officially for another hour.

6   Once in a while one of the sleepers will not awake. Like the brown wasps, he will have had his wish to die in the great droning center of the hive rather than in some

lonely room. It is not so bad here with the shuffle of footsteps and the knowledge that there are others who share the bad luck of the world. There are also the whistles and the sounds of everyone, everyone, in the world, starting on journeys. Amidst too many journeys somebody is bound to come out all right. Somebody.

7   Maybe it was on a like thought that the brown wasps fell away from the old paper nest in the thicket. You hold till the last, even if it is only to a public seat in a railroad station. You want your place in the hive more than you want a room or a place where the aged can be eased gently out of the way. It is the place that matters, the place at the heart of things. It is life that you want, that bruises your gray old head with the hard chairs; a man has a right to his place.

8   But sometimes the place is lost in the years behind us. Or sometimes it is a thing of air, a kind of vaporous distortion above a heap of rubble. We cling to a time and a place because without them man is lost, not only man but life. This is why the voices, real or unreal, which speak from the floating trumpets at spiritualist seances are so unnerving. They are voices out of nowhere whose only reality lies in their ability to stir the memory of a living person with some fragment of the past. Before the medium's cabinet both the dead and the living revolve endlessly about an episode, a place, an event that has already been engulfed by time.

9   This feeling runs deep in life; it brings stray cats running over endless miles, and birds homing from the ends of the earth. It is as though all living creatures, and particularly the more intelligent, can survive only by fixing or transforming a bit of time into space or by securing a bit of space with its objects immortalized and made permanent in time. For example, I once saw, on a flower pot in my own living room, the efforts of a field mouse to build a remembered field. I have lived to see this episode repeated in a thousand guises, and since I have spent a large portion of my life in the shade of a nonexistent tree I think I am entitled to speak for the field mouse.

10   One day as I cut across the field which at that time extended on one side of our suburban shopping center, I found a giant slug feeding from a runnel of pink ice cream in an abandoned Dixie cup. I could see his eyes telescope and protrude in a kind of dim uncertain ecstasy as his dark body bunched and elongated in the curve of the cup. Then, as I stood there at the edge of the concrete, contemplating the slug, I began to realize it was like standing on a shore where a different type of life creeps up and fumbles tentatively among the rocks and sea wrack. It knows its place and will only creep so far until something changes. Little by little as I stood there I began to see more of this shore that surrounds the place of man. I looked with sudden care and attention at things I had been running over thoughtlessly for years. I even waded out a short way into the grass and the wild-rose thickets to see more. A huge blackbelted bee went droning by and there were some indistinct scurryings in the underbrush.

11   Then I came to a sign which informed me that this field was to be the site of a new Wanamaker suburban store. Thousands of obscure lives were about to perish, the spores of puffballs would go smoking off to new fields, and the bodies of little white-footed mice would be crunched under the inexorable wheels of the bulldozers. Life disappears or modifies its appearances so fast that everything takes on an aspect of illusion—a momentary fizzing and boiling with smoke rings, like pouring dissident chemicals into a retort. Here a man was advancing, but in a few years his plaster and

bricks would be disappearing once more into the insatiable maw of the clover. Being of an archaeological cast of mind, I thought of this fact with an obscure sense of satisfaction and waded back through the rose thickets to the concrete parking lot. As I did so, a mouse scurried ahead of me, frightened of my steps if not of that ominous Wanamaker sign. I saw him vanish in the general direction of my apartment house, his little body quivering with fear in the great open sun on the blazing concrete. Blinded and confused, he was running straight away from his field. In another week scores would follow him.

12   I forgot the episode then and went home to the quiet of my living room. It was not until a week later, letting myself into the apartment, that I realized I had a visitor. I am fond of plants and had several ferns standing on the floor in pots to avoid the noon glare by the south window.

13   As I snapped on the light and glanced carelessly around the room, I saw a little heap of earth on the carpet and a scrabble of pebbles that had been kicked merrily over the edge of one of the flower pots. To my astonishment I discovered a full-fledged burrow delving downward among the fern roots. I waited silently. The creature who had made the burrow did not appear. I remembered the wild field then, and the flight of the mice. No house mouse, no *Mus domesticus,* had kicked up this little heap of earth or sought refuge under a fern root in a flower pot. I thought of the desperate little creature I had seen fleeing from the wild rose thicket. Through intricacies of pipes and attics, he, or one of his fellows, had climbed to his high green solitary room. I could visualize what had occurred. He had an image in his head, a world of seed pods and quiet, of green sheltering leaves in the dim light among the weed stems. It was the only world he knew and it was gone.

14   Somehow in his flight he had found his way to this room with drawn shades where no one would come till nightfall. And here he had smelled green leaves and run quickly up the flower pot to dabble his paws in common earth. He had even struggled half the afternoon to carry his burrow deeper and had failed. I examined the hole, but no whiskered twitching face appeared. He was gone. I gathered up the earth and refilled the burrow. I did not expect to find traces of him again.

15   Yet for three nights thereafter I came home to the darkened room and my ferns to find the dirt kicked gaily about the rug and the burrow reopened, though I was never able to catch the field mouse within it. I dropped a little food about the mouth of the burrow, but it was never touched. I looked under beds or sat reading with one ear cocked for rustling in the ferns. It was all in vain; I never saw him. Probably he ended in a trap in some other tenant's room.

16   But before he disappeared I had come to look hopefully for his evening burrow. About my ferns there had begun to linger the insubstantial vapor of an autumn field, the distilled essence, as it were, of a mouse brain in exile from its home. It was a small dream, like our dreams, carried a long and weary journey along pipes and through spider webs, past holes over which loomed the shadows of waiting cats, and finally, desperately, into this room where he had played in the shuttered daylight for an hour among the green ferns on the floor. Every day these invisible dreams pass us on the street, or rise from beneath our feet, or look upon us from beneath a bush.

17   Some years ago the elevated railway in Philadelphia was torn down and replaced by a subway system. This ancient El with its barnlike stations containing nut-vending

machines and scattered food scraps had, for generations, been the favorite feeding ground of flocks of pigeons, generally one flock to a station along the route of the El. Hundreds of pigeons were dependent upon the system. They flapped in and out of its stanchions and steel work or gathered in watchful little audiences about the feet of anyone who rattled the peanut-vending machines. They even watched people who jingled change in their hands, and prospected for food under the feet of the crowds, who gathered between trains. Probably very few among the waiting people who tossed a crumb to an eager pigeon realized that this El was like a food-bearing river, and that the life which haunted its banks was dependent upon the running of the trains with their human freight.

18   I saw the river stop.

19   The time came when the underground tubes were ready; the traffic was transferred to a realm unreachable by pigeons. It was like a great river subsiding suddenly into desert sands. For a day, for two days, pigeons continued to circle over the El or stand close to the red vending machines. They were patient birds, and surely this great river which had flowed through the lives of unnumbered generations was merely suffering from some momentary drought.

20   They listened for the familiar vibrations that had always heralded an approaching train; they flapped hopefully about the head of an occasional workman walking along the steel runways. They passed from one empty station to another, all the while growing hungrier. Finally, they flew away.

21   I thought I had seen the last of them about the El, but there was a revival and it provided a curious instance of the memory of living things for a way of life or a locality that has long been cherished. Some weeks after the El was abandoned workmen began to tear it down. I went to work every morning by one particular station, and the time came when the demolition crews reached this spot. Acetylene torches showered passers-by with sparks, pneumatic drills hammered at the base of the structure, and a blind man who, like the pigeons, had clung with his cup to a stairway leading to the change booth, was forced to give up his place.

22   It was then, strangely, momentarily, one morning that I witnessed the return of a little band of the familiar pigeons. I even recognized one or two members of the flock that had lived around this particular station before they were dispersed into the streets. They flew bravely in and out among the sparks and the hammers and the shouting workmen. They had returned—and they had returned because the hubbub of the wreckers had convinced them that the river was about to flow once more. For several hours they flapped in and out through the empty windows, nodding their heads and watching the fall of girders with attentive little eyes. By the following morning the station was reduced to some burned-off stanchions in the street. My bird friends had gone. It was plain, however, that they retained a memory for an insubstantial structure now compounded of air and time. Even the blind man clung to it. Someone had provided him with a chair, and he sat at the same corner staring sightlessly at an invisible stairway where, so far as he was concerned, the crowds were still ascending to the trains.

23   I have said my life has been passed in the shade of a nonexistent tree, so that such sights do not offend me. Prematurely I am one of the brown wasps and I often sit with them in the great droning hive of the station, dreaming sometimes of a certain tree. It

was planted sixty years ago by a boy with a bucket and a toy spade in a little Nebraska town. That boy was myself. It was a cottonwood sapling and the boy remembered it because everyone died or moved away who was supposed to wait and grow old under its shade. The boy was passed from hand to hand, but the tree for some intangible reason had taken root in his mind. It was under its branches that he sheltered; it was from this tree that his memories, which are my memories, led away into the world.

24   After sixty years the mood of the brown wasps grows heavier upon one. During a long inward struggle I thought it would do me good to go and look upon that actual tree. I found a rational excuse in which to clothe this madness. I purchased a ticket and at the end of two thousand miles I walked another mile to an address that was still the same. The house had not been altered.

25   I came close to the white picket fence and reluctantly, with great effort, looked down the long vista of the yard. There was nothing there to see. For sixty years that cottonwood had been growing in my mind. Season by season its seeds had been floating farther on the hot prairie winds. We had planted it lovingly there, my father and I, because he had a great hunger for soil and live things growing, and because none of these things had long been ours to protect. We had planted the little sapling and watered it faithfully, and I remembered that I had run out with my small bucket to drench its roots the day we moved away. And all the years since it had been growing in my mind, a huge tree that somehow stood for my father and the love I bore hiim. I took a grasp on the picket fence and forced myself to look again.

26   A boy with the hard bird eye of youth pedaled a tricycle slowly up beside me.

27   "What'cha lookin at?" he asked curiously.

28   "A tree," I said.

29   "What for?" he said.

30   "It isn't there," I said, to myself mostly, and began to walk away at a pace just slow enough not to seem to be running.

31   "What isn't there?" the boy asked. I didn't answer. It was obvious I was attached by a thread to a thing that had never been there, or certainly not for long. Something that had to be held in the air, or sustained in the mind, because it was part of my orientation in the universe and I could not survive without it. There was more than an animal's attachment to a place. There was something else, the attachment of the spirit to a grouping of events in time; it was part of our mortality.

32   So I had come home at last, driven by a memory in the brain as surely as the field mouse who had delved long ago into my flower pot or the pigeons flying forever amidst the rattle of nut-vending machines. These, the burrow under the greenery in my living room and the red-bellied bowls of peanuts now hovering in midair in the minds of pigeons, were all part of an elusive world that existed nowhere and yet everywhere. I looked once at the real world about me while the persistent boy pedaled at my heels.

33   It was without meaning, though my feet took a remembered path. In sixty years the house and street had rotted out of my mind. But the tree, the tree that no longer was, that had perished in its first season, bloomed on in my individual mind, unblemished as my father's words. "We'll plant a tree here, son, and we're not going to move any more. And when you're an old, old man you can sit under it and think how we planted it here, you and me, together."

34   I began to outpace the boy on the tricycle.

35   "Do you live here, Mister?" he shouted after me suspiciously. I took a firm grasp on airy nothing—to be precise, on the bole of a great tree. "I do," I said. I spoke for myself, one field mouse, and several pigeons. We were all out of touch but somehow permanent. It was the world that had changed.

Suggestions for Discussion or Writing

1. What parallels does Eiseley draw between the brown wasps and old men? Why does he call himself a "brown wasp"? To what other creatures of nature does Eiseley compare men?

2. In what way is the new Wanamaker store symbolic? How does Eiseley feel about the new store? How do you know?

3. What social statement is Eiseley making?

4. What relationship between the past and the present does Eiseley explore? In what way are the past and the present connected? Is it ever possible to return to the past?

5. How does Eiseley organize this essay? How does this organization affect your understanding of the essay?

The Spider and the Wasp

Alexander Petrunkevitch

Zoologist Alexander Petrunkevitch (1875–1964) was born in Russia and educated there and in Germany. He immigrated to the United States in 1903 and taught zoology at Yale from 1910 to 1944. Petrunkevitch published several scholarly research works while at Yale and became an internationally known spider expert. Two of his books are Index Catalogue of Spiders of North, Central, and South America *(1911) and* An Inquiry into the Natural Classification of Spiders *(1933). He is also known for his able translations of English and Russian poetry. The following selection reflects his fascination with spiders and the intricacies of nature.*

1   . . . In the feeding and safeguarding of their progeny insects and spiders exhibit some interesting analogies to reasoning and some crass examples of blind instinct. The case I propose to describe here is that of the tarantula spiders and their arch-enemy,

the digger wasps of the genus *Pepsis*. It is a classic example of what looks like intelligence pitted against instinct—a strange situation in which the victim, though fully able to defend itself, submits unwittingly to its destruction.

2   Most tarantulas live in the Tropics, but several species occur in the temperate zone and a few are common in the southern U.S. Some varieties are large and have powerful fangs with which they can inflict a deep wound. These formidable looking spiders do not, however, attack man; you can hold one in your hand, if you are gentle, without being bitten. Their bite is dangerous only to insects and small mammals such as mice; for a man it is no worse than a hornet's sting.

3   Tarantulas customarily live in deep cylindrical burrows, from which they emerge at dusk and into which they retire at dawn. Mature males wander about after dark in search of females and occasionally stray into houses. After mating, the male dies in a few weeks, but a female lives much longer and can mate several years in succession. In a Paris museum is a tropical specimen which is said to have been living in captivity for 25 years.

4   A fertilized female tarantula lays from 200 to 400 eggs at a time; thus it is possible for a single tarantula to produce several thousand young. She takes no care of them beyond weaving a cocoon of silk to enclose the eggs. After they hatch, the young walk away, find convenient places in which to dig their burrows and spend the rest of their lives in solitude. . . . Their sight is poor, being limited to sensing a change in the intensity of light and to the perception of moving objects. They apparently have little or no sense of hearing, for a hungry tarantula will pay no attention to a loudly chirping cricket placed in its cage unless the insect happens to touch one of its legs.

5   But all spiders, and especially hairy ones, have an extremely delicate sense of touch. Laboratory experiments prove that tarantulas can distinguish three types of touch: pressure against the body wall, stroking of the body hair and riffling of certain very fine hairs on the legs called trichobothria. Pressure against the body, by the finger or the end of a pencil, causes the tarantula to move off slowly for a short distance. The touch excites no defensive response unless the approach is from above where the spider can see the motion, in which case it rises on its hind legs, lifts its front legs, opens its fangs and holds this threatening posture as long as the object continues to move. . . .

6   The entire body of a tarantula, especially its legs, is thickly clothed with hair. Some of it is short and wooly, some long and stiff. Touching this body hair produces one of two distinct reactions. When the spider is hungry, it responds with an immediate and swift attack. At the touch of a cricket's antennae the tarantula seizes the insect so swiftly that a motion picture taken at the rate of 64 frames per second shows only the result and not the process of capture. But when the spider is not hungry, the stimulation of its hairs merely causes it to shake the touched limb. An insect can walk under its hairy belly unharmed.

7   The trichobothria, very fine hairs growing from disclike membranes on the legs, . . . are sensitive only to air movement. A light breeze makes them vibrate slowly without disturbing the common hair. When one blows gently on the trichobothria, the tarantula reacts with a quick jerk of its four front legs. If the front and hind legs are stimulated at the same time, the spider makes a sudden jump. This reaction is quite independent of the state of its appetite.

8   These three tactile responses—to pressure on the body wall, to moving of the common hair and to flexing of the trichobothria—are so different from one another that there is no possibility of confusing them. They serve the tarantula adequately for most of its needs and enable it to avoid most annoyances and dangers. But they fail the spider completely when it meets its deadly enemy, the digger wasp *Pepsis*.

9   These solitary wasps are beautiful and formidable creatures. Most species are either a deep shiny blue all over, or deep blue with rusty wings. The largest have a wing span of about four inches. They live on nectar. When excited, they give off a pungent odor—a warning that they are ready to attack. The sting is much worse than that of a bee or common wasp, and the pain and swelling last longer. In the adult stage the wasp lives only a few months. The female produces but a few eggs, one at a time at intervals of two or three days. For each egg the mother must provide one adult tarantula, alive but paralyzed. . . . The mother wasp attaches the egg to the paralyzed spider's abdomen. Upon hatching from the egg, the larva is many hundreds of times smaller than its living but helpless victim. It eats no other food and drinks no water. By the time it has finished its single gargantuan meal and become ready for wasphood, nothing remains of the tarantula but its indigestible chitinous skeleton.

10   The mother wasp goes tarantula-hunting when the egg in her ovary is almost ready to be laid. Flying low over the ground late on a sunny afternoon, the wasp looks for its victim or for the mouth of a tarantula burrow, a round hole edged by a bit of silk. The sex of the spider makes no difference, but the mother is highly discriminating as to species. Each species of *Pepsis* requires a certain species of tarantula, and the wasp will not attack the wrong species. In a cage with a tarantula which is not its normal prey the wasp avoids the spider and is usually killed by it in the night.

11   Yet when a wasp finds the correct species, it is the other way about. To identify the species the wasp apparently must explore the spider with her antennae. The tarantula shows an amazing tolerance to this exploration. The wasp crawls under it and walks over it without evoking any hostile response. The molestation is so great and so persistent that the tarantula often rises on all eight legs, as if it were on stilts. It may stand this way for several minutes. Meanwhile the wasp, having satisfied itself that the victim is of the right species, moves off a few inches to dig the spider's grave. Working vigorously with legs and jaws, it excavates a hole 8 to 10 inches deep with a diameter slightly larger than the spider's girth. Now and again the wasp pops out of the hole to make sure that the spider is still there.

12   When the grave is finished, the wasp returns to the tarantula to complete her ghastly enterprise. First she feels it all over once more with her antennae. Then her behavior becomes more aggressive. She bends her abdomen, protruding her sting, and searches for the soft membrane at the point where the spider's legs join its body—the only spot where she can penetrate the horny skeleton. From time to time, as the exasperated spider slowly shifts ground, the wasp turns on her back and slides along with the aid of her wings, trying to get under the tarantula for a shot at the vital spot. During all this maneuvering, which can last for several minutes, the tarantula makes no move to save itself. Finally the wasp corners it against some obstruction and grasps one of its legs in her powerful jaws. Now at last the harassed spider tries a desperate but vain defense. The two contestants roll over and over on the ground. It is a terrifying

sight and the outcome is always the same. The wasp finally manages to thrust her sting into the soft spot and holds it there for a few seconds while she pumps in the poison. Almost immediately the tarantula falls paralyzed on its back. Its legs stop twitching; its heart stops beating. Yet it is not dead, as is shown by the fact that if taken from the wasp it can be restored to some sensitivity by being kept in a moist chamber for several months.

13   After paralyzing the tarantula, the wasp cleans herself by dragging her body along the ground and rubbing her feet, sucks the drop of blood oozing from the wound in the spider's abdomen, then grabs a leg of the flabby, helpless animal in her jaws and drags it down to the bottom of the grave. She stays there for many minutes, sometimes for several hours, and what she does all that time in the dark we do not know. Eventually she lays her egg and attaches it to the side of the spider's abdomen with a sticky secretion. Then she emerges, fills the grave with soil carried bit by bit in her jaws, and finally tramples the ground all around to hide any trace of the grave from prowlers. Then she flies away, leaving her descendant safely started in life.

14   In all this the behavior of the wasp evidently is qualitatively different from that of the spider. The wasp acts like an intelligent animal. This is not to say that instinct plays no part or that she reasons as man does. But her actions are to the point; they are not automatic and can be modified to fit the situation. We do not know for certain how she identifies the tarantula—probably it is by some olfactory or chemo-tactile sense— but she does it purposefully and does not blindly tackle a wrong species.

15   On the other hand, the tarantula's behavior shows only confusion. Evidently the wasp's pawing gives it no pleasure, for it tries to move away. That the wasp is not simulating sexual stimulation is certain because male and female tarantulas react in the same way to its advances. That the spider is not anesthetized by some odorless secretion is easily shown by blowing lightly at the tarantula and making it jump suddenly. What, then, makes the tarantula behave as stupidly as it does?

16   No clear, simple answer is available. Possibly the stimulation by the wasp's antennae is masked by a heavier pressure on the spider's body, so that it reacts as when prodded by a pencil. But the explanation may be much more complex. Initiative in attack is not in the nature of tarantulas; most species fight only when cornered so that escape is impossible. Their inherited patterns of behavior apparently prompt them to avoid problems rather than attack them. For example, spiders always weave their webs in three dimensions, and when a spider finds that there is insufficient space to attach certain threads in the third dimension, it leaves the place and seeks another, instead of finishing the web in a single plane. This urge to escape seems to arise under all circumstances, in all phases of life, and to take the place of reasoning. For a spider to change the pattern of its web is as impossible as for an inexperienced man to build a bridge across a chasm obstructing his way.

17   In a way the instinctive urge to escape is not only easier but often more efficient than reasoning. The tarantula does exactly what is more efficient in all cases except in an encounter with a ruthless and determined attacker dependent for the existence of her own species on killing as many tarantulas as she can lay eggs. Perhaps in this case the spider follows its usual pattern of trying to escape, instead of seizing and killing the wasp, because it is not aware of its danger. In any case, the survival of the tarantula species as a whole is protected by the fact that the spider is much more fertile than the wasp.

Suggestions for Discussion or Writing

1. What motivates the differences in behavior between the spider and the wasp? Do humans have similar behavior patterns?

2. What do you think is the purpose of the essay? Does the essay achieve its purpose?

3. How does the essay use such forms as cause and effect, definition, and description? In what way are these forms effective in making meaning?

4. Considering that this is a scientific article, how do you account for such informal language as "pops out of the hole"? How would you describe "scientific" language?

5. What is the author's tone in the article? What words and phrases in the text help establish that tone?

My Wood

E. M. Forster

English novelist, essayist, and short-story writer Edward Morgan Forster (1879–1970) was born in London and received his M.A. in English from King's College, Cambridge, in 1910. His early novels include Where Angels Fear to Tread *(1905).* A Room with a View *and* Howard's End, *also early novels (1906–1910), have recently become fine motion pictures. After his initial creative burst, he wrote only a collection of short stories,* The Celestial Omnibus and Other Stories *(1911), and several journalist pieces over a fourteen-year period. His final novel,* A Passage to India *(1925), has won great literary acclaim and has also been made into a major motion picture exploring the problems of prejudice and class struggle in British-ruled India.*

1   A few years ago I wrote a book which dealt in part with the difficulties of the English in India. Feeling that they would have had no difficulties in India themselves, the Americans read the book freely. The more they read it the better it made them feel, and a cheque to the author was the result. I bought a wood with the cheque. It is not a large wood—it contains scarcely any trees, and it is intersected, blast it, by a public footpath. Still, it is the first property that I have owned, so it is right that other people should participate in my shame, and should ask themselves, in accents that will vary in horror, this very important question: What is the effect of property upon the character? Don't let's touch economics; the effect of private ownership upon

the community as a whole is another question—a more important question, perhaps, but another one. Let's keep to psychology. If you own things, what's their effect on you? What's the effect on me of my wood?

2   In the first place, it makes me feel heavy. Property does have this effect. Property produces men of weight, and it was a man of weight who failed to get into the Kingdom of Heaven. He was not wicked, that unfortunate millionaire in the parable, he was only stout; he stuck out in front, not to mention behind, and as he wedged himself this way and that in the crystalline entrance and bruised his well-fed flanks, he saw beneath him a comparatively slim camel passing through the eye of a needle and being woven into the robe of God. The Gospels all through couple stoutness and slowness. They point out what is perfectly obvious, yet seldom realized: that if you have a lot of things you cannot move about a lot, that furniture requires dusting, dusters require servants, servants require insurance stamps, and the whole tangle of them makes you think twice before you accept an invitation to dinner or go for a bathe in the Jordan. Sometimes the Gospels proceed further and say with Tolstoy that property is sinful; they approach the difficult ground of asceticism here, where I cannot follow them. But as to the immediate effects of property on people, they just show straightforward logic. It produces men of weight. Men of weight cannot, by definition, move like the lightning from the East unto the West, and the ascent of a fourteen-stone bishop into a pulpit is thus the exact antithesis of the coming of the Son of Man. My wood makes me feel heavy.

3   In the second place, it makes me feel it ought to be larger.

4   The other day I heard a twig snap in it. I was annoyed at first, for I thought that someone was blackberrying, and depreciating the value of the undergrowth. On coming nearer, I saw it was not a man who had trodden on the twig and snapped it, but a bird, and I felt pleased. My bird. The bird was not equally pleased. Ignoring the relation between us, it took fright as soon as it saw the shape of my face, and flew straight over the boundary hedge into a field, the property of Mrs. Henessy, where it sat down with a loud squawk. It had become Mrs. Henessy's bird. Something seemed grossly amiss here, something that would not have occurred had the wood been larger. I could not afford to buy Mrs. Henessy out, I dared not murder her, and limitations of this sort beset me on every side. Ahab did not want that vineyard—he only needed it to round off his property, preparatory to plotting a new curve—and all the land around my wood has become necessary to me in order to round off the wood. A boundary protects. But—poor little thing—the boundary ought in its turn to be protected. Noises on the edge of it. Children throw stones. A little more, and then a little more, until we reach the sea. Happy Canute! Happier Alexander! And after all, why should even the world be the limit of possession? A rocket containing a Union Jack, will, it is hoped, be shortly fired at the moon. Mars. Sirius. Beyond which . . . But these immensities ended by saddening me, I could not suppose that my wood was the destined nucleus of universal dominion—it is so very small and contains no mineral wealth beyond the blackberries. Nor was I comforted when Mrs. Henessy's bird took alarm for the second time and flew clean away from us all, under the belief that it belonged to itself.

5   In the third place, property makes its owner feel that he ought to do something to it. Yet he isn't sure what. A restlessness comes over him, a vague sense that he has a

personality to express—the same sense which, without any vagueness, leads the artist to an act of creation. Sometimes I think I will cut down such trees as remain in the wood, at other times I want to fill up the gaps between them with new trees. Both impulses are pretentious and empty. They are not honest movements towards money-making or beauty. They spring from a foolish desire to express yourself and from an inability to enjoy what I have got. Creation, property, enjoyment form a sinister trinity in the human mind. Creation and enjoyment are both very good, yet they are often unattainable without a material basis, and at such moments property pushes itself in as a substitute, saying, "Accept me instead—I'm good enough for all three." It is not enough. It is, as Shakespeare said of lust, "The expense of the spirit in a waste of shame": it is "Before, a joy proposed; behind, a dream." Yet we don't know how to shun it. It is forced on us by our economic system as the alternative to starvation. It is also forced on us by an internal defect in the soul, by the feeling that in property may lie the germs of self-development and of exquisite or heroic deeds. Our life on earth is, and ought to be, material and carnal. But we have not yet learned to manage our materialism and carnality properly; they are still entangled with the desire for owner-ship, where (in the words of Dante) "Possession is one with loss."

6   And this brings us to our fourth and final point: the blackberries.

7   Blackberries are not plentiful in this meagre grove, but they are easily seen from the public footpath which traverses it, and all too easily gathered. Foxgloves, too—people will pull up the foxgloves, and ladies of an educational tendency even grub for toadstools to show them on the Monday in class. Other ladies, less educated, roll down the bracken in the arms of their gentlemen friends. There is a paper, there are tins. Pray, does my wood belong to me or doesn't it? And, if it does, should I not own it best by allowing no one else to walk there? There is a wood near Lyme Regis, also cursed by a public footpath, where the owner has not hesitated on this point. He had built high stone walls each side of the path, and has spanned it by bridges, so that the public circulate like termites while he gorges on the blackberries unseen. He really does own his wood, this able chap. Dives in Hell did pretty well, but the gulf dividing him from Lazarus could be traversed by vision, and nothing traverses it here. And perhaps I shall come to this in time. I shall wall in and fence out until I really taste the sweets of property. Enormously stout, endlessly avaricious, pseudo-creative, intensely selfish, I shall weave upon my forehead the quadruple crown of possession until those nasty Bolshies come and take it off again and thrust me aside into the outer darkness.

Suggestions for Discussion or Writing

1. What do you think the author's purpose is in writing the essay? What conclusion does he come to? Does he call for action on the part of his audience?

2. What is the author's tone? What words, phrases, or anecdotes help estab-lish the tone?

3. What techniques does Forster use to organize his essay?

4. During the course of his essay, Forster alludes to several biblical passages and famous characters such as Ahab and Alexander. Of what significance are these allusions? What other allusions do you recognize? How are they pertinent to Forster's purpose?

5. Who are the Bolshies? What does Forster mean when he says "I shall weave upon my forehead the quadruple crown of possession until those nasty Bolshies come and take it off again and thrust me aside into the outer darkness"? What does Forster say about capitalism and property?

The Changing Year

Rachel Carson

Born in Springfield, Pennsylvania, Rachel Carson (1907–1964) earned her M.A. in marine biology from Johns Hopkins University in 1932 and went on to graduate study at the Marine Biological Laboratory in Woods Hole, Massachusetts. After teaching zoology at the University of Maryland, she became an aquatic biologist for the U.S. Fish and Wildlife Service until 1949 when she became the editor-in-chief for the Service. She resigned the position in 1952 to devote all her time to writing. Carson won the National Book Award for The Sea Around Us *(1957) from which "The Changing Year" comes. Her most influential and controversial book,* Silent Spring *(1962), criticizes the use of poisonous chemical fertilizers and their effects on our water supply. Among her other writings are* Under the Sea-Wind: A Naturalist's Picture of Ocean Life *(1952),* Food from the Sea: Fish and Shellfish of New England *(1943), and* The Edge of the Sea *(1955).*

1   For the sea as a whole, the alternation of day and night, the passage of the seasons, the procession of the years, are lost in its vastness, obliterated in its own changeless eternity. But the surface waters are different. The face of the sea is always changing. Crossed by colors, lights, and moving shadows, sparkling in the sun, mysterious in the twilight, its aspects and its moods vary hour by hour. The surface waters move with the tides, stir to the breath of the winds, and rise and fall to the endless, hurrying forms of the waves. Most of all, they change with the advance of the seasons. Spring moves over the temperate lands of our Northern Hemisphere in a tide of new life, of pushing green shoots and unfolding buds, all its mysteries and meanings symbolized in the northward migration of the birds, the awakening of sluggish amphibian life as the chorus of frogs rises again from the wet lands, the different sound of the wind which stirs the young leaves where a month ago it rattled the bare branches. These

things we associate with the land, and it is easy to suppose that at sea there could be no such feeling of advancing spring. But the signs are there, and seen with understanding eye, they bring the same magical sense of awakening.

2   In the sea, as on land, spring is a time for the renewal of life. During the long months of winter in the temperate zones the surface waters have been absorbing the cold. Now the heavy water begins to sink, slipping down and displacing the warmer layers below. Rich stores of minerals have been accumulating on the floor of the continental shelf—some freighted down the rivers from the lands; some derived from sea creatures that have died and whose remains have drifted down to the bottom; some from the shells that once encased a diatom, the streaming protoplasm of a radiolarian, or the transparent tissues of a pteropod. Nothing is wasted in the sea; every particle of material is used over and over again, first by one creature, then by another. And when in spring the waters are deeply stirred, the warm bottom water brings to the surface a rich supply of minerals, ready for use by new forms of life.

3   Just as land plants depend on minerals in the soil for their growth, every marine plant, even the smallest, is dependent upon the nutrient salts or minerals in the sea water. Diatoms must have silica, the element of which their fragile shells are fashioned. For these and all other microplants, phosphorus is an indispensable mineral. Some of these elements are in short supply and in winter may be reduced below the minimum necessary for growth. The diatom population must tide itself over this season as best it can. It faces a stark problem of survival, with no opportunity to increase, a problem of keeping alive the spark of life by forming tough protective spores against the stringency of winter, a matter of existing in a dormant state in which no demands shall be made on an environment that already withholds all but the most meager necessities of life. So the diatoms hold their place in the winter sea, like seeds of wheat in a field under snow and ice, the seeds from which the spring growth will come.

4   These, then, are the elements of the vernal blooming of the sea: the 'seeds' of the dormant plants, the fertilizing chemicals, the warmth of the spring sun.

5   In a sudden awakening, incredible in its swiftness, the simplest plants of the sea begin to multiply. Their increase is of astronomical proportions. The spring sea belongs at first to the diatoms and to all the other microscopic plant life of the plankton. In the fierce intensity of their growth they cover vast areas of ocean with a living blanket of their cells. Mile after mile of water may appear red or brown or green, the whole surface taking on the color of the infinitesimal grains of pigment contained in each of the plant cells.

6   The plants have undisputed sway in the sea for only a short time. Almost at once their own burst of multiplication is matched by a similar increase in the small animals of the plankton. It is the spawning time of the copepod and the glassworm, the pelagic shrimp and the winged snail. Hungry swarms of these little beasts of the plankton roam through the waters, feeding on the abundant plants and themselves falling prey to larger creatures. Now in the spring the surface waters become a vast nursery. From the hills and valleys of the continent's edge lying far below, and from the scattered shoals and banks, the eggs or young of many of the bottom animals rise to the surface of the sea. Even those which, in their maturity, will sink down to a sedentary life on the bottom, spend the first weeks of life as freely swimming hunters of the plankton. So as spring

progresses new batches of larvae rise into the surface each day, the young of fishes and crabs and mussels and tube worms, mingling for a time with the regular members of the plankton.

7   Under the steady and voracious grazing, the grasslands of the surface are soon depleted. The diatoms become more and more scarce, and with them the other simple plants. Still there are brief explosions of one or another form, when in a sudden orgy of cell division it comes to claim whole areas of the sea for its own. So, for a time each spring, the waters may become blotched with brown, jellylike masses, and the fishermen's nets come up dripping a brown slime and containing no fish, for the herring have turned away from these waters as though in loathing of the viscid, foul-smelling algae. But in less time than passes between the full moon and the new, the spring flowering of Phaeocystis is past and the waters have cleared again.

8   In the spring the sea is filled with migrating fishes, some of them bound for the mouths of great rivers, which they will ascend to deposit their spawn. Such are the spring-run chinooks coming in from the deep Pacific feeding grounds to breast the rolling flood of the Columbia, the shad moving in to the Chesapeake and the Hudson and the Connecticut, the alewives seeking a hundred coastal streams of New England, the salmon feeling their way to the Penobscot and the Kennebec. For months or years these fish have known only the vast spaces of the ocean. Now the spring sea and the maturing of their own bodies lead them back to the rivers of their birth.

9   Other mysterious comings and goings are linked with the advance of the year. Capelin gather in the deep, cold water of the Barents Sea, their shoals followed and preyed upon by flocks of auks, fulmars, and kittiwakes. Cod approach the banks of Lofoten, and gather off the shores of Iceland. Birds whose winter feeding territory may have encompassed the whole Atlantic or the whole Pacific converge upon some small island, the entire breeding population arriving within the space of a few days. Whales suddenly appear off the slopes of the coastal banks where the swarms of shrimplike krill are spawning, the whales having come from no one knows where, by no one knows what route.

10   With the subsiding of the diatoms and the completed spawning of many of the plankton animals and most of the fish, life in the surface waters slackens to the slower pace of midsummer. Along the meeting places of the currents the pale moon jelly Aurelia gathers in thousands, forming sinuous lines or windrows across miles of sea, and the birds see their pale forms shimmering deep down in the green water. By midsummer the large red jellyfish Cyanea may have grown from the size of a thimble to that of an umbrella. The great jellyfish moves through the sea with rhythmic pulsations, trailing long tentacles and as likely as not shepherding a little group of young cod or haddock, which find shelter under its bell and travel with it.

11   A hard, brilliant, coruscating phosphorescence often illuminates the summer sea. In waters where the protozoa Noctiluca is abundant it is the chief source of this summer luminescence, causing fishes, squids, or dolphins to fill the water with racing flames and to clothe themselves in a ghostly radiance. Or again the summer sea may glitter with a thousand thousand moving pinpricks of light, like an immense swarm of fireflies moving through a dark wood. Such an effect is produced by a shoal of the brilliantly phosphorescent shrimp Meganyctiphanes, a creature of cold and darkness and of the

places where icy water rolls upward from the depths and bubbles with white ripplings at the surface.

12   Out over the plankton meadows of the North Atlantic the dry twitter of the phalaropes, small brown birds, wheeling and turning, dipping and rising, is heard for the first time since early spring. The phalaropes have nested on the arctic tundras, reared their young, and now the first of them are returning to the sea. Most of them will continue south over the open water far from land, crossing the equator into the South Atlantic. Here they will follow where the great whales lead, for where the whales are, there also are the swarms of plankton on which these strange little birds grow fat.

13   As the fall advances, there are other movements, some in the surface, some hidden in the green depths, that betoken the end of summer. In the fog-covered waters of Bering Sea, down through the treacherous passes between the islands of the Aleutian chain and southward into the open Pacific, the herds of fur seals are moving. Left behind are two small islands, treeless bits of volcanic soil thrust up into the waters of Bering Sea. The islands are silent now, but for the several months of summer they resounded with the roar of millions of seals come ashore to bear and rear their young—all the fur seals of the eastern Pacific crowded into a few square miles of bare rock and crumbling soil. Now once more the seals turn south, to roam down along the sheer underwater cliffs of the continent's edge, where the rocky foundations fall away steeply into the deep sea. Here, in a blackness more absolute than that of arctic winter, the seals will find rich feeding as they swim down to prey on the fishes of this region of darkness.

14   Autumn comes to the sea with a fresh blaze of phosphorescence, when every wave crest is aflame. Here and there the whole surface may glow with sheets of cold fire, while below schools of fish pour through the water like molten metal. Often the autumnal phosphorescence is caused by a fall flowering of the dinoflagellates, multiplying furiously in a short-lived repetition of their vernal blooming.

15   Sometimes the meaning of the glowing water is ominous. Off the Pacific coast of North America, it may mean that the sea is filled with the dinoflagellate *Gonyaulax,* a minute plant that contains a poison of strange and terrible virulence. About four days after *Gonyaulax* comes to dominate the coastal plankton, some of the fishes and shellfish in the vicinity become toxic. This is because, in their normal feeding, they have strained the poisonous plankton out of the water. Mussels accumulate the *Gonyaulax* toxins in their livers, and the toxins react on the human nervous system with an effect similar to that of strychnine. Because of these facts, it is generally understood along the Pacific coast that it is unwise to eat shellfish taken from coasts exposed to the open sea where *Gonyaulax* may be abundant, in summer or early fall. For generations before the white men came, the Indians knew this. As soon as the red streaks appeared in the sea and the waves began to flicker at night with the mysterious blue-green fires, the tribal leaders forbade the taking of mussels until these warning signals should have passed. They even set guards at intervals along the beaches to warn inlanders who might come down for shellfish and be unable to read the language of the sea.

16   But usually the blaze and glitter of the sea, whatever its meaning for those who produce it, implies no menace to man. Seen from the deck of a vessel in open ocean,

a tiny, man-made observation point in the vast world of sea and sky, it has an eerie and unearthly quality. Man, in his vanity, subconsciously attributes a human origin to any light not of moon or stars or sun. Lights on the shore, lights moving over the water, mean lights kindled and controlled by other men, serving purposes understandable to the human mind. Yet here are lights that flash and fade away, lights that come and go for reasons meaningless to man, lights that have been doing this very thing over the eons of time in which there were no men to stir in vague disquiet.

17   On such a night of phosphorescent display Charles Darwin stood on the deck of the *Beagle* as she plowed southward through the Atlantic off the coast of Brazil.

> *The sea from its extreme luminousness presented a wonderful and most beautiful appearance [he wrote in his diary]. Every part of the water which by day is seen as foam, glowed with a pale light. The vessel drove before her bows two billows of liquid phosphorus, and in her wake was a milky train. As far as the eye reached the crest of every wave was bright; and from the reflected light, the sky just above the horizon was not so utterly dark as the rest of the Heavens. It was impossible to behold this plain of matter, as it were melted and consuming by heat, without being reminded of Milton's description of the regions of Chaos and Anarchy.[1]*

18   Like the blazing colors of the autumn leaves before they wither and fall, the autumnal phosphorescence betokens the approach of winter. After their brief renewal of life the flagellates and the other minute algae dwindle away to a scattered few; so do the shrimps and the copepods, the glassworms and the comb jellies. The larvae of the bottom fauna have long since completed their development and drifted away to take up whatever existence is their lot. Even the roving fish schools have deserted the surface waters and have migrated into warmer latitudes or have found equivalent warmth in the deep, quiet waters along the edge of the continental shelf. There the torpor of semi-hibernation descends upon them and will possess them during the months of winter.

19   The surface waters now become the plaything of the winter gales. As the winds build up the giant storm waves and roar along their crests, lashing the water into foam and flying spray, it seems that life must forever have deserted this place.

20   For the mood of the winter sea, read Joseph Conrad's description:

> *The greyness of the whole immense surface, the wind furrows upon the faces of the waves, the great masses of foam, tossed about and waving, like matted white locks, give to the sea in a gale an appearance of hoary age, lustreless, dull, without gleams, as though it had been created before light itself.[2]*

21   But the symbols of hope are not lacking even in the grayness and bleakness of the winter sea. On land we know that the apparent lifelessness of winter is an illusion.

[1]From *Charles Darwin's Diary of the Voyage of H.M.S. Beagle,* edited by Nora Barlow, 1934 edition, Cambridge University Press, p. 107.
[2]From *The Mirror of the Sea,* Kent edition, 1925, Doubleday-Page, p. 71.

Look closely at the bare branches of a tree, on which not the palest gleam of green can be discerned. Yet, spaced along each branch are the leaf buds, all the spring's magic of swelling green concealed and safely preserved under the insulating, overlapping layers. Pick off a piece of the rough bark of the trunk; there you will find hibernating insects. Dig down through the snow into the earth. There are the eggs of next summer's grasshoppers; there are the dormant seeds from which will come the grass, the herb, the oak tree.

22   So, too, the lifelessness, the hopelessness, the despair of the winter sea are an illusion. Everywhere are the assurances that the cycle has come to the full, containing the means of its own renewal. There is the promise of a new spring in the very iciness of the winter sea, in the chilling of the water, which must, before many weeks, become so heavy that it will plunge downward, precipitating the overturn that is the first act in the drama of spring. There is the promise of new life in the small plantlike things that cling to the rocks of the underlying bottom, the almost formless polyps from which, in spring, a new generation of jellyfish will bud off and rise into the surface waters. There is unconscious purpose in the sluggish forms of the copepods hibernating on the bottom, safe from the surface storms, life sustained in their tiny bodies by the extra store of fat with which they went into this winter sleep.

23   Already, from the gray shapes of cod that have moved, unseen by man, through the cold sea to their spawning places, the glassy globules of eggs are rising into the surface waters. Even in the harsh world of the winter sea, these eggs will begin the swift divisions by which a granule of protoplasm becomes a living fishlet.

24   Most of all, perhaps, there is assurance in the fine dust of life that remains in the surface waters, the invisible spores of the diatoms, needing only the touch of warming sun and fertilizing chemicals to repeat the magic of spring.

Suggestions for Discussion or Writing

1. Carson begins her essay with a comparison between spring on land and spring at sea. How does this set the structure for the essay? What other comparisons does she use? Where does she use them?

2. What details does Carson repeat in the essay? How is this strategy effective?

3. What seems to be Carson's purpose in writing the essay? Is she concerned more with her own feelings and thoughts or with the information itself? Does she prompt the audience to any action? If so, what?

4. Who is Carson's audience? What clues in the text reveal her intended audience?

5. Notice that Carson uses many images of light and color. How do these images enhance her meaning and purpose? What other kinds of images does she use often? Why are these an effective way to express her meaning?

The Death of the Moth

Virginia Woolf

English novelist, essayist and critic, Virginia Woolf (1882–1941) associated with many well-known writers of her time. She founded the Hogarth Press in 1917 and published many upcoming writers such as E. M. Forster, Gertrude Stein, T. S. Eliot, and Katherine Mansfield. Her most successful novel, To the Lighthouse *(1927), is filled with characters based on people in her own life. Her other work includes* Voyage Out *(1915),* Night and Day *(1919),* A Room of One's Own *(1929), and* The Waves *(1931). Woolf is known for her fine use of stream-of-consciousness and the interior monologue.*

1   Moths that fly by day are not properly to be called moths; they do not excite that pleasant sense of dark autumn nights and ivy-blossom which the commonest yellow-underwing asleep in the shadow of the curtain never fails to rouse in us. They are hybrid creatures, neither gay like butterflies nor sombre like their own species. Nevertheless the present specimen, with his narrow hay-coloured wings, fringed with a tassel of the same colour, seemed to be content with life. It was a pleasant morning, mid-September, mild, benignant, yet with a keener breath than that of the summer months. The plough was already scoring the field opposite the window, and where the share had been, the earth was pressed flat and gleamed with moisture. Such vigour came rolling in from the fields and then down beyond that it was difficult to keep the eyes strictly turned upon the book. The rooks too were keeping one of their annual festivities; soaring round the tree tops until it looked as if a vast net with thousands of black knots in it had been cast up into the air; which, after a few moments sank slowly down upon the trees until every twig seemed to have a knot at the end of it. Then, suddenly, the net would be thrown into the air again in a wider circle this time, with the utmost clamour and vociferation, as though to be thrown into the air and settle slowly down upon the tree tops were a tremendously exciting experience.

2   The same energy which inspired the rooks, the ploughmen, the horses, and even, it seemed, the lean bare-backed downs, sent the moth fluttering from side to side of his square of the window pane. One could not help watching him. One was, indeed, conscious of a queer feeling of pity for him. The possibilities of pleasure seemed that morning so enormous and so various that to have only a moth's part in life, and a day moth's at that, appeared a hard fate, and his zest in enjoying his meagre opportunities to the full, pathetic. He flew vigorously to one corner of his compartment, and, after waiting there a second, flew across to the other. What remained for him but to fly to a third corner and then to a fourth? That was all he could do, in spite of the size of the downs, the width of the sky, the far-off smoke of houses, and the romantic voice, now and then, of a steamer out at sea. What he could do he did. Watching him, it seemed as if a fibre, very thin but pure, of the enormous energy of the world had been thrust

into his frail and diminutive body. As often as he crossed the pane, I could fancy that a thread of vital light became visible. He was little or nothing but life.

3   Yet, because he was so small, and so simple a form of the energy that was rolling in at the open window and driving its way through so many narrow and intricate corridors in my own brain and in those of other human beings, there was something marvelous as well as pathetic about him. It was as if someone had taken a tiny bead of pure life and decking it as lightly as possible with down and feathers, had set it dancing and zigzagging to show us the true nature of life. Thus displayed one could not get over the strangeness of it. One is apt to forget all about life, seeing it humped and bossed and garnished and cumbered so that it has to move with the greatest circumspection and dignity. Again, the thought of all that life might have been had he been born in any other shape caused one to view his simple activities with a kind of pity.

4   After a time, tired by his dancing apparently, he settled on the window ledge in the sun, and, the queer spectacle being at an end, I forgot about him. Then, looking up, my eye was caught by him. He was trying to resume his dancing, but seemed either so stiff or so awkward that he could only flutter to the bottom of the windowpane; and when he tried to fly across it he failed. Being intent on other matters I watched these futile attempts for a time without thinking, unconsciously waiting for him to resume his flight as one waits for a machine, that has stopped momentarily, to start again without considering the reason of its failure. After perhaps a seventh attempt he slipped from the wooden ledge and fell, fluttering his wings, on to his back on the window sill. The helplessness of his attitude roused me. It flashed upon me that he was in difficulties; he could no longer raise himself; his legs struggled vainly. But, as I stretched out a pencil, meaning to help him to right himself, it came over me that the failure and awkwardness were the approach of death. I laid the pencil down again.

5   The legs agitated themselves once more. I looked as if for the enemy against which he struggled. I looked out of doors. What had happened there? Presumably it was midday, and work in the fields had stopped. Stillness and quiet had replaced the previous animation. The birds had taken themselves off to feed in the brooks. The horses stood still. Yet the power was there all the same, massed outside indifferent, impersonal, not attending to anything in particular. Somehow it was opposed to the little hay-coloured moth. It was useless to try to do anything. One could only watch the extraordinary efforts made by those tiny legs against an oncoming doom which could, had it chosen, have submerged an entire city, not merely a city, but masses of human beings; nothing, I knew, had any chance against death. Nevertheless after a pause of exhaustion the legs fluttered again. It was superb this last protest, and so frantic that he succeeded at last in righting himself. One's sympathies, of course, were all on the side of life. Also, when there was nobody to care or to know, this gigantic effort on the part of an insignificant little moth, against a power of such magnitude, to retain what no one else valued or desired to keep, moved one strangely. Again, somehow, one saw life, a pure bead. I lifted the pencil again, useless though I knew it to be. But even as I did so, the unmistakable tokens of death showed themselves. The body relaxed, and instantly grew stiff. The struggle was over. The insignificant little creature now knew death. As I looked at the dead moth, this minute wayside triumph

of so great a force over so mean an antagonist filled me with wonder. Just as life had been strange a few minutes before, so death was now as strange. The moth having righted himself now lay most decently and uncomplainingly composed. O yes, he seemed to say, death is stronger than I am.

Suggestions for Discussion or Writing

1. Initially, Woolf calls the moth "the present specimen." How does her choice of words reflect her attitude toward the moth at first? How does her attitude toward the moth change?

2. What kinds of detail does Woolf use to describe the moth? Why might she use some details but not others? How does the moth's description at the beginning differ from its description at the end? In what way is that difference significant?

3. What is the connection between what is happening to the moth and what is happening outside? Why is this connection central to Woolf's essay?

4. What does Woolf mean when she says the moth "was little or nothing but life"? How is the abstract concept of life given concreteness in the essay? What is the moth's connection with Woolf?

Hook

Walter Van Tilburg Clark

Although he was born in Maine, Walter Van Tilburg Clark (1909–1971) was reared in Nevada. After earning his M.A. in English at the University of Nevada, he went on to teach high school English and coach basketball before becoming a professor of English and teaching creative writing. His first book, Ten Women in Gale's House and Other Poems, *was published in 1932, but he is best known for* The Ox-Bow Incident *(1940). He won the O. Henry Award for the short story "The Wind and the Snow of Winter" (1945) and has published many other short stories in magazines and one collection,* The Watchful Gods *(1950). Among his other novels are* The City of Trembling Leaves *(1945) and* The Track of the Cat *(1949). "Hook" was originally published in the August 1940 issue of the* Atlantic Monthly *and, like many of his other writings, focuses on the coexistence of good and evil, pain and pleasure.*

1   Hook, the hawks' child, was hatched in a dry spring among the oaks, beside the seasonal river, and was struck from the nest early. In the drouth his single-willed parents had to extend their hunting ground by more than twice, for the ground creatures upon which they fed died by the hundreds. The range became too great for them to wish to return and feed Hook, and when they had lost interest in each other they drove Hook down into the sand and brush and went back to solitary courses over the bleaching hills.

2   Unable to fly yet, Hook crept over the ground, challenging all large movements with recoiled head, erected, rudimentary wings, and the small rasp of his clattering beak. It was during this time of abysmal ignorance and continual fear that his eyes took on the first quality of a hawk, that of being wide, alert and challenging. He dwelt, because of his helplessness, among the rattling brush which grew between the oaks and the river. Even in his thickets and near the water, the white sun was the dominant presence. Except in the dawn, when the land wind stirred, or in the late afternoon, when the sea wind became strong enough to penetrate the half-mile inland to this turn in the river, the sun was the major force, and everything was dry and motionless under it. The brush, small plants and trees alike husbanded the little moisture at their hearts; the moving creatures waited for dark, when sometimes the sea fog came over and made a fine, soundless rain which relieved them.

3   The two spacious sounds of his life environed Hook at this time. One was the great rustle of the slopes of yellowed wild wheat, with over it the chattering rustle of the leaves of the California oaks, already as harsh and individually tremulous as in autumn. The other was the distant whisper of the foaming edge of the Pacific, punctuated by the hollow shoring of the waves. But these Hook did not yet hear, for he was attuned by fear and hunger to the small, spasmodic rustlings of live things. Dry, shrunken, and nearly starved, and with his plumage delayed, he snatched at beetles, dragging in the sand to catch them. When swifter and stronger birds and animals did not reach them first, which was seldom, he ate the small, silver fish left in the mud by the failing river. He watched, with nearly chattering beak, the quick, thin lizards pause, very alert, and raise and lower themselves, but could not catch them because he had to raise his wings to move rapidly, which startled them.

4   Only one sight and sound not of his world of microscopic necessity was forced upon Hook. That was the flight of the big gulls from the beaches, which sometimes, in quealing play, came spinning back over the foothills and the river bed. For some inherited reason, the big, shipbodied birds did not frighten Hook, but angered him. Small and chewed-looking, with his wide, already yellowing eyes glaring up at them, he would stand in an open place on the sand in the sun and spread his shaping wings and clatter his bill like shaken dice. Hook was furious about the swift, easy passage of gulls.

5   His first opportunity to leave off living like a ground owl came accidentally. He was standing in the late afternoon in the red light under the thicket, his eyes half-filmed with drowse and the stupefaction of starvation, when suddenly something beside him moved, and he struck, and killed a field mouse driven out of the wheat by thirst. It was a poor mouse, shriveled and lice ridden, but in striking, Hook had tasted blood, which raised nest memories and restored his nature. With started neck plumage and shining

eyes, he tore and fed. When the mouse was devoured, Hook had entered hoarse adolescence. He began to seek with a conscious appetite, and to move more readily out of shelter. Impelled by the blood appetite, so glorious after his long preservation upon the flaky and bitter stuff of bugs, he ventured even into the wheat in the open sun beyond the oaks, and discovered the small trails and holes among the roots. With his belly often partially filled with flesh, he grew rapidly in strength and will. His eyes were taking on their final change, their yellow growing deeper and more opaque, their stare more constant, their challenge less desperate. Once during this transformation, he surprised a ground squirrel, and although he was ripped and wing-bitten and could not hold his prey, he was not dismayed by the conflict, but exalted. Even while the wing was still drooping and the pinions not grown back, he was excited by other ground squirrels and pursued them futilely, and was angered by their dusty escapes. He realized that his world was a great arena for killing, and felt the magnificence of it.

6   The two major events of Hook's young life occurred in the same day. A little after dawn he made the customary essay and succeeded in flight. A little before sunset, he made his first sustained flight of over two hundred yards, and at its termination struck and slew a great buck squirrel whose thrashing and terrified gnawing and squealing gave him a wild delight. When he had gorged on the strong meat, Hook stood upright, and in his eyes was the stare of the hawk, never flagging in intensity but never swelling beyond containment. After that the stare had only to grow more deeply challenging and more sternly controlled as his range and deadliness increased. There was no change in kind. Hook had mastered the first of the three hungers which are fused into the single, flaming will of a hawk, and he had experienced the second.

7   The third and consummating hunger did not awaken in Hook until the following spring, when the exultation of space had grown slow and steady in him, so that he swept freely with the wind over the miles of coastal foothills, circling, and ever in sight of the sea, and used without struggle the warm currents lifting from the slopes, and no longer desired to scream at the range of his vision, but intently sailed above his shadow swiftly climbing to meet him on the hillsides, sinking away and rippling across the brush-grown canyons.

8   That spring the rains were long, and Hook sat for hours, hunched and angry under their pelting, glaring into the fogs of the river valley, and killed only small, drenched things flooded up from their tunnels. But when the rains had dissipated, and there were sun and sea wind again, the game ran plentiful, the hills were thick and shining green, and the new river flooded about the boulders where battered turtles climbed up to shrink and sleep. Hook then was scorched by the third hunger. Ranging farther, often forgetting to kill and eat, he sailed for days with growing rage, and woke at night clattering on his dead tree limb, and struck and struck and struck at the porous wood of the trunk, tearing it away. After days, in the draft of a coastal canyon miles below his own hills, he came upon the acrid taint he did not know but had expected, and sailing down it, felt his neck plumes rise and his wings quiver so that he swerved unsteadily. He saw the unmated female perched upon the tall and jagged stump of a tree that had been shorn by storm, and he stooped, as if upon game. But she was older than he, and wary of the gripe of his importunity, and banked off screaming, and he screamed also at the intolerable delay.

9   At the head of the canyon, the screaming pursuit was crossed by another male with a great wing-spread, and the light golden in the fringe of his plumage. But his more skillful opening played him false against the ferocity of the twice-balked Hook. His rising maneuver for position was cut short by Hook's wild, upward swoop, and at the blow he raked desperately and tumbled off to the side. Dropping, Hook struck him again, struggled to clutch, but only raked and could not hold, and, diving, struck once more in passage, and then beat up, yelling triumph, and saw the crippled antagonist side-slip away, half-tumble once, as the ripped wing failed to balance, then steady and glide obliquely into the cover of brush on the canyon side. Beating hard and stationary in the wind above the bush that covered his competitor, Hook waited an instant, but when the bush was still, screamed again, and let himself go off with the current, reseeking, infuriated by the burn of his own wounds, the thin choke-thread of the acrid taint.

10   On a hilltop projection of stone two miles inland, he struck her down, gripping her rustling body with his talons, beating her wings down with his wings, belting her head when she whimpered or thrashed, and at last clutching her neck with his hook and, when her coy struggles had given way to stillness, succeeded.

11   In the early summer, Hook drove the three young ones from their nest, and went back to lone circling above his own range. He was complete.

12   Throughout that summer and the cool, growthless weather of the winter, when the gales blew in the river canyon and the ocean piled upon the shore, Hook was master of the sky and the hills of his range. His flight became a lovely and certain thing, so that he played with the treacherous currents of the air with a delicate ease surpassing that of the gulls. He could sail for hours, searching the blanched grasses below him with telescopic eyes, gaining height against the wind, descending in mile-long gently declining swoops when he curved and rode back, and never beating either wing. At the swift passage of his shadow within their vision, gophers, ground squirrels and rabbits froze, or plunged gibbering into their tunnels beneath matted turf. Now, when he struck, he killed easily in one hard-knuckled blow. Occasionally, in sport, he soared up over the river and drove the heavy and weaponless gulls downstream again, until they would no longer venture inland.

13   There was nothing which Hook feared now, and his spirit was wholly belligerent, swift and sharp, like his gaze. Only the mixed smells and incomprehensible activities of the people at the Japanese farmer's home, inland of the coastwise highway and south of the bridge across Hook's river, troubled him. The smells were strong, unsatisfactory and never clear, and the people, though they behaved foolishly, constantly running in and out of their built-up holes, were large, and appeared capable, with fearless eyes looking up at him, so that he instinctively swerved aside from them. He cruised over their yard, their gardens, and their bean fields, but he would not alight close to their buildings.

14   But this one area of doubt did not interfere with his life. He ignored it, save to look upon it curiously as he crossed, his afternoon shadow sliding in an instant over the chicken-and-crate-cluttered yard, up the side of the unpainted barn, and then out again smoothly, just faintly, liquidly rippling over the furrows and then over the stubble of the grazing slopes. When the season was dry, and the dead earth blew on the fields, he extended his range to satisfy his great hunger, and again narrowed it when

the fields were once more alive with the minute movements he could not only see but anticipate.

15   Four times that year he was challenged by other hawks blowing up from behind the coastal hills to scud down his slopes, but two of these he slew in mid-air, and saw hurtle down to thump on the ground and lie still while he circled, and a third, whose wing he tore, he followed closely to earth and beat to death in the grass, making the crimson jet out from its breast and neck into the pale wheat. The fourth was a strong flier and experienced fighter, and theirs was a long, running battle, with brief, rising flurries of striking and screaming, from which down and plumage soared off.

16   Here, for the first time, Hook felt doubts, and at moments wanted to drop away from the scoring, burning talons and the twisted hammer strokes of the strong beak, drop away shrieking, and take cover and be still. In the end, when Hook, having outmaneuvered his enemy and come above him, wholly in control, and going with the wind, tilted and plunged for the death rap, the other, in desperation, threw over on his back and struck up. Talons locked, beaks raking, they dived earthward. The earth grew and spread under them amazingly, and they were not fifty feet above it when Hook, feeling himself turning toward the underside, tore free and beat up again on heavy, wrenched wings. The other, stroking swiftly, and so close to down that he lost wing plumes to a bush, righted himself and planed up, but flew on lumberingly between the hills and did not return. Hook screamed the triumph, and made a brief pretense of pursuit, but was glad to return, slow and victorious, to his dead tree.

17   In all these encounters Hook was injured, but experienced only the fighter's pride and exultation from the sting of wounds received in successful combat. And in each of them he learned new skill. Each time the wounds healed quickly, and left him a more dangerous bird.

18   In the next spring, when the rains and the night chants of the little frogs were past, the third hunger returned upon Hook with a new violence. In this quest, he came into the taint of a young hen. Others too were drawn by the unnerving perfume, but only one of them, the same with which Hook had fought his great battle, was a worthy competitor. This hunter drove off two, while two others, game but neophytes, were glad enough that Hook's impatience would not permit him to follow and kill. Then the battle between the two champions fled inland, and was a tactical marvel, but Hook lodged the neck-breaking blow, and struck again as they dropped past the treetops. The blood had already begun to pool on the gray, fallen foliage as Hook flapped up between branches, too spent to cry his victory. Yet his hunger would not let him rest until, late in the second day, he drove the female to ground among the laurels of a strange river canyon.

19   When the fledglings of this second brood had been driven from the nest, and Hook had returned to his own range, he was not only complete, but supreme. He slept without concealment on his bare limb, and did not open his eyes when, in the night, the heavy-billed cranes coughed in the shallows below him.

20   The turning point of Hook's career came that autumn, when the brush in the canyons rustled dryly and the hills, mowed close by the cattle, smoked under the wind as if burning. One midafternoon, when the black clouds were torn on the rim of the sea and the surf flowered white and high on the rocks, raining in over the low cliffs,

Hook rode the wind diagonally across the river mouth. His great eye, focused for small things, stirring in the dust and leaves, overlooked so large and slow a movement as that of the Japanese farmer rising from the brush and lifting the two black eyes of his shotgun. Too late Hook saw and, startled, swerved, but wrongly. The surf muffled the reports, and nearly without sound, Hook felt the minute whips of the first shot, and the astounding, breath-taking blow of the second.

21 Beating his good wing, tasting the blood that quickly swelled into his beak, he tumbled off with the wind and struck into the thickets on the far side of the river mouth. The branches tore him. Wild with rage, he thrust up and clattered his beak, challenging, but when he had fallen over twice, he knew that the trailing wing would not carry, and then heard the boots of the hunter among the stones in the river bed and, seeing him loom at the edge of the bushes, crept back among the thicket brush and was still. When he saw the boots stand before him, he reared back, lifting his good wing and cocking his head for the serpent-like blow, his beak open but soundless, his great eyes hard and very shining. The boots passed on. The Japanese farmer, who believed that he had lost chickens, and who had cunningly observed Hook's flight for many afternoons, until he could plot it, did not greatly want a dead hawk.

22 When Hook could hear nothing but the surf and the wind in the thicket, he let the sickness and shock overcome him. The fine film of the inner lid dropped over his big eyes. His heart beat frantically so that it made the plumage of his shot-aching breast throb. His own blood throttled his breathing. But these things were nothing compared to the lightning of pain in his left shoulder, where the shot had bunched, shattering the airy bones so the pinions trailed on the ground and could not be lifted. Yet, when a sparrow lit in the bush over him Hook's eyes flew open again hard and challenging, his good wing was lifted and his beak strained open. The startled sparrow darted piping out over the river.

23 Throughout that night, while the long clouds blew across the stars and the wind shook the bushes about him, and throughout the next day, while the clouds still blew and massed until there was no gleam of sunlight on the sand bar, Hook remained stationary, enduring his sickness. In the second evening, the rains began. First there was a long, running patter of drops upon the beach and over the dry trees and bushes. At dusk there came a heavier squall, which did not die entirely, but slacked off to a continual, spaced splashing of big drops, and then returned with the front of the storm. In long, misty curtains, gust by gust, the rain swept over the sea, beating down its heaving, and coursed up the beach. The little jets of dust ceased to rise about the drips in the fields, and the mud began to gleam. Among the boulders of the river bed, darkling pools grew slowly.

24 Still Hook stood behind his tree from the wind, only gentle drops reaching him, falling from the upper branches and then again from the brush. His eyes remained closed, and he could still taste his own blood in his mouth, though it had ceased to come up freshly. Out beyond him, he heard the storm changing. As rain conquered the sea, the heave of the surf became a hushed sound, often lost in the crying of the wind. Then gradually, as the night turned toward morning, the wind also was broken by the rain. The crying became fainter, the rain settled toward steadiness, and the creep of the waves could be heard again, quiet and regular upon the beach.

25   At dawn there was no wind and no sun, but everywhere the roaring of the vertical, relentless rain. Hook then crept among the rapid drippings of the bushes, dragging his torn sail, seeking better shelter. He stopped often and stood with the shutters of film drawn over his eyes. At mid-morning he found a little cave under a ledge at the base of the sea cliff. Here, lost without branches and leaves about him, he settled to await improvement.

26   When, at midday of the third day, the rain stopped altogether, and the sky opened before a small, fresh wind, letting light through to glitter upon a tremulous sea, Hook was so weak that his good wing trailed also to prop him upright, and his open eyes were lusterless. But his wounds were hardened, and he felt the return of hunger. Beyond his shelter, he heard the gulls flying in great numbers and crying their joy at the cleared air. He could even hear, from the fringe of the river, the ecstatic and unstinted bubblings and chirpings of the small birds. The grassland, he felt, would be full of the stirring anew of the close-bound life, the undrowned insects clicking as they dried out, the snakes slithering down, heads half erect, into the grasses where the mice, gophers and ground squirrels ran and stopped and chewed and licked themselves smoother and drier.

27   With the aid of this hunger, and on the crutches of his wings, Hook came down to stand in the sun beside his cave, whence he could watch the beach. Before him, in ellipses on tilting planes, the gulls flew. The surf was rearing again, and beginning to shelve and hiss on the sand. Through the white foam-writing it left, the long-billed pipers twinkled in bevies, escaping each wave, then racing down after it to plunge their fine drills into the minute double holes where the sand crabs bubbled. In the third row of breakers two seals lifted sleek, streaming heads and barked, and over them, trailing his spider legs, a great crane flew south. Among the stones at the foot of the cliff, small red and green crabs made a little, continuous rattling and knocking. The cliff swallows glittered and twanged on aerial forays.

28   The afternoon began auspiciously for Hook also. One of the two gulls which came squabbling above him dropped a freshly caught fish to the sand. Quickly Hook was upon it. Gripping it, he raised his good wing and cocked his head with open beak at the many gulls which had circled and come down at once toward the fall of the fish. The gulls sheered off, cursing raucously. Left alone on the sand, Hook devoured the fish and, after resting in the sun, withdrew again to his shelter.

29   In the succeeding days, between rains, he foraged on the beach. He learned to kill and crack the small green crabs. Along the edge of the river mouth, he found the drowned bodies of mice and squirrels and even sparrows. Twice he managed to drive feeding gulls from their catch, charging upon them with buffeting wing and clattering beak. He grew stronger slowly, but the shot sail continued to drag. Often, at the choking thought of soaring and striking and the good, hot-blood kill, he strove to take off, but only the one wing came up, winnowing with a hiss, and drove him over onto his side in the sand. After these futile trials, he would rage and clatter. But gradually he learned to believe that he could not fly, that his life must now be that of the discharged nestling again. Denied the joy of space, without which the joy of loneliness was lost, the joy of battle and killing, the blood lust, became his whole concentration. It was his hope, as he charged feeding gulls, that they would turn and offer battle, but they

never did. The sandpipers, at his approach, fled peeping, or, like a quiver of arrows shot together, streamed out over the surf in a long curve. Once, pent beyond bearing, he disgraced himself by shrieking challenge at the businesslike heron which flew south every evening at the same time. The heron did not even turn his head, but flapped and glided on.

30   Hook's shame and anger became such that he stood awake at night. Hunger kept him awake also, for these little leavings of the gulls could not sustain his great body in its renewed violence. He became aware that the gulls slept at night in flocks on the sand, each with one leg tucked under him. He discovered also that the curlews and the pipers, often mingling, likewise slept, on the higher remnant of the bar. A sensation of evil delight filled him in the consideration of protracted striking among them.

31   There was only half of a sick moon in a sky of running but far-separated clouds on the night when he managed to stalk into the center of the sleeping gulls. This was light enough, but so great was his vengeful pleasure that there broke from him a shrill scream of challenge as he first struck. Without the power of flight behind it, the blow was not murderous, and this newly discovered impotence made Hook crazy, so that he screamed again and again as he struck and tore at the felled gull. He slew the one, but was twice knocked over by its heavy flounderings, and all the others rose above him, weaving and screaming, protesting in the thin moonlight. Wakened by their clamor, the wading birds also took wing, startled and plaintive. When the beach was quiet again, the flocks had settled elsewhere, beyond his pitiful range, and he was left alone beside the single kill. It was a disappointing victory. He fed with lowering spirit.

32   Thereafter, he stalked silently. At sunset he would watch where the gulls settled along the miles of beach, and after dark he would come like a sharp shadow among them, and drive with his hook on all sides of him, till the beatings of a poorly struck victim sent the flock up. Then he would turn vindictively upon the fallen and finish them. In his best night, he killed five from one flock. But he ate only a little from one, for the vigor resulting from occasional repletion strengthened only his ire, which became so great at such a time that food revolted him. It was not the joyous, swift, controlled hunting anger of a sane hawk, but something quite different, which made him dizzy if it continued too long, and left him unsatisfied with any kill.

33   Then one day, when he had very nearly struck a gull while driving it from a gasping yellowfin, the gull's wing rapped against him as it broke for its running start, and, the trailing wing failing to support him, he was knocked over. He flurried awkwardly in the sand to regain his feet, but his mastery of the beach was ended. Seeing him, in clear sunlight, struggling after the chance blow, the gulls returned about him in a flashing cloud, circling and pecking on the wing. Hook's plumage showed quick little jets of irregularity here and there. He reared back, clattering and erecting the good wing, spreading the great, rusty tail for balance. His eyes shone with a little of the old pleasure. But it died, for he could reach none of them. He was forced to turn and dance about awkwardly on the sand, trying to clash bills with each tormentor. They banked up squealing and returned, weaving about him in concentric and overlapping circles. His scream was lost in their clamor, and he appeared merely to be hopping clumsily with his mouth open. Again he fell sideways. Before he could right

himself, he was bowled over, and a second time, and lay on his side, twisting his neck to reach them and clappering in blind fury, and was struck three times by three successive gulls, shrieking their flock triumph.

34   Finally he managed to roll to his breast, and to crouch with his good wing spread wide and the other stretched nearly as far, so that he extended like a gigantic moth, only his snake head, with its now silent scimitar, erect. One great eye blazed under its level brow, but where the other had been was a shallow hole from which thin blood trickled to his russet gap.

35   In this crouch, by short stages, stopping repeatedly to turn and drive the gulls up, Hook dragged into the river canyon and under the stiff cover of the bitter-leafed laurel. There the gulls left him, soaring up with great clatter of their valor. Till nearly sunset Hook, broken spirited and enduring his hardening eye socket, heard them celebrating over the waves.

36   When his will was somewhat replenished, and his empty eye socket had stopped the twitching and vague aching which had forced him often to roll ignominiously to rub it in the dust, Hook ventured from the protective lacings of his thicket. He knew fear again, and the challenge of his remaining eye was once more strident, as in adolescence. He dared not return to the beaches, and with a new, weak hunger, the home hunger, enticing him, made his way by short hunting journeys back to the wild wheat slopes and the crisp oaks. There was in Hook an unwonted sensation now, that of the ever-neighboring possibility of death. This sensation was beginning, after his period as a mad bird on the beach, to solidify him into his last stage of life. When, during his slow homeward passage, the gulls wafted inland over him, watching the earth with curious, miserish eyes, he did not cower, but neither did he challenge, either by opened beak or by raised shoulder. He merely watched carefully, learning his first lessons in observing the world with one eye.

37   At first the familiar surroundings of the bend in the river and the tree with the dead limb to which he could not ascend, aggravated his humiliation, but in time, forced to live cunningly and half-starved, he lost much of his savage pride. At the first flight of a strange hawk over his realm, he was wild at his helplessness, and kept twisting his head like an owl, or spinning in the grass like a small and feathered dervish, to keep the hateful beauty of the wind-rider in sight. But in the succeeding weeks, as one after another coasted his beat, his resentment declined, and when one of the raiders, a haughty yearling, sighted his upstaring eye, and plunged and struck him dreadfully, and failed to kill him only because he dragged under a thicket in time, the second of his great hungers was gone. He had no longer the true lust to kill, no joy of battle, but only the poor desire to fill his belly.

38   Then truly he lived in the wheat and the brush like a ground owl, ridden with ground lice, dusty or muddy, ever half-starved, forced to sit for hours by small holes for petty and unsatisfying kills. Only once during the final months before his end did he make a kill where the breath of danger recalled his valor, and then the danger was such as a hawk with wings and eyes would scorn. Waiting beside a gopher hole, surrounded by the high, yellow grass, he saw the head emerge, and struck, and was amazed that there writhed in his clutch the neck and dusty coffin-skull of a rattlesnake. Holding his grip, Hook saw the great, thick body slither up after, the tip an erect,

strident blur, and writhe on the dirt of the gopher's mound. The weight of the snake pushed Hook about, and once threw him down, and the rising and falling whine of the rattles made the moment terrible, but the vaulted mouth, gaping from the closeness of Hook's grip, so that the pale, envenomed sabers stood out free, could not reach him. When Hook replaced the grip of his beak with the grip of his talons, and was free to stroke again and again at the base of the head, the struggle was over. Hook tore and fed on the fine, watery flesh, and left the tattered armor and the long, jointed bone for the marching ants.

39   When the heavy rains returned, he ate well during the period of the first escapes from flooded burrows, and then well enough, in a vulture's way, on the drowned creatures. But as the rains lingered, and the burrows hung full of water, and there were no insects in the grass and no small birds sleeping in the thickets, he was constantly hungry, and finally unbearably hungry. His sodden and ground-broken plumage stood out raggedly about him, so that he looked fat, even bloated, but underneath it his skin clung to his bones. Save for his great talons and clappers, and the rain in his down, he would have been like a handful of air. He often stood for a long time under some bush or ledge, heedless of the drip, his one eye filmed over, his mind neither asleep or awake, but between. The gurgle and swirl of the brimming river, and the sound of chunks of the bank cut away to splash and dissolve in the already muddy flood, became familiar to him, and yet a torment, as if that great, ceaselessly working power of water ridiculed his frailty, within which only the faintest spark of valor still glimmered. The last two nights before the rain ended, he huddled under the floor of the bridge on the coastal highway, and heard the palpitant thunder of motors swell and roar over him. The trucks shook the bridge so that Hook, even in his famished lassitude, would sometimes open his one great eye wide and startled.

40   After the rains, when things became full again, bursting with growth and sound, the trees swelling, the thickets full of song and chatter, the fields, turning green in the sun, alive with rustling passages, and the moonlit nights strained with the song of the peepers all up and down the river and in the pools in the fields, Hook had to bear the return of the one hunger left him. At times this made him so wild that he forgot himself and screamed challenge from the open ground. The fretfulness of it spoiled his hunting, which was not entirely a matter of patience. Once he was in despair, and lashed himself through the grass and thickets, trying to rise when that virgin scent drifted for a few moments above the current of his own river. Then, breathless, his beak agape, he saw the strong suitor ride swiftly down on the wind over him, and heard afar the screaming fuss of the harsh wooing in the alders. For that moment even the battle heart beat in him again. The rim of his good eye was scarlet, and a little bead of new blood stood in the socket of the other. With beak and talon, he ripped at a fallen log, and made loam and leaves fly from about it.

41   But the season of love passed over to the nestling season, and Hook's love hunger, unused, shriveled in him with the others, and there remained in him only one stern quality befitting a hawk, and that the negative one, the remnant, the will to endure. He resumed his patient, plotted hunting, now along a field of the Japanese farmer, but ever within reach of the river thickets.

42   Growing tough and dry again as the summer advanced, inured to the family of the farmer, whom he saw daily, stooping and scraping with sticks in the ugly, open rows of their fields, where no lovely grass rustled and no life stirred save the shameless gulls, which walked at the heels of the workers, gobbling the worms and grubs they tuned up, Hooks became nearly content with his shard of life. The only longing or resentment to pierce him was that which he suffered occasionally when forced to hide at the edge of the mile-long bean field from the wafted cruising and the restive, down-bent gaze of one of his own kind. For the rest, he was without flame, a snappish, dust-colored creature, fading into the grasses he trailed through, and suited to his petty ways.

43   At the end of that summer, for the second time in his four years, Hook underwent a drought. The equinoctial period passed without a rain. The laurel and the rabbit-brush dripped dry leaves. The foliage of the oaks shriveled and curled. Even the night fogs in the river canyon failed. The farmer's red cattle on the hillside lowed constantly, and could not feed on the dusty stubble. Grass fires broke out along the highways, and ate fast in the wind, filling the hollows with the smell of smoke, and died in the dirt of the shorn hills. The river made no sound. Scum grew on its vestigial pools, and turtles died and stank among the rocks. The dust rode before the wind, and ascended and flowered to nothing between the hills, and every sunset was red with the dust in the air. The people in the farmer's house quarreled, and even struck one another. Birds were silent, and only the hawks flew much. The animals lay breathing hard for very long spells, and ran and crept jerkily. Their flanks were fallen in, and their eyes were red.

44   At first Hook gorged at the fringe of the grass fires on the multitude of tiny things that came running and squeaking. But thereafter there were the blackened strips on the hills, and little more in the thin, crackling grass. He found mice and rats, gophers and ground-squirrels, and even rabbits, dead in the stubble and under the thickets, but so dry and fleshless that only a faint smell rose from them, even on the sunny days. He starved on them. By early December he had wearily stalked the length of the eastern foothills, hunting at night to escape the voracity of his own kind, resting often upon his wings. The queer trail of his short steps and great horned toes zigzagged in the dust and was erased by the wind at dawn. He was nearly dead, and could make no sound through the horn funnels of his clappers.

45   Then one night the dry wind brought him, with the familiar, lifeless dust, another familiar scent, troublesome, mingled and unclear. In his vision-dominated brain he remembered the swift circle of his flight a year past, crossing in one segment, his shadow beneath him, a yard cluttered with crates and chickens, a gray barn and then again the plowed land and the stubble. Traveling faster than he had for days, impatient of his shrunken sweep, Hook came down to the farm. In the dark wisps of cloud blown among the stars over him, but no moon, he stood outside the wire of the chicken run. The scent of fat and blooded birds reached him from the shelter, and also within the enclosure was water. At the breath of the water, Hook's gorge contracted, and his tongue quivered and clove in its groove of horn. But there was the wire. He stalked its perimeter and found no opening. He beat it with his good wing, and felt it cut but not give. He wrenched at it with his beak in many places, but could not tear it. Finally, in

a fury which drove the thin blood through him, he leaped repeatedly against it, beating and clawing. He was thrown back from the last leap as from the first, but in it he had risen so high as to clutch with his beak at the top wire. While he lay on his breast on the ground, the significance of this came upon him.

46   Again he leapt, clawed up the wire, and, as he would have fallen, made even the dead wing bear a little. He grasped the top and tumbled within. There again he rested flat, searching the dark with quick-turning head. There was no sound of motion but the throb of his own body. First he drank at the chill metal trough hung for the chickens. The water was cold, and loosened his tongue and his tight throat, but it also made him drunk and dizzy, so that he had to rest again, his claws spread wide to brace him. Then he walked stiffly, to stalk down the scent. He trailed it up the runway. Then there was the stuffy, body-warm air, acrid with droppings, full of soft rustlings as his talons clicked on the board floor. The thick, white shapes showed faintly in the darkness. Hook struck quickly, driving a hen to the floor with one blow, its neck broken and stretched out stringily. He leaped the still pulsing body, and tore it. The rich, streaming blood was overpowering to his dried senses, his starved, leathery body. After a few swallows, the flesh choked him. In his rage, he struck down another hen. The urge to kill took him again, as in those nights on the beach. He could let nothing go. Balked of feeding, he was compelled to slaughter. Clattering, he struck again and again. The henhouse was suddenly filled with the squawking and helpless rushing and buffeting of the terrified, brainless fowls.

47   Hook reveled in mastery. Here was game big enough to offer weight against a strike, and yet unable to soar away from his blows. Turning in the midst of the turmoil, cannily, his fury caught at the perfect pitch, he struck unceasingly. When the hens finally discovered the outlet, and streamed into the yard, to run around the fence, beating and squawking, Hook followed them, scraping down the incline, clumsy and joyous. In the yard, the cock, a bird as large as he, and much heavier, found him out and gave valiant battle. In the dark, and both earthbound, there was little skill, but blow upon blow, and only chance parry. The still squawking hens pressed into one corner of the yard. While the duel went on, a dog, excited by the sustained scuffling, began to bark. He continued to bark, running back and forth along the fence on one side. A light flashed on in an uncurtained window of the farmhouse, and streamed whitely over the crates littering the ground.

48   Enthralled by his old battle joy, Hook knew only the burly cock before him. Now, in the farthest reach of the window light, they could see each other dimly. The Japanese farmer, with his gun and lantern, was already at the gate when the finish came. The great cock leapt to jab with his spurs and, toppling forward with extended neck as he fell, was struck and extinguished. Blood had loosened Hook's throat. Shrilly he cried his triumph. It was a thin and exhausted cry, but within him as good as when he shrilled in mid-air over the plummeting descent of a fine foe in his best spring.

49   The light from the lantern partially blinded Hook. He first turned and ran directly from it, into the corner where the hens were huddled. They fled apart before his charge. He essayed the fence, and on the second try, in his desperation, was out. But in the open dust, the dog was on him, circling, dashing in, snapping. The farmer, who at first

had not fired because of the chickens, now did not fire because of the dog, and, when he saw that the hawk was unable to fly, relinquished the sport to the dog, holding the lantern up in order to see better. The light showed his own flat, broad, dark face as sunken also, the cheekbones very prominent, and showed the torn-off sleeves of his shirt and the holes in the knees of his overalls. His wife, in a stained wrapper, and barefooted, heavy black hair hanging around a young, passionless face, joined him hesitantly, but watched, fascinated and a little horrified. His son joined them too, encouraging the dog, but quickly grew silent. Courageous and cruel death, however it may afterward sicken the one who has watched it, is impossible to look away from.

50   In the circle of the light, Hook turned to keep the dog in front of him. His one eye gleamed with malevolence. The dog was an Airedale, and large. Each time he pounced, Hook stood ground, raising his good wing, the pinions newly torn by the fence, opening his beak soundlessly, and, at the closest approach, hissed furiously, and at once struck. Hit and ripped twice by the whetted horn, the dog recoiled more quickly from several subsequent jumps and, infuriated by his own cowardice, began to bark wildly. Hook maneuvered to watch him, keeping his head turned to avoid losing the foe on the blind side. When the dog paused, safely away, Hook watched him quietly, wing partially lowered, beak closed, but at the first move again lifted the wing and gaped. The dog whined, and the man spoke to him encouragingly. The awful sound of his voice made Hook for an instant twist his head to stare up at the immense figures behind the light. The dog again sallied, barking, and Hook's head spun back. His wing was bitten this time, and with a furious sideblow, he caught the dog's nose. The dog dropped him with a yelp, and then, smarting, came on more warily, as Hook propped himself up from the ground again between his wings. Hook's artificial strength was waning, but his heart still stood to the battle, sustained by a fear of such dimension as he had never known before, but only anticipated when the arrogant young hawk had driven him to cover. The dog, unable to find any point at which the merciless, unwinking eye was not watching him, the parted beak waiting, paused and whimpered again.

51   "Oh, kill the poor thing," the woman begged.

52   The man, though, encouraged the dog again, saying. "Sick him; sick him."

53   The dog rushed bodily. Unable to avoid him, Hook was bowled down, snapping and raking. He left long slashes, as from the blade of a knife, on the dog's flank, but before he could right himself and assume guard again, was caught by the good wing and dragged, clattering, and seeking to make a good stroke from his back. The man followed them to keep the light on them, and the boy went with him, wetting his lips with his tongue and keeping his fists closed tightly. The woman remained behind, but could not help watching the diminished conclusion.

54   In the little, palely shining arena, the dog repeated his successful maneuver three times, growling but not barking, and when Hook thrashed up from the third blow, both wings were trailing, and dark, shining streams crept on his black-fretted breast from the shoulders. The great eye flashed more furiously than it ever had in victorious battle, and the beak still gaped, but there was no more clatter. He faltered when turning to keep front; the broken wings played him false even as props. He could not rise to use his talons.

55   The man had tired of holding the lantern up, and put it down to rub his arm. In the low, horizontal light, the dog charged again, this time throwing the weight of his forepaws against Hook's shoulder, so that Hook was crushed as he struck. With his talons up, Hook raked at the dog's belly, but the dog conceived the finish, and furiously worried the feathered bulk. Hook's neck went limp, and between his gaping clappers came only a faint chittering, as from some small kill of his own in the grasses.

56   In this last conflict, however, there had been some minutes of the supreme fire of the hawk whose three hungers are perfectly fused in the one will; enough to burn off a year of shame.

57   Between the great sails the light body lay caved and perfectly still. The dog, smarting from his cuts, came to the master and was praised. The woman, joining them slowly, looked at the great wingspread, her husband raising the lantern that she might see it better.

58   "Oh, the brave bird," she said.

Suggestions for Discussion or Writing

1. Although a hawk is a bird of prey, many readers sympathize with and even admire Hook. Do you admire or dislike Hook? What causes you to sympathize with or dislike him? What does Clark do to create emotion for the bird?

2. How does Clark personify Hook's feelings and thoughts? How do we get inside Hook's brain and emotions?

3. What might be Clark's purpose in writing the story of Hook the hawk? How does he want the reader to respond?

4. Who is Clark's audience? How do you know?

The Birds

Daphne du Maurier

Born in London, England, Daphne du Maurier (1907–1989) was educated in France and began her writing career in 1931 with her novel of family relationships The Loving Spirit. *She is known as a fine writer of gothic fiction—romance, mystery, and suspense. She received the most acclaim for her novel* Rebecca, *which won the 1938 National Book Award and was made into the Academy Award-winning 1940 film* Rebecca. *Among her other writings are* Frenchman's Creek *(1941),* My Cousin Rachel *(1951), and* The Scapegoat *(1957), all of which have become motion pictures. She has also written short stories, biographies, a family history, screenplays, and an autobiography,* Myself When Young: The Shaping of a Writer *(1977). Her classic suspense tale, "The Birds," was adapted for the movies by Alfred Hitchcock.*

1   On December the third the wind changed overnight and it was winter. Until then the autumn had been mellow, soft. The earth was rich where the plow had turned it.

2   Nat Hocken, because of a wartime disability, had a pension and did not work full time at the farm. He worked three days a week, and they gave him the lighter jobs. Although he was married, with children, his was a solitary disposition; he liked best to work alone.

3   It pleased him when he was given a bank to build up, or a gate to mend, at the far end of the peninsula, where the sea surrounded the farmland on either side. Then, at midday, he would pause and eat the meat pie his wife had baked for him and, sitting on the cliff's edge, watch the birds.

4   In autumn great flocks of them came to the peninsula, restless, uneasy, spending themselves in motion; now wheeling, circling in the sky; now settling to feed on the rich, new-turned soil; but even when they fed, it was as though they did so without hunger, without desire.

5   Restlessness drove them to the skies again. Crying, whistling, calling, they skimmed the placid sea and left the shore.

6   Make haste, make speed, hurry and begone; yet where, and to what purpose? The restless urge of autumn, unsatisfying, sad, had put a spell upon them, and they must spill themselves of motion before winter came.

7   Perhaps, thought Nat, a message comes to the birds in autumn, like a warning. Winter is coming. Many of them will perish. And like people who, apprehensive of death before their time, drive themselves to work or folly, the birds do likewise; tomorrow we shall die.

8   The birds had been more restless than ever this fall of the year. Their agitation more remarked because the days were still.

9   As Mr. Trigg's tractor traced its path up and down the western hills and Nat, hedging, saw it dip and turn, the whole machine and the man upon it were momentarily lost in the great cloud of wheeling, crying birds.

10   Nat remarked upon them to Mr. Trigg when the work was finished for the day.

11   "Yes," said the farmer "there are more birds about than usual. I have a notion the weather will change. It will be a hard winter. That's why the birds are restless."

12   The farmer was right. That night the weather turned.

13   The bedroom in the cottage faced east. Nat woke just after two and heard the east wind, cold and dry. It sounded hollow in the chimney, and a loose slate rattled on the roof. Nat listened, and he could hear the sea roaring in the bay. He drew the blanket round him, leaned closer to the back of his wife, deep in sleep. Then he heard the tapping on the windowpane. It continued until, irritated by the sound, Nat got out of bed and went to the window. He opened it; and as he did so something brushed his hand, jabbing at his knuckles, grazing the skin. Then he saw the flutter of the wings and the thing was gone again, over the roof, behind the cottage.

14   It was a bird. What kind of bird he could not tell. The wind must have driven it to shelter on the sill.

15   He shut the window and went back to bed, but feeling his knuckles wet, put his mouth to the scratch. The bird had drawn blood.

16   Frightened, he supposed, bewildered, seeking shelter, the bird had stabbed at him in the darkness. Once more he settled himself to sleep.

17   Presently the tapping came again—this time more forceful, more insistent. And now his wife woke at the sound, and turning in the bed said to him, "See to the window, Nat; it's rattling."

18   "I've already been to it," he told her. "There's some bird there, trying to get in."

19   "Send it away," she said. "I can't sleep with that noise."

20   So he went to the window for the second time, and now when he opened it there was not one bird on the sill but half a dozen; they flew straight into his face.

21   He shouted, striking out at them with his arms, scattering them; like the first one, they flew over the roof and disappeared.

22   He let the window fall and latched it.

23   Suddenly a frightened cry came from the room across the passage where the children slept.

24   "It's Jill," said his wife, roused at the sound.

25   There came a second cry, this time from both the children. Stumbling into their room, Nat felt the beating of wings about him in the darkness. The window was wide open. Through it came the birds, hitting first the ceiling and the walls, then swerving in midflight and turning to the children in their beds.

26   "It's alright. I'm here," shouted Nat, and the children flung themselves, screaming, upon him, while in the darkness the birds rose, and dived, and came for him again.

27   "What is it, Nat? what's happened?" his wife called. Swiftly he pushed the children through the door to the passage and shut it upon them, so that he was alone in their bedroom with the birds.

28   He seized a blanket from the nearest bed, and using it as a weapon, flung it to right and left about him.

29   He felt the thud of bodies, heard the fluttering of wings; but the birds were not yet defeated, for again and again they returned to the assault, jabbing his hands, his head, their little stabbing beaks sharp as pointed forks.

30   The blanket became a weapon of defense. He wound it about his head, and then in greater darkness, beat at the birds with his bare hands. He dared not stumble to the door and open it lest the birds follow him.

31   How long he fought with them in the darkness he could not tell; but at last the beating of the wings about him lessened, withdrew; and through the dense blanket he was aware of light.

32   He waited, listened; there was no sound except the fretful crying of one of the children from the bedroom beyond.

33   He took the blanket from his head and stared about him. The cold gray morning light exposed the room.

34   Dawn and the open window had called the living birds; the dead lay on the floor.

35   Sickened, Nat went to the window and stared out across his patch of garden to the fields.

36   It was bitter cold, and the ground had all the hard, black look of the frost that the east wind brings. The sea, fiercer now with turning tide, whitecapped and steep, broke harshly in the bay. Of the birds there was no sign.

37   Nat shut the window and the door of the small bedroom and went back across the passage to his own room.

38   His wife sat up in bed, one child asleep beside her; the smaller one in her arms, his face bandaged.

39   "He's sleeping now," she whispered. "Something must have cut him; there was blood at the corners of his eyes. Jill said it was the birds. She said she woke up and the birds were in the room."

40   His wife looked up at Nat, searching his face for confirmation. She looked terrified, bewildered. He did not want her to know that he also was shaken, dazed almost, by the events of the past few hours.

41   "There are birds in there," he said. "Dead birds, nearly fifty of them." He sat down on the bed beside his wife.

42   "It's the hard weather," he said. "It must be that; it's the hard weather. They aren't the birds, maybe, from around here. They've been driven down from upcountry."

43   "But Nat," whispered his wife, "it's only this night that the weather turned. They can't be hungry yet. There's food for them out there in the fields."

44   "It's the weather," repeated Nat. "I tell you, it's the weather."

45   His face, too, was drawn and tired, like hers. They stared at one another for a while without speaking.

46   Nat went to the window and looked out. The sky was hard and leaden, and the brown hills that had gleamed in the sun the day before looked dark and bare. Black winter had descended in a single night.

47   The children were awake now. Jill was chattering, and young Johnny was crying once again. Nat heard his wife's voice, soothing, comforting them as he went downstairs.

48   Presently they came down. He had breakfast ready for them.

49   "Did you drive away the birds?" asked Jill.

50   "Yes, they've all gone now," Nat said. "It was the east wind brought them in."

51   "I hope they won't come again," said Jill.

52   "I'll walk with you to the bus," Nat said to her.

53   Jill seemed to have forgotten her experience of the night before. She danced ahead of him, chasing the leaves, her face rosy under her pixy hood.

54   All the while Nat searched the hedgerows for the birds, glanced over them to the fields beyond, looked to the small wood above the farm where the rooks and jackdaws gathered; he saw none. Soon the bus came ambling up the hill.

55   Nat saw Jill onto the bus, then turned and walked back toward the farm. It was not his day for work, but he wanted to satisfy himself that all was well. He went to the back door of the farmhouse; he heard Mrs. Trigg singing, the wireless making a background for her song.

56   "Are you there, missus?" Nat called.

57   She came to the door, beaming, broad, a good-tempered woman.

58   "Hullo, Mr. Hocken," she said. "Can you tell me where this cold is coming from? Is it Russia? I've never seen such a change. And it's going on, the wireless says. Something to do with the Arctic Circle."

59   "We didn't turn on the wireless this morning," said Nat. "Fact is, we had trouble in the night."

60   "Kiddies poorly?"

61   "No." He hardly knew how to explain. Now, in daylight, the battle of the birds would sound absurd.

62   He tried to tell Mrs. Trigg what had happened, but he could see from her eyes that she thought his story was the result of nightmare following a heavy meal.

63   "Sure they were real birds?" she said, smiling.

64   "Mrs. Trigg," he said, "there are fifty dead birds—robins, wrens, and such—lying now on the floor of the children's bedroom. They went for me; they tried to go for young Johnny's eyes."

65   Mrs. Trigg stared at him doubtfully. "Well, now," she answered. "I suppose the weather brought them; once in the bedroom they wouldn't know where they were. Foreign birds maybe, from that Arctic Circle."

66   "No," said Nat. "They were the birds you see about here every day."

67   "Funny thing," said Mrs. Trigg. "No explaining it, really. You ought to write up and ask the *Guardian*. They'd have some answer for it. Well, I must be getting on."

68   Nat walked back along the lane to his cottage. He found his wife in the kitchen with young Johnny.

69   "See anyone?" she asked.

70   "Mrs. Trigg," he answered. "I don't think she believed me. Anyway, nothing wrong up there."

71   "You might take the birds away," she said. "I daren't go into the room to make the beds until you do. I'm scared."

72   "Nothing to scare you now," said Nat. "They're dead, aren't they?"

73   He went up with a sack and dropped the stiff bodies into it, one by one. Yes, there were fifty of them all told. Just the ordinary, common birds of the hedgerow; nothing as large even as a thrush. It must have been fright that made them act the way they did.

74   He took the sack out into the garden and was faced with a fresh problem. The ground was frozen solid, yet no snow had fallen; nothing had happened in the past

hours but the coming of the east wind. It was unnatural, queer. He could see the white-capped seas breaking in the bay. He decided to take the birds to the shore and bury them.

75   When he reached the beach below the headland, he could scarcely stand, the force of the east wind was so strong. It was low tide; he crunched his way over the shingle to the softer sand and then, his back to the wind, opened up his sack.

76   He ground a pit in the sand with his heel, meaning to drop the birds into it; but as he did so, the force of the wind lifted them as though in flight again, and they were blown away from him along the beach, tossed like feathers, spread and scattered.

77   The tide will take them when it turns, he said to himself.

78   He looked out to sea and watched the crested breakers, combing green. They rose stiffly, curled, and broke again; and because it was ebb tide, the roar was distant, more remote, lacking the sound and thunder of the flood.

79   Then he saw them. The gulls. Out there, riding the seas.

80   What he had thought at first were the whitecaps of the waves were gulls. Hundreds, thousands, tens of thousands.

81   They rose and fell in the troughs of the seas, heads to the wind, like a mighty fleet at anchor, waiting on the tide.

82   Nat turned; leaving the beach, he climbed the steep path home.

83   Someone should know of this. Someone should be told. Something was happening, because of the east wind and the weather, that he did not understand.

84   As he drew near the cottage, his wife came to meet him at the door. She called to him, excited. "Nat," she said, "it's on the wireless. They've just read out a special news bulletin. It's not only here, it's everywhere. In London, all over the country. Something has happened to the birds. Come listen; they're repeating it."

85   Together they went into the kitchen to listen to the announcement.

86   "Statement from the Home Office, at eleven A.M. this morning. Reports from all over the country are coming in hourly about the vast quantity of birds flocking above towns, villages, and outlying districts, causing obstruction and damage and even attacking individuals. It is thought that the Arctic air stream at present covering the British Isles is causing birds to migrate south in immense numbers, and that intense hunger may drive these birds to attack human beings. Householders are warned to see to their windows, doors, and chimneys, and to take reasonable precautions for the safety of their children. A further statement will be issued later."

87   A kind of excitement seized Nat. He looked at his wife in triumph. "There you are," he said. "I've been telling myself all morning there's something wrong. And just now, down on the beach, I looked out to sea and there were gulls, thousands of them, riding on the sea, waiting."

88   "What are they waiting for, Nat?" she asked.

89   He stared at her. "I don't know," he said slowly.

90   He went over to the drawer where he kept his hammer and other tools.

91   "What are you going to do, Nat?"

92   "See to the windows and the chimneys, like they tell you to."

93   "You think they would break in with the windows shut? Those wrens and robins and such? Why, how could they?"

94   He did not answer. He was not thinking of the robins and the wrens. He was thinking of the gulls.

95   He went upstairs and worked there the rest of the morning, boarding the windows of the bedrooms, filling up the chimney bases.

96   "Dinner's ready." His wife called him from the kitchen.

97   "All right. Coming down."

98   When dinner was over and his wife was wahing up, Nat switched on the one o'clock news. The same announcement was repeated, but the news bulletin enlarged upon it. "The flocks of birds have caused dislocation in all areas," said the announcer, "and in London the mass was so dense at ten o'clock this morning that it seemed like a vast black cloud. The birds settled on rooftops, on window ledges, and on chimneys. The species included blackbird, thrush, the common house sparrow, and as might be expected in the metropolis, a vast quantity of pigeons, starlings, and that frequenter of the London river, the blackheaded gull. The sight was so unusual that traffic came to a standstill in many thoroughfares, work was abandoned in shops and offices, and the streets and pavements were crowded with people standing about to watch the birds."

99   The announcer's voice was smooth and suave; Nat had the impression that he treated the whole business as he would an elaborate joke. There would be others like him, hundreds of them, who did not know what it was to struggle in darkness with a flock of birds.

100   Nat switched off the wireless. He got up and started work on the kitchen windows. His wife watched him, young Johnny at her heels.

101   "What they ought to do," she said, "is to call the Army out and shoot the birds."

102   "Let them try," said Nat. "How'd they set about it?"

103   "I don't know. But something should be done. They ought to do something."

104   Nat thought to himself that "they" were no doubt considering the problem at that very moment, but whatever "they" decided to do in London and the big cities would not help them here, nearly three hundred miles away.

105   "How are we off for food?" he asked.

106   "It's shopping day tomorrow, you know that. I don't keep uncooked food about. Butcher doesn't call till the day after. But I can bring back something when I go in tomorrow."

107   Nat did not want to scare her. He looked in the larder for himself and in the cupboard where she kept her tins.

108   They could hold out for a couple of days.

109   He went on hammering the boards across the kitchen windows. Candles. They were low on candles. That must be another thing she meant to buy tomorrow. Well, they must go early to bed tonight. That was, if—

110   He got up and went out the back door and stood in the garden, looking down toward the sea.

111   There had been no sun all day, and now, at barely three o'clock a kind of darkness had already come; the sky was sullen, heavy, colorless like salt. He could hear the vicious sea drumming on the rocks.

112   He walked down the path halfway to the beach. And then he stopped. He could see the tide had turned. The gulls had risen. They were circling, hundreds of them, thousands of them, lifing their wings against the wind.

113   It was the gulls that made the darkening of the sky.

114   And they were silent. They just went on soaring and circling, rising, falling, trying their strength against the wind. Nat turned. He ran up the path back to the cottage.

115   "I'm going for Jill," he said to his wife.

116   "What's the matter?" she asked. "You've gone quite white."

117   "Keep Johnny inside," he said. "Keep the door shut. Light up now and draw the curtains."

118   "It's only gone three," she said.

119   "Never mind. Do what I tell you."

120   He looked inside the tool shed and took the hoe.

121   He started walking up the lane to the bus stop. Now and again he glanced back over his shoulder; and he could see the gulls had risen higher now, their circles were broader, they were spreading out in huge formation across the sky.

122   He hurried on. Although he knew the bus would not come before four o'clock, he had to hurry.

123   He waited at the top of the hill. There was half an hour still to go.

124   The east wind came whipping across the fields from the higher ground. In the distance he could see the clay hills, white and clean against the heavy pallor of the sky.

125   Something black rose from behind them, like a smudge at first, then widening, becoming deeper. The smudge became a cloud; and the cloud divided again into five other clouds, spreading north, east, south, and west; and then they were not clouds at all but birds.

126   He watched them travel across the sky, within two or three hundred feet of him. He knew, from their speed, that they were bound inland; they had no business with the people here on the peninsula. They were rooks, crows, jackdaws, magpies, jays, all birds that usually preyed upon the smaller species, but bound this afternoon on some other mission.

127   He went to the telephone call box, stepped inside, lifted the receiver. The exchange would pass the message on. "I'm speaking from the highway," he said, "by the bus stop. I want to report large formations of birds traveling upcountry. The gulls are also forming in the bay."

128   "All right," answered the voice, laconic, weary.

129   "You'll be sure and pass this message on to the proper quarter?"

130   "Yes. Yes." Impatient now, fed up. The buzzing note resumed.

131   She's another, thought Nat. She doesn't care.

132   The bus came lumbering up the hill. Jill climbed out.

133   "What's the hoe for, Dad?"

134   "I just brought it along," he said. "Come on now, let's get home. It's cold; no hanging about. See how fast you can run."

135   He could see the gulls now, still silent, circling the fields, coming in toward the land.

136   "Look, Dad; look over there. Look at all the gulls."

137   "Yes. Hurry now."

138   "Where are they flying to? Where are they going?"

139   "Upcountry, I dare say. Where it's warmer."

140   He seized her hand and dragged her after him along the lane.

141   "Don't go so fast. I can't keep up."

142   The gulls were copying the rooks and the crows. They were spreading out in formation, across the sky. They headed, in bands of thousands, to the four compass points.

143   "Dad, what is it? What are the gulls doing?"

144   They were not intent upon their flight, as the crows, as the jackdaws, had been. They still circled overhead. Nor did they fly so high. It was as though they waited upon some signal; as though some decision had yet to be given.

145   "I wish the gulls would go away." Jill was crying. "I don't like them. They're coming closer to the lane."

146   He started running, swinging Jill after him. As they went past the farm turning, he saw the farmer backing his car into the garage. Nat called to him.

147   "Can you give us a lift?" he said.

148   Mr. Trigg turned in the driver's seat and stared at them. Then a smile came to his cheerful, rubicund face. "It looks as though we're in for some fun," he said. "Have you seen the gulls? Jim and I are going to take a crack at them. Everyone's gone bird crazy, talking of nothing else. I hear you were troubled in the night. Want a gun?"

149   Nat shook his head.

150   The small care was packed, but there was room for Jill on the back seat.

151   "I don't want a gun," said Nat, "but I'd be obliged if you'd run Jill home. She's scared of the birds."

152   "Okay," said the farmer. "I'll take her home. Why don't you stop behind and join the shooting match? We'll make the feathers fly."

153   Jill climbed in, and turning the car, the driver sped up the lane. Nat followed after. Trigg must be crazy. What use was a gun against a sky of birds?

154   They were coming in now toward the farm, circling lower in the sky. The farm, then, was their target. Nat increased his pace toward his own cottage. He saw the farmer's car turn and come back along the lane. It drew up beside him with a jerk.

155   "The kid had run inside," said the farmer. "Your wife was watching for her. Well, what do you make of it? They're saying in town the Russians have done it. The Russians have poisoned the birds."

156   "How could they do that?" asked Nat.

157   "Don't ask me. You know how stories get around."

158   "Have you boarded your windows?" asked Nat.

159   "No. Lot of nonsense. I've had more to do today than to go round boarding up my windows."

160   "I'd board them now if I were you."

161   "Garn. You're windy. Like to come to our place to sleep?"

162   "No, thanks all the same."

163   "All right. See you in the morning. Give you a gull breakfast."

164   The farmer grinned and turned his car to the farm entrance. Nat hurried on. Past the little wood, past the old barn, and then across the stile to the remaining field. As he jumped the stile, he heard the whir of wings. A black-backed gull dived down at him from the sky. It missed, swerved in flight, and rose to dive again. In a moment it was joined by others—six, seven, a dozen.

165   Nat dropped his hoe. The hoe was useless. Covering his head with his arms, he ran toward the cottage.

166   They kept coming at him from the air—noiseless, silent, save for the beating wings. The terrible, fluttering wings. He could feel the blood on his hands, his wrists, upon his neck. If only he could keep them from his eyes. Nothing else mattered.

167   With each dive, with each attack, they became bolder. And they had no thought for themselves. When they dived low and missed, they crashed, bruised and broken, on the ground.

168   As Nat ran he stumbled, kicking their spent bodies in front of him.

169   He found the door and hammered upon it with his bleeding hands. "Let me in," he shouted. "It's Nat. Let me in."

170   Then he saw the gannet, poised for the dive, above him in the sky.

171   The gulls circled, retired, soared, one with another, against the wind.

172   Only the gannet remained. One single gannet, above him in the sky. Its wings folded suddenly to its body. It dropped like a stone.

173   Nat screamed; and the door opened.

174   He stumbled across the threshold, and his wife threw her weight against the door.

175   They heard the thud of the gannet as it fell.

176   His wife dressed his wounds. They were not deep. The backs of his hands had suffered most, and his wrists. Had he not worn a cap, the birds would have reached his head. As for the gannet—the gannet could have split his skull.

177   The children were crying, of course. They had seen the blood on their father's hands.

178   "It's all right now," he told them. "I'm not hurt."

179   His wife was ashen. "I saw them overhead," she whispered. "They began collecting just as Jill ran in with Mr. Trigg. I shut the door fast, and it jammed. That's why I couldn't open it at once when you came."

180   "Thank God the birds waited for me," he said. "Jill would have fallen at once. They're flying inland, thousands of them. Rooks, crows, all the bigger birds. I saw them from the bus stop. They're making for the towns."

181   "But what can they do, Nat?"

182   "They'll attack. Go for everyone out in the streets. Then they'll try the windows, the chimneys."

183   "Why don't the authorities do something? Why don't they get the Army, get machine guns?"

184   "There's been no time. Nobody's prepared. We'll hear what they have to say on the six o'clock news."

185   "I can hear the birds," Jill said. "Listen Dad."

186   Nat listened. Muffled sounds came from the windows, from the door. Wings brushing the surface, sliding, scraping, seeking a way of entry. The sound of many bodies pressed together, shuffling on the sills. Now and again came a thud, a crash, as some bird dived and fell.

187   Some of them will kill themselves that way, he thought, but not enough. Never enough.

188   "All right," he said aloud. "I've got boards over the windows, Jill. The birds can't get in."

189   He went and examined all the windows. He found wedges—pieces of old tin, strips of wood and metal—and fastened them at the sides of the windows to reinforce the boards.

190   His hammering helped to deafen the sound of the birds, the shuffling, the tapping, and—more ominous—the splinter of breaking glass.

191   "Turn on the wireless," he said. He went upstairs to the bedrooms and reinforced the windows there. Now he could hear the birds on the roof—the scraping of claws, a sliding, jostling sound.

192   He decided the whole family must sleep in the kitchen and keep up the fire. He was afraid of the bedroom chimneys. The boards he had placed at their bases might give way. In the kitchen they would be safe because of the fire. He would have to make a joke of it. Pretend to the children they were playing camp. If the worst happened and the birds forced an entry by way of the bedroom chimneys, it would be hours, days perhaps, before they could break down the doors. The birds would be imprisoned in the bedrooms. They could do no harm there. Crowded together, they would stifle and die. He began to bring the mattresses downstairs.

193   At sight of them, his wife's eyes widened in apprehension.

194   "All right," he said cheerfully. "We'll all sleep together in the kitchen tonight. More cozy, here by the fire. Then we won't be worried by those silly old birds tapping on the windows."

195   He made the children help him rearrange the furniture, and he took the precaution of moving the dresser against the windows.

196   We're safe enough now, he thought. We're snug and tight. We can hold out. It's just the food that worries me. Food and coal for the fire. We've enough for two or three days, not more. By that time—

197   No use thinking ahead as far as that. And they'd be giving directions on the wireless.

198   And now, in the midst of many problems, he realized that only dance music was coming over the air. He knew the reason. The usual programs had been abandoned; this only happened at exceptional times.

199   At six o'clock the records ceased. The time signal was given. There was a pause, and then the announcer spoke. His voice was solemn, grave. Quite different from midday.

200   "This is London," he said. "A national emergency was proclaimed at four o'clock this afternoon. Measures are being taken to safeguard the lives and property of the population, but it must be understood that these are not easy to effect immediately, owing to the unforeseen and unparalleled nature of the present crisis. Every householder must take precautions about his own building. Where several people live together, as in flats and hotels, they must unite to do the utmost that they can to prevent entry. It is absolutely imperative that every individual stay indoors tonight.

201   "The birds, in vast numbers, are attacking anyone on sight, and have already begun an assault upon buildings; but these, with due care, should be impenetrable.

202   "The population is asked to remain calm.

203   "Owing to the exceptional nature of the emergency, there will be no further transmission from any broadcasting station until seven A.M. tomorrow."

204   They played "God Save the Queen." Nothing more happened.

205   Nat switched off the set. He looked at his wife. She stared back at him.

206   "We'll have supper early," suggested Nat. "Something for a treat—toasted cheese, eh? Something we all like."

207   He winked and nodded at his wife. He wanted the look of dread, of apprehension, to leave her face.

208   He helped with the supper, whistling, singing, making as much clatter as he could. It seemed to him that the shuffling and the tapping were not so intense as they had been at first, and presently he went up to the bedrooms and listened. He no longer heard the jostling for place upon the roof.

209   They've got reasoning powers, he thought. They know it's hard to break in here. They'll try elsewhere.

210   Supper passed without incident. Then, when they were clearing away, they heard a new sound, a familiar droning.

211   His wife looked up at him, her face alight.

212   "It's planes," she said. "They're sending out planes after the birds. That will get them. Isn't that gunfire? Can't you hear guns?"

213   It might be gunfire, out at sea. Nat could not tell. Big naval guns might have some effect upon the gulls out at sea, but the gulls were inland now. The guns couldn't shell the shore because of the population.

214   "It's good, isn't it," said his wife, "to hear the planes?"

215   Catching her enthusiasm, Jill jumped up and down with Johnny. "The planes will get the birds."

216   Just then they heard a crash about two miles distant. Followed by a second, then a third. The droning became more distant, passed away out to sea.

217   "What was that?" asked his wife.

218   "I don't know," answered Nat. He did not want to tell her that the sound they had heard was the crashing of aircraft.

219   It was, he had no doubt, a gamble on the part of the authorities to send out reconnaissance forces, but they might have known the gamble was suicidal. What could aircraft do against birds that flung themselves to death against propeller and fuselage but hurtle to the ground themselves?

220   "Where have the planes gone, Dad?" asked Jill.

221   "Back to base," he said. "Come on now, time to tuck down for bed."

222   There was no further drone of aircraft, the naval guns had ceased. Waste of life and effort, Nat said to himself. We can't destroy enough of them that way. Cost too heavy. There's always gas. Maybe they'll try spraying with gas, mustard gas. We'll be warned first, of course, if they do. There's one thing, the best brains of the country will be on it tonight.

223   Upstairs in the bedrooms all was quiet. No more scraping and stabbing at the windows. A lull in battle. The wind hadn't dropped, though. Nat could still hear it roaring in the chimneys. And the sea breaking down on the shore.

224   Then he remembered the tide. The tide would be on the turn. Maybe the lull in battle was because of the tide. There was some law the birds obeyed, and it had to do with the east wind and the tide.

225   He glanced at his watch. Nearly eight o'clock. It must have gone high water an hour ago. That explained the lull. The birds attacked with the flood tide.

226   He reckoned the time limit in his head. They had six hours to go without attack. When the tide turned again, around 1:20 in the morning, the birds would come back.

227   He called softly to his wife and whispered to her that he would go out and see how they were faring at the farm, see if the telephone was still working there so that they might get news from the exchange.

228   "You're not to go," she said at once, "and leave me alone with the children. I can't stand it."

229   "All right," he said, "all right. I'll wait till morning. And we can get the wireless bulletin then, too, at seven. But when the tide ebbs again, I'll try for the farm; they may let us have bread and potatoes."

230   His mind was busy again, planning against emergency. They would not have milked, of course, this evening. The cows would be standing by the gate, waiting; the household would be inside, battened behind boards as they were here at the cottage.

231   That is, if they had had time to take precautions.

232   Softly, stealthily, he opened the back door and looked outside.

233   It was pitch-dark. The wind was blowing harder than ever, coming in steady gusts, icy, from the sea.

234   He kicked at the step. It was heaped with birds. These were the suicides, the divers, the ones with broken necks. Wherever he looked, he saw dead birds. The living had flown seaward with the turn of the tide. The gulls would be riding the seas now, as they had done in the forenoon.

235   In the far distance on the hill, something was burning. One of the aircraft that had crashed; the fire, fanned by the wind, had set light to a stack.

236   He looked at the bodies of the birds. He had a notion that if he stacked them, one upon the other, on the window sills, they would be added protection against the next attack.

237   Not much, perhaps, but something. The bodies would have to be clawed at, pecked and dragged aside before the living birds gained purchase on the sills and attacked the panes.

238   He set to work in the darkness. It was queer. He hated touching the dead birds, but he went on with his work. He noticed grimly that every windowpane was shattered. Only the boards had kept the birds from breaking in.

239   He stuffed the cracked panes with the bleeding bodies of the birds and felt his stomach turn. When he had finished, he went back into the cottage and barricaded the kitchen door, making it doubly secure.

240   His wife had made him cocoa; he drank it thirstily. He was very tired. "All right," he said, smiling, "don't worry. We'll get through."

241   He lay down on his mattress and closed his eyes.

242   He dreamed uneasily because, through his dreams, ran the dread of something forgotten. Some piece of work that he should have done. It was connected, in some way, with the burning aircraft.

243   It was his wife, shaking his shoulder, who awoke him finally.

244   "They've begun," she sobbed. "They've started this last hour. I can't listen to it any longer alone. There's something smells bad too, something burning."

245   Then he remembered. He had forgotten to make up the fire.

246   The fire was smoldering, nearly out. He got up swiftly and lighted the lamp.

247   The hammering had started at the windows and the door, but it was not that he minded now. It was the smell of singed feathers.

248   The smell filled the kitchen. He knew what it was at once. The birds were coming down the chimney, squeezing their way down to the kitchen range.

249   He got sticks and paper and put them on the embers, then reached for the can of kerosene.

250   "Stand back," he shouted to his wife. He threw some of the kerosene onto the fire.

251   The flame roared up the pipe, and down into the fire fell the scorched, blackened bodies of the birds.

252   The children waked, crying. "What is it?" asked Jill. "What's happened?"

253   Nat had no time to answer her. He was raking the bodies from the chimney, clawing them out onto the floor.

254   The flames would drive the living birds away from the chimney top. The lower joint was difficult though. It was choked with smoldering, helpless bodies of the birds caught by fire.

255   He scarcely heeded the attack on the windows and the door. Let them beat their wings, break their backs, lose their lives, in the desperate attempt to force an entry into his home. They would not break in.

256   "Stop crying," he called to the children. "There's nothing to be afraid of. Stop crying."

257   He went on raking out the burning, smoldering bodies as they fell into the fire.

258   This'll fetch them, he said to himself. The draft and the flames together. We're all right as long as the chimney doesn't catch.

259   Amid the tearing at the window boards came the sudden homely striking of the kitchen clock. Three o'clock.

260   A little more than four hours to go. He could not be sure of the exact time of high water. He reckoned the tide would not turn much before half past seven.

261   He waited by the range. The flames were dying. But no more blackened bodies fell from the chimney. He thrust his poker up as far as it could go and found nothing.

262   The danger of the chimney's being choked up was over. It could not happen again, not if the fire was kept burning day and night.

263   I'll have to get more fuel from the farm tomorrow, he thought. I can do all that with the ebb tide. It can be worked; we can fetch what we need when the tide's turned. We've just got to adapt ourselves, that's all.

264   They drank tea and cocoa, ate slices of bread. Only half a loaf left, Nat noticed. Never mind, though; they'd get by.

265   If they could hang on like this until seven, when the first news bulletin came through, they would not have done too badly.

266   "Give us a smoke," he said to his wife. "It will clear away the smell of scorched feathers."

267   "There's only two left in the packet," she said. "I was going to buy you some."

268   "I'll have one," he said.

269   He sat with one arm around his wife and one around Jill, with Johnny on his lap, the blankets heaped about them on the mattress.

270   "You can help admiring the beggars," he said. "They've got persistency. You'd think they'd tire of the game, but not a bit of it."

271   Admiration was hard to sustain. The tapping went on and on; and a new, rasping note struck Nat's ear, as though a sharper beak than any hitherto had come to take over from its fellows.

272   He tried to remember the names of birds; he tried to think which species would go for this particular job.

273   It was not the tap of the woodpecker. That would be tight and frequent. This was more serious; if it continued long, the wood would splinter as the glass had done.

274   Then he remembered the hawk. Could the hawks have taken over from the gulls? Were these buzzards now upon the sills, using talons as well as beaks? Hawks, buzzards, kestrels, facons; he had forgotten the birds of prey. He had forgotten the gripping power of the birds of prey. Three hours to go; and while they waited, the sound of the splintering wood, the talons tearing at the wood.

275   Nat looked about him, seeing what furniture he could destroy to fortify the door.

276   The windows were safe because of the dresser. He was not certain of the door. He went upstairs; but when he reached the landing, he paused and listened.

277   There was a soft patter on the floor of the children's bedroom. The birds had broken through.

278   The other bedroom was still clear. He brought out the furniture to pile at the head of the stairs should the door of the children's bedroom go.

279   "Come down, Nat. What are you doing?" called his wife.

280   "I won't be long," he shouted. "I'm just making everything ship-shape up here."

281   He did not want her to come. He did not want her to hear the pattering in the children's bedroom, the brushing of those wings against the door.

282   After he suggested breakfast, he found himself watching the clock, gazing at the hands that went slowly around the dial. If his theory was not correct, if the attack did not cease with the turn of the tide, he knew they were beaten. They could not continue through the long day without air, without rest, without fuel.

283   A crackling in his ears drove away the sudden, desperate desire for sleep.

284   "What is it? What now?" he said sharply.

285   "The wireless," said his wife. "I've been watching the clock. It's nearly seven."

286   The comfortable crackling of the wireless brought new life.

287   They waited. The kitchen clock struck seven.

288   The crackling continued. Nothing else. No chimes. No music.

289   They waited until a quarter past. No news bulletin came through.

290   "We heard wrong," he said. "They won't be broadcasting until eight o'clock."

291   They left the wireless switched on. Nat thought of the battery, wondered how much power was left in the battery. If it failed, they would not hear the instructions.

292   "It's getting light," whispered his wife. "I can't see it but I can feel it. And listen! The birds aren't hammering so loud now."

293   She was right. The rasping, tearing sound grew fainter every moment. So did the shuffling, the jostling for place upon the step, upon the sills. The tide was on the turn.

294   By eight there was no sound at all. Only the wind. And the crackling of the wireless. The children, lulled at last by the stillness, fell asleep.

295   At half past eight Nat switched the wireless off.

296   "We'll miss the news," said his wife.

297   "There isn't going to be any news," said Nat. "We've got to depend upon ourselves."

298   He went to the door and slowly pulled away the barricades. He drew the bolts, and kicking the broken bodies from the step outside the door, breathed the cold air.

299   He had six working hours before him, and he knew he must reserve his strength to the utmost, not waste it in any way.

300   Food and light and fuel; these were the most necessary things. If he could get them, they could endure another night.

301   He stepped into the garden; and as he did so, he saw the living birds. The gulls had gone to ride the sea, as they had done before. They sought sea food and the buoyancy of the tide before they returned to the attack.

302   No so the land birds. They waited, and watched.

303   Nat saw them on the hedgerows, on the soil, crowded in the trees, outside in the field—line upon line of birds, still, doing nothing. He went to the end of his small garden.

304   The birds did not move. They merely watched him.

305   I've got to get food, Nat said to himself. I've got to go to the farm to get food.

306   He went back to the cottage. He saw to the windows and the door.

307   "I'm going to the farm," he said.

308   His wife clung to him. She had seen the living birds from the open door.

309   "Take us with you," she begged. "We can't stay here alone. I'd rather die than stay here alone."

310   "Come on, then," he said. "Bring baskets and Johnny's pram. We can load up the pram."

311   They dressed against the biting wind. His wife put Johnny in the pram, and Nat took Jill's hand.

312   "The birds," Jill whimpered. "They're all out there in the fields."

313   "They won't hurt us," he said. "Not in the light."

314   They started walking across the field toward the stile, and the birds did not move. They waited, their heads turned to the wind.

315   When they reached the turning to the farm, Nat stopped and told his wife to wait in the shelter of the hedge with the two children. "But I want to see Mrs. Trigg," she protested. "There are lots of things we can borrow if they went to market yesterday, and—"

316   "Wait here," Nat interrupted. "I'll be back in a moment."

317   The cows were lowing, moving restlessly in the yard, and he could see a gap in the fence where the sheep had knocked their way through to roam unchecked in the front garden before the farmhouse.

318   No smoke came from the chimneys. Nat was filled with misgiving. He did not want his wife or the children to go down to the farm.

319   He went down alone, pushing his way through the herd of lowing cows, who turned this way and that, distressed, their udders full.

320   He saw the car standing by the gate. Not put away in the garage.

321   All the windows of the farmhouse were smashed. There were many dead gulls lying in the yard and around the house.

322   The living birds perched on the group of trees behind the farm and on the roof of the house. They were quite still. They watched him. Jim's body lay in the yard. What was left of it. His gun was beside him.

323   The door of the house was shut and bolted, but it was easy to push up a smashed window and climb through.

324   Trigg's body was close to the telephone. He must have been trying to get through to the exchange when the birds got him. The receiver was off the hook, and the instrument was torn from the wall.

325   No sign of Mrs. Trigg. She would be upstairs. Was it any use going up? Sickened, Nat knew what he would find there.

326   Thank God, he said to himself, there were no children.

327   He forced himself to climb the stairs, but halfway up he turned and descended again. He could see Mrs. Trigg's legs protruding from the open bedroom door. Beside her were the bodies of blackbacked gulls and an umbrella, broken. It's no use doing anything, Nat thought. I've only got five hours; less than that. The Triggs would understand. I must load up with what I can find.

328   He tramped back to his wife and children.

329   "I'm going to fill up the car with stuff," he said. "We'll take it home and return for a fresh load."

330   "What about the Triggs?" asked his wife.

331   "They must have gone to friends," he said.

332   "Shall I come and help you then?"

333   "No, there's a mess down there. Cows and sheep all over the place. Wait; I'll get the car. You can sit in the car."

334   Her eyes watched his all the time he was talking. He believed she understood. Otherwise she certainly would have insisted on helping him find the bread and groceries.

335   They made three journeys altogether, to and from the farm, before he was satisfied they had everything they needed. It was surprising, once he started thinking, how many things were necessary. Almost the most important of all was planking for the windows. He had to go around searching for timber. He wanted to renew the boards on all the windows at the cottage.

336   On the final journey he drove the car to the bus stop and got out and went to the telephone box.

337   He waited a few minutes, jangling the hook. No good, though. The line was dead. He climbed onto a bank and looked over the countryside, but there was no sign of life at all, nothing in the fields but the waiting, watching birds.

338   Some of them slept; he could see their beaks tucked into their feathers.

339   You'd think they'd be feeding, he said to himself, not just standing that way.

340   Then he remembered. They were gorged with food. They had eaten their fill during the night. That was why they did not move this morning.

341   He lifted his face to the sky. It was colorless, gray. The bare trees looked bent and blackened by the east wind.

342   The cold did not affect the living birds, waiting out there in the fields.

343   This is the time they ought to get them, Nat said to himself. They're a sitting target now. They must be doing this all over the country. Why don't our aircraft take off now and spray them with mustard gas? What are all our chaps doing? They must know; they must see for themselves.

344   He went back to the car and got into the driver's seat.

345   "Go quickly past that second gate," whispered his wife. "The postman's lying there. I don't want Jill to see."

346   It was a quarter to one by the time they reached the cottage. Only an hour to go.

347   "Better have dinner," said Nat. "Hot up something for yourself and the children, some of that soup. I've not time to eat now. I've got to unload all this stuff from the car."

348   He got everything inside the cottage. It could be sorted later. Give them all something to do during the long hours ahead.

349   First he must see to the windows and the door.

350   He went around the cottage methodically, testing every window and the door. He climbed onto the roof also, and fixed boards across every chimney except the kitchen's.

351   The cold was so intense he could hardly bear it, but the job had to be done. Now and again he looked up, searching the sky for aircraft. None came. As he worked, he cursed the inefficiency of the authorities.

352   He paused, his work on the bedroom chimney finished, and looked out to sea. Something was moving out there. Something gray and white among the breakers.

353   "Good old Navy," he said. "They never let us down. They're coming down channel; they're turning into the bay."

354   He waited, straining his eyes toward the sea. He was wrong, though. The Navy was not there. It was the gulls rising from the sea. And the massed flocks in the fields, with ruffled feathers, rose in formation from the ground and, wing to wing, soared upward to the sky.

355   The tide had turned again.

356   Nat climbed down the ladder and went inside the cottage. The family were at dinner. It was a little after two.

357   He bolted the door, put up the barricade, and lighted the lamp.

358   "It's nighttime," said young Johnny.

359   His wife had switched on the wireless once again. The crackling sound came, but nothing else.

360   "I've been all round the dial," she said, "foreign stations and all. I can't get anything but the crackling."

361   "Maybe they have the same trouble," he said. "Maybe it's the same right through Europe."

362   They ate in silence.

363   The tapping began at the windows, at the door, the rustling, the jostling, the pushing for position on the sills. The first thud of the suicide gulls upon the step.

364   When he had finished dinner, Nat planned, he would put the supplies away, stack them neatly, get everything shipshape. The boards were strong against the windows

and across the chimneys. The cottage was filled with stores, with fuel, with all they needed for the next few days.

365   His wife could help him, and the children too. They'd tire themselves out between now and a quarter to nine, when the tide would ebb; then he'd tuck them down on their mattresses, see that they slept good and sound until three in the morning.

366   He had a new scheme for the windows, which was to fix barbed wire in front of the boards. He had brought a great roll of it from the farm. The nuisance was, he'd have to work at this in the dark, when the lull came between nine and three. Pity he had not thought of it before. Still, as long as the wife and kids slept—that was the main thing.

367   The smaller birds were at the windows now. He recognized the light tap-tapping of their beaks and the soft brush of their wings.

368   The hawks ignored the windows now. They concentrated their attack upon the door.

369   Nat listened to the tearing sound of splintering wood, and wondered how many million years of memory were stored in those little brains, behind the stabbing beaks, the piercing eyes, now giving them this instinct to destroy mankind with all the deft precision of machines.

370   "I'll smoke that last cigarette," he said to his wife. "Stupid of me. It was the one thing I forgot to bring back from the farm."

371   He reached for it, switched on the cracking wireless.

372   He threw the empty packet onto the fire and watched it burn.

Suggestions for Discussion or Writing

1. What is the predominant mood of the story? What words, phrases, and sentences help create that mood? How does the description of the birds' behavior contribute to the mood?

2. What do the birds remember in their "little brains"? Do you think it is the "Russians" or some other force directing the birds?

3. When do you first feel that humanity is doomed to some ill fate? What words, phrases, and incidents foreshadow the events of the story, particularly what happens at the Trigg farm and on the news bulletin?

4. What do you think du Maurier's purpose is in writing this story? Does she call for some action on the reader's part?

5. What might the "crackling wireless" represent? What final outcome does it suggest?

6. Compare this story with the depiction of birds in "Hook."

The Fish

Mary Oliver

Born in Cleveland, Ohio, Mary Oliver (1935–) attended Ohio State and Vassar College. She became a poet but worked as a secretary to sustain herself. She later became the chairwoman of the Writing Department of the Fine Arts Work Center in Massachusetts and a visiting professor at Case Western Reserve University. She has won numerous poetry awards including the Poetry Society of America first prize for "No Voyage" (1962) and the Devil's Advocate Award for "Christmas, 1966" (1968). Her other work includes The River Styx, Ohio, and Other Poems *(1972),* The Night Traveler *(1978),* Sleeping in the Forest *(1979), and* American Primitive *(1983) for which she won the 1984 Pulitzer Prize for poetry. Many of her poems, like "The Fish," express the mythic, mysterious quality of nature.*

The first fish I ever caught
would not lie down
quiet in the pail
but flailed and sucked
5   at the burning
amazement of the air
and died
in the slow pouring off
of rainbows. Later
10   I opened his body and separated
the flesh from the bones
and ate him. Now the sea
is in me: I am the fish, the fish
glitters in me; we are
15   risen, tangled together, certain to fall
back to the sea. Out of pain,
and pain, and more pain
we feed this feverish plot, we are nourished
by the mystery.

Suggestions for Discussion or Writing

1. What natural cycle does the poem describe?

2. Of what significance is the fact that the fish "would not lie down quiet in the pail"?

3. What is meant by "the slow pouring off of rainbows," "this feverish plot," and the "mystery"?

4. In what way is the sea symbolic?

5. In what ways are we all "nourished by the mystery"?

Wild Swans

Edna St. Vincent Millay

Edna St. Vincent Millay (1892–1950) received a degree from Vassar College. Her first book of poems Renascence and Other Poems *was published in 1917. She received a Pulitzer Prize in 1923 for her book* The Harp Weaver and Other Poems. *She also wrote plays,* King's Henchman *(1926) and others, and acted with the Provincetown Players during the 1920s. During the thirties, she wrote many poems in conventional form and was particularly noted for her sonnets. Some of her later poems were concerned with social issues and war, although she wrote very little during the 1940s. Her* Collected Poems *was published after her death.*

I looked in my heart while the wild swans went over.
And what did I see I had not seen before?
Only a question less or a question more;
Nothing to match the flight of wild birds flying.
5   Tiresome heart, forever living and dying,
House without air, I leave you and lock your door.
Wild swans, come over the town, come over
The town again, trailing your legs and crying!

Suggestions for Discussion or Writing

1. What metaphor is Millay using for the flying swans?

2. How effective is Millay's use of repetition: "a question less/a question more" and "come over the town, come over the town"? What is she trying to achieve by the repetition?

3. Why is the flight of the birds symbolic?

4. How does the tone of this poem compare to the story by Clark? to du Maurier?

5. What is the "house without air"?

The Groundhog

Richard Eberhart

The poet and educator Richard Eberhart (1904–) earned his bachelor's degree at Dartmouth, an M.A. in lyrical poetry from Cambridge in 1933, and went on to graduate work at Harvard. He served as the private tutor for the son of King Prajadhipok of Siam, was the master of Engish at St. Mark's School in Massachusetts, and worked as a professor of English at Dartmouth for 28 years. Eberhart won the Bollinger Prize in Poetry from Yale University in 1962 and has since won the Pulitzer Prize for his Selected Poems: 1930 –1965 *(1966) and the National Book Award for* Collected Poems: 1930 –1976. *Eberhart, named the Poet Laureate of Dartmouth College (an honor also bestowed on Robert Frost), as well as the Poet Laureate of New Hampshire, has written several other poetry collections, including* Fields of Grace *(1972) and* Ways of Light *(1980), and several plays, including "The Apparition" (1951) and "The Bride from Mantua" (1964).*

In June, amid the golden fields,
I saw a groundhog lying dead.
Dead lay he; my senses shook,
And mind outshot our naked frailty.
5   There lowly in the vigorous summer
His form began its senseless changes,
And made my senses waver dim
Seeing nature ferocious in him.
Inspecting close his maggots' might
10   And seething cauldron of his being,
Half with loathing, half with a strange love,
I poked him with an angry stick.
The fever arose, became a flame
And Vigour circumscribed the skies,
15   Immense energy in the sun,
And through my frame a sunless trembling.
My stick had done nor good nor harm.
When stood I silent in the day
Watching the object, as before;
20   And kept my reverence for knowledge
Trying for control, to be still,
To quell the passion of the blood;
Until I had bent down on my knees
Praying for joy in the sight of decay.
25   And so I left; and I returned

In Autumn strict of eye, to see
The sap gone out of the groundhog,
But the bony sodden hulk remained.
But the year had lost its meaning,
30   And in intellectual chains
I lost both love and loathing,
Mured up in the wall of wisdom.
Another summer took the fields again
Massive and burning, full of life,
35   But when I chanced upon the spot
There was only a little hair left,
And bones bleaching in the sunlight
Beautiful as architecture;
I watched them like a geometer,
40   And cut a walking stick from a birch.
It has been three years, now.
There is no sign of the groundhog.
I stood there in the whirling summer,
My hand capped a withered heart,
45   And thought of China and of Greece,
Of Alexander in his tent;
Of Montaigne in his tower,
Of Saint Theresa in her wild lament.

Suggestions for Discussion or Writing

1. What is the author's attitude toward the decay of the groundhog? What might the groundhog symbolize for the author? What words, phrases, or images illustrate the author's attitude?

2. What image of summer does the author present? What part do the images of light, energy, and flame play in the poem?

3. Why does the person poke the dead groundhog? What might he hope to accomplish?

4. What is the tone of the poem? What words, phrases, images help establish the tone?

5. Why does the person lose "both love and loathing"? Of what? What are his "intellectual chains"? What is the relationship between intellectual chains and nature?

6. Of what significance are the final allusions to China, Greece, Alexander, Montaigne, and Saint Theresa?

7. Compare Eberhart's attitude toward nature with that of Clark and Oliver.

The World in Transition
Using Technology to Know
About Science

Introduction

H uman technology marks our decades of life with ever-increasing knowledge. One of the most exciting recent developments is in the investigation of chaos. Almost every discipline has been touched by this challenge to certainties of the past. James Gleick's book, from which we took the first article in this chapter, details the development of theories of chaos in several different fields of study. Stephen W. Hawking's monumental study in theoretical physics, clearly written and suited to the lay audience, is introduced next in this chapter.

Dangers in our environment and explorations into geology are the subject of three other articles and a poem. Radon has been shown to be a hidden threat that creeps into homes and businesses without warning. A product of uranium disintegration, radon is produced when the motion of a fault can metamorphose the rock, causing radon to be released into structures that are built above the area. Other rocks are not so threatening. James Bailey discusses the phenomenon rocks can create—triboluminescence—a phenomenon that is also discussed in Richard Feynman's article in Chapter 6, and Jeanette Harris describes amber, organic material turned into rock. Walter McDonald's poem gives examples of the uses of glass, from the beautiful to the frightening.

The missile silos of McDonald's poem bring us to the topic of four other selections from this chapter. The destruction of the earth is a topic that has challenged and frightened us for decades. Whether from an external force, such as the one Robert Nichols postulates—collision with an extraterrestrial object—or from our own misuse of nuclear weapons, as is investigated in Walter Van Tilburg Clark's story and the two poems by Robert Frost and Richard Armour, we feel ourselves uneasy and at risk.

In a time of great luxury and convenience, the developed countries of the world must look at both the positive and negative aspects of our high technology. We live better than the kings of the past: our homes are warmer; our food is grown, stored, and prepared with amazing efficiency; and our transportation and communications are astonishingly sophisticated. Recent developments in science and physics have been opening whole new perspectives, and research has produced new depths of knowledge to our already overflowing store. Yet we have the power to destroy it all. The ultimate question is: Will we?

Prologue

from *Chaos: Making a New Science*

James Gleick

Born in New York City, James Gleick graduated from Harvard University in 1976. He has been an editor, writer, and science reporter for the New York Times *for over ten years. In addition to his book* Chaos *(1988) from which this article comes, he recently published* Genius: The Life and Science of Richard Feynman *(1992), a biographical sketch of another essayist in our collection.*

1   The police in the small town of Los Alamos, New Mexico, worried briefly in 1974 about a man seen prowling in the dark, night after night, the red glow of his cigarette floating along the back streets. He would pace for hours, heading nowhere in the starlight that hammers down through the thin air of the mesas. The police were not the only ones to wonder. At the national laboratory some physicists had learned that their newest colleague was experimenting with twenty-six-hour days, which meant that his waking schedule would slowly roll in and out of phase with theirs. This bordered on strange, even for the Theoretical Division.

2   In the three decades since J. Robert Oppenheimer chose this unworldly New Mexico landscape for the atomic bomb project, Los Alamos National Laboratory had spread across an expanse of desolate plateau, bringing particle accelerators and gas lasers and chemical plants, thousands of scientists and administrators and technicians, as well as one of the world's greatest concentrations of supercomputers. Some of the older scientists remembered the wooden buildings rising hastily out of the rimrock in the 1940s, but to most of the Los Alamos staff, young men and women in college-style corduroys and work shirts, the first bombmakers were just ghosts. The laboratory's locus of purest thought was the Theoretical Division, known as T division, just as computing was C division and weapons was X division. More than a hundred physicists and mathematicians worked in T division, well paid and free of academic pressures to teach and publish. These scientists had experience with brilliance and with eccentricity. They were hard to surprise.

3   But Mitchell Feigenbaum was an unusual case. He had exactly one published article to his name, and he was working on nothing that seemed to have any particular promise. His hair was a ragged mane, sweeping back from his wide brow in the style of busts of German composers. His eyes were sudden and passionate. When he spoke, always rapidly, he tended to drop articles and pronouns in a vaguely middle European way, even though he was a native of Brooklyn. When he worked, he worked obsessively. When he could not work, he walked and thought, day or night, and night was best of all. The twenty-four-hour day seemed too constraining. Nevertheless, his experiment in personal quasiperiodicity came to an end when he decided he could no longer bear waking to the setting sun, as had to happen every few days.

4   At the age of twenty-nine he had already become a savant among the savants, an ad hoc consultant whom scientists would go to see about any especially intractable problem, when they could find him. One evening he arrived at work just as the director of the laboratory, Harold Agnew, was leaving. Agnew was a powerful figure, one of the original Oppenheimer apprentices. He had flown over Hiroshima on an instrument plane that accompanied the *Enola Gay,* photographing the delivery of the laboratory's first product.

5   "I understand you're real smart," Agnew said to Feigenbaum. "If you're so smart, why don't you just solve laser fusion?"

6   Even Feigenbaum's friends were wondering whether he was ever going to produce any work of his own. As willing as he was to do impromptu magic with their questions, he did not seem interested in devoting his own research to any problem that might pay off. He thought about turbulence in liquids and gases. He thought about time—did it glide smoothly forward or hop discretely like a sequence of cosmic motion-picture frames? He thought about the eye's ability to see consistent colors and forms in a universe that physicists knew to be a shifting quantum kaleidoscope. He thought about clouds, watching them from airplane windows (until, in 1975, his scientific travel privileges were officially suspended on grounds of overuse) or from the hiking trails above the laboratory.

7   In the mountain towns of the West, clouds barely resemble the sooty indeterminate low-flying hazes that fill the Eastern air. At Los Alamos, in the lee of a great volcanic caldera, the clouds spill across the sky in random formation, yes, but also not-random, standing in uniform spikes or rolling in regularly furrowed patterns like brain matter. On a stormy afternoon, when the sky shimmers and trembles with the electricity to come, the clouds stand out from thirty miles away, filtering the light and reflecting it, until the whole sky starts to seem like a spectacle staged as a subtle reproach to physicists. Clouds represented a side of nature that the mainstream of physics had passed by, a side that was at once fuzzy and detailed, structured and unpredictable. Feigenbaum thought about such things, quietly and unproductively.

8   To a physicist, creating laser fusion was a legitimate problem; puzzling out the spin and color and flavor of small particles was a legitimate problem; dating the origin of the universe was a legitimate problem. Understanding clouds was a problem for a meteorologist. Like other physicists, Feigenbaum used an understated tough-guy vocabulary to rate such problems. *Such a thing is obvious,* he might say, meaning that a result could be understood by any skilled physicist after appropriate contemplation and calculation. *Not obvious* described work that commanded respect and Nobel prizes. For the hardest problems, the problems that would not give way without long looks into the universe's bowels, physicists reserved words like *deep.* In 1974, though few of his colleagues knew it, Feigenbaum was working on a problem that was deep: chaos.

9   Where chaos begins, classical science stops. For as long as the world has had physicists inquiring into the laws of nature, it has suffered a special ignorance about disorder in the atmosphere, in the turbulent sea, in the fluctuations of wildlife populations, in the oscillations of the heart and the brain. The irregular side of nature, the discontinuous and erratic side—these have been puzzles to science, or worse, monstrosities.

10   But in the 1970s a few scientists in the United States and Europe began to find a way through disorder. They were mathematicians, physicists, biologists, chemists, all seeking connections between different kinds of irregularity. Physiologists found a surprising order in the chaos that develops in the human heart, the prime cause of sudden, unexplained death. Ecologists explored the rise and fall of gypsy moth populations. Economists dug out old stock price data and tried a new kind of analysis. The insights that emerged led directly into the natural world—the shapes of clouds, the paths of lightning, the microscopic intertwining of blood vessels, the galactic clustering of stars.

11   When Mitchell Feigenbaum began thinking about chaos at Los Alamos, he was one of a handful of scattered scientists, mostly unknown to one another. A mathematician in Berkeley, California, had formed a small group dedicated to creating a new study of "dynamical systems." A population biologist at Princeton University was about to publish an impassioned plea that all scientists should look at the surprisingly complex behavior lurking in some simple models. A geometer working for IBM was looking for a new word to describe a family of shapes—jagged, tangled, splintered, twisted, fractured—that he considered an organizing principle in nature. A French mathematical physicist had just made the disputatious claim that turbulence in fluids might have something to do with a bizarre, infinitely tangled abstraction that he called a strange attractor.

12   A decade later, chaos has become a shorthand name for a fast-growing movement that is reshaping the fabric of the scientific establishment. Chaos conferences and chaos journals abound. Government program managers in charge of research money for the military, the Central Intelligence Agency, and the Department of Energy have put ever greater sums into chaos research and set up special bureaucracies to handle the financing. At every major university and every major corporate research center, some theorists ally themselves first with chaos and only second with their nominal specialties. At Los Alamos, a Center for Nonlinear Studies was established to coordinate work on chaos and related problems; similar institutions have appeared on university campuses across the country.

13   Chaos has created special techniques of using computers and special kinds of graphic images, pictures that capture a fantastic and delicate structure underlying complexity. The new science has spawned its own language, an elegant shop talk of *fractals* and *bifurcations, intermittencies* and *periodicities, folded-towel diffeomorphisms* and *smooth noodle maps.* These are the new elements of motion, just as, in traditional physics, quarks and gluons are the new elements of matter. To some physicists chaos is a science of process rather than state, of becoming rather than being.

14   Now that science is looking, chaos seems to be everywhere. A rising column of cigarette smoke breaks into wild swirls. A flag snaps back and forth in the wind. A dripping faucet goes from a steady pattern to a random one. Chaos appears in the behavior of the weather, the behavior of an airplane in flight, the behavior of cars clustering on an expressway, the behavior of oil flowing in underground pipes. No matter what the medium, the behavior obeys the same newly discovered laws. That realization has begun to change the way business executives make decisions about insurance, the way astronomers look at the solar system, the way political theorists talk about the stresses leading to armed conflict.

15   Chaos breaks across the lines that separate scientific disciplines. Because it is a science of the global nature of systems, it has brought together thinkers from fields that had been widely separated. "Fifteen years ago, science was heading for a crisis of increasing specialization," a Navy official in charge of scientific financing remarked to an audience of mathematicians, biologists, physicists, and medical doctors. "Dramatically, that specialization has reversed because of chaos." Chaos poses problems that defy accepted ways of working in science. It makes strong claims about the universal behavior of complexity. The first chaos theorists, the scientists who set the discipline in motion, shared certain sensibilities. They had an eye for pattern, especially pattern that appeared on different scales at the same time. They had a taste for randomness and complexity, for jagged edges and sudden leaps. Believers in chaos—and they sometimes call themselves believers, or converts, or evangelists—speculate about determinism and free will, about evolution, about the nature of conscious intelligence. They feel that they are turning back a trend in science toward reductionism, the analysis of systems in terms of their constituent parts: quarks, chromosomes, or neurons. They believe that they are looking for the whole.

16   The most passionate advocates of the new science go so far as to say that twentieth-century science will be remembered for just three things: relativity, quantum mechanics, and chaos. Chaos, they contend, has become the century's third great revolution in the physical sciences. Like the first two revolutions, chaos cuts away at the tenets of Newton's physics. As one physicist put it: "Relativity eliminated the Newtonian illusion of absolute space and time; quantum theory eliminated the Newtonian dream of a controllable measurement process; and chaos eliminates the Laplacian fantasy of deterministic predictability." Of the three, the revolution in chaos applies to the universe we see and touch, to objects at human scale. Everyday experience and real pictures of the world have become legitimate targets for inquiry. There has long been a feeling, not always expressed openly, that theoretical physics has strayed far from human intuition about the world. Whether this will prove to be fruitful heresy or just plain heresy, no one knows. But some of those who thought physics might be working its way into a corner now look to chaos as a way out.

17   Within physics itself, the study of chaos emerged from a backwater. The mainstream for most of the twentieth century has been particle physics, exploring the building blocks of matter at higher and higher energies, smaller and smaller scales, shorter and shorter times. Out of particle physics have come theories about the fundamental forces of nature and about the origin of the universe. Yet some young physicists have grown dissatisfied with the direction of the most prestigious of sciences. Progress has begun to seem slow, the naming of new particles futile, the body of theory cluttered. With the coming of chaos, younger scientists believed they were seeing the beginnings of a course change for all of physics. The field had been dominated long enough, they felt, by the glittering abstractions of high-energy particles and quantum mechanics.

18   The cosmologist Stephen Hawking, occupant of Newton's chair at Cambridge University, spoke for most of physics when he took stock of his science in a 1980 lecture titled "Is the End in Sight for Theoretical Physics?"

19   "We already know the physical laws that govern everything we experience in everyday life. . . . It is a tribute to how far we have come in theoretical physics that it now takes enormous machines and a great deal of money to perform an experiment whose results we cannot predict."

20   Yet Hawking recognized that understanding nature's laws on the terms of particle physics left unanswered the question of how to apply those laws to any but the simplest of systems. Predictability is one thing in a cloud chamber where two particles collide at the end of a race around an accelerator. It is something else altogether in the simplest tub of roiling fluid, or in the earth's weather, or in the human brain.

21   Hawking's physics, efficiently gathering up Nobel Prizes and big money for experiments, has often been called a revolution. At times it seemed within reach of that grail of science, the Grand Unified Theory or "theory of everything." Physics had traced the development of energy and matter in all but the first eyeblink of the universe's history. But was postwar particle physics a revolution? Or was it just the fleshing out of the framework laid down by Einstein, Bohr, and the other fathers of relativity and quantum mechanics? Certainly, the achievements of physics, from the atomic bomb to the transistor, changed the twentieth-century landscape. Yet if anything, the scope of particle physics seemed to have narrowed. Two generations had passed since the field produced a new theoretical idea that changed the way nonspecialists understand the world.

22   The physics described by Hawking could complete its mission without answering some of the most fundamental questions about nature. How does life begin? What is turbulence? Above all, in a universe ruled by entropy, drawing inexorably toward greater and greater disorder, how does order arise? At the same time, objects of everyday experience like fluids and mechanical systems came to seem so basic and so ordinary that physicists had a natural tendency to assume they were well understood. It was not so.

23   As the revolution in chaos runs its course, the best physicists find themselves returning without embarrassment to phenomena on a human scale. They study not just galaxies but clouds. They carry out profitable computer research not just on Crays but on Macintoshes. The premier journals print articles on the strange dynamics of a ball bouncing on a table side by side with articles on quantum physics. The simplest systems are now seen to create extraordinarily difficult problems of predictability. Yet order arises spontaneously in those systems—chaos and order together. Only a new kind of science could begin to cross the great gulf between knowledge of what one thing does—one water molecule, one cell of heart tissue, one neuron—and what millions of them do.

24   Watch two bits of foam flowing side by side at the bottom of a waterfall. What can you guess about how close they were at the top? Nothing. As far as standard physics was concerned, God might just as well have taken all those water molecules under the table and shuffled them personally. Traditionally, when physicists saw complex results, they looked for complex causes. When they saw a random relationship between what goes into a system and what comes out, they assumed that they would have to build randomness into any realistic theory, by artificially adding noise or error. The modern study of chaos began with the creeping realization in the 1960s that quite simple

mathematical equations could model systems every bit as violent as a waterfall. Tiny differences in input could quickly become overwhelming differences in output—a phenomenon given the name "sensitive dependence on initial conditions." In weather, for example, this translates into what is only half-jokingly known as the Butterfly Effect—the notion that a butterfly stirring the air today in Peking can transform storm systems next month in New York.

25   When the explorers of chaos began to think back on the genealogy of their new science, they found many intellectual trails from the past. But one stood out clearly. For the young physicists and mathematicians leading the revolution, a starting point was the Butterfly Effect.

Suggestions for Discussion or Writing

1. Why does the prologue begin with the description of Mitchell Feigenbaum? How does his examination of the topic reflect the topic of chaos itself?

2. How did the questions on chaos from several different disciplines coincide?

3. What definition of chaos is given in this section? According to some advocates of chaos, how important is the concept behind chaos?

4. What is the connection with chaos and the theories of Stephen Hawking?

5. Why has chaos created such a stir in the scientific community?

Our Picture of the Universe

from *A Brief History of Time:*
From the Big Bang to Black Holes

Stephen W. Hawking

Stephen W. Hawking, born 1942 in Oxford, England, is a British physicist, educator, editor, and writer. Victim of Lou Gehrig disease, he has overcome extreme handicaps to become known as one of the finest minds of our century. He is a Lucasion Professor of Mathematics at Cambridge University, a tradition-honored position once held by Sir Isaac Newton. He has received many honors, among them the Royal Astronomical Society Gold Medal (1985) and the Paul Dirac Medal and Prize from the Institute of Physics (1987). Recent books include Three Hundred Years of Gravitation *(1987) and* Formation and Evolution of Cosmic Strings *(1990).*

1   A well-known scientist (some say it was Bertrand Russell) once gave a public lecture on astronomy. He described how the earth orbits around the sun and how the sun, in turn, orbits around the center of a vast collection of stars called our galaxy. At the end of the lecture, a little old lady at the back of the room got up and said: "What you have told us is rubbish. The world is really a flat plate supported on the back of a giant tortoise." The scientist gave a superior smile before replying, "What is the tortoise standing on?" "You're very clever, young man, very clever," said the old lady. "But it's turtles all the way down!"

2   Most people would find the picture of our universe as an infinite tower of tortoises rather ridiculous, but why do we think we know better? What do we know about the universe, and how do we know it? Where did the universe come from, and where is it going? Did the universe have a beginning, and if so, what happened *before* then? What is the nature of time? Will it ever come to an end? Recent breakthroughs in physics, made possible in part by fantastic new technologies, suggest answers to some of these longstanding questions. Someday these answers may seem as obvious to us as the earth orbiting the sun—or perhaps as ridiculous as a tower of tortoises. Only time (whatever that may be) will tell.

3   As long ago as 340 B.C. the Greek philosopher Aristotle, in his book *On the Heavens,* was able to put forward two good arguments for believing that the earth was a round sphere rather than a flat plate. First, he realized that eclipses of the moon were caused by the earth coming between the sun and the moon. The earth's shadow on the moon was always round, which would be true only if the earth was spherical. If the earth had been a flat disk, the shadow would have been elongated and elliptical, unless the eclipse always occurred at a time when the sun was directly under the center of the disk. Second, the Greeks knew from their travels that the North Star appeared lower in the sky when viewed in the south than it did in more northerly regions. (Since the North Star lies over the North Pole, it appears to be directly above an observer at the North Pole but to someone looking from the equator, it appears to lie just at the horizon.) From the difference in the apparent position of the North Star in Egypt and Greece, Aristotle even quoted an estimate that the distance around the earth was 400,000 stadia. It is not known exactly what length a stadium was, but it may have been about 200 yards, which would make Aristotle's estimate about twice the currently accepted figure. The Greeks even had a third argument that the earth must be round, for why else does one first see the sails of a ship coming over the horizon, and only later see the hull?

4   Aristotle thought that the earth was stationary and that the sun, the moon, the planets, and the stars moved in circular orbits about the earth. He believed this because he felt, for mystical reasons, that the earth was the center of the universe, and that circular motion was the most perfect. This idea was elaborated by Ptolemy in the second century A.D. into a complete cosmological model. The earth stood at the center, surrounded by eight spheres that carried the moon, the sun, the stars, and the five planets known at the time, Mercury, Venus, Mars, Junipter, and Saturn. The planets themselves moved on smaller circles attached to their respective spheres in order to account for their rather complicated observed paths in the sky. The outermost sphere carried the so-called fixed stars, which always stay in the same positions relative to

each other but which rotate together across the sky. What lay beyond the last sphere was never made very clear, but it certainly was not part of mankind's observable universe.

5   Ptolemy's model provided a reasonably accurate system for predicting the positions of heavenly bodies in the sky. But in order to predict these positions correctly, Ptolemy had to make an assumption that the moon followed a path that sometimes brought it twice as close to the earth as at other times. And that meant that the moon ought sometimes to appear twice as big as at other times! Ptolemy recognized this flaw, but nevertheless his model was generally, although not universally, accepted. It was adopted by the Christian church as the picture of the universe that was in accordance with Scripture, for it had the great advantage that it left lots of room outside the sphere of fixed stars for heaven and hell.

6   A simpler model, however, was proposed in 1514 by a Polish priest, Nicholas Copernicus. (At first, perhaps for fear of being branded a heretic by his church, Copernicus circulated his model anonymously.) His idea was that the sun was stationary at the center and that the earth and the planets moved in circular orbits around the sun. Nearly a century passed before this idea was taken seriously. Then two astronomers—the German, Johannes Kepler, and the Italian, Galileo Galilei—started publicly to support the Copernican theory, despite the fact that the orbits it predicted did not quite match the ones observed. The death blow to the Aristotelian/Ptolemaic theory came in 1609. In that year, Galileo started observing the night sky with a telescope, which had just been invented. When he looked at the planet Jupiter, Galileo found that it was accompanied by several small satellites or moons that orbited around it. This implied that everything did *not* have to orbit directly around the earth, as Aristotle and Ptolemy had thought. (It was, of course, still possible to believe that the earth was stationary at the center of the universe and that the moons of Jupiter moved on extremely complicated paths around the earth, giving the *appearance* that they orbited Jupiter. However, Copernicus's theory was much simpler.) At the same time, Johannes Kepler had modified Copernicus's theory, suggesting that the planets moved not in circles but in ellipses (an ellipse is an elongated circle). The predictions now finally matched the observations.

7   As far as Kepler was concerned, elliptical orbits were merely an ad hoc hypothesis, and a rather repugnant one at that, because ellipses were clearly less perfect than circles. Having discovered almost by accident that elliptical orbits fit the observations well, he could not reconcile them with his idea that the planets were made to orbit the sun by magnetic forces. An explanation was provided only much later, in 1687, when Sir Isaac Newton published his *Philosophiae Naturalis Principia Mathematica,* probably the most important single work ever published in the physical sciences. In it Newton not only put forward a theory of how bodies move in space and time, but he also developed the complicated mathematics needed to analyze those motions. In addition, Newton postulated a law of universal gravitation according to which each body in the universe was attracted toward every other body by a force that was stronger the more massive the bodies and the closer they were to each other. It was this same force that caused objects to fall to the ground. (The story that Newton was inspired by an apple hitting his head is almost certainly apocryphal. All Newton himself ever said

was that the idea of gravity came to him as he sat "in a contemplative mood" and "was occasioned by the fall of an apple.") Newton went on to show that, according to his law, gravity causes the moon to move in an elliptical orbit around the earth and causes the earth and the planets to follow elliptical paths around the sun.

8   The Copernican model got rid of Ptolemy's celestial spheres, and with them, the idea that the universe had a natural boundary. Since "fixed stars" did not appear to change their positions apart from a rotation across the sky caused by the earth's spinning on its axis, it became natural to suppose that the fixed stars were objects like our sun but very much farther away.

9   Newton realized that, according to his theory of gravity, the stars should attract each other, so it seemed they could not remain essentially motionless. Would they not all fall together at some point? In a letter in 1691 to Richard Bentley, another leading thinker of his day, Newton argued that this would indeed happen if there were only a finite number of stars distributed over a finite region of space. But he reasoned that if, on the other hand, there were an infinite number of stars, distributed more or less uniformly over infinite space, this would not happen, because there would not be any central point for them to fall to.

10   This argument is an instance of the pitfalls that you can encounter in talking about infinity. In an infinite universe, every point can be regarded as the center, because every point has an infinite number of stars on each side of it. The correct approach, it was realized only much later, is to consider the finite situation, in which the stars all fall in on each other, and then to ask how things change if one adds more stars roughly uniformly distributed outside this region. According to Newton's law, the extra stars would make no difference at all to the original ones on average, so the stars would fall in just as fast. We can add as many stars as we like, but they will still always collapse in on themselves. We now know it is impossible to have an infinite static model of the universe in which gravity is always attractive.

11   It is an interesting reflection on the general climate of thought before the twentieth century that no one had suggested that the universe was expanding or contracting. It was generally accepted that either the universe had existed forever in an unchanging state, or that it had been created at a finite time in the past more or less as we observe it today. In part this may have been due to people's tendency to believe in eternal truths, as well as the comfort they found in the thought that even though they may grow old and die, the universe is eternal and unchanging.

12   Even those who realized that Newton's theory of gravity showed that the universe could not be static did not think to suggest that it might be expanding. Instead, they attempted to modify the theory by making the gravitational force repulsive at very large distances. This did not significantly affect their predictions of the motions of the planets, but it allowed an infinite distribution of stars to remain in equilibrium—with the attractive forces between nearby stars balanced by the repulsive forces from those that were farther away. However, we now believe such an equilibrium would be unstable: if the stars in some region got only slightly nearer each other, the attractive forces between them would become stronger and dominant over the repulsive forces so that the stars would continue to fall toward each other. On the other hand, if the stars got a bit farther away from each other, the repulsive forces would dominate and drive them farther apart.

13   Another objection to an infinite static universe is normally ascribed to the German philosopher Heinrich Olbers, who wrote about this theory in 1823. In fact, various contemporaries of Newton had raised the problem, and the Olbers article was not even the first to contain plausible arguments against it. It was, however, the first to be widely noted. The difficulty is that in an infinite static universe nearly every line of sight would end on the surface of a star. Thus one would expect that the whole sky would be as bright as the sun, even at night. Olbers's counterargument was that the light from distant stars would be dimmed by absorption by intervening matter. However, if that happened the intervening matter would eventually heat up until it glowed as brightly as the stars. The only way of avoiding the conclusion that the whole of the night sky should be as bright as the surface of the sun would be to assume that the stars had not been shining forever but had turned on at some finite time in the past. In that case the absorbing matter might not have heated up yet or the light from distant stars might not yet have reached us. And that brings us to the question of what could have caused the stars to have turned on in the first place.

14   The beginning of the universe had, of course, been discussed long before this. According to a number of early cosmologies and the Jewish/Christian/Muslim tradition, the universe started at a finite, and not very distant, time in the past. One argument from such a beginning was the feeling that it was necessary to have "First Cause" to explain the existence of the universe. (Within the universe, you always explained one event as being caused by some earlier event, but the existence of the universe itself could be explained in this way only if it had some beginning.) Another argument was put forward by St. Augustine in his book *The City of God*. He pointed out that civilization is progressing and we remember who performed this deed or developed that technique. Thus man, and so also perhaps the universe, could not have been around all that long. St. Augustine accepted a date of about 5000 B.C. for the Creation of the universe according to the book of Genesis. (It is interesting that this is not so far from the end of the last Ice Age, about 10,000 B.C., which is when archaeologists tell us that civilization really began.)

15   Aristotle, and most of the other Greek philosophers, on the other hand, did not like the idea of a creation because it smacked too much of divine intervention. They believed, therefore, that the human race and the world around it had existed, and would exist, forever. The ancients had already considered the argument about progress described above, and answered it by saying that there had been periodic floods or other disasters that repeatedly set the human race right back to the beginning of civilization.

16   The questions of whether the universe had a beginning in time and whether it is limited in space were later extensively examined by the philosopher Immanuel Kant in his monumental (and very obscure) work, *Critique of Pure Reason,* published in 1781. He called these questions antinomies (that is, contradictions) of pure reason because he felt that there were equally compelling arguments for believing the thesis, that the universe had a beginning, and the antithesis, that it had existed forever. His argument for the thesis was that if the universe did not have a beginning, there would be an infinite period of time before any event, which he considered absurd. The argument for the antithesis was that if the universe had a beginning, there would be an infinite period of time before it, so why should the universe begin at any one particular

time? In fact, his cases for both the thesis and the antithesis are really the same argument. They are both based on his unspoken assumption that time continues back forever, whether or not the universe had existed forever. As we shall see, the concept of time has no meaning before the beginning of the universe. This was first pointed out by St. Augustine. When asked: What did God do before he created the universe? Augustine didn't reply: He was preparing Hell for people who asked such questions. Instead, he said that time was a property of the universe that God created, and that time did not exist before the beginning of the universe.

17   When most people believed in an essentially static and unchanging universe, the question of whether or not it had a beginning was really one of metaphysics or theology. One could account for what was observed equally well on the theory that the universe had existed forever or on the theory that it was set in motion at some finite time in such a manner as to look as though it had existed forever. But in 1929, Edwin Hubble made the landmark observation that wherever you look, distant galaxies are moving rapidly away from us. In other words, the universe is expanding. This means that at earlier times objects would have been closer together. In fact, it seemed that there was a time, about ten or twenty thousand million years ago, when they were all at exactly the same place and when, therefore, the density of the universe was infinite. This discovery finally brought the question of the beginning of the universe into the realm of science.

18   Hubble's observations suggested that there was a time, called the big bang, when the universe was infinitesimally small and infinitely dense. Under such conditions all the laws of science, and therefore all ability to predict the future, would break down. If there were events earlier than this time, then they could not affect what happens at the present time. Their existence can be ignored because it would have no observational consequences. One may say that time had a beginning at the big bang, in the sense that earlier times simply would not be defined. It should be emphasized that this beginning in time is very different from those that had been considered previously. In an unchanging universe a beginning in time is something that has to be imposed by some being outside the universe; there is no physical necessity for a beginning. One can imagine that God created the universe at literally any time in the past. On the other hand, if the universe is expanding, there may be physical reasons why there had to be a beginning. One could still imagine that God created the universe at the instant of the big bang, or even afterwards in just such a way as to make it look as though there had been a big bang, but it would be meaningless to suppose that it was created *before* the big bang. An expanding universe does not preclude a creator, but it does place limits on when he might have carried out his job!

19   In order to talk about the nature of the universe and to discuss questions such as whether it has a beginning or an end, you have to be clear about what a scientific theory is. I shall take the simple-minded view that a theory is just a model of the universe, or a restricted part of it, and a set of rules that relate quantities in the model to observations that we make. It exists only in our minds and does not have any other reality (whatever that might mean). A theory is a good theory if it satisfies two requirements: It must accurately describe a large class of observations on the basis of a model that contains

only a few arbitrary elements, and it must make definite predictions about the results of future observations. For example, Aristotle's theory that everything was made out of four elements, earth, air, fire, and water, was simple enough to qualify, but it did not make any definite predictions. On the other hand, Newton's theory of gravity was based on an even simpler model, in which bodies attracted each other with a force that was proportional to a quantity called their mass and inversely proportional to the square of the distance between them. Yet it predicts the motions of the sun, the moon, and the planets to a high degree of accuracy.

20   Any physical theory is always provisional, in the sense that it is only a hypothesis: you can never prove it. No matter how many times the results of experiments agree with some theory, you can never be sure that the next time the result will not contradict the theory. On the other hand, you can disprove a theory by finding even a single observation that disagrees with the predictions of the theory. As philosopher of science Karl Popper has emphasized, a good theory is characterized by the fact that it makes a number of predictions that could in principle be disproved or falsified by observation. Each time new experiments are observed to agree with the predictions the theory survives, and our confidence in it is increased; but if ever a new observation is found to disagree, we have to abandon or modify the theory. At least that is what is supposed to happen, but you can always question the competence of the person who carried out the observation.

21   In practice, what often happens is that a new theory is devised that is really an extension of the previous theory. For example, very accurate observations of the planet Mercury revealed a small difference between its motion and the predictions of Newton's theory of gravity. Einstein's general theory of relativity predicted a slightly different motion from Newton's theory. The fact that Einstein's predictions matched what was seen, while Newton's did not, was one of the crucial confirmations of the new theory. However, we still use Newton's theory for all practical purposes because the difference between its predictions and those of general relativity is very small in the situations that we normally deal with. (Newton's theory also has the great advantage that it is much simpler to work with than Einstein's!)

22   The eventual goal of science is to provide a single theory that describes the whole universe. However, the approach most scientists actually follow is to separate the problem into two parts. First, there are the laws that tell us how the universe changes with time. (If we know what the universe is like at any one time, these physical laws tell us how it will look at any later time.) Second, there is the question of the initial state of the universe. Some people feel that science should be concerned with only the first part; they regard the question of the initial situation as a matter for metaphysics or religion. They would say that God, being omnipotent, could have started the universe off any way he wanted. That may be so, but in that case he also could have made it develop in a completely arbitrary way. Yet it appears that he chose to make it evolve in a very regular way according to certain laws. It therefore seems equally reasonable to suppose that there are also laws governing the initial state.

23   It turns out to be very difficult to devise a theory to describe the universe all in one go. Instead, we break the problem up into bits and invent a number of partial theories. Each of these partial theories describes and predicts a certain limited class of

observations, neglecting the effects of other quantities, or representing them by simple sets of numbers. It may be that this approach is completely wrong. If everything in the universe depends on everything else in a fundamental way, it might be impossible to get close to a full solution by investigation of parts of the problem in isolation. Nevertheless, it is certainly the way that we have made progress in the past. The classic example again is the Newtonian theory of gravity, which tells us that the gravitational force between two bodies depends only on one number associated with each body, its mass, but is otherwise independent of what the bodies are made of. Thus one does not need to have a theory of the structure and constitution of the sun and the planets in order to calculate their orbits.

24   Today scientists describe the universe in terms of two basic partial theories—the general theory of relativity and quantum mechanics. They are the great intellectual achievement of the first half of this century. The general theory of relativity describes the force of gravity and the large-scale structure of the universe, that is, the structure on scales from only a few miles to as large as a million million million million (1 with twenty-four zeros after it) miles, the size of the observable universe. Quantum mechanics, on the other hand, deals with phenomena on extremely small scales, such as a millionth of a millionth of an inch. Unfortunately, however, these two theories are known to be inconsistent with each other—they cannot both be correct. One of the major endeavors in physics today, and the major theme of this book [*A Brief History of Time: From the Big Bang to Black Holes*], is the search for a new theory that will incorporate them both—a quantum theory of gravity. We do not yet have such a theory, and we may still be a long way from having one, but we do already know many of the properties that it must have. And we shall see, in later chapters, that we already know a fair amount about the predictions a quantum theory of gravity must make.

25   Now, if you believe that the universe is not arbitrary, but is governed by definite laws, you ultimately have to combine the partial theories into a complete unified theory that will describe everything in the universe. But there is a fundamental paradox in the search for such a complete unified theory. The ideas about scientific theories outlined above assume we are rational beings who are free to observe the universe as we want and to draw logical deductions from what we see. In such a scheme it is reasonable to suppose that we might progress ever closer toward the laws that govern our universe. Yet if there really is a complete unified theory, it would also presumably determine our actions. And so the theory itself would determine the outcome of our search for it! And why should it determine that we come to the right conclusions from the evidence? Might it not equally determine that we draw the wrong conclusion? Or no conclusion at all?

26   The only answer that I can give to this problem is based on Darwin's principle of natural selection. The idea is that in any population of self-reproducing organisms, there will be variations in the genetic material and upbringing that different individuals have. These differences will mean that some individuals are better able than others to draw the right conclusions about the world around them and to act accordingly. These individuals will be more likely to survive and reproduce and so their pattern of behavior and thought will come to dominate. It has certainly been true in the past that what we call intelligence and scientific discovery has conveyed a survival advantage. It is not

so clear that this is still the case: our scientific discoveries may well destroy us all, and even if they don't, a complete unified theory may not make much difference to our chances of survival. However, provided the universe has evolved in a regular way, we might expect that the reasoning abilities that natural selection has given us would be valid also in our search for a complete unified theory, and so would not lead us to the wrong conclusions.

27   Because the partial theories that we already have are sufficient to make accurate predictions in all but the most extreme situations, the search for the ultimate theory of the universe seems difficult to justify on practical grounds. (It is worth noting, though, that similar arguments could have been used against both relativity and quantum mechanics, and these theories have given us both nuclear energy and the micro-electronics revolution!) The discovery of a complete unified theory, therefore, may not aid the survival of our species. It may not even affect our life-style. But ever since the dawn of civilization, people have not been content to see events as unconnected and inexplicable. They have craved an understanding of the underlying order in the world. Today we still yearn to know why we are here and where we came from. Humanity's deepest desire for knowledge is justification enough for our continuing quest. And our goal is nothing less than a complete description of the universe we live in.

Suggestions for Discussion or Writing

1. What theories for the shape of the earth are given in this article? What reasons are given for these theories? Have you ever heard of Ptolemy's model? What else can you tell about the Ptolemaic theory of astronomy?

2. What is significant about Copernicus's and Kepler's theories? How did these theories influence Newton?

3. What is the theory of "first cause," and does it differ according to various theorists?

4. What was Edwin Hubble's contribution to our picture of the universe?

5. Give your understanding of the general theory of relativity and quantum mechanics. How does this article help you understand—in simple terms—these complex theories? Why are physicists searching for a unified theory?

Hidden Hazards of Radon

Linda C. S. Gundersen

Linda C. S. Gundersen received her B.S. in geology from the State University of New York at Stony Brook in 1979 and is working on a doctoral dissertation on the Reading Prong. She is a uranium geologist with the U.S. Geological Survey in Denver, Colorado.

1   In late 1984 I was mapping the geology of a group of old mines in New York State for the U.S. Geological Survey (USGS), hoping to gain a better understanding of the distribution of uranium in the region. But the nature of my job and the entire field of uranium geology were suddenly changed when a construction engineer in Pennsylvania made a terrifying discovery.

2   The engineer, Stan Watras, was working on the final stages of the construction of the Limerick Generating Station, a nuclear power plant near Pottstown, Pennsylvania. From time to time, his work brought him to the Unit One reactor, which although not yet turned on, already contained some radioactive material. Guarding the gate to the reactor was a set of radiation detectors to make sure departing workers didn't accidentally take traces of radioactivity away with them. During December 1984, Watras began setting the detectors off. After eleven years of working in nuclear power plants, Watras could not understand why he was suddenly contaminating himself, and he began to suspect that the source of the contamination was not in the power plant.

3   On December 15, Watras put his suspicion to a test. He went straight to Unit One, walked in, then turned around immediately, and left through the detector portal. The alarm went off. The plant obviously was not the source of the contamination.

4   Subsequent tests of his home in nearby Boyertown revealed that the air contained more than 1,000 picocuries per liter of the radioactive gas radon—several hundred times the level at which the Environmental Protection Agency now recommends taking steps to fix the problem. On January 5, 1985, the engineer and his family were told to leave their home. They would not be able to return for six months, and removing the threat cost tens of thousands of dollars. But to stay in the house, they were told, would have meant a risk of lung cancer equal to smoking 135 packs of cigarettes a day.

5   It's a chilling story, and one that understandably caused a lot of concern—even panic—among the people of Boyertown and the surrounding area. But immediately after the Watras discovery, geologists and other scientists began to gain a better understanding of radon contamination of homes. Now it is possible to respond to the threat of indoor radon calmly and to fix the problem with relatively little expense. Removing the threat from the Watras house today probably would cost only a few hundred dollars.

6   Radon is a colorless, odorless, radioactive gas produced when uranium molecules eject some of the protons and neutrons from their nuclei. In the process, the molecules change first into thorium, then radium, then radon. But radon isn't the end of this chain. Radon itself decays into polonium and eventually into a stable isotope of lead. As it decays, it emits radiation in the form of high-energy photons, electrons, and clusters of protons and neutrons known as alpha particles. Much of this radiation—especially the alpha particles—can cause random chemical changes as they pass through the body. Doctors can harness this effect to destroy tumors, but it is far more commonly harmful. Many experts now question the early assessments of the health risks posed by radon, including the comparisons of radon levels to packs of cigarettes smoked. Still, the EPA and the Surgeon General currently estimate that exposure to radon in buildings causes between 5,000 and 20,000 cases of lung cancer each year.

7   When state geologists and environmental officials first came to the aid of the Watras family, they already had some understanding of radon and the health risks it

could pose. In the 1970s, scientists discovered that uranium miners exposed to radon at work were at increased risk of developing lung cancer. Radon also had been found in homes, but only in those built on landfills containing radioactive waste or constructed of radioactive materials. There was no evidence of either of these circumstances in Boyertown, and this led to a disturbing and surprising conclusion: the radon had to have a natural source.

8   In November 1985, as the uranium geologist for USGS, I joined a group of colleagues from the Pennsylvania Geological Survey and other northeastern state agencies in an effort to solve the mystery.

Searching for the Source

9   When I arrived in Boyertown, my colleagues had already linked the area's radon problems to the Reading Prong, a band of highlands that extends from Reading, Pennsylvania, to Fairfield County, Connecticut. Some of the rocks in the prong contain uranite, titanite, and several other minerals that include uranium either as a main constituent or as an impurity. Geologists told the public that not all the Reading Prong posed a risk, but the press dubbed the region "Radon Alley." It was clear that we would have to come up with a fuller understanding of the geologic processes affecting the distribution of the radon if we were going to calm the public.

10   The observant people of Boyertown had already noticed an important clue to the situation there: the houses that turned out to have the worst radon problems were all clustered along one narrow strip. The Pennsylvania Geological Survey suspected that a geologic fault might underlie the strip and that the fault might somehow help radon move from the rocks into the houses. I was able to confirm this suspicion as soon as I examined the area's bedrock. It was composed of mylonite, a fine-grained metamorphic rock that forms only along faults. I had already studied mylonite as part of my research at the New York uranium mines, which are also located on the Reading Prong.

11   Mylonite forms when the shearing motion of a fault heats and compresses the rock on either side of the fault line. In this case, one side of the fault consisted of a quartz-biotite gneiss, which contained between 5 and 25 parts per million of uranium. (In other words, each kilogram of rock contained 5 to 25 milligrams of uranium.) When this material was metamorphosed into mylonite, the concentration increased to 50 parts per million. The uranium in the gneiss had been trapped in tiny inclusions inside the quartz crystals of the gneiss. The shearing forces partially melted these crystals, allowing the uranium to migrate to the crystal surfaces. This meant that when uranium decayed into radon, the radon would find itself not locked inside a crystal but located in the relatively permeable space between the grains of the rock. The shearing also changed the size of the grains: coarse-grained gneiss became fine-grained mylonite. This made the whole rock more permeable to radon. These effects helped make the mylonite a much greater source of radon gas than the original gneiss had been.

12   Now the other geologists and I understood why homes in this particular part of the Reading Prong contained such high levels of radon. But shearing isn't the only way to get high-uranium soils, and quartz-biotite gneiss isn't the only source of uranium in Earth's crust. We began searching for other places across the country where radon from naturally occurring uranium could be posing health problems. This effort

has taken up a large part of my time for the last seven years and is still far from over. But we have found that a great many different geologic situations present threats of varying severity all across the United States.

13   Earth's supply of uranium ultimately originated in novas and supernovas (the explosive deaths of stars). Only in these incredible bursts of energy could the more quotidian constituents of the universe, such as hydrogen, helium, and iron, fuse with one another to form uranium and the other heavy elements. These elements were flung across space, along with all the substance of the exploding stars. After many millions of years, they condensed into new stars and planets. When our planet was formed, it received a certain amount of uranium. This supply has been decreasing ever since as the uranium gradually decays into lighter elements.

14   The average concentration of uranium in Earth's crust is 2.8 parts per million. But within the crust, different rock types have different, predictable concentrations of uranium. Uranium has moved from place to place during Earth's 4.5-billion-year history, and geological, chemical, and biological processes have concentrated it in certain rocks. Black shale, for example, has 10 parts per million, while basalt has only 0.5. This is because black shale contains oil—a mixture of many organic compounds. These organic compounds were once part of living things that accumulated uranium in their bodies. Coal and some kinds of limestone have acquired high concentrations of uranium in much the same way. Basalt, on the other hand, forms when magmas derived from Earth's mantle cool and solidify. As magma cools, it separates into materials of different weights and chemical properties, and different fractions of the magma produce different rock types. Basalt happens to form from a magma fraction that is chemically unsuitable to the crystallization of uranium.

15   Once radon forms, it can take many different routes into a home. The Watras house was built directly onto the bedrock, so the gas was able to diffuse directly from the rock through cracks in the foundation into the basement. Usually though, the radon or its precursors must pass through a layer of soil, and this can complicate the picture. Some areas with relatively high concentrations of uranium in the bedrock may end up with very little radon getting into homes because the soil is relatively impermeable. But other areas with less uranium may develop a serious radon problem simply because the soil is extremely permeable.

Radon in the United States

16   By considering both bedrocks and soils, we have been able to identify the principal rock types and geographic areas of the United States with high geologic radon potential. These include:

17   ▪ Uranium-containing rocks that have metamorphosed, allowing the uranium to migrate and concentrate locally within the rock. These metamorphic rocks can be derived from sediments, volcanic rocks, or granite intrusives, but if they have been highly deformed or sheared, they may contain high concentrations of uranium. Shear zones cause the worst indoor radon problems in the United States—including those in Boyertown. Shear zones are found in the Piedmont of the eastern

United States, in New England, the Adirondacks, the Rocky Mountains, the Sierra Nevada, and parts of the California coastal mountains.

18   ▪ Glacial lake deposits and glacial deposits derived from uranium-bearing rocks and sediments. Clay-rich tills and lake clays emit high levels of radon because they have high surface-area-to-volume ratios and because they crack into pieces when they dry out, making them very permeable. Eskers, moraines, and coarse-grained tills often have high permeability and in many areas are derived from uranium-bearing rock. These deposits are found across the northern United States from New England to northern Washington. The geologic radon potential of these deposits varies.

19   ▪ Marine black shales. The majority of organic-rich black shales are only moderately uranium-bearing but may emanate relatively large amounts of radon because they are very permeable. These rocks are found in the Appalachian Mountains, the Appalachian Plateau, the Appalachian Valley and Ridge, the Atlantic Coastal Plain, and the Great Plains.

20   ▪ Soils derived from carbonate rocks. Although most carbonates are low in uranium, the soils derived from them are often high in uranium and radium. This is because carbonates are soluble in water. The rain washes away much of the carbonate material, leaving concentrated uranium behind. These soils are found in the Appalachian Valley and Ridge, the Appalachian Plateau, and parts of the Great Plains.

21   ▪ Uranium-containing sediments deposited in ancient rivers, deltas, lakes, and seas. Much of the nation's reserve uranium ore is contained within these deposits, which dominate the stratigraphy of the western United States. These rocks are found throughout the Great Basin and Colorado Plateau as well as in the Mesozoic basins of the Piedmont and in the Devonian and Mississippian-age rocks of the Appalachian Plateau.

22   Other rock and soil types are less likely to cause radon problems. Among the sedimentary rocks, these include marine quartz sands, nonorganic shales and sandstones, and some clays and river sediments—generally speaking, those without a high organic, phosphate, or heavy mineral composition and not derived from uranium-containing parent materials. Among the metamorphic, igneous and volcanic rocks, those composed of dark—or mafic—materials are the least likely to produce radon. But there are exceptions within these general rock groups. Localized uranium deposits may form within any kind of rock if ground water carries the uranium into it or if uranium-rich magmas intrude. These deposits can produce radon even if they are completely surrounded by uranium-free rocks. Still, this knowledge gives us a "first cut" on rock types likely to cause radon problems. Any rock type with over 2 parts per million is considered a likely source of indoor radon problems.

Radon and Health

23   After a decade of research on radon in homes, scientists, engineers, and architects have a good grasp on the general extent of indoor radon problems in the United States and ways to mitigate them. Medical researchers, however, are still arguing the magnitude of the health risks posed by radon.

24   Researchers have recognized how radon might cause lung cancer. When radon decays, it produces two short-lived isotopes: polonium-218 and polonium-214. Both are solids and tend to attach to dust and aerosols in the air that you can inhale easily. The contaminated dust can lodge in your lungs, where alpha particles emitted by the polonium can cause harm.

25   It is the tissues of your lungs' bronchial tubes that will bear the brunt of this radiation. These tissues contain many stem cells, precursors of a number of different kinds of cells. These precursor cells divide frequently and must therefore make many copies of their DNA. Every time the DNA is copied there is an opportunity for mutation. Alpha particles increase the likelihood of a mutation, and some mutations can cause or promote cancer.

26   National and international committees of experts have calculated that 1 to 3 percent of people exposed to 4 picocuries per liter for their entire lives will die of lung cancer induced by radon. (The EPA estimates that 10 percent of lung cancer cases involve radon.) This is an average rate that includes both smokers and non-smokers. If you smoke, your risk is higher than the average; if you do not smoke, your risk is lower.

27   These risk estimates, based on studies of miners who were exposed to large amounts of radon on the job, are uncertain. It will take more study to get a more precise estimate of the risk posed by radon.

28   The data from the research on underground miners does have one important positive message: after the miners left their high-radon work environment, their excess lung cancer risk declined. Their bodies seemed to recover from the radiation. By testing for radon and taking any necessary steps to lower your home's radon level, you can not only avoid future damage to your health, but also begin to undo any damage you may already have sustained.

Suggestions for Discussion or Writing

1. What is radon and what effect does it have on humans? How dangerous is it?

2. How does radon get into a home? How can it be detected?

3. What kinds of rocks have high geologic radon potential? Where are these kinds of rocks found?

4. How are smoking and radon linked?

5. How do we reduce the risk of having problems with radon?

Will We Be Ready . . . When Worlds Collide?

Robert G. Nichols

Robert G. Nichols is an award-winning freelance writer whose specialty is space science and technology. Born in 1953 in Boston, Nichols received his B.A. in psychology at University of Massachusetts and his M.S. in study of the future at the University of Houston. Currently a technical writer with data communications, he was a contractor at the NASA Johnson Space Center during the early days of the shuttle program. His articles have appeared in Technology Review, Air and Space, *and* Sky and Telescope. *Nichols currently resides in Brockton, Massachusetts.*

1 In celestial terms, it was a "near miss." On March 22, 1989, an asteroid, perhaps as much as a quarter of a mile wide, brushed within 400,000 miles of Earth. The event didn't prompt worldwide panic—there was no rioting in the streets, the stock market didn't crash and people didn't clamor to get into air raid shelters. Yet for astronomers, it was an unpleasant reminder that our planet might be living on borrowed time. While the chance of such an object colliding with Earth is statistically very low, the possibility cannot be ruled out entirely. If an asteroid that size had actually struck our planet, it would have carried the force of more than 2,000 megatons of exploding TNT, the equivalent of more than 130,000 Hiroshima bombs.

2 If all of this sounds a bit far-fetched, take a moment to ponder the fate of the dinosaurs. In a now-famous paper published by Walter and Luis Alvarez in 1980, it was suggested that the great dinosaur extinction since 65 million years ago was caused by the impact of a huge asteroid at least five or six miles across. When that asteroid collided with our planet, it threw up enough dust and debris into the atmosphere to cause a global climate change that wiped out most species of terrestrial and marine life.

3 In addition to spawning a renewed interest in dinosaurs, the Alvarez paper also made people realize that such a catastrophe could happen again. Indeed, similar events, albeit small ones, have occurred in the more recent past. In 1908, an object—now believed to be the fragment of a comet or a loose conglomoration of rocky material—came crashing to Earth near the Tunguska River in a remote region of Siberia. Measuring only about 160 feet in diameter, the object exploded nearly four miles above the ground, leveling trees in a 750-square-mile area.

4 Perhaps the most famous asteroid impact is the Meteor Crater in Arizona. About 50,000 years ago, an iron asteroid between 130 and 160 feet in diameter came careening towards our planet. Because this asteroid was metallic, not rocky or icy like the one at Tunguska, it plowed through the atmosphere and struck the ground, leaving a crater three-quarters of a mile wide and 600 feet deep.

5   To date, scientists have found some 130 craters caused by an extraterrestrial object hitting the earth. One of these—a 125-mile-wide crater in Mexico's Yucatan peninsula—was created by an asteroid eight miles in diameter. It might have been the one that brought about the extinction of the dinosaurs.

6   Though the vast majority of asteroids reside in a belt between Jupiter and Mars, astronomers have known since the 1930s that some asteroids cross Earth's orbit. Known collectively as Apollo asteroids, the largest of them is Ganymed (not to be confused with Ganymede, one of Jupiter's moons) which is nearly 24 miles across. (Take heart, however, calculations indicate Ganymed and Earth will not collide anytime in the forseeable future.)

7   Estimates vary, but astronomers believe there are close to 2,000 near-Earth objects that are one kilometer (three-fifths of a mile) or larger. So far, only about 100 of these have actually been catalogued.

8   "As we go to smaller sizes, the numbers of these objects increase rapidly," explains Tom Gehrels, a planetary scientist at the University of Arizona. Gehrels says that there could be a million near-Earth objects measuring 100 meters (about 300 feet) or larger. In the case of objects ten meters (about 30 feet) or larger, the total might be as high as one billion.

9   If a ten-meter object were to fall towards Earth, chances are it would break apart and never reach the surface. Unless an asteroid were made of a very dense material—such as the metallic object that created Meteor Crater—it would have to be at least 150 meters (about 500 feet) wide in order to survive the descent through our atmosphere. A 150-meter object would strike the Earth with a force of 250 megatons of TNT, creating a crater three kilometers wide.

10   When objects reach the one-kilometer range, their effects become global rather than local. With an impact force equal to 75,000 megatons of TNT, an enormous volume of dust would be spewed into the atmosphere, reducing the amount of sunlight reaching the Earth's surface. The temperature of the planet would drop, plants would die, and there would be widespread starvation. If the object were big enough and the global cooling lasted long enough, many plant and animal species, including homo sapiens, could go the way of the dinosaurs.

11   The growing concern and unease about asteroid collisions eventually reached the attention of the United States Congress, which ordered NASA to set up two workshops to look into the matter. The first of these, the Near-Earth Object Detection Workshop, was "charged with determining how best to discover the population of near-Earth objects that could do catastrophic damage," according to Don Yeomans, a research astronomer at the Jet Propulsion Laboratory in Pasadena, California, and one of the 23 members of the NEO Detection workshop.

12   Because of the danger from asteroids a kilometer across and larger, the NEO Detection Workshop tried to determine the best way to locate such objects. In a report sent to NASA and Congress earlier this year, the Workshop recommended that a network of six observatories be constructed around the world. The observatories would use scanning telescopes and charged-couple devices (CCDs)—electronic detectors that can produce images with much higher resolution than conventional cameras. Over a period of an hour or so, the telescope scans a portion of the sky several times. Images

produced by the CCD are then analyzed by computers in order to detect objects that moved during the multiple scans. Anything that moved during the time between the scans must be relatively close by. By observing these nearby objects, astronomers would plot their orbit to determine if they pose a danger to Earth.

13   A prototype of just such a system has been up and running at the Kitt Peak Observatory as part of the Spacewatch program since September 1990. Spacewatch was created to develop new techniques for locating near-Earth objects. According to Gehrels, who is the principal investigator for the program, the Spacewatch telescope has been locating about three near-Earth objects each month. At this rate, only a fraction of the near-Earth objects could ever be catalogued.

14   By constructing the six-telescope network, it may be possible to locate virtually all the larger near-Earth objects within 10 to 15 years. However, it is not enough to simply find the objects. They must also be monitored. Because they cross the orbits of the planets, near-Earth objects tend to have unstable orbits that change over time. Astronomers have already lost track of as many as one-third of the near-Earth objects that had been located.

15   The network of six observatories could be constructed for about $70 million and maintained for about $15 million a year. Acknowledging the budget constraints facing NASA and Congress. Yeomans speculated that, to save funds, "we could go to the Spacewatch system and improve its CCD detectors, make them a little bit larger so they could scan more of the sky." Demonstrating the system on the Spacewatch telescope will give NASA a chance to try out the technology before committing itself to the more costly worldwide facilities.

16   Not only could the six observatories locate asteroids that might be headed for Earth, they could also generate a tremendous amount of data for study purposes. Using the information to determine when an asteroid will pass close to Earth, astronomers can select the best opportunity to study the object from Earth-bound telescopes. NASA could also use the information when planning missions for unmanned space probes. Probes destined for the outer planets, for example, could be diverted to pass close by a near-Earth asteroid. This was done with NASA's Galileo space probe. Galileo's trajectory to Jupiter was plotted so that it would pass close by two asteroids: Gaspra (which it photographed last October) and Ida (scheduled for a 1993 rendezvous). The observatories will likely find other asteroid and comet candidates for unmanned missions in the future.

17   In addition to the NEO Detection Workshop, NASA also set up the Near-Earth Object Interception Workshop, charged with determining what can be done when an asteroid is headed for Earth. The NEO Interception Workshop had its first meeting in January and will present its report and recommendations to NASA in April.

18   What kinds of things can be done to avert an asteroid collision? John Rather, the Assistant Director of Space Technology at NASA headquarters, said that "there are a broad range of choices depending on the warning time." Rather, who is also chairman of the NEO Interception Workshop, explained that if "you have years or decades for doing something, you can go about it in a very methodical fashion." Nuclear or conventional explosives and various types of exotic technology could be used to divert an object from its collision course with Earth.

19   Even a very large asteroid, several kilometers across, could be diverted by using a "relatively modest nuclear bomb," explained Dr. Clark Chapman of the Planetary Science Institute in Tucson, Arizona. Anchored to the surface of the asteroid, a bomb with a yield of just a couple of kilotons would shove the asteroid into a new trajectory. "Detailed engineering studies haven't been done," Chapman cautions, "but there don't seem to be any unsolvable problems."

20   Another option, assuming we had significant lead time, would be to place an electromagnetic mass driver on the asteroid. This idea was popularized by space colony advocates in the mid-1970s as a way to ship raw material from the surface of the Moon to space factories in Earth orbit. The mechanism is a sort of high-velocity conveyor belt. Large open vehicles (often referred to as "buckets") travel along a guideway, propelled by powerful magnetic coils. When the buckets reach the end of the guideway, they abruptly slow down. The material inside (not affected by the magnetic drive coils) continues to travel at high speed and flies out the open end of the bucket. A mass driver, powered by either solar panels or a nuclear power plant, could take chunks of an asteroid and fling them off into space. By shooting material out at high velocity for many years, the mass driver could maneuver the asteroid into a new, safer trajectory.

21   Objects that are relatively small—say a few hundred feet in diameter—could be moved around in a variety of ways. For example, rocket motors placed on the surface of an asteroid could steer the object away from Earth. It might even be feasible to blow up the object into several smaller pieces that would either miss the Earth or be small enough to burn up in the atmosphere.

22   If an object is spied only a few weeks or months before impact, there may be no time to do anything to prevent the collision. However, in the case of smaller objects, it might be possible to lessen the collision's aftermath. People living near ground zero (where the object will strike) could be evacuated to a safe location. This would be a relatively simple undertaking if the object were headed for sparsely populated areas, but could be a nightmare if it were aimed at New York City or Beijing. If the object were going to hit the ocean (a 75 percent chance, since three-fourths of the Earth's surface is water), people in coastal areas would have to be evacuated because the resulting tidal wave would probably reach around the globe.

23   The prospects are less encouraging if an object one kilometer or larger is sighted only months before impact. The only option would be to try to weather the catastrophe that is sure to follow.

24   With all the concern about the catastrophic results of a collision with a large asteroid, it's vital to remember that the odds of a collision are extremely low. Statistically speaking, the Earth will be struck by an asteroid one or two kilometers in diameter once very 300,000 years. A smaller asteroid, say the size of the one that made Meteor Crater, will slam into our planet once every few centuries.

25   Unfortunately, these long odds argue against spending the resources necessary to search out and monitor near-Earth objects, and to develop the technology to deflect them away from Earth. Understandably, people have a difficult time preparing for a disaster that probably won't occur in their lifetime, or their children's lifetime, or their grandchildren's lifetime. . . .

26   Nonetheless, if even a relatively small asteroid slammed into a populated area, the results would almost certainly be disastrous. It would be doubly tragic if that disaster could have been averted. With this in mind, the $70 million price tag for the network of six observatories seems like a small price to pay to prevent such a calamity. Tom Gehrels may have summed it up best: "It would be stupid for humanity to let itself be eliminated by a rock."

Suggestions for Discussion or Writing

1. If the chance of being hit by an rogue asteroid is fairly low, why are people uneasy about the prospects?

2. Science fiction writers delight in painting a scenario of disaster caused by an asteroid collision. What changes do you think such an incident would create?

3. What is being done to prepare in case of such a catastrophe? Could anything avert a collision?

4. How do we know that asteroids have already hit the earth in earlier times?

5. Would prevention be worth the financial investment involved?

Uncommon Light from Common Rocks

James Bailey

James Bailey, an evaluation engineer working in industrial control design and a freelance writer from Milwaukee, Wisconsin, contributes articles on photography, electronics, science, and technology regularly to various journals and magazines. He was a contributing editor to Modern Photography *from 1976 to 1988 before moving to that post at* Popular Photography. *He has received nine U.S. patents. He has also published* How to Select and Use Electronic Flash *(1983).*

1   Lying unnoticed in the gravel you trample underfoot are ordinary-looking rocks holding a power known to only a few.

2   No, this isn't an excerpt from a fantasy novel about magic crystals and shards that save mythical kingdoms from evil tyrants—it's fact! I have been regaling folks with "magic" rocks for years. It never fails to get their attention.

3   The power, or property, of these particular rocks and minerals is the fascinating ability to produce light in response to various stimuli.

4   The most common light-producing phenomenon is called triboluminescence (TRY-bow-loo-mih-NES-ence). This poorly understood phenomenon occurs when certain materials, such as minerals in rocks, flash with a mysterious but distinct light when rubbed together. You can also release this light by crushing the materials or holding them against a spinning grinding wheel.

5   Triboluminescence is in no way related to the sparks you see when striking a piece of steel against flint or holding steel against a grinding wheel. These actions tear tiny chips from the steel and make them red hot, which is why you can start fires using flint and steel. In contrast, triboluminescence produces cold light, similar in appearance to the bioluminescence of certain mushrooms or even fireflies.

6   The most common rocks that will light up every time are quartz and quartzite. These are the milky or honey-colored glassy rocks found in gravel and road cuts. Some are sharp-edged; others are rounded and satiny. Choose rocks that are translucent. Test by holding the rock up to light. (Don't look toward the sun; you may injure your eyes!) If you can see light—even dimly—through the rock, it is worth taking for your experiments. For ease of handling, try to find rocks that are at least one-half inch or one centimeter in diameter. Smaller rocks flash just as well but are more difficult to grasp. Hand-sized rocks are the easiest to manipulate.

7   If you can't find suitable quartz rocks underfoot, you can purchase them inexpensively at rock shops or by mail. Or go to a supplier of landscaping stone. Ask for silica rock if quartz is not the advertised name. Such stone is usually sold by the bushel or cubic yard, but you can probably get a handful for the asking, especially if you explain your purpose. ("What? Rocks that light up?")

8   Other minerals that exhibit triboluminescence are petrified wood, lepidolite (a form of mica), sphalerite (an ore of zinc), rose quartz, and chlorophane (a green variety of fluorite). (I have had no luck lighting up common white or violet fluorite.) Chlorophane is much more fragile than quartz and quickly breaks into tiny pieces before scattering far from its natural source. Unless you live near a mine, it is more convenient to buy inexpensive rough pieces of green fluorite for your experiments. Tell the rock dealer what you plan to do and ask for the lowest-priced specimens. You don't need prize show pieces; your rocks are going to get nicked when you knock them together. You might ask to try before you buy. (Always ask permission before banging someone else's specimens together. Better yet, ask the dealer to demonstrate.) Rose quartz and chlorophane are translucent, so you'll see their light easily. It is more difficult to see the light produced by petrified wood, lepidolite, and sphalerite because they are opaque. You see the light only at the point of contact, not through the specimen.

9   Take your rocks into a dark room or closet. Wait a minute or so for your eyes to acclimate. Wear safety goggles because small chips may break off and injure your eyes. It isn't necessary to look closely for the flashes. They will be quite obvious!

10   If you have small rocks, tap them together quickly, repeatedly, and with force. You should see a flash of light each time the rocks make contact. With larger rocks, scrub one against the other for a rapidly repeating string of flashes.

11   Some common household items exhibit slight triboluminescence. Sugar does so best, but it doesn't work nearly as well as quartz. Salt shows the effect rarely, with rock salt performing a bit better than table salt. To see light from these substances, you'll need a glass mortar and pestle. (It's difficult to see the flashes in the porcelain type—you need a container you can see through.) A simple substitute is a sturdy glass custard dish and a stainless steel teaspoon. Do not use a glass beaker—it is too thin and likely to break under this rough handling.

12   Put a teaspoonful of sugar or salt in the mortar or dish. In a dark room vigorously grind the crystals with the pestle or the back of the spoon. You'll see a few flashes at the point where the pestle pulverizes the crystals against the mortar. Watch carefully— not only are the flashes few and momentary, they are dim. You'll get the best flashes from a piece of wintergreen-flavored Lifesavers candy. In a dark room, simply grab one of the little rings with a pair of pliers and crush. You'll see a very bright flash. Grind the broken pieces with the mortar and pestle for a real visual treat!

13   The actual mechanism that makes some rocks and crystals flash varies among different minerals or chemicals. In each material, though, the friction of rubbing causes electrons in the mineral's atoms to be temporarily dislodged from their orbits. When the electrons jump back to their normal resting place, some form of energy is released.

14   Some minerals release light when electrons return to a stable orbit. Others dissipate energy as an electrical discharge. The discharge ionizes minute amounts of nitrogen gas within tiny cracks in the rocks or along freshly broken surfaces as the crystals fall to pieces. The latter is what happens in salt and sugar crystals. In still other minerals, ultraviolet radiation from the ionized nitrogen causes the mineral to fluoresce, just as it does under an ultraviolet lamp. Wintergreen Lifesavers react this way. The breaking sugar crystals produce electric discharges which ionize the surrounding nitrogen. (Remember, the atmosphere is mostly nitrogen.) The resulting ultraviolet radiation causes the oil of wintergreen flavoring, methyl salicylate, to fluoresce vividly.

15   Why some samples of certain substances flash this way and others don't remains a puzzle. Scientists propose many causes of triboluminescence, but somehow they always find materials that refute the proposals. What we do know is that trace amounts of certain impurities apparently make it easier for more electrons to be knocked out of their orbits. In a paper published in the *Journal of Physical Chemistry* in 1989, B. P. Chandra and others describe a series of triboluminescence experiments using synthetically grown sodium chloride and lithium fluoride crystals. The experimenters doped their crystals with traces of impurities, including barium, lead, strontium, and calcium, to increase triboluminescence.

16   That is not to say that impurities guarantee triboluminescence. I tried salt crystals containing traces of lead and manganese from the Salton Sea in California. They failed to light at all when crushed in my mortar. And some organic compounds triboluminesce only when they're pure. Nor is there a clear connection between fluorescence and triboluminescence. Those same California salt crystals fluoresce a brilliant red under shortwave ultraviolet radiation. Perhaps there are several independent causes of triboluminescence.

17   Another way to release "mysterious light" from rocks is by thermoluminescence. As you can tell from the prefix *thermo,* this is light released when a substance is heated. Not many minerals exhibit this property, but when you find some that do, the light will be quite showy—much more so than the light you get from knocking rocks together. Most fragments of calcite crystals thermoluminesce a beautiful bright yellow. Chlorophane fluorite glows a pale but bright green, while white and violet fluorite shine more yellow.

18   You need not heat the rocks until they are red hot. Red heat is incandescence, not thermoluminescence. All materials not destroyed by high temperature will incandesce. For thermoluminescence you need only heat the right minerals 150°–250°C to make them glow beautifully. You need no flame. A soldering iron works perfectly for small specimens. I heat small chips of the minerals on an old soldering iron that has its tip filed flat on one side. The flat surface provides a secure place for rock samples to rest. It's no fun if they fall off in the dark! You may want to secure the iron in a vise for added safety and convenience. Be sure to point the tip away from the edge of the bench or table so you won't brush against it.

19   To protect your fingers, use long-nosed pliers to place the rock chip on the iron. Turn off the lights and let the specimen heat up for a minute or so. Non-metallic minerals are relatively poor conductors of heat, so it takes awhile for the whole chip to become sufficiently hot for the top surface to glow. Some minerals crack, and broken pieces may fly off explosively. Fragments of fluorite seem particularly prone to imitating popcorn. Once again, wear safety glasses.

20   If you often experiment with thermoluminescence, you may want to plug your soldering iron into a dimmer switch or a motor speed control. Then you can set the iron hot enough to activate the rocks but cool enough to retard corrosion of the tip.

21   The mechanism behind thermoluminescence is a bit different from that of triboluminescence. According to Professors F. Daniels and R. A. Alberty in their textbook *Physical Chemistry,* some minerals have extra electrons trapped within their crystal structure. The electrons were produced by eons of radioactive decay of extremely minute amounts of uranium within the rocks.

22   Such crystals, when heated above a certain threshold, free the electrons that produce light as they find their way to stable orbits. If you take the crystal off the heat, it continues to glow until it cools below the threshold.

23   Thermoluminescent minerals glow for only a few minutes. Heat releases most of the trapped electrons and no more light will be given off after they stabilize. This is a good reason to heat only tiny chips off your specimens—you won't get a repeat performance from a used chip. You need a new chip for each attempt.

24   Frequently a certain specimen may give off light when heated, while others that look just like it won't. I've had one specimen of ordinary white marble—the type commonly used for garden decoration—in my basement for years. It glowed nicely with thermoluminescence, and it fluoresced brightly under ultraviolet illumination. A second piece of seemingly similar marble that I picked up recently failed to light or fluoresce at all. The puzzle persists. And I'll let the scientists work on that. My fun is in the pursuit of these special rocks. Now that you know about the lights hidden in roadside rocks, experiment for yourself and share the secret with some budding scientists on your next camping trip—they'll love it!

Suggestions for Discussion or Writing

1. What is triboluminescence?

2. Can you identify some of the types of rocks that are successful in exhibiting triboluminescence? What types are common in your locale?

3. Have you tried triboluminescence with wintergreen candies? What suggestions does the article make to produce the effect?

4. What is thermoluminescence? What is the process given to see this effect?

5. What is the value of teaching the phenomenon on triboluminescence to others? How did Feynman (Chapter 6) use this phenomenon in his teaching?

Forever Amber: The Rebirth of Baltic Gold

Jeanette M. Harris

Born in Berlin, West Germany, in 1948, Jeanette Harris was raised in Canada and earned a B.A. and M.A. at the University of Toronto, where she received many honors for her scholarship and writing. She has worked as a writer, editorial assistant, and U.S. agent for Camera Press London. In addition to her many journal articles, Harris has written Canada: The Land and Its People *and* Mined It! A Fairy Tale with Mineral Content.

1   In Europe the treasure hunt for amber is on again. Once upon a time in the early 1700s the Prussian King Friedrich Wilhelm I presented Russia's Peter the Great with a magnificent Amber Room; it was a masterpiece of large amber wall panels and decorations which became part of a palace that Peter built for his wife, the future Empress Catherine I, at Tsarskoye Selo. The Germans captured the village outside St. Petersburg during World War II and the great treasure disappeared. The search for the $150 million plus Amber Room has continued over forty years complete with a special task force, a mysterious death, intriguing comments by Boris Yeltsin and recent speculation in the press. What else was buried with it?

2   More than a pretty resin with a past, amber has held other fascinating secrets. Inclusions of organic material both vegetable and animal have revealed much about ancient flora and fauna. A veritable preservation chamber of insect life, amber has frozen species that go back to the dinosaur period. It has highlighted the evolution of

ants in particular; one such interesting specimen of a wasplike ant was found by rock collectors in a New Jersey clay formation and is now at Harvard. Small wonder that in his recent bestseller *Jurassic Park* Michael Crichton uses the idea of isolating dinosaur DNA from biting insects preserved in amber.

3   Amber deposits occur wherever trees producing resin grew. Simply put, the soft sticky resin dropped to the ground, occasionally trapping insects, etc., hardened, and became buried; it is eventually unearthed in a rocklike state perhaps with an interesting cargo. Much of this fossil resin dates from the Oligocene epoch of the Tertiary Period 40 million years ago. The greatest deposit has been along the southeastern shores of the Baltic sea especially around the former Samland of old East Prussia. There it is enshrined in a marine glauconitic sand, known as blue earth, in the Lower Oligocene strata. Between 1885 and 1914 a million pounds of this northern gold was mined in the area around the fabled Königsberg and more recently dubbed Kaliningrad, which the Soviets closed after World War II. Not surprisingly Baltic peoples have always had a soft spot for amber. Other European sources have been Scandinavia, the Netherlands, Czechoslovakia, Romania, and Sicily, while it is also found in the U.S., Canada, Mexico, Chile and Burma; the Dominican Republic has been a good source lately.

4   Warm to the touch, this is indeed a beautiful and unique organic gem which is pleasantly light to wear. It ranges from transparent to translucent, from golden to brown; blue amber, colored by pyrite, is rare. Found in variously shaped nodules, "icicles," runs or lumps, amber can also occur rounded into pebbles or grains when in alluvial sand or gravel, but then no longer has the opaque coating. Singly refractive with an index of about 1.54, amber has a very low density ranging from 1.05 to 1.10 g/cc and so can float in a concentrated salt solution. With a hardness of about 2.5, a little greater than that of gypsum and harder than most resins, it is reasonably workable. Chemically amber is composed of hydrocarbons with the approximate formula $C_{10}H_{16}O$. Softening and starting to decompose at 150°C, it melts at 250°C. The aromatic fumes from burning amber may remind one of pine tree resin due to succinic acid which is greatest in the pale opaque or "bony" varieties.

5   The ancients sensed amber's resinous origin. Greek legend attributes it to the tears of Phaethon's sisters who were transformed into poplars when they grieved for his death. The name comes from the Arabic anbar and the Romans called it succinum, since they believed it came from tree sap. (Don't confuse it with ambergris, which is from sperm whales and used in perfumes.) Thales of Miletus, that ancient Greek sage, discovered its power of attraction when subjected to friction and indeed the word electricity itself is derived from the Greek word elektron, which is associated with amber and also an alloy of gold and silver.

6   This organic gem has been with us since Neolithic times. Found in Mycenaen tombs, ancient European lake dwellings, and even at Stonehenge, it was traded across Europe in the Bronze Age and in classical times. American amber was used by the Maya and Aztecs as ornaments and incense. A decoration and talisman, it was later transformed into religious objects in the Middle Ages. More recently it has been carved into everything from figurines to cigarette holders. It was even used as a medicine up until the 19th century.

7   While European amber has an Old World cachet, much fine production comes from the Dominican Republic recently. Unlike the more readily accessible (physically if not politically!) Baltic amber found in shoreline deposits and on beaches after storms, this variety is embedded in sandstone in the rugged northern highlands. Miners look for it carefully with shovels and picks. The crude amber is bought by the pound and jewelers work it in Santo Domingo to make the most of eye-catching inclusions of air and insects.

Ersatz Amber: The Beguiling Fakes

8   Alas, imitations have damaged amber's image and value. Plastic is a great pretender; with its high specific gravity, however, it sinks in concentrated salt solutions while amber does not. Kauri gum or copal resin, a recent and less valuable resin from the Kauri pine of New Zealand, has also been substituted; it melts far more readily than amber. Ambroid or pressed amber, which is made by heating small pieces and pressing them together, also confuses the issue; it can be distinguished from true amber by a "flow structure" and elongate bubbles; the mosaic effect is visible with a lens on polished surfaces and heightened when immersed in alcohol. Forget the old electric trick of picking up pieces of paper after rubbing amber on material, since copal and plastic do the same. It has been suggested that simple body heat releases a slight camphor smell from amber, but that could just be your deodorant! So caveat emptor.

9   Pliny's time has long passed when a small carved figure was worth more than a slave in the marketplace. Nevertheless, prices do vary dramatically. Modest earrings may cost a mere $25 and a pleasant enough necklace anything up to $300, while a piece with curious patterns or insects or in a chic setting may fetch quite a bit more; the price of antique ornaments and sculptures depends, of course, on their workmanship and age. The semi-opaque brown color is the least valuable. Estate sales are always worth exploring for those who prefer to buy rather than beachcomb and delve. The new more open Russian situation should prove interesting for amber supplies and make it the politically correct gem of the decade. Like the popular novel of the thirties, *Forever Amber*, this organic gem was in vogue when this century was still young, romantic, and struggling; has its time come again?

Suggestions for Discussion or Writing

1. What is amber and how is it produced? Why is it valuable?

2. Have you ever seen something carved out of amber? What qualities would you expect to see?

3. Why can plastic imitate amber? What characteristics are similar in both plastic and amber? What other imitations are possible? How can you tell if something is really amber?

4. Much amber was stolen and hidden during World War II. What other art treasures have disappeared during wars or political upheaval? Have any been recovered?

5. Why should we learn about amber and other natural substances from the earth? Of what value is this knowledge?

The Portable Phonograph

Walter Van Tilburg Clark

Although he was born in Maine, Walter Van Tilburg Clark (1909–1971) was reared in the West. After earning his M.A. in English at the University of Nevada, he went on to teach high school English and coach basketball before becoming a professor of English and teaching creative writing. His first book, Ten Women in Gale's House and Other Poems, *was published in 1932, but he is best known for* The Ox-Bow Incident *(1940). He has won the O. Henry Award for the short story "The Wind and the Snow of Winter" (1945) and has published many other short stories in magazines and one collection,* The Watchful Gods *(1950). Among his other novels are* The City of Trembling Leaves *(1945) and* The Track of the Cat *(1949). "The Portable Phonograph" was originally published in the winter 1943 issue of the* Yale Review *and, like many of his other writings, focuses on the coexistence of good and evil, pain and pleasure.*

1 The red sunset with narrow, black cloud strips like threads across it, lay on the curved horizon of the prairie. The air was still and cold, and in it settled the mute darkness and greater cold of night. High in the air there was wind, for through the veil of the dusk the clouds could be seen gliding rapidly south and changing shapes. A queer sensation of torment, of twosided, unpredictable nature, arose from the stillness of the earth air beneath the violence of the upper air. Out of the sunset, through the dead, matted grass and isolated weed stalks of the prairie, crept the narrow and deeply rutted remains of a road. In the road, in places, there were crusts of shallow, brittle ice. There were little islands of an old oiled pavement in the road too, but most of it was mud, now frozen rigid. The frozen mud still bore the toothed impress of great tanks, and a wanderer in the neighboring undulations might have stumbled, in this light, into large, partially filled-in and weed-grown cavities, their banks channelled and beginning to spread into badlands. These pits were such as might have been made by falling meteors, but they were not. They were the scars of gigantic bombs, their rawness already made a little natural by rain, seed, and time. Along the road, there were rakish remnants of fence. There was also just visible, one portion of tangled and multiple barbed wire still erect, behind which was a shelving ditch with small caves, now very quiet and empty, at intervals in its back wall. Otherwise there was no structure or remnant of a structure visible over the dome of the darkling earth, but only, in sheltered hollows, the darker shadows of young trees trying again.

2   Under the wuthering arch of the high wind a V of wild geese fled south. The rush of their pinions sounded briefly, and the faint, plaintive notes of their expeditionary talk. Then they left a still greater vacancy. There was the smell and expectation of snow, as there is likely to be when the wild geese fly south. From the remote distance, towards the red sky, came faintly the protracted howl and quick yap-yap of a prairie wolf.

3   North of the road, perhaps a hundred yards, lay the parallel and deeply intrenched course of a small creek, lined with leafless alders and willows. The creek was already silent under ice. Into the bank above it was dug a sort of cell, with a single opening, like a reflection or a deception of the imagination. The light came from the chary burning of four blocks of poorly aged peat, which gave off a petty warmth and much acrid smoke. But the precious remnants of wood, old fence posts and timbers from the long-deserted dugouts, had to be saved for the real cold, for the time when a man's breath blew white, the moisture in his nostrils stiffened at once when he stepped out, and the expansive blizzards paraded for days over the vast open, swirling and settling and thickening, till the dawn of the cleared day when the sky was thin blue-green and the terrible cold, in which a man could not live for three hours unwarmed, lay over the uniformly drifted swell of the plain.

4   Around the smoldering peat, four men were seated crosslegged. Behind them, traversed by their shadows, was the earth bench, with two old and dirty army blankets, where the owner of the cell slept. In a niche in the opposite wall were a few tin utensils which caught the glint of the coals. The host was rewrapping in a piece of daubed burlap four fine, leather-bound books. He worked slowly and very carefully, and at last tied the bundle securely with a piece of grass-woven cord. The other three looked intently upon the process, as if a great significance lay in it. As the host tied the cord, he spoke. He was an old man, his long, matted beard and hair gray to nearly white. The shadows made his brows and cheekbones appear gnarled, his eyes and cheeks deeply sunken. His big hands, rough with frost and swollen by rheumatism, were awkward but gentle at their task. He was like a prehistoric priest performing a fateful ceremonial rite. Also his voice had in it a suitable quality of deep, reverent despair, yet perhaps at the moment, a sharpness of selfish satisfaction.

5   "When I perceived what was happening," he said, "I told myself, 'It is the end. I cannot take much; I will take these.' "

6   "Perhaps I was impractical," he continued, "But for myself, I do not regret, and what do we know of those who will come after us? We are the doddering remnant of a race of mechanical fools. I have saved what I love; the soul of what was good in us is here; perhaps the new ones will make a strong enough beginning not to fall behind when they become clever."

7   He rose with slow pain and placed the wrapped volumes in the niche with his utensils. The others watched him with the same ritualistic gaze.

8   "Shakespeare, the Bible, *Moby Dick, The Divine Comedy,*" one of them said softly. "You might have done worse, much worse."

9   "You will have a little soul left until you die," said another harshly. "That is more than is true of us. My brain becomes thick, like my hands." He held the big, battered hands, with their black nails, in the glow to be seen.

10   "I want paper to write on," he said. "And there is none."

11   The fourth man said nothing. He sat in the shadow farthest from the fire, and sometimes his body jerked in its rags from the cold. Although he was still young, he was sick and coughed often. Writing implied a greater future than he now felt able to consider.

12   The old man seated himself laboriously, and reached out, groaning at the movement, to put another block of peat on the fire. With bowed heads and averted eyes, his three guests acknowledged his magnanimity.

13   "We thank you, Doctor Jenkins, for the reading," said the man who had named the books.

14   They seemed then to be waiting for something. Doctor Jenkins understood, but was loath to comply. In an ordinary moment he would have said nothing. But the words of *The Tempest,* which he had been reading, and the religious attention of the three made this an unusual occasion.

15   "You wish to hear the phonograph," he said grudgingly.

16   The two middle-aged men stared into the fire, unable to formulate and expose the enormity of their desire.

17   The young man, however, said anxiously, between suppressed coughs, "Oh, please," like an excited child.

18   The old man rose again in his difficult way, and went to the back of the cell. He returned and placed tenderly upon the packed floor, where the firelight might fall upon it, an old portable phonograph in a black case. He smoothed the top with his hand, and then opened it. The lovely green-felt-covered disk became visible.

19   "I have been using thorns as needles," he said. "But tonight, because we have a musician among us"—he bent his head to the young man, almost invisible in the shadow—"I will use a steel needle. There are only three left."

20   Two middle-aged men stared at him in speechless adoration. The one with the big hands, who wanted to write, moved his lips, but the whisper was not audible.

21   "Oh, don't!" cried the young man, as if he were hurt. "The thorns will do beautifully."

22   "No," the old man said. "I have become accustomed to the thorns, but they are not really good. For you, my young friend, we will have good music tonight."

23   "After all," he added generously, and beginning to wind the phonograph, which creaked, "they can't last forever."

24   "No, nor we," the man who needed to write said harshly. "The needle, by all means."

25   "Oh, thanks," said the young man. "Thanks," he said again in a low, excited voice, and then stifled his coughing with a bowed head.

26   "The records, though," said the old man when he had finished winding, "are a different matter. Already they are very worn. I do not play them more than once a week. One, once a week, that is what I allow myself."

27   "More than a week I cannot stand it; not to hear them," he apologized.

28   "No, how could you?" cried the young man. "And with them here like this."

29   "A man can stand anything," said the man who wanted to write, in his harsh, antagonistic voice.

30   "Please, the music," said the young man.

31   "Only the one," said the old man. "In the long run, we will remember more that way."

32   He had a dozen records with luxuriant gold and red seals. Even in that light the others could see that the threads of the records were becoming worn. Slowly he read out the titles and the tremendous dead names of the composers and the artists and the orchestras. The three worked upon the names in their minds, carefully. It was difficult to select from such a wealth what they would at once most like to remember. Finally, the man who wanted to write named Gershwin's "New York."

33   "Oh, no," cried the sick young man, and then could say nothing more because he had to cough. The others understood him, and the harsh man withdrew his selection and waited for the musician to choose.

34   The musician begged Doctor Jenkins to read the titles again, very slowly, so that he could remember the sounds. While they were read, he lay back against the wall, his eyes closed, his thin, horny hand pulling at his light beard, and listened to the voices and the orchestras and the single instruments in his mind.

35   When the reading was done he spoke despairingly. "I have forgotten," he complained; "I cannot hear them clearly.

36   "There are things missing," he explained.

37   "I know," said Doctor Jenkins. "I thought that I knew all of Shelley by heart. I should have brought Shelley."

38   "That's more soul than we can use," said the harsh man. "*Moby Dick* is better.

39   "We can understand that," he emphasized.

40   The Doctor nodded.

41   "Still," said the man who had admired the books, "we need the absolute if we are to keep a grasp on anything.

42   "Anything but these sticks and peat clods and rabbit snares," he said bitterly.

43   "Shelley desired an ultimate absolute," said the harsh man. "It's too much," he said. "It's no good; no earthly good."

44   The musician selected a Debussy nocturne. The others considered and approved. They rose to their knees to watch the Doctor prepare for the playing, so that they appeared to be actually in an attitude of worship. The peat glow showed the thinness of their bearded faces, and the deep lines in them, and revealed the condition of their garments. The other two continued to kneel as the old man carefully lowered the needle onto the spinning disk but the musician suddenly drew back against the wall again, with his knees up, and buried his face in his hands.

45   At the first notes of the piano the listeners were startled. They stared at each other. Even the musician lifted his head in amazement, but then quickly bowed it again, strainingly, as if he were suffering from a pain he might not be able to endure. They were all listening deeply, without movement. The wet, blue-green notes tinkled forth from the old machine, and were individual, delectable presences in the cell. The individual, delectable presences swept into a sudden tide of unbearably beautiful dissonance, and then continued fully the swelling and ebbing of that tide, the dissonant inpourings, and the resolutions, and the diminishments, and the little, quiet wavelets of interlude lapping between. Every sound was piercing and singularly sweet. In all

the men except the musician, there occurred rapid sequences of tragically heightened recollection. He heard nothing but what was there. At the final, whispering disappearance, but moving quietly so that the others would not hear him and look at him, he let his head fall back in agony, as if it were drawn there by the hair, and clenched the fingers of one hand over his teeth. He sat that way while the others were silent, and until they began to breathe again normally. His drawn-up legs were trembling violently.

46   Quickly Doctor Jenkins lifted the needle off, to save it and not to spoil the recollection with scraping. When he had stopped the whirling of the sacred disk, he courteously left the phonograph open and by the fire, in sight.

47   The others, however, understood. The musician rose last, but then abruptly, and went quickly out at the door without saying anything. The others stopped at the door and gave their thanks in low voices. The Doctor nodded magnificiently.

48   "Come again," he invited, "in a week. We will have the 'New York.'"

49   When the two had gone together, out towards the rimed road, he stood in the entrance, peering and listening. At first, there was only the resonant boom of the wind overhead, and then far over the dome of the dead, dark plain, the wolf cry lamenting. In the rifts of clouds the Doctor saw four stars flying. It impressed the Doctor that one of them had just been obscured by the beginning of a flying cloud at the very moment he heard what he had been listening for, a sound of suppressed coughing. It was not near-by, however. He believed that down against the pale alders he could see the moving shadow.

50   With nervous hands he lowered the piece of canvas which served as his door, and pegged it at the bottom. Then quickly and quietly, looking at the piece of canvas frequently, he slipped the records into the case, snapped the lid shut, and carried the phonograph to his couch. There, pausing often to stare at the canvas and listen, he dug earth from the wall and disclosed a piece of board. Behind this there was a deep hole in the wall, into which he put the phonograph. After a moment's consideration, he went over and reached down his bundle of books and inserted it also. Then, guardedly, he once more sealed up the hole with the board and the earth. He also changed his blankets, and the grass-stuffed sack which served as a pillow, so that he could lie facing the entrance. After carefully placing two more blocks of peat upon the fire, he stood for a long time watching the stretched canvas, but it seemed to billow naturally with the first gusts of a lowering wind. At last he prayed, and got in under his blankets, and closed his smoke-smarting eyes. On the inside of the bed, next to the wall, he could feel with his hand the comfortable piece of lead pipe.

Suggestions for Discussion or Writing

1. When does the story take place? What clues in the text tell you so?

2. The old man says to his companions about the four carefully wrapped books, "I have saved what I love; the soul of what was good in us is here." Based on that statement, what does the old man seem to value?

3. What four books would you salvage? Why?

4. What do each of the other three men value? What do their values tell you about their personalities?

5. Why does the author not give the four men names? How does he refer to them instead? What effect does this have on the story?

6. Why does the old man conceal his phonograph and books and sleep with a lead pipe? How do his actions contrast with his earlier courtesy?

7. Why are the fine arts important to the four men? How essential to humanity are the arts?

A Brief History of Glass

Walter McDonald

A creative writer and university professor, Walter McDonald (born in 1934) works at Texas Tech University in Lubbock, Texas. He received his Ph.D. at the University of Iowa (1965) and was a U.S. Air Force career officer from 1957 to 1971. He has written, among other things, A "Catch-22" Casebook (1973), Caliban in Blue and Other Poems *(1976),* One Thing Leads to Another *(1978), and* Burning the Fence *(1981), as well as the volume of poems from which the selection was taken,* Anything Anything *(1980). He has received several awards including the 1976 Voertman's Poetry Award from the Texas Institute of Letters.*

Egyptians fired the first glass
as glaze for alabaster jars.
Mary the sister of Lazarus bought, broke
one of these flasks for the feet of Jesus.
5   For Cleopatra they could make mirrors
smooth as the Nile, thread
viscous spools of glass delicate
as the hair of Isis, blow
silica replicas of rams' horns
10 and coil tiny asps with fangs of glass.

In 1500, Venetian artisans
were sealed in the island fortress
of Murano, the penalty for sharing
the spun secrets of Venetian glass

15   death. Elizabeth's Raleigh arranged asylum
        for three: in eight years English artists
        were the Venetians' equals. When Drake burned
        the Spanish Armada, glass lions everywhere
        became the sign of sovereignty, of Empire.

20   Today in Pier One shops throughout the world
        Hong Kong glass swans swim on shelves,
        their long necks arching smooth,
        their vacant eyes dimpled.
        Post-Dresden dolls, their rose skin
25   seared with fire, line other shelves
        like bodies in a morgue, their glass eyes
        open, almost like mirrors,
        polished like the glass luster
        on the shoes of serious young men, down
30   deep in the missile silos of Kansas.

Suggestions for Discussion or Writing

1. Why has glass had such a long history? Why is it a valuable commodity for trade?

2. What metaphors and similes do you find in this poem?

3. How has glass reflected the events of history, according to this poem? What same manifestations have you seen in the use of glass?

4. When does the tone of this poem change? What irony is suggested in the poem?

5. What allusions are suggested? How do these allusions add to the meaning of the poem?

Fire and Ice

Robert Frost

American poet Robert Frost (1874–1963) was the most popular poet in America during his own lifetime. He won the Pulitzer Prize for poetry in 1924, 1931, 1937, and 1943. Born in San Francisco, Frost attended Dartmouth and Harvard and worked as a farmer, editor, and schoolteacher. These experiences provided the basis for his poetry. His first collection of poetry, A Boy's Will *(1913), sent him on his way to worldwide acclaim. He read his poem "The Gift Outright" at John F. Kennedy's inauguration. Frost is known for his plain language, straightforwardness, conventional form, and layered meanings, all of which are exhibited by some of his best-loved poems: "Mending Wall," "Design," "Stopping by Woods on a Snowy Evening," "Birches," and "After Apple-Picking."*

Some say the world will end in fire,
Some say in ice.
From what I've tasted of desire
I hold with those who favor fire.
5   But if it had to perish twice,
I think I know enough of hate
To say that for destruction ice
Is also great
And would suffice.

Suggestions for Discussion or Writing

1. Is Frost discussing more than the end of the world? How do you know?

2. In what way are fire and ice symbolic in the poem?

3. What type of figurative langauge does Frost use in the poem? How does the figurative language enhance the meaning?

4. What words don't rhyme with "fire" or "ice"? How might that difference be significant? How does the structure of the poem contribute to the meaning?

Hiding Place

Richard Armour

*Born in San Pedro, California, Richard Armour (1906–   ) earned his M.A.
(1928) and Ph.D. (1933) from Harvard. He became a professor of English,
toured Europe and Asia as a lecturer, became the dean of faculty at Scripps
College in Claremont, California, and taught as a visiting professor at a
number of universities. Among his writings are* Coleridge the Talker *(1940),*
Young Voices *(1941), and* Writing Light Verse and Prose Humor *(1971).
Armour is known for his prose humor and satire. His series of "It All Started
With . . . " books illustrates his humorous approach:* It All Started with
Columbus *(1953),* It All Started with Eve *(1956),* It All Started with Stones
and Clubs *(1967), and* It All Started with Freshman English *(1973).*

*A speaker at a meeting of the New York Frozen Food Locker Association
declared that the best hiding place in event of an atomic explosion is a frozen
food locker, where "radiation will not penetrate."*   —News Item

> Move over, ham
>   And quartered cow,
> My Geiger says
>   The time is now.
>
> 5   Yes, now I lay me
>   Down to sleep,
> And if I die,
>   At least I'll keep.

Suggestions for Discussion or Writing ▬▬▬▬

1. Could this poem be considered dark humor? Why or why not? What elements within the poem give it a darker side?

2. What is the relationship of the poem to the news item quoted just before it? How does the news item enhance the poem's meaning?

3. What words are personified? What is the effect of this personification?

4. What prayer is alluded to in the second stanza? What words of the prayer have been changed? What is the effect of including a prayer in the poem? What is the effect of the altered prayer?

5. What seems to be the poet's purpose in composing this short poem? What is his tone? What clues in the text let you know how the poet feels about the subject?

Literary Credits

"Silent Snow, Secret Snow" from: THE COLLECTED SHORT STORIES OF CONRAD AIKEN. Copyright © 1960 by Conrad Aiken. Reprinted by permission of Brandt & Brandt Literary Agents, Inc.

"Uncommon Light from Common Rocks" by James Bailey. Copyright © 1992 by James Bailey. Reprinted by permission of EARTH Magazine.

"What is the Truth about Global Warming?" by Robert J. Bidinotto. Reprinted with permission from the February 1990 Reader's Digest. Copyright © 1990 by The Reader's Digest Assn., Inc.

"Books" by Allan Bloom. Copyright © 1987 by Allan Bloom. Reprinted by permission of Simon & Schuster, Inc.

"Homestead in Idaho" from IDEAS OF ORDER by Marion B. Brady and Ray K. Bird. Copyright © by permission of Clinton F. Larson.

"Killing Our Future" by Sarah Brady. Reprinted by permission of Sarah Brady.

"The Changing Year" from *The Sea Around Us,* Revised Edition, by Rachel L. Carson. Copyright © 1961 by Rachel L. Carson; renewed 1989 by Roger Christie. Reprinted by permission of Oxford University Press, Inc.

"Apart from the Animals" by Paul Chance. Copyright © 1988 by Paul Chance. Reprinted with permission from *Psychology Today Magazine.* Copyright © 1988 (Sussex Publishers, Inc.)

"The Huddled Masses" by Alistair Cooke. From ALISTAIR COOKE'S AMERICA by Alistair Cooke. Copyright © 1973 by Alistair Cooke. Reprinted by permission of Alfred A. Knopf, Inc.

"next to of course god america i" is reprinted from IS 5 Poems by e.e. cummings, Edited by George James Firmage, by permission of Liveright Publishing Corporation. Copyright © 1985 by e.e. cummings Trust. Copyright © 1926 by Horace Liveright. Copyright © 1954 by e. e. cummings. Copyright © 1985 by George James Firmage.

"Dandelions" by John Davies. Reprinted by permission of John Davies. Copyright © 1993.

"Heaven and Earth in Jest" from PILGRIM AT TINKER CREEK by Annie Dillard. Copyright © by Annie Dillard. Reprinted by permission of HarperCollins Publishers Inc.

Index

Notes